REASONS AND LIVES IN BUDDHIST TRADITIONS

Studies in Indian and Tibetan Buddhism

This series was conceived to provide a forum for publishing outstanding new contributions to scholarship on Indian and Tibetan Buddhism and also to make accessible seminal research not widely known outside a narrow specialist audience, including translations of appropriate monographs and collections of articles from other languages. The series strives to shed light on the Indic Buddhist traditions by exposing them to historical-critical inquiry, illuminating through contextualization and analysis these traditions' unique heritage and the significance of their contribution to the world's religious and philosophical achievements.

STUDIES IN INDIAN AND TIBETAN BUDDHISM

Reasons and Lives in Buddhist Traditions

Studies in Honor of Matthew Kapstein

Edited by
Dan Arnold, Cécile Ducher,
and Pierre-Julien Harter

Wisdom

Wisdom Publications, Inc.
199 Elm Street
Somerville, MA 02144 USA
www.wisdomexperience.org

Library of Congress Cataloging-in-Publication Data
Names: Kapstein, Matthew, honoree. | Arnold, Daniel Anderson, 1965– editor. | Ducher, Cécile, editor. | Harter, Pierre-Julien, editor.
Title: Reasons and lives in Buddhist traditions: studies in honor of Matthew Kapstein / edited by Dan Arnold, Cécile Ducher, and Pierre-Julien Harter.
Description: Somerville, MA: Wisdom Publications, Inc., 2019. | Series: Studies in Indian and Tibetan Buddhism | Includes bibliographical references. |
Identifiers: LCCN 2019014019 (print) | LCCN 2019014990 (ebook) | ISBN 9781614295501 (ebook) | ISBN 9781614295280 (hardcover: alk. paper)
Subjects: LCSH: Buddhism. | Philosophy, Asian.
Classification: LCC BQ120 (ebook) | LCC BQ120 .R43 2019 (print) | DDC 294.3—dc23
LC record available at https://lccn.loc.gov/2019014019

ISBN 978-1-61429-528-0   ebook ISBN 978-1-61429-550-1

23 22 21 20 19   5 4 3 2 1

Typesetting by Tony Lulek. Design by Gopa&Ted2. Set in DGP 11/13.
Cover image courtesy of Bonhams.

Printed on acid-free paper that meets the guidelines for permanence and durability of the Production Guidelines for Book Longevity of the Council on Library Resources.

Printed in the United States of America.

Contents

Matthew Kapstein, 1985, at the meeting of the International
Association of Tibetan Studies in Munich.
Photo by Janet Gyatso.

Preface

THIS VOLUME OF ESSAYS in Buddhist and Tibetan Studies celebrates the contributions and influence of Matthew Kapstein on the occasion of his seventieth birthday. In the course of a career of teaching at Columbia University (1989–96), the University of Chicago (1986–89, 1996–present), and the École Pratique des Hautes Études in Paris (2002–18), Matthew Kapstein has been a prolific intellectual historian of Tibetan civilization and a philosophically inclined scholar of Indian and Tibetan traditions of thought, and his scholarship and teaching have influenced a generation or two of scholars in religious studies, art history, philosophy, and other disciplines, particularly as they pertain to Indology, Tibetology, and Buddhist studies. The essays included herein were solicited specifically for this volume, and all therefore represent original contributions written particularly by way of honoring Matthew's considerable role in the intellectual lives of the contributors, all of whom have variously been students, collaborators, and/or colleagues of his.

These disciplinarily various essays in Tibetan and Buddhist studies reflect something of the intellectually wide-ranging character of Matthew's own scholarship and teaching, which is also reflected in the four different books by Matthew that have lent their titles to this volume's parts. Part 1 takes its title from *The Tibetan Assimilation of Buddhism: Conversion, Contestation, and Memory* (Oxford University Press, 2000), an erudite monograph comprising case studies in the historical development of Tibet's broad domain of religious thought. Part 2 is titled after *The Tibetans* (Blackwell, 2006), which, despite its concise title, represents a magisterial synthesis comparable in scope and significance to R. A. Stein's 1962 *Civilisation tibétaine*. Part 3 takes its name from *The Rise of Wisdom Moon*, an elegant translation (for the Clay Sanskrit Library, 2009) of a Sanskrit philosophical play by the eleventh-century Vedāntin Kṛṣṇamiśra. Part 4 is named after *Reason's Traces: Identity and Interpretation in Indian and Tibetan Buddhist Thought* (Wisdom Publications, 2001), a widely appreciated collection of essays that incisively engage a broad range of the sophisticated philosophical traditions of

India and Tibet. The thematically and methodologically various contributions to this volume are grouped according to the one among these works by Matthew to which they most nearly correspond; however, it is in the nature of the case, given the breadth of Matthew's own scholarly work as well as the differing North American and European contexts in which he has influenced so many different students and colleagues, that much of the work herein resists such straightforward characterization. Nonetheless, it is reasonable to hope that everyone who has admired any of Matthew's work will find in the present volume something of the thematic interests and scholarly virtues that inspired their admiration.

In addition to thanking all of the contributors for their timely provision of scholarly essays befitting Matthew's influence (and also for their patience with our editorial predilections), the editors would like to thank the two anonymous referees who read the manuscript for Wisdom Publications for their close attention and helpful comments. The editors would also particularly like to thank David Kittelstrom, editor extraordinaire, whose careful and thoughtful work on this volume are typical of a career dedicated to ensuring the consistently high quality of books from Wisdom Publications. The editors would also like, finally, to note the untimely passing of one of the most noted contributors to the volume: the University of Chicago's Steven Collins, a world-renowned scholar of Pali Buddhism (and longtime colleague to Matthew) who died in February of 2018. Happily for us, Steve had already by then submitted his contribution, well in advance of the original due date for contributors; we are, then, fortunate in being able to include an essay—"What Is Buddhist Wisdom?"—that affords a glimpse of Steve's last book, which he had finished shortly before his untimely passing, and which is to be posthumously published by Columbia University Press as *Civilization, Wisdom, Practices of Self: Theravāda Buddhism Seen Anew*. While the present collection of essays is by way of honoring the scholarly contributions of Matthew Kapstein, we would like to dedicate any further merit to the continued flourishing of the clarity of thought typical not only of Matthew but also of Steven Collins; the world is surely much in need of it. As for the proceeds, royalties from this volume will be donated to Karuna-Shechen (karuna-shechen.org), which does important work in a part of the world much loved by Matthew.

A Note on Transliteration and Phonetics

In hopes of ameliorating the alienating effect of Tibetan orthography on non-Tibetanists, select common words have been rendered phonetically throughout this volume: Lhasa, Dergé, thangka, Nyingma, Kadam, Kagyü, Sakya, Geluk, Jonang, Bön, Ü, Tsang, Kham, Amdo, Kangyur, Tengyur, Dalai Lama, Paṇchen Lama, and Karmapa. Within each essay, recurrently used Tibetan names and terms are also rendered phonetically, with Wylie transliteration supplied on the first usage. In the interest of precision for the specialist reader, however, all other Tibetan is rendered in Wylie transliteration, with words capitalized according to initial letter rather than root letter.

By Way of an Introduction: A "Discussion of the Person" Who Is Matthew Kapstein

Dan Arnold

Brief Thoughts, Preliminary to a Discussion of One Person, on Personalism in Indian Buddhist Philosophy

In the "Note Concerning History and Chronology" with which he prefaces his highly regarded *Reason's Traces*, Matthew Kapstein says that the "Personalist Controversy"—the Indian Buddhist tradition's critical engagement, that is, with the Personalist (*pudgalavāda*) school of thought, which figured centrally in works like the Pali *Kathāvatthu* and in chapter 9 of Vasubandhu's *Abhidharmakośabhāṣyam*—"represents the beginning of formal debate and argument in Buddhist circles, and so is of particular importance for the history of Indian philosophy" (2001, xvii). Given the Indian Buddhist tradition's orienting concern to elaborate the doctrine that persons are "without selves" (*anātmavāda*), it stands to reason that the tradition's great contributions to philosophical thought would centrally involve attention to the idea that while *selves* do not exist, something must nevertheless be said about *persons*. The point is arguably reflected in the Buddhist tradition's many discussions of the two truths, which is an idea that surely originated in response to what was a basically hermeneutical version of this problem: despite all that Buddhist sūtras say by way of claiming that there are no *selves*, the same sūtras are nevertheless replete with the stories, actions, and teachings of sometimes richly characterized persons.

The avowedly Personalist (*pudgalavāda*) school represents what would become one of the Indian tradition's more contentious expressions of debate on these issues. Indeed, this is a school that many contemporary readers are perhaps most apt to know as the target of a sustained attack by Vasubandhu—that of the "Treatise on the Negation of the Person," which Vasubandhu appended to his *Abhidharmakośabhāṣyam* (and which many will know in

Matthew's translation; see Kapstein 2001, 347–75). While that text reflects what became a broad consensus among Indian Buddhists to the effect that Personalism was an unorthodox doctrine that was rightly marginalized, the Chinese pilgrim Xuanzang is said to have calculated, at the time of his travels in India in the seventh century, that some 25 percent of the subcontinent's Buddhists were avowed adherents of Personalist schools. Something of the influence of this supposedly marginal school is arguably evident, as well, in the works of Nāgārjuna and of some of his successor Mādhyamikas. In the course of the 1987 dissertation that gave early expression to his own abiding interest in the philosophical study of personal identity, Matthew himself ventured in this regard that it is compellingly likely that "Nāgārjuna drew heavily on the literature of the Personalist controversy as a major element in his philosophical background."[1] Since that is a thought I have been increasingly apt to entertain in recent years, it seems fitting to begin this introduction to *the person who is "Matthew Kapstein"* with some brief reflections—in conversation with some prominent Indian Buddhists, and by way of homage to Matthew—on what can reasonably be said, by proponents of the Buddhist no-self doctrine, about just what a "person" might be.

Now, insofar as Personalism came to be widely regarded as unorthodox, contemporary readers are not unreasonably predisposed to accept that anything in the vicinity of Personalist views must, of course, be problematic—predisposed to think that if, according to one's interpretation, such-and-such a Buddhist thinker turns out to have held what look to be "Personalist" views, that would, *ipso facto*, be reason to doubt the interpretation. Nevertheless, I have come to think the Personalist trend of thought, which too often is anachronistically reified as a "school" defined in terms of later doxographical consensus, may have had a more influential afterlife than is typically appreciated. I would argue, in particular, that a philosophical case for the reasonableness of Personalism turns out to suggest real affinities with Madhyamaka as that was elaborated by Nāgārjuna and (perhaps even more strikingly) Candrakīrti. On one hermeneutically charitable reading of Personalism, in other words, it turns out that a central insight of Personalism may closely resemble one of Madhyamaka's guiding impulses—a point that becomes all the more clear if

1. Kapstein 1987, 100, where he cites Conze (1967, 130ff.) and Murti (1955, 205ff.) as having recognized some of the relevant affinities. For his overall engagement with *pudgalavāda* (including his consideration of Nāgārjuna's manifest affinities thereto), see Kapstein 1987, 88–114. On Nāgārjuna vis-à-vis *pudgalavāda*, see also Vetter 1982, Vetter 1992, and Walser 2005, 245–53 (and passim). On Xuanzang's calculation, see Williams et al. 2012, 92. On Pudgalavāda more generally, see Cousins 1994 and Priestley 1999. For sensitive reflections on the supposedly unorthodox (but *not* "heretical") nature of Pudgalavāda, see Carpenter 2015, 5.

we closely consider Candrakīrti's recurrent and emphatic use of a formulation that, as Candrakīrti may not himself have been aware, clearly had "Personalist" roots.

Before we get to an exegetical case for that conclusion, though, consider the basic sense it could make for a Mādhyamika to embrace ideas comparable to those affirmed by some Personalists. Nāgārjuna and Candrakīrti, I think it not terribly controversial to say, were chiefly concerned to refute characteristically Ābhidharmika elaborations of the two truths. In particular, they aimed to show that the *dharmas* theorized in the Abhidharma literature—the supposedly basic existents to which Ābhidharmikas would show persons to be reducible—cannot, in fact, make sense as being "ultimately existent" (*paramārthasat*). These Mādhyamikas argued, indeed, that the Abhidharma literature's *dharmas* are not finally any more real than the conventionally existent (*saṃvṛtisat*) phenomena they were posited to explain. By arguing as much, Mādhyamikas effectively recommended a recuperation of conventional truth; for if what is "ultimately true" is just that *there are no ultimately real existents*, it stands to reason that "conventionally real" (*saṃvṛtisat*) existents are the only kind that remain in play.[2]

Now consider that *persons* are arguably the most salient of all those things thought to be conventionally existent. As Wilfrid Sellars says in terms of what he christened the "manifest image"—which may be thought analogous to Buddhists' "conventional truth," just as Sellars's contrasting "scientific image" is analogous to ultimate truth—"there is an important sense in which the primary objects of the manifest image are *persons*" (Sellars 1991, 9). *Pace* Sellars, the characteristically Madhyamaka recuperation of conventional truth can, then, be characterized as the recuperation of a *personal* level of description—which is perhaps not so far from what the Personalists were on about.

By way of now exploring this idea (which is sure to be resisted by many students of Madhyamaka), let us start with one of the texts that Matthew himself makes available, in *Reason's Traces*, as well exemplifying debates between Buddhists and Brahmanical philosophers on the issue of personal identity: Vasubandhu's *Treatise on the Negation of the Person*, to give the title according to Matthew's translation of Vasubandhu's aforementioned appendix to his magisterial *Abhidharmakośabhāṣyam*.[3] While Vasubandhu's text is ostensibly

2. I here allude to a formulation of Mādhyamika understandings of ultimate truth that is widely attributed to Mark Siderits; for a closer consideration of that (in particular, of the difference it makes whether the expression is interpreted in the *semantic* terms favored by Siderits), see Arnold 2012, 231–33.

3. Matthew's translation of this, the only chapter in Vasubandhu's *Abhidharmakośabhāṣyam*

concerned more generally to refute *selves*, and while it occasioned response from the Nyāya school of Brahmanical philosophy, the text almost immediately launches into the intramural matter of an extended critique of Personalism. Vasubandhu frames this critique with the question of whether the kind of *person* affirmed by this doctrine exists in either of the two ways admitted by Ābhidharmikas: "This must be examined: do they hold it to be substantial or to be conceptually constructed?"[4]

While Vasubandhu, like most Ābhidharmikas, had no problem affirming the latter idea (that "persons" are practically useful conceptual constructs), he thought the former idea (that persons are *substantially* real) cannot be made coherent. In this regard, as Matthew wrote in the dissertation that influentially introduced Derek Parfit's reductionism to students of Buddhist philosophy, Vasubandhu was much like Parfit, who held that *reductionism* and *non-reductionism* "are two mutually exclusive alternatives, and that between them there is no *tertium quid*" (Kapstein 1987, 95). Vasubandhu held, in other words, that if Personalism's *persons* were neither "substantially" real nor "conceptually constructed," then they just couldn't be talking about anything at all.

Vasubandhu represents his Personalist interlocutors, however, precisely as eschewing both alternatives and as instead affirming this: "Depending upon the bundles which are inwardly held now, the person is conceptually constructed."[5] It is not immediately obvious how or whether this differs from Vasubandhu's own view that persons are "conceptually constructed"; a lot will depend on how we understand just what is added by the qualification of this construction as "depending upon the bundles." If the claim can be understood, however, to express a viable alternative to Vasubandhu's putatively exhaustive options, it would (as Matthew says in his dissertation) "be troubling for Parfit's thesis, no less than for that of [the Personalists'] Buddhist opponents."[6] What epitomizes Personalism, on Vasubandhu's represen-

---

that consists entirely of prose, is included in *Reason's Traces*, chapter 14: "Vasubandhu and the Nyāya Philosophers on Personal Identity" (Kapstein 2001, 347–91). The same chapter includes translated selections from, inter alia, Vātsyāyana and Uddyotakara on *Nyāya Sūtra* 1.1.10. Curiously, Duerlinger's 2003 translation and study of Vasubandhu's text seems to reflect no awareness of Matthew's translation.

4. Kapstein 2001, 351; Vasubandhu's Sanskrit is available in the edition of Pradhan (1975, 461): *vicāryaṃ tāvad etat: kiṃ te dravyata icchanty, āhosvit prajñaptitaḥ.*

5. Kapstein 2001, 351, and Pradhan 1975, 461: *nâiva hi dravyato 'sti, nâpi prajñaptitaḥ; kiṃ tarhi, ādhyātmikān upāttān varttamānān skandhān upādāya pudgalaḥ prajñapyate.*

6. Kapstein 1987, 95. Well appreciating the comparative philosophical implications here, Matthew thus concludes that "with the elimination of the Personalists' attempt to go through the

tation thereof, is precisely the view that there is, in fact, a viable *tertium quid* here: *persons* do not exist in either of the only two ways Ābhidharmikas had said that anything could exist; rather, they are "conceptually constructed"—as I will translate, they "become manifest"—*depending upon the bundles.*[7]

Leaving aside, for the moment, the question of what (if any) sense this makes as an alternative to the options Vasubandhu allows, I would first emphasize that precisely the same formulation—the paradigmatically Personalist claim that persons "become manifest depending upon the bundles"—figures centrally in the writings of the Mādhyamika Candrakīrti, who wrote a century or two after Vasubandhu. Among the several places where Candrakīrti emphatically uses just this formulation is in concluding a celebrated discussion typically represented as advancing his *critique* of the "person": the discussion at *Madhyamakāvatāra* 6.150–63, which riffs on the idea (long familiar to the Buddhist tradition) that the reductionist analysis of persons is helpfully analogized to the similar analysis of chariots.

In this famous discussion, Candrakīrti refutes all of the seven options that he takes to exhaust the possible ways in which chariots and their parts could be related; none of these possibilities, Candrakīrti argues, turns out to be coherent.[8] But having argued as much, Candrakīrti then concludes at *Madhyamakāvatāra* 6.158 that there nonetheless remains something to be said about chariots and their parts: "Even though it is not made intelligible (either ultimately or ordinarily) in any of seven ways, a chariot does—in ordinary terms alone, not subject to rigorous analysis—*become manifest relative to* its parts."[9] The concluding, italicized phrase renders exactly the expression that

horns of the dilemma, Indian scholastic philosophy during the first half of the first millennium . . . was left with two viable alternatives: the soul-theories of the Brahmanical pluralist schools and the logical constructivism of the Buddhist Abhidharmists; i.e., the choices available to classical Indian thinkers were essentially similar to those offered by Parfit."

7. The word *bundle* is Kapstein's favored translation for the word *skandha*, which is more familiarly translated as "aggregate." On my preference for translating "become manifest," see note 10 below.

8. The possibilities are given at verse 6.151: "A chariot, for example, is not admitted as distinct from its parts, nor as indistinct, nor as possessing them. It is not in its parts, nor are the parts in it; it is not a mere collection of them either, nor is it their arrangement." (I have translated from Li 2014, 22–23: *svāṅgebhya iṣṭo na ratho yathânyo, na câpy ananyo na ca nāma tadvān / nâṅgeṣu nâṅgāny api tatra nâpi, saṃghātamātraṃ na ca sanniveśaḥ //.*) In his dissertation, Matthew briefly summarizes Candrakīrti's arguments in this regard (Kapstein 1987, 159–63) but prescinds from considering what Candrakīrti affirms in the wake of his critical onslaught—and it is in Candrakīrti's positive proposal that the expression we are considering figures.

9. Translated from Li 2014, 23: *na tattvato nâiva ca lokataś ca, sa saptadhā yady api yāti siddhim / svāṅgāny upādāya vinā vicāraṃ, prajñapyate lokata eva câiṣa //.*

Vasubandhu took to express the Personalist claim; the claim, as in Matthew's translation, that a *person* "is conceptually constructed depending upon its parts" can also be understood as the claim that a person *shows up* relative to those.[10]

Not only, though, does Candrakīrti thus embrace the very statement that Vasubandhu took to typify Personalism, but indeed he says a lot about how just this statement epitomizes (not Personalism but) *Madhyamaka*. Indeed, anyone whose acquaintance with Madhyamaka is chiefly by way of Candrakīrti's *Madhyamakāvatāra* might reasonably suppose that the real target of Vasubandhu's critique of Personalism was, in fact, Madhyamaka; for the formulation that Vasubandhu perhaps most closely scrutinizes will be eminently familiar to Candrakīrti's readers as one of his most characteristic turns of phrase.[11] While it is perhaps unlikely that Vasubandhu really had Nāgārjuna in his sights, scholars like Tilmann Vetter and Joseph Walser have, like Matthew himself, argued for a historical connection to Personalism on the part of Candrakīrti's predecessor Nāgārjuna.[12] What's more, their case for that conclusion centers on Nāgārjuna's characteristic handling not only of the same expression we have so far noted, but also of the Sanskrit word *upādāna*—a word that turns out to be deeply implicated in the expression at issue.

Basically denoting any act (as on Matthew's translation) of "acquisition," the word *upādāna* will be familiar to students of Buddhism as naming the ninth link in the twelvefold chain of dependent origination. In that con-

10. Like many who follow the Tibetan translation of the term *prajñapyate* (Tibetan, *'dogs pa*), Matthew translates this as "is conceptually constructed." This suggests, however, that Candrakīrti is making a basically *idealist* claim—one to the effect that (as on David Burton's reading of Madhyamaka), "if the mind's activity of conceptual construction did not occur, there would be no entities" (Burton 1999, 68). I take it, however, that as derived from the causative stem of *pra-jñā* ("to know"), the term *prajñapyate* is better rendered as denoting any case of something's being "made known"—of anything's "coming into view" or "becoming manifest." The term applies, then, to anything at all that *shows up* for us. To be sure, it will be chief among Candrakīrti's points that what shows up for us inexorably implicates our conceptual "taking" of things. Lest such mental activity be thought a privileged factor, however, he will also emphasize that how we "take" things is itself dependent, in turn, on what is there *to be taken*. There is, to that extent, more to the world than conceptual constructions thereof, even if it is only through such constructions that any of it is available to us.

11. That Vasubandhu might really have been targeting Madhyamaka was once suggested to me by Dan Lusthaus, in conversation many years ago. Notwithstanding the plausibility of the suggestion, Vasubandhu explicitly names the target of his critique as the Vātsīputrīyas, one of a couple of schools taken to have upheld *pudgalavāda*, and the commentarial tradition is unanimous in taking Vasubandhu to be concerned with *pudgalavāda*.

12. See note 1, above.

text, *acquisition* (*upādāna*), itself caused by *desire* (*tṛṣṇā*), in turn gives rise to *being* (*bhava*), which in turn causes *birth*. The same word is commonly used in connection with the *bundles* (*skandha*), which are often referred to in the tradition specifically as the "acquisitive *skandhas*" (*upādāna-skandhas*), which are so called because "they form the causal basis for the future states of the continuum that they constitute" (Kapstein 2001, 25n39). Quintessentially Ābhidharmika categories such as the *skandhas*, in other words, can be characterized as "what is acquired" (*upādāna*) in the sense that these are the essentially impersonal kinds of existents and events that uniquely count, in the Abhidharma literature, as ultimately real. These represent, as it were, the "stuff" from which experience emerges—whatever is "taken up" or "acquired" (whether as content or predecessor cause) whenever a moment of experience occurs, thus perpetuating the cycle of *saṃsāra*.

With just this sense of the word in mind, Nāgārjuna and Candrakīrti alike use *upādāna* as shorthand for all the impersonal categories (*skandhas*, *dhātus*, *āyatanas*, etc.) said in Abhidharma literature to constitute the ultimately existent entities to which such conventionally real things as persons can be reduced—shorthand for all the kinds of entities, in Sellars's idiom, that have their place in the "scientific image," as against the *manifest image* in terms of which things like "persons" make sense. Similarly, the *skandhas* ("bundles" or "aggregates") were shorthand for all Ābhidharmika categories, as in the expression Vasubandhu takes to epitomize Personalism: "relative to the *skandhas*, a 'person' comes into view" (*skandhān upādāya pudgalaḥ prajñapyate*). But if, with Nāgārjuna and Candrakīrti, we substitute *upādāna* for *skandha*, we now have an expression involving two forms of the same verbal root (*upa+ā+√dā*, "to acquire"): *upādāna*, and the gerund *upādāya*, which I have translated as "relative to" (and Matthew as "depending upon"). This gerund was indeed used with that sense, but it is significant that the phrase we now have—*upādānam upādāya prajñapyate*—literally means persons show up only "having *taken up*" (*upādāya*)[13] what is there "*to be taken*" (*upādāna*, i.e., the impersonal constituents of Abhidharma analysis). In a passage (at *Madhyamakāvatāra* 6.161–62) widely taken as definitively expressing his view, Candrakīrti shows why this matters: now the phrase clearly implies reference

13. This form will be familiar to those who have read much in the interpretive literature on Nāgārjuna's *Mūlamadhyamakakārikā*, and particularly to those who have obsessed over *Mūlamadhyamakakārikā* 24.18. That verse's much-discussed phrase *upādāya prajñapti* corresponds exactly to Candrakīrti's phrase (also used by Vasubandhu's Personalists), which differs from *Mūlamadhyamakakārikā* 24.18 only in using the finite verbal form *prajñapyate*. Of the considerable body of literature that might be cited on the verbal form *upādāya* as it figures in these much-discussed phrases, I would particularly recommend Salvini 2011.

to a whole "situation" or "event" of *acquiring* or *taking up*—and that means that nothing can show up unless there is also (*inter alia*) a "*taker*."

And that, for Candrakīrti, is finally the most salient point about Abhidharma's categories: none of them makes sense except in the context of some constitutive process—except relative (we might also say) to a particular description, which must itself be presupposed if the categories are to make sense. Consider, then, how Candrakīrti exploits the fact that we now have in play a couple of variations on the same word: For him and the Personalists alike, something centrally at issue is said to make sense only *upādānam upādāya* ("having taken up what is to be taken up"); and what is most salient about this expression for Candrakīrti is that any reference to an act of "taking up" (*upādāna*) necessarily presupposes *all* the component parts of any act (as theorized by the Sanskrit grammarians). Among other things, this means there must be some *agent* of the act in question—in this case, an "acquirer" or "appropriator" (*upādātṛ*).

This is just as Candrakīrti says at *Madhyamakāvatāra* 6.159ac: "The usage common to everyone has it that a chariot is at once a *whole*, a *possessor of its parts*, and an *agent*, also well known to everyone as being the *acquirer* [of what is acquired]."[14] Here, it is striking not only that Candrakīrti thus affirms precisely the kinds of abstractions typically refuted by Buddhists (who will generally have no truck with the idea of real "wholes" that somehow exist over and above their parts), but also that he again says just what Vasubandhu took the Personalists to say. On the Personalists' account, too, persons are figured as the "appropriators" or "acquirers" (*upādātṛ*) of the bundles; it is because persons keep grasping at the bundles that they (persons) are bound in *saṃsāra*. Among the ways, then, in which Vasubandhu's refutation of Personalism finds expression is as the claim that "there is no acquirer of the bundles"—nor, Vasubandhu adds, anyone "who casts them off."[15] Affirming, against that view, what he takes as "the usage common to everyone," Candrakīrti seemingly sides with the Personalists, and takes it as philosophically significant that any reference to something "acquired" necessarily presupposes some "acquirer" thereof.

Now, Candrakīrti's point in affirming this is not, of course, to affirm that "acquirers" (or "wholes," "agents," etc.) are *ultimately* existent; indeed, Candrakīrti's is quite the converse point: while of course "acquirers" and the like are just conventionally existent, the basic constituents (*dharmas*) to which

14. *Madhyamakāvatāra* 6.159ac, translated from the Sanskrit as given in Li 2014, 23: *aṅgī sa evâvayavī sa kartā, rathaḥ sa evêti jane niruktiḥ / siddho 'py upādātṛtayā janānāṃ*.

15. Kapstein 2001, 362, and Pradhan 1975, 468: *tasmān nâsti skandhānāṃ kaścid upādātā, nâpi nikṣiptā*.

Ābhidharmikas would reduce these are not, it turns out, any *more* real than those. And chief among the reasons for this is that Ābhidharmika categories invariably turn out themselves to be intelligible only relative to the very things they were posited to explain. Candrakīrti says as much in commenting on *Madhyamakāvatāra* 6.159ac:

> Insofar as they mistakenly understand the meaning of scripture, some mistakenly explain everyone's settled convention like this: "Only collections of parts exist, but *wholes* do not exist in any way at all, since they are not apprehended over and above the parts. Likewise, only parts exist, but not part-possessors; only actions exist, but not actors; only what is appropriated exists, not the appropriators thereof—and this because in each case the latter is not apprehended over and above the former." This reasoning entails, however, that *parts themselves* do not exist, either.[16]

The very idea of parts, in other words, is intelligible only relative to some "whole." That means, however, that any reductionist analysis that aims to show the complete unreality of the latter unwittingly renders the former unintelligible as well.

For Candrakīrti, the right conclusion to draw from this can be expressed (as here in concluding *Madhyamakāvatāra* 6.159) as an exhortation that epitomizes his understanding of Madhyamaka: "Do not annihilate the convention that is familiar to everyone!"[17] Only by maintaining conventional usage, Candrakīrti argues, can we make any sense at all of either chariots or their parts.[18] His arguments to this effect clearly amount to a development of the generally Mahāyāna idea that not only *persons* but also Abhidharma's *dharmas* are "selfless."[19] That familiar idea is to be understood, on Candrakīrti's account, as meaning that putatively ultimate *dharmas* can no more withstand

16. Translated from La Vallée Poussin 1970, 278, lines 9–18.

17. Li 2014, 23: *mā saṃvṛtiṃ nāśaya lokasiddhām.*

18. Nāgārjuna makes much the same point, I think, in one of the many verses in which he likewise rings the changes on the word *upādāna* in clearly *pudgalavāda* ways: "The self is not other than what is appropriated, nor is it the case that it just *is* what is appropriated, nor does it exist without what is appropriated. Nor, however, are we entitled to the judgment that it does not exist" (*Mūlamadhyamakakārikā* 27.18: *evaṃ nânya upādānān na côpādānam eva sa / ātmā nâsty anupādāna nâpi nâsty eva niścayaḥ*). This is among the passages quoted by Murti (1955, 206) in the discussion Matthew cites as relevant to his thoughts on Nāgārjuna's indebtedness to *pudgalavāda* (see note 12, above).

19. It is regularly said in Mahāyāna texts that while the traditions of Buddhism that they

ultimate scrutiny than persons can. Abhidharma's explanatory categories are themselves intelligible only as conventionally existent, and nothing at all, therefore, is "ultimately" existent.

Now, the Personalists, as against this, are often taken to have affirmed the *ultimate* reality of persons. If that's right, Candrakīrti clearly would part company with them, and Madhyamaka's affinities with Personalism might come to seem more misleading than illuminating. Here, though, I would follow Amber Carpenter in suggesting that Personalists may not, in fact, have held that persons are ultimately existent. To be sure, the Personalists characteristically affirmed that persons are *avaktavya*, or "inexpressible"—a characterization, redolent of the mystifying idea of "ineffability," that is surely apt to be understood as suggesting something like "ultimacy." In a philosophically sensitive reconstruction of the case for Personalism, though, Amber Carpenter (2015) has cogently argued that what the Personalists meant in calling persons "inexpressible" is only that the status of persons cannot be expressed *in the terms allowed by Ābhidharmikas*.

As is suggested (we saw) by Vasubandhu's initial response to his Personalist interlocutor, anything at all that one can refer to must, according to the terms allowed in Abhidharma, be either "substantially" or "conceptually" existent; as logically contradictory alternatives, these (Vasubandhu thinks) exhaust the possibilities. Against that idea, the Personalists can be understood to have recognized that while persons (as all Buddhists agree) are not, of course, *substantially* existent, Abhidharma's austere alternatives make it impossible to allow that the category of *persons* is nonetheless uniquely basic. Persons, on this reading, are not ultimately existent, but that cannot coherently be understood as an *eliminative* claim; for it turns out a complete account of the Buddhist path cannot be made intelligible without reference to persons.

What makes Personalism a reasonable position, Carpenter argues, is attention to the problem of how or whether Ābhidharmikas could be entitled to an idea that figures centrally in their account, in light of the no-self doctrine, of the problems of personal identity: the idea, in particular, that the basic constituents to which persons can be reduced (i.e., Abhidharma's *dharmas*) occur in discrete causal series or "continua" (*santāna*). Ābhidharmikas appealed to the idea of *continua* in order to make sense of phenomena like memory; the reason, for example, why I remember only "my" experiences and not "yours" is that only some of the past's innumerable causally efficacious events are in the

disparage as Hīnayāna taught only *pudgalanairātmya* (the "selflessness of persons"), Mahāyāna additionally teaches *dharmanairātmya* (the "selflessness of [Abhidharma's] *dharmas*").

same continuum that constitutes "me." However, the idea that we can identify discrete causal series arguably begs the questions most centrally at issue in theorizing personal identity. The problem generally has to do with whether Buddhist reductionists, for whom really existent wholes can never be found over and above the parts that constitute them, can justifiably help themselves to the idea of discrete *continua* of causally related events. After all, how is a continuum any different, conceptually, from a whole? From the Personalists' perspective, the specific problem is that it seems we can individuate any such continuum only with reference to precisely the *personal* level of description that the reductionist aims to explain away; it is only as a person that any series of causes can so much as come into view as an identifiable continuum. As Carpenter puts it, Personalism was thus motivated by "the fact that the ultra-minimalist Buddhist view inevitably *presumes* the individuation of person-constituting aggregates and person-constituting streams" (2015, 16). In fact, Candrakīrti can here make common cause with the Personalists; for his own critique of Abhidharma's appeal to continua likewise charges Ābhidharmikas with begging the question and might, to that extent, be enlisted as part of a case for Personalism.[20]

If, then, we eschew the reflexive tendency to dismiss the idea on account of the received view of Personalism as manifestly unorthodox, it seems there is good reason to think that Personalist insights may, perhaps unbeknownst to Candrakīrti himself, have figured importantly in Candrakīrti's characteristic understanding of Madhyamaka.[21] And, if we appreciate that Candrakīrti's Madhyamaka thus represents a way to argue for the ineliminable character of

20. Candrakīrti critiques the idea of discrete continua at *Madhyamakāvatāra* 6.15 and again at 6.59–61. At 6.15, he first introduces the idea of *continua* as meant to circumvent a problem he has shown with regard to the idea that causation consists in the arising of anything from something "other"—the problem, i.e., that the property of *being other* applies not only to what one seeks to identify as a "cause," but also to everything else in the world that is not the "effect" in question. Regarding this, the Ābhidharmika can rejoin that a "cause" is not just *anything* that is other than the effect; it is, rather, something "other" that is nevertheless *within the same continuum* of events. Candrakīrti lengthily argues at *Madhyamakāvatāra* 6.59–61, though, that if the problem is to specify *which* of the innumerable "other" things is sufficiently closely related to some existent to count as its cause, it is no help to say that *it's the one in the same continuum*. After all, the continua here invoked are likewise "different" from one another, and so one now has the problem of specifying, without begging the question, *which* continuum is the right one. Quoting *Madhyamakāvatāra* 6.61, Matthew aptly comments in his dissertation (Kapstein 1987, 203) that Candrakīrti thus saw the idea of a *continuum* as "another effort, in reaction to the Buddha's rejection of the persisting self, to reintroduce such a thing through the back door, as it were."

21. For contrasting thoughts on what distinguishes Madhyamaka from Pudgalavāda, see, inter alia, Garfield 2015, 110.

a *personal* level of description, we may, after all, be on the trail of something like a viable *tertium quid* between the alternatives that (as Matthew convincingly shows) Vasubandhu and Derek Parfit similarly took to be exhaustive. On my reading, Candrakīrti's viable alternative consists in recognizing that characteristically Ābhidharmika analyses do indeed show the self-theories (*ātmavāda*) of Brahmanical schools to be incoherent, but that Abhidharma's reductionist analyses likewise run aground on their pretension to have arrived at an *ultimately true* alternative. Claims to that effect—to the effect, that is, that Abhidharma has identified mind-independently real existents that ultimately *explain* "merely conventional" phenomena, which can in contrast be recognized as having a deficient status—can never be sustained, just because any explanation proposed as ultimately true will inexorably be shot through with our own explanatory interests and conceptual capacities. That is precisely to say, however, that there *is* no truth that is altogether independent of conventional truth; the conventionally real world in which *persons* make sense is, to that extent, as "real" as anything *can* be. Conventional truth is, indeed, an ineliminable condition of the possibility of our recognizing what is ultimately true,[22] which is just that there *is* nothing any more real than all this; "there is no difference at all between *saṃsāra* and *nirvāṇa*."[23]

Matthew Kapstein: A "Pudgalavāda"

Whatever one decides about how best to understand Madhyamaka in light of all this, it is clear at least that all of the Buddhist positions scouted above—the Personalists' idea that reference to causal continua turns out to run proxy for reference to *persons*; Vasubandhu's challenge to explain the existential status of this "person" that is supposedly distinct from a "self"; and Candrakīrti's thought that Abhidharma's putatively basic existents turn out to be no more real than the conventional existents they were supposed to explain—are variously wrestling with a problem that philosopher David Wiggins has identified in making a case for *sortalism*. It is apt, in this regard, to invoke a time-honored Buddhist trope: just like different moments of flame in the continued burning of a lamp, different moments in the career of any continuant—a moment as the infant child Matthew Kapstein, for example, as compared with a moment as the adult and accomplished scholar of that name—are "neither the same as nor different from" one another. Wiggins's sortalism is motivated by the recognition that a locution like this makes sense only given some answer to the

22. So *Mūlamadhyamakakārikā* 24.8–10.

23. *Mūlamadhyamakakārikā* 25.19.

question: "same *what*?"[24] Following Wiggins, I suggest that the "personalist controversy"—which represents, as Matthew put it, "the beginning of formal debate and argument in Buddhist circles"—reflects the significance of Wiggins's insight. Even for proponents of the no-self doctrine, the time-honored Buddhist trope can only mean "neither the same nor a different *person*." That it is hard to do away with all reference to persons was clearly a point of interest to Buddhist philosophers.

There is, of course, much more to be said about all this. Here, however, I have sketched something of the Indian Buddhist tradition's philosophically rich discourse on the category of the person by way of introducing a different sort of *pudgalavāda*: a "discussion" (*vāda*), in particular, of the person (*pudgala*) whom we honor with this volume. That person, whose scholarly achievements were recognized with his 2018 induction into the National Academy of Arts and Sciences (his fellow inductees included the likes of Tom Hanks, Barack Obama, and Ta-Nehisi Coates), is neither the same as nor different from the Matthew Tom Kapstein who was born in New York City on December 15, 1949.

Matthew Kapstein, circa 1967.
Drawing by bandmate Chris Cheney.

24. So Wiggins: "Sortalism is the position which insists . . . that, where it is asked whether *x* and *y* are the same, it has to be asked *what are they*—what kind of thing is *x* and what kind of thing is *y*?" (2016, x).

As a young New Yorker, Matthew Kapstein attended first the Horace Mann School and then the Elisabeth Irwin High School. As a teenager in New York in the 1960s, Matthew the younger was much invested in the Greenwich Village music scene, involved at least one band including Matthew. His high school friends included renowned musician Nick Katzman, and two of Woody Guthrie's children were classmates. Young Matthew's mother, a senior editor at *Seventeen* magazine,[25] once sought her son's teenaged perspective on the best band for her to book to perform at a media event; at his cheeky recommendation, she booked The Fugs. (Those who do not immediately appreciate how amusing this recommendation was are encouraged to have a listen to *The Fugs First Album*.) To this day, few things get the vastly erudite Professor Kapstein as excited as discussing music by the likes of Reverend Gary Davis and Mississippi John Hurt, whose playing was much in the air in the New York of his youth.

After graduating from high school, the young Matthew Kapstein began his undergraduate studies at the University of Wisconsin in Madison, where Richard Robinson had not long before established North America's first doctoral program in Buddhist studies—a storied program that produced a couple of generations' worth of the field's preeminent scholars. In the event, Matthew would spend only a year at Wisconsin (the academic year 1968–69), but it befits the scholar he would eventually become that Matthew should thus have begun his studies in Sanskrit and Buddhist studies at a school that would surely have an honored place in any pilgrimage of North American Buddhist sites.

In search, perhaps, of a more vibrant music scene, Matthew transferred to the University of California at Berkeley, where he was a student from 1971–73. At Berkeley, he continued his studies in Sanskrit with Robert Goldman—the acknowledgments to Goldman's widely used Sanskrit primer, *Devavāṇīpraveśikā*, thank Matthew for having "corrected the copy and [written] out, in a clear and elegant hand, all the *devanāgarī* for the first working text" (Goldman 1980, xviii)—and in Buddhist studies with Lewis Lancaster (and, later, Padmanabh Jaini). Matthew's cohort at Berkeley included such other future Buddhologists as Rob Kritzer and Janet Gyatso, who at that time were graduate students there. Clearly, the continuum of mental events conveniently designated as "Matthew Kapstein" continued to be infused with such *vāsanā*s as could ripen into distinguished work in Buddhist studies.

As one can learn from the title page of his 1987 doctoral dissertation, Matthew's Berkeley bachelor's degree is dated 1981; for while he had completed

25. See http://tinyurl.com/yxultsdx.

his undergraduate studies at Berkeley in the early 1970s, Matthew felt no compelling need to finalize the necessary administrative niceties until he decided to embark on his doctoral studies in 1981. In between, Matthew finished out his twenties mostly in Nepal. There, he cultivated astonishing breadth and depth of knowledge regarding pretty much all aspects of Tibetan civilization. Supporting himself as a book importer and translator, Matthew lived mostly in the Solukhumbu region of Nepal, where he studied from 1974 to 1976 at the Serlo Monastery (in Junbesi) under Khenpo Sangyé Tenzin (1924–90), the renowned Sherpa scholar who had founded Serlo in 1959.[26] During the years

Matthew Kapstein, second from left, at Serlo Monastery in Nepal in 1975. *Photo courtesy of Tulku Pema Tharchin.* See also plate 1.

he spent living among Tibetan scholars, Matthew also studied with the Sixteenth Karmapa Rangjung Rikpai Dorjé (1927–81), Dilgo Khyentsé Rinpoché (1910–92), Kalu Rinpoché (1905–89), and Deshung Rinpoché (1906–87), and also with Düdjom Rinpoché Jikdral Yeshé Dorjé (1904–87), whose monumental *Rnying ma'i bstan pa'i rnam bzhag*, published in 1991 as *The Nyingma School of Tibetan Buddhism: Its Fundamentals and History*, was edited and translated by Gyurme Dorje in collaboration with Matthew.[27] Somewhere, there is surely a rich photographic record of the Nepal years; photography is

26. On Gser lo Monastery and Mkhan po Sangs rgyas bstan 'dzin, see now Berg 2017.

27. See Dudjom Rinpoche 1991.

among Matthew's countless interests, and his more recent photographic work in Nepal and Tibet in the 1990s and 2000s can be seen in a number of places.[28]

By the time he technically completed his BA and began his doctoral studies in 1981, Matthew—at this point in his early thirties, and neither the same person who eagerly followed the Greenwich Village music scene circa 1967 nor yet the distinguished fellow of the National Academy of Arts and Sciences whom we now honor—had already developed unexcelled knowledge of Tibetan civilization and also of the Indian Buddhist traditions to which it was heir. When he decided, then, to begin preparing for a career as a scholar, Matthew saw little point in pursuing a PhD in Buddhist studies. Strikingly, the man known to many readers of the present book chiefly as director of Tibetan studies at the École Pratique des Hautes Études earned his PhD not in Tibetology but in a department of Western philosophy[29]—that of Brown University, where he studied with the likes of Roderick Chisholm, Philip Quinn, Ernest Sosa, and James Van Cleve (all of them, among contemporary philosophers, names to conjure with).

At Brown, thirty-something Matthew did keep a foot in the world of Indology; he worked with A. L. Basham (who was for a time a visiting professor there), and Robert Thurman (at that time a professor at Amherst College) was an outside reader of his dissertation. Matthew's studies were chiefly focused, though, on the curriculum of a first-rate philosophy department—one that was, much to its credit, eminently open to the kind of comparative work Matthew aimed to pursue. Matthew's state-of-the-art philosophical education is abundantly evident in the aforementioned dissertation, from which my preliminary reflections on Buddhist personalism took their bearings: "Self and Personal Identity in Indian Buddhist Scholasticism: A Philosophical Investigation." Addressed to "those who have come to question whether the modern philosophical problem of personal identity is the product only of the unique cultural-historical situation of the post-Cartesian West, or whether it reflects more general human reflection on the human condition" (1987, vii), Matthew's dissertation represents an important milestone; exemplary of the kind of philosophically sophisticated work in Buddhist studies that has only in recent decades begun to flourish, it makes accessible to philosophers something of the richness and rigor of several streams of Indian philosophy (chiefly, Abhi-

28. See, for example, Kapstein 2016, which publishes photographs taken in connection with the work Matthew published as "A Pilgrimage of Rebirth Reborn" (Kapstein 1998). See, as well, https://www.himalayanart.org/pages/Kapstein/kapstein.html. Some of Matthew's photos from Nepal were exhibited in the University of Chicago's Foster Hall in 1997.

29. With a tip of the hat to Garfield and Van Norden 2016.

dharma and Yogācāra, but also the work of Naiyāyika critics of Buddhist philosophers), even as it represents a philosophical contribution to the study of personal identity in its own right. The category of the *person*, then, has long been of interest to this noted scholar of Buddhist studies.[30]

Matthew receiving his doctorate degree at Brown University. *Photo courtesy of Christine Mollier*

As a newly minted PhD, Matthew's first academic position was at the University of Chicago, where he was appointed in the Department of South Asian Languages & Civilizations from 1986 to 1989. It was at Chicago that I first met Matthew, when, as a prospective student scouting graduate programs in the winter of 1989, I conversed with him one winter day in Foster Hall. I instead ended up attending Columbia (the weather having been much nicer in New York City when I visited there a week later)—where, as it turned out,

30. One might, in this regard, easily get a feel for this enduring preoccupation on Matthew's part by considering Kapstein 1986, which represents a seminal effort at putting Buddhist reductionists in conversation with Derek Parfit. Matthew recently revisited the 1986 essay in memory of Steve Collins, whose untimely passing in February 2018 is much lamented by contributors to the present volume; see Kapstein 2018.

I would study for a few years with Matthew, who had left Chicago just a few months after I met him there for a position in Columbia's Religion Department, wherein he taught from 1989 to 1996. (Among the classes I had with Matthew at Columbia was one on the problem of evil as that figures in philosophy of religion. The class was called, simply, "Evil"; Matthew said it ought to have had a lab practicum.) In 1996, Matthew returned to the University of Chicago, where he has been associated with the Divinity School ever since. Having fallen in love, though, with French Sinologist Christine Mollier, Matthew remained a regular member of the Divinity School faculty for only a decade or so; in 2002, he assumed a position on the faculty of the École Pratique des Hautes Études in Paris, marrying Christine in 2006. For most of the years since then, his continued involvement in Chicago has been as an annual visitor under the aegis of the Numata Foundation's visiting professorships in Buddhist studies. In Paris, meanwhile, he has, among other things, directed a research team in Tibetan studies at the Centre de Recherche sur les Civilisations de l'Asie Orientale.[31] Matthew has bridged these worlds through such collaborative ventures as his presently ongoing project on Tibetan manuscript studies, which was advanced by a 2015 workshop (involving a number of contributors to the present volume) at the University of Chicago Paris Center. It is in Paris and/or in Chicago that Matthew has taught or otherwise worked with most of the contributors to the present volume.[32]

As fascinatingly circuitous as his intellectual trajectory has been, it doesn't seem quite sufficient to explain the astonishing breadth and depth of Matthew's knowledge and erudition, which are abundantly evident in an extraordinary facility with languages as well as in a deep and humble respect for the historical traditions of learning that it has been his life's work to engage. There seems little point in enumerating the languages in which Matthew comfortably moves (not just Tibetan and Sanskrit, but Hindi, Nepali, Chinese, German, Hebrew . . .); he will probably have learned another by the time one gets to the end of the list. His deep involvement in Parisian academic life has been facilitated by his love of France and his ability to live and teach in French—strengths that have informed his ongoing efforts at reviving the distinguished tradition of French Tibetology typified by the likes of R. A. Stein and Jacques

31. Among the projects of the formidable team of scholars he has directed is one concerning "les manuscrits sanscrits dans les régions tibétaines de la Chine"—an arena in which Matthew himself has made notable contributions. Other projects have concerned the history of Bhutan and studies in Bön and Tibet's other ancient indigenous traditions.

32. Having taken my own circuitous route back to Chicago, I was advised by Matthew on the dissertation I completed there in 2002.

His Holiness the Dalai Lama meeting with Matthew in Dharamsala, India,1985.
Photo courtesy of Christine Mollier

Bacot (whose work Matthew greatly admires). As those who have studied with him in North America and Europe well know, Matthew has, in this regard, always encouraged his students to respect and learn from the achievements of past scholars. Many will have heard him express deeply informed admiration for, say, Stcherbatsky's dated and eccentric but brilliant *Buddhist Logic*, and it seems Matthew is always ready with a touching anecdote or a penetrating insight about, say, the personal life of Sylvain Lévi—or, for that matter, about the sartorial elegance of Arnold Toynbee, or the vicissitudes of the German edition of Freud's works, or the Tibetan-language textbooks used by Tibetan high-school students in India and in China's Tibet Autonomous Region.

Matthew's intellectually generous recognition of the scholarly achievements of others is reflected, as well, in the decade he spent as editor of SUNY Press's long-distinguished (though now regrettably defunct) series in Buddhist studies, for which he midwifed such widely respected and varied books as Georges Dreyfus's *Recognizing Reality* (1997), John Makransky's *Buddhahood Embodied* (1997), Matthieu Ricard's *Life of Shabkar* (1994), and Cyrus Stearns's *Buddha from Dolpo* (1999). A few vectors in Matthew's life trajectory interestingly come together in one such volume: Richard Kohn's *Lord of the Dance* (2001), the posthumous publication of which was overseen by Matthew. This was fitting given Matthew's own role in the book's genesis; Kohn's initial orientation to Nepal's Solukhumbu region, where he would research the Mani Rimdu festival, was provided by Matthew, whom Kohn met in New York before undertaking his own travels to Nepal (whence Matthew had just returned) in 1978.

The far-ranging character of Matthew's interests is amply reflected both in his prolific scholarship and in his teaching, and is but partially reflected in the wide range of offerings included in the present volume. Nevertheless, the following essays well attest to the influence of Matthew's abiding attention to such diverse subjects as the thought of Vasubandhu and other Ābhidharmikas (consider the essays by Brennan, Gold, Kachru, Kumagai); art history, particularly in connection with ritual theory (see the essays of Davidson, Debreczeny, Heller); hermeneutics (Collins, Harter, Nance); manuscriptology and textual analysis (Phuntsho, van der Kuijp); the study of religious experience and of transformative "technologies of the self"[33] (Deroche, Dreyfus, Meyers); the intellectual history of the Jonangpas (Mathes, Sheehy) and of other Tibetan and Indian sects or lineages (Achard, Ducher, Ehrhard, Eltschinger, Forgues, Ramble); and the career of Tibetan Buddhist traditions in such profoundly different contexts as seventeenth-century Bhutan (Deleplanque) and twentieth-century China and Taiwan (Jagou).

With this volume's contributions in mind, then, consider now how significantly all of the foregoing concerns figure in the work of the *one person* (as both the Personalists and Candrakīrti make it unproblematic to say) who is Matthew Kapstein. In the probing historical essays of *The Tibetan Assimilation of Buddhism* (2000), for example, Matthew's engagement with seminal Tibetan texts such as the *Sba bzhed* makes vividly available a sense of Tibet's indigenous historiography, even as he ranges over Chinese, Greek, Nestorian Christian, and Manichaean influences thereon. All the while, the book exhibits historiographical sensibilities keenly informed by R. G. Collingwood's recognition that the historian "re-enacts the past in his mind: but in this reenactment it does not become a present or an actuality. The actuality is the actual thought of the historian that reenacts it."[34] In *The Tibetans* (2006), Matthew has given us what has justly been called "the best single overview of Tibetan cultural history currently available"[35]—a book "so comprehensive,

33. This will be familiar to many as an expression of Foucault's (1988), but I first came across the idea by way of Matthew's appropriation of it in his contribution to a volume whose index I prepared (Kapstein 1996).

34. Collingwood 1994, 444. Collingwood's *Idea of History* has long been a touchstone for Matthew's thinking, which clearly bears the imprint of Collingwood's conception of historical thought as eminently *interpretive*; one will have to look elsewhere for naively positivistic historical work.

35. Huber 2009, 972.

well informed, beautifully written and majestically sensitive"[36] as to clearly supersede such magisterial syntheses as R. A. Stein's *Civilisation Tibétaine* (1962), even as Matthew frames his by judiciously interrogating the very idea of any such synthesis: "'Tibet' is not now and never has been a monolithic entity, and the Tibetan people, far from being homogeneous, are diverse in terms of life-style, language, religion, and indeed most areas of culture." Despite this, he says, "we can still speak sensibly, if tentatively, of a Tibetan civilizational sphere, focusing upon that which has at least the appearance of greatest universality within it" (Kapstein 2006, xii). Not to be overlooked, when it comes

Matthew in Tibet, near Lhasa, 2004.
Photo courtesy of Christine Mollier

to Matthew's considerable contributions to the study of Tibetan intellectual history, is his role in making available the *Collected Works* (*gsung 'bum*) of the fourteenth-century Jonangpa scholar Dölpopa Sherab Gyaltsen. Long known to history chiefly as the target of withering attacks by influential Gelukpa critics, Dölpopa's *Collected Works* were recovered (and acquired for the US Library of Congress) by Matthew in the course of studies in Sichuan province in 1990.[37] At the same time, Matthew is one of the rare Tibetanists who is also a crack Sanskritist, as evident in his elegant translation, for the regrettably

36. Adams 2007, 153–54.

37. See Kapstein 1992.

defunct Clay Sanskrit Library, of Kṛṣṇamiśra's *Prabodhacandrodaya*, whose title Matthew renders as *The Rise of Wisdom Moon* (2009).

The foregoing and many other works represent the scholarship of a perceptive and vastly learned historian of civilizations and of religions. And yet, Matthew also remains every bit a philosopher. The many dissertations he has supervised at the University of Chicago were chiefly in the Divinity School's Philosophy of Religions program, in which Matthew's *Reason's Traces* is widely revered as a model of philosophically engaged work that is at once ambitious and rigorous. That book, which incorporates large parts of Matthew's 1987 dissertation, comprises such gems as "Mereological Considerations in Vasubandhu's 'Proof of Idealism,'"[38] which is widely regarded as one of the best philosophical studies of Vasubandhu's hugely influential *Viṃśikā*. The same book also includes an introduction, entitled "What Is 'Buddhist Philosophy'?," that stands as an exemplary reflection on what it means to engage the works of culturally and temporally remote thinkers in light of the fact that *all* thinking is, necessarily, at once constrained and enabled by one's location in some historical tradition(s). So far as I am aware, it is this essay that influentially introduced the thought of Pierre Hadot to scholars of Buddhist studies, for whom it is now familiar to apply to Buddhist thought the conception (invoking the title of Hadot 1995) of *Philosophy as a Way of Life*.[39] Matthew's philosophical work invariably reflects, in general, a hermeneutically sensitive appreciation of the fact that any scholarly "realization"—any instance of *adhigama*, or of something's "coming through" to us—necessarily depends on *āgama*, which Matthew nicely distinguishes as "what *comes down* to us."[40]

As he has effected such deep soundings in the history of human thought across many centuries and several civilizations, skillfully adopting a wide range of disciplinary approaches as he engages all manner of material and literary expressions thereof, Matthew Kapstein has all along done work that is singularly and above all distinguished by its sheer *humaneness*. I have long thought this most poignantly reflected in the passage with which he concludes the aforementioned study of Vasubandhu's *Viṃśikā*: "When we begin to appreciate Vasubandhu's insights from the vantage point of our own phil-

38. Kapstein 2001, 181–204.

39. See Kapstein 2001, 7–15. See, too, the essay by Deroche in the present volume.

40. As Matthew says, then, of this pair of terms that figures centrally in structuring (inter alia) Vasubandhu's *Abhidharmakośabhāṣyam*, "the transmitted doctrine [*āgama*] is that which *comes down* to us, while realization is that which *comes through* [*adhigama*] when the transmission is rightly understood." (2001, 335) On whether or not it is apt to borrow the term *adhigama* for reference to *scholarly* (rather than spiritual) realization, see Jonathan Gold's essay in this volume.

osophical understanding, what is most human about us leaps through centuries, rushes across continents, and greets what is most human in what had formerly been alien. We meet Vasubandhu face-to-face, incline towards one another, and commune in our perennial capacity to puzzle over what is real" (2001, 197). These beautiful sentences give eloquent expression to an all-too-rare intellectual selflessness—a humane intellectual generosity that recognizes in the achievements of others a condition of the possibility of one's "own" understanding.

Like all of us, of course, the person whose work and teaching this volume now honors—Matthew Kapstein, Tibetologist and Sanskritist, historian and philosopher, professor and fellow of the National Academy of Arts and Sciences—is selfless in another sense, too. Though it be distinguished, his name denotes nothing at all like an enduring *self.* To that extent, the Matthew whom we now honor is neither the same as nor different from any or all of the other things he has been—teenage musician, student at a Sherpa monastery, connoisseur of Himalayan art, blues enthusiast, historian, philosopher, photographer, littérateur. As the Indian Buddhist tradition's Personalists understood, however—and as the Mādhyamika Candrakīrti's recuperation of conventional truth (in perhaps unwitting testament to the influence of the Personalists) makes it reasonable for Buddhists to say—it is nonetheless true that we honor an extraordinary *person*. Relative to the bundles—and relative, as well, to the life worlds and intellectual achievements of scholars and saints spanning countless centuries and several civilizations—the person who is Matthew Kapstein has become vividly manifest. With this volume of essays, we express—inadequately, no doubt, but nevertheless genuinely—our deep appreciation for this person's having come into view for all of us.

Works Cited

Adams, Vincanne. 2007. [Review of Matthew Kapstein, *The Tibetans.*] *The China Journal*, 58 (July): 153–55.

Arnold, Dan. 2012. *Brains, Buddhas, and Believing: The Problem of Intentionality in Classical Buddhist and Cognitive-scientific Philosophy of Mind*. New York: Columbia University Press.

Berg, Eberhard. 2017. *Khenpo Sangye Tenzin and the Career of Serlo Shedrup Zungdrel Ling Gonpa, That Evolved into One of the Most Important Monasteries of the Sherpas of NE Nepal*. Lumbini: Lumbini International Research Institute.

Burton, David F. 1999. *Emptiness Appraised: A Critical Study of Nāgārjuna's Philosophy*. London: Curzon Press.

Carpenter, Amber. 2015. "Persons Keeping Their *Karma* Together: The Reasons for the *Pudgalavāda* in Early Buddhism." In *The Moon Points Back*, edited by Koji Tanaka et al., 1–44. New York: Oxford University Press.

Collingwood, R. G. 1994. *The Idea of History*. Rev. ed. New York: Oxford University Press.

Conze, Edward. 1967. *Buddhist Thought in India*. Ann Arbor: University of Michigan Press.

Cousins, L. S. 1994. "Person and Self." In *Buddhism into the Year 2000: International Conference Proceedings*, 15–31. Bangkok and Los Angeles: Dhammakaya Foundation.

Dreyfus, Georges. 1997. *Recognizing Reality: Dharmakīrti's Philosophy and Its Tibetan Interpretations*. Albany: State University of New York Press.

Dudjom Rinpoche. 1991. *The Nyingma School of Tibetan Buddhism: Its Fundamentals and History*. Translated and edited by Gyurme Dorje and Matthew Kapstein. Boston: Wisdom Publications.

Duerlinger, James. 2003. *Indian Buddhist Theories of Persons: Vasubandhu's "Refutation of the Theory of a Self."* New York: RoutledgeCurzon.

Foucault, Michel. 1988. *Technologies of the Self: A Seminar with Michel Foucault*. Edited by Luther H. Martin et al. Amherst: University of Massachusetts Press.

Garfield, Jay L. 2015. *Engaging Buddhism: Why It Matters to Philosophy*. New York: Oxford University Press.

Garfield, Jay L., and Bryan W. Van Norden. 2016. "If Philosophy Won't Diversify, Let's Call It What It Really Is." *New York Times*, May 11, 2016, http://tinyurl.com/lfoapck.

Goldman, Robert P., with Sally J. Sutherland. 1980. *Devavāṇīpraveśikā: An Introduction to the Sanskrit Language*. Berkeley: Center South and Southeast Asian Studies, University of California.

Hadot, Pierre. 1995. *Philosophy as a Way of Life: Spiritual Exercises from Socrates to Foucault*. Edited by Arnold Davidson, translated by Michael Chase. Oxford: Blackwell Publishing.

Huber, Toni. 2009. [Review of Matthew Kapstein, *The Tibetans*.] *The Journal of Asian Studies*, 68.3 (August): 970–72.

Kapstein, Matthew T. 1986. "Collins, Parfit, and the Problem of Personal Identity in Two Traditions." *Philosophy East and West* 36.3: 289–98.

———. 1987. "Self and Personal Identity in Indian Buddhist Scholasticism: A Philosophical Investigation." PhD dissertation. Providence, RI: Brown University.

———. 1992. *The 'Dzam-thang Edition of the Collected Works of Kun-mkhyen Dol-po-pa Shes-rab Rgyal-mtshan: Introduction and Catalogue*. Delhi: Shedrup Books.

———. 1996. "*gDams ngag:* Tibetan Technologies of the Self." In *Tibetan Literature: Studies in Genre*, edited by José Ignacio Cabezón and Roger R. Jackson, 275–89. Ithaca, NY: Snow Lion Publications.

———. 1998. "A Pilgrimage of Rebirth Reborn: The 1992 Celebration of the Drigung Powa Chenmo." In *Buddhism in Contemporary Tibet: Religious Revival and Cultural Identity*, edited by Melvyn C. Goldstein and Matthew T. Kapstein, 95–119. Berkeley: University of California Press.

———. 2000. *The Tibetan Assimilation of Buddhism: Conversion, Contestation, and Memory*. New York: Oxford University Press.

———. 2001. *Reason's Traces: Identity and Interpretation in Indian and Tibetan Buddhist Thought*. Boston: Wisdom Publications.

———. 2006. *The Tibetans*. Malden, MA: Blackwell Publishing.

———. 2009. *The Rise of Wisdom Moon, by Krishna-mishra*. Clay Sanskrit Library 52. New York: New York University Press / JCC Foundation.

———. 2016. *The Great Transference at Drikung: Its Last Traditional Performance, 6–13 August 1992*. Munich: Garchen Stiftung.

———. 2018. "Collins and Parfit Three Decades On." *Sophia* 57.2: 207–10.

Kohn, Richard J. 2001. *Lord of the Dance: The Mani Rimdu Festival in Tibet and Nepal*. Albany: State University of New York Press.

La Vallée Poussin, Louis de, ed. 1970. *Madhyamakāvatāra par Candrakīrti: Traduction tibétaine*. Bibliotheca Buddhica 9. Osnabrück: Biblio Verlag. (Reprint.)

Li Xuezhu, ed. 2014. "*Madhyamakāvatāra-kārikā* Chapter 6." *Journal of Indian Philosophy* 43: 1–30.

Makransky, John. 1997. *Buddhahood Embodied: Sources of Controversy in India and Tibet*. Albany: State University of New York Press.

Murti, T. R. V. 1955. *The Central Philosophy of Buddhism: A Study of the Mādhyamika System*. London: George Allen & Unwin.

Pradhan, Prahlad, ed. 1975. *Abhidharmakośabhāṣyam of Vasubandhu*. Patna: K. P. Jayaswal Research Institute.

Priestley, Leonard C. D. C. 1999. *Pudgalavāda Buddhism: The Reality of the Indeterminate Self*. Toronto: University of Toronto Centre for South Asian Studies.

Ricard, Matthieu, trans. 1994. *The Life of Shabkar: The Autobiography of a Tibetan Yogin*. Albany: State University of New York Press.

Salvini, Mattia. 2011. "*Upādāyaprajñaptiḥ* and the Meaning of Absolutives: Grammar and Syntax in the Interpretation of Madhyamaka." *Journal of Indian Philosophy* 39: 229–44.

Sellars, Wilfrid. 1991. *Science, Perception and Reality*. Atascadero, CA: Ridgeview Publishing.

Stein, R. A. 1961. *Civilisation Tibétaine*. Paris: Dunod. (English translation by J. E. Stapleton Driver. London: Faber, 1972.)

Stearns, Cyrus. 1999. *The Buddha from Dolpo: A Study of the Life and Thought of the Tibetan Master Dolpopa Sherab Gyaltsen*. Albany: State University of New York Press.

Vetter, Tilmann, 1982. "Zum Problem der Person in Nāgārjunas Mūla-Madhyamaka-Kārikās." In *Offenbarung als Heilserfahrung im Christentum, Hinduismus und Buddhismus*, edited by Walter Strolz, Shizuteru Ueda, et al., 167–85. Freiberg: Herder.

———. 1992. "On the Authenticity of the Ratnāvalī." *Asiatische Studien / Études Asiatiques* 46.1: 492–506.

Walser, Joseph. 2005. *Nāgārjuna in Context: Mahāyāna Buddhism and Early Indian Culture*. New York: Columbia University Press.

Wiggins, David. 2016. *Continuants: Their Activity, Their Being, and Their Identity*. New York: Oxford University Press.

Williams, Paul, with Anthony Tribe and Alexander Wynne. 2012. *Buddhist Thought: A Complete Introduction to the Indian Tradition*. New York: Routledge.

Part 1
The Tibetan Assimilation of Buddhism

The Ten Virtues and the Tibetan Assimilation of Buddhism

Sam van Schaik[1]

One of the most impressive features of Matthew Kapstein's work is its range. Among other topics, he has written on history, ritual, philosophy, and codicology, all with equal fluency. I have been lucky enough to work with him on the early manuscripts and history of Tibetan Buddhism, where our interests have often coincided. Even before this, my own work was influenced and informed by his masterful book *The Tibetan Assimilation of Buddhism*, published in 2000. In this work covering a huge range of topics, Matthew looked at the evidence of the earliest Tibetan manuscripts, those found in the Dunhuang library cave in Chinese Central Asia.

Drawing on his extensive knowledge of previous scholarship on the Dunhuang manuscripts, Matthew was able to make some important statements about how the conversion of Tibet to Buddhism was carried out during the imperial period. In particular, he identified what he called the "emphatic propagation of the karma-saṃsāra cosmology" as the main feature of this conversion project:

> The Dunhuang Tibetan documents provide striking evidence of the active promotion of the Buddhist teachings of karma and saṃsāra among the Tibetans during the last centuries of the first millenium. The implication of the texts concerned seems to be that these doctrines were to some extent still contested or were at least felt in some ways to be problematic. Though emphatic propagation of the karma-saṃsāra cosmology would always remain a prominent dimension of Tibetan Buddhist doctrinal instruction, in both its

1. The research for this paper was carried out with the support of the European Research Council in the project *Beyond Boundaries: Religion, Region, Language and the State* (ERC grant agreement no. 609823).

> popular and scholastic facets, later Tibetan historians mostly seem to have forgotten that the conceptions of karma and saṃsāra were once controversial.[2]

In my own work on the Tibetan Buddhist manuscripts from Dunhuang, I have returned to these words again and again, finding them confirmed in new ways. This paper is a small gift in return, a discussion of a group of manuscripts on the ten Buddhist virtues that is clearly part of the project to instill the karma-saṃsāra cosmology in the Tibetan empire.

According to traditional Tibetan histories, one of the key features in the conversion of Tibet to Buddhism is a text called the *Sūtra of the Ten Virtues* (*Dge ba bcu'i mdo*), often abbreviated to the *Ten Virtues*. This text plays a key role in the narrative of how the seventh-century emperor Songtsen Gampo (Srong btsan sgam po, r. 605?–49) formulated Tibet's law code, as well as in the stories of the conversion of the eighth-century emperor Tri Songdetsen (Khri Srong lde btsan, r. 742–ca. 800) to Buddhism. For example, one of the earliest Tibetan histories of Buddhism, composed by Bsod nams rtse mo, states that Songtsen Gampo "formulated the laws based on the *Ten Virtues*."[3] The semi-mythical narrative of the arrival of Buddhism in Tibet during the imperial period contained in the *Maṇi Bka' 'bum* has a similar statement: "Then in order to lead Tibet to the dharma, [Songtsen Gampo] made the laws based on the *Sūtra of the Ten Virtues*."[4]

Slightly more details are given in another early historical narrative, the *Testimony of Ba* (*Sba/Dba' bzhed*). Here, we are told how the *Ten Virtues* was brought to Tibet by Thon mi Saṃbhota, who had been sent to India to develop a Tibetan alphabet:

> [Songtsen Gampo] gave an order and dispatched Thon mi Saṃbhota to bring back books containing the dharma and writing system of India. He returned, having found the *Ratnameghasūtra* and the *Ten Virtues*, bringing with him Kaṃśadatta, an Indian man of letters.[5]

2. Kapstein 2000, 34.

3. Dge ba bcu las brtsams te khrim bcas / (*Sa skya bka' 'bum* 2:343.2).

4. Dge ba bcu'i mdo la brten nas khrims bcas te / (*Ma ṇi bka' 'bum* 1:188b).

5. Rgya gar gi chos dang yi ge'i dpe len par thon mi gsam po ra la bka' stsal te btang nas / yig mkhan rgya gar gyi li byin zhes bgyi ba zhig kyang khrid de mchis/ chos dkon mchog sprin dang dge ba bcu btsal nas mchi te/ (*Dba' bzhed* MS, fol. 1v–2r). The manuscript of the *Dba' bzhed* contains an interlinear note listing some other texts as well.

And as in the other stories, the text of the *Ten Virtues* then forms the basis of the Tibetan system of law:

> Having conferred with the four close attendants who were learning to read and write, and having considered it for four months, the emperor devised a legal system with fundamentals derived from the *Ten Virtues* and had it written down.[6]

In some versions of the *Testimony of Ba*, the *Sūtra of the Ten Virtues* also plays a role in the Buddhist education of Tri Songdetsen, as suggested by the Korean Chan monk Reverend Kim:[7]

> First the king should read the *Sūtra of the Ten Virtues*, and from that he will develop faith and understand correct activity. Next he should read the *Vajracchedikā*, in order to understand the correct view and develop great faith. Next he should read the *Śālistamba* in order to understand the fusion of activity and view, which will result in his faith in the dharma.[8]

The text also features in later histories of Buddhism that draw on these foundational works. Thus it is surprising that the *Sūtra of the Ten Virtues* did not survive to be included in the Tibetan Buddhist canon. We might wonder whether it actually existed, or was another semi-mythical element of these early narratives, an idealized text as an emblem of the teaching of the ten virtues. Clues that some such text did exist are found in two imperial library catalogues, the *Ldan dkar ma* and *'Phang thang ma*. These works list a text under the name the *Extracted Sūtra of the Ten Virtues* (*Dge ba bcu dang blang ba'i mdo*).[9] This

6. Zha bring nang pa yi ge bslabs bzhi dang mol te / btsan pos dgongs nas zla ba bzhi'i bar du bka' khrims dge ba bcu las gzhi blangs mdzad de yi ge bris so / (*Dba' bzhed* MS, f.2r).

7. In the *Testimony of Ba*, Reverend Kim (Gyim hwa shang) gives advice to Tri Songdetsen's emissaries on the eve of their journey to China to investigate Buddhism there; see Wangdu and Diemberger 2000, 48–49. Some of Kim's Chan teachings were translated into Tibetan and survived; see van Schaik 2015, 13–14 and 51–52.

8. Dang po dge ba bcu'i mdo bklags/ de la rgyal po dad pa skyes/ spyod pa dag par go de nas rdo rje gcod pa bklags/ de lta ba dag par go dad pa cher skyes/ de nas sa lu ljang pa bklags/ lta spyod zung 'brel du go nas chos la yid ches (*Sba bzhed*, p.15.)

9. This is number 266 in the *Ldan dkar ma*, where it is in the section on sūtras translated from the Chinese. In the *'Phang thang ma* (fol. 21), the title is *'Phags pa dge ba bcu dang du blang ba'i mdo* and occurs in the section on texts taken from rare, old manuscripts; see Lalou 1953 and *Dkar chag 'phang thang ma*.

is an odd title, suggesting that the text in question was taken (*blang ba*) from a larger text. As we will see, this is one mystery that we can probably solve.

The text of the *Ten Virtues* itself seems not to have survived in Tibet's received tradition; I have not found the text in any canonical or extra-canonical collections. However, there are several manuscripts containing texts on the ten virtues that were preserved in the Dunhuang library cave. Among these, the most common is simply called the *Ten Virtues* (*Dge ba bcu*), of which five copies survive.[10] Another text, surviving only in one manuscript copy, has a longer descriptive title, *Sūtra of the Ten Virtues, Derived from the Ārya Daśabhūmika* (*'Phags pa sa bcu pa gnyis kyi nang nas dge ba bcu 'byung ba'i mdo*).[11] As the title suggests, this is an extract from the *Daśabhūmika Sūtra* (hereafter referred to as the *Derived Sūtra*).[12] Given the similarity of this title to the one found in the imperial catalogues, the two texts might in fact be the same.

The language and orthography of the manuscripts containing the *Ten Virtues* tends to conform less to the translation standards established in the early ninth century, suggesting that it was translated or composed before that time.[13] The *Derived Sūtra*, on the other hand, is clearly extracted from the version of the *Daśabhūmika Sūtra* that is found in the Tibetan canon, dating from after the reforms in translation terminology.

Some of the manuscript copies of the *Ten Virtues* also give an impression of antiquity. The scroll IOL Tib J 606 is written in a semi-cursive style similar to that seen in official documents from the imperial period.[14] The pecha folio Pelliot tibétain 968 has the same dimensions as the folios used for the copying of the *Perfection of Wisdom Sūtra* for the Tibetan emperor Tri Tsukdetsen (Khri Gtsug lde btsan, r. 815–41). While the paper might have been used

10. The five manuscripts that contain the text called the *Ten Virtues* are IOL Tib J 606 and 660; Pelliot tibétain 4/7, 968, and 971. Some of these are fragmentary and missing titles and colophons but clearly contain the same text as the more complete copies. There are a number of other manuscripts with different texts on the ten virtues, but because all of these are fragmentary, it is not clear whether they come from texts on the ten virtues specifically or whether the ten virtues appear as part of a broader topic. These are Pelliot tibétain 969, 972, 973, and 974.

11. This manuscript is Pelliot tibétain 970. I am not sure of the meaning of *gnyis* in this colophon. Stein (1986, 183n35) seems to have missed the derivation from the *Daśabhūmika sūtra*. Stein (1986, 183n35) also seems to suggest that Pelliot tibétain 971, 972, 973 and 974 contain the same text, but this is not the case.

12. *Daśabhūmikasūtra*, Dergé *bka' 'gyur*, 36:187b–190b.

13. Scherrer-Schaub 2002, 313–16.

14. On the style of the imperial-period official manuscripts, see van Schaik 2013, 123–24 and 130.

The ten nonvirtues in the Dunhuang texts and the Mahāvyutpatti

	Sūtra of the Ten Virtues	*Derived Sūtra*	*Mahāvyutpatti*
1. killing	srog gcod	srog gchod	srog gcod
2. stealing	dku ba	ma byin par len pa	ma byin par len pa
3. sexual misconduct	g.yem ba	log par g.yem	log par g.yem pa
4. lying	rdzun smra	rdzun du smra ba	rdzun du smra ba
5. slander	pra ma	phra ma'i tshig	phra mar smra ba
6. harsh words	ngag rtsub	zhe gcod pa'i tshigs†	tshig rtsub po smra ba
7. gossip	tshig gyal	tshig khyal ba	tshig bkyal ba
8. covetous thoughts	chags par sems pa*	chag sems†	brnab sems
9. malevolent thoughts	ngan du sems pa*	gnod sems	gnod sems
10. wrong views	log par lta ba	log lta	log par lta ba

* The order of these two is reversed in the *Ten Virtues*

† These forms are also found in the canonical *Daśabhūmika Sūtra.*

in later years, the writing style is also comparable with the scribal style that was used in these sūtras.[15] Some other manuscripts of the *Ten Virtues*—IOL Tib J 660, Pelliot tibétain 971—may have been written in the mid-ninth century as well.[16] By contrast, the single manuscript of the *Derived Sūtra* shows a style that is only seen in later manuscripts, probably from the latter part of the tenth century.[17]

15. The folio is 20 x 70 cm, placing it in the type II category of *Perfection of Wisdom* manuscripts, as discussed in Iwao 2012. These were probably made locally in Dunhuang itself.

16. One of the complete versions, Pelliot tibétain 4, part of a compendium in a concertina format manuscript, is probably from the tenth century.

17. The style is similar to that of the scribe responsible for several manuscripts containing mahāyoga tantric texts; see van Schaik and Dalton 2004.

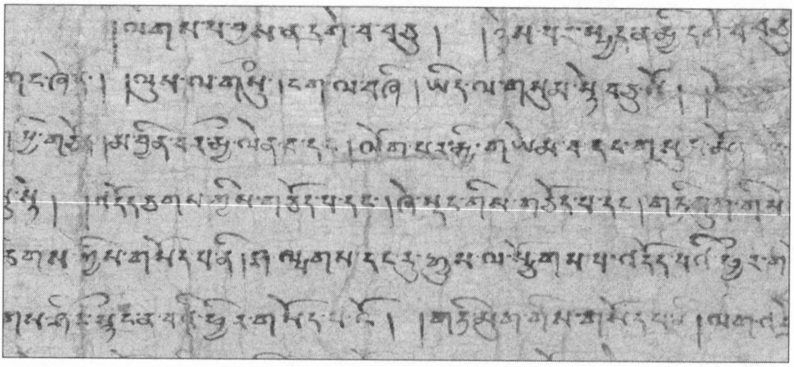

Detail of the scroll IOL Tib J 606.

As for the text of *The Ten Virtues*, it is not presented as a sūtra and reads more like a treatise, though no author is mentioned in any of the colophons. The colophon in IOL Tib J 606 simply calls the text the *Ten Virtues* (*Dge ba bcu*), while the colophon in Pelliot tibétain 4, probably a later copy, calls it *An Extended Treatise on the Ten Virtues* (*Dge ba bcu rgyas par bcad*). The discussion of the ten virtues in the text is fairly standard; it offers a description of the ten negative actions to avoid, subdividing some of these actions in more specific categories.

Some of the descriptions of the negative actions are culturally interesting. For example, the discussion on killing mentions hunting:

> "Killing because of desire" means killing due to desire for meat and hide, or for horn and wool, and so on.[18]

The discussion of lying mentions sharp practices used by merchants:

> "Stealing by trickery" means things like making weights and measures, disputing and rejecting the payment, then making new ones, selling the goods elsewhere, and making a profit.[19]

18. *De la ’dod chags gyis gsod ces bya ba ni / sha lpags dang / ru rgyus la stsogs pa ’dod pa’i phyir gsod pa’o /.* This passage contains the archaic term *ru rgyus*, which also appears in *Old Tibetan Chronicle* (Pelliot tibétain 1287, l.415).

19. *De la sgyus brku zhes bya ba ni / bye srang bco zhing / shags dang rtsis dor dang / khe spogs gsar byed la stsogs pa byed pa’o /.*

The discussion of sexual misconduct mentions three kinds of "protected" women with whom it is improper to have sex:

> Of these, "protected by dharma" means that the dharma prohibits sleeping with one's mother, sister, or with animals. "Protected by the king" means that it is not permissible to have sex with the wife of a ruler. "Protected by the parents" means that for a male or female relative, or anyone in a similar role to have sexual relations with children, is totally improper and not permitted.[20]

The discussion of lying includes those who lie about their spiritual achievements in order to claim the status of a teacher; such people are said to include the *bon po* and the *bon mo*. Something called "necessary lying" is also mentioned and is defined as lying because one's life and position are endangered (*srog srid la bab*). This is an Old Tibetan legal term, which appears in a number of early inscriptions, including the Zhol pillar.[21] These and other features of the text suggest that it was composed, or possibly translated from an unknown source, during the Tibetan imperial period, before the standardization of translation terminology in the early ninth century.[22]

This brief codicological and orthographic survey of *Ten Virtues* does suggest that the text was in circulation during the Tibetan imperial period. I will conclude this paper by looking at some further supporting evidence for the composition and circulation of a text on the ten Buddhist virtues during the Tibetan imperial period.

In the extended edict by Tri Songdetsen on establishing Buddhism in Tibet, it is said:

> If one behaves well through body, speech, and mind, that is virtue; if one behaves badly, that is sin . . . What is virtue? Primarily, it is the ten virtues. What is nonvirtue? Primarily, it is the ten nonvirtues.[23]

20. *De la chos gyis bsrung zhes bya ba ni / ma dang bu sring dang / byol song la chos gyis myi nyal ba'o / / rgyal pos bsrung zhes bya ba ni / myi dbang ba'i bud myed la byi ba byed du myi gnang ba'o / / pha mas bsrung zhes bya ba ni / bu tsa phos mos gang yang 'dra ste / log shig tu g.yem tu myi gnang ba'o /.*

21. See Coblin 1991, 316.

22. Other archaic terms in the text include *lha dpal* for *phan yon*—see Stein 1984, 263; *lce mchin*, an archaic term meaning "eloquence" that also appears in Pelliot tibétain 1283; *g.yog bran*, a term for servants or bondsmen that appears in Pelliot tibétain 1071, 1072, and 1283.

23. *Lus dang ngag dang yid gsum nas legs par spyad to cog ni dge ba 'gyur / nyes pa spyad to cog ni*

Compare the opening words of the *Ten Virtues*:

> It is said: "If one acts well, that is ten virtues; if one acts badly, that is the ten nonvirtues." What then are the ten nonvirtues?[24]

The source of this quote that opens the *Ten Virtues* is not specified, and it may not be from any specific text. It is not, however, dissimilar to Tri Songdetsen's edict. This edict also contains a reference to a text supposedly composed to give the correct interpretation of the dharma for the Tibetans:

> A council was held about how the right path should not be altered and how it could be spread wider. Thus an excellent summary of the dharma was made.[25]

I am not suggesting that this is a reference to the composition of the *Ten Virtues* itself, but it does indicate that brief summaries (*mdo*) of the key points of the dharma were written during Tri Songdetsen's time as part of his project to install Buddhism as the religion of his state. Given the evidence that we have reviewed above for the existence of the text of the *Ten Virtues* in the imperial period, the text seems to be one of the outcomes of this aspiration.

Another link between the Tibetan imperium and the *Ten Virtues* can be found in a Chinese manuscript from Dunhuang.[26] This scroll contains a copy of a text called *Dasheng jing zuanyao yi* 大乘經纂要義, or *Summary of the Essential Points of the Mahāyāna Sūtras*.[27] The following colophon, also in Chinese, comes at the end of the text:

> 壬寅六月大蕃國有　讚普印信, 并此十善經本, 傳流諸州, 流行讀誦, 後八月十六日寫畢記
>
> In the sixth month of the water-tiger year, a letter sealed with the Tibetan emperor's seal of Great Tibet, with a copy of the *Sūtra*

sdig par 'gyur / . . . dge ba gang zhe na dge ba bcu la bstsogs pa'o / mi dge ba gang zhe na / mi dge bcu la bstsogs pa'o / (text from Richardson 1998, 97).

24. *Legs par byas na dge ba bcu / nyes par spyad na myi dge ba bcu zhes bya'o // myi dge ba bcu gang zhe na /.*

25. *De lam legs par ni ji ltar mi 'gyur ched ni ji ltar che zhe na/ chos kyi mdo ni legs su bgyi bas /* (text from Richardson 1998, 98).

26. Or.8210/S.3966.

27. Another scroll, Or.8210/S.553, contains the earlier part of the same text. The sūtra is also found in Pelliot chinois 2298. The canonical reference is Taishō 85.2817.1183a–1184a.

> *of Ten Virtues*, was sent to every prefecture to be circulated and recited. On the sixteenth day of the following eighth month, this copy was made.

As Daishun Ueyama pointed out, this water-tiger year can only be the year 822. Therefore, the emperor who is mentioned here must be Tri Tsukdetsen.[28] On the face of it, this looks like a striking confirmation of the promotion of the text of the *Ten Virtues* by the Tibetan imperium.[29] And this seems to be supported by the fact that we have at least five copies of the *Ten Virtues*, some of which appear to date to the imperial period.

Unfortunately it is not quite that simple. While the above-quoted colophon mentions a *Sūtra of Ten Virtues* (*Shi shan jing* 十善經), this is not the text of which it is the colophon, since it comes after a Chinese text called the *Summary of the Essential Points of the Mahāyāna Sūtras*.[30] The Chinese text does have a section on the ten virtues, so perhaps in this case the Chinese *Summary of the Essential Points of the Mahāyāna Sūtras* was copied by a Chinese scribe living in Dunhuang instead of the Tibetan *Ten Virtues*, to fulfill the emperor's order.[31]

It is a rare thing in the study of early Tibet to be able to link the traditional narratives about a text with contemporaneous evidence of the circulation of that text, and rarer still to have manuscript examples of the text itself available to us. So while the content of the *Ten Virtues* is nothing out of the ordinary, the way that it brings together these different strands of historiography is really quite extraordinary. We probably have to remain skeptical about the claim in the traditional histories that the text of the *Ten Virtues* formed the basis for Tibetan lawmaking in the reign of Songtsen Gampo. Nevertheless, the very fact that this became the accepted narrative was an important factor

28. See Ueyama 1990, 314–23.

29. Thanks to an imperial-period Sino-Tibetan glossary from Dunhuang, we can confirm that *shi shan* 十善 was considered equivalent to *dge ba bcu*. This appears in Pelliot tibétain 1257, 7a, l.7, column 3. See Apple and Apple 2017, 132.

30. A detailed summary of this text is given in Ueyama 1990, 320–31.

31. There is no *Sutra of Ten Virtues* (*Shishan jing* 十善經) in the Chinese Buddhist canon, though there are similarly titled texts: *Shishanye dao jing* 十善業道經 (Taishō 15.600) and *Shou shishanjie jing* 受十善戒經 (Taishō 24.1486). Neither seems to be related to the Tibetan text of the *Ten Virtues* or the text derived from the *Daśabhūmika*. Stein 1986, 183n35, references two Dunhuang manuscripts containing the *Shou shishanjie jing*: S.5175.2 and S.2565.2, though in fact this is only one manuscript: Or.8210/S.2565 (the second text); the number 5175 is the reference number for the same manuscript used by Lionel Giles in his catalogue of Chinese Buddhist manuscripts from Dunhuang (Giles 1957).

in the way Tibetans came to understand their legal system.[32] The number of copies of the *Ten Virtues* among the Tibetan Dunhuang collections, and their antiquity, is interesting enough; taken together with Tri Songdetsen's statement about writing a summary of the dharma, and Tri Tsukdetsen's order to have the *Sūtra of the Ten Virtues* copied and circulated throughout the empire, we can really begin to see how this text (and others like it) were part of the project to embed the *karma-saṃsāra* cosmology in Tibetan culture.

32. See Pirie 2013 and Charles Ramble's paper in this volume.

Works Cited

Apple, James, and Shinobu Apple. 2017. "A Re-evaluation of Pelliot tibétain 1257: An Early Tibetan-Chinese Glossary from Dunhuang." *Revue d'Études Tibétaines* 42: 68–180.

Coblin, W. S. 1991. "A Study of the Old Tibetan Shangshu Paraphrase." *Journal of the American Oriental Society* 111: 303–22 and 523–39.

Giles, Lionel. 1957. *Descriptive Catalogue of the Chinese Manuscripts from Tun-huang in the British Museum*. London: The British Museum.

Iwao, Kazushi. 2012. "The Purpose of Sūtra Copying in Dunhuang Under the Tibetan Rule." In *Dunhuang Studies: Prospects and Problems for the Coming Century of Research*, edited by Irina Popova and Liu Yi, 102–5. Saint Petersburg: Slavia.

Kapstein, Matthew T. 2000. *The Tibetan Assimilation of Buddhism: Conversion, Contestation, and Memory*. New York: Oxford University Press.

Lalou, Marcelle. 1953. "Les Textes Bouddhiques au Temps du Roi Khri-sroṅ-lde-bcan." *Journal asiatique* 241: 313–54.

Pirie, Fernanda. 2013. "Law and Religion in Historic Tibet." In *Religion in Disputes*, edited by F. and K. von Benda-Beckmann, M. Ramstedt, and B. Turner, 231–47. London: Palgrave Macmillan.

Richardson, Hugh. 1998. *High Peaks, Pure Earth: Collected Writings on Tibetan History and Culture*. London: Serindia Publications.

van Schaik, Sam. 2013. "Dating Early Tibetan Manuscripts: A Paleographical Method." In *Scribes, Texts and Rituals in Early Tibet and Dunhuang*, edited by B. Dotson, K. Iwao, and T. Takeuchi, 119–35. Wiesbaden: Reichert Verlag.

———. 2015: *Tibetan Zen: Discovering a Lost Tradition*. Boston: Snow Lion Publications.

van Schaik, Sam, and Jacob Dalton. 2004. "Where Chan and Tantra Meet: Buddhist Syncretism in Dunhuang." In *The Silk Road: Trade, Travel, War and Faith*, edited by Susan Whitfield, 61–71. London: The British Library Press.

Scherrer-Schaub, Cristina. 2002. "Enacting Words: A Diplomatic Analysis of the Imperial Decrees (*bkas bcad*) and Their Application in the *Sgra sbyor bam po gñis pa* Tradition." *Journal of the International Association of Tibetan Studies* 25.1–2: 263–340.

Stein, R. A. 1984. "Tibetica Antiqua II. L'usage de métaphores pour des distinctions honorifiques à l'époque des rois tibétains." *Bulletin de l'École française d'Extrême-Orient* 73: 257–72.

———. 1986. "Tibetica Antiqua IV. La tradition relative au début du bouddhisme au Tibet." *Bulletin de l'École française d'Extrême-Orient* 75: 169–96.

Ueyama Daishun. 1990. *Tonkō bukkyō no kenkyū* [*Studies on Buddhism in Dunhuang*]. Kyōto: Hōzōkan.

Wangdu, Pasang, and Hildegard Diemberger. 2000. *dBa' bzhed: The Royal Narrative Concerning the Bringing of the Buddha's Doctrine to Tibet.* Vienna: Verlag der Österreichischen Akademie der Wissenschaften.

Tibetan Sources

Dba' bzhed MS, reproduced in Wangdu and Diemberger 2000.

Dkar chag 'phang thang ma / Sgra sbyor bam po gnyis pa. Beijing: Mi rigs dpe skrun khang, 2003.

Ma ṇi bka' 'bum. Edited by Trayang and Jamyang Samten. Delhi: n.p., 1975.

Sa skya bka' 'bum. Tokyo: The Tōyō Bunko, 1968.

Sba bzhed. Edited by Gonpo Gyaltsen. Beijing: Mi rigs dpe skrun khang, 1980.

Manuscript Collections

IOL Tib J. Tibetan manuscripts from Dunhuang in the Stein collection, British Library, London.

Or.8210/S. Chinese manuscripts from Dunhuang in the Stein collection, British Library, London.

Pelliot tibétain. Tibetan manuscripts from Dunhuang in the Pelliot collection, Bibliothèque nationale de France, Paris.

Pelliot chinois. Chinese manuscripts from Dunhuang in the Pelliot collection, Bibliothèque nationale de France, Paris.

The Legal Foundations of Tibetan Religious Thought[1]

Charles Ramble

Introduction

Almost all Tibetan legal codes from the post-imperial period explicitly derive their legitimacy from the Buddhist values they purport to enshrine. The source to which the later Tibetan accounts refer is the *Mi chos gtsang ma bcu drug*, attributed to Srong btsan sgam po and said to be based on the *Sūtra of the Ten Virtues* (*Daśakuśalasūtra*), and lawmakers ever thereafter have presented their tracts as measures for the realization of these basic principles. The conviction among Tibetans that the legal system of the Ganden Phodrang (Dga' ldan pho brang) government was founded in Buddhist tenets remains deeply entrenched. An idea of the tenacity of this belief may be obtained from the work of Rebecca French, whose study of the Central Tibetan legal system conveys the conviction of her principal informant, a diaspora Tibetan who had practiced law in the pre-1959 era, concerning the religious underpinnings of his profession.

In the absence of evidence to the contrary, most researchers have considered the *Sūtra of the Ten Virtues* as a late fabrication aimed at giving a Buddhist legitimacy to an essentially secular institution.[2] In his important contribution to the present volume, however, Sam van Schaik demonstrates that the *Sūtra of the Ten Virtues* and similar texts were in fact widely circulated during the imperial period. According to van Schaik, even if the work is unlikely to have been the basis of lawmaking in the time of Srong btsan sgam po, it was "clearly part of the project to instill the *karma-saṃsāra* cosmology in the Tibetan empire," and was "an important factor in the way Tibetans came to understand their legal system" at a period earlier than is generally supposed.

1. Owing to limitations of space, the Tibetan text of passages cited here has not been included. For an extended version of this article, see www.kalpa-bon.com/articles/legal-foundations-tibetan-religious-thought.

2. See, for example, Schuh 1984, 300.

The antiquity of the *Sūtra of the Ten Virtues* notwithstanding, the visibility of the debate over the degree to which Buddhism may or may not have influenced legal thinking in Tibet may have eclipsed certain fundamental aspects of the relationship between Tibetan law and religion, to the extent of blinding us to the existence of important structural properties that they share. In this article, I will go so far as to suggest that a significant area of Tibetan religious belief is actually *based on* legal principles. In order to explore this possibility further, however, we need to adopt a more comprehensive understanding of both religion and law.

Aleatoric Devices

Ritual may not be exclusive to religion—indeed, several studies have been devoted to establishing the validity of the idea of secular ritual[3]—or even intrinsic to it, but ritual nevertheless forms a significant part of religion. It also forms an important part of Tibetan law. Among the different types of rituals that feature in both domains, perhaps the most salient is the use of procedures that manifest the will of a divine agency. These aleatoric techniques may be used in the selection of officials, in determining the outcome of a dispute, or for assessing the efficacy of a ritual. Here I shall compare the use of two such devices as they are used in judicial and religious contexts.

In their study of Sakya principality, Cassinelli and Ekvall state that there were "three standard methods used . . . to resolve stalemates" in legal cases.[4] It is the second and third of these methods that are of particular interest here. One, "involving least tension and apprehension for the contestants," entailed taking a stone out of a jar of opaque oil:

> The jar contained one white and one black pebble. The accused drew a single pebble and then replaced it; then his accuser drew a single pebble. The drawing continued until one draw one man drew white and the other black. The issue was then incontrovertibly resolved in the favor of the man who had drawn white.[5]

The other procedure involved rolling dice, and the authors illustrate its application with reference to a particular case from the 1940s. A man was found

3. See, for example Moore and Meyerhoff 1977.

4. Cassinelli and Ekvall 1969, 175.

5. Cassinelli and Ekvall 1969, 176n15.

murdered in a village, and his brother accused a neighbor of being the perpetrator. Since the case involved a homicide, it was taken to the capital for trial.

> The Law Officials ordered that a yak be killed and its hide spread, bloody side up, on the courtroom floor. The accused, without clothes and with his hair let down knelt on one edge and his accuser, normally attired, knelt facing him on the other edge. . . .The total of the accused's roll was higher than that of his accuser, and so he won the first round. He lost the second round, but won the third, and was thereupon declared innocent of the killing.[6]

In both these cases gods are invoked not as judges, much less as agents of retribution, but rather to vindicate the position of the respective parties; they are summoned as witnesses.

The use of black and white stones and also the rolling of dice are integral parts of certain Tibetan religious ceremonies, notably the ritual for the retrieval of lost souls (*bla 'gugs*). In the course of the ceremony, a representative of the patient performs certain procedures to determine whether his or her soul has been restored.[7] A copper cauldron is set on a stand and filled with water to which milk and calendula petals are added. The officiant places at the bottom of the cauldron six white and six black stones that are referred to respectively as "soul stones" (*bla rdo*) and "demon stones" (*bdud rdo*). At a certain point an assistant plunges his hand into the murky water and extracts a stone. A white stone signifies that that soul has been retrieved, whereas a black one means that this part of the ritual must be performed again.

The patient must then play a game of dice with the soul's demonic captor. A representative of the patient rolls a pair of white dice on a white mat, using his right hand. The demon is represented by a dough figure, and a pair of black dice are rolled on a black mat on his behalf by a woman, using her left hand. Each side has three throws, but the patient has only to win one round in order for the ritual to be considered successful. Before the dice are thrown, various supernatural powers are invoked:

> Hey! May the lama and the tutelary divinity be impartial witnesses; may the divine protectors of Bon be impartial witnesses; may the dakinis and the treasure guardians be impartial witnesses; and may

6. Cassinelli and Ekvall 1969, 176.

7. For two descriptions of this ritual, see Karmay 1998 and Ramble 2010.

> the territorial gods, the earth lords and the eight classes of demigods act as impartial witnesses today![8]

Far from being entreated to take the side of the patient and to coerce the demon into giving up the soul, the divinities are being asked to remain neutral and simply to bear witness to the outcome of the game.

Oaths and Truth

The procedures described above for establishing the guilt or innocence of a suspected criminal are similar to the protocols for certain oaths. John Claude White describes the measures for swearing an oath that entail the use of hot—rather than simply opaque—oil. A black stone and a white stone of similar size were put into a pot containing boiling oil, and the pot arranged so that the stones could not be seen. The person on trial would extract one stone. If he removed the white stone without any burning, he would be declared innocent, guilty if he picked the black stone. There is no suggestion that any divinities are to be invoked here as enforcers.[9]

The procedure is a trial by ordeal, but as Schuh has pointed out, Tibetan does not distinguish between oath-swearing and undergoing an ordeal. The treatment of the murder suspect described by Cassinelli and Ekvall also finds its parallels in an oath. A document from south Mustang, undated but probably from the nineteenth century, records the procedure whereby an agreement was reached over the pasture boundaries of four contiguous territories.

> Having invited [*lacuna*] as witness(es), in order to establish their pasture boundaries . . . [representatives of] the four commmunities spread out a fresh hide as a seat; they wore red copper vessels on their heads, and came out naked, with black yak-hair ropes tied around their necks, and after swearing an oath, they established the boundaries as follows . . .[10]

There is no mention either here, or anywhere later in the document, of any divine enforcers, only the opening reference to calling someone or something as witness.

An oath is a declaration of truth; that is to say, an actual state of affairs.

8. Ramble 2010, 215.

9. Cited in Schuh 1984, 294.

10. Ramble 2008a, document HMA/Te/Tib/56.

The etymological and conceptual connection between the Sanskrit terms for "truth" and "being" have been discussed by the recipient of the present volume, Matthew Kapstein, with whom it has been my privilege to work in close association at the École Pratique des Hautes Études for almost a decade. It is the importance of this correspondence, as he points out, that has led some authors to render the term *satya*, "truth," as "reality."[11] For Giorgio Agamben, it is precisely in this adequation between the signifier (the word) and the signified (the reality) that the force of the oath lies. Suggesting that language originated *pari passu* with ethos, he argues that "the oath expresses the demand . . . for the speaking animal to put its nature at stake in language and to bind together in an ethical and political connection words, things and actions."[12] The involvement of divinities is a later elaboration. A component of many Tibetan rituals is the procedure knowns as *bden pa bdar*, the "invocation of the truth," or "truth telling." This is an illocutionary act in which the priest ensures the efficacy of the rite he is performing by formally declaring the truth of certain divinities whom he names, or indeed of the doctrine itself. Here is an example of such an invocation from a nineteenth-century Bönpo work:

> The invocation of the truth: . . . by relying on the power and might of the truth of the Buddha's word, the truth of the word of Bön, the truth of Gshen rab and of the eternity-beings (i.e., bodhisattvas) . . . may all [harmful beings] instantly be summoned into this effigy as helplessly as if they were sparrows pursued by a hawk.[13]

Here, the force of the ritual derives from the truth of Bön and its divinities, and it is this that renders demons compliant with the intention of the ritual. The Tibetan procedure of *bden pa bdar* has antecedents not only in Indian Buddhism but in Indian religion more generally, where it appears under a variety of names such as *satyavacana*, *satyavādya*, *satyavākya*, and so forth.[14] In a classic study of the subject, E. W. Burlingame makes the important point that, although the power of truth is often closely associated with the power of righteousness (goodness, merit, and so forth) and also—as in the extract from Bönpo work cited above—with "the superhuman might of spirits, deities and Buddhas,"

11. Kapstein 1997, 421.

12. Agamben 2011, 69.

13. Gsang sngags gling pa 1998, 478.

14. Brown 1972, 252.

> such mention does not mean, however, that the Act of Truth in any way depends for its efficacy upon the co-operation of these other forces, powerful though they are. Truth, in and by itself all-powerful and irresistible, is essentially distinct from them, and operates independently of them.[15]

The gods, then, are not integral to the efficacy of the act of truth, however much they may appear to be in certain, especially later, works. There are two possible mechanisms whereby both ritual and the act of truth operate: one—purportedly later—is through the agency of gods who are induced or coerced into action by the ritual; and the other spontaneously, through the intrinsic force of the performance itself, which is "powerful in its own right." Now, what is of particular interest here is the intriguing suggestion, to be found in several works, that the impeccable execution of a ritual is itself no guarantee of its efficacy, either through the power of the performance or through the secondary agency of the gods. Two examples will serve here by way of illustration of a strikingly different understanding of the ritual dynamic. The first is from the mythic narrative (*smrang*) section of a ritual for the subjugation of "vampires of loss" (*god sri*), a category of demon that preys on livestock.

> First, secure the support of the gods; invoke them as witnesses, then summon the vampire of loss and diffuse it [into the effigies]. If there is an assistant, perform the invocation of the truth and then say as follows: one day all the gods and demons of the phenomenal world . . . failed to appreciate this as the truth. The eight haughty ones of the phenomenal world did not support it. At the beginning of the world ages, in the sky, the demons caused hail to fall, and on earth many creatures died. . . . From the bones of horses that were left in the houses, the following year there came vampires of loss of horses.[16]

The disturbing implication of the passage seems to be the following: the utterance of the truth has no intrinsic power, and neither does it have the ability to coerce the gods who are present into implementing it. The gods act not as enforcers but as witnesses to the truth that has been enunciated, and it is their dereliction of this duty that has resulted in the rise of vampires.

The second example, from the collection of Bönpo funerary texts known

15. Burlingame 1917, 432.

16. *God sri*, fols. 1v–2r.

as the *Mu cho'i khrom 'dur*, reinforces the notion that the ritual has no intrinsic power:

> Protect the near and dear of our benefactor, and witness that we have performed the repulsion of external adversities. If we perform the "driving away" of our enemies and they do not leave, if we perform the "repulsion" and they are not repelled, if we perform the "subjugation" and they are not tamed but continue to harm us, fulfill your role as mediators and witnesses![17]

Just as, in the previous example, the gods were at liberty to endorse or to ignore the declaration of truth, in the present case the proper execution of the rite does not automatically elicit the compliance of the demons that are to be expelled. They may decide not to comply, but in this case, the text seems to say, they are in transgression of the law, and it is the duty of the gods—who are, again, present as witnesses—to testify that the ritual was performed as it should be, and that the priest is in the right.

The two examples given here are not anomalies but manifestations of a cultural understanding of ritual as a legal process. The following section will pursue this line of inquiry by exploring a principle that has been underestimated in discussions of Tibetan law, and is also crucial to our understanding of ritual. This is the notion of precedent.

Res judicata *and* Stare decisis

To make a claim for the importance of precedent in Tibetan law may seem surprising in the light of Rebecca French's insistence that the legal system made no provision for it, and that each case was considered on its own merits. This claim invites closer scrutiny. French suggests that Tibetan law did not observe the principles—present in British and American legal systems, for example—of *stare decisis* and *res judicata* (1995, 139). Leaving aside the latter, let us consider the status of *stare decisis*. The formulation, an abbreviation of the phrase *stare decisis et non quieta movere*, "to stand by decisions and not disturb the undisturbed," supports the principle that cases should be assessed in the light of comparable examples from the past.

If the examples of actual cases cited below categorically contradict Rebecca French's argument, I do not think that that is because her claim is wrong. The legal universe from which French derives her conclusions is the official

17. *Sngags kyi mdo 'dur*, pp. 81–82.

judiciary connected with the Ganden Phodrang government, and the premises underlying this institution were not ubiquitous. In her study of legal anthropology, Fernanda Pirie reminds us that a single nation or even a small-scale society may be host to a multiplicity of legal systems, even without the spurious extension of the label "law" to systems of social regulation such as kinship (Pirie 2013, 14). The examples cited below are from Mustang, in Nepal, but they are not significantly different from similar documents from Central Tibet. In both cases, we know that local communities tried to settle disputes internally, without recourse to national structures, since such engagements were invariably costly and intrusive, and often brutal.

Legal decisions and undertakings are not *always* made on the basis of precedent. However, when there is a departure from established models, we find a clause stating that this is the case. Explicit breaks with the past are uncommon and are situation-specific rather than the "default" procedure. Two examples may be cited. In 1910, a family of priestly rank was ordered by the council of the commoner village on whose territory it lived to provide one member for public labor. The family contested the levy by citing an earlier incident when the local lord had requisitioned labor for building his palace and demanded a representative from each household. The same family had argued that, as priests, they had always been exempt from corvée, and the lord had accepted their position. In 1910 they were able to use this case as successful grounds for exemption from public labor.[18]

In another case from 1890, two villages had a dispute about usufruct of a salina that they had traditionally shared. The document reasserts the right of both communities to use the salt. The basis for this decision entails two established precedents. First, there is an appeal to deep antiquity—the resource has been shared "since ancient times, and this shall endure till the end of the world age." The second precedent is more recent and refers to the confirmation of this traditional arrangement by the king of Jumla. Since Jumla's hold over Mustang was broken by the Gorkhas in 1789, the point of reference must be prior to this date. The fact that here, as in the previous example, several precedents are invoked is significant, and by no means unusual.[19]

These cases serve to underscore the point that Tibetan law, as represented by these documents from a culturally Tibetan enclave, set a high value on the need to "stand by decisions and not disturb the undisturbed;" courses of action were legitimized by reference to similar procedures that had been followed in the past.

18. Ramble 2016, document HMA/LTshognam/Tib/07.

19. Ramble 2008a, document HMA/Te/Tib/43.

Tibetan Ritual

There are, as Karmay says, broadly two types of Tibetan ritual, *sādhana* (*sgrub thabs*) and *gto*. The *gto* ritual, which is concerned with curing illnesses and healing more general natural afflictions by propitiating gods and demons,

> was often concerned with the everyday life of the people. It functions to create social cohesion and moral obligation among the members of the village community. It encourages communal organization centering upon the cult of the local spirits connected with water, soil, rocks, and mountains. The defining feature of these rituals is the mythical antecedent, *smrang* or *rabs*. Thus *gto* rituals generally begin with a reference to a preceding action or a sort of event that is supposed to have taken place in the distant past. It appears that without this precedent, the ritual itself does not seem to have much significance regarding the effect that it is intended to have.[20]

The evocation of precedents in mythic narratives is particularly striking in the ritual literature from Dunhuang. For now, let us consider the particular example of numerous precedents in one text, PT1285. The text, relating to a ritual for healing victims of poisoning, consists of an extensive narrative, the *smrang*, which contains examples of how the ritual has been successful in the past. There is not just one story but at least nine. It is, as Rolf Stein says, a sort of jurisprudence: it lists all the examples of resolution in the history of this type of case.[21] The point is that, in archaic rituals, successful outcomes are achieved if the procedure followed accords with the established precedents. *Gto* rituals are formulated according to the idiom of bringing harmony where there was discord, and the crucial figure in all this is a priestly figure who acts as mediator.

Priests and Mediators

As in the case of the documents cited above, signatories to the resolution of disputes invariably include mediators, known as *bar mi*. Minor matters may feature just one person in this role, whereas more serious issues are likely to list several. The importance of the mediator in Tibetan law has been pointed out in several publications, including a recent study, by Fernanda Pirie, of a

20. Karmay 2010, 54.

21. Stein 1971, 504.

law code in which an entire section is devoted to the principles according to which mediators should act.[22]

As is well known, the character of Shenrab Miwo (Gshen rab mi bo), the legendary founder of the Bön religion, is most developed in three hagiographical works dating from about the eleventh to the fourteenth century: the *Mdo 'dus*, the *Gzer mig*, and the *Gzi brjid*. Shenrab also appears in a few Bön works that are earlier than these biographies, as well as in ritual texts from more recent times. In these accounts, he is presented not as a buddha figure but as a hero who resolves disputes. One cache of such texts found in Dga' thang 'bum pa, a large stūpa in Lho kha, has been studied by a number of researchers.[23] Of particular relevance to us here is the mythic narrative (*smrang*) of a *byol*, a type of ransom ritual. In this case, it concerns a story about the resolution of a murder case involving nonhuman protagonists. A young *klu*, Klu Rab bzang to re, falls in love with a woman of the Smra category, Smra lcam Si le ma. Her brother, Smra then pa, kills Klu Rab bzang to re and the latter's father, Klu rje zin brtsan, vows to take revenge. Because of Smra then pa's magical powers, Klu rje zin brtsan is unable to kill him, and he is forced to resort to adjudication to claim compensation for his son's death. The figure is set at 770,000 *srang* of gold, an impossibly high figure that Smra then pa is unable to pay. In desperation, Smra then pa turns to Shenrab Miwo to save him from his enemies. Shenrab agrees to do this and invites two other figures to join him in performing the *byol* ritual whereby Klu rje zin brtsan accepts substitutes for the 770,000 *srang*. These substitutes include a monkey, a sheep, and a bird. The text informs us that this event was the historical precedent for both the ransom ritual and the custom of blood money.[24]

In his study of this text, Bellezza points out that Shenrab is not a buddha figure so much as a priest. He certainly is a priest, to the extent that he performs the ritual that restores harmony between parties who are engaged in an epic dispute. More specifically, however, his position is that of a *mediator*, who restores peace between warring groups of nonhuman beings—the Smra on one side and the *klu*, the *srin*, the *bdud*, the *yi dwags*, and the *ltas ngan* on the other. He achieves this by negotiating a reasonable figure for the blood money demanded by the injured party; a figure that, in the performance of the ritual, is represented by certain animals and substitutes.

Although the primary role of Shenrab as a mediator has been superseded in the later Bön literature, it is interesting to note that some Buddhist works doc-

22. Pirie, Forthcoming.

23. Pa tshab Pa sangs dbang 'dus and Glang ru Nor bu tshe ring 2007.

24. Bellezza 2010, 72–90.

ument the role of the Bönpo hero as being primarily one of ritual and mediation. A passage in one text states that the corresponding figure "could mediate in disputes between humans on the one hand and gods and demons on the other."[25] The role of the priest as a legal figure is also alluded to in a work by 'Jig rten mgon po (1143–1217), which was the basis for the much better-known treatise on Bön by the Gelukpa scholar Thu'u bkwan Blo bzang chos kyi nyi ma (1737–1802). According to this account, the figure who corresponds to Shenrab was abducted by demons and instructed by them for up to to twelve years, before being reintroduced to the human realm. Following the death of King Gri gum, he was invited to perform the *gri gshid* ritual to counter the effects of a violent death but replied, "Although I know a great many of these rituals, they can be reduced to three categories: suppressing demons and vampires, making offerings to the revered gods on high, and reciting the methods of the law in the middle."[26]

The examples given so far reveal two themes common to legal and ritual procedures: the importance of precedent in establishing the legitimacy or efficacy of the procedure, and the role of the mediator in restoring harmony. In legal texts, the harmony is social, and in the ritual texts it concerns relations between humans and nonhumans or between different categories of nonhumans.

To conclude, I would like to draw attention to one of the very few texts of which I am aware that deals with the actual application of the law. Only five folios—found in a cave in Mustang, Nepal—are available, and since they are numbered from 46–48, 50, and 52, they were clearly part of a larger work. The language is archaic and difficult to understand, with many words that are not found in dictionaries. The work relates to a society in which there is no supreme authority that can enforce laws. This, I believe, was characteristic of most of Tibet for most of its history, either because there was no such authority or else because people preferred to sort out their issues without approaching official judicial authorities.

How, then, were the two parties to come to an agreement about the extent of the compensation to be paid; or, if the sums in question are actually specified in the missing part of the text, how is the guilty party to be persuaded to pay it? The text in question is a remarkable one because it is a legal manual that has features of archaic ritual texts. First of all, it establishes a series of precedents for disputes and reconciliation that are said to have occurred among humans, gods, and animals:

25. Nyang 1988, 160–61.

26. 'Bri gung 'Jig rten mgon po, *Dam chos*, fols. 20r–v.

> Once upon a time, the gods and demigods fought because they did not reach an agreement over the wish-fulfilling tree; the serpent spirits fought because they did not reach an agreement over a jewel; . . . the emperors fought because they could not agree over their dominions; dogs (?) fought over food. Generally, then, there is conflict even in the realm of the gods, while resolution may be achieved [even] in the realm of the demons. If there is no possibility of reconciliation, that is because the enemies are karmic enemies: the snake and the weasel are karmic enemies, as are the crow and the owl, the sparrowhawk and the sparrow, the sheep and the wolf. The fault is due to the fact that they have inferior intelligence. But we humans have intelligence, and even if there is conflict, we must reconcile.[27]

Here we see a striking case of the human world of legal reparation being compared to disputes in the nonhuman realms of both animals and gods. The dispute that is currently taking place is nothing new; it is a feature of life in the world. But just as disputes are natural, so too is their resolution, even among demons. In the absence of a supreme ruler, resolution is achieved by a mediator, called *bar spyi*. On the one hand the mediator must try to persuade the aggrieved party not to demand an impossibly high compensation. He is advised to say: "Something that has caused no more harm than the point of a needle doesn't demand recompense as great as a sword." And at the same time he must persuade the offender that peace can only be achieved if he actually pays the compensation: "there can be no reconciliation without discussion, or without the payment of the compensation."

The mediator is not more powerful than the disputing parties, and he even acknowledges this fact, warning them that they have nothing to gain from harming him:

> If you kill me, you are the one who will suffer tormented feelings; if you beat me, your laughter will be in tears; if you scratch me, it's your nails that will hurt. . . . Since you are proud and powerful, and I, the mediator, am weak, the two of you should not compete in strength.[28]

There is even a hint that the role of the mediator is a priestly one, since his healing role is compared to that of the Buddha: "We are feeling unwell, as if we

27. *Mardzong K*, fol. 46v.

28. *Mardzong K*, fol. 47v.

were in a sickbed; we are as if in a prison pit. If you are arrogant and unwise, I, the mediator, would be like the buddha whose medicine has little benefit when he comes."

Conclusion

There are several well-known sets of laws and systems of legislation in Tibetan literature, as well as established procedures for trying criminal cases. Both for the purpose of legitimizing these law codes and also to establish standards for making legal judgments, it was essential to have precedents. In order to achieve such resolutions, it was, and is, important to have mediation. The examples of case records we have seen show that disputes were resolved not by the judgment of a higher authority but thanks to the mediation of a respected outsider who could persuade people to heal their own social problems.

Having established that this is a basic principle of Tibetan legal thinking, we can see that indigenous Tibetan rituals are understood in exactly the same way: social and physical ills are the result of disharmony between humans or nonhumans, and the purpose of the ritual is to restore this harmony. The central figure in these myths is not the tantric practitioner who subjugates demons and forces them to do his bidding but the priestly mediator. He is explicitly compared with a legal mediator, who persuades the warring parties that nothing will be gained from their conflict, and that compensation for wrongs committed must be paid in the form of sacrificial offerings but this compensation must be reasonable. The assurance that the mediation will be successful is provided by a history of cases, whether in this world or in a supernatural realm, in which a similar process of conciliation has led to the restoration of harmony.

Works Cited

Agamben, Giorgio. 2011 [2008]. *The Sacrament of Language: An Archaeology of the Oath.* Stanford, CA: Stanford University Press.

Bellezza, John. 2008. *Zhang Zhung: Foundations of Civilization in Tibet: A Historical and Ethnoarchaeological Study of the Monuments, Rock Art, Texts, and Oral Tradition of the Ancient Tibetan Upland.* Vienna: Verlag der Österreichischen Akademie der Wissenschaften.

———. 2010. gShen-rab myi-bo: His Life and Times According to Tibet's Earliest Literary Sources. *Revue d'Études Tibétaines* 19: 31–118.

'Bri gung 'Jigs rten mgon po. *Dam chos dgongs gcig pa'i rtsa tshig rdo rje'i gsung brgya lnga bcu pa dang / lhan thabs gsung bzhi bcu ba / chings rnam pa bzhi / tshoms bdun go rim gyi rnam dbye dang bcas pa.* Dehra Dun: Drikung Kagyu Institute, Jangchub Ling.

Brown, W. N. 1972. "Duty as Truth in India." *Proceedings of the American Philosophical Society* 116: 252–86.

Burlingame, E. W. 1917. "The Act of Truth (Saccakiriya): A Hindu Spell and Its Employment as a Psychic Motif in Hindu Fiction." *Journal of the Royal Asiatic Society*, 429–67.

Cassinelli, C. W., and Robert B. Ekvall. 1969. *A Tibetan Principality: The Political System of Sakya*. Ithaca, NY: Cornell University Press.

French, Rebecca. 1995. *The Golden Yoke: The Legal Cosmology of Buddhist Tibet*. Ithaca, NY: Cornell University Press.

God sri mnan pa bzhugs pa legs so. Manuscript of five folios owned by Lama Tsultrim of Lubrak, Mustang.

Gsang sngags gling pa. 1998. *Yang snying gsang ba'i thugs sgrub las / bsad pa dgra srog spu gri. G.yung drung bon gyi bka' brten*, 38: 465–93. Lhasa: Dkar ru grub dbang sprul sku bstan pa'i nyi ma. TBRC.org ID: W30498.

Kapstein, Matthew T. 1997. "Buddhist Perspectives on Ontological Truth." In *A Companion to World Philosophies*, edited by E. Deutsch and R. Bontekoe, 420–33. Oxford: Blackwell Publishing.

Karmay, Samten. 1998. "The Soul and the Turquoise: A Ritual for Recalling the *bla*." In *The Arrow and the Spindle: Studies in History, Myths and Beliefs in Tibet*. Kathmandu: Mandala Books, 310–38.

———. 2010. "Tibetan Indigenous Myths and Rituals with Reference to the Ancient Bön Text: the *Nyenbum* (*Gnyan 'bum*)." In *Tibetan Ritual*, edited by José Cabezón, 53–68. New York: Oxford University Press.

Mardzong K. Manuscript of five folios (fols 46–49, 50, 52) from Mardzong Caves, Lo Monthang, Nepal.

Moore, Sally Falk, and Barbara Myerhoff, eds. 1977. *Secular Ritual*. Amsterdam: Van Gorcum.

Nyang Nyi ma 'od zer. 1988. *Chos 'byung me tog snying po sbrang rtsi'i bcud*. Lhasa: Bod ljongs mi dmangs dpe skrun khang.

Pa tshab Pa sangs dbang 'dus and Glang ru Nor bu tshe ring, 2007. *Gtam shul dga' thang 'bum pa che nas gsar du rnyed pa'i bon gyi gna' dpe bdams bsgrigs*. Lhasa: Bod ljongs bod yig dpe rnying dpe skrun khang.

Pirie, Fernanda. 2013. *The Anthropology of Law*. Oxford: Oxford University Press.

———. Forthcoming. "The Making of Tibetan Law: The *Khrims gnyis lta ba'i me long*." In *On a Day of a Month of the Fire Bird Year: Festschrift for Peter Schwieger on his 65th Birthday*, edited by Jeannine Bischoff, Petra Maurer, and Charles Ramble. Kathmandu: Lumbini International Research Institute.

Ramble, Charles. 2007. "The Aya: Fragments of an Unknown Tibetan Priesthood." In *Pramāṇakīrtiḥ: Papers Dedicated to Ernst Steinkellner on the Occasion of his 70th Birthday*, edited by Birgit Kellner et al., 2:681–718. Vienna: Wiener Studien zur Tibetologie und Buddhismuskunde.

———. 2008a. *Tibetan Sources for a Social History of Mustang, Nepal, Volume 1: The Archive of Te*. Halle: International Institute for Tibetan and Buddhist Studies.

———. 2008b. *The Navel of the Demoness: Tibetan Buddhism and Civil Religion in Highland Nepal*. New York: Oxford University Press.

———.2010. "Playing Dice with the Devil: A Bonpo Soul-Retrieval Ritual Attributed to Kong rtse 'phrul rgyal and Its Interpretation in Mustang, Nepal." In *Bon: The*

Indigenous Source for Tibetan Religion, edited by Samten Karmay and Donatella Rossi. *East and West* 59: 203–32.

———. 2016. *Tibetan Sources for a Social History of Mustang, Nepal, Volume 2: The Archives of the Tantric Lamas of Tshognam*. Andiast: International Institute for Tibetan and Buddhist Studies.

Schuh, Dieter. 1984. "Recht und Gesetz in Tibet." In *Tibetan and Buddhist Studies Commemorating the 200th Anniversary of the Birth of Alexander Csöma de Körös*, edited by L. Ligeti, 291–311. Budapest: Akadémiai Kiadó.

Snellgrove, David. 1967. *The Nine Ways of Bon*. London Oriental Series 18. Oxford: Oxford University Press. (Repr. Boulder: Prajñā, 1980.)

Sngags kyi mdo 'dur mu cho'i khrom 'dur chen mo las / lha yon 'bul ba thams cad len (lan) brda' sprod. In *G.yung drung bon gyi bka' brten*, compiled by *Dkar ru grub dbang sprul sku Bstan pa'i nyi ma*, 6:79–82. Lhasa: Sog sde sprul sku bstan pa'i nyi ma, 1998.

Stein, Rolf. 1971. "Du récit au rituel dans les manuscrits tibétains de Touen-houang." In *Études tibétaines dédiées à la mémoire de Marcelle Lalou*, edited by Ariane Macdonald, 479–547. Paris: Adrien Maisonneuve.

Thu'u bkwan Blo bzang chos kyi nyi ma. 1985. *Grub mtha' thams cad kyi khungs dang 'dod tshul ston pa legs bshad shel gyi me long*. Lanzhou: Kan su'u mi rigs dpe skrun khang.

Rivalry and Identity: A Record of Tibetan and Chinese Artists Competing in Early Seventeenth-Century Amdo

Karl Debreczeny[1]

A BRIEF ACCOUNT OF an incident that took place in 1611 of local Tibetan artists of Sengé Shong (Seng ge gshong) and Chinese artists competing side by side in the building and ornamenting of a monastery in Amdo, Drotsang (Gro tshang) Monastery, located on the Sino-Tibetan border, can be found in the *Impartial Comprehensive View of Reb gong Genealogies and Clan Histories* (*Reb gong rus mdzod lta ba mkha' khyab phyogs bral*, hereafter referred to as the *Rebgong Chronicle*), a record of Rebgong history going back to the Yuan dynasty, attributed to Rgya bza'i dge shes 'Jam dbyangs grags pa.[2] This is not only a fascinating account of ethnic rivalry between two artistic communities in early seventeenth-century Amdo but also an interesting account of questions of Tibetan identity along the Sino-Tibetan frontier. The account, barely one and a half folios long, reads as follows:[3]

> In the iron-pig year of the tenth cycle (1611), when Li kyā Shes rab mchog ldan [hereafter Likyā Sherab Chokden] established Drotsang Monastery, many artists of Sengé Shong in Rebgong, were invited. When they built the Drotsang assembly hall, the Drotsang

1. In the spirit of *Buddhism Between Tibet and China* and Matthew Kapstein's enduring interest in exploring the complex Tibeto-Chinese encounter, this small contribution to a well-deserved recognition of his contributions to the field is a means to add personal thanks to my professor and dissertation committee member.

2. This text was first brought to my attention by 'Jigs med bsam grub. Pema Bhum, director of Latse Library in New York, kindly shared a copy of a handwritten unpublished manuscript in the collection of the library, and I thank them both. I first presented a less-developed version of this material in my dissertation: Debreczeny 2007, 208–14 and 432–33. The text was later published in 2010 by the Nationalities Publishing House with support from the Trace Foundation.

3. *Rebgong Chronicle*, unpublished ms., fols. 266v–267v. See appendix 1 below for the Tibetan.

great chapel, and the Drotsang chapel for *brtsan* spirits, they spent over a year and several months making images, wall paintings, painted wood furnishings, goldwork, clay tile roofs, and gilt tile roofs.[4]

At this time, the famous Chinese artist Krang po[5] said: "What do foolish Tibetans know?" and [the Chinese artists] thus looked down on [Tibetan artists]. When the Chinese and Tibetans vied over skill, Tibetan and Chinese goldsmiths competed in goldsmithing, painters competed in painting, and sculptors competed in sculpting and erecting statues. Because the Tibetan artists prevailed in two [categories] and the Chinese in one, the Chinese artists praised them, saying, "It is difficult to compete against the Tibetans." Nevertheless, the Chinese artists spoke behind their backs saying, "If you consider these artists' way of speaking, much of it is unlike the language of foolish Tibetans. They must be Chinese."

The Chinese artists went to the precious guru Likyā Sherab Chokden and asked, "Likyā Rinpoché, these artists who erected religious images together with us speak various languages [mixed together]. We do not understand, what race are they?"

In answer to the question, Likyā Sherab Chokden answered: "As for them, they are descendants of army officers of one of the eighteen great tribes, Stong tsha,[6] [sent] to Amdo by the Tibetan imperial ruler. As for their race, they are Tibetans. As for their homeland, it is Ü-Tsang. As for their home base, it is Rebgong Gser mo ljongs. Sengé [Shong] has a reputation as a "place of learning."[7] Because they are famous for skill in craft, they are reputed as unrivaled in the world. The great ones do not leave their own land to go to other places [as itinerant artists]."

The Chinese artists were amazed that a race of foolish Tibetans was well skilled in craft like that, and they asked, "Where were they trained?"

He [Likyā] answered accordingly: "As for the skill earned through hard work by those bearing the name Sengé: who can compete with the teaching lineage of craftsmanship learned from the

4. *Gser tog* can also be gilt roof ornaments.

5. *Rebgong Chronicle* 2010, 711, transcribes the Chinese name as Grang bo.

6. *Rebgong Chronicle* 2010, 712: Ldong tsha.

7. *Rig pa 'byung ba'i gnas*, or "place of learning," is an epithet of Seng ge gshong.

> Nepalese: sculpture, drawing, how to[8] dye with pigment and mixing colors, the composition of wall paintings, the forging of copper and gold of the goldsmith, and the application of liquid gold (gilding) [learned] from eminent Nepalese, from the middle of the *me mkha' rgya mtsho* period (624–1026)[9] up until its end? As for the practice of these, because there are various unusual distinctive qualities, it is difficult to explain."
>
> The historical accounts of this, which tell of the arts in which Chinese artists and Tibetan artists vied in skill, and of the victory of the famous Tibetan artists of Sengé [Shong], is outlined on the surface of the wall paintings opposite to the two great [guardian] kings on the right side of the main door of the great chapel of Drotsang Dorjé Chang (Gro tshang rdo rje 'chang). This history that cannot be erased is now made clear.

This account is translated from a facsimile of a handwritten manuscript kept at Latse Library that entered their collection in 2003. The *Rebgong Chronicle* published in 2010 was published with substantial emendations. It is difficult to tell what is original to the text and what has been added later; nonetheless the published version adds some interesting information. For instance, it states in the first sentence that the accomplished artists of Sengé Shong are descendants of the three who bore the name Sengé who came from La stod, in Tsang, and were trained in the techniques from the region of Nepal:

> In the iron-gig year of the tenth cycle (1611), when Likyā Sherab Chokden established Drotsang Monastery, many accomplished artists of the lineage and descendants of the three renowned as Sengé who studied their craftsmanship from the region of Nepal, the ones from Tsang La stod who resided in Rebgong Gser mo ljongs, were invited.[10]

It is also more specific in the outcome of the competition: "The Tibetans prevailed in goldsmithing and sculpture. The Chinese prevailed in painting."[11]

The modern Rebgong scholar 'Jigs med bsam grub made use of this story

8. Here, *tshad*, emended to *tshul*.

9. *Me mkha' rgya mtsho* was a Tibetan dating system used before the *rab byung* sixty-year cycle.

10. *Rebgong Chronicle* 2010, 711.

11. *Rebgong Chronicle* 2010, 711.

in several publications on the history of Rebgong and Tibetan art but omitted the passage that recounts the tension between Chinese and Tibetan artists as well as the debate on the ethnic identity of the Rebgong artists. He also changed the outcome of the competition:

> Because many renowned Chinese artists looked down on Tibetan artists, when Chinese and Tibetans vied over skill, Tibetan and Chinese goldsmiths competed in goldsmithing, painters competed in painting, and sculptors competed in sculpture. In the end, Tibetan artists prevailed in all respects, and because of that, the renowned Chinese artists were chastened.[12]

It is unclear whether these differences are because 'Jigs med bsam grub was reading another manuscript edition of this text, such as the aforementioned private printing made in the 1970s said to be the original printed text, or whether he simply changed the text for his own purposes.

It should be mentioned at this point that this chronicle as a whole is a problematic historical document containing many questionable dates that contradict established chronologies of other historical events. The text was first mentioned in modern scholarship by the respected Amdo scholar 'Jigs med theg mchog in 1988.[13] Even the dates of the author are unclear. According to the 2010 version, the dates of Rgya bza'i dge shes 'Jam dbyangs grags pa's were 1486–1572(?), and he was born in Rebgong in Amdo.[14] According to other local accounts, he was sent to Amdo from Central Tibet by the Fifth Dalai Lama in the seventeenth century. Within this context, it must be remarked that several Tibetan spelling variants accord with the local Rebgong dialect, thus suggesting a local author, unless these passages are later interpolations. For instance, *tshad*, meaning "model" or "measure," is a misspelling of *tshul*, "how"; both words are pronounced the same way in the local Rebgong dialect, and their spellings are often confused.[15]

It is difficult to find corroborating evidence of this incident outside of this chronicle. Neither Tibetan nor Chinese accounts of Drotsang Monastery's founding refer to this story.[16] An abbreviated version of the event appears in

12. Reb gong pa 'Jigs med bsam grub 2002a, 127; 2002b, 89; and 2005, 48–50.

13. 'Jigs med theg mchog, 1988.

14. *Rebgong Chronicle* 2010, 1.

15. Thanks to Pema Bhum for pointing this local linguistic variant out to me.

16. For instance: Dkon mchog bstan pa rab rgyas 1987, 173, Skya tsa sgom pa tshe ring, 1989, 60–64, and Pu Wencheng, 1990, 120–21.

Amdo Regional Tibetan Cultural Arts (安多地区藏族文化艺术), a local modern publication on Tibetan art written in Chinese by a Tibetan author. It recounts:

> In the metal-dog year of the tenth cycle of the Tibetan calendar (1611), when Likyā Sherab Chokden built Drotsang Monastery, [he] invited many artisans from Rebgong Wutun. They built Drotsang Monastery's great sūtra hall, great Buddha hall, and protector chapel. This took a little over a year. While constructing its interior, with its wall paintings, woodcarvings, lacquerwork, carved brickwork, precious vessels, and so on, they competed in crafts with many renowned Chinese artisan painters. The Tibetan master painters achieved victory and gained great acclaim.[17]

Interestingly this author gives a higher status to Tibetan painters, calling them "master painters" (藏族画师), than to Chinese painters, who are only "artisan painters" (汉族画匠), a distinction not reflected in the Tibetan. The results of the competition, with the Tibetan painters victorious, also follows more closely 'Jigs med bsam grub's version, where the Tibetans prevailed in all three categories. As the author, Danqu, does not cite his source however, it is possible that he is drawing on another version of the same chronicle, indirectly through another secondary source, or on a local oral tradition.[18]

A more recent Chinese study of Rebgong painting briefly mentions the 1611 competition with Chinese painters but focuses on the question of the artists' language and the village of Sengé Shong's ancestral identity:

> In 1611 in Qinghai, Ledu (乐都) painters and Chinese painters competed, and the Chinese painters' technique was different. They said: "The language you speak, it is not [of the] Tibetans (藏族). They are [descendants of] military ancestors who have become painting artists." [The villagers of] Sengé Shong (桑格雄) are the descendants of a fighting people, due to their ancestors being soldiers. The graves

17. 藏历第十绕迥金狗年(公元1611),李家谢热却典修建卓仓寺时,迎请了热贡五屯的许多工匠,修建了卓仓寺大经堂,大佛殿,护法殿,历时年余,修建其中的内供,壁画,木雕,油漆,砖雕,宝瓶等时,与许多知名的汉族画匠比赛工艺,藏族画师取胜且名声大振。Danqu 1997, 183. Note Tibetan sources give the iron-pig year; the iron-dog year is 1610.

18. Danqu lists both Tibetan and Chinese sources in his bibliography, but the *Rebgong Chronicle* is not among them. Danqu's book came out some five years before 'Jigs med bsam grub's articles, so 'Jigs med bsam grub's articles are unlikely to be the source of this story, unless they shared material.

here are horseshoe-shaped, and moreover sickles hang like banners over every household's doorway.[19]

In essence, the Chinese artists are saying that people of Sengé Shong are not Tibetans but descendants of Mongolian troops—that is to say, Monguors. Interestingly, this Chinese author asserts that this passage is based on a Tibetan handwritten manuscript, a Wutun (Sengé Shong) record (记录), that was discovered in 1958 in a monastery in Wutun.[20] If this is true, this would be the only other historical document corroborating the event. While the manuscript is not named, the content is different enough from the *Rebgong Chronicle* to suggest that it is not another version of that text.

Questions of Ethnic and Cultural Identity

The story takes place in an interethnic borderland where Tibetans, Mongolians, Chinese, Monguors, and other peoples continually negotiate complex cultural relationships. Rebgong (Tongren) is a famous center of Tibetan artists in modern-day Qinghai near the southern Gansu border, known to this day for a style that draws heavily from Chinese painting.[21] Linguistically people of the Rebgong area speak a Tibetan dialect with many Chinese loanwords, which might explain the Chinese artists' confusion as to the local artists' language and identity. Regarding their language, the 2010 version of this clan history states that the Chinese artists slandered the Tibetan artists, saying: "As for the language of these artists who resemble foolish Tibetans, because they speak [a mix of] various languages such as Chinese, Mongolian (*sog skad*), Monguor (*hor skad*), and Tibetan, much of it does not fit with Tibetan language. As for their race, they must be Chinese."[22]

Several villages are inhabited by a distinct ethnic population that specialized for centuries in thangka painting, now called Monguors in this area, including Upper and Lower Sengé Shong, Sgo dmar, and Gnyan thog, and who claim descent from Mongolian soldiers.[23] As pointed out by Gray Tuttle,

19. Chen Naihua 2013, 85.

20. Chen Naihua 2013, 85.

21. Linrothe 2001.

22. *De nas rgya'i bzo bo rnams kyis kyang bod mi blun po dang 'dra ba'i bzo ba 'di rnams kyi skad rigs ni rgya skad dang sog skad/ hor skad bod skad sogs skad rigs sna tshogs bshad pas bod skad dang mi mthun pa mang po 'dug pa'i mi 'di rigs ni rgya rigs yin pa sha stag red ces lkog lab brgyab/*. *Rebgong Chronicle* 2010, 712.

23. Sonam Tsering and Sonam Tsering 2011; Dhondup 2011, 35.

Monguors have their own ethnic identity, history, and language going back to the garrisons of the Mongol empire in the thirteenth century but are too often considered identical to Tibetans.[24] To complicate matters further, while the people of the villages of Sengé Shong and Gnyan thog are both classified as Monguor, they speak languages that are mutually unintelligible.[25] The Monguor are known in the official Chinese classification system as the Tu 土族, but such ethnonyms do not delineate a group with clear linguistic or cultural identity.[26] The PRC classification of nationalities is based on the idea of blood kinship and seemingly driven by a need for "indigenous" groups of a region. This led to the creation of largely artificial groupings, such as the Tu, which itself simply derives from the Chinese term *turen* 土人, or "native people."[27]

Furthermore, three villages in the area of Sengé Shong—Upper Sengé, Lower Sengé, and Rgya tsang ma—were classified by the Chinese government as their own ethnic group Wutun 吴屯, but local people petitioned to have themselves reclassified as Tibetan in the 1980s. One part of the argument was related to aspects of the Tibetan language spoken in the area being closer to that of Central Tibet than to local dialects.

According to local oral tradition, the Tibetan inhabitants of this region are said to be the descendants of army officers and their troops who were sent from Central Tibet during the imperial period, as mentioned by Likyā Rinpoche in this narrative.[28] Origin stories of Tibetan communities in border regions, including Amdo, are often associated with the expansion of the Tibetan Empire.[29] The 2010 published edition of the *Rebgong Chronicle* adds, "As for the clan (*rus*) of these artists, they are of . . . Dar stong Rgyal mtshan, a person of La stod, in Tsang,"[30] and again reiterates a few lines later that they are "descendants from the two, Ü and Tsang."[31] Indeed, the 2010 text mentions the artists' ancestry in Central Tibet four times, whereas the earlier manuscript mentions it only once. While it is unclear where the additional

24. Tuttle 2006, 37–43.

25. Dhondup 2011, 51.

26. Samuel 2013, 6.

27. Samuel 2013, 9; Cooke and Goodman, 2010.

28. One of the communities in Reb gong called Mgar rtse claims they are descendants of minister Mgar. See Sonam Tsering and Sonam Tsering 2011.

29. Dge 'dun chos 'phel (1903–51), Tsepon Skakabpa, and Samten Karmay make similar statements about the origins of Tibetans in Amdo. See Dhondrup 2011, 37, and Samuel 2013, 7.

30. *Reb gong Chronicle* 2010, 712.

31. *Reb gong Chronicle* 2010, 712.

information comes from, it seems likely that the new emphasis on Central Tibetan origins in the later text is related to the recent local assertion of a Tibetan identity.

Much could also be said about the Indic cultural affiliations implied by the statement that these artists' Central Tibetan ancestors' craft has its roots in Nepal rather than China. If the narrative is to be believed, this training happened in the ancient past: "[learned] from eminent Nepalese, from the middle of the *me mkha' rgya mtsho* period (624–1026) up until its end." Nepalese art was of great importance in Central Tibet, especially after the decline of Buddhism in India, and Newari artists were often imported for important commissions. As reflected in this narrative, the region of Tsang was especially associated with Nepalese art, where it became one of the dominant styles from the thirteenth to sixteenth centuries.[32] Even well into the seventeenth century, when this account purportedly occurred, the Panchen Lama was recorded to have brought in Nepalese artists at Bkra shis lhun po Monastery in Tsang.[33]

Questions of Monastery Identity

Initially the identity of the temple discussed in the *Rebgong Chronicle* also appears unclear. While it bears the same distinctive Tibetan name Drotsang as the famous Ming-period Drotsang Dorjé Chang, or Qutansi 瞿昙寺, and is located in the same area, there is a major chronological problem with the two being the same temple. On the one hand, the *Rebgong Chronicle* states that Drotsang Monastery was founded in 1611, by Likyā Sherab Chokden, a Gelukpa incarnate lama from a local Monguor ruling family, the Li *jia* 李家.[34] Gro tshang rdo rje 'chang on the other hand, was a Kagyü institution founded in 1392 with close ties to the Sakya order. It changed sectarian affiliation to the Geluk circa 1450.[35]

While the Likyā incarnations were involved in later renovations at Qutansi,[36] evidence for the identity of this Drotsang Monastery, and the circumstances for its establishment, can be found in a nineteenth-century source, the *Religious History of Amdo* (*Mdo smad chos 'byung*, 1865):

32. Jackson 2010.

33. Bareja-Starzyńska 2015, 86, and Smith in Blo bzang chos kyi rgyal mtshan 1969, 6 and 76.

34. Blo bzang 'phrin las 2002, 2330, also mentions Li kya Shes rab mchog ldan founding Gro tshang Monastery in 1611.

35. Sperling 2001, 80. This is also reflected in the *Mdo smad chos 'byung*, 172.

36. See for instance *Mdo smad chos 'byung*, 172–73.

> The *jina* Bsod nams rgya mtsho [the Third Dalai Lama; 1543–88] was invited. Because the Vajradhara (Dorjé Chang) chapel was mixed in with the village, based on the request concerning the need to establish a monastery downhill, a solitary place was [sought out in] prophecy and given the name Bkra shis lding kha. . . .
>
> In the earth-sheep year (1619),[37] the third year since the Great Fifth [Dalai Lama's] birth in the fire-snake year (1617), the *nang so*[38] Dpal ldan rgya mtsho and Chos rgyal phun tshogs acted as donors. The Bsam blo Li kya *rab 'byams pa* Shes rab mchog ldan built the temple Gro tshang dgon Bkra shis lhun po in Lhas sngo ting according to the prophecy of the previous *jina*. According to the *Skal ldan chos 'byung*: "The *dharmasvāmin* Shes rab mchog ldan set up a *grwa tshang* and reestablished the monastery in Gro tshang, in the female earth-sheep year. Since then thirty-four years have passed." Based on what is written in the *Kun mkhyen bstan rtsis re'u mig*, it is genuinely evident and appears to also say that this was in the iron-pig year (1611).[39]

It states that because Drotsang Dorjé Chang (Qutansi) had become mixed in (or tainted by) the secular community that had grown up around it, a need was seen to establish a more secluded monastery. Thus the Likyā incarnation founded a branch monastery that bears its mother institution's name, Drotsang, in a more remote area chosen by the Third Dalai Lama's previous divination. Because the two temples share the name Drotsang, their identity is often confused.[40] Some Chinese scholars for instance suggested that Rebgong artists painted later renovations to Qutansi, without providing any evidence for their argument, mixing up the two temples.[41]

37. Three years after the fire-snake year should be the iron-monkey year (1620), not the earth-sheep year (1619).

38. Title of the main ruler of Reb gong, with their seat in Rong bo, until their weakening in the early seventeenth century. See Dhondup 2011, 38–42.

39. Dkon mchog bstan pa rab rgyas 1987, 173, and Wu Jun 1989, 168–69.

40. As a result, Li kya Shes rab mchog ldan is sometimes credited with a major renovation of Qutansi. Gruschke (2001, 29) and Gyurme Dorje (1996, 583) both say it was in 1564.

41. For instance, Qian Zhengkun (1995, 58 and 63) describes the wall paintings of Qutan Hall (Qutandian 瞿曇殿) as "works that carry on the style of Qinghai's 'Reb gong art.'"

Gro tshang dgon Bkra shis lhun po

The stage for this narrative, Gro tshang dgon Bkra shis lhun po, called Yaocaotaisi 藥草台寺 in Chinese, is located in the present-day village of Shipogou 石坡溝村, about seven kilometers from its mother monastery Qutansi. Its former satellite status is confirmed in a 1762 Chinese gazetteer, the *Xining fu xin zhi* 西寧府新志, which calls the temple "a sub-temple of Qutansi" (瞿曇寺下院).[42] Gro tshang dgon Bkra shis lhun po became one of Drotsang Dorjé Chang's (Qutansi) major subsidiary monasteries and a sūtra study college in the late Ming, growing quickly to a substantial size of about four hundred monks and its own incarnate lamas. Drotsang's growth into branch monasteries can also be understood in the larger context of large-scale expansion of Geluk monasteries in Amdo in the sixteenth to eighteenth centuries, linked both to monks and lamas trained in the main Geluk seats of power in Central Tibet and supported by local Mongolian and Monguor patronage.

According to Father Louis Schram, a Catholic missionary who interviewed incarnate lamas from both these monasteries circa 1911–22, because most of their lamas were of Monguor origin, their monasteries declined after Sku 'bum byams pa gling (Ta'ersi 塔尔寺) and Dgon lung (Youning si 佑宁寺) were built in 1506 and 1604 and the Monguor lamas went over to these monasteries.[43] In 1885, the branch declared its independence and claimed possession of the pastures, farms, and forests. In retaliation, the monks of the mother monastery burned Yaocaotaisi's temples.[44] Drotsang Monastery was destroyed again during the Cultural Revolution in 1967 and reopened in 1984.[45] Thus, the artworks at Drotsang Monastery that stood as testaments to early seventeenth-century Rebgong craftsmanship and Sino-Tibetan artistic exchange appear to be lost.

Conclusion

The *Rebgong Chronicle* is a problematic historical document. According to Latse Library director Pema Bhum, when the manuscript of the *Rebgong*

42. Yang Yingju and Shen Yunlong 1966, 8.

43. Schram 1957, 315. For the digital version of Schram's texts, edited by Charles Kevin Stuart in 2006, see http://hdl.handle.net/1811/24312.

44. Schram 1957, 315–16.

45. See Nian Zhihai and Bai Gengdeng 1993, 112–13. Gruschke 2001, 46, says it was destroyed in 1967. For more on the history of the rebuilding of Yaocaotaisi see the *Chongjian zhou cang gongqin jian zhi* (Unknown author 2004).

Chronicle was acquired in 2003, the owner insisted on being paid by the page and therefore had an incentive to add to the original manuscript. What is original to the text is therefore unclear. Moreover, while the 2010 publication is supposed to be based on this manuscript, the source of the changes and additions is also unclear. The editors may have obtained other editions. Given the regional context of identity politics in the last few decades, however, it seems likely that the new emphasis on Central Tibetan origins of the artists is related to the recent local claim of a Tibetan identity by villagers of Sengé Shong, which is being projected back into historical sources. Hopefully, further corroborating sources such as the local record discovered in a Sengé Shong monastery in 1958, will surface. Most of the photographs taken by Father Louis Schram during his research on the Monguors in the region were also lost during the social upheavals in China in 1948.[46] Surveys made by the provincial Cultural Affairs Bureaus (文化局) across China in the 1950s may also document something of the monastery's pre–Cultural Revolution state and, if made available, may afford some glimpse of these once-rich materials.

Appendix 1. An Excerpt from the Rebgong Chronicle

Rgya bza'i dge shes 'Jam dbyangs grags pa, *Reb gong rus mdzod lta ba mkha' khyab phyogs bral*, unpublished manuscript in the Latse Library, New York, fols. 266v–267v.

(266v) རབ་བྱུང་བཅུ་བའི་ལྷུངས་པགལོ། ལི་ཀུ་ཧླིས་རབ་མཆོག་ལྡན་གྱིས་གྲོ་ཚང་དགོན་པ་བཏབ་སྐབས། རེབ་གོང་སེངེ་ཤྐཤོང་གི་ལྷ་བཟོ་མང་པོ་གདན་དྲངས་ནས་གྲོ་ཚང་འདུ་ཁང་དང་། གྲོ་ཚང་ལྷ་ཁང་ཆེན་མོ་དང་། གྲོ་ཚང་བརྟན་ཁང་རྣམས་ལོ་གཅིག་དང་ཟླ་བ་འགའི་རིང་ནང་རྟེན་དང་། གདུམ་རིས། ཤིང་ཚན་དང་གསེར་ཚོན། སྐུ་ཐིག་དང་གསེར་ཏོག་རྣམས་བཞེངས་སྐབས་སུ། རྒྱའི་ལྷ་བཟོ་གྲགས་ཆེན་ཀྲང་པོ་ཡིས་གཙོས་བོད་མི་ཁྲུན་པོའི་ཅི་ཤེས་ཟེར་ནས་མཐོང་ཆུང་མཛད་དེ། རྒྱ་བོད་གཉིས་ཀྱིས་ལག་རྩལ་འགྲན་པའི་སྐབས་སུ། བོད་རྒྱ་གཉིས་ནས། གསེར་མགར་བའི་གསེར་མགར་ནས་ (267r) །འགྲན་པ་དང་། རི་མོ་བའི་རི་མོ་བྲིས་ནས་འགྲན་པ་དང་། འཛིམ་བཟོ་བའི་རྟེན་བཞེངས་པའི་འཇིམ་བཟོའི་རྩལ་འགྲན་པས། ཕྱོགས་གཉིས་ནས་བོད་རྒྱལ་བ་དང་། ཕྱོགས་གཅིག་པ་རྒྱ་རྒྱལ་བས། རྒྱ་མི་ལྷ་བཟོ་བ་རྣམས་ཀྱིས་བོད་མི་ལ་འགྲན་པར་དཀའ་ཞེས་གཟེངས་བསྟོད་མཛད། འོན་ཀྱང་རྒྱ་མའི་ལྷ་བཟོ་བའི། ལྷ་བཟོ་འདི་རྣམས་ཀྱི་སྐད་རིགས་ལ་བལྟས་ན་བོད་མི་ཁྲུན་པོའི་སྐད་རིགས་ལ་མི་མཐུན་པ་མང་པོ་འདུག་པའི་རྒྱའི་རིགས་ཡིན་པ་ཤ{ར}་སྣང་རེད་ཅེས་སྙིག་ལབ་རྒྱབ་སྟེ། རྒྱའི་ལྷ་བཟོ་བ་རྣམས་ཀྱིས་བླ་མ་རིན་པོ་ཆེ་ལི་ཀུ་ཧླིས་རབ་མཆོག་ལྡན་པའི་སྐུ་མདུན་སོང་དེ། ལི་ཀུ་རིན་པོ་ཆེ་ལགས། ང་ཚག་དང་ལྷན་དུ་སྐུ་གསོང་ [sic] (= གསུང་) ཐུགས་རྟེན་བཞེངས་པའི་ལྷ་བཟོ་འདི་རྣམས་ཀྱིས་སྐད་རིགས་སྣ་ཚོགས་བཤད་པར་གོ་རྒྱུ་མི་འདུག་པའི་འདི་ཚོའི་མི་རིགས་གང་ལ་གཏོགས་པ་རེད་ཞེས་ཞུས་པའི། ལན་དུ། ལི་ཀུ་ཧླིས་རབ་མཆོག་ལྡན་པས་གསུངས་དོན། འདི་རྣམས་ནི་བོད་རྒྱལ་བཙན་པོས་མདོ་སྨད་དུ་ཆ་ཆེན་བཅོ་བརྒྱད་ཀྱི་ནང་ཚན་ སྟོང་ཚའི་དམག་དཔོན་གྱི་མི་རྒྱུད་སྟེ། རིགས་ནི་བོད། ཡུལ་ནི་དབུས་

46. Schram 1954, 24.

གཙང་། གཞི་འཛིན་ས་ནི་རེབ་གོང་གསེར་མོ་ལྗོངས་སྟེ། རིག་པ་འབྱུང་བའི་གནས་སུ་སེངྒེ་གླིང་ཙན་ཞེས་ལག་རྩལ་གྱི་སྙན་པས་འཛིག་ (267v) རྟེན་འགྲན་ཟླ་དང་བྲལ་བའི་གྲགས་ཆེ་བ་རྣམས་རང་ཡུལ་ནས་ས་ཕྱོགས་གཞན་ལ་མི་ཕེབས་པར་འདུག་གོ་ཅེས་གསུངས་པས། རྒྱའི་ལྷ་བཟོ་བ་རྣམས་ཧ་ལས་པའི་བོད་མི་རྣུན་པོའི་རིགས་སུ་འདི་འདྲ་ལག་རྩལ་ཡག་པོ་ཡོད་པ་གང་ནས་བསླབ་པ་རེད་ཞེས་ཞུ་བས། ལན་དུ། ཁོང་གིས་གསུངས་དོན། སེངྒེ་གླིང་ཙན་རྣམས་ཀྱིས་དཀའ་བ་སྤྱད་པའི་ལག་རྒྱུན་ནི། མི་མཁའ་རྒྱ་མཚོའི་དཀྱིལ་ནས་མཇུག་གི་བར་དུ། བལ་པོའི་བཟོ་ཤུལ་བྱུང་ཙན་རྣམ་པའི་མདུན་ནས། རྟེན་བཞེངས་དང་། རི་མོ། ཚོན་གྱིས་མདོག་རྒྱུར་ཚད་ [sic] (=ཚུལ་) དང་མདངས་ཤུལ་ཚད་ [sic] (=ཚུལ་) །གདུམ་རིས་ཀྱི་སྟེབ་སྦྱོར། གསེར་མགར་གྱི་ཐིངས་གསེར་རྟུང་ཚད་[sic] (=ཚུལ་) དང་། ཆབ་བྱུག་ཐསད་རྣམས་བལ་པོ་ནས་བསླབ་པའི་ལག་རྒྱུན་བཟང་པོ་དེའི་སློབ་རྒྱུད་ལ་སུས་འགྲན་ནུས། འདི་རྣམས་ཀྱི་ལག་རྒྱུན་ནི་ཐུན་མོང་མ་ཡིན་པའི་ཁྱད་ཆོས་སྣ་ཚོགས་ཡོད་པས་བཤད་པའི་འཛད་པར་དཀའོ་ཞེས་གསུངས་སོ།། འདིའི་ལོ་རྒྱུས་རྣམས་ཀྱི་ཚང་རྗོ་རྗེ་འཆང་གི་ལྷ་ཁང་ཆེན་མོའི་སྒོ་ཆེན་གྱི་གཡས་ཕྱོགས་སུ་རྒྱལ་ཆེན་གཉིས་ཁ་སྦྲོད་དུ་ཡོད་པའི་གདུམ་རིས་དེའི་ངོས་ན། རྒྱའི་ལྷ་བཟོ་དང་། བོད་ལྷ་བཟོའི་ལག་རྩལ་འགྲན་པའི་གཟུངས་རིས་དང་། བོད་མིའི་ལྷ་བཟོ་སེངྒེ་གླིང་ཙན་རྣམས་རྒྱལ་སོང་ཞེས་པའི་ཟིན་བྲིས་རྣམས། ལོ་རྒྱུས་སུབ་ཐུབ་མེད་པར་ད་ལྟ་གསལ་བར་སྣང་ངོ།

Works Cited

Bareja-Starzyńska, Agata. *The Biography of the First Khalkha Jetsundampa Zanabazar by Zaya Pandita Luvsanprinlei: Studies, Annotated translation, Transliteration and Facsimile.* Warsaw: Dom Wydawniczy ELIPSA, 2015.

Blo bzang chos kyi rgyal mtshan. 1969. *The Autobiography of the First Panchen Lama Blo-bzang-chos-kyi-rgyal-mtshan.* English introduction by E. Gene Smith. New Delhi: Ngawang Gelek Demo.

Blo bzang 'phrin las. 2002. *Bod rig pa'i tshig mdzod chen mo shes bya rab gsal* ("Dungkar Great Tibetological Dictionary"). Beijing: Zhongguo Zangxue yanjiu zhongxin.

Chen Naihua 陈乃华. 2013. *Wu ming de zao shen zhe: Regong tangka* yiren *yanjiu* 无名的造神者热贡唐卡艺人研究. The Anonymous: Regong thangkha painters research. Beijing: Shijie tushu chuban gongsi.

Danqu 丹曲. 1997. *Anduo diqu Zangzu wenhua yishu* 安多地区藏族文化艺术 ("Amdo Regional Tibetan Cultural Arts"). Lanzhou: Gansu Mizu chubanshe.

Debreczeny, Karl. 2007. "Ethnicity and Esoteric Power: Negotiating the Sino-Tibetan Synthesis in Ming Buddhist Painting." PhD dissertation. Chicago: University of Chicago.

Dhondup, Yangdon. 2011. "Reb kong: Religion, History and Identity of a Sino-Tibetan borderland town." *Revue d'Études Tibétaines* 20: 33–59.

Dkon mchog bstan pa rab rgyas. 1987. *Mdo smad chos 'byung* ("Religious History of Amdo," 1865). Gansu: Minzu chubanshe.

Gruschke, Andreas. 2001. *The Cultural Monuments of Tibet's Outer Provinces: Amdo.* Bangkok: White Lotus Press.

Jackson, David P. 2010. *The Nepalese Legacy in Tibetan Painting.* New York: The Rubin Museum of Art.

'Jigs med theg mchog. 1988. *Rong bo dgon chen gyi gdan rabs* ("Abbatial Succession of Rong bo Monastery"). Xining: Qinghai Minzu chubanshe.

Kapstein, Matthew. 2009. *Buddhism Between Tibet and China.* Boston: Wisdom Publications.

Linrothe, Rob. 2001. "Creativity, Freedom and Control in the Contemporary Renaissance of Reb gong Painting." *The Tibet Journal* 26.3–4: 5–90.

Nian Zhihai 年治海 and Bai Gengdeng 白更登. 1993. *Qinghai Zangzhuan fojiao siyuan mingjian* 青海藏传佛教寺院明鉴. Lanzhou: Gansu Renmin chubanshe.

Pu Wencheng 蒲文成. 1990. *Gan Qing Zang chuan fojiao siyuan* 甘青藏传佛教寺院. Xining: Qinghai renmin chubanshe.

Qian Zhengkun. 1995. "Qinghai Ledu Qutansi bihua yenjiu" 青海乐都瞿昙寺壁画研究. *Meishu Yenjiu* 美术研究 5: 57–63.

Reb gong pa 'Jigs med bsam grub. 2002a. "Bod du sku gzugs bris 'bur sogs kyi byung 'phel skor rags tsam gleng ba" ("A Brief Discussion of the Origin and Spread of Paintings and Sculpture in Tibet"). *Krung go'i bod kyi shes rig* 58.2: 113–31.

———. 2002b. "Bod kyi bris 'bur sgyu rtsal gyi byung 'phel skor bshad pa" ("The Origin and Development of Tibetan Painting and Sculpture"). *Bod ljongs zhib 'jug* 81.2: 80–90.

———. 2005. *Reb gong seng ge gshong gi lo rgyus gangs ri'i chu rgyun zhes bya ba* ("A History of Rebgong Sengé Shong, Snow Mountains and Rivers"). Beijing: Mi rigs dpe skrun khang.

Rebgong Chronicle:

Rgya bza'i dge shes 'Jam dbyangs grags pa. *Reb gong rus mdzod lta ba mkha' khyab phyogs bral* ("Impartial Comprehensive View of Reb gong Genealogies and Clan Histories"). Facsimile of an unpublished handwritten manuscript at Latse Library, New York, fols. 266v–267v.

———. 2010. *Reb kong rus mdzod lta ba mkha' khyab phyogs bral* (热贡族谱*Reb-koṅ rus mdzod bźugs so* / Rgya-bza'i Dge-bśes 'Jam-dbyaṅs-bsod-nams-grags-pas mdzad ("History and Records of Clans in Rebgong, Including Local Rulers and Ministers"). Beijing: Mi rigs dpe skrun khang.

Samuel, Geoffrey. 2013. "Reb kong in the Multiethnic Context of A mdo: Religion, Language, Ethnicity, and Identity." In *Monastic and Lay Traditions in North-Eastern Tibet*, edited by Geoffrey Samuel and Yangdon Dhondup, 5–20. Leiden and Boston: Brill.

Schram, Louis. 1954. *The Monguors of the Kansu-Tibetan Frontier, I*, Transactions of the American Philosophical Society, new series, vol. 44, part 1.

———. 1957. *The Monguors of the Kansu-Tibetan Frontier, II*, Transactions of the American Philosophical Society, new ser., vol. 47, part 1.

———. 1961. *The Monguors of the Kansu-Tibetan frontier, III*, Transactions of the American Philosophical Society, new ser., vol. 51, part 3.

Skya tsa sgom pa tshe ring. 1989. "Gro tshang gi chos srid byung rim mthong gsal me long." ("The Arising of Gro tshang's Clerical Government: A Clearly Seen Mirror"). *Sbrang char* 4: 60–64.

Sonam Tsering and Sonam Tsering. 2011. "The Historical Polity of Repgong." http://places.thlib.org/features/23751/descriptions/1225.

Sperling, Elliot. 2001. "Notes on the Early History of Gro-tshang Rdo-rje-'chang and Its Relations with the Ming Court." *Lungta* 14: 77–87.

Tuttle, Gray. 2006. "The Middle Ground: The Monguor Place in History, Between China and Tibet." In *The Monguors of the Kansu-Tibetan Frontier, I–III*, edited by Charles Kevin Stuart and Louis Schram, 37–43. http://hdl.handle.net/1811/24312.

Unknown author. 2004. *Chongjian zhou cang gongqin jian zhi* 重建卓仓贡钦简志 ("A Record of Rebuilding [Yaocaotaisi 藥草台寺]"). No publication information provided.

Wu Jun 吴均. 1989. *Anduo zheng jiao shi* 安多政教史 ("The Political and Religious History of Amdo"). Gansu: Gansu renmin chubanshe. (A Chinese translation of Dkon mchog bstan pa rab rgyas 1865.)
Yang Yingju 楊應琚 and Shen Yunlong 沈雲龍. 1966 [1762]. *Xining fu xin zhi* 西寧府新志 ("New Gazetteer of Xining Prefecture"). *Chuan* 15, vol. 2. Taipei: Wen hai chubanshe.

Revisiting the *Mañjuśriyamūlakalpa*'s Painting Chapters

Ronald M. Davidson[1]

MATTHEW KAPSTEIN'S INTEREST in painting extends back to his time in the Shar Khumbu region, when he knew the Sherpa painting teacher Au Leshi, and continued on with his contribution on the *paṭa* preparatory rites found in the *Mañjuśriyamūlakalpa*'s rituals on painting.[2] One of the longest of Indian Buddhist tantras—and one that continued to accrete chapters over time—the *Mañjuśriyamūlakalpa* is taken by some traditions as foundational for the association of some wrathful deities and the bodhisattva Mañjuśrī. Yet the text features painting rituals in many of its chapters, and Matthew saw some of these rites reconsidered in modern Tibetan writings. Matthew stayed with me a few times upon returning from India and Nepal, and at one point gave my daughter Stephanie a thangka of Green Tārā, which I seem to recall him describing as having been painted by Au Leshi as a teaching piece. The painting now graces my daughter's home in Berkeley.

In his investigation of the cloth-preparation ritual delineated in chapter 4 of the received *Mañjuśriyamūlakalpa*, Kapstein laments caricatures of the Buddhist artist, described on the one hand as a simple artisan creating formulaic materials for meditators and on the other hand as a virtuoso yogin expressing his personal vision of a divinity. Rightly, Kapstein indicates that the artist in Buddhist cultures is better understood as collaborating with his tradition and patrons in a larger project that involves creating the world. The bare artisan model, in particular, he found to be "a distorted one, obscuring an ongoing project of world-construction in which artist and dharma master (and possibly also king, patron, and poet) were collaboratively engaged."[3] Kapstein goes on to examine the preparatory rites found in four of the fifteen painting

1. I thank Richard Payne for assistance in the romanization of Japanese titles and Dan Arnold for editorial suggestions.

2. Kapstein 1995.

3. Kapstein 1995, 244.

rituals in the *Mañjuśriyamūlakalpa*, most of whose rites had been previously described by Marcelle Lalou.[4]

Kapstein explores neither the spectrum of rituals, nor the entire longest (*jyeṣṭha*) painting rite, but instead concentrates on the preparatory aspects: the collection of cotton, its weaving by a virgin, and the consecration of the cloth onto which the painting is to be made. He argues that the gathering of materials, as well as their arrangement and consecration, replicate a pattern of ritual behavior that is representative of much of Mahāyāna ideology. He goes on to observe that, by the time of the nineteenth-century recasting of the ritual in the work of Jam mgon 'Ju Mi pham, aspects of the ritual—especially the weaving of the cloth—had been subject to an "extreme condensation" (p. 259), given that Tibetans did not typically gather cotton and weave it into cloth. Kapstein's point is that, while ritual details in the consecration of the painting appear optional, nonetheless "Tibetan artistic practice traditionally remained continuous with the ritual ethos of Pāla Buddhism, wherein the creation of art was valued above all for its contribution to the ordering of and introduction of divine agency into our world" (p. 261). In this regard, Kapstein argues that the process of painting is a constructive social and religious project, one that not only stretches back to the Pāla artistic legacy but that also constitutes a practice that exhibits a rolling dynamic in its continual reformulation of religious culture, given specific sociocultural parameters, material availability, and institutional requirements.

Kapstein's point is a good one, but it may be somewhat narrowly focused on the painting rituals specific to the early chapters of the *Mañjuśriyamūlakalpa*, in two ways. First, I would acknowledge that his articulation of something akin to Bourdieu's idea of *habitus* applied to Buddhist ritual execution is appealing; nevertheless, both the textual and Buddhist ritual contexts would seem to beg for further exploration. Second, I believe that Kapstein's focus has drawn our gaze to one set of *Mañjuśriyamūlakalpa* painting rites without engaging either the breadth or the stratigraphy of *paṭa* rituals in that work. Contributions to these desiderata will occupy this essay.

Ritual as the Will to Creation

If I were to expand on Kapstein's point, I would concur that—like the envisioning of a maṇḍala from nothingness or like the creation of a pure land from previous vows (*pūrvapraṇidhāna*)—Buddhist cosmology provides an ideological subtext voicing a strong version of moral intention and execution as the basis for the efflorescence of reality. In this view, the apparent firmness of physical

4. Lalou 1930.

reality is misleading, for reality is a quasi-fluid medium that may be modified over time, based on the aspiration of the ritual agent and the spiritual ability exercised toward his or her goals. The *telos* of a ritual act may implicate various strategies for the officiant to exercise his discretion in executing summation, excision, expansion, deletion, inversion, and a number of other ritual modifications required for the successful completion of the creative act. That does not mean, however, that the sense of the ritual is lost, for the elasticity of the ritual enterprise has been one of the hallmarks of Indian and Tibetan rituals generally, and this enterprise has been understood as such by the tradition.

While this general point is true, that does not mean either that the specific outcomes rightly identified by Kapstein actually result from conscious intellectual decisions or that they can be found validated in prior Buddhist scholastic treatises. Indian models of either the individual or collective moral universe are broadly understood under the rubric of karma, in which the creation of specific world systems (*lokadhātu*) is the consequence of the residual moral force from previous actions extending back through beginningless time. As the *Abhidharmakośa* so succinctly declares, "All the diversity of the world arises from karma, which is will, and that which is created by it" (*Abhidharmakośa* 4.1ab *karmajaṃ lokavaicitraṃ cetanā tatkṛtaṃ ca tat*). Commenting on this verse, Yaśomitra's *Sphuṭārthāvyākhyā* explains that cosmic diversity is "differentiated by cosmic level, destiny, species, and so on" (*dhātugatiyonyādibhedena*). Given that the Buddhist project focuses on personal conduct, the relationship between will and the creation of the world is only dealt with tangentially in this context, although sections of the Sarvāstivāda *Prajñaptiśāstra*, as well as related sections of other Abhidharma texts, are necessarily more explicit in the differentiation of these elements. Nonetheless, the emphasis in Buddhist thought has overwhelmingly been on the categories of wholesome/unwholesome conduct in the individual (*kuśalākuśalakarmapatha*) and on the problematic of how karmic residues (*avijñapti*) or their emotional traces (*anuśaya*) may be preserved in a stream of being. This latter problematic was perceived to be the central crux of the doctrine of karma, given the concomitant Buddhist commitment to both the doctrines of non-self and transmigration. Coupled with the ubiquitous idea that, for the most part, the ripening of karma—and thus the construction of the world—happens in a subsequent life rather than the current one, these doctrines would seem to constrain Buddhists to pay less attention to the immediate consequences of ritual and more to meditative consequences (e.g., *Abhidharmakośa* 4.56).

Yet this is again only partly true, since both the foundation and the maintenance of the saṃgha utterly depend on the lineage of ordination, and thus on the continued efficacy of the discipline of the Vinaya vows (*prātimokṣasaṃvara*), which was extended to include lay vows as well (*Abhidharmakośa* 4.17–34).

This dependence partly accounts for the peculiar Sarvāstivāda doctrine of "imperceptible matter" (*avijñaptirūpa*), an element proposed to act as the continued support of the act of ordination, a support that operates throughout the life of the individual. Thus, while most moral action has physical consequences in the subsequent life, *avijñaptirūpa* is the consequence of a specific action in this life, and indeed does not carry over into the subsequent life, since ordination—if not surrendered at some point—only perdures until the point of death. In this way, Buddhist thinkers elaborated a kind of consequence for which there was scant space within the architecture of karma. At the same time, they developed an intellectual justification for the obvious fact that ordination changes both the physical and moral dynamic of the individual, predisposing him or her to beneficial states of being. Yet in this instance, the act of *avijñaptirūpa* creation is not specifically "karmic" in the same way as other results are—nor is *avijñaptirūpa* described with the formal language of "karmic result"—but is instead modeled with language focusing on its dependence on the "natural outflow" great elements, and on the mind and its accompanying mental events (*Abhidharmakośabhāṣya* to 4.6ab: *naiḥṣyandikāni eva bhūtāny upādāya cittacaittāni copādāyāvijñaptir bhavati*). Such models avoided the complex implications of karma and its maturation while still allowing the Sarvāstivāda thinkers a justification for the effects of ordination.

Consequently, if we are looking for a specific model on the relationship between the performative (artistic or ritual) will to create and the universe created thereby—a model positing a real-time operation—Buddhist scholastic thought, indeed most of Buddhist thought overall, would seem to present an incongruous system. For example, both Dharmaśrī's *Abhidharmahṛdaya* (T 1550.28.812c15) and its commentary *Miśrakābhidharmahṛdayaśāstra* (T 1552.28.888c28) relegate artistic accomplishment (*śilpasthāna* or *śilpakalā*) to the category of "indeterminate action that is not associated with defilements" (*anivṛtāvyākṛta*).[5] There seems to be little to suggest that the ideology of artistic ritual in the manner outlined in the *Mañjuśriyamūlakalpa*—with supreme rewards for one performing the elaborate preparation, for one performing the painting rituals, and for one simply glancing at the painting[6]—might be grounded in ideas of ritual action supported within the Abhidharma corpus. Nor does the section on virtue in the *Bodhisattvabhūmi* yield more accommodating results in its construction of the ritual of the bodhisattva's vow. While it affirms that the bodhisattva who has taken the ritual of *bodhisattvasaṃvara*

5. Willemen 1975, 29, and Ryose 1987, 139.

6. *Mañjuśriyamūlakalpa*, 59 and 65–67.

is esteemed in this life, the discourse mostly amplifies the benefits of wholesomeness beyond the grave into succeeding lives.[7]

The extraordinary powers—articulated in the *Mañjuśriyamūlakalpa* and elsewhere in the esoteric textual corpus—said to be achieved by ritual means are instead accessible, according to most prior Buddhist texts, primarily by meditative means: they are effected through the contemplations yielding the attainment of supernormal cognition, particularly the five forms of superknowledge (*pañcābhijñā*) or other forms of *ṛddhi*.[8] As a result, whether we examine Śrāvaka or Bodhisattva sources, prior ideologies of Buddhist ritual in fact support a rather modest model of ritual efficacy; ritual serves the purpose of accelerating the growth and maturation of the roots of goodness, with little to suggest the more baroque benefits extolled in the tantric texts. Yet it is clear that Buddhists accepted the idea of real-time benefits at some level and at some time, even if this inchoate value received scant justification in intellectual circles.[9]

In pursuit of the antecedents of the Buddhist painting rituals, we might cast a glance at the preeminent Indian ritual tradition, the Vedic system of the domestic rituals and their development in the *dharmaśāstra* and *vidhāna* literature. These ritual procedures certainly have left traces in the parts of the *Mañjuśriyamūlakalpa* examined by Kapstein and Lalou. The young virgin weaving the cloth for the painting, for example, is to be drawn from one of the twice-born castes (*Mañjuśriyamūlakalpa*, 56.1–2) and is to exhibit the qualities of a good woman described in the *śāstras* (*strīlakṣaṇaupraśastacihna*). Both she and the officiant are to be fed *haviṣyāhāra*, identifying food used in fire oblations.[10] The signs to be noticed for determining whether to continue or discontinue the preparatory rite extend from the well-developed *Dharmaśāstra* and related literature, largely concerning the recitation of the Vedas by a student, and have been conveniently tabulated by Olivelle (2006).

Structurally, the Abhidharma ideology of a complete karmic act—a preparation (*prayoga*), the basic act (*maulakarmapatha*), and the subsequent follow-through (*pṛṣṭa*)—might seem to suggest the notion of ritual preparation, execution, and signs of accomplishment seen in the ritual in question. However, in reality the structure of preparation, execution, and success has been part of Vedic ritual literature since the *Brāhmaṇas* were composed. And in fact we should note that the term *karma* is applicable in both instances,

7. *Bodhisattvabhūmi*, 155–57, Tatz 1986, 62, and *Bodhisattvaśīlaparivarta-ṭīkā*, fols. 202b7–204a3.

8. Gómez 1977.

9. See, for example, Davidson 2014, 29–30.

10. *Mañjuśriyamūlakalpa*, 57.5–6.

for ritual action in the Vedic system is also known as *karma*, albeit in a quite different sense than the personal or collective moral value identified in the *śramaṇa* traditions. This is also one reason why ritual confession is so different within the two systems: confession and repair (*prāyaścitta*) in Vedic usage is necessary in the case of ritual or purity indiscretions, whereas confession (*deśanā*) in Buddhist rites focuses on ethical breeches in the paths of karma.

So it is not surprising that the idea of a preparatory enterprise (*puraścaraṇa*) for consecration of images is well established in texts allied to Vedic schools. In the *Baudhāyana-gṛhyapariśiṣṭa* (2.13), for example, the brahman is to feed other brahmans, construct an image of Viṣṇu, consecrate a place, and wrap the image, placing it overnight in a watercourse of some variety. Following that, there is the full ritual of consecration. Similar procedures have found their way into the medieval sectarian literatures of several traditions[11] and are ultimately drawn from such rites of passage (*naimittika-saṃskāra*) as the second-birth consecration (*upanayana*) of a young boy, generally between the age of eight and fourteen, depending on caste and tradition.

Lest it seem questionable that painting rituals might in some way be related to the Brahmanical rites of passage, the *Parāśara-dharmasaṃhitā* invokes their similarity in an explicit simile in its discussion of why a brahman without the rites of passage (especially one without the *upanayana* and a firm grasp of the recitation of the *Gāyatrī*) is a brahman in name only. For Parāśara, as in the case of other Brahmanical theoreticians, humans must be ritually cultivated prior to being considered entirely real, and he uses the image of a painter and painting to discuss the officiant and the boy in these rites.

> *citrakarma yathānekair aṅgair unmīlyate śanaiḥ* |
> *brāhmaṇyam api tadvad dhi saṃskārair mantrapūrvakaiḥ* || 8.19
>
> *iti* | *citrakāraḥ prathamaṃ paṭādau maṣīrekhābhiḥ sarvāvayavasampūrṇāni manuṣyādirūpāṇi likhati* | *na ca tāni tāvatā darśanīyatvam āpadyante* | *punas tāny eva rūpāṇi nānāvidh avarṇaprakṣepeṇonmīlitāni darśanīyatām āpadyante* | *evaṃ jātibrāhmaṇyaṃ śāstrīyasaṃskārair utkṛṣyate* | *mantrasaṃskāreṇa vidyādayo 'py upalakṣyante* | (Śâstri, vol. 2, part 1, p. 221)
>
> Just as the act of painting gradually, through several colors, is revealed,
> So too, the condition of being a Brahman is indeed revealed by the rites of passage associated with mantras.

11. Keul 2017.

Sāyaṇa Mādhavācārya explains:

> So the painter first draws on the cloth the forms of the humans complete with their limbs through the use of lines of ink, but they are not yet so attractive. Yet again those forms (of the limbs, etc.) become rendered attractive, having their appearance revealed by the application of different varieties of color. Analogously, the condition of being a brahman at birth is exalted through the textually prescribed rites of passage, for knowledge and so on are defined by the rite of refinement through mantras (*mantrasaṃskāreṇa*).

In support, Mādhavācārya then quotes a couplet communicating almost exactly the same substance, attributing it to the *ṛṣi* Aṅgiras, a sage to whom is ascribed versions of an *Āṅgirasasmṛti*; one received recension contains the verses in question.[12] The use of the painting metaphor in the *Dharmaśāstras* of Parāśara and Aṅgiras, and elaborated in Mādhavācārya's commentary on the former, perhaps signals that the trope was popular for its creative and aesthetic dimensions. Rather than creation *ex nihilo* through ritual means, though, this metaphor stresses the image of inherence: just as the potential form innate in the cloth is brought to life by the action of the painter, analogously the condition of being *vipra*, a "knowledgeable one," is inherent in a brahman boy, only to be revealed by the conferral of the *saṃskāra*s with the Vedic mantras.

It appears, then, that we are on solid ground in saying that the domestic rituals of the *varṇāśramadharma*, which Buddhists sometimes categorized as "worldly," provided some of the ideology, impetus, and methods of performance for the later *dhāraṇī* texts and, following them, the Buddhist tantras. The areas of selective influence include: when the result of a ritual may be observed, what that result may be, the qualifications of the performers, and the ritual architecture. But perhaps more significant than this is the very idea that ritual action can bring about soteriological results in this life, and that certain kinds of material media can operate as transformative substances through the constructive, ritual engagement with those materials. Given this emphasis on the substances of the physical world (not just in the instance of painting), it easily follows that the spectrum and specificity of material components required in the Buddhist tantric ritual exceed those found in all the other forms of Buddhism combined.

Yet, one distinctive Buddhist aspect of this ritual system is exactly its employment of painting, especially on cloth, as a soteriological enterprise; painting receives much less attention in Brahmanical literature (with the exception of

12. Mādhavācārya's quote is found in *Āṅgirasasmṛti* 2.4.9–10; Aiyangar 1953, 133–34.

the *Viṣṇudharmottarapurāṇa*) than it does in Buddhist works. Indeed, the centrality of the rituals of painting—whether on cloth (*paṭa*), walls (*kuḍyā*), maṇḍalas,[13] or painting boards (*phalaka*)—is a distinctive attribute of later Buddhist scripture, especially the *Mañjuśriyamūlakalpa*, and finds its greatest commonality with the descriptions and treatment of painting in Sanskrit drama and in the literature of the secular world. The centrality of painting rituals within esoteric Buddhist texts represents something of a problem for those positing a strong model of a "shared ritual syntax" between the *Mañjuśriyamūlakalpa* and other tantric texts, as recently affirmed by Goodall and Isaacson (2016); the situation appears somewhat more complex than their analysis suggests.

The Paṭa Lineage

There is much more to be said on the topic of materiality in Buddhist ritual, and I have in a small measure alluded to some of it elsewhere;[14] space, however, requires that the topic be revisited on another occasion. Now, I would like to engage very briefly the other major area needing attention: the language of the painting rituals. Whereas Shinohara's (2014) examination of painting texts is exclusively through the vehicle of Chinese translations, this is best done through the investigation of the surviving Sanskrit texts.

The earliest of our surviving painting ritual texts, the fifth chapter in the **Mūlamantra* found in the Gilgit fragments, sets out the performative and linguistic parameters:

> *athāta paṭalavidhānaṃ vakṣye sarvakāryeṣu sādhakaṃ | paṭe acchinnadaśake keśāpagate | ekahastaṃ dvihastaṃ vā samantena caturaśrakaṃ poṣadhikena citrakareṇa navabhājane na śleṣair aṃgair buddhaṃ bhagavantaṃ citrāpayitavyam siṃhāsanasyoparinisạṇṇaṃ sarvālaṃkāravibhūṣitaṃ kūṭāgāraparivṛtaṃ dharmaddeśayamānaṃ |*

> Now, I will explain the procedure for painting the cloth. On new cotton cloth with the fringe not yet cut and devoid of hair, whether of one or two cubits, but square all around, the Lord Buddha is to be painted by a painter who has observed the *poṣadha* rules with colors not [combined] with *śleṣa*. [The Buddha] is rendered seated

13. Macdonald 1962.

14. Davidson 2017a and Davidson 2017b.

on a lion throne, endowed with every ornament, surrounded by his palace, and teaching the Dharma.

The text found on Gilgit ms. side no. 1731 (56v) is replicated on 1732 (57r), indicating that the scribe forgot where he had left off and recopied the same material, or that the previous scribe had done so; the two folia sides do not appear to be written by different hands, and the text of the two sides is virtually identical. Consequently, we would conclude that this is not the autograph but paleographically a sixth-century copy of an earlier text. This lends support to Zhīsheng's estimate that the earliest Chinese version is an early sixth-century translation made during the Liáng dynasty (502–57),[15] a date that would place it as our earliest work employing a painting ritual, one of many ritual actions described in this intriguing work.

In the above passage, *śleṣa* is a notable term, probably technical, and variously spelled as either *śleṣa* or *śleṣaka* in the *Mañjuśriyamūlakalpa*[16] and *śleṣaka* in the *Amoghapāśamahākalparāja* manuscript (fol. 45a1). Edgerton, following Lalou's *couleurs franches*, believed the term to signify "unmixed," which may be correct.[17] But *saṃśleṣaṇa* indicates a "glue" or "cement," and this is how the translation of the term into Tibetan is sometimes handled, "colors without glue."[18] However, in Amoghavajra's translation of this same passage, the term is glossed as meaning "without hide glue,"[19] and this, I think, is probably the correct interpretation. Using hide glue on the cloth would involve dead animal products left as residue on the image of the Buddha, unacceptable in such early works, which are quite concerned with purity.

Be that as it may, this textual pericope from the **Mūlamantra* exhibits a textual pattern replicated in several other painting texts in the Buddhist corpus, and is especially notable for its similarity of language to some of the painting sections in the *Mañjuśriyamūlakalpa*. The difficulty in understanding something of the historical development of these specific *Mañjuśriyamūlakalpa* painting sections is actually facilitated by the **Mūlamantra* material. In the received *Mañjuśriyamūlakalpa*, there are fifteen sections that describe—whether briefly or in greater detail—painting procedures, generally including rituals

15. Davidson 2017a, 129.

16. *Mañjuśriyamūlakalpa*, 68.8, 74.22, 131.16, 289.11, 304.15, 318.7, 322.20, 567.25, 699.17, and 702.6.

17. Edgerton 1953, 81a, and Lalou 1930, 30.3.

18. E.g., **Mūlamantra*, D 506, fol. 305b4, and S468, fol. 485b3: *tshon spyin med pas.*

19. T 1005A.19.628b4: *wùyòng píjiāo* 勿用皮膠.

surrounding the preparation of the cloth, attributes of the painter, and the painting's iconography. These are tabulated here:[20]

Sastri Sanskrit edition	Tibetan texts	Chinese texts
A. *jyeṣṭha-paṭa*, chap. 4, pp. 55.22–66.18	D 129b2–136b4; S 168a4–178b2	T 1191.20.859b7–862a17
B. *madhyama-paṭa*, chap. 5, pp. 68.5–69.21	D 137a5–138a7; S 179a7–181a2	T 1191.20.862b9–c13
C. *kanyasa-paṭa*, chap. 6, p. 71.4–25	D 138b7–139a6; S 181a6–182b1	T 1191.20.862c28–863a11
D. *mantra-paṭa*, chap. 7, pp. 74.18–77.2	D 141a1–142b1; S 184b5–187a1	T 1191.20.863c18–864b17
E. *paṭavidhānamaṇḍala*, chap. 14, pp. 131.16–133.9	D 174a2–b6; S 233b6–235a2	T 1191.20.876b4–28
F. *paṭanirdeśa*, chap. 26, p. 289.10–15	D 206a7–b1; S 283a1–5	T 1191.20.888c1–6
G. *amitāyuḥ-paṭavidhāna*, chap. 27, pp. 304.11–305.21	D 217a2–218a4; S 299a2–300b5	T 1191.20.892c16–893a24
H. *paṭavidhāna*, chap. 28, p. 311.11–23	D 222a1–6; S 306a7–b7	T 1191.20.894a28–b12
I. *dvitīyaṃ paṭavidhānaṃ*, chap. 28, p. 315.18–21	D 225a3–5; S 311a3–6	T 1191.20.895b22–27
J. *pañcamaṃ paṭavidhānam*, chap. 28, p. 318.7–17	D 227a1–6; S 313b6–314a5	T 1191.20.896b7–17
K. *mañjuśrīpaṭavidhānam*, chap. 29, p. 322.20–26	D 229b1–3; S 317b1–4	T 1191.20.897b15–25
L. chap. 51, pp. 552.8–553.23	D 274b4–275a7; S 387a7–388b1	T 1216[a].21.77b19–78a3
M. chap. 52. pp. 567.24–568.3	D 284a7–b2; S 401b5–7	Ø
N. chap. 55, p. 699.16–18	Ø	Ø
O. chap. 55, p. 702.4–6	Ø	Ø

Among these sections, it is item K., the "rite for painting Mañjuśrī," that is the closest to the language of the **Mūlamantra*, essentially substituting the

20. Cf. Yoshitoshi 2015, 1–69.

great bodhisattva of wisdom for the **Mūlamantra*'s Buddha Śākyamuni in the painting, although the **Mūlamantra* painting also includes many other figures not found in section K. An extended discussion of the **Mūlamantra*'s painting text must wait for another opportunity, but it is fair to observe that the principal similarity of language in the **Mūlamantra* is neither with the earlier (A–D) nor later (L–O) parts of the *Mañjuśriyamūlakalpa* but with those in the middle. Items L through M, representing the chapters 51–52 of the received *Mañjuśriyamūlakalpa*, were transmitted independently, as has already been observed by Matsunaga (1985, 884); sections N and O in chapter 55 constitute later additions of independent origin and are not found in the eleventh-century translations into either Chinese or Tibetan.

It is interesting that in all likelihood the oldest *paṭa* painting section in the *Mañjuśriyamūlakalpa* occurs in the later chapters of the core material translated during the eleventh century. As a result, it may be worthwhile to revisit assumptions on how Buddhist tantras were aggregated into the lengthy texts we have today, especially pertaining to three of the largest: the *Mañjuśriyamūlakalpa*, the *Amoghapāśamahākalparāja*, and the *Dhāraṇīsaṃgraha* (T 901). The hodgepodge nature of their compilation suggests that "textual strategy" may in places be perhaps too strong a term to capture the manner in which these pericopes were placed together, and we may (as in our case) find some of the oldest material located toward the end of the earliest aggregate text.

Conclusion

Matthew Kapstein has returned our attention to a ritual program focused on painting and, at the same time, examined the rite in light of some modern presumptions surrounding painters in Pāla India and medieval Nepal; his analysis emphasized the continuity of traditional culture connecting the two. The other side of the coin, however, is the manner in which this traditional Buddhist painting culture was initially formed, and how its maturation necessitated departure from some of the suppositions of earlier Buddhist intellectual culture, in which artistic ability and the painted surface were not accorded such spiritual powers as described in esoteric Buddhist texts. The two areas seemingly most influential in Buddhist painting's divergence from earlier Buddhist practices are indigenous Indian traditions of painting on cloth and the Brahmanical ritual systems. The former was implicated by the medium itself, while the latter furnished ideologies of this-life ritual soteriology, a marked penchant for rituals to become inflated, distinctive qualifications of the ritual participants, envisioned signs of success, and an emphasis on ritual purity. This essay is but a first approximation of some of the thornier questions involved in such an extraordinary transformation of the Buddhist enterprise in early medieval India.

Works Cited

Abbreviations

D Ui, Hakuju, et al, eds. 1934. *A Complete Catalogue of the Tibetan Buddhist Canons (Bkaḥ-ḥgyur and Bstan-ḥgyur)*. Sendai: Tōhoku Imperial University.

S Skorupski, Tadeusz, ed. 1985. *A Catalogue of the Stog Palace Kanjur*. Bibliographia Philologica Buddhica, Series Maior 4. Tokyo: The International Institute for Buddhist Studies.

T *Taishō Shinshū Daizōkyō*. Takakusu Junjirō and Watanabe Kaikyoku, eds. 1924–35. Tokyo: Daizōkyōkai.

Abhidharmakośa. Swami Dwarikadas Shastri, ed. *Abhidharmakośa & Bhāṣya of Ācārya Vasubandhu with Sphuṭārthā Commentary of Ācārya Yaśomitra*. 5 parts. Bauddha Bharati Series 5. Varanasi: Bauddha Bharati, 1970.

Abhidharmahṛdaya. T 1551. See Willemen 1975 and Ryose 1987.

Amoghapāśamahākalparāja. Kimura Takayasu, ed. "Transcribed Sanskrit Text of the Amoghapāśakalparāja." *Taishō Daigaku Sōgō Bukkyō Kenkyūjo Nenpō* (大正學綜合佛教研究所年報) vol. 20 (1998): 1–58; vol. 21 (1999): 81–128; vol. 22 (2000): 1–64; vol. 23 (2001): 1–76; vol. 26 (2004): 120–83; vol. 32 (2010): 170–207; vol. 33 (2011): 32–64. T 1092; D 686. Translated by Bodhiruci II in 707 CE.

Āṅgirasasmṛti. A. N. Krishna Aiyangar, ed. 1953. *Āṅgirasasmṛti*. The Adyar Library Series 84. Adyar, Chennai: The Adyar Library.

Baudhāyana-gṛhyapariśiṣṭa. Pieter Nicolaas Bubbo Harting. 1922. *Selections from the Baudhāyana-Gṛhyapariśiṣṭasūtra*. Amersfoort: J. Valkhoff & Co.

Bodhisattvabhūmi. Unrai Wogihara, ed. 1971. *Bodhisattvabhūmi—A Statement of Whole Course of the Bodhisattva (Being Fifteenth Section of Yogācārabhūmi)*. Tokyo: Sankibo Buddhist Book Store.

Bodhisattvaśīlaparivarta-ṭīkā. D 4046.

Davidson, Ronald M. 2014. "Studies in *Dhāraṇī* Literature II: Pragmatics of *Dhāraṇīs*." *Bulletin of the School of Oriental and African Studies* 77.1: 5–61.

———. 2017a. "Studies in Dhāraṇī Literature IV: A Nāga Altar in 5th Century India." In Keul 2017, 123–70.

———. 2017b. "Magicians, Sorcerers and Witches: Considering Pretantric, Non-Sectarian Sources of Tantric Practices." *Religion* 18.188; doi:10.3390/rel8090188.

Edgerton, Franklin. 1953. *Buddhist Hybrid Sanskrit Grammar and Dictionary, Vol. II: Dictionary*. New Haven: Yale University Press.

Gómez, Luis O. 1977. "The Bodhisattva as Wonder-Worker." In *Prajñāpāramitā and Related Systems: Studies in Honor of Edward Conze*, edited by Lewis Lancaster and Luis O. G Gómez, 221–61. Berkeley: Asian Humanities Press.

Goodall, Dominic, and Harunaga Isaacson. 2016. "On the Shared 'Ritual Syntax' of the Early Tantric Traditions." In *Tantric Studies: Fruits of a Franco-German Collaboration on Early Tantra*, 1–76. Pondichéry: Institut Français de Pondichéry.

Kapstein, Matthew T. 1995. "Weaving the World: The Ritual Art of the *Paṭa*' in Pāla Buddhism and Its Legacy in Tibet." *History of Religions* 34.3: 241–62. [Reprinted as chapter 10 of *Reason's Traces*.]

Keul, István, ed. 2017. *Consecration Rituals in South Asia*. Leiden and Boston: Brill.

Lalou, Marcelle. 1930. *Iconographie des Étoffes Peintes (Paṭa) dans le Mañjuśrīmūlakalpa*. Buddhica—Documents et Travaux pour l'Étude de Bouddhisme 4. Paris: Librairie Orientaliste Paul Geuthner.

Macdonald, Ariane. 1962. *Le Maṇḍala du Mañjuśrīmūlakalpa*. Paris: Adrien-Maisonneuve.

Mañjuśriyamūlakalpa. T. Ganapati Sastri, ed. 1920–23. *Āryamañjuśrīmūlakalpaḥ*. Trivandrum Sanskrit Series 70, 76, and 84. Trivandrum: Oriental Manuscripts Library of the University of Travancore. D 543, S 503, T 1191.

Matsunaga, Yūkei. 1985. "On the Date of the *Mañjuśrīmūlakalpa*." *Tantric and Taoist Studies in Honour of R. A. Stein*, vol. 3. *Mélanges chinoises et bouddhiques* 22.3: 882–94.

Miśraka-abhidharmahṛdaya-śāstra. T 1552. See Ryose 1987.

**Mūlamantra*. Matsumura, H. 1983. "A Text on Esoteric Iconography from the Gilgit Manuscripts." *Mikkyo Zuzo* 2: 71–79. Vira, Raghu, and Lokesh Chandra, eds. 1995. *Gilgit Buddhist Manuscripts*, fols. 1724–33. Bibliotheca Indo-Buddhica Series 150–52. Delhi: Sri Satguru Publications. T 1005a, T 1006, T. 1007, D 506, S 468.

Olivelle, Patrick. 2006, "When Texts Conceal: Why Vedic Recitation Is Forbidden at Certain Times and Places (Presidential Address)." *Journal of the American Oriental Society* 126.3: 305–22.

Parāśara-dharmasaṃhitā. Paṇḍit Vâman Śâstri Islâmapurkar, ed. 1893–1919. *Parâśara Dharma Saṃhitâ, or Parâśara Smṛiti, with the Commentary of Sâyaṇa Mâdhavâchârya*. 3 vols. in 6 parts. Bombay Sanskrit Series 47. Bombay: Government Central Book Depot.

Ryose, Wataru S. 1987. *A Study of the* Abhidharmahṛdaya*: The Historical Development of the Concept of Karma in the Sarvāstivāda Thought*. PhD dissertation. Madison: University of Wisconsin.

Shinohara, Koichi. 2014. *Spells, Images, and Maṇḍalas*. New York: Columbia University Press.

Tatz, Mark. 1986. *Asanga's Chapter on Ethics with the Commentary of Tsong-Kha-Pa, The Basic Path to Awakening, The Complete Bodhisattva*. Lewiston and Queenston, NY: The Edwin Mellen Press.

Willemen, Charles. 1975. *The Essence of Metaphysics—Abhidharmahṛdaya*. Brussels: L'Institut Belge des hautes études Bouddhiques.

Yoshitoshi Otsuka (大塚恵俊). 2015. *"Monjushiri-kompon-gikikyō" shosetsu no pata no mikkyō girei ni tsuite* (『文殊師利根本儀軌経』所説のパタの密教儀礼について). PhD dissertation. Tokyo: Taishō University.

The Chinese Disciples of Gangkar Rinpoché (1893–1956)

Fabienne Jagou

A biographical approach allows for the analysis of individual lives as integral to collective processes. Biography can thus be conceived not only as charting an individual path through a microhistory but also as attempting to understand a community. While researching the biography of Shen Shuwen 申書文, a.k.a. Elder Gongga (*Gongga Laoren* 貢噶老人, 1903–97)—a Buddhist laywoman who was first a disciple of Gangkar Rinpoché ('Bo gangs dkar Rin po che Karma chos kyi seng ge 1893–1956) in China in the 1940s and later a lay Buddhist master in Taiwan after migrating there in the 1960s—I realized that others among Gangkar Rinpoché's disciples had followed a similar spiritual path. Elder Gongga was part of a Chinese Buddhist lay community whose members derived their legitimacy from their relationship with their Tibetan master. Of the almost forty such disciples whom I have identified by name, eight are well-known Chinese disciples of Gangkar Rinpoché who claimed to be Vajrācārya (*Jingang shi* 金剛師), famous because of their achievements outside of China and thanks to biographical and autobiographical sources available today. There were monks: Miaokong 妙空, a.k.a. Fahai Lama 法海喇嘛 (1920–91),[1] Mankong 満空 (dates unknown), Pujing 普淨 (1902–86), and Puqin普欽 (d. 1960). At least four, though, were lay Buddhists: Zhang Chengji張澄基 (1920–88), who would become widely known as Garma C. C. Chang; Chen Jianmin 陳建民 (1906–87), who would be known in the West under the name of Yogi Chen; Chen Jibo 陳濟博 (1899–1993);[2] and Elder Gongga.

In this paper, I will analyze this community of Chinese followers of Gangkar Rinpoché who migrated to Taiwan in the 1960s and who became famous

1. Concerning Miaokong, see Esposito 2008.

2. Chen Jibo later entered university and became a member of various administrative offices in Sichuan. Information related to Chen Jibo is too scarce to include him further in this analysis.

either in Asia or in the West. They all assumed their authority from their relationship with Gangkar Rinpoché, whose teachings they adapted to their own audiences. I will consider three factors, common to the lives of these individuals, as motivating their actions and making their careers possible: (1) a concern to establish of a self-styled community; (2) their decision to seek spiritual experience in the Bo Gangkar ('Bo Gangs dkar) Monastery in Mi nyag (in the Tibetan province of Kham) in the 1940s; and (3) the foundation of social networks based on their experiences at Bo Gangkar Monastery at this time. Studying their individual paths in all their complexity, I hope both to determine commonalities and to appreciate the outstanding individual achievements of three of these people in particular—Zhang Chengji, Chen Jianmin, and Elder Gongga. In this way, my aim is to facilitate some understanding of the history of a community, and more generally to evaluate the importance of networks created in Tibet in the 1940s for some accomplishments realized in Taiwan from the 1980s onward—accomplishments that have contributed significantly to the development of Tibetan Buddhism in Taiwan and in North America.

The Fame of Gangkar Rinpoché and His Relations with Gara Lama

Political events in Tibet spurred the migration of Tibetan Buddhist masters from Central Tibet to China starting in the 1920s, among whom the Ninth Paṇchen Lama Thub bstan chos kyi nyi ma (1883–1937) was preeminent.[3] Others from the Tibetan province of Kham, still adjoining China's Sichuan province in the 1930s and '40s, were in turn eager to receive Chinese monks and lay practitioners and, more generally, to participate in exchanges of Buddhist learning between China and Tibet. One of those involved in such exchanges was Gangkar Rinpoché.

Gangkar Rinpoché was well known in China for a variety of reasons.[4] First, he was the ninth reincarnation of the Gangkar lineage. One of his masters was the Eleventh Si tu Rin po che, Padma dbang mchog rgyal po (1886–1952), and he received teachings from the Fifteenth Karmapa, Mkha' khyab rdo rje (1871–1922). He became the junior tutor of the Sixteenth Karmapa, Rang byung rig pa'i rdo rje (1924–81). In addition to these prestigious masters, he was also close to Gara Lama (Mgar ra bla ma Bsod nams rab brtan, 1865–1936), who invited him to come to China to teach.[5] He went to China in 1936, after

3. On the Ninth Panchen Lama, see Tuttle 2005 and Jagou 2011.

4. Meinert 2009, 216.

5. Mi nyag Mgon po 1997, 60–61.

the death of Gara Lama, with the aim of building a *stūpa* dedicated to him at Mount Lu 廬山 in Jiangxi province. From then on, his work included the teaching of Tibetan Buddhism in China, and he helped in China's efforts at stabilizing her political situation by performing rituals and also in training future Chinese intellectuals in Tibetan studies. He would stay in China from 1946 to 1949 and again from 1953 to 1956. Like every Tibetan master then resident in China, he became close to members of the Chinese government (such as Li Zongren 李宗仁, 1891–1969) as well as to warlords (such as Long Yun 龍雲 from Yunnan, 1884–1962), and he was granted titles by the Nationalist government. According to Carmen Meinert, Gangkar Rinpoché eventually accepted the role of successor to Gara Lama, thus taking on Gara Lama's many Chinese disciples.[6]

The precise nature of the relationship between Gara and Gangkar is obscure, but they seem to have known each other for a long time. It is difficult to draw a portrait of Gara Lama due to the scarcity of information about him and his actions in China.[7] Even his name is a subject of speculation. He was called Gara Lama in Tibetan texts and Nuona Lama (諾那喇嘛) or Nuona Hutuketu (諾那呼圖克圖) in Chinese texts. Having come from Ri bo che, in Kham province, he arrived in Beijing in 1924. He is said to have escaped from prison in Lhasa, where he had been detained six years.[8] In China, he served in both political and religious roles. His political position involved the establishment of offices in Nanking and in Dar rtse mdo, then considered as the capital of the administrative region that would come to be called Xikang province, in 1927. He seems to have had his own political agenda, which aimed at creating an independent kingdom in his native Tibetan province. He taught

6. Meinert 2009, 216–24. Gangs dkar Rin po che received the title of "teacher of the Chinese nation" (*rgyal khab kyi bla ma*) and also that of "omniscient meditation master, a benefactor spreading Buddhism" (*bstan pa spel ba'i bshes gnyen kun mkhyen bsam gtan gyi slob dpon*) in 1947.

7. 'Jam dpal rgyal mtshan 1985, 207–33.

8. 'Jam dpal rgyal mtshan 1985, 211–20. According to Skal bzang bkra shis, quoted by Carmen Meinert (2009, 233n13), Mgar ra bla ma was first recognized by the Tibetan cabinet to be the Thirteenth Dalai Lama Thub bstan rgya mtsho (1876–1933), but the recognition was then withdrawn. According to Xu Qinting, Mgar ra was involved in the war between the Kuomintang and the Tibetan armies in Kham. After the Chinese general was unable to protect Chab mdo, he sent his own army (more than seven thousand men) to resist the Tibetan army. Mgar ra was defeated and sent to Lhasa to be imprisoned for six years. Xu Qinting gives an account of the conditions of his imprisonment: a cell was dug in the ground, and Mgar ra was fed into it through a hole. During the six years of his imprisonment, he dug until he was able to escape his cell. He then lived as a beggar until someone recognized him and helped him get to India. Skal bzang bkra shis 1996, 113–22, and Xu Qinting 1997, chaps. 1 and 5–7.

texts of the Nyingma and Kagyü schools, and his disciples were numerous.[9] He was the seventh of his lineage; no subsequent incarnation has since been recognized.

How Gara Lama and Gangkar Rinpoché first met is unclear, but according to Meinert they were friends.[10] According to Xu Qinting, Gara Lama, while in Kham, entrusted Gangkar Rinpoché in 1935 with the duty of teaching Buddhism. However, Xu Qinting's statement to this effect is vague and does not specify any evidence for his claim.[11] Wang Desheng, the son of a disciple of Gangkar Rinpoché, confirms that Gara Lama invited Gangkar to come and meet him in Dar rtse mdo that same year (1935).[12] Meinert refers to a wish pronounced by Gara that Gangkar Rinpoché would come to China.[13]

Gara Lama's confidence in Gangkar Rinpoché is very important, as the Chinese disciples of the former were enabled by this to carry on with the work Gara Lama and Gangkar Rinpoché had begun together, while Gangkar Rinpoché, for his part, was ensured an audience from the beginning. Together, they engendered and inspired a generation of Chinese lay disciples, some of whom acted as translators, secretaries, and lay Buddhist masters.

The Political and Historical Context of Sichuan as a Place for Devotees of Tibetan Buddhism

The Chinese lay disciples endured much social, economic, and political upheaval. The retreat of the Nanking government to Sichuan in 1938, followed by Buddhist masters both Chinese (Taixu 太虛, 1889–1947) and Tibetan (Lcang skya Qutuγtu Blo bzang dpal ldan bstan pa'i gron me, 1891–1957), together with the proximity of Sichuan to Tibet, allowed for the emergence of a Sino-Tibetan Buddhist community. Many Chinese Buddhist laymen became interested in Tibetan Buddhism as a result of this migration to Sichuan. This was the case for Elder Gongga. She is said to have been devoted to a Buddhist life from an early age. In 1939, she met Taixu, who advised her first to enter the Institute for the Study of Sino-Tibetan Buddhism (*Han Zang jiaoli*

9. His teachings were compiled and published in Taipei in 1998. See Xu 1997 and Meinert 2009, 219–20.

10. Meinert 2009, 218.

11. Xu Qinting 1997, 24, says, of the limits of his knowledge in this regard, that "he knows this only because of their ancient link from a previous life" (*zi zhi yinyuan yi le* 自知因緣已了).

12. Wang Desheng 2006, 71.

13. Meinert 2009, 221.

yuan 漢藏教理院) in Chongqing and then to go to Tibet for further study.[14] She is just one of many who went to Sichuan to follow the Kuomintang government and got involved in Tibetan religious life once there.

The Chinese Devotees' Experience in Bo Gangkar

It must have required determination for Chinese young people to go to Tibet to study with a Tibetan Buddhist master. It is not always easy to know much about their experience there. Some left testimonies that have been transcribed by their disciples, but many others did not. Zhang Chengji, Chen Jianmin, Chen Jibo, and Elder Gongga were all at Bo Gangkar at the same time, in the early 1940s. None of them is said to have been a student at the Mi nyag Institute for the Study of Mahāyāna and Vajrayāna Buddhism (*Muya xian mi foxueyuan* 木雅顯密佛學院), which was founded at Bo Gangkar Monastery in 1939 and dedicated to the Han disciples of Gangkar Rinpoché. This suggests that they were all there pursuing their own initiative and that each followed his or her own way. Although they were there at the same time, they scarcely mention each other in their testimonies, only occasionally naming their fellow practitioners.

The meeting of Gangkar Rinpoché and these Chinese disciples coincided with the building of the Gara stūpa from 1936 to 1939, and this was a time of confluence for the community. For example, Mi nyag Mgon po, the Tibetan biographer of Gangkar Rinpoché, reports that Mankong was already accompanying Gangkar Rinpoché in China in 1936, without specifying how they had met before then.[15] Wang Desheng, the Chinese biographer of Gangkar Rinpoché, reports that Mankong, who was from Chongqing, studied with Taixu from the early 1930s. As he knew the Tibetan language (it is unknown how he learned it), Mankong began to work as a translator in the Institute for the Study of Sino-Tibetan Buddhism. There, he could have met Gangkar Rinpoché and become his disciple when the latter came to visit the institute. According to Wang Desheng, Mankong became the interpreter of Gangkar in China.[16] Contrary to Mi nyag Mgon po's claim, Wang Desheng adds that Han Dazai 韓大哉 (1884–1975) accompanied Gangkar when the latter first came

14. Wang Shisheng 2002, 78–79.

15. Mi nyag Mgon po (1997, 59) was a disciple of the Ninth Gangs dkar Rin po che.

16. Wang Desheng 2006, 81. Wang Desheng's father was a disciple of the Ninth Gangs dkar Rin po che and has written a book about Gangs dkar Rin po che and his Chinese disciples, but he does not cite his sources.

to China, as Han Dazai was already the interpreter and translator of Gara.[17] Mankong and Han Dazai supervised the construction of the stūpa of Gara with Gangkar and stayed with him until its consecration in 1939.[18] Mankong served Gangkar in Kham and in China until the death of the master in 1956. Han Dazai disappeared during the Cultural Revolution.

Hu Yalong (胡亚龙, 1915–81), a Chinese woman who first introduced herself to Gangkar by directly addressing him in Tibetan, began to accompany Mankong as his co-interpreter from 1939. Mankong and Hu Yalong were arrested in 1951, after Bo Gangkar Monastery fell under the scrutiny of the authorities.[19] Mankong was shortly freed and returned to his work as an interpreter and translator, while Hu Yalong remained imprisoned till 1976, a few years before her death.[20] It is unclear what eventually happened to Mankong, though we can say that he was an active agent of Gangkar Rinpoché among the latter's community of Chinese devotees. Zhang Chengji and Chen Jianmin were there too. Both received teachings from Gangkar during the three years in which the stūpa was being constructed.

Connections during this period among the Chinese disciples who were together later in Taiwan can be drawn. Although Elder Gongga does not mention the importance of Chen Jianmin's role at Bo Gangkar in connection with her decision to go to there, others report that she decided to go to Bo Gangkar after learning that Chen Jianmin was conducting a spiritual retreat there.[21] She was in any case influenced by General Zhu Qinglan朱慶瀾將軍 (1874–1941), a friend of her father who was well known as a laymen active in the revival of Buddhism in northwestern China.[22] It was he who invited Elder Gongga to go to Xian (西安) to meet Taixu.[23]

According to the testimony of one of her Taiwanese disciples, Elder Gongga confirmed that Chen Jianmin and Zhang Chengji had been in the monastery while she was there, saying that the former looked serious and wrote down everything he heard from Gangkar Rinpoché, while the latter was young and

17. Wang Desheng 2006, 76.

18. Wang Desheng 2006, 85–88.

19. Apparently, Gangs dkar Rin po che was worried about the increasing number of Chinese people in his monastery (there were eighty in 1952), supposing that some of them were not well intentioned; see Meinert 2009, 226, and Wang Desheng 2006, 218.

20. Wang Desheng 2006, 218–19.

21. Wang Desheng 2006, 124.

22. Shi Dongchu 1992, 1:329–37, and Xiao Yin 2000, 3:58–61.

23. Wang Shisheng 2002, 78–79; Shi Dongchu 1992, 331, confirms that Taixu was in Xian in 1931.

far less serious. According to this disciple's testimony, however, Elder Gongga did not confirm that Chen Jianmin had been on retreat at the same time as her; she preferred, rather, to dwell on the difficult conditions of her own reclusion.[24] It seems certain that Elder Gongga was the only woman in Bo Gangkar who conducted a three-year solitary retreat there.

Chen Jianmin was a married father of two, and his father-in-law, Chen Xunlin, was a lay disciple of Gara Lama who among others helped supervise the construction of the stūpa of Gara. Chen Jianmin himself became a disciple of Gara after having studied with Taixu. In 1937, he became a teacher of Chinese language in the Institute for the Study of Sino-Tibetan Buddhism in Chongqing. He would retire from this work to go assist in the building of the stūpa at Mount Lu, where he met and received esoteric teachings from Gangkar, whom he then followed to Kham. Gangkar at first denied Chen Jianmin's request to join him, because of Chen Jianmin's role as head of a family of four. But Chen Jianmin found a protector in Fan Changyou 藩昌猷, a Chongqing bank director who agreed to take care of his family while Chen Jianmin was in Kham, and so he was finally able to go to Bo Gangkar.[25] There, he received a number of teachings from Gangkar Rinpoché, though we know nothing about his retreat or realization.[26]

Chen Jianmin had first met Zhang Chengji at Mount Lu, and the two met again at Bo Gangkar. Zhang Chengji, like Chen Jianmin, first became close with Gangkar Rinpoché at Mount Lu. When Zhang Chengji was eighteen years old, his father Zhang Dulun 張篤倫—a disciple of Gara who would become the mayor of Chongqing a few years later—gave him financial assistance so he could go to Kham and live there. He studied with Gangkar Rinpoché and chose to have a family. He married a Tibetan woman, with whom he had two sons. Together with Chen Jianmin, he received teachings from Gangkar, and when Chen Jianmin undertook a retreat, Zhang Chengji supported him. In the 1960s, Zhang Chengji went to Hong Kong, to Taiwan, and then to the United States; there, he became known, under the name Garma C. C. Chang, as the first translator of the songs of Mi la ras pa.[27]

So, these three Chinese disciples—Chen Jianmin, Elder Gongga, and Zhang Chengji—were in Bo Gangkar together in the early 1940s, all of them having benefited from the support of Chinese lay Buddhist protectors.

24. Weng Hanliang, interview.

25. Wang Desheng 2006, 72–115.

26. Concerning Chen Jianmin, see Jagou, Forthcoming.

27. Wang Desheng 2006, pp. 111, 113–14, 118, and 121; Chang 1962.

Zhang Chengji and Chen Jianmin were friends, while nothing is said about any kind of relationship between Elder Gongga and either Zhang Chengji or Chen Jianmin. Indeed, Elder Gongga is absent from all of the sources I have consulted regarding the Bo Gangkar lay Buddhist community, except for the biography of Gangkar Rinpoché written by Wang Desheng and her own published autobiographies.

Chen Jianmin, Elder Gongga, and Zhang Chengji, as well as Mankong and Hu Yalong, followed various paths to their common destination. It would be illuminating to know more about how the teachings were organized within the institute Gangkar Rinpoché founded in his monastery in 1939. The three main disciples here discussed seem to have had personal encounters only with Gangkar except that two were friends, and Elder Gongga reminisced about both of the others. These disciples never raised the question of the language of communication between their master and themselves. Obviously Mankong, Hu Yalong, and Han Dazai, who knew Tibetan, would have played an important role in facilitating the relationships between the Tibetan master and his Chinese disciples, and he should thus be considered as central to the network of Gangkar Rinpoché's Chinese disciples because of his position as interpreter.[28] However, it seems that Gangkar Rinpoché could speak Chinese, as Zhang Chengji attributed to him the Chinese translation of the *Essentials of Mahāmudrā* that he later published in English.[29]

Becoming Buddhist Lay Masters in Asia and in the West

Following their time at Bo Gangkar, the paths of the three disciples we have discussed at first diverged. Zhang Chengji stayed in Kham with his Tibetan family, while Elder Gongga is said to have begun teaching in China; Chen Jianmin is supposed to have received additional teachings from thirty-seven other Tibetan masters.

Eventually, though, all three of them retreated first to Hong Kong and then, at the beginning of the 1960s, to Taiwan. In Taiwan, they were immediately recognized as esoteric Buddhist lay masters, filling a gap that had been left when Japanese Shingon masters returned to Japan from Taiwan in 1945. Gangkar's Chinese disciples were welcomed by the Taiwanese Buddhist lay

28. For example, Zhang Chengji (Chang 1963, 16) wrote that Mankong translated the *Six Yogas* of Dwags po Bkra shis rnam rgyal into Chinese.

29. Chang 1963, 37–46. The *Essentials of Mahāmudrā* original Tibetan text is *Phyag rgya chen po'i sgom rim gsal bar byed pa legs bshad zla ba'i od zer*, written by Dwags po Bkra shis rnam rgyal (1511–87).

community, which contributed to their settlement on the island. Although their public teachings were limited to a small circle of disciples because of the martial law imposed on Taiwan by the Kuomintang (which included a ban on public religious practices), they were able to establish institutes from early on, and they were supported by various Buddhist lay communities thanks to their connection with disciples of Gara Lama and Gangkar Rinpoché already living in Taiwan. These included Qu Yingguang (屈映光, 1883–1973), Wu Runjiang (吳潤江 , 1909–79), Han Tong (韓同, 1900–1994), and Liu Ruizhi (劉銳之 1914–97), who were already well known within the circumscribed circle of the Buddhist lay community.[30] They, too, contributed to the development of Tibetan Buddhism in Taiwan: Qu Yingguang created the Vajrayana Buddhist Institute in 1971, Wu Runjiang founded the Nuona Institute (*Nuona Jingshe* 諾那精舍) in 1975, Han Tong was the master of the Lotus Buddhist Institute (*Lianhua jingshe* 蓮花精舍), and Liu Ruizhi founded the Vajrayana Association (*Jingangsheng xuehui* 金剛乘學會).

Chen Jianmin (or his disciples) created the center Adi Buddha Mandala (*fo jiao yujia shi* 佛教瑜伽士) in California, and a small monastery called *Puxian wang rulai tancheng* 普賢王入來壇城 was built in Taipei by his disciples. He wrote *Buddhist Meditation: Systematic and Practical*, which was first published in Malaysia in 1966 under the direction of British monk Bhikkhu Khantipalo (b. 1932). It was later (1980) published in Taiwan in a Chinese translation entitled *Fundamentals of Chan Buddhism* (*Fojiao chan ding* 佛教禪定). Moreover, Chen Jianmin wrote more than a hundred pocket-sized booklets, the first of which was entitled *A Talk on Preaching* (*Tan fo fa zhi hong hua* 談佛法之弘化).

Zhang Chengji, as we have seen, was also a prolific writer of Buddhist books. Under the name Garma C. C. Chang, he published such books as *The Practice of Zen* (1959), *The Hundred Thousand Songs of Milarepa* (1962), and *Teachings of Tibetan Yoga: An Introduction to the Spiritual, Mental and Physical Exercises of the Tibetan Religion* (1963). Chen Jianmin helped select and introduce the distillation of the Milarepa translation in the *Sixty Songs of Milarepa*, also published in 1966 under the direction of Khantipalo; thus the link between Zhang Chengji and Chen Jianmin was maintained.

Elder Gongga established two monasteries in Taiwan and facilitated the invitation of the first Tibetan masters from the Karma Kagyü and Nyingma schools to visit Taiwan. These Tibetan visitors established Taiwanese branches

30. Before 1986, religious groups had to be registered with Taiwan's Ministry of Interior Affairs, and the number of new monks and nuns was reported by the Buddhist Association of the Republic of China every year.

of their main monasteries in India or in the Himalayas, thus allowing a propitious development of their teachings and the foundation of a Buddhist network including their Taiwanese centers and devotees.

This prosopographic analysis is still limited to a very small number of Gangkar Rinpoché's disciples, as it remains difficult to research the lives of all these Chinese Buddhists. Many more lay Chinese who went to Gangkar Rinpoché's institute in Kham are still to be discovered, and their lives and contributions to the development of Tibetan Buddhism warrant further study. It is clear, however, that most of the Chinese Buddhist laypersons who taught Tibetan Buddhism in Taiwan from the 1960s onward were disciples of Gara Lama or Gangkar Rinpoché. This testifies to the fact that the network established between Gara and Gangkar worked well, surviving in exile to the present day, even as the teachings of the Chinese successors to these influential Tibetans evolved toward a hybrid Sino-Tibetan Buddhism suited to a Taiwanese audience.

Works Cited

Chang, Garma C. C. 1959. *The Practice of Zen*. New York: Harper & Row.

———. 1962. *The Hundred Thousand Songs of Milarepa*. New Hyde Park, NY: University Books.

———. 1963. *Teachings of Tibetan Yoga: An Introduction to the Spiritual, Mental, and Physical Exercises of the Tibetan Religion*. New Hyde Park, NY: University Books. (Later published as *The Six Yogas of Naropa and Teachings on Mahamudra*. Ithaca, NY: Snow Lion Publications, 1986.)

Esposito, Monica. 2008. "rDzogs chen in China: From Chan to Tibetan Tantrism in Fahai Lama's (1921–1991) Footsteps." In *Images of Tibet in the 19th and 20th centuries*, edited by Monica Esposito, 2:473–548. Études thématiques 22. Paris: École française d'Extrême-Orient.

Jagou, Fabienne. 2011. *The Ninth Panchen Lama: A Life at the Crossroads of Sino-Tibetan Relationships*. Chiang Mai: Silkworm/EFEO.

———. Forthcoming. "The Chen Jianmin (1906–87) Legacy: An 'Always on the Move' Buddhist Practice." In *Translocal Lives and Religion: Connections between Asia and Europe in the Late Modern World,* edited by Philippe Bornet. Sheffield: Equinox Publishing.

'Jam dpal rgyal mtshan. 1985. *Khams ri bo che dgon dang rje drung sprul sku gong ma mgar ra bla ma bcas kyi lo rgyus rags bsdus* [Short Biographies of the Rje drung Sprul sku Gong ma and Gara Lama, Two Reincarnate Masters of Ri bo che Monastery in Kham]. *Bod kyi lo rgyus rig gnas dpyad gzhi'i rgyu cha bdams bsgrigs* 6: 207–33. (TBRC.org ID: W00KG01666)

Meinert, Carmen. 2009. "Gangkar Rinpoche between Tibet and China: A Tibetan Lama among Ethnic Chinese in the 1930s to 1950s." In *Buddhism between China and Tibet*, edited by Matthew Kapstein, 215–38. Boston: Wisdom Publications.

Mi nyag Mgon po. 1997. *'Bo gangs dkar sprul sku'i rnam thar dad pa'i pad dkar bzhugs so* [White Lotus of Faith: A Biography of Bo Gangkar Rinpoché]. Beijing: Mi rigs dpe skrun khang.

Shi Dongchu 釋東初. 1992. *Zhongguo fojiao jin dai shi* 中國佛教近代史 [History of Buddhism during the Modern Period]. Taipei: Dongchu chubanshe 東初出版社.

Skal bzang bkra shis. 1996. "'Mgar ra bla mas lu'u cun dmag khams khul 'byor skabs mnyam 'brel dang go min tang skabs bod sog u yon lhan khang gi u yon sogs byas skor [The affairs of the Mongolian and Tibetan Affairs Commission when Liu's army arrived in Kham and Gara Lama rejoined the Kuomintang]." *Bod kyi lo rgyus rig gnas dpyad gzhi'i rgyu cha bdams bsgrigs* 10: 113–22.

Tuttle, Gray. 2005. *Tibetan Buddhists in the Making of Modern China*. New York: Columbia University Press.

Wang Desheng 王德生. 2006. *Gongga huofo* 貢噶活佛 [Gangkar Rinpoché]. Kunming: Yunnan minzu chubanshe.

Wang Shicheng 王世成. 2002. "Gongga laoren zhuan lüe" 貢噶老人傳略 [Biographical Notice of Elder Gongga]. In *Bai yun jian de zhuanqi: Jingang Shangshi Gongga laoren xueshan xiuxing ji (Gongga laoren kou shu)* 白雲間的傳奇：金剛上師貢噶老人雪山修行記 (貢噶老人口述) [Marvelous Story among the White Clouds: Narrative of the Vajra Master Elder Gongga's Religious Practice in the Snowy Mountains (according to Her Oral Testimony)], edited by Long Zhaoyu 龍昭宇, 75–100. Zhonghe: Zheng fa yan.

Xiao Yin 小隱. 2000. "Xinhai yuanlao cishan xianqu—Zhu Qinglan jiangjun de yisheng 辛亥元老慈善先驅 — 朱慶瀾將軍的一生 [Senior Statesman of the Revolution of 1911, Pioneer of Charity: General Zhu Qinglan's Whole Life]." *Dang'an yu shi xue* 檔案與史學 3: 58–61.

Xu Qinting 徐芹庭. 1997. *Nuona fawang hongjiao baozang* 諾那法王紅教寶藏 [Precious Buddhist Teachings of the Nyingma Master Nuona]. Taipei: Shenghuan tushu.

From Poti to Pixels: Digitizing Manuscripts in Bhutan

Karma Phuntsho

THE KINGDOM OF BHUTAN has come to be seen as the last bastion of Himalayan Buddhist civilization after the decline of Buddhism in Tibet and other parts of the Himalayas. With its long history and undisturbed continuity, Bhutan's far-flung temples and monasteries today represent a literary and cultural treasure that is largely unharmed and still unexplored. The literary collections in these temple and monastic repositories, which brought Professor Matthew Kapstein on his most recent trip to Bhutan, remained unknown and all but impossible to access, and their values unappraised and unstudied. Despite the spiritual, academic, and artistic significance of these collections to the local communities, scholars, and practitioners, they remain in precarious condition, vulnerable to damage and even destruction.

This paper describes a program of digital documentation of the manuscripts that has the twin aims of preserving the manuscripts in digital copies and making them broadly accessible. It briefly discusses the intent and processes of preserving and disseminating rare manuscripts in digital copies, and the outcome and impact of such a program in the context of the widespread change that Bhutan is undergoing. It reveals both the urgency of digitization of archives and the expedience of digital technology in duplicating and disseminating texts from secluded areas.

Bhutan's Remote Archives

The second half of the twentieth century was the most tumultuous period in the history of Himalayan Buddhist literature. The rich literary wealth of Tibet underwent widespread destruction and dispersal during the Communist takeover of Tibet and Mongolia and the Cultural Revolution. In recent years, numerous projects of reproduction, documentation, and digitization of texts have arisen as corrective efforts to preserve and consolidate the damaged and dispersed texts. The Himalayan literary heritage has never before seen such massive and systematic reproduction and distribution as is happening today through institutions both in the Himalayan countries and in the West. Their works have significantly reshaped our understanding of the Tibetan literary landscape and the overall accessibility to the materials.

Bhutan, however, has remained largely aloof from the events that reshaped the literary landscape of the Tibetan Buddhist world elsewhere. Due to its long isolation and independence and its conservative cultural and political policies, Bhutan generally managed to avoid the ravages of political turmoil and unbridled change outside its borders, and it is seen today as a unique repository of the cultural and religious wealth of the Buddhist Himalaya. The country has now shed its isolation and is undergoing a rapid transformation through the forces of modernization and globalization. (See plate 3.)

The temple libraries of Bhutan are perhaps some of the world's most secluded collections of books. Most of the temple archives are located in remote areas at high elevations and still not connected by motor roads. Some of them are at several days of hiking distance and rarely visited by people outside the local communities. Official records list about 2,200 temples in the country, out of which an estimated two hundred have substantial collections of books. The earliest temples are said to have been established in the seventh century, and some claim to have books produced as early as the eighth century, although the archival collections generally date from the fourteenth to the twentieth century, and the vast majority of books were created during the medieval period of Bhutan's history, from the seventeenth to the twentieth century.

While most of the libraries belong to monastic centers and were created by religious hierarchs, some are private family collections, accumulated by the members of the family and passed down as heirlooms. The manuscripts were mostly produced locally, and some establishments also had small xylographic printeries. The abundance of Daphne and Edgeworthia plants, from which paper was made, not only made book publishing vibrant in Bhutan but also allowed Bhutan to export paper to Tibet. Bhutanese travelers often brought huge reams of paper to Tibet to print books such as the Kangyur scriptural collection, as no Kangyur woodblocks were available in Bhutan itself. The collections in Bhutan thus include handwritten manuscripts and local xylographic prints made in Bhutan, as well as books printed in Tibet.

As items of great spiritual significance and use in religious rituals, the books are treasured by the local communities as a cultural heritage. They are normally wrapped in layers of "clothes" (*na bza'*), sometimes bound between wooden covers with special "belts" (*sku bcing*), and stacked on shelves or cupboards in the shrine rooms. The books are typically stored conscientiously yet are nonetheless exposed to dust, dampness, worms, and in some cases rodents. Not uncommonly, books are brittle and worn due to age and intensive use.

Thus the books lie vulnerable to damage despite being cherished and cared for. The local communities have neither the resources nor the knowledge and skills for preservation. For example, the temples are not properly protected against fire. An accidental fire from ubiquitous butter lamps and incense could instantly reduce a library to ashes, as has happened numerous times throughout Bhutan's history. Today, with Bhutan's hydropower boom and amateur electrification in many locales, short circuits have become a major cause of temple fires. In the past decade alone, Wangdi Phodrang (*dbang 'dus pho brang*), an eminent fortified monastic and political center founded in the seventeenth century, and Pagar (*spa sgar*) Temple, a vibrant monastery well known for book production in medieval times, were both destroyed by fire alleged to have been caused by a short circuit. Temples may also be damaged by windstorm or earthquake, not infrequent in the region. The devastating earthquake of September 2011 affected 339 temples in western Bhutan, with seventeen destroyed beyond repair.

In addition, Bhutan is undergoing sweeping social and cultural change due to its engagement with the rest of the world. Materialism is spreading across the country, and the voracious markets for religious antiquities in the West and the Far East have led to increased commodification of religious antiques, including books. Thieves hunting for religious treasures have broken open almost all the stūpas in the country, many of which had been left vulnerable by the widespread migration from rural villages to urban areas that has left the cultural heartlands empty and unprotected. (See plate 4)

The Digitization Process

The book in Bhutan and the culture associated with it are today in a state of transition. Aware of their spiritual, educational, social, cultural, and academic value and of the urgency to safeguard some of the precious collections, I embarked on a mission of exploration and digitization of Bhutan's archival collections. A more detailed narrative of my initial adventures of digitization is published elsewhere.[1] What follows is a briefer account.

My first quest for rare manuscripts began in 2003 after Rob Mayer asked me to find for him copies of two Vajrakīla tantras from *Rnying ma rgyud 'bum* (Collected Tantras of the Nyingma) manuscripts kept in Gangteng (*sgang steng*) Monastery. I was then traveling across Bhutan with my teacher, His

1. Karma Phuntsho 2010.

Holiness Penor Rinpoché (*pad nor rin po che*). We halted at Gangteng Monastery, where His Holiness conducted a public ceremony for over ten thousand people, and I visited the monastic library with its elegant *Rnying ma rgyud 'bum* manuscripts. I requested Gangteng Tulku to allow me to photograph them, but as I expected, he replied with a vague "no" and polite smile. Although he understood the virtues of documenting such rare books and the use academic scholars could make of the photos, he was unsure about the overall benefit of such reproduction.

His response betrayed the influence of the religious conservatism associated with traditional restrictions on esoteric knowledge typically held by traditional lamas, and the general cultural protectionism that the Bhutanese state strongly enforced.[2] There was understandably a felt worry among lamas that sacred texts may be "disturbed" by the act of photography and that, once in digital form, their sanctity would diminish through wide and easy replication, rendering inapplicable the restrictions traditionally imposed on access to the esoteric content of books such as the *Rnying ma rgyud 'bum*, which fall within the highest category of Buddhist tantric teachings.[3]

Less evident perhaps was also the concern that such malleable and reproducible formats as digital images may undermine the unique ownership of the texts and the socio-religious legitimacy and authority they held. Moreover, he was also aware of the problematic and often controversial nature of the academic study of such sacred texts, as critical scientific analyses carried out by academics and their conclusions often contravened long-held traditional beliefs and stories about the texts and their applications.

I was fully aware of such cultural sensitivities and religious agendas but keen to play the game correctly, with investment of time and effort. So I persisted with my requests in the following months, giving all the good reasons I could think of. After a long test of persuasion and endurance that lasted months, I managed to win his consent to document the *Rnying ma rgyud 'bum* collections. My association with prominent religious masters such as Penor Rinpoché, then the head of the Nyingma order, and my own stature among the monastic communities as an author no doubt helped my dogged determination.

2. A few weeks before our encounter, he was reprimanded by the Minister for Home Affairs for footage showing the inside of the protector chapel (*mgon khang*) in a documentary produced in the UK. The filming had taken place during his absence.

3. Such open access can be paramount to the serious violation of tantric *samaya* precepts generally known as the "open proclamation of secrets" (*gsang bsgrags*). One root precept of esoteric Vajrayāna Buddhist practice is to refrain from divulging the secret teachings and practices to people who have not been initiated.

With his permission, I made my first journey to photograph the books on a grueling country bus crammed with farmers and sacks of rice. I was equipped with many packets of presents, the latest Minolta camera, a laptop, CDs and batteries. The bus broke down twice with punctures during the ten-hour journey. At Gangteng, I stayed with my former colleagues, who were then teaching in the monastic college as abbots. Their friendship and support was a great asset for my work, from finding the caretaker of the monastic library and assistant monks to providing me with timely and comforting meals.

The images I produced for Rob Mayer in 2003 were produced almost single-handedly using a Konica Minolta Dimage F200. I spent approximately ten hours every day taking photos of the voluminous books. The configuration was basic, with a board on which to place the texts and a camera with a tripod. I initially focused using the LCD screen but soon found out that the screen view did not exactly match the resultant images. I also discovered later that the view from the viewfinder did not match the images produced. Hence, the best method was to set the camera and texts in the position to produce a good sample and thereafter maintain the same position.

The greatest challenge was the lack of electricity in Gangteng at that time. The monastic college ran a power generator for three hours in the evening. During this time, I had not only to charge the computer fully but also to create backup CDs. The scarcity of electricity taught me how to run my computer power efficiently and at times also seriously obstructed the photography, as I ran out of computer power to download the images from the camera cards. Worse, the power from the generator was not strong enough to recharge the camera battery. I tried to use another generator in the village that its owner kindly lent to me, carrying it on my back to the monastery, but unfortunately it could not recharge the batteries either. Thus, when all batteries were empty, I had to leave Gangteng after a couple of weeks. The following spring, I returned to Gangteng armed with a bag full of lithium CR-V3 batteries and resumed the photography of the forty-six volumes of *Rnying ma rgyud 'bum*. Wrapped with a blanket in the cold temple hall, I took almost a thousand images each day making optimal use of daylight. After completion of each volume, I downloaded the card onto the computer, checked the images for defects, and saved them in multiple copies. All the images were produced in a fine jpeg format of roughly 1.20MB that Rob Mayer later claimed to be the best *Rnying ma rgyud 'bum* copies produced to date.

However, it was only in November 2004 that a major initiative to digitize the entire collection of manuscripts in Gangteng was planned. The Lisbet Rausing Charitable Trust had given the British Library a generous fund to start the Endangered Archives Programme. The aim was to document endangered archives around the world. Although I learned about the competition for funds only two days before the deadline, my application for funds to photograph the entire collection of manuscripts at Gangteng was successful. With funding in place, I labored again to get the written permission to document the entire collection. Thanks to my prior work in building connections and confidence, the permission was granted without much delay.

Funded by the Endangered Archives Programme, I set off to Gangteng on my third trip under the aegis of the Gangteng Tulku. I was fully equipped this time with two laptops, two Canon cameras, several rechargeable batteries, camera cards, card reader, external hard drives, and DVDs for storage. In Gangteng, we built an outdoor station and began photography in earnest with the assistance of six monks from the monastic college. Two of the monks prepared the folios for photography, two laid the texts on the board, and two of them took the pictures. At lunch break and in the evening, two of them helped me download the images from the cards, sort the files, and make backups. To overcome the electricity problem, I financially contributed to the acquisition by the monastic college of a much larger kerosene generator able to recharge batteries and run for several hours. (See plate 5.)

When we finished the photography of the entire collection of manuscripts in Gangteng, there was 1,476GB of data comprising over 284,300 images of some 500 volumes of texts. The images were produced in duplicate copies of jpeg and raw formats, each with the size of roughly 2MB and 7MB respectively. The jpeg files are good for easy access and distribution. Although the file size is not large, the quality of the images is enough for reading purposes while being easily transferable. Raw images on the other hand are in a proprietary format and thus require specific software to open them. However, they retain the maximum data captured by the camera and allow shooting parameters to be changed even after the photo is taken. Using the proprietary software, these files can be converted into other formats such as tiff and jpeg of varying capacities.

This short description of my initial foray into digitization captures the various cultural, logistical, and technological challenges one faces in successfully digitizing an archival collection. The first challenge, obviously, is to find out what the collections hold. Without any comprehensive inventory or catalogues for archives, it is often by word of mouth or through a pilot visit that one finds out whether a temple has a significant collection. In this regard, the incomplete list generated by the National Library and Archives of Bhutan (2006) for some temples was of immense help.

The lack of information on the collection is made worse by the physical remoteness of the temples. One is lucky if the temple is accessible by motor road. Most temples are not, and when they are, the roads are perilous. On the way to Bonbji, the team had to drive over a wobbly wooden bridge over a big river. Similarly, the road to Thadrak was blocked by a vast stretch of ice that the team had to break to proceed with the project.

Once on site, the temple heads are often not around to give access, and if they are, they are unwilling to grant it due to their lack of knowledge about digital documentation, fear of extra work, and a general cultural conservatism. While enhanced mobile connectivity has helped reach people to seek prior permission and support, my own connection to the monastic world as well as the official backing from the Departure of Culture and Central Monastic Body helped us gain access to most archives. Thanks to a growing awareness of the benefits of cultural documentation, and also to recommendations from archive owners who have benefited from our work, access to collections has now become much easier.

The next challenge, after obtaining permission, is to find a suitable space for the photography. Temple interiors are mostly dark, while most places outside have poor or no protection against direct sun and wind. A space with the right lighting condition is crucial as digital cameras were used instead of scanners. Digital photography is indeed the most effective and economic approach to preservation under the circumstances prevailing in Bhutan, and it is the best method to make the resources speedily available to a wider audience. It is preferred over microfilms, as the latter, almost always in monochrome, have a considerable level of data loss and are constrained in distribution, while color digital images capture and retain a maximum degree of similarity to the original, which helps the reader understand the text better. They are also more easily duplicable, convertible, and distributable. (See plate 6.)

Moreover, the remote archives lack stable electric power, thus the use of a scanner, photocopier, or any other devices requiring stable power are not feasible. Even if there is electricity, most available scanners do not have sufficient width to accommodate a traditional *poti* leaf, and the alternative of a feed-sheet scanner is not suitable for fragile books. Besides, such equipment is difficult to transport, while digital cameras are easy to transport and use with computers and rechargeable batteries. The digital SLRs we used thus far also produce simultaneously crisp and clear raw images of compact data, for archival purposes, and jpeg images, which are easily distributable. The raw images can be easily converted into tiff images of various sizes.

Photography is carried out mostly outdoors in the shade with good natural light. Transparent plastic covers and curtains are sometimes used to diffuse strong sunlight and protect the texts from sudden rain or wind. Wooden boards are used as backgrounds to hold the texts and are covered with gray cloths for balancing color. As it is difficult to find copy stands with sufficient horizontal arm length to photograph texts lying face up from above, we photographed the books as one would take a portrait of a person. The texts rest on small pins on the wooden board, and the camera is tilted on the tripod to a parallel degree. The pins are relocated according to the width of the leaves, and as many leaves as fit on the camera's picture frame are placed on the board simultaneously. In later projects, a color card to facilitate color correction was added on the board. Since our work in Drametse (*dgra med rtse*) in 2007, measuring tape has been placed horizontally and vertically to capture the physical dimensions of the books during digitization in various places.

Once the camera is set, the shutter is released with an external shutter trigger in order to avoid pressure on the camera. The focus and frames are set each time the camera is moved for changing card or battery. To get sharp images, it is often useful to zoom in and set the focus before taking the shots. As discussed above, the frame and brightness of the picture seen through the viewfinder, on the LCD and on a computer screen differ slightly, so it is important to check the images on a computer screen before finalizing the setting. Such practical experience, gained heuristically from trial and error, was as useful as training in the control of camera settings and photographic skills.

The photography since the project in Drametse and Ogyen Choling (*o rgyan chos gling*) was mostly undertaken by a group of dedicated and talented staff led by a chief proficient in the Tibetan Buddhist textual tradition, digital photography, and computing. The staffs consist of learned individuals, conversant with the texts and familiar with digital photography. They take the pictures, check the images, make final copies, and create the list and catalogue.

Local monks or lay priests were hired as assistants to help set up the station, move, unwrap and wrap the enormous bundles of texts, put the pages in order, and turn the folios during photography. This helped young people associated with the temples to gain exposure to and learn from the processes of documentation. Employing them ensures that members of the host community gain basic knowledge of digital data and their use. Many of these assistants later joined the team as full-time staff.

Despite the utmost care given to the equipment, problems with the cameras and digital tools were inevitable. We had one serious incident while working in Drametse, some twenty-five hours' drive from Thimphu, the nearest place with limited access to technical support. One of the cameras displayed a mysterious "error 99" and refused to take pictures when the shutter was released. The pictures it did take were fuzzy, dark, out of focus, and distorted. The camera had to be sent to the Canon service center in Bangkok, which was unable to identify the cause of this malfunction but replaced the entire mirror box, shutter frame, and three other interior parts. It most likely succumbed to the severe trial it was going through, one that Canon engineers may not have expected.

Another technical problem occurred when one of the hard drives started to malfunction and show rainbow-colored lines on the images. Fortunately, this problem was noticed before substantial data loss. The faulty hard drive was returned to the agent in Thimphu, but this put the team under severe storage constraints. This problem of digital storage shortage was faced during most projects as we produced more data than expected, and the size of the images increased with each new generation of cameras.

Outcomes of the Program

Since 2005, a total of forty-four archives have been digitized, including twenty-one archives through funding from the Endangered Archives Programme (EAP039, EAP105, EAP310, and EAP570) and ten temple archives associated with the tradition of Bhutan's foremost saint, Pema Lingpa (1450–1521), through a project at Cambridge University funded by the UK's Arts and Humanities Research Council. The projects have focused on handwritten manuscripts and printed books if they were rare and, particularly, if the woodblocks were lost. The map provided (see plate 7) shows the coverage and digital outcomes of the digitization.

Copies of the images, in raw and jpeg formats, have been deposited in the National Library and Archives of Bhutan for safekeeping and shared with archive owners when they requested copies. Copies are also retained in the Loden Foundation, an educational charity in Bhutan, and shared with the archive owners, Central Monastic Body, the Institute of Language and Cultural Studies, and many scholarly or religious persons who approach us with requests for copies of rare books needed for study or religious services.

A detailed catalogue based on the master template of the British Library is being written. Some of the collections are available online through the EAP website. Besides digitally preserving the books that are in precarious condition and making them easily available, the digitization program also helped enhance the awareness of cultural preservation using digital technology. The Loden Foundation has since 2013 carried out a complementary project of audio-visual documentation of the intangible cultures of Bhutan in order to preserve the dying cultures as well as obtain a comprehensive understanding of Bhutan's past.

Most of the collections photographed are outstanding literary holdings in their size, quality, antiquity, and integrity. For the world at large and Bhutan in particular, they represent an astounding heritage of enormous value and significance. The digital reproduction of the collections not only fulfilled our dual objectives of conserving the unique collections in digital surrogates and of making them easily accessible but has also helped us vastly enhance our understanding of the literary history and culture of the Himalayas in general and the individual archives in particular. Through several discoveries and insights revealed by the projects that cannot be discussed here for lack of space, the process helped us unravel the underlying assumptions about Bhutan's literary past and assess its significance as a whole.

Major Collections Digitized

Collection	Provenance of manuscripts digitized
Bka' 'gyur	Gangteng, Nephug, Thadrak, Chizhi, Dongkarla, Phajoding, Dodedra
'Bum	Dongkarla, Drametse, Yagang, Tsakaling, Mendru Gonpa, Dodedra
Rnying rgyud	Gangteng, Drametse, Tshamdra, Pagar, Dongkarla
Dgong 'dus	Phurdrub Gonpa, Lama Sa-nga, Dongkarla
Gter mdzod	Prakar
Mdzod bdun	Prakar
Rdor gling chos skor	Ogyen Choling
Pad dkar gsung 'bum	Phajoding
Pad gling chos skor	Tsakaling, Gangteng

In addition to a great number of manuscript renditions of well-known canons and other collections, the projects have also brought to light many unknown titles. A general analysis of the content and the provenance of the collections also gives insight into the religious and socioeconomic history of different parts of Bhutan and the extent of the transmission of ideas and practices within Bhutan and with other parts of the Himalayan region. A glance at the collections of the archives also revealed that the *mgyogs yig* script that Bhutan claims as its unique national script was not so common before the twentieth century, while the *dbu med 'bru tsha* script, which the Bhutanese today consider a Tibetan script and are generally unable to read, was widely used for writing noncanonical manuscripts.

Transformation of the Book-View

The culture of the book in Bhutan and the Buddhist Himalayas is witnessing unprecedented changes today as the traditional *poti* format is being quickly replaced by other formats. As mentioned, the second half of the twentieth century was perhaps one of the most dramatic chapters in the history of the book in the Tibetan Buddhist world, involving destruction and dispersal, but also efforts at preservation and revival. During that critical period, book culture also encountered modernity and its technological advantages, which in many ways facilitated its resurgence both in the Himalayas and abroad, while also bringing about far-reaching changes both in the physical production and the perception of the book.

With the influx of modern goods and practices, mass-produced industrial paper has replaced traditional handmade paper, modern metal nibs have supplanted local bamboo pens, and modern metal typesetting has replaced xylographic blocks. In terms of format, the bound codex format has become more popular than the traditional *poti* style, and along with this, books have increasingly come to be seen as literary and educational tools rather than as sacred objects with transcendent value.

The meeting of Himalayan book culture with the dominant Western tradition of the book and modern printing has not been without problems and challenges. It has led to dramatic changes in the ways people construct, organize, reproduce, access, and disseminate knowledge and information. With books increasingly published in bound codex, some among the conservative quarters of Bhutanese society fear that the sanctity of texts and cultural practices involving the traditional book could be lost. As most of the bound books that the Bhutanese initially encountered were on mundane and secular topics, the Bhutanese people did not associate modern books with sacred literature. Thus, when the Buddhist canons are printed in the bound format, they do not inspire the same kind of awe and respect as they do in the *poti* format. Thus, the change in physical appearance has led to a significant shift in the perception of books and their transcendental and ritual use.

If the Bhutanese book culture is going through a significant change through its convergence with modernity and the bound-book tradition, a fundamental shift in people's attitude, approach, and use of books is unfolding with the convergence of Bhutan's cultural world with digital technology. With IT facilities reaching even the most remote parts of the country, and Facebook and WeChat gripping its people, the book culture is witnessing yet another new chapter. Like bound books, digital books stored in CDs and hard drives inspire an even lower sense of sanctity, and also cannot perform the same role as traditional books in rituals and ceremonies.

Digital technology has transformed the way we organize and seek knowledge today. In nearly a decade of efforts to preserve Bhutanese archives in digital copies, I have reproduced some forty-four libraries, which now fit in a few pocket-sized external hard drives. Ancient scriptures available on a shimmering screen at the click of a mouse instil a very different perception and approach than illuminated tomes in a rustic temple. Digitization certainly has its advantages. For instance, it allows unprecedented access to collections located in the remotest corners of the country and provides unprecedented ease of access for codicological, historical, philological, and bibliographic use. Besides access, the digital copies are also highly portable, convertible, and adaptable according to the needs of one's study. The digital zoom facility, which allows easy magnification of small print, is but one advantage of digital copies over the original books.

However, the full ramifications of this transition from solid *poti* to malleable pixels of digital data are yet to be seen. Digitization is certainly bringing changes to the cultural system of thinking. Although with traditional books we do not face much of the common issues of copyright violations, plagiarism, and so forth, the Bhutanese book culture is confronted by other cultural problems, such as the loss of sacred instrumentality and uncontrolled access to esoteric teachings mentioned above.

Despite these problems, the Bhutanese literary world on the whole is enamored by digital technology and ready to embrace its advantages. This is visible in lay priests carrying tablets containing texts for their rituals and village elders using WeChat for community connections. It may not be too farfetched to imagine hard drives adorning the temple shelves and being paraded across valleys, DVDs replacing the scrolls filling prayer wheels, and micro SD cards containing hundreds of sacred texts being worn as amulets. Indeed, if the book culture takes such a turn, digital books would take on a special ritual function. Yet it is also quite possible that the non-literary functions of the Bhutanese book will be largely lost. At this critical juncture, it may be worth asking whether or not the book will survive and be of expedient use in its traditional *poti* format, and what major changes will reshape the Bhutanese view of books.

Works Cited

Butterworth, Jody, Andrew Pearson, Patrick Sutherland, and Adam Farquhar, eds. 2018. *Remote Capture: Digitising Documentary Heritage in Challenging Locations*. Cambridge: Open Book Publishers.

Gedun Rinchen. 1972. *Dpal ldan 'brug pa'i gdul zhing lho phyogs nags mo'i ljongs kyi chos 'byung blo gsar rna ba'i rgyan*. Thimphu: Tango Drubde.

Karma Phuntsho. 2009. "Gangtey's Untold Treasures." In *Written Treasures of Bhutan: Mirror of the Past and Bridge of the Future—Proceedings of the First International Conference on the Rich Scriptural Heritage of Bhutan*, edited by John Ardussi and Sonam Tobgay, 267–85. Thimphu: National Library and Archives of Bhutan.

———. 2010. "Unravelling Bhutanese Treasures." In *Ancient Treasures, New Discoveries: Proceedings of the XIth Seminar of International Association for Tibetan Studies*, edited by Hildegard Diemberger and Karma Phuntsho, 120–40. Leiden: Brill.

———. 2012. "Reflections on Multidisciplinary Approach in Himalayan Studies: The Case of the Book." In *Buddhist Himalaya: Studies in Religion, History and Culture*, edited by Alex Mckay and Anna Denjongpa, 1:17–28. Gangtok: Namgyal Institute of Tibetology.

National Library and Archives of Bhutan. 2006. *List of Books in Temples and Monasteries in Seven Dzongkhags Collected through Literary Survey by the National Library of Bhutan*. Thimphu: National Library and Archives of Bhutan.

Part 2
The Tibetans

The Case of the Missing Shangpas in Tibet

Michael R. Sheehy

IN HIS NEXT LIFE, Matthew Kapstein might very well make a great private eye. As his prodigious scholarship demonstrates, he not only wields tenacious criticality, but has an uncanny knack for investigating evidence, examining records, detecting clues, and solving intellectual crimes. Matthew, like any good detective of Tibetology, has gone in search of what's missing in Tibetan Buddhism. From my first encounter with Matthew as a graduate student, and over the years, I have admired his scholarship on the missing traditions of Tibetan Buddhism. No doubt a reflection of my own interests, I have gained a particular respect for Matthew's contributions to the study and preservation of the Jonang (*jo nang*) and Shangpa (*shangs pa*), two Tibetan Buddhist traditions that have to date received scant scholarly attention. The Shangpa and Jonang traditions seemingly vanished (or at least, disappeared from normative historical narratives), yet thanks to patient scholarship, fieldwork, and preservation efforts—largely pioneered by Matthew Kapstein—these traditions are now on the Tibetan studies map.

In honor of Matthew's contributions to the study of the Shangpa, and as an extension of Jonang history, this essay builds on research for which Matthew laid the foundation in his 1980 essay "The Shangs-pa bKa'-brgyud: An Unknown School of Tibetan Buddhism."[1] It aims to contribute to our working knowledge of the institutional history of the Shangpas in Tibet, based on Tibetan lineage records and fieldwork that the author conducted to locate Shangpa historical sites in the Shangs and 'Phan po valleys of central

1. Kapstein 1980. Matthew's essay, along with E. Gene Smith's 1970 historical introduction to Kalu Rinpoche's Tibetan language reproduction of the *Golden Rosary of the Shangs pa*, continue to be the mesial building-blocks for Shangs pa studies. Smith 2001 is a reprint of the introduction in Karma Rang byung kun khyab 1970. For early Western scholarship on the Shangs pa, see chapter 9 of George Roerich's 1949 translation of 'Gos Lo tsā ba's *Blue Annals*, and the outline of the Kagyü in Li An-che 1949, 52–53. See also Thuken Losang Chökyi Nyima 2009, 118–20. Note that the originally intended *bKa'* in the title belongs to a different transliteration system.

Tibet during the summer of 2014, providing clues in the case of the missing Shangpas.[2]

The Shangpas serve as a particularly fascinating case to trace transmission history in Tibet. Because of their multifarious transmissions across the Tibetan traditions, the Shangpas have a history that is riddled with questions about identity and presence that pertain to their loose social networks of knowledge exchange and elusive institutional order. As Matthew elegantly described, the Shangpas are like "some vine that adorns a whole forest without being able to stand by itself," so much so that it "may strike one who follows its twists and turns as being virtually an omnipresent element in Tibetan Buddhism." Nevertheless, while the aim to trace the twists and turns of the Shangpas' entangled Buddhist history is beyond the scope of this brief essay, we ask, "What is Kagyü?" and, "Where were the Shangpas located in Tibet?"

Kagyü Lineage Streams

To face the abstract identity of the Shangpas, we must first give attention to the simple question, "What is Kagyü?" This is a question of critical importance in the investigation regarding the Shangpas, for as Matthew writes, "If there is any statement concerning the Shangs-pa made with sufficient frequency to be termed commonplace, it is that the Shangs-pa bKa'-brgyud is a branch of the larger bKa'-brgyud school . . ."[3]

To approach this search for identity, Matthew makes explicit a useful hermeneutical distinction between an "order" or "sect" (*lugs*, *srol*), on the one hand, and a "lineage" (*brgyud*), on the other.[4] According to this model, the difference is that an order is an organized institution with structures of authority and property; a lineage is a continued stream of the transmission of knowledge and practices. Lineages can be subsumed and sustained by institutional religious orders, while orders can dissipate into multifarious transmission lineages. While by no means a clean-cut distinction, it serves our current purpose for investigating the historical identity of the Shangpas.

2. Among Shangs pa historical and biographical sources, a guiding text in my reconstruction of Shangs pa historical networks up to the sixteenth century has been Kun dga' Grol mchog's *gsan yig*, or record of teachings received, *A Bounty of Teachings* (*Bstan pa'i nor bdzas*). Kung dga' Grol mchog, *Dam pa'i chos*, fols. 243–51. Kapstein identified eight sites of importance in his 1980 article, (1) Zhang zhong, (2) Gnas rnying, (3) Rmog lcog, (4) 'Bal skyer sgang, (5) Ri gong, (6) 'Jags, (7) Bsam sdings, (8) Rtag rdo rje gdan. Kapstein 1980, 143n12. Note that 'Phan po is the modern iteration of 'Phan yul, which is more common in early Shangs pa sources.

3. Kapstein 1980, 138.

4. Kapstein 1980, 139.

The Tibetan term Bka' brgyud (Kagyü) literally means "transmissions that are spoken," referring to a lineage (*brgyud*) of oral instructions.[5] The term came into broad use in Tibet starting in the eleventh century, conveying the claim of a continuity of spoken instructions from Indic sources. The nomenclature gave form to a multiplicity of Kagyü streams, including the Dga' ldan Bka' brgyud, for esoteric teachings of the Geluk tradition, and Padma'i Bka' brgyud, for the oral tradition of the Nyingma.[6] Kagyü is also frequently used as the proper name for the traditions that emerged from Lo tsā ba Mar pa Chos kyi blo gros (1012–1100) and subsequently his disciple Mi la ras pa (1040–1123). The association of the Shangpa Kagyü with this usage of Kagyü, and its implication that the Shangpas belong to a branch of the Mar pa Bka' brgyud, is a source of repeated misrepresentation.[7]

In organizing the Kagyü as part of his project to categorize the Tibetan traditions, the *ris med* synthesizer 'Jam mgon Kong sprul (1813–99) divides the Kagyü into four major lineages:

1. Kam tshang or Karma Bka' brgyud, founded by the First Karma pa Dus gsum mkhyen pa (1110–93)
2. 'Ba' rom Bka' brgyud, founded by Dar ma dbang phyug (1127–99)
3. Tshal pa Bka' brgyud, founded by Bla ma Zhang Brtson 'grus grags pa (1123–93)[8]
4. Phag gru Bka' brgyud, founded by Phag mo gru pa Rdo rje rgyal po (1110–70)

There are also eight minor lineages:

1. 'Bri gung Bka' brgyud, founded by 'Bri gung 'Jig rten mgon po (1143–1217)
2. Stag lung Bka' brgyud, founded by Stag lung Thang pa bkra shis dpal (1142–1210)

5. Matthew here references a definition of *bka' brgyud* by Thu'u bkwan: *bka' babs kyi gdams pa'i brgyud 'dzin*. Kapstein 1980, 138 and n5. Thuken Losang Chökyi Nyima 2009, 117–56. Smith 2001, 40. Tāranātha makes the point in the introduction to his history of Shangs pa teachings that the Shangs pa tradition is Kagyü because it is a continuous stream of masters who have transmitted the teachings. Tāranātha, *Rgyal ba'i bstan pa*, 417–18.

6. Kapstein 1980, 138.

7. Matthew makes mention of this misrepresentation by both Stein and Tucci in the secondary literature. Kapstein 1980, 138.

8. Also known as the Zhang tshal Bka' brgyud.

3. Khro phu Bka' brgyud, founded by Rgyal tsha Rin chen mgon (1118–95) and Kun ldan ras pa (1148–1217)
4. 'Brug pa Bka' brgyud, founded by Gling rje ras pa Padma rdo rje (1128–88) and Gtsang pa rgya ras Ye shes rdo rje (1161–1211)[9]
5. Smar pa Bka' brgyud, founded by Smar pa grub thob Shes rab seng ge (d.u.)
6. Yel pa Bka' brgyud, founded by Sangs rgyas yel pa Ye shes brtsegs (1134–94)
7. G.ya' bzang Bka' brgyud, founded by Zwa ra skal ldan Ye shes seng ge (1168–1207)
8. Shug gseb Bka' brgyud, founded by Gyer sgom Tshul khrims seng ge (1144–1204)

Kong sprul does not include the Shangpa lineage in his taxonomy of the Kagyü because it does not flow from Mar pa Chos kyi blo gros.[10] Though the lineages are well known and accepted models of Kagyü subdivisions originating with Mar pa, this classification is a taxonomy ascribed to Kong sprul.[11] Subsumed among these later Kagyü lineage divisions, there are yet further substreams of Kagyü, demonstrating the complexity and granularity of the historically intertwined Kagyü lineage networks, such as:

- Zur mang Bka' brgyud, a substream of the Kam tshang Bka' brgyud
- Gnas mdo Bka' brgyud, a substream of the Kam tshang Bka' brgyud, founded by Karma Chags med (1613–78)
- Rgyal ston Bka' brgyud, a substream of the Kam tshang Bka' brgyud
- Lha nang pa Bka' brgyud, a substream of the 'Bri gung Bka' brgyud, associated with Lha nang pa Sangs rgyas rin chen (1164–1224)
- 'Ba' ra ba Bka' brgyud, a substream of the 'Brug pa Bka' brgyud or Gling ras Bka' brgyud

9. Extensions of the 'Brug pa Bka' brgyud are its divisions of the Stod, Smad, and Bar Bka' brgyud, all associated with Gling ras pa and Gtsang pa rgya ras.

10. Thu'u bkwan Blo bzang chos kyi nyi ma makes a clear distinction between the Kagyü lineage of 'Khyung po rnal 'byor pa and that of Mar pa, stating that the Kagyü is twofold: (1) the Shangs pa Bka' brgyud and the (2) Dwags po Bka' brgyud. Thuken Losang Chökyi Nyima 2009, 117–18. On Kong sprul's classification of the Shangs pa, see Kapstein 1996.

11. This division of the four major and eight minor lineages predates Kong sprul and can be found in a brief supplication liturgy by the fifteenth-century Karma Kam tshang author 'Jam dpal bzang po, a disciple of the Sixth Karmapa, where it reads, "*che bzhi chung brgyad brgyud*..." 'Jam dpal bzang po 2009, 177.

- G.ya' yak Bka' brgyud, a substream of the 'Brug pa Bka' brgyud or Gling ras Bka' brgyud[12]
- Gsal stong sho sgom Bka' brgyud, a substream of the 'Ba' rom Bka' brgyud

An earlier categorization of the Kagyü is found in the writings of the eclectic Shangpa, Jonang, and Sakya scholar Kun dga' grol mchog (1507–65), who divides the Kagyü into three streams:[13]

1. Nāro Paṇchen (Nāropa)
   a. Mar pa Chos kyi blo gros
   b. Rngog Lo tsā ba (1036–1197)[14]
   c. Mi la ras pa
   d. Sgam po pa (1079–1153)
   e. Karma pa Dus gsum mkhyen pa (1110–93)
   f. Phag mo gru pa
   g. 'Bri gung
   h. Stag lung
   i. Bla ma Zhang
2. Ḍākinī Ni gu ma
3. Siddha
   a. Emperor Srong btsan Sgam po (617–50)
   b. Padmasambhava
   c. Rgwa Lo tsā ba Gzhon nu dpal (twelfth century)
   d. Gter ston Dung mtsho ras pa (d. 1329)

In historical supplements to his compilation, *One Hundred and Eight Instructions of the Jonang*, Grol mchog describes twenty-five transmission lineages that stream from the ḍākinī Ni gu ma.[15] Though Kong sprul delineates

12. This substream originated from disciples of Gtsang pa rgya ras Ye shes rdo rje.

13. Kapstein 1980, 142n5. Kun dga' grol mchog 1981c, 359.

14. In all likelihood, this refers to Rngog Chos sku rdo rje, a disciple of Mar pa Chos kyi blo gros, and not to Rngog Lo tsā ba Blo ldan shes rab (1059–1109). For details about the life and the place of Rgnog Chos sku rdo rje in the Kagyü lineage, see Ducher 2017, 221–46.

15. According to Kun dga' grol mchog 1981b, 63–64, the teachings that stream from Ḍākinī Ni gu ma are summed up in the seminal practices of the Four Golden Dharmas (*gser chos bzhi*): (1) the Six Dharmas of Ni gu ma (*chos drug*), (2) Mahāmudra (*phyag chen*), (3) Integration onto the Path (*lam khyer*), and (4) Deathless Mind (*'chi med*). And the fifth golden dharma is the white and red Khecharī. Kapstein 1980, 144n22. Kapstein 1992. Harding,

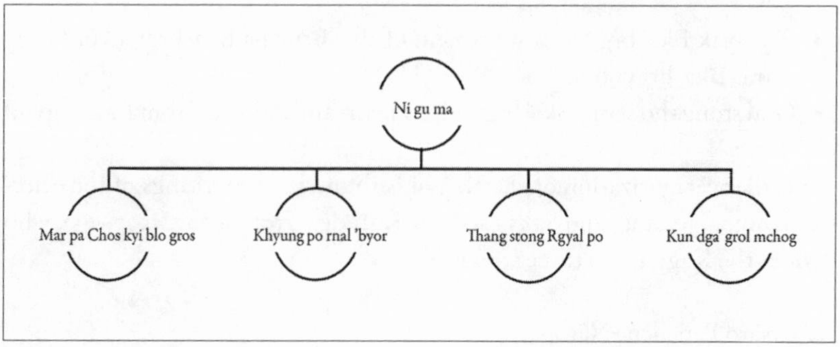

The Lineal Descendants of Ni gu ma

the Kagyü lineages that stream from Mar pa Chos kyi blo gros as Mar pa Bka' brgyud, and as being different than the Shangpa Kagyü lines that stream from Khyung po rnal 'byor, "the yogin of the Khyung clan"—both Mar pa and Khyung po rnal 'byor are registered by Grol mchog as having received transmissions from ḍākinī Ni gu ma.[16]

Locating Shangpa Sites in Tibet

The mystery of the Shangpas, however, does not so much concern its lineal streams and matrices but rather its historical identity as an institutional order. Now that we have identified Shangpa Kagyü as a distinct order, we can surmise where its lineage networks were geographically located on the Tibetan plateau.

As we find in Khyung po rnal 'byor's hagiography, the Shangpa order was institutionalized when he founded Zhang zhong Monastery in the Shangs Valley, one of 108 sites that he reputedly established over a three-year period.[17] Matthew notes in his 1980 article that the Shangpas "lost the one opportunity they ever had to create a unified sect" when his disciples cremated Khyung

30–33. For Grol mchog's condensed instructions on the Ni gu chos drug, Kun dga' grol mchog 1981a, 283–88. See also Kapstein 1997, 184–87.

16. See streams from Grol mchog above, note 13. For a discussion of the historical relation between the Six Dharmas of Nāropa, Six Dharmas of Ni gu ma, and Six Dharmas of Sukhasiddhī, see Tāranātha, 102–5. See Kapstein 2005 for a discussion of Khyung po rnal 'byor's dates and why Matthew assigns him a date a half century earlier, spanning roughly the period from 1050–1140, rather than 978/990–1127. On the origins of the Shangs pa, including translations by Matthew, see Schaeffer 2013, 230–42.

17. Karma Rang byung kun khyab. 1970, 114. As Matthew notes, the Tibetan term for sites (*gnas dgon*) used in this context is meant to include not only monasteries but also hermitages, stūpas, etc. Kapstein 1980, 143n7.

po rnal 'byor's corpse and divided the relics rather than enshrining them at Zhang zhong.[18] Though many of Khyung po rnal 'byor's disciples founded their own sites, this disunity of the order persisted throughout Shangpa history. We can deduce that while these sites likely remained independent institutions, the Shangpas had a significant institutional presence in central Tibet during their founder's lifetime through the early twelfth century.

The following list builds on field research conducted by the author at Shangpa sites in Tibet and is structured around the four site types that Matthew introduced in his 1980 article, supplemented with relevant historical site data and GIS location coordinates, which are provided in the notes where available.[19]

A. Sites founded by a Shangpa master:

1. Shangs Zhang zhong rdo rje gdan: founded by Khyung po rnal 'byor in 1021[20] (see plate 8)
2. Jog mda' 'Chad kha dgon: founded by Khyung po rnal 'byor in 1090[21] (see plate 9)
3. Sngags Khyung dgon: founded by Khyung po rnal 'byor.[22]

18. Kapstein 1980, 139.

19. Kapstein 1980, 139–40. A simple working taxonomy of Tibetan sites includes: (A) monastery (*dgon pa*), monastic seat (*dgan sa*), satellite monastery (*dgon lag*); (B) mountain retreat (*ri khrod*), meditation cave (*sgrub phug*), nunnery (*btsun ma'i dgon*); (C) stūpa (*mchod rten*). Other possibly relevant categories that are not included in this list of Shangs pa sites would be birth places or residences. GIS data provided in the notes below was gathered by the author in Tibet and subsequently entered into the place databases of Harvard World Map, TibetMap (http://worldmap.harvard.edu/maps/tibet), Buddhist Digital Resource Center (www.tbrc.org/#!places/), and Jonang Foundation (www.jonangfoundation.org/list/sites). See these online resources for research tools and maps. Some GIS locations are approximate to county seat.

20. Alternative names, Zhong zhong dgon or Zhang zhang dgon. Active. Recently rebuilt, home to approximately thirty monks. Located in Rnam gling County, Shangs (29° 40' 620" N, 89° 08' 228" E). For an account of Zhang zhong Monastery, see Kaḥ thog Si tu 03 Chos kyi rgya mtsho's (1880–1925) pilgrimage guidebook, Chos kyi rgya mtsho 2001, 452, and for further description, see 'Jam dbyangs Mkhyen rtse'i dbang po 1980, 510–13, Rdo rje tshe dbang 2014, 135–59, and for an analysis of the variation of site name, 38–139.

21. Alternative names, 'Phan yul Chad kha dgon or Jog po 'Chad dkar. Ruined. Located in the 'Phan po Valley (29° 30' 42.12" N, 91° 9' 15.48" E). Not to be confused with the early Kadam monastery of the same name, later converted to a Geluk monastery, founded by Dge shes 'Chad kha ba, located in Lha sa municipal district. An occasion of Khyung po rnal 'byor staying at 'Phan yul 'Chad khar monastery after his return from India is recorded in his hagiography. Nam mkha' Bsam grub rgyal mtshan 1996, 37–38.

22. Located in Gnya' nang County. Currently operating as a Nyingma monastery. Rdo rje tshe dbang 2014, 52–453.

4. Gnas rnying dgon: founded by Khyung po rnal 'byor's disciple La stod pa Dkon mchog mkhar in approximately 1050.[23] Gnas rnying Kagyü transmissions of the Shangpa tradition continued here through Gnas rnying A'i seng ge, a disciple of Sangs rgyas Ston pa Brtson 'grus seng ge (1207–78).
5. Rmog lcog dgon pa: founded by Khyung po rnal 'byor's disciple Rmog lcog Rin chen brtson 'grus (1110–70) in 1150.[24] Continued with an active line of tulku reincarnations until the 1940s.[25]
6. Sku lugs dgon: founded by Rmog lcog Rin chen brtson 'grus[26]
7. Yol phu Ri gong dgon pa: founded by Sangs rgyas gnyan ston chos kyi shes rab (1175–1255)[27]
8. Yol phu Brag rtsa dgon: founded by Sangs rgyas ston pa brtson 'grus seng ge[28]
9. 'Jag chung Dpal dgon: founded by Gtsang ma Shangs ston in 1290.[29] Primary seat of the 'Jag pa transmissions of the Shangpa

23. Located in Khang dmar County (28° 49' 0.012" N, 89° 39' 0" E). Currently operating as a Geluk monastery. Rdo rje tshe dbang 2014, 453–55. For a description of an occasion when La stod pa Dkon mchog mkhar arrived at Gnas rnying dgon with Khyung po rnal 'byor, see the *Gnas rnying chos 'byung*, 12b–13a.

24. Alternative name, Lha phu Rmog lcog dgon. Located in Lha phu district, Shangs (29° 40' 56.3844" N, 89° 5' 57.246" E). Ruined. Both this and Sku lugs dgon are located in the vicinity of Rmog lcog's birthplace, Lha phu spang rtsa. The author heard that there are recent attempts to rebuild. Rdo rje tshe dbang 2014, 456–57.

25. Smith 2001b, 54.

26. Alternative names, Skugs lung or Lkugs lung dgon pa. Located in Lha phu district, near Shangs. Rdo rje tshe dbang 2014, 457–60.

27. Also spelled Yol bu Ri gung dgon pa or Yol ri gong gi dgon. Located in Chu shur County. Matthew lists this monastery as founded by Gtsang ma Shangs ston (Kapstein 1980, 143n12), but it was founded by Sangs rgyas gnyan ston chos kyi shes rab and inherited by his disciple Brtson 'grus seng ge (1207–78) as well as Gser gling pa Bkra shis dpal and Sangs rgyas ston pa (Rdo rje tshe dbang 2014, 462–65). This site is where Gser gling pa Bkra shis dpal continued the Gnas rnying Bka' brgyud transmissions of the Shangs pa. Transmission streams through Gser gling pa at Ri gong Monastery became known as the "lower tradition" based on its geographical location. This was the seat where Phag mo gru pa Rdo rje rgyal po (1110–70) and later Kam tshang lineage holders received transmission. The so-called "upper tradition" of Ri gong, the Ri gong stod rgyud, continued the transmission of the Lcags zam tradition.

28. Located in Chu shur County. Founded by Sangs rgyas ston pa brtson 'grus seng ge after meeting Sangs rgyas gnyan ston and receiving Shangs pa transmissions at Yol phu Ri gong monastery. As Rdo rje tshe dbang indicates, the exact location of this historic site is not yet found, *da lta dgon shul nges gtan ma rnyed*. Rdo rje tshe dbang 2014, 450–52.

29. Also spelled 'Jags chung dpal dgon. Ruined. Located in Rnam gling County, Shangs [29° 40' 56.3844" N, 89° 5' 57.246" E]. Matthew lists this as founded by Gtsang ma Shangs ston.

10. 'Jag chen Dpal dgon: founded by Gtsang ma Shangs ston's disciple, 'Jag chen Rgyal mtshan 'bum and his disciple, 'Jag chen 'Jam pa dpal[30]
11. Nyang smad Bsam sdings dgon: founded by Gzhon nu grub in 1300.[31] Seat of the Nyang smad Bsam sdings transmissions of the Shangpas
12. Rta nag Sa rdo rje gdan dgon: founded by Pha rgod Kun dga' bzang po in 1375.[32] Seat of the Rta nag Shangpa transmissions. Monastery where the Second Dalai Lama Dge 'dun rgya mtsho (1475–1542) was born[33]
13. Ri bo che dgon: stūpa founded in the year 1386, later rebuilt in 1426 by Thang stong rgyal po (1361–1485).[34] Seat of the Lcags zam transmissions of the Shangpa and the re-embodiments of Thang stong rgyal po (see plate 10)
14. Lcags zam Chu bo ri dgon: site of the Lcags zam transmissions of the Shangpas, associated with Thang stong rgyal po.[35] Primary seat of the successive Lcags zam tulku lineage

---

Kapstein 1980, 143n12. It is an early Shangs pa site where Gtsang ma Shangs ston lived for most of his lifetime. Also, site of 'Jag chen Rgyal mtshan 'bum, 'Jag chen Byams pa dpal, 'Jag chen Shes rab tshul khrims, and 'Jag chen Kun dga' dpal bzang. Rdo rje tshe dbang 2014, 466–69.

30. Also spelled 'Jags chen dgon. Located in Rnam gling County, Shangs. Site of Gtsang ma Shangs ston's disciple 'Jag chen Rgyal mtshan 'bum and his disciple 'Jag chen Byams pa dpal. Rdo rje tshe dbang 2014, 469–70.

31. Alternate name, Pa snam Bsam sdings dgon. Ruined. Located in Pa snam County (29° 3' 38.664" N, 89° 9' 9.6876" E). This Bsam sdings Monastery is not to be confused with Yar 'brog Bsam sdings, located in Sna dkar rtse County (28°58, 442; 90° 28, 364), the Bo dong pa monastery and seat of the Bsam sdings Rdo rje phag mo lineage. This is an emendation to Kapstein 1980, 144n23 (Rdo rje tshe dbang 2014, 470–76; Sangs rgyas rgya mtsho 1998, 252).

32. Located near Rnam gling County, Rta nag Valley, Shangs (29° 40' 56.3844" N, 89° 5' 57.246" E). Rdo rje tshe dbang 2014, 47778.

33. Pha rgod Kun dga' bzang po, the founder of this monastery, was the grandfather of Sreg ston Kun dga' rgyal mtshan (1432–81), who was also a Shangs pa lineage-holder and the father of the Second Dalai Lama Dge 'dun rgya mtsho. Interestingly enough, the Second Dalai Lama returned throughout his life to Rta nag Monastery, where he composed several works, including praises in verse to Tsong kha pa and his father.

34. Alternative names, Dpal Ri bo che dgon E wam dga' 'khyil or Cung Ri bo che or Gcung Ri bo che. Active. Located in Gtsang (29° 6' 55.26" N, 86° 21' 36" E). Rdo rje tshe dbang writes that a Kangyur and Tengyur were housed at this site in the year 1434 and that the stūpa was established two years later, in 1436 (Rdo rje tshe dbang 2014, 482–83). For a discussion on the lifespan of Thang stong Rgyal po, see Stearns 2007, 1–14.

35. Alternative name, Chi bo ri Tshe chu grub sde. Ruined. Located in Gzad chu shul, Chu bo ri. Associated with Thang stong Rgyal po and the seat of the Lcags zam tulku lineage. Sangs rgyas rgya mtsho 1998, 407–8. On the Lcags zam tulkus, see Chab spel 1991, 294–95.

15. Lcags zam Mo brag dgon: site of the Lcags zam transmissions of the Shangpas, founded by the fifteenth-century figure Yar lung pa Tshul khrims 'gyur med. Converted to a Geluk monastery in 1698[36]
16. Rin dga' Chos sde dgon: founded circa 1050.[37] Converted to a Geluk site circa 1600
17. Mgon po dgon: originally a Shangpa site, founded in 1400.[38] Converted to a Karma Kagyü site in 1673
18. Rta nag Ri mkhar dgon: founded by the fourteenth-century master Mus chen Nam mkha'i rnal 'byor.[39] Later converted to a Geluk monastery
19. Bong shod Ri bo che'i dgon: originally a Shangpa site, founded by Byang chub rgyal mtshan.[40] Converted to a Nyingma monastery and later a Geluk monastery
20. Rdzong shod dgon: Shangpa site located in Kham, founded by 'Jam mgon Kong sprul in 1877[41]
21. Mtsho kha dgon: Shangpa site in Kham, founded in 1890.[42] Seat of the twentieth-century master 'Dzi sgar Kong sprul Blo gros rab 'phel (1901–58), one of the five re-embodiments of 'Jam mgon Kong sprul[43]

36. Located in Lha rtse County, Mang mkhar phu shang (29° 4' 53.976" N, 87° 38' 13.3476" E). According to *Dga' ldan chos 'byung*, there were thirty-two monks residing there in 1698. Sangs rgyas rgya mtsho 1998, 263 (Rdo rje tshe dbang 2014, 485–88).

37. Active. Located in Bzhad mthong smon County (29° 28' 59.988" N, 88° 34' 0.012" E).

38. Active. Located in Nang chen County, Khams (32° 19' 3" N, 95° 36' 4.68" E).

39. Located in Bzhad mthong smon County. Mus chen Nam mkha'i rnal 'byor's disciple was Byang sems sbyin pa bzang po, who transmitted the Shangs pa line to Thang stong Rgyal po, associating this place with the Thang lugs of the Shangs pa (Rdo rje tshe dbang 2014, 478–80).

40. Located in Ding ri County. This figure Byang chub gyal mtshan is uncertain. According to the *Dga' ldan chos 'byung*, there were twenty-seven monks residing there in 1698. (Sangs rgyas rgya mtsho 1998, 270; Rdo rje tshe dbang 2014, 484–85).

41. Alternative name, Rdzong shod Bde gshegs 'dus pa'i pho brang. Active. Located in Dpal yul County, Khams (31° 22' 0.012" N, 99° 5' 60" E). Alternative dates for its founding by Kong sprul are 1857 or 1867. There are approximately thirty monks currently in residence. See 'Jigs med bsam grub 1995, 3 and 310–12.

42. Located in Ri bo che County, Chab mdo, Khams (31° 7' 29.0208" N, 96° 21' 36.7128" E).

43. Smith 2001a, 271. 'Jam mgon Kong sprul is said to have made prayers for his rebirth at this monastery, Tshe dbang bkra shis 2004, 67.

B. Sites inherited via hereditary connection:

22. 'Bal Skyer sgang dgon: ancestral monastery inherited by Skyer sgang Chos kyi seng ge (1154–1217) in 1200.[44] Affiliated with the *Zhi byed* practice tradition. Chos kyi seng ge was a disciple of Rmog lcog pa and dedicated this site to him.

C. Hermitage sites where yogins dwelled:

23. Lan pa Spyil po ri khrod: Khyung po rnal 'byor's retreat site[45]
24. Khyung ri sgrub khang: Khyung po rnal 'byor's retreat site[46]
25. Bzhad khyung sgrub khang: Khyung po rnal 'byor's retreat site[47]
26. Rmog lcog ri khrod: founded by Rmog lcog Rin chen brtson 'grus in 1150.[48] Currently operating as a Geluk site under the governance of 'Bras spungs Monastery

D. Other sites associated with Shangpa masters:

27. Mus rta dgongs dgon: Site of the early fourteenth-century master Mus chen Rgyal mtshan dpal bzang[49]
28. Mus sdi lung dgon: site of the fourteenth-century master Mus chen Nam mkha'i rnal 'byor[50]
29. Zhe dgon pa: Site of sixteenth-century master Rje btsun Bsod nam tshe mo[51]

44. Alternative name, Stod lung Skyer sgang dgon. Ruined. Located in Gtsang (29° 23' 6.6768" N, 91° 0' 5.9796" E) (Rdo rje tshe dbang 2014, 460–62).

45. Ruined. Located in Lhun grub County.

46. Alternative name, Khyung 'dul ri. Ruined. Located in Bzhad mthong smon County (Rdo rje tshe dbang 2014, 450–52).

47. Bzhad khyung 'dul ri'i khyung po byas brten sgrub khang.

48. Alternative name, Mnyes (snye) thang rmog lcog. Active. Located in Mnyes thang khul (29° 19' 51.9456" N, 90° 45' 35.7336" E). This is a small monastery, referenced as both a hermitage (*ri khrod*) and a monastery (*dgon pa*), being categorized as a hermitage here. According to the 1999 regional gazetteer of the area, there were eight monks residing there in 1959 (Chu shur rdzong 1999, 39–40; Rdo rje tshe dbang 2014, 480–82).

49. Mus chen Gnyags ston rgyal mtshan dpal bzang was a disciple of Gtsang ma Shangs ston.

50. Mus chen Nam mkha'i rnal 'byor was a disciple of Mus chen Gnyags ton rgyal mtshan dpal bzang.

51. Bsod nams rtse mo was a teacher of Kun dga' grol mchog and 'Gyur med bde chen. Began to teach 'Gyur med bde chen in 1552.

30. Tshar tshar dgon: Karma Kagyü monastery in Khams, founded in 1575.[52] Currently operating as a Shangpa site
31. 'Bo dkar dgon: originally a Karma Kagyü monastery, founded in 1850.[53] Currently operating as a Shangpa site

The Shangpas Found

A search for the missing Shangpas reveals (1) that the Shangpas were an independent order of Tibetan Buddhism, distinct from Kagyü lineages that originated from Mar pa, and (2) that this order of Tibetan Buddhism historically had a significant institutional identity, asserting its presence in central Tibet up through the sixteenth century with numerous monasteries, hermitages, and stūpas.[54]

Starting with the establishment of Zhang zhong Monastery, Shangpa sites continued to be built through the fourteenth century, while a curtailed institutional presence continued up to the sixteenth century. Based on this preliminary site list, we estimate that there were nearly thirty sites claimed by the Shangpa tradition in central Tibet up through the sixteenth century, rivaled by the Jonang, whose site presence was also approximately

52. Alternative name, Rdza Tshar tshar dgon. Active. Located in Sde dge County, Khams (32° 23' 60" N, 98° 58' 59.988" E). Founded by Karma Bka' brgyud master Tshar tshar Sgrub rgan grags pa rgyal mtshan (b. 1526).

53. Alternative name, 'Bo ('bur) dkar Glang dgon Bkra shis rab brtan gling. Active. Located in Mnga' ris (31° 26' 60" N, 84° 24' 36" E).

54. Other sites not well identified include: (1) Byang Rdo rje ldan, site of Byang sems 'Byin pa bzang po; (2) Dge 'phel chos kyi pho brang, site of 'Jam dbyang bsod nams rgyal mtshan; (3) Gsang ngags bde chen, a hermitage site of Ngag dbang bstan pa dar rgyas; (4) Rdo rje brag rdzong, site of 'Jam mgon Rdo rje rin chen, and Lcog po rtse Monastery.

Key of Shangpa Sites in Tibet

1. Shangs Zhang zhong rdo rje gdan	13. Ri bo che dgon	25. Bzhad khyung sgrub khang†
2. Jog mda' 'Chad kha dgon	14. Lcags zam Chu bo ri dgon*	26. Rmog lcog ri khrod
3. Sngags Khyung dgon*	15. Lcags zam Mo brag dgon	27. Mus rta dgongs dgon*
4. Gnas rnying dgon	16. Rin dga' Chos sde dgon	28. Mus sdi lung dgon*
5. Rmog lcog dgon pa	17. Mgon po dgon	29. Zhe dgon pa†
6. Sku lugs dgon*	18. Rta nag Ri mkhar dgon*	30. Tshar tshar dgon
7. Yol phu Ri gong dgon pa*	19. Bong shod Ri bo che'i dgon*	31. 'Bo dkar dgon
8. Yol phu Brag rtsa dgon*	20. Rdzong shod dgon	* County marker only; precise location unknown
9. 'Jag chung Dpal dgon*	21. Mtsho kha dgon	† Location unknown
10. 'Jag chen Dpal dgon*	22. 'Bal Skyer sgang dgon	
11. Nyang smad Bsam sdings dgon	23. Lan pa Spyil po ri khrod*	
12. Rta nag Sa rdo rje gdan dgon	24. Khyung ri sgrub khang*	

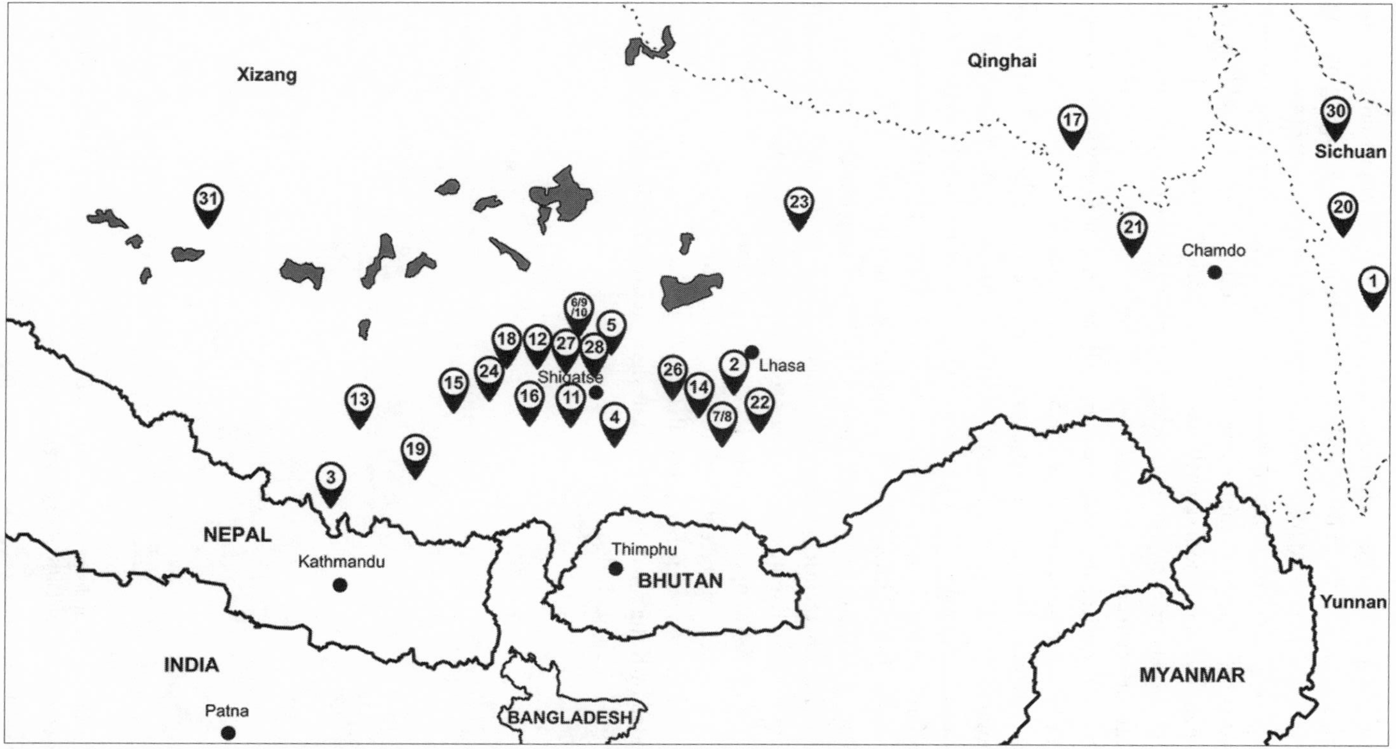

Map of Shangpa Sites in Tibet

thirty.[55] In his 1980 essay, Matthew infers that many Shangpa sites became inactive or changed sectarian affiliation before Dpa' bo Gtsug lag phreng ba (1504–64) composed his history, *A Feast for Scholars* (*Chos 'byung mkhas pa'i dga' ston*), because the author notes that only a few adherents remained at that time.[56] This is an important observation that suggests that Shangpa sites had fizzled by the sixteenth century, even prior to the mass subsumption of monasteries by the Dga' ldan Pho brang government in the mid-seventeenth century.

Of the historical sites surveyed, many lie in ruin, and only a few remain extant in contemporary Tibet. The Shangpa tradition in Tibet does, however, continue to remain intrinsically entwined in Tibetan Buddhism through its various transmission lines, most actively via the Jonang tradition in Amdo. Jonang transmissions of the Shangpa practice lineage flowed from Grol mchog through his successor Tāranātha (1575–1635), all the way to present-day Jonang lineage-holders, and via a parallel lineage from Tāranātha through the Nyingma exemplar Rig 'dzin Tshe dbang nor bu (1698–1755). In the late nineteenth century, 'Jam mgon Kong sprul established several Shangpa sites in Kham as part of the broader *ris med* renaissance. Today, several Shangpa sites operate inside Tibet, most notably, (1) Zhang zhong rdo rje gdan, which was recently rebuilt; (2) Thang stong Rgyal po's Ri bo che stūpa, which was recently renovated; (3) Tshar tshar dgon; (4) Rdzong shod, founded by Kong sprul; (5) Mtsho kha dgon, founded by Kong sprul's disciple; and (6) 'Bo dkar dgon.

55. Up through the mid-seventeenth century there were approximately thirty-three significant Jonang sites in central Tibet (*dbus gtsang*).

56. Kapstein 1980, 140.

Works Cited

Chab spel Tshe brtan phun tshogs and Mi 'gyur rdo rje. 1991. *Bod kyi gal che'i lo rgyus yig cha gdams bsgrigs.* TBRC.org ID: W19220. Lhasa: Bod ljongs mi dbangs dpe skrun khang.

Chos kyi rgya mtsho. 2001. *Dbus gtsang gnas yig.* Chengdu: Si khron mi rigs dpe skrun khang.

Chu shur rdzong. 1999. *Grong khyer lha sa'i lo rgyus rig gnas.* Lhasa: Grong khyer lha sa'i gzhung.

Ducher, Cécile. 2017. "A Lineage in Time: The Vicissitudes of the rNgog pa bka' brgyud from the 11th through 19th c." PhD dissertation. Paris: École Pratique des Hautes Études.

Ehrhard, Franz-Karl. 2012. "'Flow of the River Ganga': The Gsan-yig of the Fifth Dalai Bla-ma and Its Literary Sources." In *Studies on the History and Literature of Tibet and the Himalaya*, edited by Roberto Vitali, 79–96. Kathmandu: Vajra Publications.

Gnas rnying chos 'byung. Skyes bu dam pa rnams kyi rnam par thar pa rin po che'i gter mdzod. Unpublished woodblock. TBRC.org ID: W1CZ897.

Harding, Sarah. 2007. *Niguma, Lady of Illusion.* Boston and London: Snow Lion Publications.

'Jam dbyangs Mkhyen rtse'i dbang po. 1980. *Bod yul gsang sngags gsar rnying gi gdan rabs ngo mtshar padmo'i dga' tshal.* In *Mkhyen brtse'i dbang po gsung 'bum*, vol. 18. Gangtok: Gonpo Tseten.

'Jam dpal bzang po. 2009. *Gsol 'debs rdo rje 'chang thung ma.* In *Zhal 'don gces btus*, 175–78. Rumtek: Dhorphen Publication.

'Jigs med bsam grub. 1995. *Dkar mdzes khul gyi dgon sde so so'i lo rgyus gsal bar bshad pa.* Beijing: Krung go'i bod kyi shes rig dpe skrun khang.

Kapstein, Matthew T. 1980. "The Shangs-pa bKa'-brgyud: An Unknown School of Tibetan Buddhism." In *Tibetan Studies in Honour of Hugh Richardson: Proceedings of the International Seminar on Tibetan Studies,* edited by Michael Aris and Aung San Suu Kyi, 138–44. Warminster, England: Aris and Phillips.

———. 1992. "The Illusion of Spiritual Progress: Remarks on Indo-Tibetan Buddhist Soteriology." In *Paths to Liberation: The Mārga and Its Transformations in Buddhist Thought*, edited by Robert Buswell and Robert Gimello, 193–224. Honolulu: University of Hawai'i Press.

———. 1996. "gDams ngag: Tibetan Technologies of the Self." In *Tibetan Literature: Studies in Genre*, edited by José I. Cabezón and Roger R. Jackson, 275–89. Ithaca, NY: Snow Lion Publications.

———. 1997. "The Journey to the Golden Mountain." In *Religions of Tibet in Practice*, edited by Donald S. Lopez Jr., 178–87. Princeton, NJ: Princeton University Press.

———. 2005. "Chronological Conundrums in the Life of Khyung po rnal 'byor: Hagiography and Historical Time." *Journal of the International Association of Tibetan Studies* 1: 1–14.

Karma Rang byung kun khyab. 1970. *Shangs pa gser 'phreng: A Golden Rosary of Lives of Masters of the Shangs-pa Dkar-brgyud-pa Schools.* Leh: Sonam W. Tashigang.

Kun dga' grol mchog. 1981a. *Zab khrid brgya dang brgyad kyi yi ge.* In *Gdams ngag mdzod*, vol. 18. Paro: Lama Ngodrup and Sherab Drimey.

———. 1981b. *Khrid brgya'i spyi chings rnam par spel ba ngo mtshar chos kyi sgo mang*. In *Gdams ngag mdzod*, vol. 18. Paro: Lama Ngodrup and Sherab Drimey.

———. 1981c. *Khrid brgya'i sa 'grel ya mtshan 'phrul gyi lde mig*. In *Gdams ngag mdzod*, vol. 18. Paro: Lama Ngodrup and Sherab Drimey.

———. *Dam pa'i chos kyi thob yig bstan pa'i nor bdzas*. Unpublished woodblock print.

Li An-che. 1949. "The Bkah-brgyud sect of Lamaism." *Journal of the American Oriental Society*, 69, 51–59.

Nam mkha' bsam grub rgyal mtshan. 1996. *Shangs pa bka' brgyud bla rabs kyi rnam thar*. Lhasa: Bod ljongs mi dmangs dpe skrun khang.

Ngag dbang kun dga' bsod nams. 2000. "Chos kyi rje dpal ldan bla ma dam pa rnams las dam pa'i chos ji ltar thos tshul legs par bshad pa zab rgyas chos kun gsal ba'i nyin byed ces bya ba las khyab bdag 'khor lo'i mgon po rgyal ba mus pa chen po rdo rje 'chang sangs rgyas rgyal mtshan gyis rjes su bzung ba'i tshul gyi sarga." In *A mes zhabs ngag dbang kun dga' bsod nams kyi bka' 'bum*, 2:7–252. Kathmandu: Sa skya rgyal yongs gsung rab slob gnyer khang.

Rdo rje tshe dbang. 2014. *Dpal ldan shangs pa bka' brgyud kyi chos 'byung*. Lhasa: Bod ljongs mi dmangs dpe skrun khang.

Riggs, Nicole, trans. 2000. *Like An Illusion: Lives of the Shangpa Kagyu Masters*. Eugene: Dharma Cloud Publishing.

Roerich, George, trans. 1949 (1976 reprint). *The Blue Annals*. Delhi: Motilal Banarsidass.

Sangs rgyas rgya mtsho. 1998. *Dga' ldan chos 'byung baidūrya ser po*. Beijing: Krung go bod kyi shes rig dpe skrun khang.

Schaeffer, Kurtis R., Matthew T. Kaptein, and Gray Tuttle, ed. 2013. *Sources of Tibetan Tradition*. New York: Columbia University Press.

Smith, E. Gene. 2001a. "'Jam mgon Kong sprul and the Nonsectarian Movement." In *Among Tibetan Texts: History and Literature of the Himalayan Plateau,* 235–72. Boston: Wisdom Publications.

———. 2001b. "The Shangs pa bka' brgyud Tradition." In *Among Tibetan Texts: History and Literature of the Himalayan Plateau*, 53–57. Boston: Wisdom Publications.

Stearns, Cyrus. 2007. *King of the Empty Plain: The Tibetan Iron-Bridge Builder Tangtong Gyalpo*. Boston: Snow Lion Publications.

Tāranātha. 1981. "Khrid brgya'i brgyud pa'i lo rgyus kha skong." In *Gdams ngag mdzod*, vol. 18. Paro: Lama Ngodrup and Sherab Drimey.

———. "Rgyal ba'i bstan pa rin po che spyi'i rnam bzhag las 'phros pa'i dpal ldan shangs pa'i chos skor gyi 'byung khung yid kyi mun sel." In *Rje btsun tā ra nā tha'i gsung 'bum,* vol. 17. 'Dzam thang, 199?.

Thuken Losang Chokyi Nyima. 2009. *The Crystal Mirror of Philosophical Systems: A Tibetan Study of Asian Religious Thought*. Library of Tibetan Classics. Translated by Geshé Lhundub Sopa et al. Edited by Roger R Jackson. Boston: Wisdom Publications.

Tshe dbang bkra shis. 2004. *Shar phyogs sprul pa'i sbas gnas chen po rdzong shod bde 'dus pho brang chen mo'i byung ba rags bsdus skal bzang dad pa'i gsos sman*. TBRC.org ID: W1CZ2486.

van der Kuijp, Leonard. 1995. "Fourteenth Century Tibetan Cultural History VI: The Transmission of Indian Buddhist Pramānavāda According to the Early Tibetan Gsan yig-s*." In *Asiatische Studien: Zeitschrift der Schweizerischen Asiengesellschaft*. Études asiatiques: Revue de la Société Suisse-Asie 49.

The *Treasury of Kagyü Mantra*: A Nineteenth-Century Collection of Marpa's Tantric Teachings

Cécile Ducher

IN 1976 IN Kathmandu, the Sixteenth Karmapa transmitted a major set of empowerments, the *Treasury of Kagyü Mantra* (*Bka' brgyud sngags mdzod*, henceforth *Treasury*), to an assembly of a thousand followers. Among the few Westerners gathered in the Ka-Nying Shedrub Ling Monastery (*Bka' rnying bshad sgrub gling*) for the occasion was a young American devotee, Upāsaka Kamalaśīla, also known as Matthew Kapstein. He and another American, Vajranātha (John Reynolds), together wrote an unpublished, thirty-three-page "Introduction to the *Kadjy Ngakdzø*," explaining in great detail where this set of initiations comes from, the meaning of the various phases of empowerments, and the visualizations of the deities the collection contains. Forty years later, this Kamalaśīla—by then the Directeur d'Étude at the École Pratique des Hautes Études in Paris—directed the present author's dissertation on the history of the Ngokpa Kagyü (*Rngog pa Bka' brgyud*) lineage, which relies heavily on the *Treasury*. In the course of the defense of that dissertation, Professor Kapstein stated that since he had had the great privilege of receiving these empowerments in 1976, all his work on tantrism and Tibetan rituals had been like footnotes to that experience. Although, as is common in the case of Tibetan literature, some degree of hyperbole cannot be excluded (as witnessed by the breath of Professor Kapstein's oeuvre), it is nonetheless a great pleasure for me to honor him with the following thoughts on the *Treasury*'s significance in Tibet's religious history, which includes a short overview of its contents.

Secret Mantrayāna occupies a central role in Tibetan Buddhism. Most Tibetan lineages are constituted by the transmission of empowerments, which are considered the entrance door to the Vajrayāna. Among the four main Tibetan orders that developed in Tibet, the Kagyü lineage traces back to a Tibetan translator, Marpa (Mar pa Chos kyi blo gros, 1002?–1081?), famous for having received in India the transmission of several major highest yoga

Matthew Kapstein in Kathmandu in 1976 for the *Bka' brgyud sngags mdzod* empowerments.
Photo by Edward Henning

tantras (*niruttaratantra, bla na med pa'i rgyud*) from two of the most important masters of the time, Nāropa and Maitripa, and for having brought back to Tibet empowerments and instructions for these major tantras.[1] Marpa had four main disciples. One of them, Mi la ras pa (1028?–1111?), was followed by Sgam po pa (1079–1153), and from the latter all the Kagyü sub-orders developed.[2] Despite the preeminence of these Kagyü traditions today, Marpa's tantric teachings were also preserved by his other disciples, chief among them Rngog Chos rdor (1023–90) and Mtshur ston Dbang nge (eleventh century).[3] Their lineages, however, did not survive as independent orders for more than a few centuries and, as a result, are not very well known. Because of this, several tantras that Marpa brought to Tibet and that were originally propounded

1. See Ducher 2017a, 301–6, for references to Marpa's lifespan.

2. Except for the Shangs pa Bka' brgyud, which comes from Khyung po rnal 'byor. See Sheehy article in the present volume for details.

3. For details on the Rngog lineage, see Ducher 2017b, especially pages 186–206, for an account of the life story and transmissions received by each of Mar pa's four main disciples.

by Rngog and Mtshur ston were on the verge of extinction by the nineteenth century. It was to avert their loss and to spread once more Marpa's traditions that the great nineteenth-century polymath Jamgön Kongtrul ('Jam mgon Kong sprul Blo gros mtha' yas, 1813–99) compiled the *Treasury*. Thanks to Kongtrul's efforts and the subsequent continuation of his lineage, particularly in the Karma Kagyü and Drikung Kagyü orders, most of Marpa's traditions remain alive today, although some of them are very seldom practiced.

The Collection

The original volumes of the *Treasury* were xylographed in Dpal spungs, Kongtrul's monastery in eastern Tibet. There remain today in the old Dpal spungs printing house some woodblocks dating to that period. The collection was then organized in three bulky volumes. A copy of this original edition is now available in the Namgyal Institute in Gangtok (Sikkim, India). The volumes were divided into two and first republished as six volumes in India in 1974. A few years later, a calque of the Dpal spungs xylograph was ordered by Dil mgo Mkhyen rtse Rin po che, and this new edition was published in 1982 in eight volumes.[4] This version, abridged here as *Treasury*, is the one described in the present article as it is the most widespread in the Tibetan and academic communities and has been reordered according to Kongtrul's catalogue, thus reflecting accurately the form Kongtrul intended to give to his work.[5]

As in his other treasuries, Kongtrul gathered many sources for his collection. The *Treasury* thus contains texts composed by Kongtrul, reprints of previous works by identified authors, and anonymous works. In the catalogue, Kongtrul states that his first sources are Indian texts. This refers to the tantras themselves as well as to the commentaries and rituals elaborated by Indian masters. These texts gave rise to various Indian traditions that were imported to Tibet and became the sources of the ensuing traditions. Marpa received his main tantric transmissions from several masters (the Padmavajra tradition of *Hevajra* from Nāropa, the Ārya tradition of *Guhyasamāja* from Jñānagarbha, the Kukuripa tradition of *Mahāmāyā* from Śāntibhadra, and so on) and again with key instructions from Nāropa and Maitripa. In the catalogue, Kongtrul

4. The last two volumes are additions by Dil mgo Mkhyen rtse on the transmission of Vajrapāṇi.

5. See a description of the various editions of the *Treasury* in Ducher 2017b, 74–77. Kongtrul's catalogue is 1:1–53. Other sources used in order to assess the collection are the records of teaching received by Mdil mgo Mkhyen rtse (*Gsung 'bum*, 25:48–66, TBRC.org ID: W21809) and Bdud 'joms Rinpoche (*Gsung 'bum*, 20:253–78, W20869).

then classifies his Tibetan sources in five chronological stages. His description reads as follows:[6]

1. First are the earliest Tibetan texts such as the *Mdo sbyar* and the *Gur gyi srog shing* by Marpa [commentaries on *Hevajra* and *Pañjara*]; the manuals composed by Rngog Mdo sde as well as his commentary on the *Hevajratantra*, called *Likeness of a Precious Ornament* (*Rin chen rgyan 'dra*); the *Collected Works* of Mgar and Rtsags [Rngog Mdo sde's main disciples]; the *Old Ngok Maṇḍalas* (*Rngog dkyil rnying*), manuals compiled by later Ngokpas such as Kun dga' rdo rje (1145–1222), Thogs med grags pa (1108–44), and Rin chen bzang po (1243–1319).[7]
2. The manuals composed by the Third Karmapa (1284–1339) on *Hevajra*, *Cakrasaṃvara*, *Guhyasamāja*, *Mahāmāyā*, and so on, and by his successors the Sixth Karmapa (1416–1453), the Seventh Karmapa (1454–1506), the Eighth Karmapa (1507–54), the Great 'Jam dbyangs from Mtshur phu (fourteenth to fifteenth centuries),[8] and so on, represent the main Kam tshang tradition, in which many manuals on most tantras of the Mar Ngok tradition were composed.
3. The *Manuals on Ngok Maṇḍalas* (*Rngog dkyil yig cha*) composed by Lo chen Bsod nams rgya mtsho (1424–82) provide outlines and clarify practices on the basis of the *Old Ngok Maṇḍalas*. Based on them, the manuals of the Fourth Shamar (Zhwa dmar Chos grags ye shes, 1453–1524) have a wise vision endowed with the two forms of knowledge that thoroughly remove the stains of errors.
4. Tāranātha (1575–1634) cleaned the general hybridations and crossovers in the Ngok practices and composed manuals that purely and unmistakably expound the Indian root texts and Marpa's interpretation.
5. Karma Chags med (1613–1618) summarized the extensive initiation

6. *Treasury*, 1:6–7. See transliteration in Ducher 2017b, 71–72. In the present translation, I use the widespread version of the authors' names rather than the alternative titles or names given by Kongtrul.

7. For details on the identity of these masters of the Rngog lineage, see Ducher 2017b, chap. II.3, pp. 222–327.

8. 'Jam dbyangs Don grub 'od zer, the abbot of Mtshur phu for forty-five years, was a disciple of the Fifth Karmapa (1384–1415) and a master of Lo chen Bsod nams rgya mtsho (Ehrhard 2002, 45–46).

> texts of the *Old Ngok Maṇḍalas* and unified the self- and front-generation stages, thus speeding up the empowerment.
>
> Although the empowerments and reading transmissions of the latter three are uninterrupted, I mainly based my renderings on the writings of the Fourth Shamar and of Tāranātha, which are unmistaken as to the meaning and have a majestic blessing.

Among the sources used by Kongtrul, many are now available and can thus be compared to the version included in the *Treasury*. For most maṇḍalas, the first texts written were the versions of rituals and commentaries composed within the Ngok lineage, that is to say by the descendants of Rngog Chos rdor, especially his son Rngog Mdo sde. They were the most prolific commentators of Marpa's tradition and are considered the main holders of his "exegetic lineage" (*bshad brgyud*), as opposed to Mi la ras pa's "practice lineage" (*sgrub brgyud*). Several volumes of commentaries and practice rituals composed by members of the Ngok family were found in the concealed library of 'Bras spungs's Gnas bcu Temple and have been published.[9] The second phase is represented by various works dispersed in the collected works of the Karmapas. The third phase is represented by the writings of Lo chen Bsod nams rgya mtsho. He was a student of 'Gos Lo tsā ba, himself one of the major students of the last important Ngok master, Byang chub dpal (1360–1446). Lo chen was responsible, with his master 'Gos Lo tsā ba and the former's disciple, the Fourth Shamar, for the successful transition of the transmissions from the Ngok family to the other Kagyü lineages.[10] Although stored in the Gnas bcu Temple, Lo chen's complete works have not been published yet. The writings of his disciple, the Fourth Shamar, are available and contain several rituals and commentaries related to the Ngok traditions, as are those of Tāranātha and Karma Chags med that similarly contain Ngok traditions. Among these, Kongtrul considers that the most appropriate cycles (that is to say the texts containing everything necessary for the practice of a specific tantra—empowerment ritual, main *sādhana* and related rites, as well as commentaries and explanations) are the ones by the Fourth Shamar and Tāranātha because they are loaded with spiritual influence, have the appropriate length, are easy to use, and are free of errors. He therefore used those as references, sometimes including the original documents in the *Treasury*, sometimes editing them in order to compose texts of his own.

9. Ducher 2017b, 40–47.

10. Ehrhard 2002, Fermer 2017, and Ducher 2017b, chap. II.4.

Its Contents

The contents of the six volumes of the *Treasury* can be divided into three groups that Kongtrul calls, respectively, the "initial virtue," "middling virtue," and "concluding virtue." The main source of my presentation is Kongtrul's catalogue of the *Treasury*—previously described in my dissertation on the Ngok history—as well as fieldwork in Bodhgaya undertaken in early 2018 that allowed me to witness the way the collection was handed over, thus combining textual and anthropological analysis.[11]

For twenty days, Be ru Mkhyen rtse Rinpoché (b. 1947) led the actual transmission of this set of empowerments in his monastery.[12] Although the event was mainly dedicated to his son, the Fourth Kongtrul (born 1995), approximately seventy lamas and monks as well as forty Western and Asian disciples were in attendance. Be ru Mkhyen rtse prepared the empowerment of the day every morning, starting around 6:00 a.m., and transmitted it to the assembly in the afternoon. The transmission of the whole cycle started with the "initial virtue"—that is to say, the authorizations of practice for Marpa's three special deities—on the first day. The empowerments for the fifteen major maṇḍalas of the collection, the "middling virtue," began on the second day, with the preparation (*rta mgon*) for the Hevajra empowerment, the first of the yoginī tantras, followed on the next day by the actual transmission of Hevajra. The subsequent yoginī tantras were then transmitted each on one day, without a specific preparation day. Another day was dedicated to the preparation of the empowerment of the first mahāyoga tantra, the Guhyasamāja. It was followed by the actual empowerment of the Guhyasamāja and the other mahāyoga tantras on the following days. Authorizations of practice for Vajrapāṇi and other protectors were given on the penultimate day, and long-life deities on the last, thus combining in two days seven authorizations from both the "initial" and "final" virtues, the latter term referring to protectors. On some days reading transmissions (*lung*), generally related to the empowerment of the day, were

11. *Treasury*, 1:1–53. See the content of the collection in Ducher 2017b, 437–43, and a more detailed description of its history and content on pages 69–84 of the same.

12. Under the umbrella term *empowerment* are two kinds of transmissions. The *great empowerment* (*dbang* or *dbang chen*) matures the mind of the disciple and introduces him or her to the maṇḍala of a specific tantra by way of four initiations (vase, secret, wisdom, and name). "Authorizations of practices" (*rjes gnang*) authorize the disciple to practice a specific deity. As pointed out by Kongtrul (*Treasury*, 1:12.3–4), one cannot receive an authorization fully without having previously had one's mind matured by an empowerment. Hence he advises to start with the Hevajra empowerment, in case the disciple has not received any empowerment yet.

offered, but the complete *lung* of the *Treasury* was not transmitted during the event.

The Initial Virtue

The first of the six volumes contains what Kongtrul considers auspicious for a beginning—that is to say, the transmissions for the long-life deities of White Tārā and Amitāyus. It also includes the cycles associated to Marpa's three special deities—Uṣṇīṣavijaya, Green Tārā, and Vajrasattva from King Jaḥ. Although Vajrapāṇi is counted among the "thirteen highest yoga tantras" from the middling virtue, the ritual included by Kongtrul is an authorization of practice coming from the collection compiled by the Ninth Karmapa, "Knowing One Liberates All" (*Cig shes kun grol*), not a complete empowerment. The reason it figures within the initial virtue is to dispel obstacles.

Kongtrul also includes in the initial virtue a "ritual for worshiping the master" (*bla ma mchod pa'i cho ga*) in order, he says, "to open the doors of blessing." This particular practice, composed by Gling ras pa (1128–88), is mostly constituted of praises and verses of offering and is considered spoken by Vajradhara himself. In his supplement to the text, Kongtrul states that Gling ras pa clarifies the meaning of three Indian scriptures as well as of the instructions of Nāropa and Tilopa, as they were mediated by Marpa. Thus this specific text fits as an introduction for transmissions of the Indian esoteric treasury that Marpa imported to Tibet.[13]

The Middling Virtue

Volumes 2 to 5 contain the heart of the collection: fifteen transmissions associated with "thirteen highest yoga tantras." In traditional accounts given by Tibetan masters, these thirteen tantras are paradigmatic of Marpa's teaching. In fact, not all of them come from Marpa, and only twelve tantras are contained in the middling virtue of the *Treasury*; the thirteenth, Vajrapāṇi,

13. *Treasury*, 1:480: *rgya gzhung gsum gyi bstan don te lo nā ro'i gdams ngag mar pa las brgyud cing gling rje ras pas gsal bar mdzad pa bla ma mchod pa'i cho ga* [...]. I thank Matthew Kapstein for pointing out to me how strange it might seem at first glance to include this particular practice in the collection (one could have expected a guruyoga of Marpa for instance) and for clarifying, a few weeks later, why, after all, it was not odd at all, substantiating his opinion by solid lines of arguments, though not the exact quotes underlying them. After ten years of studying with him, I learned this is the way of great teachers: setting the question in an enigmatic manner, letting the student look for answers, answering himself the question in a slightly less enigmatic fashion, and letting the student search further in order to understand the answer.

is only partially presented, since Kongtrul only provides the authorization of practice. It is included in volume 1, since it generally contains the initial virtue.[14]

The term *tantra* is the general designation of a text of (usually) Indian origin. It can be a *root* tantra (the *Two Segments* for instance, under which name the root *Hevajratantra* is known) or an *explanatory* tantra (the *Vajrapañjāratantra* for instance, which is the uncommon explanatory tantra of the *Hevajratantra*).

The same tantra can include multiple maṇḍalas, which explains why several transmissions can develop on the basis of a single tantra. For instance, the *Treasury* contains two maṇḍalas associated with the *Hevajratantra*, that of the main male deity, Hevajra, and that of his consort, Nairātmyā. Similarly, the *Cakrasaṃvaratantra* and *Catuṣpīṭhatantra* are associated with two maṇḍalas, centered on the male and female figures of these tantras.

When tantras spread in India, they were practiced by people who gained "accomplishments" (*siddhi*s), which is why they were called *siddha*s. These siddhas created specific rites associated with these tantras, which gave rise to "traditions" (*lugs*, also called *bka' srol*). The practice of Hevajra, for instance, developed in eight main traditions in India. In Tibet, it flourished in the tradition that Marpa received from Nāropa and in the one that 'Brog mi Lo tsā ba received from Gayādhara, initially coming from Virūpa.[15] The main traditions included in the *Treasury* are Marpa's and are thus associated with his masters Nāropa, Maitripa, Śāntibhadra, and their own masters. These traditions are particularly famous for their pith instructions (practical instructions given from master to disciple), considered to be particularly efficient for reaching siddhis.

Each cycle included in the *Treasury* comprises several texts that Kongtrul chose from among a large pool of rites and commentaries penned by the authors mentioned above.[16] In general, there is for each cycle an empowerment rite used by the vajra master when empowering a disciple to practice a specific tantra. The empowerment consists of several phases through which the disci-

14. This may be one of the reasons for the inclusion by Dil mgo mkhyen rtse of an actual empowerment in volume 7 of the 1982 edition.

15. Kongtrul 2008, 161–66, and Sobisch 2008, 30–49.

16. In the collection, there are 126 texts. Out of these, seventy were authored by Kongtrul (55.6 percent), thirty-seven by other identified authors (29.3 percent), two are tantras (1.6 percent), and sixteen (13.5 percent) are anonymous. Among texts by other authors, five come from Tāranātha, but none come from the Fourth Zhwa dmar or Karma Chags med. Most others were composed by Karma Kagyü hierarchs, three by Bu ston Rin chen grub (1290–1364), and eight by Rngog masters.

ple is introduced to the maṇḍala of the deities and is thus empowered by their spiritual strength. It corresponds to the *path of maturation* (*smin lam*). Once a disciple is empowered, he or she can practice the deities in question, thus following the *path of liberation* (*grol lam*). The latter is divided into two phases, the *creation phase* (*bskyed rim*) and the *perfection phase* (*rdzogs rim*).[17]

The creation phase is practiced by means of various ritual texts. The most common is the practice ritual called a *sādhana* (*sgrub thabs*, literally "methods of practice"); this is the text a practitioner uses to practice the deity he or she has been empowered to embody. Rituals can be of several types, depending on the aim of the practice, and can be more or less extensive. There can be further rites aimed at specific activities, such as fire offerings (*sbyin sreg*). Kongtrul includes rituals for the creation phase and instructions (*khrid*) on the perfection phase for the main transmissions associated with Marpa, excepting those related to the *Cakrasaṃvaratantra*, which, he says, are well preserved elsewhere.

According to Kongtrul, the tantras of the middling virtue are all of the highest yoga tantra class. Although many systems of teaching were introduced in Tibet by various translators and paṇḍitas, the ones gathered in the *Treasury* trace back to Marpa and his main disciples, Rngog Chos rdor (the seven maṇḍalas), Mtshur ston (Guhyasamāja and Buddhakapāla) and Mi la ras pa (Cakrasaṃvara). They were later propagated in all Kagyü schools, foremost among them the Karma and 'Bri gung.

A traditional distinction in highest yoga tantras is between tantras that focus particularly on methods (*thabs*)—called "father" (*pha rgyud*), or *mahāyoga* tantras—and those that focus particularly on wisdom (*shes rab*), the "mother" (*ma rgyud*), or *yoginī* tantras.[18] Most of Marpa's transmissions (*Hevajra*, *Cakrasaṃvara*, *Buddhakapāla*, *Mahāmāyā*, and *Catuṣpīṭha*) are yoginī tantras. These are further divided in "families" (*rigs*). The first four belong to the Akṣobhya family. The fifth, *Catuṣpīṭha*, to the Vairocana family.

The first three transmissions in the collection (the Hevajra maṇḍala with nine deities, the Nairātmyā maṇḍala with fifteen deities and the Pañjāra one with five Hevajra maṇḍalas relating to the five buddha families, hence forty-nine deities) belong to the Hevajra cycle. The perfection phase associated with it is called *merging and transference* (*bsre 'pho*). Hevajra was Marpa's main practice and is the one expounded in most detail in the *Treasury*.

Four maṇḍalas (Peaceful Cakrasaṃvara Vajrasattva from the *Saṃpuṭatantra*, Five-Deity Cakrasaṃvara and Five-Deity Vajravārāhī from the

17. Kongtrul 2005, 203.

18. For a less traditional presentation, see Isaacson and Sferra 2015.

Cakrasaṃvara Root Tantra, and Six-Cakravartin Cakrasaṃvara from the *Abhidhānottaratantra*) are associated with the *Cakrasaṃvaratantra*. Their perfection phase is called the Six Dharmas of Nāropa (*nā ro chos drug*). Following in the footsteps of Mi la ras pa and many of the Karmapas, most practitioners of the various Kagyü schools rely on *Cakrasaṃvara* as their main practice, and this practice is therefore not on the verge of extinction. For this reason, Kongtrul does not include instructions on the topic in the collection.

Mahāmāyā is expounded through both the main maṇḍala with five deities and instructions on the perfection phase,[19] as is *Buddhakapāla*, with a maṇḍala of twenty-five deities and its perfection phase.[20] As far as *Catuṣpīṭha* is concerned, there are the two maṇḍalas of Yogāmbara (the male deity) and Jñānaḍākinī (the female deity) together with the perfection phase of that tantra.[21]

After the yoginī tantras, Kongtrul includes in volumes 4 and 5 two transmissions of Marpa that belong to the mahāyoga class, namely *Guhyasamāja* and the *Nāmasaṃgīti*. Tantras in that class are distinguished according to the three poisons—desire, ignorance, and anger. *Guhyasamāja* belongs to the desire class. The cycle expounded in the *Treasury* is that of *Guhyasamāja* with thirty-three deities of the Ārya Nāgārjuna tradition, together with its perfection phase, called the Five Stages (*rim lnga*). This transmission was especially cherished by Marpa and carried a particularly high symbolic capital in Tibet in the eleventh century, as demonstrated by the fact that most of Marpa's biographies insist on his eagerness to be one of the first to spread it widely in Tibet.

The *Nāmasaṃgīti*, or *Mañjuśrīnāmasaṃgīti*, is one of the most central tantras in Tibet, and there exist several traditions, associated with all classes of tantras. The one in the *Treasury* is said to belong to the mahāyoga class and to be related to ignorance. Although the transmission Marpa received from Maitripa indeed belongs to that class, Rngog Chos rdor also received the *Nāmasaṃgīti* from other masters. The particular tradition he spread is called *Gsang ldan*.[22] It comes from Vilāsavajra and is generally associated with the yoga tantra level.[23]

Kongtrul includes two more mahāyoga cycles in order to cover the "anger

19. Described in Kongtrul 2008, 183–86.

20. Kongtrul 2008, 186–87.

21. Kongtrul 2008, 179–82.

22. The Sanskrit version of *Gsang ldan*, if one is to believe the Sanskrit title (in Tibetan letters) provided in Agrabodhi's commentary (Dergé 2584, 63:214), may be *Guhyāpanna. This is the name given in most publications. As it is not attested, the Tibetan appellation is kept here (see Ducher 2017b, 114).

23. Tribe 2016.

type," although these transmissions do not come from Marpa. These are the cycles of Five-Deity Yamāntaka according to Virūpa's tradition and Nine-Deity Vajrabhairava according to Mal Lo tsā ba's tradition. Only the practice and empowerment rituals are included in the *Treasury*, without any specific perfection phase.

At the end of the fifth volume are several Marpa Kagyü rituals that do not rely on one tantra in particular but explain more general aspects of Marpa's transmissions such as *gaṇacakra*s (*tshogs mchod*, more generally called *tshogs 'khor*), consecrations (*rab gnas*), empowerments, and so on. Kongtrul does not explicitly mention these texts in the catalogue, hence they tend to be displaced or lost in the various editions.

The Final Virtue

The sixth volume contains four cycles of protective deities, two of them particularly associated with Marpa. One of these is Vajramahākāla, also called Tent Protector (*gur mgon*). *Gur*, "tent," is a translation of the Sanskrit *pañjara* and refers to the fact that he is the protector of the *Pañjaratantra*. This transmission is also known as the "aural transmission of Marpa" (*mar pa'i / lho brag pa'i snyan rgyud*) because it was "very secret." The other is the cycle of Dud sol ma.[24] Although her cult is initially derived from the *Catuṣpīṭhatantra*, she became the central protective deity of the Mar Ngok teachings, hence of most of the transmissions collected in the *Treasury*, chief among them *Hevajra*.

Another cycle, not particularly related to Marpa, is that of the wisdom-protector Four-Armed Mahākāla with thirteen deities. It comes from the tradition of Rgwa Lo tsā ba Gzhon nu dpal (twelfth century) and is one of the main Karma Kagyü protectors. Closing the collection are a few texts related to the five Bkra shis Tshe ring ma, a group of female protectors particularly associated with Mi la ras pa and the "lineage of practice."

Legacy

Kongtrul completed the first version of the *Treasury* in the summer of 1854.[25] He then revised the collection several times (in 1856, 1881, and 1886), enriching it with the new transmissions he was receiving from various masters. He transmitted it completely for the first time in the spring of 1860 to the Fourteenth Karmapa (1798–1868) and again to the Fifteenth Karmapa (1871–1922) in his

24. Her name in Sanskrit is Dhūmāṅgārī (see Ducher 2017b, 110n385).

25. All the data in this paragraph comes from Barron 2003.

hermitage of Tsa 'dra in 1887. On the latter occasion, so many lamas came to receive the transmission that the hermitage was completely full. Another occasion was in 1882, when 'Jam dbyangs Blo gter dbang po (1847–1914), the abbot of Ngor Thar rtse Monastery, sojourned in Tsa 'dra for several months, also receiving Kongtrul's *Treasury of Instructions* (*Gdams ngag mdzod*) and several other transmissions. Blo gter dbang po was a disciple of 'Jam dbyangs Mkhyen rtse dbang po (1820–92). Together they compiled a massive collection of rituals, the *Compendium of Sādhanas* (*Sgrub thabs kun btus*), and Blo gter dbang po later collected an even more massive set of tantric transmissions, the *Compendium of Tantras* (*Rgyud sde kun btus*). Both collections rely on the *Treasury of Kagyü Mantra* for Marpa's traditions, reproducing the commentaries and rituals authored by Kongtrul.[26] In all, Kongtrul transmitted the complete collection on seven occasions, thus ensuring its diffusion and playing an instrumental role in the revival of Tibetan Buddhism in eastern Tibet. He describes in his *Autobiography* how during his life he actively collected and practiced all transmissions available, many of which were on the verge of disappearance. He systematized them in his *Five Treasuries* and taught them widely and repeatedly to those that requested them. Thanks to these colossal efforts, many traditions, including Marpa's, were effectively saved. In the late 1950s and early 1960s, many Kagyü, Nyingma, and Sakya masters from Kham fled Tibet. Some, like the Sixteenth Karmapa (1924–81), Bdud 'joms Rin po che, and Dil mgo Mkhyen rtse Rin po che, held these traditions and transmitted them in exile to fellow Tibetans and to Westerners and also republished the precious sets of texts they had brought with them. Thus Marpa's tradition even survived the tribulations Tibet suffered in the twentieth century.

Despite the importance of the *Treasury* as the representative of Marpa's teaching, it is far from being well known today. No Western study goes beyond a general outline of contents, and very few individuals practice the central transmissions of the collection, *Hevajra* and *Nairātmyā*, let alone other cycles such as *Mahāmāyā* and *Catuṣpīṭha*. The present contribution is a mere scratching of the surface of the oceanic wealth contained in the collection. Fruitful future endeavors may include clarifying the specificities of Marpa's transmissions, particularly when compared to those developed by Mi la ras pa, Sgam

26. Blo gter dbang po commissioned a set of paintings of the 139 maṇḍalas of the *Rgyud sde kun btus*. Hiroshi Sonami—the Ngor abbot who brought these paintings into exile in the 1960s—and Musashi Tachikawa published schemas of these maṇḍalas in 1989 and 1991, and Tachikawa, together with Ragu Vira and Lokesh Chandra, also took part in the publication of line drawings of the 139 maṇḍala in 2006. These reproductions are helpful tools to visualize the specificities of the Rngog transmissions as they are codified in the *Treasury* (see, for instance, Bsod rnam rgya mtsho and Tachikawa 1989).

po pa, and their heirs on the one hand and, on the other, to those traditions of the same deities whose lineage did not go through Marpa.

Works Cited

Barron, Richard (Chökyi Nyima), trans. 2003. *The Autobiography of Jamgön Kongtrul: A Gem of Many Colors*. Ithaca, NY: Snow Lion Publications.

Bsod nams rgya mtsho and Musashi Tachikawa. 1989. *The Ngor Mandalas of Tibet: Plates*. Bibliotheca Codicum Asiaticorum 2. Tokyo: The Centre for East Asian Cultural Studies.

Ducher, Cécile. 2017a. *Building a Tradition: The Lives of Mar-pa the Translator*. Munich: Indus Verlag.

———. 2017b. "A Lineage in Time: The Vicissitudes of the rNgog pa bka' brgyud from the 11th through 19th Centuries." PhD dissertation. Paris: École Pratique des Hautes Études.

Ehrhard, Franz-Karl. 2002. *Life and Travels of Lo-Chen Bsod-Nams Rgya-Mtsho*. Lumbini, Nepal: Lumbini International Research Institute.

Fermer, Mathias. 2017. "Putting Yar rgyab on the Map." In *Fifteenth Century Tibet: Cultural Blossoming and Political Unrest*, edited by Volker Caumanns and Marta Sernesi, 63–96. Lumbini, Nepal: Lumbini International Research Institute.

Isaacson, Harunaga, and Francesco Sferra, 2015. "Tantric Literature: Overview South Asia." In: *Brill's Encyclopedia of Buddhism*, edited by Jonathan Silk et al., 307–19. Leiden: Brill.

Kapstein, Matthew. 1995. "gDams-ngag: Tibetan Technologies of the Self." In *Tibetan Literature: Studies in Genre*, edited by Roger Jackson and José Cabezón, 275–89. Ithaca, NY: Snow Lion Publications.

———. 2007. "Tibetan Technologies of the Self, Part II: The Teachings of the Eight Great Conveyances." In *The Pandita and the Siddha: Tibetan Studies in Honour of E. Gene Smith*, edited by Ramon Prats, 110–29. Dharamsala, India: Amnye Machen Research Institute.

Kongtrul [Kong sprul Blo gros mtha' yas]. 1982. *Bka' brgyud sngags mdzod*. Paro, Bhutan: Lama Ngodrup and Sherab Drimey. TBRC.org ID: W20876.

———. 2003. *The Autobiography of Jamgön Kongtrul: A Gem of Many Colors.* Translated by Richard Barron. Ithaca, NY: Snow Lion Publications.

———. 2005. *The Treasury of Knowledge, Book 6, Part 4: Systems of Buddhist Tantras*. Translated by Elio Guarisco and Ingrid McLeod. Ithaca, NY: Snow Lion Publications.

———. 2008. *The Treasury of Knowledge, Book 8, Part 3: The Elements of Tantric Practice*. Translated by Elio Guarisco and Ingrid McLeod. Ithaca, NY: Snow Lion Publications.

Sobisch, Jan-Ulrich. 2008. *Hevajra and Lam 'bras Literature of India and Tibet as Seen through the Eyes of A-mes-zhabs*. Wiesbaden: Reichert Verlag.

Tribe, Anthony. 2016. *Tantric Buddhist Practice in India: Vilāsavajra's Commentary on the Mañjuśrīnāmasaṃgīti*. London: Routledge.

Historic and Iconographic Identification of a Thangka of the Ngor Lineage

Amy Heller

As a gesture of homage to my esteemed friend and colleague Matthew, I would like to present a succinct study of a thangka representing numerous eminent scholars and lamas, in a prestigious lineage, allowing for reflection on the subtle distinctions in apparel and portrait characteristics employed to differentiate among categories of Buddhist hierarchs, both lay and monastic. The identification of the subjects portrayed and the chronology of the creation of the thangka may be securely established by the Tibetan inscriptions. As an abbatial commission of the late sixteenth century, it is the epitome of aesthetic refinement, elegance, and opulence, immediately to be associated with the paintings produced in Ngor Monastery in that period. The striking palette of brilliant primary tones of red, blue, and green contrasts with the abundant use of gold in the inscriptions, fabrics, and thrones. The colors are masterfully applied with delicate brushstrokes to render intricate textile patterns and floral buds and leaf tendrils, while the background of opaque color fields in vivid tones of red and blue creates a visual enhancement of the central portraits of the two Buddhist hierarchs.

According to the gold inscription in elegant calligraphy written in the lower register on the front of the thangka, this was dedicated to honor the eleventh abbot of Ngor, Sangs rgyas seng ge (1504–69).[1] As discussed below, the first

1. The thangka was published in Bonhams auction catalogue for March 16, 2015 (http://www.bonhams.com/auctions/22316/lot/15/), with research by the present writer, Jeff Watt, and Ulrich von Schroeder. Jeff Watt listed this painting and a summary description; see HAR 41215 (https://www.himalayanart.org/items/41215). I thank Edward Wilkinson of Bonham's for his kind authorization to publish the painting and my research on it, Ulrich von Schroeder for kindly supplying the additional photograph, and Jörg Heimbel for sharing many references with me. I am grateful to Ven. Lama Kunga Thartse Rinpoche of Ngor (Evam Choden Tibetan Buddhist Center, Kensington, California), and to Jörg Heimbel and the anonymous reviewers for their suggestions on the translation of the prayer on the front of the thangka.

sections of the inscription include a wordplay on the syllables of the names of the ninth abbot, Lha mchog seng ge (1468–1535), and the tenth, Dkon mchog lhun grub (1497–1557). It is thus apparent that these two abbots are the subjects portrayed at center (see plate 11).

Among the names of those portrayed are mahāsiddhas—as spiritual ancestors—and several abbots of Ngor, commencing with the founder, Ngor chen. There is relatively little indication of any naturalistic portraiture. The iconography of deities and mahāsiddhas conforms to usual norms, while the faces of the Sakya and Ngor hierarchs present some tendencies to indicate personal facial features (receding hairline, bald, big nose, plump/thin face, beard) instead of simply a repetitive norm of hieratic portraits. The extent to which the individuation of the features was naturalistic or corresponded to artistic whims is uncertain at present. It would be necessary to compare paintings representing the same members of the Ngor lineage to determine whether these features are based on historic records of personal appearance.

The lineage represented on the thangka is rather uncomplicated until the eighth abbot, Sangs rgyas rin chen (r. 1501–16, P16). The uniform garment of red and orange monastic robes and the presence or absence of hats is the norm. The identification of the latter members of the lineage is somewhat more complicated, however. Sangs rgyas rin chen is followed in the lineage by P17, Sa skya Lo tsā ba. He was the twenty-second chief hierarch of Sakya *bdag chen*, represented with a long red monastic hat draped over his head and shoulders as well as monastic robes. The next in the lineage is P18, Bya btang rje, also wearing monastic robes but no hat. Bya btang pa literally means "the renunciate," but in this case it refers to the epithet-cum-nickname "Bya btang chos rje," who was a teacher of both the ninth and tenth abbots of Ngor.[2]

The inscription refers to figure P19 as Grags pa blo gros, and he deserves some attention here, as two men are known by this name. According to David Jackson, a monk named Grags pa blo gros was the rival of Dkon mchog lhun grub for the position of tenth abbot.[3] Another illustrious Sakya hierarch also named Grags pa blo gros (1563–1617) served as chief administrator of Sakya Monastery, a role in which he succeeded his father, Kun dga' rin chen (d. 1584). When the thangka was first studied, the individual P19 was considered to be a simple monk. However, a close observation of his garments, pose, and hair

2. Powers and Templeman 2012, 210. Heimbel 2017, 351–52n602, gives his full name as Kun dga' mchog ldan. He was a disciple of Go rams pa (see Heimbel, Forthcoming).

3. Jackson 1989, 53: "gNyan lo Grags pa blo gros wanted the appointment of *gdan sa pa*, but to his disappointment, Dkon mchog lhun grub was installed."

leads us to question this assessment (see plate 12). Unlike the other monks portrayed, Grags pa blo gros is seated in three-quarter profile, his chest frontally positioned with the hands in the mudrā of meditation, the two thumbs touching. The hands rest in his lap, which is fully covered by his outer shawl in red brocade. His short-sleeved V-neck monastic robe is hidden beneath the outer robe, the upper hem visible horizontally at the level of his heart. Among other figures in the lineage, only one, P12, the second abbot of Ngor, Mus chen (see plate 13), is represented performing this mudrā, with his outer shawl draped to reveal an additional long-sleeved orange jacket. His hair is short, and he has no beard. The hairline of Grags pa blo gros is clearly receding, he has a short beard, and due to the three-quarter profile of his head, the hair of the nape of his neckline is emphasized. Is this monastic tonsure? This may be indicative of a change in vows. For example, the chief Sakya hierarch Kun dga' rin chen had lay and novice monastic ordination, which he subsequently renounced in order to sire heirs, keeping vows as a lay practitioner (*sngags 'chang*, "upholder of mantra").[4] He was succeeded first by his eldest son and then his younger son, *sngags 'chang* Grags pa blo gros rgyal mtshan in the position of chief hierarch of Sakya, who also later had three children, born between 1588 and 1597. One may therefore wonder whether the master Grags pa blo gros portrayed in this thangka ought to be identified with the chief hierarch of Sakya or with the earlier monk from Ngor?

Comparison with an inscribed sculpture of a major Sakya hierarch preserved in the Musée Guimet is helpful. This is the portrait of a teacher identified as Ngag dbang bsod nams dbang phyug (1638–85, plates 14 and 15).[5] He served as chief hierarch of Sakya, as had his father, the direct nephew of Grags pa blo gros. The portrait shows a man dressed in the short-sleeved monastic robes with the upper hem at heart level, the outer shawl covering his shoulders. To show that he is a ritual practitioner, he has a *phur bu* dagger tucked in the upper hem of his garment. His facial expression is both alert and sensitive. The lower lobes of his ears have holes indicating that he once wore now-lost earrings. The back of the statue, however, is more revealing of his religious status: he wears his hair in a long braid, carefully combed. This indicates that this is an early seventeenth-century portrait of the chief hierarch of Sakya, who, as a devout practitioner, wears his hair long and does not abide by the monastic vows that require tonsure.

4. Tucci 1949, vol. 2, table I, refers to sngags 'chang dbang po kun dga' rin chen.

5. Béguin 1991, 91, "The Fifth Dalai Lama (?)," and color plate 25, MG 24 472. Photography courtesy of the Musée Guimet. I thank Nathalie Bazin, curator of the Himalayan collections, for her help and authorization to publish these photographs.

To conclude this brief historical and iconographical essay, in the context of the Ngor lineage portrait of the ninth and tenth abbots, it is tempting to consider that the lineage concludes with Grags pa blo gros of Sakya, as an emphasis on the strong relationship between Ngor and Sakya over the centuries. This tentative identification shows the difficulties inherent in identification based on inscriptions and visual examination of the front of an image only, as in general only the front is visible in painted icons. Additional criteria are thus required to gain a fuller understanding of the painted portrait, as may be afforded by the image sculpted in the round.

Transliteration of the Inscriptions

bla ma rnams dang lhag pa'i lha tshogs la /
mchog tu dad pas tshul bzhin mnyes byas nas /
rgyud dang man ngag du ma'i mdzod bzung ste /
ji bzhin smra ba'i seng ge de la 'dud /

dkon mchog gsum dngos yongs 'dzin mgon gyis bzung /
khrims ldan thos bsam bsgom pa'i nor gyis phyug /
lhun grub phrin las phyogs brgya spel mkhas pa'i /
blo ldan dge ba'i bshes la gsol ba 'debs /

rtsa brgyud kyi bla ma rnams kyis rig pa 'dzin pa sangs rgyas seng ge la byin gyis brlab tu gsol / mangalam //

Translation

Pleasing the assembly of the many lamas and deities
with the highest faith, I bow to Lha mchog seng ge,
who like Mañjuśrī upholds the treasury
of the numerous teachings and tantra.

Praise to the wise teacher Dkon mchog lhun grub,
who richly embodies the values of the Triple Jewels in discipline, hearing, thought, and contemplation,
who skillfully spreads in all directions
the spontaneously enlightened activities (of the Buddha and his teachings).

May the lineage of all the lamas make praise and benediction to *vidyādhara* Sangs rgyas seng ge (upholder of the knowledge of the Buddha's teachings). May it be auspicious!

Names as Inscribed on the Thangka

P – person
D – deity
M – mahāsiddha
G – goddess

P1	P2	D1	M1	M2	P3	P4	P5
P6	D2	D3	D4	P7			
P8							P9
P10							P11
P12							P13
P14		P20			P21		P15
P16							P17
P18							P19
G1	G2	G3	G4	G5	G6	G7	G8

P1 Sa pa Blo gros bzang (?)
P2 Darpaṇa Ācārya, eleventh–twelfth century
D1 Yama (inscription: Dpal 'dzin)
M1 Virūpa
M2 Ḍombipa and consort
P3 Blo bzang snying po, the Indian paṇḍita Sumatigarbha, tenth century
P4 Blo bo Lo tsā ba, translator and student of Darpaṇa
P5 Mchog ldan Legs pa'i blo gros, thirteenth century
P6 Dpal ldan seng ge, thirteenth century, teacher of Bu ston
D2 Mañjuśrī
D3 Rakta Yamāri and consort, emanation of Mañjuśrī
D4 Yama Dharmarāja
P7 Bu ston (Rin chen grub, 1290–1364), abbot of Zha lu
P8 Dpal ldan Bla ma Dam pa (1312–75), fourteenth hierarch of Sakya, also student and teacher of Bu ston
P9 Phyogs las rnams rgyal (1306–86), student of Bu ston
P10 Ye shes rgyal mtshan, student of Bla ma Dam pa and teacher of Ngor chen

P11 Rdo rje 'chang (Vajradhara), epithet for Ngor chen Kun dga' bzang po (1382–1456), Ngor founder and first abbot of Ngor Monastery
P12 Mus chen (Sems dpa' chen po Dkon mchog rgyal mtshan, 1388–1469, r. 1456–62), second abbot of Ngor
P13 Kun dga' dbang phyug (1424–78), fourth abbot of Ngor and nephew of Ngor chen
P14 Kun mkhyen ("the omniscient"), epithet referring to Go rams pa Bsod nams seng ge, sixth abbot of Ngor (1429–89)
P15 Dkon mchog 'phel, seventh abbot of Ngor (1475–1514)
P16 Sangs rgyas rin chen, eighth abbot of Ngor (1450–1524)
P17 Sa skya Lo tsā ba (1485–1533, r. 1496–1533), twenty-second Sakya hierarch
P18 Bya btang rje (dates unknown), teacher of Lha mchog seng ge and Dkon mchog lhun grub at Ngor
P19 Grags pa blo gros (1563–1617, r. 1589–1617), son of Kun dga' rin chen and twenty-fourth Sakya hierarch
P20 Lha mchog seng ge (1468–1535), ninth abbot of Ngor
P21 Dkon mchog lhun grub (1497–1557), tenth abbot of Ngor
G1–G8 Eight goddesses of offerings

Works Cited

Béguin, Gilles. 1991. *Tibet Art et Méditation*. Paris: Edition Findakly.

Bonhams. March 16, 2015. "A Lineage Portrait Thangka of the Ninth and Tenth Abbots of Ngor Monastery." http://www.bonhams.com/auctions/22316/lot/15/.

Heimbel, Jörg. 2017. *Vajradhara in Human Form: The Life and Times of Ngor Chen Kun dga' bzang po*. Lumbini, Nepal: Lumbini International Research Institute.

____. Forthcoming. "In Need of Donations: A Letter Written by Go rams pa to Encourage the Collecting of Offerings in Eastern Tibet." In *On A Day of a Month of the Fire Bird Year: Festschrift for Peter Schwieger on Occasion of his 65th Birthday*, edited by Jeannine Bischoff, Petra Maurer, and Charles Ramble. Lumbini, Nepal: Lumbini International Research Institute.

Henss, Michael. 2004. Book review of *Dating Tibetan Art: Essays on the Possibilities and Impossibilities of Chronology from the Lempertz Symposium* by Ingrid Kreide-Damani. *The Tibet Journal* 29.4: 75–106.

Jackson, David. 1989. "Sources on the Chronology and Succession of the Abbots of Ngor Ewam-chos-ldan." *Berlin Indologische Studien* 4.5: 49–94.

Powers, John, and David Templeman. 2012. *Historical Dictionary of Tibet*. Lanham, MD: Scarecrow Press.

Tucci, Giuseppe. 1949. *Tibetan Painted Scrolls*, 2 vols. Rome: La Libreria dello Stato.

Watt, Jeff. "Item: Teacher (Lama) – Lhachog Sengge." Himalayan Art Resource 41215, March 2015. https://www.himalayanart.org/items/41215.

From Tibet to Bhutan: The Life and Legacy of Tsang Khenchen Jamyang Palden Gyatso

Jetsun Deleplanque

I CANNOT THINK OF a better way to pay homage to my illustrious teacher, Matthew Kapstein, than to commemorate the life and legacy of another great polymath, Jamyang Palden Gyatso ('Jam dbyangs dpal ldan rgya mtsho, 1610–84), more popularly known in Tibet and Bhutan as Tsang Khenchen (Gtsang Mkhan chen). Surprisingly, besides a few passing references in literature relating to the founding of the Bhutanese state in the seventeenth century, little is known about the great scholar from Tsang. He is generally remembered in Bhutanese and Western sources as a Karma Kagyüpa scholar who fled from persecution in Tibet following the rise of the Ganden Phodrang (Dga' ldan pho brang) government and settled in the Paro (Spa gro) Valley of western Bhutan, where he penned the authoritative and much celebrated biography of Bhutan's founding figure, the Drukpa ('Brug pa) hierarch Shabdrung Ngawang Namgyal (Zhabs drung Ngag dbang rnam rgyal, 1594–1651). More recent scholarship has however begun to hint at the contours of some other aspects of his life, including his artistic contributions in Bhutan and his relationship to the Tenth Karmapa hierarch, Chöying Dorjé (Chos dbyings rdo rje, 1604–74), of whom he also produced a biography.[1] Such treatments remain terse, however, and our overall picture of his life fragmentary. It is also unfortunate that a number of misconceptions regarding this great figure, such as his almost unanimous identification as a Karma Kagyü scholar, have arisen, although they do not appear to be attested in Tibetan sources. Tsang Khenchen did share a strong affinity toward the Karma Kagyü sect and generally espoused a nonsectarian approach to Buddhist learning, but he undoubtedly identified with the Sakya milieu in which he was ordained and trained.

1. For Gtsang Mkhan chen's artistic contributions in Bhutan, see Ardussi 2008 and Maki 2017. For his relationship with and biography of the Karmapa, see Mengele 2012.

Fortunately, Tsang Khenchen left behind a detailed autobiography of over 450 folios,[2] which, besides clarifying many aspects of his life, is a treasure trove for the student of the tumultuous seventeenth century. Drawing from Tsang Khenchen's autobiography, this article has three aims: (1) to provide a brief biographical sketch of the great scholar's life, (2) to clarify his relationship with the Tenth Karmapa hierarch, and (3) to underline his significance for the founding of the Bhutanese state and our general understanding of Tibet's seventeenth century. In so doing, it is my hope that a greater extent of Tsang Khenchen's legacy and influence in Tibet and Bhutan may be appreciated.

The Autobiography

In his pioneering work on the history of Bhutan, Michael Aris has characterized Tsang Khenchen's biography of Shabdrung Ngawang Namgyal as "one of the most deeply frustrating works in the historical literature of Bhutan," mostly owing to the numerous and complicated categories of Buddhist thought that, in his opinion, end up obscuring the biographical subject. Aris proceeded to comment that it is in Tsang Khenchen's own autobiography that the forces of this literary style are most apparent, where "an inconceivable wealth of Buddhist concepts have been applied to the story of his experience."[3] Tsang Khenchen's autobiography is a long and difficult undated work in manuscript form comprising 458 folios in two volumes and written in highly ornate Tibetan.[4] While Aris is certainly right that Buddhist abstractions abound in parts of the autobiography, Tsang Khenchen equally displays a very clear documentary style in other places. The first volume, recounting the first thirty years of the scholar's life in Tibet before his flight to Bhutan, offers rare and lucid descriptions of life under the Tsangpa hegemony leading up to the war that eventually toppled his primary patron, the Desi (Sde srid) Karma bstan skyong dbang po (1606–42). As such, Tsang Khenchen's autobiography becomes an invaluable source for the history of the period, providing

2. 'Jam dbyangs dpal ldan rgya mtsho 1975 (hereafter *Autobiography*). I would like to express my heartfelt gratitude to Shar gzhon Tshe ring zla ba of the Minzu Daxue in Beijing for his assistance in reading through some of the difficult passages of this text.

3. Aris 1979, 203–4.

4. Although the autobiography is undated, its composition can be roughly attributed to the mid 1670s, since it was composed before the biography of Zhabs drung Ngag dbang rnam rgyal. The narrative is unfinished and ends abruptly after Gtsang Mkhan chen's return from his second trip to India. The remaining ten folios of the text are penned by one of Gtsang Mkhan chen's close disciples, presumably Grags pa rgya mtsho (1646–1719), who recounts the final activities and eventual death of his teacher.

an alternate version of events from mainstream accounts. His descriptions of the Tsangpa court or the carnage at the hands of Mongol troops in 1641–42, for example, stand in sharp contrast to later Geluk narratives and represent what the late Elliot Sperling has called a "picture from the margins."[5]

That said, as stated in the introduction to his work, Tsang Khenchen's primary impetus for writing about his life is didactic. The inconceivable wealth of Buddhist concepts that populate his narrative are indeed very real attempts on his part to illustrate the Buddhist truths he strived to embody. His persistent recourse to Buddhist theory and imagery in order to explain the phenomena that surrounded him also has the merit of offering his reader rare glimpses into the unique *mentalité* of the religious elite of the period. His reflections on the violence that occurred through much of his life, for example, are illustrative of the struggle of religious individuals such as himself to frame and rationalize these events along Buddhist lines. At other times, Tsang Khenchen's narrative is deeply personal and indulges his reader in the little details that often make for great storytelling. His ornate poetry, punctuating much of the text, appears to function as much as a means of guiding his reader through the vicissitudes of his own introspections as it does to himself. What emerges is thus a rich and complex narrative that is at times normative and at other times deeply idiosyncratic. The vacillation between these two modes is at once representative of Tsang Khenchen's depth of erudition and character.

The Life of Tsang Khenchen Jamyang Palden Gyatso

Tsang Khenchen was born in 1610 at his family's estate[6] in the Upper Nyang (Myang stod) Valley of Tsang on the auspicious fifteenth day of the fourth month at sunrise and given the name Nor bu bzang po. His father, Sngags 'chang Dge bsnyen bzang po, was an important administrator from the Nubs clan and a tantric practitioner in the lineage of Ratna gling pa.[7] His mother, Tshe dbang khye'u 'dren, was also a practitioner and belonged to the

5. Debreczeny and Tuttle 2016, 9.

6. Gtsang Mkhan chen's family possessed a large estate called Bkra shis rab tu brtan pa'i khang bzang situated in Gtsang dga' in the Upper Myang Valley. A number of important religious teachers were hosted there. For a description of the estate, see *Autobiography* 1:91a.

7. Gtsang Mkhan chen's father was considered to be the incarnation of the founder of the Za'u Temple in the lineage of Ratna gling pa. He was also a fervent follower of the Drukpa sect and a disciple of the Fourth Rgyal dbang 'Brug chen Kun mkhyen padma dkar po, from whom he received his name. For a full description of his religious affiliations, see *Autobiography* 1:103a–104b.

prestigious Lce clan.[8] Her brother, Tsang Khenchen's maternal uncle, Byang chub dpal rig 'dzin gu ru rin po che, was a well-known artist and master craftsman.[9] Tsang Khenchen was the last of three children, after his brother Tshe'i dbang po and his sister Rnam par rgyal ma.[10] Because two other elder siblings had died in infancy, his parents engaged in various pious activities before his birth and during his infancy, including visits to religious centers and receiving blessings from important lineage holders of the region, such as the Sixth Shamarpa (Zhwa dmar pa) Gar dbang chos kyi dbang phyug (1584–1629) and Jonang Tāranātha (1575–1635), among others.

Tsang Khenchen began his religious education under the tutelage of his parents, both of whom he refers to as bodhisattvas. While his mother was the first to introduce him to the fundamentals of Mahāyāna Buddhism, his father transmitted to him the mantra of Vajrakīlaya from the moment he was able to speak. Especially inclined to the religious life from a very young age, Tsang Khenchen was coveted by a number of religious institutions and rumored to be the reincarnation of some important figures.[11] When, at the age of five, he started reading under the tutelage of the monk Blo gros rin chen, his exposure to Buddhist avadānas confirmed his desire to dedicate his life to the Buddhist path. It is at the tender age of seven, however, that his aspirations fully transpired, when he met for the first time Khenchen Lunkrik Kunga Gyatso (Mkhan chen Lung rigs kun dga' rgya mtsho, b.u.–1639), the celebrated Sakyapa scholar who was at the time abbot of the nearby monastery of Spos khang chos sde and who would become the most important figure in his life.[12]

8. Gtsang Mkhan chen's mother was considered to be an incarnation of the mother of the Jonang prelate Kun dga' grol mchog and was often referred to as a *ḍākinī*. See *Autobiography* 1:15a.

9. Unfortunately, Gtsang Mkhan chen's autobiography fails to mention at any point where and with whom he studied Tibet's artistic traditions. We are told however that his drawing and painting began at a very young age and can therefore presume that his maternal uncle had a hand in transmitting this knowledge to him.

10. Gtsang Mkhan chen mentions in the *Autobiography* (1:270a) that a younger brother of his was killed in the war of 1641–42. His early descriptions of his childhood, however, make no mention of a younger brother. It is probably fair to assume that the individual in question was rather a close relative of Gtsang Mkhan chen.

11. Probably owing to his affiliation to the Lce clan and an incident that occurred at Dpal 'khor chos sde, Gtsang Mkhan chen was rumored to be the reincarnation of the sixth abbot of Zhwa lu, Drung gnas Bzang po rgyal mtshan (*Autobiography* 1:23a). For a discussion of the previous incarnations that Gtsang Mkhan chen was believed to have taken, see *Autobiography* 1:9a–b. Regarding the various individuals and institutions that coveted Gtsang Mkhan chen, see *Autobiography* 1: 52a.

12. Spos khang chos sde, also known as Spos khang tshogs pa or Spos khang tshogs sde, was founded in 1213 by Paṇḍita Śākyaśrībhadra's disciple Byang chub dpal bzang po. The monastery

Instantly struck by unwavering faith and devotion toward this teacher, Tsang Khenchen took refuge and novice vows in his presence. Although he strongly desired to join the community of monks and had the support of the majority of his relatives, Tsang Khenchen's father, a tantric householder practitioner, was reluctant to let his son be ordained. Finally, through the intervention of Lungrik Gyatso himself, his father acquiesced, and Tsang Khenchen was ordained by his root teacher on the fifteenth day of the first month of 1622, at the age of thirteen, and given the name Jamyang Palden Gyatso.

Soon after Tsang Khenchen's ordination, Lungrik Gyatso was promoted by the Tsang Desi to become abbot of the important Dpal 'khor chos sde Monastery in Rgyal rtse. Tsang Khenchen spent the next three years studying under his teacher at Dpal 'khor chos sde and accompanying him on his travels in Ü (Dbus) and Tsang. At the age of fifteen, he spent the *dbyar gnas* retreat at his family estate, where Mkhan po Bsam gtan rin chen, who succeeded Lungrik Gyatso as abbot of Spos khang, was in residence. There, Tsang Khenchen gave his first sermon to an assembly of monks on the subject of epistemology. Everyone present was impressed by his aptitude and eloquence and encouraged him to continue his studies at a monastic college. It is also during these years that Tsang Khenchen received his first teachings from the Sixth Shamarpa, while the latter was visiting the Nyang Valley and was hosted at the family estate.

At the age of sixteen, Lungrik Gyatso arranged for Tsang Khenchen to be enrolled at the prestigious Gser mdog can Monastery, where the young monk could continue his training in sūtra and tantra in the tradition of Paṇ chen Shākya mchog ldan (1428–1507). There, Tsang Khenchen studied under the renowned Paṇḍita Shākya bstan 'dzin, who became his second-most important teacher.[13] Tsang Khenchen excelled at his wide-ranging studies, quickly making a name for himself. Besides focusing extensively on the major subjects of Tibetan scholasticism, including Prajñāpāramitā literature, Pramāṇa, Abhidharma, Vinaya, Madhyamaka, and Yogācāra, his studies at Gser mdog can also included Sanskrit, grammar, and poetics. By the age of twenty he began touring the major religious institutions of the Tsang region for his debate rounds and gathered much fame and recognition, including the favor of the Tsang ruler, for his mastery of epistemology. These years were also marked by many trips to Rgyal rtse and Gzhis ka rtse, where Tsang Khenchen

acted as the seat of one of Śākyaśrībhadra's original four monastic communities, the Jo gdan tshogs sde bzhi. For more on Śākyaśrībhadra's four monastic communities, see Heimbel 2013.

13. For a full list of teachings (*gsan yig*) that Gtsang Mkhan chen received from Shākya bstan 'dzin, see *Autobiography* 1:231a–251b.

would meet with his lama Lungrik Gyatso to receive various tantric empowerments and sādhanas.[14]

At the age of twenty-five, in 1634, through the recommendation of Lungrik Gyatso and by order of the Tsang Desi, Tsang Khenchen was enthroned as the abbot of Spos khang Monastery. Now responsible for one of the major seats of Paṇ chen Śākyaśrībhadra's lineage, he spent the following years occupied with important administrative duties and a busy teaching schedule. Although he worked tirelessly for the welfare of his community, Tsang Khenchen longed to live a life of retreat far away from the hustle and bustle of Tibet's powerful religious institutions. Life would have it differently however, and in 1638, after having led the community of Spos khang for four years, Tsang Khenchen was summoned to Bsam 'grub rtse and recruited by the Tsang ruler to become the abbot of a new religious center at the capital.[15] Unable to refuse such a prestigious offer from the Desi, Tsang Khenchen acquiesced and became, overnight, one of the most influential figures in the Tsang kingdom. Ill suited to a life of riches and prestige, however, Tsang Khenchen became increasingly disillusioned with his position in the capital. The political turmoil engulfing the region and the sudden death of his root teacher made his longing for a life of retreat in remote locations all the more pronounced.

When the Mongol troops of Gushri Khan ravaged the Tsang region in 1641, Tsang Khenchen was on a visit to his ancestral home in the Nyang Valley. Caught in the chaos and carnage of the war, he fled southward in the cover of night with a small retinue that included his brother and sister. Taking all kinds of detours to avoid running into an army patrol, the party eventually arrived at a site on the banks of the Yar klung gtsang po, where, coincidentally, the Tenth Karmapa Chöying Dorjé had set up camp. Thus, amid the chaos of war, Tsang Khenchen was to have one of the most significant encounters of his life. Instantly struck with immense faith and devotion to the Karma Kagyü hierarch, the two spent much time discussing religious matters, and both parties traveled together as far as Tsa ri. At this point, Tsang Khenchen contemplated whether to return to his home in Tsang or to continue his journey southward to the forests of Lho mon. Knowing that his position as lama

14. For a full list of teachings (*gsan yig*) that Gtsang Mkhan chen received from Lung rigs rgya mtsho, see *Autobiography* 1:158b–169b.

15. Although Gtsang Mkhan chen does not name the center in question, this can be none other than the monastery of Bde chen chos skor, built by Karma bstan skyong dbang po in 1637–38 and completely destroyed in 1642 by Mongol forces. Gtsang Mkhan chen tells us that the center included a college for each of the major sects of Tibetan Buddhism and was built in an effort to mirror the activities of the kings of the Yar klung dynasty. For a description of the center, see *Autobiography* 1: 201a–b and 218b–222a.

to the Tsang king almost surely meant persecution for him and his followers at the hands of the new Ganden Phodrang government, he eventually chose exile and embarked on the arduous journey to the Bhutanese border.

Tsang Khenchen entered Bhutan through northern Gasa (Mgar sa), using the same route that Shabdrung Ngawang Namgyal had taken some twenty-five years earlier. His descriptions of the lush forests, wild animals, and flowers of the southern land stand in sharp contrast to the war-ravaged and desolate landscape he left behind. Soon after crossing the border, he left his party and entered a solitary retreat not far from present-day Gasa.[16] Later, while giving some teachings and empowerments to the general public at the Dgon tshe phug cave, he was invited to proceed southward to the Bhutanese capital of Punakha (Spu na kha) and meet with Shabdrung Ngawang Namgyal at the Spung thang bde ba chen palace. This would be the first of many meetings that Tsang Khenchen had with the Drukpa hierarch, the two forging a special bond that would last until the latter's final retreat and death in 1651.

Tsang Khenchen saw in the person of Shabdrung Ngawang Namgyal a true incarnation of the bodhisattva Avalokiteśvara and revered him with the same fervor he did his teacher Lungrik Gyatso. Although his original intention was to spend only a short time in Bhutan and continue on his travels to Sikkim and India, Tsang Khenchen ended up spending the remainder of his life in the Drukpa state as a cherished guest of the Drukpa hierarch and his successors. For the Shabdrung, Tsang Khenchen was also an important asset to his state-building project. The breadth of his erudition and his previous standing at the Tsang court made him a welcome addition to the ranks of the newly founded theocratic state. In particular, his knowledge of logic and epistemology was especially sought after, and he was quickly recruited to train the monks of the state monastic body at the Punakha rdzong. Although he was instrumental in the founding of a college of dialectics (*mtshan nyid grwa tshang*) by composing commentaries of Indian treatises for its use and even teaching there for a month, Tsang Khenchen's long-held desire for a life of retreat was granted and respected. While it would appear that he spent the first ten years of his stay in Bhutan in the Punakha region, he eventually settled at the small hermitage of Sman chu nang in the Paro Valley, where, besides three short trips to India, he remained for the rest of his life.

From his seat at Sman chu nang, Tsang Khenchen trained a whole generation of prominent Bhutanese scholars and artists, including the celebrated

16. Gtsang Mkhan chen's brother and sister continued on their journey to Sikkim, while the rest of the party appears to have returned to Tibet. His brother eventually traveled to Bhutan to meet him, while his sister stayed in Sikkim and eventually died there.

artist Grags pa rgya mtsho (1646–1719) and the Third Rje mkhan po Pad dkar lhun grub (1640–99). His most lasting contributions however are arguably the many volumes that he penned while in Bhutan. From tantric exegeses, commentaries on Indian and Tibetan philosophical treatises, works on grammar and poetics, and numerous biographies, the breadth of Tsang Khenchen's literary activity is immediately apparent. His biography of the Buddha, comprising over one thousand pages, has been characterized by Kurtis Schaeffer as perhaps the largest life of the Buddha ever composed in Tibetan, a "veritable encyclopedia of Buddhist-lore, with citations from seemingly every conceivable scriptural source that touches upon the Buddha's story."[17] His most enduring work however remains his biography of Shabdrung Ngawang Namgyal that the latter personally requested him to write and that served as the base text for all later biographies of the Drukpa hierarch and founder of the Bhutanese state.

On the eighth day of the sixth month of the wood-mouse year (1684), at the age of seventy-five, Tsang Khenchen passed away while in retreat at Sman chu nang. It appears that his death was precipitated by an ailment to his foot that had first developed while in Tsang and later flared up again in Bhutan. His death was accompanied by many auspicious signs.

Tsang Khenchen's Relationship with the Tenth Karmapa

Up until recently, not much was known about the life of one of the most important figures of Tibet's seventeenth century, the Tenth Karmapa hierarch Chöying Dorjé. The last decade has however seen a wave of scholarship on the great artist-practitioner, uncovering many details of his life and artistic contributions.[18] One subject that has puzzled scholars relates to the identity of the Karmapa's ever-faithful attendant, going by the name of Kuntu Sangpo (Kun tu bzang po), to whom a number of the Karmapa's biographical compositions are addressed. In a monograph on the life of the hierarch, Irmgard Mengele has advanced the hypothesis that Tsang Khenchen and Kuntu Sangpo may be one and the same person. Besides the fact that both individuals share the same birth year and lifespans, Mengele bases this assumption on four points related to Tsang Khenchen and the Karmapa's autobiographical writings.[19] Mengele however concludes that despite the evidence presented, a

17. See Schaeffer's introduction to Chögyel 2015.

18. See Mengele 2012, Shamar Rinpoche 2012, Debreczeny and Tuttle 2016, and Debreczeny 2012.

19. The four points sustaining Mengele's argument are the following: (1) Gtsang Mkhan chen's

number of questions still need to be answered through a more careful study of the life of Tsang Khenchen. It will perhaps suffice to say here that besides the evidence being thin,[20] a careful study of Tsang Khenchen's life overwhelmingly refutes this hypothesis.

The only surviving biographical information that we have on Kuntu Sangpo is related in Si tu and 'Be lo's history of the Karma Kagyü sect. In it, we learn that Kuntu Sangpo was born in the G.yor po Valley of Lho kha. He was ordained by the Sixth Shamarpa and began his studies at the age of fifteen at the Karma Kagyü monastery of Thub bstan nyin byed gling in Kong po. He met the Karmapa while the latter was visiting Lho brag and became his personal attendant serving him for the next thirty-five years. Kuntu Sangpo was with the Karmapa when his encampment was attacked in 1645 and fled with him into exile in Lijiang.[21] In light of Tsang Khenchen's biographical sketch given above, the shared identity of these two individuals is

autobiography cites in full a passage from the beginning of the Karmapa's biographical composition the *Wish-Fulfilling Cow* (*Byang chub sems dpa'i rtogs brjod pa zhing kun tu rang nyid 'ong ba gdul bar bya ba kun gyi 'dod pa 'jo ba'i ba mo*) in which the latter describes their meeting. At the end of this passage, the Karmapa refers to Gtsang Mkhan chen by the term *rim gro ba* ("attendant"), the name by which he addressed Kun tu bzang po. (2) Mengele understands a passage in Gtsang Mkhan chen's autobiography to be referring to him receiving a secret tantric name by the Karmapa. (3) Another passage in the autobiography recounts a meeting between Gtsang Mkhan chen and the Sixth Zhwa dmar pa, Fifth Si tu pa, and Fifth Rgyal tshab. The three tell him that if he were to go in the presence of the Karmapa, the latter would be pleased by his knowledge. (4) Three biographical compositions of the Karmapa that he had entrusted in the care of Kun tu bzang po were mistakenly published in Bhutan in 1976 as part of the collected works of Gtsang Mkhan chen. See Mengele 2012, 287–89.

20. For the sake of brevity, I shall address each of Mengele's points in the order that they appear: (1) The Karmapa does indeed refer to Gtsang Mkhan chen as *rim gro ba* in his *Wish-Fulfilling Cow*. This term however is not exclusive to Kun tu bzang po. In the previous page, for example, the Karmapa refers to himself as the Zhwa dmar pa's *rim gro ba*. (2) The passage in question mentions the conferral of a secret tantric name to Gtsang Mkhan chen by Zhabs drung Ngag dbang rnam rgyal at the Spu na kha rdzong, not by the Karmapa. (3) Gtsang Mkhan chen does recount a meeting in his youth with the three Kagyü figures, whereupon they encouraged him to meet with the Karmapa. He even recounts that he replied with the aspiration, "May I be fortunate enough to be in the presence of the Karmapa." This, however, does not substantiate the claim that Gtsang Mkhan chen became the Karmapa's attendant for thirty-five years. (4) The fact that the Karmapa's biographical compositions were accidentally published in the collected works of Gtsang Mkhan chen is puzzling. Attributing this curious mistake to the possibility that Gtsang Mkhan chen was indeed Kun tu bzang po is a far stretch, however. More probable is the possibility that given Gtsang Mkhan chen's relationship with the Karmapa, the Karmapa's writings were kept in proximity to his, and the editors failed to separate them.

21. See Si tu and 'Be lo 1972, 2:174a.

simply not possible. It is unfortunate that this hypothesis has been uncritically adopted in subsequent scholarship.[22]

The fact that Tsang Khenchen was not the Karmapa's beloved attendant Kuntu Sangpo does not diminish in any way the strong affinity shared between these two individuals. Tsang Khenchen did write a biography of the Karma Kagyü hierarch from his seat in Paro and felt unwavering devotion toward him. His autobiography recounts numerous dreams and visions of the Karmapa during his retreats in Bhutan and even posits that he was probably a disciple of the Seventh and Eighth Karmapas in previous lives.[23]

Tsang Khenchen's Legacy and Significance

As mentioned above, Tsang Khenchen's autobiography remains an invaluable source for the complicated processes taking place during Tibet's turbulent seventeenth century. In particular, his descriptions of the Tsang court and the activities of his primary patron the Tsang Desi Karma bstan skyong dbang po are a welcome addition to our knowledge of this otherwise little known and short-lived hegemony. While Karma bstan skyong dbang po has been characterized by some as somewhat of an irreverent and hawkish ruler,[24] Tsang Khenchen's descriptions of the Tsang Desi however could not be more contradictory. The picture that emerges from his interactions with the ruler is one of a deeply pious individual who spent much of his time and resources sponsoring the various Buddhist sects prevalent in Tsang.[25] The Tsang court was strongly invested in the promotion of an ecumenical approach to Buddhist patronage and the religious center at the capital for which Tsang Khenchen was recruited to become the abbot stands as a clear example of this inclination. The center included a college for each of the Kadam, Sakya, Nyingma,

22. In her work on the artistic legacy of Gtsang Mkhan chen, Ariana Maki, for example, wholly takes up Mengele's hypothesis, describing the life of Gtsang Mkhan chen as if he were Kun tu bzang po. See Maki 2017.

23. See *Autobiography* 1:9b.

24. David Templeman, one of the leading scholars on the period, has characterized Karma bstan skyong dbang po as a hot-headed individual with pretensions to grandeur and a flippant dismissal of lamas in general. These observations appear to be primarily drawn from the testimonies of the Third Yol mo sprul sku (1589–1644) and the First Paṇchen Lama Blo bzang chos kyi rgyal mtshan (1567–1662). See Debreczeny and Tuttle 2016, 19.

25. During his audiences with the Gtsang ruler, Gtsang Mkhan chen describes in detail the courtesy that he is accorded, including the ruler lowering his throne so that he is seated at the same height as his guest, and so on. See, for example, *Autobiography* 1:145b–146b, 1:177a, and 1:201b.

Kagyü, and Jonang traditions and regularly hosted monks and *mkhan pos* from the important centers of each sect. Tsang Khenchen himself stood at the forefront of this nonsectarian movement, striving to foster dialogue and cooperation among the various traditions surrounding him. Idealized as they are, his descriptions of the final years of the Tsangpa hegemony, especially in comparison to the wide-scale destruction that ensued, evoke almost something of a golden age, a return to the old days of the Tibetan dynasty ruled by devout bodhisattva kings.

It is against the backdrop of the activities taking place in Tsang before and after the rise of the Ganden Phodrang government that the state-building project of Shabdrung Ngawang Namgyal can be best understood. As John Ardussi has claimed, the Drukpa state was initially probably something of a clone of the situation at Rwa lung, the Shabdrung's ancestral monastic seat in Tsang, with a few officials and a network of patrons and properties.[26] As the Bhutanese state expanded, however, its apologists extensively drew on previous Tibetan models of governance to lay its theoretical foundations. There is no more significant contribution to this effort than Tsang Khenchen's biography of Shabdrung Ngawang Namgyal. Again, as Ardussi has claimed, far from a piece of unvarnished biography or history, Tsang Khenchen's biography acted essentially as a political statement. The many categories of Buddhist thought that Michael Aris so abhorred were rather careful attempts by Tsang Khenchen to articulate a justification for the state-building efforts of the Shabdrung in the language of intellectual debate current at the time.[27] There can be little doubt that Tsang Khenchen's experience at the Tsang court and the subsequent rise to power of the Ganden Phodrang government deeply influenced his views on the Shabdrung's state-building effort. Wholly convinced by the promise of a Buddhist realm governed by a bodhisattva in which persecuted religious individuals like him could find shelter, Tsang Khenchen rallied behind this vision and became one of its primary literary architects. His biography of the Shabdrung has and continues to act as an enduring emblem of the Bhutanese state, providing a template for numerous Bhutanese scholars and historians to continue the work of formulating a Bhutanese identity. It should come as no surprise, then, that the illustrious eighteenth-century Bhutanese scholar and Ninth Rje mkhan po, Shākya rin chen (1710–59), whom Karma Phuntsho

26. Ardussi 2004, 15.

27. Ardussi 2004, 11.

has characterized as one of the principal expounders of a Bhutanese national identity,[28] was considered to be a reincarnation of Tsang Khenchen.

It is my hope that albeit brief, this biographical sketch of Tsang Khenchen gives a taste of the remarkable scope of his activities and influence in Tibet and Bhutan. In the often-dark recesses of Tibet's seventeenth century, Tsang Khenchen stands out as a great luminary. As a founding figure of the Bhutanese state, his legacy both encompasses and stretches far beyond his role as a talented scholar, teacher, biographer, and artist.

28. Phuntsho 2013, 340.

Works Cited

Ardussi, John. 2004. "Formation of the State of Bhutan ('Brug gzhung) in the 17th Century and Its Tibetan Antecedents." *Journal of Bhutan Studies* 2.2: 10–32

———. 2008. "Gyalse Tenzin Rabgye (1638–1696), Artist Ruler of 17th Century Bhutan." In *The Dragon's Gift: The Sacred Arts of Bhutan,* edited by Terese Tse Bartholomew and John Johnston, 88–99. Boston: Serindia Publications.

Aris, Michael. 1979. *Bhutan: The Early History of a Himalayan Kingdom.* London: Aris & Phillips.

Chögyel, Tenzin. 2015. *The Life of the Buddha.* Translated by Kurtis R Schaeffer. New York: Penguin Books.

Debreczeny, Karl, ed. 2012. *The Black Hat Eccentric: Artistic Vision of the Tenth Karmapa.* New York: Rubin Museum of Art.

Debreczeny, Karl, and Gray Tuttle, eds. 2016. *The Tenth Karmapa and Tibet's Turbulent 17th Century.* Chicago: Serindia Publications.

Heimbel, Jörg. 2013. "The Jo gdan tshogs sde bzhi: An Investigation into the History of the Four Monastic Communities in Śākyaśrībhadra's Vinaya Tradition." In *Nepalica-Tibetica: Festgabe for Christoph Cüppers,* edited by Franz-Karl Ehrhard and Petra Maurer, 1:187–242. Andiast: International Institute for Tibetan and Buddhist Studies.

'Jam dbyangs dpal ldan rgya mtsho. 1974. *Dpal 'brug pa rin po che ngag dbang rnam rgyal gyi rnam thar rgyas pa chos kyi sprin chen po'i dbyangs.* Delhi: Topden Tsering.

'Jam dbyangs dpal ldan rgya mtsho. 1975. *Bstan pa 'dzin pa'i skyes bu thams cad kyi rnam par thar pa la gus shing rje su 'jug pa'i rtogs brjod pha rol tu phyin pa dang gzungs dang ting nge 'dzin gyi sgo mang po rim par phye ba'i gtam.* 2 vols. Thimphu: Kunsang Tobgay.

Karma pa Chos dbyings rdo rje. 1976. *Byang chub sems dpa'i rtogs brjod pa zhing kun tu rang nyid 'ong ba gdul bar bya ba kun gyi 'dod pa 'jo ba'i ba mo zhes bya ba bzhugs so.* Thimphu: Kunsang Tobgay.

Maki, Ariana. 2017. "A Visual Transmission: Bhutanese Art & Artists from the 17th–19th Centuries." In *Mandala of 21st Century Perspectives: Proceedings of the International Conference on Tradition and Innovation in Vajrayana Buddhism,* edited by Dasho Karma Ura, Dorji Penjore, and Chhimi Dem, 102–21. Thimphu: Centre for Bhutan Studies.

Mengele, Irmgard. 2012. *Riding a Huge Wave of Karma: The Turbulent Life of the Tenth Karma-pa.* Kathmandu: Vajra Publications.

Phuntsho, Karma. 2013. *The History of Bhutan.* Noida, India: Random House India.

Shamar Rinpoche. 2012. *A Golden Swan in Turbulent Waters: The Life and Times of the Tenth Karmapa Choying Dorje.* Lexington, VA: Bird of Paradise Press.

Si tu Paṇ chen Chos kyi 'byung gnas and 'Be lo Tshe dbang kun khyab. 1972. *Sgrub brgyud karma kam tshang brgyud pa rin po che'i rnam par thar pa rab 'byams nor bu zla ba chu shel gyi phreng ba.* Delhi: D. Gyaltshan and Kesang Legshay.

"A Good Life for Me, the Little Bhadanta": A Song of Spiritual Experience

Franz-Karl Ehrhard

For Matthew and in commemoration of our teacher Sangs rgyas bstan 'dzin (1924–90)

IT HAS BEEN noted that the personal, subjective strain in the Tibetan poetical tradition is most evident in the "songs of experience" (*nyams mgur*), which can be described as songs about the way in which experiential realization arises from one's having meditated according to the guru's instruction. These poems express feelings of joy, their tone being primarily positive and celebratory, but they also contain recollections of obstacles along the way to enlightenment. If one looks into the broad corpus of this literary genre of Tibetan Buddhism, one finds in these songs, in particular, accounts of the poet's education and training, which allude to the difficulties he had to overcome, reported in such a way as to inspire others. Still, there is a great variety among them in terms of content, tone, and style, and it has been suggested that one can unite them by a common theme—personal spiritual experience.[1]

In the following a song will be presented that takes up the above-mentioned themes, and structures the individual verses into an autobiographical account. It provides dates, starting with the author's birth and ending with his age

1. For more concerning this view of "songs of experience," see Jackson 1996, 377–83. The poems examined therein range in time from the eleventh to the twentieth century, and include the authors Mi la ras pa (1052–1135), Tsong kha pa Blo bzang grags pa (1357–1419), 'Brug pa Padma dkar po (1527–92), the Sixth Dalai Lama Tshangs dbyangs rgya mtsho (1683–1705), Geshe Rabten (1920–86), and Chögyam Trungpa (1939–87). Consult Kapstein 2003, 769–73, for Tibetan yogic poetry as exemplified in the songs of Mar pa Chos kyi blo gros (1012–97). He argues that these songs, although connected with Indian literature, the tradition of the mahāsiddhas, and the symbols derived from the tantras, remain nevertheless a decidedly Tibetan genre, drawing freely upon well-established conventions of oratory and bardic recitation.

when the poem was completed. Its main focus is on the spiritual training, the individual teachers, and the doctrines they transmitted. The author is Ngawang Namgyal (Ngag dbang rnam rgyal, b. 1628), a Buddhist teacher from northern Dolpo in the Nepalese Himalayas. The course of his life has already been sketched on the basis of his *Record of Teachings Received* (*Thob yig*), but no concerted attention has been paid so far to his *Collected Spiritual Songs* (*Mgur 'bum*).[2] This latter collection contains about one hundred poems of various lengths, the first ones dating from the year 1658, when the author began a three-year retreat at a site called Sgom phug. Further places of his spiritual practice are mentioned, including Chos lung rab brtan, Ri bo 'brug sgra, and, especially, Gnam gung. It is this last site, in northern Dolpo, that is mainly associated with the name of Ngawang Namgyal, and it must have served as his residence in the later part of his life.

~

Praise to the guru!

The teachers, the superior personal deity and the Jina together with his
 sons—the three kinds of jewels—
in the precious palace of my own mind,
rest inseparable from me: please confer the highest and common siddhis!

Having taken me, someone of minor deeds, as an authority,
some faithful ones, very diligent in their respect,
said that by all means there is a need for a biography of me.
I myself, having the outer appearance of a monk but without the true
 dharma, having been born at the end of times,
with the power of only minor spiritual strength acquired through virtue
 accumulated previously,

2. The record of Ngag dbang rnam rgyal has been used in order to investigate the transmission of treasure cycles of the Rnying ma school; see Ehrhard 2013, 314–24 and 329–30. His collection of spiritual songs was quite widely disseminated, and it was filmed by the Nepal-German Manuscript Project (NGMPP) on two occasions (NGMPP reel-nos. L 62/4 & L 411/3). Both the record and songs have been published on the basis of a rare manuscript from western Nepal (see sources cited below), and it is the edition used for this presentation of the autobiographical song. The collection bears the title *Disconnected Gibberish: Songs of Experience, [Containing] the Renunciate Ngag dbang rnam rgyal's Personal Recollections*. For a song describing the special qualities of Gnam gung, see *Mgur 'bum*, 167.5–172.1.

whose discriminative awareness in this life is small and whose discipline is weak,
whose intellect is deluded and who has no conscious awareness of the door to learning,
who has not trained in words [heard while] listening to the sūtras and tantras,
devoid of reflecting on and cultivating the reality of the profound creation and completion stages,
and who does not understand the words of instruction and the crucial points of meditation:
how could there exist [in my case] the story of a life [that is a source] of great astonishment?

But when you said that it is necessary by all means,
[I can only answer] that the story of my life from the time my mother bore me till the present when I am sixty-four
does not exist, in accordance with the true dharma;
[nevertheless,] the means by which I sustained the life of this worldly existence
I will explain shortly: listen carefully!

On the border between the two, Nepal and Tibet, where are different people,
in the presence of the Self-Arisen [Ārya] Wa ti bzang po,
in a dragon year [=1628], on the twenty-fifth day of the *dbyu gu* lunar mansion (i.e., the eighth Tibetan month)
I was born to a faithful religious mother—so it is said:
All this meant a good life for me, the little bhadanta! (1)

At the meeting grounds of Khyung rdzong dkar po, [the capital of] Mnga' ris [Gung thang],
from [Yol mo ba Sprul sku] Bstan 'dzin nor bu (1598–1644)
and from the lord of the Sūtra- and Mantrayāna, the great *upādhyāya* of Gzhad ri [Monastery],
I heard as if mere peripheral activity the profound doctrine:[3]

3. According to the record, these early meetings with the Third Yol mo ba Sprul sku occurred at the age of two, i.e., 1630, and the one with the scholar from Gzhad ri Monastery followed one year later; see *Thob yig*, 3.1–4.1. Bstan 'dzin nor bu was staying in the region of Mang yul Gung thang around this same period; see Bogin 2013, 241–45. Gzhad ri, also known as Skyed [mo]

All this meant a good life for me, the little bhadanta! (2)

At glorious Mtha' dkar, the pilgrimage site of spiritual realization,
together with Chos skyong dpal bzang, the noble highest guide,
I established to some extent a connection with the profound doctrine,
including the empowerment of the long-life practice [and] the empowerment [and] reading authorization of Guhyapati (i.e., Vajrapāṇi):[4]
All this meant a good life for me, the little bhadanta! (3)

The way to found monasteries, produce statues, books, and stūpas,
to confer empowerments upon others when resting on a teaching throne,
and to show up to make offerings on the auspicious tenth day and so forth—
I performed [these playful] acts of a child to some degree in accordance with the doctrine:
All this meant a good life for me, the little bhadanta! (4)

In order to purify, the minor residual karma connected with previous training was revealed:
a simple lack of concern with devotion toward other profound doctrines;
[but] when I heard the name of the instructions of the cycles of the
Three [Wish-Fulfilling] Gems[5]
it sounded pleasant, like thunder in the ears of a peacock:
All this meant a good life for me, the little bhadanta! (5)

---

tshal 'og ma, was one of the six great monastic institutions resulting from the activities of the Sa skya pa master Sangs rgyas 'phel (1411–85) from Gtsang; it was founded by one of his disciples in the early sixteenth century; see Akester 2017, 527.

4. For the studies with Chos skyong dpal bzang at Mtha' dkar in northern Dolpo at the age of seven, i.e., in the year 1635, see *Thob yig*, 4.1–3. It is stated that this was in the home region of Ngag dbang rnam rgyal. The monastery of Mtha' dkar had been founded by Bsod nams blo gros (1516–81), the first abbot of Dmar sgom and a follower of the Ngor pa tradition of the Sa skya school; see Ehrhard 2013, 315n4. The transmission of teachings included the biography and spiritual songs of Chos skyong dpal bzang, which remain unavailable. The latter individual was also one of the masters of Yon tan rgyal mtshan (1590–1674), a Buddhist teacher from southern Dolpo; see Ehrhard 2015, 15n16.

5. The teachings of the Aural Transmissions of Saṃvara (*bde mchog snyan brgyud*) are traditionally grouped into three main cycles, called *wish-fulfilling gems*; these are the Lineage Wish-Fulfilling Gem (*brgyud pa yid bzhin nor bu*), the Wish-Fulfilling Gem of the Maturation Path" (*smin lam yid bzhin nor bu*), and the Wish-Fulfilling Gem of the Liberation Path" (*grol lam yid bzhin nor bu*); see Sernesi 2011, 183. In the fifteenth century the Aural Transmissions were taken up by the 'Brug pa Bka' brgyud school; see Sernesi 2011, 190.

Once my sixteenth year was upon me [= 1643], it was in the presence of the teacher Ras chen [Blo 'phel dpal bzang],
with the devotion of a pure intent, that I dwelled at the threshold of this noble doctrine,
well adorned with the discipline of an upāsaka [vow conferred by] the mentor.
Thus, from then on, the peak of my aspiration for happiness was established:[6]
All this meant a good life for me, the little bhadanta! (6)

With the refined gold of the heart essence of the mighty Jina,
the sun and moon above and below were joined through untiring effort and zeal in regard to such instruction;
the bliss heat spread throughout my body, and I was released from the dread of coldness:
All this meant a good life for me, the little bhadanta! (7)

The path of liberation, mahāmudrā, and the path of skillful means, the instructions of the six doctrines of Nāropa,
the sādhanas of guru[-yoga], the outer, inner, and secret ones, and so forth—
just a small share of the instructions of ripening and liberation did I obtain:
All this meant a good life for me, the little bhadanta! (8)

The current of the river of the tradition of the glorious 'Brug pa—
in order to cleanse the obscurations of body, my number of prostrations was 600,000, and some [recitations] slipped from my mouth as well:
All this meant a good life for me, the little bhadanta! (9)

In order to cleanse the obscuration of speech, [I performed] the hundred-syllable [mantra of Vajrasattva], the maṇḍala [offering], the seven-limbed [pūjā], and a succession of prayers;

6. The same year, i.e., 1643, is also given in the record as the time when the doctrine of the Aural Transmissions was received for the first time; see *Thob yig*, 6.1–7.1. In the following year further teachings were transmitted, starting with liturgical manuals of the 'Brug pa Bka' brgyud school; see *Thob yig*, 7.1–9.4. There special mention is made of the cycle of the Aural Transmission of the Ḍākinīs (*mkha' 'gro snyan brgyud*) and the reading authorizations of hagiographical literature, including the biography of Gtsang smyon He ru ka (1452–1507). The master also conferred treasure teachings of the Rnying ma school, especially the cycle Profound Instructions on Vajravārāhī (*Rdo rje phag mo zab khrid*) of Rig 'dzin Bstan gnyis gling pa (1480–1535); see *Thob yig*, 9.4–11.3.

in order to cleanse the obscuration of mind, [I attended to] the means of upholding the view and
approaching and realizing [the personal deity] and so forth—a custom I had merely begun:
All this meant a good life for me, the little bhadanta! (10)

On one occasion, when I was in the presence of the teacher [Ras chen Blo 'phel dpal bzang],
[I underwent] scolding, hunger, thirst, exhaustion, and so forth,
but the only attitude I had toward his admonishment
was that it was a means of cleansing my faults and obscurations:
All this meant a good life for me, the little bhadanta! (11)

From Mahāsattva Dpal ldan don grub [I obtained]
profound treasures: the instructions of [the cycle] *Guru* [*che mchog*] *dmar po*,
the sādhana of Mahākaruṇika, the *gcod yul* [practice], the peaceful and wrathful deities, and so forth;
the tradition of [the teachers of] glorious Dmar sgom [monastery], father [and] sons—
up to now its spiritual practice has not deviated even a little:[7]
All this meant a good life for me, the little bhadanta! (12)

Glorious Lhasa, the Dharmacakra [site] that is the most excellent Vajrāsana of Jambudvīpa's Tibet,
and the special pilgrimage places of Dbus, [epicenter] of the land of snows—
in a dream-like illusory fashion I encountered them for a brief moment:
All this meant a good life of me, the little bhadanta! (13)

At the pilgrimage site Brag dkar [rta so], at Chos sdings, and so forth,
from the most excellent guide [Ras chen] Karma chos 'phel (d. 1671),

7. For the transmission of teachings by Dpal ldan don grub, see *Thob yig*, 11.3–17.1. This particular teaching tradition is called in the record "the long transmission of Chos skyabs dpal bzang, father and sons, the Dharmarājas of glorious Dmar sgom" (*dpal dmar sgom chos kyi rgyal po chos skyabs dpal bzang yab sras kyi ring lugs*). This phrase refers to Chos skyabs dpal bzang (1536–1625) and the following abbots of Dmar sgom; the first abbot was a disciple of Bsod nams blo gros, the founder of this monastery in northern Dolpo. The cycle *Guru che mchog dmar po* is one of the treasures of Nyang ral Nyi ma'i 'od zer (1124–92); concerning this transmission and further treasure teachings received from Dpal ldan don grub, see Ehrhard 2013, 315–20. One of the spiritual songs of Ngag dbang rnam rgyal is addressed to the "great monk community of Dmar sgom" (*dmar bsgom [=sgom] 'dus sde chen po*); see *Mgur 'bum*, 426.1–433.3.

the evenly dispersed [fruit of the] doctrine of the sūtras and tantras came
forth,
including the coemergent [mahāmudrā], the six doctrines of Nāropa,
hagiographies of the Kagyü [masters], and the temporary vows:[8]
All this meant a good life for me, the little bhadanta! (14)

In the presence of Dpal ldan bzang po, the mighty conqueror,
I obtained the rule of the Vinaya *pratimokṣa*, the root of the doctrine,
the two sets of instructions on the realization of deathlessness,
the profound path of *gcod yul*, the instructions of *'pho ba* and so forth;
and in addition, many scattered pieces of advice:[9]
All this meant a good life for me, the little bhadanta! (15).

Although some people into whose heart vileness had entered
introduced the poison of bad food [into me], and so did [me] harm,
through a lucky combination of circumstances—a medical examination,
yoga, [and rituals to] remove misfortune—
I felt like a peacock released from a snare:
All this meant a good life for me, the little bhadanta! (16)

From the final rebirth of Snubs chen Nam mkha' snying po, Karma Blo
bzang, the head of a hundred spiritual lineages,
I received the Three Wish-Fulfilling Gems together with the branch
instructions,
the combined pair of [instructions on] ripening and liberation, [which were
like] a vessel filled to the brim:
All this meant a good life for me, the little bhadanta! (17)

8. According to the record, the first visit to Brag dkar rta so in Mang yul, the famous site of the great yogin Mi la ras pa, occurred at the age of twenty-nine years, i.e., in 1657; for this date and the teachings transmitted, especially those of the Karma Kaṃ tshang Bka' brgyud pa, see *Thob yig*, 17.1–20.2. A biographical sketch of this master, the sixth abbot of Brag dkar rta so, can be found in Chos kyi dbang phyug: *Gdan rabs*, 563.2–566.4. At Chos sdings, also located in Mang yul, Ngag dbang rnam rgyal intoned a further spiritual song of his; see *Mgur 'bum*, 252.1–254.2.

9. Ngag dbang rnam rgyal had first met Dpal ldan bzang po at the age of ten, in the year 1638, at the latter's residence in Hrab in northern Dolpo; concerning this early visit and the obtaining of the mentioned teachings on a later occasion, see *Thob yig*, 4.3–5.3. On the foundation of the monastery of Hrab by Dpal ldan blo gros (1527–96), who was a further disciple of Bsod nams blo gros and another abbot of Dmar sgom, see Ehrhard 2013, 315n5. Dpal ldan bzang po is also known for having been one of the masters of Dpal ldan rdo rje (1647–1723), a Buddhist teacher from southern Dolpo and contemporary of Ngag dbang rnam rgyal; see Ehrhard 2015, 15n16.

I obtained [the cycles] *Yang zab* [*dkon mchog spyi 'dus*] and *Zhi khro* [*nges don snying po*], which are the combined sections of the mother and son [treasures],
the teaching cycles *Thugs* [*rje*] *chen* [*po*] *nam mkha' rgyal po* [*ngan song rang grol*], *Tshe dpag med* [*gnam lcags rdo rje*] and *Rta phag* [*yid bzhin nor bu*], together with the *Gsang lam bla* [*ma*] *sgrub* [*pa*] [doctrine];
moreover, many scattered [instructions on] ripening and liberation:[10]
All this meant a good life for me, the little bhadanta! (18)

When I reached my thirty-fifth year [= 1662]—whether owing to previous karma or immediate circumstances—
I was struck by the mouth-vapor of a poisonous nāga, master of the territory;
severe leprosy ground my body and mind to dust;
the pain of my body was like a fish out of water,
and the suffering of my mind was like a bird whose nest has been destroyed:
All this meant a good life for me, the little bhadanta! (19)

The methods for benefiting this [sickness] were completely worn out,
and it was certain that it was the bad karma, collected in a series of [previous] lifetimes;
nevertheless, like the exemplary lives of the Jina's sons, the great beings,
I engaged in the giving and taking of virtue and sin, an exchange wherein one's self and others are made equal:
All this meant a good life for me, the little bhadanta! (20)

The king of methods is to dedicate one's personal aggregates to the masses,
sacrificing whatever is held dear and abandoning completely the grasping at a self;
when this has become the most excellent of medicines, one enjoys sickness and takes delight in dying—

10. An overview of the life of Karma Blo bzang can be found in Ehrhard 2013, 229–35. He is counted as the fifth abbot of Brag dkar rta so; see Chos kyi dbang phyug: *Gdan rabs*, 554.1–563.2, and the translation in Sernesi, Forthcoming. The record of teachings received lists first the teachings of the Aural Transmission, followed by the treasure cycles; see *Thob yig*, 20.2–28.5 and 28.5–35.5. These cycles including the final one are all finds of Rig 'dzin 'Ja' tshon snying po (1586–1656). This final doctrine is called a "special doctrine" (*khyad chos*) from Dvags lha sgam po and refers to the *Dvags po gsang lam bla sgrub*; see the works in Schwieger 1990, 230–34 [= nos. 360–69]. The encounter with Karma Blo bzang is placed by Ngag dbang rnam rgyal in his thirty-second year, i.e., 1660. One of the spiritual songs is dedicated to the memory of Karma Blo bzang, having been written after news of his passing at Brag dkar rta so was received; see *Mgur 'bum*, 148.1–154.3.

a great wonder indeed if by bad circumstances good fortune is reached:
All this meant a good life for me, the little bhadanta! (21)

Long did I abandon the tumult of worldly towns;
at practice sites in the lower or upper parts [of valleys] and blessed by previous [masters],
uninvolved in nonreligious acts of the three doors,
I took up the tradition of practice for eleven years [= 1662–73]:
All this meant a good life for me, the little bhadanta! (22)

Among the three—mountain retreats, strict seclusion, and abstaining from speech—
each month in autumn and spring I stayed for two months in mountain retreats,
and for four or three months in winter I abstained from speech,
and during all these periods, it was exclusively in strict seclusion:
All this meant a good life for me, the little bhadanta! (23)

With O rgyan dpal bzang (1617–77), he who was prophesied by Padmasambhava,
there were several connections in regard to material things and teachings,
including the *Sprul sku snying thig*, the heart essence of the profound treasures;
and the Sky Doctrine, the heart-treasure mine:[11]
All this meant a good life for me, the little bhadanta! (24)

The offering materials from faithful living and dead [followers]:
in order that they might grasp the essence of illusory riches,
I made a thousandfold offering to gods and men under the eyes of the noble ones—
extensive clouds of butter lamp offerings:
All this meant a good life for me, the little bhadanta! (25)

11. The *Sprul sku snying thig* is a treasure cycle of Rig 'dzin Bdud 'dul rdo rje (1615–72), while the *Gnam chos* is among the revelations of Gter ston Mi 'gyur rdo rje (1645–67). In the record, these two cycles are listed in the same order as here, and the meeting with O rgyan dpal bzang is assigned to the year 1677; see *Thob yig*, 36.5–49.4. For a biographical sketch of O rgyan dpal bzang, a native of southern Mustang and founder of Sku tshab gter lnga Monastery, see Ehrhard 2013, 220–23; both mentioned cycles were obtained by him from the two treasure discoverers personally during an extended journey to Khams in eastern Tibet.

For the benefit of male and female donors having a connection with me,
for my father and mother, and for all living and dead beings,
I intoned an extensive dedication-of-merit prayer so that the threefold cycle (i.e., agent, action, and object) [might be one]
and that the extent of their connection would bind them to virtue—how delightful!
All this meant a good life for me, the little bhadanta! (26)

At a most isolated place, the pilgrimage site Ling nga brag [dmar rdzong],
in the presence of Gzil gnon rdo rje, a descendant of the Rgyal thang family,
I listened merely a little bit to the instructions of profound teachings,
namely the complete collected writings of Mahāvidyādhara ['Ja' tshon snying po]
and the cycle *Bka' lung chos [kyi] sgron [ma]*, together with the profound *gcod yul* [practice] and so forth:[12]
All this meant a good life for me, the little bhadanta! (27)

To the feet of Gar dbang rdo rje (1640–85), a second Padmasambhava,
I held the crown of my head, and his mind and my own mingled into one;
in a manner proper to the joyful experience of a father meeting his son,
he cared [for me] with the instructions of ripening and liberation [according to his] profound teachings:[13]
All this meant a good life for me, the little bhadanta! (28)

12. According to the record, the encounter with Zil gnon rdo rje occurred at the age of fifty-one, i.e., in the year 1679; see *Thob yig*, 49.4–51.1. The transmission of the collected writings of 'Ja' tshon snying po had been received previously by Zil gnon rdo rje from the above-mentioned O rgyan dpal bzang; the cycle titled *Bka' lung chos kyi sgron ma* is identified in the corresponding lineage as a treasure of Gter ston Rin chen gling pa (fourteenth century). Concerning Zil gnon rdo rje, further members of the Rgyal thang family, and the Mi la ras pa site Ling nga brag dmar rdzong in Mang yul, see Ehrhard 2008, 103–4. Another record of teachings received, that of Nor bu bde chen (b. 1617) from the Gur rigs Mdo chen tradition, lists the same cycle of Rin chen gling pa as obtained from Zil gnon rdo rje; see Ehrhard 2008, 113–14.

13. The encounter with Rig 'dzin Gar dbang rdo rje at the latter's residence Dpal gyi shel phug in Gung thang can again be situated in the year 1679; for this date and the transmission of teachings, see *Thob yig*, 51.5–61.4. The record lists the cycles *Rdor sems thugs kyi me long*, *Padma'i snyan brgyud*, *Thugs rje chen po rtsa gsum snying thig*, and *Rdo rje phur pa spu gri reg gcod* as having been received from the treasure discoverer of Mnga' ris Gung thang; for a study of his life and findings, see Solmsdorf 2014, 77–144. The record exhibits no colophon, and as a final item the reading authorization for the extended extracanonical version of the *Jātakamāla* written by the Third Karma pa Rang byung rdo rje (1284–1339) is mentioned.

In order to clear away hindrances to the completion of my own and others' accumulations [of merit and wisdom],
I accomplished some things in line with the tradition of qualified craftsmanship—
statues of the sugatas, stūpas, books, and so forth:[14]
All this meant a good life for me, the little bhadanta! (29)

The very essence of the most excellent deity Mahākaruṇika—
the six syllables—I executed in relief on immutable stone
a little more than twenty-four thousand times:
All this meant a good life for me, the little bhadanta! (30)

From the age of forty [= 1667] up to now at sixty-four [= 1691],
I conferred upon some followers faithful in their devotion
empowerments and instructions of ripening and liberation:
All this meant a good life for me, the little bhadanta! (31)

It is only the pronouncements and the practices of the previous ones;
there is not anything else at all—self-fabricated adulteration or a desire to know—that exists [in me];
[my] sole [concern] is not to be in contradiction with the reality of the profound tantras:
All this meant a good life for me, the little bhadanta! (32)

Thus is it said.

14. A pictorial representation of the Aural Transmission with Karma Blo bzang as the central figure has survived and is now in the Rubin Museum of Art, New York. The officiant figure portrayed at the bottom center can be identified as Ngag dbang rnam rgyal; in the same function, he is also depicted on a thangka of White Amitayus that contains images of other teachers of his mentioned above. For details, see Sernesi, Forthcoming. A seventeenth-century print of Gtsang smyon's *Life of Milarepa* lists Ngag dbang rnam rgyal, the master of the monastery of Nam gung, as one of its main donors; see Sernesi, Forthcoming. The xylograph in question was produced at Chos sdings in Mang yul; concerning this site, see note 8 above.

Bya bral ngag dbang rnam rgyal gyi rang gi dran so'i (= bso'i) nyams dbyangs 'brel med kyi 'khyal (= 'chal) gtam, 436.2–445.5

namo guru /

bla ma rnams dang yi dam lhag pa'i lha /
rgyal ba sras bcas dkon mchog rnam pa gsum /
kho bo'i citta rin chen pho brang du /
'bral med bzhugs la mchog 'thun (= mthun) dngos grub bstsol (= stsol) /

dbyas (= byas) chung dag la tshad mar 'dzin pa yis /
gus shin 'dun pa'i (= dun pa'i) dad ldan 'ga' yar rnams /
kho bos (= kho bo'i) rnam thar cis nas dgos so zer /
dus mthar skye pa'i chos med ser gzugs ngas /
sngon bsags dkar po'i byang stobs chung ba'i 'thus (= mthus) /
tshe 'dir shes rab chung zhing btul pa gzhan (= zhan) /
blo gros rmongs shing shes sgo'i rnam rig med /
mdo rgyud thos pa'i tshig la ma sbyangs shing /
bsam bsgom bskyed rdzogs zab mo'i don las dbyen (= dben) /
bslabs (= bslab) shes tshig dang bsgom pa'i gnad [437] ma shes /
ngo mtshar che ba'i rnam thar ci nas yod /

'on kyang khyed cag cis kyang dgos zer na /
ma las skyes nas ding sang re bzhi'i bar /
chos dang 'thun pa'i (= mthun pa) rnam thar ma mchis so /
'jig rten 'di yi tshe phyid byas tshul rnams /
'dor sdus (= mdor bsdus) bshad do legs par gsan mdzod cig /

mi rigs mi cig (= gcig) bal bod gnyis kyi 'tshams (= mtshams) /
rang 'byon (= byon) wa ti bzang po'i sku zhabs su /
'brug lo nyer lnga rgyu skar dbyig gu (= dbyu gu) la /
chos 'thun (= mthun) dad ldan ma las btsas zhes zer /
de kun bhan chung bdag gi rnam thar legs / (1)

mnga' ris khyung rdzong dkar po'i 'dun sa ru /
padma'i rnam sprul *bstan 'dzin nor bu* dang /
mdo sngags mnga' bdag *gzhad ri mkhan chen* las /
zab mo chos kyi bka' 'chid (= mchid) zur tsam thos /
de kun bhan chung bdag gi rnam thar legs / (2)

grub pa'i gnas chen dpal gyi mtha' dkar du /
'dren mchog dam pa chos skyong dpal bzang las /
tshe grub dbang dang gsang bdag dbang lung dang /
rje nyid [438] rang gi rnam 'gur (= mgur) rags sdus (= bsdus) sogs /
zab mo'i chos la 'brel pa cung zad bzhag /
de kun bhan chung bdag gi rnam thar legs / (3)

dgon gnas 'debs dang sku gsung thugs rten bzhengs /
chos khrir 'dug nas gzhan la dbang bskur tshul /
dus bzang tshes bcu mchod pa'i tshul snang sogs /
byis pa'i bya byed chos dang 'thun (= mthun) tsam byas /
de kun bhan chung bdag gi rnam thar legs / (4)

sngon sbyangs 'brel pa'i las 'phro bag tsam sang (= gtsang) /
zab chos gzhan la gus pa lhod pa tsam /
nor bu skor gsum gdams pa'i mtshan thos tshe /
rma bya'i rna bar dbyar skyes rnga ltar snyan /
de kun bhan chung bdag gi rnam thar legs / (5)

bcu drug lon tsher *ras chen bla ma*'i drung /
lhag bsam dad pa'i (= dad pas) dam pa'i chos sgor bzhugs /
yongs 'dzin dge snyen (= bsnyen) khrim (= khrims) kyi (= kyis) legs pa'i brgyan /
'di phyir skyid pa'i 'dun mgo de nas tshugs /
de kun bhan chung bdag gi rnam thar legs / (6)

rgyal dbang thugs tig gser gyi yang zhun gyis /
steng 'og nyi zla kha sbyor gdams pa la /
brtson [439] 'grus lhod pa med pa'i 'bad brtsol (= rtsol) gyis /
bde drod lus rgyas grang ba'i 'jigs las grol /
de kun bhan chung bdag gi rnam thar legs / (7)

grol lam lta ba phyag rgya chen po dang /
thab (= thabs) lam gdams pa na ro'i chos drug dang /
bla ma'i grub (= sgrub) thabs phyi nang gsang ba sogs /
smin grol gdams pa'i go skal zur tsam thob /
de kun bhan chung bdag gi rnam thar legs / (8)

dpal ldan 'brug pa'i ring lugs chu bo'i rgyun /
lus kyi sgrib pa 'dag phyir phyag grangs ni /

'bum phrag drug dang kha 'char 'ga' re btang /
de kun bhan chung bdag gi rnam thar legs (9)

ngag sgrib sbyang phyir yig brgya maṇḍal dang /
yang lag 'dun pa (= bdun pa) gsol 'debs rims pa (= rim pa) dang /
yid sgrib sbyong phyir lta ba'i skyong thabs dang /
snyen (= bsnyen) grub (= sgrub) la sogs bka' srol ma 'tshugs (= tshugs) tsam /
de kun bhan chung bdag gi rnam thar legs / (10)

bla ma'i drung na 'dug pa'i gnas skabs su /
bka' bskyon (= bkyon) bkres skom ngal dub la sogs pa /
sdig sgrib 'dag pa'i thabs ni ma togs pa (= gtogs pa) /
bka' ba'i rnam 'gyur de tsam ma byas pa /
de kun bhan chung [440] bdag gi rnam thar legs / (11)

sems dpa' chen po *dpal ldan don 'grub (= grub)* nas /
zab gter gu ru sngon dmar gdams pa dang /
thugs chen grub (= sgrub) thabs bcod (= gcod) yul bzhi (= zhi) drag sogs /
dpal ldan dmar bsgom (= sgom) yab sras bka' srol rnams /
ding sang bar du nyams len ma 'chugs (= 'chug) tsam /
de kun bhan chung bdag gi rnam thar legs / (12)

'dzam gling bod kyi rdo rje gdan mchog gi /
chos 'khor dpal gyi lha sa la sogs pa /
gangs can dbus kyi gnas chen khyad par rnams /
rmi lam sgyu ma'i 'tshul (= tshul) yud tsam 'jal (= mjal) /
de kun bhan chung bdag gi rnam thar legs (13)

gnas chen brag dkar chos sdings la sogs su /
bdag gi 'dren mchog *karma chos 'phel* las /
lhan cig skyes sbyor na ro'i chos drug dang /
bka' rgyud (= brgyud) rnam thar snyen (= bsnyen) gnas la sogs /
mdo sngags chos kyi thang ma legs par rdal (= brdol) /
de kun bhan chung bdag gi rnam thar legs / (14)

thub dbang gnyis pa *dpal ldan bzang po*'i drung /
bstan rtsa so thar 'dul ba'i bslab sbya (= bya) dang /
'chi med grub [441] pa'i gdams pa rnam gnyis dang /
bcod (= gcod) yul zab lam 'pho ba'i gdams pa sogs /

gzhan yang kha 'thor zhal lung mang dag thob /
de kun bhan chung bdag gi rnam thar lags (= legs) / (15)

tha rang (= tha ram) snying la bzhugs pa (= zhugs pa) 'ga' zhig gis /
zas ngan gdug gi sbyor bas tho tsam (= mtho 'tsham) yang /
sman spyad (= dpyad) 'phrul 'khor bgegs sel rten 'brel gyis /
bar chad las grol rma bya'i ngang tshul rgyas /
de kun bhan chung bdag gi rnam thar legs / (16)

snubs chen nam mam mkha'i snying po skye mtha' ni /
rigs brgya'i gtso bo *karma blo bzang* nas /
nor bu skor gsum cha lag zhal gdams bcas /
smin grol bzung (= zung) 'jug bum pa gang byos lon /
de kun bhan chung bdag gi rnam thar legs / (17)

yang zab bzhi (= zhi) 'khro (= khro) ma bu cha sdebs (= bsdebs) dang /
thugs chen nam mkha'i rgyal po tshe dpag med /
rta phag chos bskor (= skor) gsang lam bla grub (= sgrub) dang /
gzhan yang smin grol kha 'thor (= thor) mang zhig thob /
de kun bhan chung bdag gi rnam thar legs / (18)

so lnga lon dus sngon las 'phral [442] rkyen gyis /
sa bdag klu gnyan gdug pa'i kha rlangs phog /
mdze nad drag po'i (= drag pos) lus sems rdul du brlag /
lus kyi na tsha nya mo chu bral 'dra /
sems kyi mya ngan bya mo tshang brlag 'dra /
de kun bhan chung bdag gi rnam thar legs /(19)

de la phan pa'i thabs ni kun du rdugs /
tshe rabs bsags pa'i las ngan yin par nges /
'on kyang rgyal sras sems dpa'i rnam thar ltar /
dge sdig btong (= gtong) len bdag gzhan mnyam brje byas /
de kun bhan chung bdag gi rnam thar legs / (20)

thabs kyi rgyal po phung po tshogs su bsngos /
bces (= gces) 'dzin blos btang bdag 'dzin rtsa nas spangs /
sman gyi mchog gyur na dga' shi skyid btang /
nyams len dkyus su 'jug pa'i bskul mar byung /
rkyen ngan g.yang du lon pa ngo mtshar che /
de kun bhan chung bdag gi rnam thar legs / (21)

'jig rten grong gi 'du'i 'dzi ring du spangs /
gong ma'i byin brlabs grub gnas phu mda' ru /
sgo gsum chos min las dang ma 'dres par /
mi lo [443] bcu gcig grub pa'i srol kha bzung /
de kun bhan chung bdag gi rnam thar legs / (22)

ri mtshams ldag (= 'dag) sbyar smra bcad gsum gyi khongs /
ston dpyid zla re zla gnyis ri mtshams dang /
dgun zla bzhi'am gsum re smra ba bcad /
dus rnams kun du ldag (= 'dag) sbyar kho na'i lugs /
de kun bhan chung bdag gi rnam thar legs / (23)

padma'i lung bstan *o rgyan dpal bzang* nas /
zab gter thugs bcud sprul sku snying thig dang /
gnam chos thugs kyi gter kha la sogs pa /
chos dang zang zing 'brel ba 'ga' tsam yod /
de kun bhan chung bdag gi rnam thar legs / (24)

dad ldan gson gshin rnams kyi phul ba'i rdzas /
sgyu ma nor la snying po blang ba'i phyir /
lha mi'i mchod stong 'phags pa'i spyan lam du /
mar me mchod pa'i sprin phung rgya chen phul /
de kun bhan chung bdag gi rnam thar legs / (25)

bdag la 'brel yod yon bdag pho mo dang /
pha ma gson [444] gshin sems can kun don du /
'khor gsum yod (= yon) bdag bsngo smon rgyas 'debs zhus /
'brel tshad dge la sbyar pa a la la /
da (= de) kun bhan chung bdag gi rnam thar legs / (26)

gnas chen ling nga brag gi yang dbyen (= dben) du /
rgyal thang gdung 'dzin *gzil gnon rdo rje*'i drung /
rigs (= rig) 'dzin chen po'i bka' 'bum yongs rdzogs dang /
bka' lung chos gron (= sgron) yang zab bcod (= gcod) yul sogs /
zab chos gdams pa'i 'brel pa zur tsam thos /
de kun bhan chung bdag gi rnam thar legs / (27)

pad 'byung gnyis pa *gar dbang rdo rje*'i zhabs /
spyi bor rten (= brten) zhing thugs yid gcig tu 'dres /
pha bu 'phrad pa'i dga' nyams tshul bzhin du /

zab gter smin grol gdams pas rjes su bzung /
de kun bhan chung bdag gi rnam thar legs (28)

bdag gzhan tshogs rdzogs sgrib pa sbyang slad du /
bde gshegs sku gzugs [445] mchod rten glegs bam sogs /
bzo khyad lugs dang 'thun pa (= mthun pa) 'ga' re sgrubs (= bsgrubs)
de kun bhan chung bdag gi rnam thar legs (29)

lha mchog thugs rje chen po'i yang snying ste /
mi 'gyur rdo la yig drug 'bur sdod (= dod) ni /
khri phrag gnyis dang bzhi stong lhag tsam bzhengs /
de kun bhan chung bdag i rnam thar legs / (30)

bzhi bcu'i tshe nas ding sang re bzhi'i bar /
dad ldan mos pa'i rjes 'jug 'ga' re la /
smin grol dbang dang gdams pa'i rjes su bzung /
de kun bdag i bhan chung rnam thar legs (31)

gong ma'i gsung dang phyag len ma gtogs pa /
rang bzo'i lhad dang shes 'dod bstan (= gtan) nas med /
rgyud sde zab mo'i don dang ma 'gal tsam /
de kun bhan chung bdag gi rnam thar legs (32)

ces so //

Works Cited

Akester, Matthew. 2017. *Jamyang Khyentsé Wangpo's Guide to Central Tibet*. Chicago: Serindia Publications.

Bogin, Benjamin. 2013. *The Illuminated Life of the Great Yolmowa*. Chicago: Serindia Publications.

Chos kyi dbang phyug, Brag dkar rta so sprul sku (1775–1837). 2011. "Grub pa'i gnas chen brag dkar rta so'i gnas dang gdan rabs bla ma brgyud pa'i lo rgyus mos ldan dad pa'i gdung sel drang srong dga' ba'i dal gtam. " In *Kun-mkhyen Brag-dkar-ba Chos-kyi dbang-phyug gi gSung-'bum Rin-po-che*, 10:485–594. Kathmandu: Śrī Gautam Vihāra. [= *Gdan rabs*]

Ehrhard, Franz-Karl. 2008. *A Rosary of Rubies: A Chronicle of the Gur-rigs mdo-chen Tradition from South-West Tibet*. Collectanea Himalayica 2. Munich: Indus Verlag.

———. 2013. *Buddhism in Tibet & the Himalayas: Texts and Traditions*. Kathmandu: Vajra Publications.

———. 2015. "'Throne-Holders of the Middle Valley': Buddhist Teachers from Southern Dolpo." *Bulletin of Tibetology* (Special Issue: Buddhist Himalaya: Perspectives on the Tibetan Cultural Area) 51.1–2: 7–45.

Jackson, Roger R. 1996. "'Poetry' in Tibet: Glu, mGur, Snyan ngag, and 'Songs of Experience.'" In *Tibetan Literature: Studies in Genre*, edited by José I. Cabezón and Roger R. Jackson, 368–92. Ithaca, NY: Snow Lion Publications.

Kapstein, Matthew T. 2003. "The Indian Literary Identity in Tibet". In *Literary Cultures in History*, 747–802. Berkeley: University of California Press.

Ngag dbang rnam rgyal (b. 1628). 1976. "Sprang bhan ngag dbang rnam rgyal bdag gi zab chos kyi thob yig dgos 'dod kun 'byung." In *The Collected Songs of Esoteric Experience of Bya-bral Ṅag-dbaṅ-rnam-rgyal*, 1–61. TBRC.org ID: W20509. Dolanji, HP: Tibetan Bonpo Monastic Centre. [= *Thob yig*]

———. 1976. "Bya bral ngag dbang rnam rgyal gyi rang dran so'i (= gso'i) nyams dbyangs 'brel med kyi 'khyal (= 'chal) gtam." In *The Collected Songs of Esoteric Experience of Bya-bral Ṅag-dbaṅ-rnam-rgyal*, , 62–489. Dolanji, HP: Tibetan Bonpo Monastic Centre. [= *Mgur 'bum*]

Schwieger, Peter. 1990. *Tibetische Handschriften und Blockdrucke, Teil 10: Die mTshur-phu-Ausgabe der Sammlung Rin-chen gter-mdzod chen-mo, Bände 1–14.* Verzeichnis der orientalischen Handschriften in Deutschland 11:10. Stuttgart: Franz Steiner Verlag.

Sernesi, Marta. 2011. "The Aural Transmission of Saṃvara: An Introduction to Neglected Sources for the Study of the Early bKa' brgyud." In *Mahāmudrā and the bKa' brgyud Tradition*, edited by Roger R. Jackson and Matthew T. Kapstein, 179–209. Beiträge zur Zentralasienforschung 25. Andiast: International Institute for Tibetan and Buddhist Studies.

———. Forthcoming. *Re-Enacting the Past: A Cultural History of the School of gTsang smyon Heruka*. Contributions to Tibetan Studies 13. Wiesbaden: Reichert Verlag.

Solmsdorf, Nikolai. 2014. *Treasure-Traditions of Western Tibet: Rig-'dzin Gar-dbang rdo-rje snying-po (1640–1685) and His Activities in Mang-Yul Gung-thang.* Collectanea Himalayica 4. Munich: Indus Verlag.

Are We All Shentongpas?

Gregory Forgues

I first met Matthew Kapstein in Paris in 2014 while participating in the conference he organized on Ge sar of Gling at the Collège de France. I was already well acquainted with his research and was impressed by his rigorous and creative approach to Tibetan Buddhist thought and culture. A few months after the conference, as I had already started my PhD on 'Ju Mi pham rnam rgyal rgya mtsho's (1846–1912, hereafter Mipham) interpretation of Madhyamaka, I asked him to be my examiner. Needless to say, Professor Kapstein's comments proved invaluable to enhancing the quality of my research. Some of his remarks led me to reconsider some key issues and explore areas I would have neglected had I not benefited from his vast knowledge of Tibetan scholastic traditions. Among his many excellent publications, one article came to be a particularly influential source of inspiration for my own research. In "We Are All Gzhan stong pas," Professor Kapstein discusses Paul Williams's *Reflexive Nature of Awareness*, a monograph analyzing the dispute between Mipham and Geluk scholars with regard to the refutation of reflexive awareness (*svasaṃvedana*, *rang rig*) in Śāntideva's *Bodhicaryāvatāra* 9.20–26. In his review, Professor Kapstein makes the following central points for anyone interested in analyzing Tibetan Buddhist doctrines and hermeneutical debates:

1. "Given our present knowledge of Tibetan doctrinal history doxographic labels such as *gzhan stong pa* and *rang stong pa* are best avoided, except of course where they are used within the tradition itself";
2. "Our primary task must be to document and interpret precise concepts and arguments, and in many cases the recourse to overly broad characterizations seems only to muddy the waters."[1]

1. Kapstein 2000, 21.

Professor Kapstein's apt recommendation that we approach concepts and arguments in terms of their own context, without superimposing broad categorizations upon the doctrines of Buddhist authors, is methodologically invaluable. In the spirit of "We Are All Gzhan stong pas," I will illustrate this by looking into the work of Mipham, one of the most important and researched Tibetan Buddhist scholars. Based on a commentary in which he highlights his interpretation of Klong chen pa's (1308–64, hereafter Longchenpa) view on *sugatagarbha*, I intend to demonstrate the value of Professor Kapstein's comments.

Mipham is known to have found in Longchenpa's works a major source of inspiration when it comes to expounding the ultimate view of the highest path as understood in the Nyingma tradition.[2] In one of his most personal and central works on Madhyamaka, the *Dbu ma rgyan gyi rnam bshad*, a commentary on Śāntarakṣita's *Madhyamakālaṃkāra*, Mipham's introductory discussion of the root text refers twice to Longchenpa's *Treasury of Wish-Fulfilling Jewels* (*Yid bzhin mdzod*). Mipham is also the only Tibetan author who attempted to comment on this text in a series of short commentaries.[3] Mipham's commentary on chapter 18 of the *Treasury of Wish-Fulfilling Jewels* presents the nonconceptual and nondual unity of the two truths from a perspective clearly influenced by Dzokchen,[4] as well as a detailed elucidation of the notion of *tathāgatagarbha* as understood in his tradition—presentations that are independent of disputations related to the *gzhan stong–rang stong* distinction. The root text of the eighteenth chapter of the *Treasury of Wish-Fulfilling Jewels*, together with the commentaries thereon by Longchenpa and Mipham, are therefore essential documents for understanding Mipham's ultimate position on what came to be termed *buddha nature*.[5] Accordingly, I will here focus on the following texts:

2. See Kapstein 2000, 118, and Wangchuk 2012, 21n10. Although Mipham appears to synthesize the thoughts of Longchenpa and Go rams pa, his ultimate intention appears to be closer to the views of the former. For example, just like Longchenpa but unlike Go rams pa, Mipham accepts the last two turnings of the wheel as definitive.

3. *Yid bzhin mdzod kyi grub mtha' sdus pa*, *Yid bzhin rigs gsal*, *Yid bzhin phreng ba*, *Le'u bco brgyad pa'i tshig 'grel ba*. See Arguillère 2007, 11.

4. As a side note, these texts show that Mipham formalized in a more scholastic language Longchenpa's esoteric poetic instructions, a fact supported by the translations below in which one can read Longchenpa's own commentary on chapter 18 of his own *Yid bzhin mdzod*.

5. On Mipham's position with regard to the *gzhan stong–rang stong* distinction in relation to his interpretation of *de bzhin gshegs pa'i snying po*, see Williams 1998, Pettit 1999a, Pettit 1999b, Williams 1999, Kapstein 2000, Duckworth 2008, Kapstein 2009, and Wangchuk 2012. Mipham's works focusing on this topic are *Gzhan stong khas len seng ge'i nga ro* (English

- Longchenpa's root text: *Treasury of Wish-Fulfilling Jewels*[6]
- Longchenpa's autocommentary: *White Lotus* (*Theg pa chen po'i man ngag gi bstan bcos yid bzhin rin po che'i mdzod kyi 'grel ba padma dkar po*)
- Mipham's commentary: *Commentary on Chapter 18* (*Le'u bco brgyad 'grel*)

In the introductory paragraphs to his commentary, Longchenpa explains that chapter 18 is a pith instruction on the inconceivable and nondual fundamental sameness (*mnyam nyid*) in the sense of the nonconceptual gnosis of luminosity (*'od gsal*), the indivisible truth (*bden pa dbyer med*) itself. This teaching on the inconceivable nature of reality is declared to be given from the perspective of the resultant Vajra Vehicle by both Longchenpa and Mipham. In short, it is the highest view according to this tradition. Analyzing Longchenpa's root text, Mipham summarizes the content of chapter 18 of the *Treasury of Wish-Fulfilling Jewels* by stressing the centrality of "indivisibility"[7] as a principle that structures Longchenpa's entire vision of reality and by grounding it within a soteriological program:[8]

> First, the ground (*gzhi*) is ascertained as the indivisible truth; [second], the path is the practice of the indivisibility of saṃsāra and nirvāṇa; [third], that which is to be attained is resolved as the indivisibility of the ground and the result.

In the three texts, Longchenpa and Mipham emphasize four main points:[9]

1. The ground is the primordially luminous gnosis (*ye shes*), also called *sugata nature*, in which two aspects are indivisible: emptiness (*stong cha*) and cognition (*mkhyen cha*).[10] Mipham explains that these respectively correspond to the unconditioned natural state (*rang*

---

translation in Pettit 1999a) and *Bde gshegs snying po'i stong thun chen mo seng ge'i nga ro* (English translation in Duckworth 2008).

6. This text was translated by Thurman 1997, 172ff., and Butters 2006, 757ff., in both cases without references to Longchenpa's *White Lotus* or Mipham's *Commentary on Chapter 18*.

7. Equivalent terms for *dbyer med* are *zung 'jug* or *gnyis med*, see Forgues, Forthcoming. The concept of indivisibility entails the rejection of the position in which the two truths are seen as distinct realms.

8. Mipham, *Commentary on Chapter 18*, 566.

9. For details, see translations of extracts of the three texts below.

10. Both Longchenpa and Mipham use the term *sugatagarbha* (*bde bar gshegs pa'i snying po*) instead of *tathāgatagarbha* (*de bzhin gshegs pa'i snying po*) in the three texts mentioned.

bzhin) and to spontaneous presence (*lhun grub*) as awareness (*rig pa*). The ground is presented as the indivisible truth.

2. However, conventional words and concepts belong to the level of "conventional" or "concealing" truth (*saṃvṛtisatya*, *kun rdzob kyi bden pa*), which cannot be established when analyzed. On the level of the ground, there is in fact no duality in terms of saṃsāra and nirvāṇa, appearance and emptiness, fault and virtue. As a consequence, the ground is utterly free from mental proliferations (*spros bral*) such as indivisible and divisible, same and other, and so on.[11]
3. This approach therefore delineates two epistemic spheres: the adventitious realm of conceptuality and duality typical of conditioned mind (*rnam shes* or *sems*) and the realm of profound peace characterized by nonconceptual and nondual gnosis (*ye shes* or *rig pa*). This way of defining the two truths corresponds to the *mthun mi mthun* model, according to which the distinction between the concealing and the ultimate is not established in terms of emptiness (*stong nyid*) and appearance (*snang ba*) but rather on the basis of a concordance (or lack thereof) between the way things are and the way things appear.[12] As Mipham explains, the distinction between the ultimate and the concealing truths is in this case based on an analysis of the validity of conventions from an epistemic perspective. This account of the two truths clearly concerns the epistemic status of cognition, not the ontological status of phenomena. The conventional, or concealing, truth corresponds to a distorted cognitive state, whereas the ultimate truth denotes an unfabricated form of cognition. Longchenpa gives the example of the hallucinations perceived by a person who has ingested datura as an a metaphor for the concealing.[13]
4. The disjunction between these two spheres has the propaedeutic function of distinguishing conditioned mind (*sems*) from nonconceptual nondual awareness (*rig pa*). On the highest level, Mipham refutes any presentation of the two truths in which these are distinct,[14]

11. Mipham makes a widespread use of the distinction between the nominal and actual ultimates (*rnam grangs pa'i don dam* vs. *rnam grangs ma yin pa'i don dam*) in his interpretation of Madhyamaka (see, for example, *Dbu ma rgyan gyi rnam bshad* 34.5ff., *'Jug 'grel* 576.5ff., and *Shes rab ral gri* 804.3ff.).

12. See Kapstein 2009, 64.

13. See paragraph 6: *Treasury of Wish-Fulfilling Jewels*, 50.2–4, *White Lotus*, 645.4–5, and *Commentary on Chapter 18*, 569.1–5.

14. *Commentary on Chapter 18*, 570.3–6.

> while agreeing with Longchenpa that distinguishing positive actions from negative ones in the context of the path is nevertheless necessary insofar as causality is a fact from the perspective of delusion.[15] According to Mipham and Longchenpa, the discourse on the two truths itself belongs to the level of conceptualization; ultimately, the truth cannot be divided into separate elements.[16]

This last point is made obvious in the third part of Longchenpa's verses and commentaries. After giving the three classic examples illustrating the meaning of *sugatagarbha*,[17] Longchenpa goes on to explain that these conventional expressions are merely used to dispel confusion by pointing at something that is by nature beyond concepts and dualistic thought.[18] In the following paragraph, Longchenpa shows that the natural condition (*gnas lugs*, lit. "the way things are") is taught through synonymous expressions corresponding to well-established Buddhist terms (e.g., *dhātu*, [*sugata*]*garbha*, *paramārtha*, *prabhāsvara*, *prajñāpāramitā*, *satya*, *dharmatā*, and *tathatā*). These expressions, which actually have the same referent, are used to illustrate various aspects of inexpressible reality.[19] Mipham takes the didactic use of these synonymous terms to be justified as long as the supreme absolute beyond mental proliferations (*spros bral*) is not recognized. In his view, such expressions are useful for teaching particular aspects of reality, even if they necessarily fail to capture the nonconceptual nature of this ultimate. In fact, since none of these conventional ways of referring to the nondual, nonconceptual ultimate can themselves transcend discursive thought, the same is true, *a fortiori*, for the doxographic concept of *gzhan stong*, which presupposes the dichotomous notions of self and other. As explained by Professor Kapstein:[20]

> Even those who favor a pro–*gzhan stong* interpretation of Mipham seem to agree that in the last analysis this must give way to a

15. See paragraph 11: *Treasury of Wish-Fulfilling Jewels*, 50.6–7, *White Lotus*, 648.1–4, and *Commentary on Chapter 18*, 571.1–3.

16. *Commentary on Chapter 18*, 567.4–568.1, as well as 569.5–570.1.

17. See paragraphs 14–18. Two of these three examples are found in the *Ratnagotravibhāga* (the buried treasure, see RGV 1.112–13; the sugata in the lotus, see RGV 1.99), one is from Nāgārjuna's *Dharmadhātustava* (the light inside a pot, see Dergé 2314, fol. 255a).

18. See paragraph 19: *Treasury of Wish-Fulfilling Jewels*, 51.6–7, and *White Lotus*, 651.3–6.

19. See paragraph 20: *Treasury of Wish-Fulfilling Jewels*, 51.7–52.2, *White Lotus*, 652.1–653.2, and *Commentary on Chapter 18*, 572.6–573.1.

20. Kapstein 2000, 118–19.

radical freedom from conceptual elaborations (*spros bral*) and that the latter expression, and not *gzhan stong*, surely represents Mipham's preferred idiom.

In the present case, Mipham's and Longchenpa's discussions of the inexpressible reality in terms of an epistemic disjunction between two cognitive modes are soteriologically motivated. Even if some of the technical terms used in this context are also bases for doxographic classifications, and thus become objects of hermeneutical debates in the Indo-Tibetan philosophical context, their *raison d'être* is to delineate the contours of a journey toward liberation. While this point may appear trivial, it has important methodological consequences along the lines suggested by Professor Kapstein's comments.

The question is to determine the extent to which doxographic categorization (or for that matter any research methodology) can contribute to our understanding of an author's particular thought. First, and most basically, discourses framed in terms of broad doxographic terms such as *gzhan stong* may play only a limited role, if any, in the doctrinal landscape of a specific author. To that extent, analyzing an author's doctrine through a predetermined choice of lens may induce a methodological bias, particularly with respect to the task of characterizing the author's doctrine. While the resulting investigation may be informative with regard to the chosen topic, this may lead to a premature narrowing of focus on specific aspects of the author's thought, possibly precluding attention to potentially important themes. Second, the meaning and import of an author's use of technical terms may depend on considerations pertaining to a fundamental soteriological movement or scheme, as made clear when Mipham summarizes Longchenpa's chapter 18 as a teaching on the indivisibility of reality in the soteriological context of the ground, path, and result. Analyzing doctrinal aspects through predetermined technical or doxographic terms, independently of their relation to the notion of path, therefore amounts to a choice of methodological lens that risks obscuring the underlying soteriological movement of an author's view, which, in a Buddhist context, should be a real concern.[21]

In the case of Mipham, for example, various studies have been structured around the concepts of *śūnyatā*, *tathāgatagarbha*, or *yuganaddhavāda*.[22] These excellent contributions have allowed us to better grasp various dimensions of Mipham's thought. As a further step in our exploration of this author's works,

21. On Mipham's four stages of realization of nonconceptual gnosis in the context of Madhyamaka, see Phuntsho 2005, 150.

22. Phuntsho 2005, Duckworth 2008, Wangchuk 2012.

I have here tried to reevaluate Mipham's doctrinal project without presupposing the putative centrality of doxographic notions or technical terms in the corpus of his Collected Works. Instead, encouraged by Professor Kapstein's insight, I have relied on the entire corpora of texts themselves; following a traditional philological approach complemented by corpus-linguistic methods, I have looked for frequent collocations, patterns of intertextuality and synonymy, as well as clusters of meaning units across Mipham's works in order to determine Mipham's own understanding of doctrinal concepts and ideas in his writings.[23] In this context, it is important to keep in mind that this web of concepts paradoxically forms a discourse on the nonconceptual. As Professor Kapstein reminds us with regard to Mipham's philosophical project,[24]

> There is an important sense in which the ultimate cannot be in the scope of thought, and even such notions as "freedom from the proliferation of dichotomous categories" and "accord between reality and appearance" must be themselves understood as elements of conventional reasoning, which generates conceptual models in order to think an absolute that it can never attain.

The aim of my forthcoming publication, *Radical Nondualism in the Works of 'Ju Mi pham rNam rgyal rGya mtsho*, is therefore to document the interplay of these conceptual models of reality and the soteriological notion of liberation in Mipham's philosophical discourse. By examining his works as well as other relevant texts such as the eighteenth chapter of the *Yid bzhin mdzod* and its commentaries, I hope to contribute to a better understanding of the interaction between semantic networks of concepts and the overarching soteriological movement toward the nonconceptual absolute that Mipham perceived as foundational for his doctrinal approach.

Translations

1. The Ground as the Indivisible Truth[25]

Longchenpa's *Treasury of Wish-Fulfilling Gems*, chap. 18, paragraph 3:

> The nature of this [indivisible truth] is luminosity, gnosis.

23. See Forgues, Forthcoming.

24. Kapstein 2009, 64.

25. This heading corresponds to Mipham's outline.

Supreme peace[26] since beginningless time, naturally free from mental proliferations,
spontaneously present like the sun and unconditioned like the sky's expanse,
it is the primordially abiding pure and vast nature
and, thus, the indivisibility of appearance and emptiness, without affirmation or negation, coming or going.

Longchenpa's *White Lotus*, chap. 18, fols 643.1–643.6:

The essential nature of the spontaneously occurring innate awareness is luminous natural purity. The genuine self, free from mental proliferations since beginningless time, adorned with the complete maṇḍala of [awakened] qualities that is like the unobscured sun, is the state that does not waver from the basic space, the nature of phenomena, the fundamental nature that is like the sky. Since the unconditioned primordially abides as great spontaneous presence, the completely pure natural state abides as the indivisibility of appearance and emptiness. It is said in the *Mañjuśrīnāmasaṃgīti* [6.5]: "[He is] the one without a beginning, the one whose self is free from mental proliferations . . ."[27]

Mipham's *Commentary on Chapter 18*, fols. 566.4–567.4:

As for the first of these three decisive experiences,[28] what is the nature of reality labeled "indivisible truth?" It is that which is called "primordially luminous gnosis" or "sugata nature." In relation to the word *luminosity* [Longchenpa gives] the example of what is both free from obscurity and endowed with light, [the sun].[29] Likewise, this is a name for that which is endowed with the sublime cog-

26. The root text reads *rab zhi* instead of *rang bzhin*.

27. Wayman's edition is slightly different from Longchenpa's quote: / *thog ma med spros med bdag* / / *de bzhin nyid bdag dag pa'i bdag* / *anādhir niṣprapañcātmā śuddhātmā tathatātmakaḥ* // See Wayman 1985, 75. Cf. Longchenpa's *White Lotus*, 643.2: *rang bzhin gyis ni dag pa'i bdag* / *thog ma med nas spros med bdag*.

28. *La bzla ba*. Literally "to cross a mountain pass." Mipham refers here to the ground as the indivisible truth, the path as the indivisibility of saṃsāra and nirvāṇa and the indivisibility of the ground and the result (see *Commentary on Chapter 18*, 566).

29. This refers to the example of the sun given by Longchenpa in the verses above.

nizing aspect of gnosis, being uncovered by obscurations. Therefore it is called the gnosis free from obscurations. This is explained from the perspective of awareness, the sublime cognizing aspect [of gnosis]. Moreover, it has not remained as any extreme whatsoever since beginningless time, meaning from the very beginning. Being complete peace, it is thus the [genuine] self or natural abiding. With this, the aspect of emptiness has been explained. The example for both awareness and emptiness is the luminous orb of the sun and the unobscured sky's expanse, corresponding respectively to the spontaneously present sublime cognizing aspect and the unconditioned natural state. This basic space that is the unity of awareness and emptiness is naturally completely pure, regardless of any effort to make [it pure]. Further, since it is not even attained by means of the two imperfections consisting in the conditioned saṃsāra and the partly peaceful unconditioned, it is total and complete purity. As it primordially abides as that which is possessed of the fundamental state, appearance and emptiness are indivisible within the essential nature. Nirvāṇa is not to be established as a truth, while the truth of saṃsāra must also not be refuted. Therefore, there is no going and coming with regard to faults and virtues.[30] In the present case, the application of conventional words and concepts as well as mental proliferations belonging to the [level of the] concealing truth is completely cut off in the absence of coming and going. No consideration whatsoever based on words and concepts, such as saṃsāra and nirvāṇa, appearance and emptiness, fault and virtue, is established as withstanding analysis. Such considerations are therefore concealing. All the coming and going of these [mental proliferations] is complete peace.

Longchenpa's *Treasury of Wish-Fulfilling Gems*, chap. 18, paragraph 4:[31]

Because it exceeds the concealing, the sphere of divisions and partitions,
it is the pacification of all mental proliferations.
As it surpasses the two truths that are fabrications,
the indivisible truth is neither established nor unestablished.

30. This sentence refers to the last verse of the stanza above.

31. *Treasury of Wish-Fulfilling Gems*, 49.7–50.1, and *White Lotus*, 643.6–7.

> Within basic space indivisible is the nature of appearance and
> emptiness.
> Therefore this truth is proclaimed to be indivisible.

Longchenpa's *White Lotus*, chap. 18, fols. 643.7–644.5:

> Compared to gnosis, which is luminosity, the concealing truth, saṃsāra, resembles clouds. Thus, because the concealing truth cannot be cognized, it cannot be established even as a mere illusory appearance. If this [concealing truth] is not established, the ultimate [itself] in the sense of a consideration about the emptiness of the manifoldness is [also] not established. Since these two are not established, the distinction between the two truths taken as a philosophical system is not established as anything at all. Since the [two truths] do not exist, passing beyond the two truths that are superimposed by the intellect in terms of truth and falsity, the appeasement of all mental proliferations, is proclaimed to be the indivisible truth as no conceptual truth is established. That which is established as concealing [truth], being ultimately not established, is ineffable. Thus the gnosis of the luminous basic space is called the spontaneously present great purity. However, it does not exist at all as these two truths of appearance and emptiness according to which philosophical systems are conceptualized.... If truth is indivisible on the level of this manifoldness of the two truths, which are conventionally imputed, how much more so from the perspective of the fundamentally unconditioned luminosity!

Mipham's *Commentary on Chapter 18*, fols. 567.4–568.1:

> This being so, [the indivisible truth] exceeds the domain of distinctions, such as, "This is the concealing [truth] and that is the ultimate truth." Therefore, arising on account of the conceptualization of philosophical systems, [the two truths] are designated as the concealing that is appearance and the ultimate that abides without arising. Since no[thing] is posited as even the two truths that are conceptual fixations, all mental proliferations such as clinging to existence or nonexistence and so forth are completely pacified. The reason for this is the indivisibility of the two truths into separate elements from the perspective of the way things are. This key point consists in the indivisibility [of the two truths] into separate

elements such as "This is established on the level of the concealing [truth]" or "This is ultimately not established." To recapitulate, the nature of appearance and emptiness is nondual within the dharmadhātu. Since there is nothing to be done dualistically, even these two truths of the concealing and the ultimate are nothing but verbalizations by way of sounds and words.

Longchenpa's *Treasury of Wish-Fulfilling Gems*, chap. 18, paragraph 5:[32]

> If we analyze conventions through the approach of the two truths,
> since in this case all saṃsāric phenomena of false appearances are untrue and deceptive,
> they represent the concealing truth,
> whereas the phenomena related to nirvāṇa, [such as] profound peace or luminosity,
> are accepted as the immutable nature, ultimate truth.

Longchenpa's *White Lotus*, chap. 18, fols. 644.7–645.3:

> Thus the subliminal consciousness consisting in the various mental predispositions obscuring the luminous ultimate heart essence, the appearances that are the mental predispositions of the eight consciousnesses, the various appearing objects such as external forms, and all aspects of internal mind are saṃsāric. Therefore, since what is deceptive is essenceless, this is posited as the concealing truth, while the luminous ground is determined as the spontaneously present ultimate truth. It is like in the example of the sun and the clouds. The luminous object that is obscured is the ultimate truth. The phenomena of saṃsāra obscuring [this luminous object]—the aggregates, the basic constituents, and the sources of cognitions—are the concealing truth. The appearance of this [concealing] truth is not established. As a consequence, since luminosity does not exist substantially, one does not merge [appearance and luminosity] out of the necessity to differentiate or merge [the two truths] as if they were one or separate. Therefore truth is understood as indivisible.

Mipham's *Commentary on Chapter 18*, fols. 568.1–569.1:

32. *Treasury of Wish-Fulfilling Gems*, 50.1–2, and *White Lotus*, 644.6.

> Although the dharmadhātu is understood as being [nondual],[33] when, in reliance upon the way things appear, one establishes distinctions through a mere conventional approach, [these distinctions] are included in deceptive appearance. When one analyzes the entire set of phenomena of saṃsāric appearances, which are conceptualized in terms of subject and object, nothing is [found to be] true. Being unstable, they are impermanent. Therefore a phenomenon bearing this deceptive property is a concealing truth. Profound because difficult to understand, the complete pacification of all mental proliferations is the luminous gnosis of sublime knowing. All phenomena are included within the great nirvāṇa because all suffering has been left behind. Since it surpasses infinitesimal particles and momentary phenomena, the freedom from the uneasiness of change that is imbued with an immutable nature is asserted as the ultimate truth. This way of positing the concealing and the ultimate is set forth on account of how things appear and how things are. They are determined from the perspective of appearance and emptiness. Therefore, [these two truths] correspond to saṃsāra and nirvāṇa. However, in the present case, the method consists in positing the concordance between the way things are and the way things appear as the ultimate [truth] and the non-concordance between the way things are and the way things appear as the concealing [truth]. This great approach in which [the two truths] remain as two [separate realms] is found in a great number of sūtras. Therefore one should not mix [them] with one another. Regarding the latter way of defining the two truths, the method of defining them relies on establishing distinctions between that which is correct or incorrect by means of valid cognitions analyzing conventions.

2. *The Path as the Practice of Indivisibility of Saṃsāra and Nirvāṇa*[34]

Longchenpa's *Treasury of Wish-Fulfilling Gems*, chap. 18, paragraph 9:[35]

> Although saṃsāra manifests, it is not established.
> Therefore, it is without inherent nature.

33. See this end of the previous section of Mipham's commentary above.

34. Longchenpa's *Treasury of Wish-Fulfilling Gems*, 50.5–6, Longchenpa's *White Lotus*, 646.6–647.2, and Mipham's *Commentary on Chapter 18*, 570.3–6.

35. *Treasury of Wish-Fulfilling Gems*, 50.5–6, and *White Lotus*, 646.6–7.

Because the ultimate of dharmadhātu and individually distinguished phenomena do not exist,
the indivisibility of saṃsāra is taught as this very fundamental sameness.

Longchenpa's *White Lotus*, chap. 18, fols. 646.7–647.2:

> The aspect of being unestablished both of unestablished saṃsāric appearances and of the dharmadhātu, the real nature of phenomena, are incompatible with the fact that they are one within the immaculate ultimate. However, [saṃsāric appearances and the dharmadhātu] are not blended together. Because it is not stained by saṃsāra, reality is indivisible on account of being explained as the complete purity of the real nature itself.

Mipham's *Commentary on Chapter 18*, fols. 570.3–6:

> Thus, the dyad of the emptiness [aspect], the dharmadhātu, and the luminosity [aspect], gnosis, does not exist dualistically. It is not divisible into two [separate elements]. Therefore the mode of appearance [of things] is appearance itself in the sense of saṃsāra. The mode of being [of things] (*gnas tshul*) is that which naturally abides in nirvāṇa. However, in the fundamentally unconditioned nature, saṃsāra and nirvāṇa do not exist dualistically. Truth is indivisible into two [separate elements]. . . . This very saṃsāra, when analyzed by means of reasoning, is not established. Therefore defiled [phenomena], the nature of saṃsāra, does not exist in the slightest. Primordial purity, the ultimate of the dharmadhātu, the ground that one differentiates, and phenomena that are divisions of aspects are not established in the real sense. As a consequence, inasmuch as saṃsāra and nirvāṇa are indivisible, peace is taught as fundamental sameness.

3. The Indivisibility of Ground and Result[36]

Longchenpa's *Treasury of Wish-Fulfilling Gems*, chap. 18, paragraph 12:[37]

36. Longchenpa's *Treasury of Wish-Fulfilling Gems*, 50.7–51.1, Longchenpa's *White Lotus*, 648.4–649.4, and Mipham's *Commentary on Chapter 18*, 571.3–572.5.

37. *Treasury of Wish-Fulfilling Gems* 50,7 & *White Lotus* 648,4.

The nature of the immutable ultimate truth
is the spontaneously present sugata nature that is luminosity,
the nature of phenomena that is the indivisibility of emptiness,
luminosity, and awareness.

Longchenpa's *White Lotus*, chap. 18, fols. 648.4–5:

This primordially unconditioned gnosis that must be known for oneself is [the indivisibility of] emptiness and luminosity, the freedom from mental proliferations, the sugata nature. It is said in the *Uttaratantra* [RGV 1.51cd]:[38] "It has immutability as its nature, being afterward as it was before."[39]

Mipham's *Commentary on Chapter 18*, fols. 571.3–5:

Luminosity, the nature of the ultimate truth, the sugata nature, primordially abides [as it is] and is spontaneously present since it does not depend on causes and conditions. If you ask what the attributes of the [nature of the ultimate truth] are, [the answer is that] it is empty of essence and luminous by nature. Awareness, or gnosis, being the opposite of not knowing, is imbued with a spontaneously luminous nature because the indivisibility of luminosity and emptiness is free from any objective factor. This is the nature of phenomena, the indivisibility of luminosity, emptiness, and awareness.

Longchenpa's *Treasury of Wish-Fulfilling Gems*, chap. 18, paragraph 13:[40]

This very [nature of the sugata] is the maṇḍala of the spontaneously present nature.
Imbued with the primordially and spontaneously perfect quintessence of awakening,
it is pure, free from mental proliferations, free from falling into any [limited] position.

38. Compare with Dergé 4024, fol. 57a: */ ji ltar sngar bzhin phyis de bzhin / / 'gyur ba med pa'i chos nyid do /* (corresponding to *yathā pūrvaṃ tathā paścād avikāritvadharmatā*). Johnston's Sanskrit edition slightly differs from the quoted text.

39. The logical subject of the sentence is *tathāgatadhātu*; see RGV 1.49.

40. *Treasury of Wish-Fulfilling Gems*, 50.7–51.1, and *White Lotus*, 648.6.

Profound and peaceful, it is beyond the union or separation of the *kāya*s and gnosis.

Longchenpa's *White Lotus*, chap. 18, fols. 648.6–649.4:

The qualities of the *kāya*s and gnosis are primordially perfect in the inexpressible essential nature, which, abiding in all beings, is naturally cognizant luminosity, spontaneously present, free from mental proliferations. Thus the quintessence of awakening present in oneself is the maṇḍala of the spontaneously present ground.

Mipham's *Commentary on Chapter 18*, fols. 571.5–572.5:

When this answer is explained in detail, [the quintessence of awakening is considered to be a maṇḍala], because it is endowed with the supreme renunciation: it is pure in the primordial absence of any stain of defiling obscurations, and being free from all falling into extremes or biased positions, it is free of the proliferation of conceptualizations, the cause of these stains. [It is a maṇḍala] because it possesses this very dharmadhātu, the awakened *kāya* of that which is difficult to understand: the gnosis that is the pacification of all conceptualities—namely, the great realization primordially beyond union and separation. Although [this maṇḍala] is beyond union and separation with regard to the five awakened *kāya*s, it does not appear from the perspective of ordinary beings, just like the natural radiance of a gem [is imperceptible] in the absence of [suitable] conditions. Since it cannot be realized just as it is by way of an intellectual investigation, it is profound. The natural radiance of luminosity, the cognitive aspect that is gnosis, is [always] present, unceasing. However, it is extremely difficult for those who [naturally] abide in the state in which all mental proliferations are pacified to realize this as long as they remain ensnared by conceptualizations in terms of the four extremes.

Works Cited

Arguillère, Stéphane. 2007. *Profusion de la vaste sphère, Klong-chen rab-'byams (Tibet, 1308–1364). Sa vie, son oeuvre, sa doctrine*. Leuven: Peeters.

Butters, Albion M. 2006. *The Doxographical Genius of Klong chen rab 'byams pa*. PhD dissertation. New York: Columbia University.

Duckworth, Douglas S. 2008. *Mipam on Buddha Nature*. Albany: State University of New York Press.

Forgues. 2020. *Radical Nondualism in the Works of 'Ju Mi pham rNam rgyal rGya mtsho (1846–1912): The Interplay of Knowledge and Liberation in a Tibetan Philosophical Discourse on Yuganaddha.*

Kapstein, Matthew. 2000. "We Are All Gzhan stongs pas." *Journal of Buddhist Ethics* 7: 105–25.

———. 2009. "Mipam Namgyel: The Lion's Roar Affirming Extrinsic Emptiness." In *Buddhist Philosophy: Essential Readings*, edited by William Edelglass and Jay L. Garfield. New York: Oxford University Press.

Johnston E. H., ed. 1950. *Ratnagotravibhāga Mahāyānottaratantraśāstra by Asaṅga*. Patna: Bihar Research Society.

Longchenpa (Klong chen pa). [*White Lotus.*] *Theg pa chen po'i man ngag gi bstan bcos yid bzhin rin po che'i mdzod kyi 'grel ba padma dkar po lde ba.* In *Mdzod bdun*, vol. 1: *Yid bźin mdzod*. Gangtok: Sherab Gyaltsen and Khyentse Labrang, 1983.

———. [*Treasury of Wish-Fulfilling Gems.*] *Yid bzhin mdzod kyi don khrid zab don do rje snying po ldeb.* In *Mdzod bdun*, vol. 1: *Yid bźin mdzod*. Gangtok: Sherab Gyaltsen and Khyentse Labrang, 1983.

Mipham (Mi pham). *'Jam mgon 'ju mi pham rgya mtsho'i gsung 'bum*. Paro: Palri Parkhang, 1984–93. TBRC.org ID: W23468

———. *Dbu ma la 'jug pa'i 'grel ba zla ba'i zhal lung dri med shel 'phreng*, 1:497–816.

———. *Bde gshegs snying po'i stong thun chen mo seng ge'i nga ro*, 4:563–608.

———. *Don rnam par nges pa shes rab ral gri*, 4:787–820.

———. *Gzhan stong khas len seng ge'i nga ro*, 12:359–99.

———. *Dbu ma rgyan gyi rnam bshad 'jam dbyangs bla ma dgyes pa'i zhal lung*, 13:1–416.

———. *Spyod 'jug shes rab kyi le'u'i tshig don go sla bar rnam par bshad pa nor bu ke ta ka*, 14:1–96.

———. *Yid bzhin mdzod kyi grub mtha' sdus pa*, 21:439–500.

———. *Yid bzhin rin po che'i mdzod kyi dka' gnad ci rigs gsal bar byed pa*, 21:501–63.

———. [*Commentary on Chapter 18*] [*Yid bzhin*] *le'u bco brgyad pa'i tshig 'grel ba*, 21:565–78.

———. *Yid bzhin mdzod kyi sa bcad bsdus sdom ku mu da'i phreng ba*, 21:579–611.

Pettit, John. 1999a. *Mipham's Beacon of Certainty*. Boston: Wisdom Publications.

———. 1999b. "Review of *Altruism and Reality*." *Journal of Buddhist Ethics* 6: 120–37.

Phuntsho, Karma. 2005. *Mi pham's Dialectics and the Debate of Emptiness*. New York: RoutledgeCurzon.

Thurman, Robert A. F. 1997. *Essential Tibetan Buddhism*. Edison, NJ: Castle Books.

Wangchuk, Dorji. 2012. "Was Mi-pham a Dialectical Monist? On a Recent Study of Mi-pham's Interpretation of the Buddha-Nature Theory." *Indo-Iranian Journal* 55: 15–38.

Wayman, Alex. 1985. *Chanting the Names of Mañjuśrī: The Mañjuśrī-Nāma-Saṃgīti: Sanskrit and Tibetan Texts.* Boston: Shambhala Publications.

Williams, Paul. 1998. *The Reflexive Nature of Awareness*. Richmond, UK: Curzon Press.

———. 1999. "A Response to John Pettit." *Journal of Buddhist Ethics* 6: 138–53.

Part 3
The Rise of Wisdom Moon

What Is Buddhist Wisdom?

†*Steven Collins*

I FIRST MET MATTHEW Kapstein in 1986, and in the more than thirty years since then it has been a great pleasure to have had him as a friend and also, fortunately, during a large part of that period, as a colleague. I have thus been able to learn a great deal from his voluminous knowledge, not only of Buddhism but of many other things, and I am happy to have the opportunity to contribute this small piece in his honor.

This paper derives, typically, from a brief remark of his, made in passing at a conference entitled "Madness and Wisdom," held at the University of Chicago in 2014. The papers were on aspects of Hinduism and Tibetan Buddhism. It turned out that almost all the instances of apparently mad behavior and speech discussed at the conference were in fact performances by people who were actually quite sane, with the "madness" undertaken as a form of teaching. Rarely, if ever, was real madness seen as a form of enlightenment, as it was, for example, in the anti-psychiatry movement of the 1960s, perhaps most famously exemplified by Thomas Szasz in the USA (Szasz 1961) and R. D. Laing in the UK (Laing 1969). For them, the experience of schizophrenics and other psychotics afforded access to a kind of reality and truth which (in their view) so-called "sane" people were denied. Whether this was ever true of the so-called "holy madmen" of India and Tibet (and elsewhere) remains, to me at least, an open question. Personally I doubt it. One finds an analogous phenomenon in Christianity: "The holy fool." Of course the word *holy* is a Christian term of art (the whole phrase is also derived from Christian theology) that should be used with great care and self-awareness in the study of Buddhism. I think one should avoid such borrowings altogether. It would be interesting to pursue research into whether such "enlightened," "holy" figures would be classed as mad by contemporary scientific psychiatrists or whether it was always a teaching device constructed and used by sane people. In Mahāyāna Buddhism this performed madness is categorized as an instance of skill in means (*upāyakauśalya*). Anything goes.

But be all that as it may, Matthew's remark was something like this: "Compared to ordinary, everyday virtue and common-sense wisdom, enlightenment is pretty much 'out there,' anyway," by which he meant it was analogous to madness, or mad behavior. This set me thinking of *wisdom* (Pali *paññā*, Sanskrit *prajñā*), as the term figures in Buddhist sayings and texts (called *nīti*) about ordinary, everyday virtue and common sense; in proverbs on prudence, good policy, and what is well spoken (*subhāṣita*); and in all (so-called, but most often mistakenly) fables, morality tales, and the like, circulated by people whom we call, and who no doubt sometimes call themselves, Buddhists, Hindus, and Jains. These contain many examples of wisdom.[1]

Consider verses 26–27 from the *Lokanīti*;[2] as these are also found in the *Mahābhārata*, the wisdom of the "wise man" (*paṇḍita*) cannot represent a specifically Buddhist doctrine. I translate *dhamma* (*dharma*) in many, indeed most contexts, as "what is right":

> Even if a fool pays respect to a wise man all his life,
> he will not understand what is right, as a spoon does not (know) the flavor of a curry.
> If a discerning man (*viññū*) pays respect to a wise man even for a moment,
> he will understand what is right, as the tongue (knows) the flavor of a curry.

The kind of Buddhist wisdom usually thought of (and written about) is what the *Oxford English Dictionary* defines as "Knowledge (esp. of a high or abstruse kind); enlightenment." This is textualized, for example, in the Perfection of Wisdom (*prajñāpāramitā*) literature. (I think "perfection" is a mistranslation, on which more below.) Within the tradition, this is indeed what everyone is or should eventually be aiming at, where *prajñā* is equivalent to *bodhi*, "enlightenment." For an outsider such as myself, this is just mythology, something thought up by the human imagination as a discursive artifact. There is no such thing as enlightenment. It is often said to be beyond discourse, ineffable. This notion is just a plaything, inserted by traditions where it has a useful role at certain points. Outside of discourse, ineffability means nothing. Within discourse, which is the only thing an existential, ideology-free form of description and analysis can accept as existing, ineffability is a counter used at certain points in a game, a *Glass Bead Game* perhaps. Nat-

1. Much of what follows is taken from Collins, Forthcoming.

2. Bechert and Braun 1981.

urally, each tradition thinks that its discourse is the only way to get to this ineffability.

So if this kind of wisdom is just a mute counter in a game, what of the kinds of thing called "wisdom" in ordinary life? I do not want to define this. Contemporary psychologists and philosophers who study wisdom, for their own purposes legitimately, do have to try to do so. But students of Buddhist literature, taken in a comprehensive sense, do not. We can be content with other senses and synonyms found also in the *Oxford English Dictionary*:

> *Wisdom.* capacity of judging rightly in matters relating to life and conduct; soundness of judgment in the choice of means and ends; sometimes, less strictly, sound sense, esp. in practical affairs; opp. to folly.
> *wise.* having or exercising sound judgment or discernment; capable of judging truly concerning what is right or fitting, and disposed to act accordingly; having the ability to perceive and adopt the best means for accomplishing an end; characterized by good sense and prudence; opp. to foolish.
> *wise man.* a man who is wise, a man of good judgment or discernment; a discreet or prudent man (often opposed to fool).
> *sage.* of a person: wise, discreet, judicious. Practically wise, rendered prudent or judicious by experience.

It is useful also to remember the French:

> *sage.* sound, sensible, wise, good (= well-behaved), sober, moderate, restrained, tame.
> *sagesse.* wisdom, good sense, soundness, good behavior, moderation.

One says to a child *sois sage*, meaning "behave yourself."

All of these senses can be understood to apply to and to be used in everyday life, and all of them are found in Buddhist texts: proverbs, fables, morality tales, and the like. The three examples of stories I shall give here are taken from the collection of stories redacted in Pali as the *Jātaka*s, birth stories (of the Buddha Gotama's past lives). These stories are often said, by other Pali texts as well as ubiquitously by modern scholars, to illustrate Gotama's fulfillment of what is usually translated as "perfections" (Pali *pāramī*, Sanskrit *pāramitā*). There are ten of these according to Theravāda tradition, and they are not sequential—this as opposed to the six in Mahāyāna, which culminate in *prajñāpāramitā*. In Pali, *paññā* as a *pāramī* (sometimes *pāramitā*) is the fourth. Other Pali texts, such as the introduction (*nidāna*) to the Jātaka collection, which is obviously a later editorial addition, do refer to the birth stories as exemplifying each of the *pāramīs*, but these references are often not borne out by the texts, which generally seem to have nothing to do with wisdom in any sense of the word. Texts that purport to exemplify the *pāramīs*—texts said at the outset to be "about" (*ārabbha*) them—are in fact scarce, and in some cases not found. The exception is *paññā-pāramī*, which has, out of the over five hundred stories, ten (by my reckoning) that begin *paññā-pāramiṃ ārabbha*. I have studied all of these, and also as many of the texts as I can which use the word (sometimes as part of a proper noun) *paṇḍita*—there are so very many occurrences of this word, which is also often translated as "wise," although this often seems perfunctory.

(It is very unfortunate, by the way, that all of the *Jātaka* stories were translated over a hundred years ago by a team of Oxbridge Classicists, in six volumes now usually available in three. The translations are simply awful, with the same words translated differently, different words translated the same way, delicate psychological and sociological subtleties entirely lost, the very frequent comedy entirely absent, and so on. The always difficult and sometimes beautiful verses are rendered into English rhyming verse, which turns them into doggerel. In order to achieve the rhyme, Pali words are often omitted or English words added. Most nonspecialists, and even Buddhist studies scholars who don't know Pali, or at least (like most of them) not enough of it, have been condemned for over a century to this horror, and I don't suppose anyone now is going to translate them all anew. It would be a life's work, and who would get tenure for it? Fortunately, some good translations have recently appeared, with very helpful introductions.)[3]

Before giving some examples of the stories, I will explore, philologically, some of the more important words used in the context of these stories.

bodhisattva/bodhisatta. The usual form used in English is the Sanskrit *bodhisattva*, sometimes spelled in inscriptions *bodhisatva*. This

3. Over the years, one or two better translations of individual *Jātaka*s have appeared in journals. Margaret Cone's accurate and elegant translation of the *Vessantara Jātaka* appeared in 1977, reprinted in 2011. In 2006, Sarah Shaw's excellent selection of twenty-six *Jātaka* stories appeared in a Penguin Classics edition of *The Jātakas*. Particularly welcome is Naomi Appleton and Sarah Shaw's (2015) two-volume translation of the ten last and longest stories, *The Ten Great Birth Stories of the Buddha: The Mahānipāta of the Jātakātthavaṇṇanā*. These new translations, along with their sometimes quite extensive introductions, are now by far the best point of entry into the birth stories. Some scholars have published books on particular subjects in this literature, some of which contain useful summaries of the stories (though not extensive translations) of them.

is, however, a grammatically incoherent term, the Sanskrit compound being as bizarre as the literal English translation "enlightenment being." The Sanskrit *sattva* can indeed be equivalent to Pali (or some other form of Middle Indo-Aryan) *satta*, "being." In compound, however, with *bodhi*, the word must in fact be one of two words *satta*, both past participles. One is from √*sañj*, "to be attached to" or "intent on": thus *bodhisatta* would mean "(someone) intent on enlightenment." It could also be from √*śak/sak*, "to be able": *bodhisatta* would thus mean "(someone) capable of enlightenment." There is no way to choose between these two, so I use the interpretive phrase "future buddha."

pāramī/pāramitā. *Para*, or *pāra*, both have the same range of meanings: "highest, supreme," "the utmost reach or fullest extent." *Pāramī* and *pāramitā* are both nominal forms, called in Sanskrit *vṛddhi* (strengthened) derivatives from *para* or *pāra*, from the root √*pṛ*, among whose meanings are "get over, overcome, bring to an end." *Pāramī* and *pāramitā* therefore mean, among other things, "highest state" (as given in Monier-Williams's Sanskrit dictionary). Edgerton's *Buddhist Hybrid Sanskrit Dictionary* gives "supremacy, mastery." (Monier-Williams, following Sanskrit texts, takes *-ita* to be a past-passive participle from √*i*, to go, and *pāra* as "further shore," which is possible, and so translates *pāramitā* as "gone to the opposite shore"; given, however, that the Pali *pāramī* is a synonym, this must be wrong.) Why on earth "perfection" was chosen as a translation I don't know. That word has a background in Christian theology, so no doubt this is another example of Christian contamination. Someone, no doubt in the nineteenth century, chose "wisdom," and because of lethargy in translation we are stuck with that as a general term. What can "perfection" mean when used, non-mythologically, of a human being in the modern world? I prefer "excellence." (OED: "The state or fact of excelling; the possession chiefly of good qualities in an eminent or unusual degree; surpassing merit, skill, virtue, worth, etc.; dignity, eminence.") Given the variety of meanings of "wisdom" in English, as also *paññā* in Pali, I will ignore the polysemy of both *wisdom* and *paññā* and translate *paññā–pāramī* (*-itā*) as "excellence in wisdom."

paññā/prajñā. It has recently been claimed[4] that both *paññā* (*prajñā*) and *paṇḍita* came, originally, from the same root, but this is not

4. Aklujkar 2001.

> important to me. The root of the former is √*jñā*, basically meaning "to know." With the prefix *pra* (Pali *pa-*) in Sanskrit, one gets *prajñā*, in Pali *paññā*. In Pali sometimes the *j* is dropped—hence, √*ñā*, from which the noun *ñāṇa*. The *Dictionary of Pali* gives for *paññā* "understanding, cleverness, discriminative knowledge, true, profound understanding," and for *ñāṇa* "knowledge, understanding." The words *paññā* and *ñāṇa* are as wholly unspecific and heterogeneous, as of course are the words given in English dictionaries as synonyms or senses for them. The English monk-translator Ñāṇamoli preferred "understanding" for *paññā*. The contemporary American monk-translator Thanissaro prefers, at least in the systematic texts he standardly translates, "discernment." This is accurate and useful in those contexts, but readers without Pali will not know that this is the same concept standardly translated as "wisdom" in other texts.

When translating, one is between a rock and a hard place: a traditional, standard rendering might be vague or inappropriate to the text one is dealing with, but making one's own choice risks being idiosyncratic, so that readers depending on translations (that is, almost everyone) would have to take each translated text on its own, without being able to make connections with others using the standard rendering. Translation is both necessary and impossible.

The only birth story that has anything remotely connected with what we might call "philosophical" skill is the *Mahābodhi Jātaka*, a strange story that shows that the context of possessing wisdom does not have to be moral. The future Buddha is an ascetic who lives in a royal park for twelve years. The king has five advisors, each of whom holds a different philosophical and ethical doctrine. As judges, they all accept bribes. The future Buddha takes over as judge and makes judgments according to what is right. The previous advisors persuade the king that Mahābodhi, the future Buddha, is the king's enemy, plotting to kill him, and one day the king agrees. A dog, thinking in language, stands at the door as the future Buddha is about to enter the palace and barks. The future Buddha, "by his knowledge of the meaning of all sounds," returns first to the park, then to the Himalayas, and then to a forest in a frontier village. The advisors kill the queen and say that Mahābodhi has done it. Knowing what is going on, Mahābodhi eats the flesh of a monkey, dries its skin, and wears it as clothing. He returns to the royal park and sits on a stone slab. The king arrives, and Mahābodhi, the future Buddha, tells him what he has done with the monkey skin, and how it has been of great service to him. The five advisors accuse him of murder (*pāṇatipāta*, "attacking living [breathing] beings," as in the first precept). The future Buddha asks them how he is guilty according to each of their doctrines, which are explained briefly, and he refutes them all. The king ties the advisors up with dog leashes, sprinkles cow dung over them, and exiles them. The future Buddha stays on for a few days, advising the king to be diligent, and returns to the Himalayas.

The five doctrines are analogous to (but not the same as) a much-discussed sutta, the *Sāmaññaphala*, the "Fruits of Asceticism" (*Dīgha-nikāya* 2). (The passage also has analogs elsewhere.) That text begins by presenting a series of six positions, expressed in clumsy or even incorrect Pali, to which the Buddha opposes a long and elegant account of the Buddhist path. This sutta has usually been taken, in a positivist historiographical manner, as a straightforward record of the imagined "ideological ferment" that characterized the sudden growth of asceticism and ascetical sects at the time of the second urbanization of India. I disagree. The linguistic and conceptual clumsiness of these so-called "heretical" views is such that I think they are deliberately meant to be satirical; these so-called "teachers" are so stupid that they can't even speak or reason properly. (I am not the first person to say this.) Be that as it may be, the story of Mahābodhi as a whole is also decidedly odd. Is a wise man apt to kill a monkey and use its skin as trickery to (seem to) refute opponents? Make of the story what you will—it apparently purports, in any case, to be "about excellence in wisdom."

The second story is less dramatic, less baffling, but, to me anyway, very interesting. It is the "Birth Story about a Barley-Meal Bag" (*Sattubhasta Jātaka*). The "story of the present" that frames this birth story says it is "about excellence in wisdom" (*paññā-pāramiṃ ārabbha*). Monks praise the Buddha, in a series of common epithets, as having different kinds of *paññā*: "great wisdom, wide-ranging wisdom, joking wisdom, quick[-witted] wisdom, sharp wisdom, crushing contrary views." Before telling the story of the past, the Buddha remarks, as often, "Now I have *paññā*, but in the past when my knowledge (*ñāṇa*) was not ripe [or, not cooked], I was wise to the extent that I was practicing for the sake of knowing enlightenment." In the story of the past, the future Buddha becomes minister-advisor to a king. When he speaks, "it is as if the time of a Buddha had arisen throughout the kingdom . . . he spoke with the elegance of a Buddha." Then the real story starts.

A young brahman wife with an old husband is sexually dissatisfied and takes a lover. She sends her old husband to get money enough to hire a maid, giving him a leather bag with barley meal, some made into cakes and some not so. He gets the money then turns back. At a place where there is pleasant (presumably clear) water, he eats some barley, then without tying up the bag goes to get some water. While he is gone a black snake gets into the bag and eats some barley. The brahman comes back, ties up the bag, and goes off. A tree spirit sees him and offers a riddle: "Brahman, if you stay on the road, you yourself will die. If you go home today, your wife will die." The spirit disappears.

The brahman, unable to see the spirit, "terrified with fear of death," goes to Benares. People tell him that wise Senaka (Senakapaṇḍita), the future Buddha, is about to teach *dhamma*, what is right, with the elegance of a Buddha and with a sweet voice. He does so, and Senaka sees the brahman sorrowing and asks him why he is upset. The brahman tells him what the spirit said. Wise Senaka reflects on the different kinds of death, and as he does so realizes that there must be a snake in the brahman's bag. He knows this precisely by his knowledge of skill in means (*upāyakosallanāṇen' eva*) and knows, "*as if* seeing with a divine eye," what has happened and what the spirit's words mean: if the brahman stays on the road and opens the bag again to eat and puts his hand in it, the snake will bite him fatally; if he goes home, his wife would do the same thing. Cross-examining the brahman about what has happened, wise Senaka tells him to undo the bag and hit it with a stick. The commentary to a verse in the text here cites a proverb or maxim:

> The skillful ("good," *kusalā*) say that *paññā* is best,
> like the moon among the stars.
> Virtue, good fortune, goodness, and what is right
> are followers of a wise man (*paññavato*).

The brahman hits the snake, which comes out and is caught by a snake charmer, who sets it free in the forest. The brahman speaks some verse in praise of Senaka and says that it was a good thing for him to have found Senaka and to have seen that the latter possessed "good wisdom" (*sādhupaññaṃ*). He then offers Senaka money, which Senaka refuses; instead, Senaka has the brahman's bag filled with a thousand coins and tells him to go home. Cross-examined again about the reason for his journey, the brahman tells him. Senaka devises a strategy by which the brahman can go home, keep his money, and get rid of his wife's lover, in all of which he is successful.

In what does Senaka's wisdom consist? He does not know by supernatural means, since the text clearly says he worked out what had happened *as if* (*viya*) by a divine eye. One could use that overworked and entirely vague word "intuition," which doesn't explain anything. I think the text is like a detective story. From the initially obscure and, to the rest of us, indecipherable tree-spirit's riddle, the future Buddha works out, in a Sherlock Holmesian or Philip Marlowe–like manner, what the tree spirit's enigmatic words mean; in this he is inordinately skillful, but his is an empirical deduction. In later giving the brahman advice (and practical assistance) on how to punish his wife and get rid of her lover, is he wise? Savvy? Smart? Surely all of these. (The solving of riddles, by the way, is a very common skill of wise men, the world over.)

One last story, perhaps the most surprising to those who think wisdom in Buddhism is only of one kind. It is the birth story about Sulasā (#419 *Sulasā Jātaka*). The main story is told in the story of the present. A female servant of Anāthapiṇḍika named Sulasā goes to a park wearing an expensive ornament. A thief, intending to kill her and take it, plies her with fish, meat, and alcohol. He takes her from the garden to somewhere more private. Realizing his intention, she asks him to get her some water from a well. As he is leaning over the well, she pushes him in; thinking this may not be enough to kill him, she drops a large brick on his head. She tells the story to Anāthapiṇḍika's wife, who tells it to Anāthapiṇḍika, who tells it to the Buddha. The Buddha says, "Now is not the first time that this slave girl has been endowed with wisdom (*paññā*: shrewdness?) occurring (in a way) appropriate to a situation . . . in the past also she killed him."

In the story of the past, then, Sulasā is a madam with a brothel of five hundred women. A thief terrorizes the people of the town. The townspeople catch him and are taking him to the place of execution when Sulasā, standing at a window, sees him and falls in love with him. Thinking that if she could free him, she could give up her disreputable life and live with him, she frees him by sending a thousand coins to the chief constable. She and the thief marry. But after three or four months of marriage, he decides he can no longer live there and plans to kill her and take all her expensive jewelry. He tries to trick her by saying that he owes a lot of money to a tree spirit and that they should go repay him. When the two of them get to the tree spirit, the latter tells her the truth: her husband wants to kill her and steal her jewelry. Conceiving a plan to kill her husband rather than be killed, she pretends to walk around him in reverence but pushes him from behind over a steep cliff. He is crushed to pieces and dies. The spirit who lives on the mountaintop—who is in fact the future Buddha—speaks verses that begin thus:

> It is not only a man who can be *paṇḍita*; a woman is *paṇḍitā* if
> she is attentive in all circumstances.
> It is not only a man who can be *paṇḍita*; a woman is *paṇḍitā* if
> she can quickly discern what is useful.

I cite this story not because a woman is said to be *paṇḍitā*; despite the misogyny that is ubiquitous in the stories, this is actually said quite often elsewhere. I cite this, rather, because here being *paṇḍita* consists in committing murder when necessary. Some people would dismiss this as "worldly wisdom." That, however, is an English (Christian) category, not a Buddhist one.

So, Buddhist wisdom is a many-splendored thing. These are just a few of many examples from the birth stories of the kind of everyday virtue and common-sense Wisdom, relative to which Matthew characterized the wisdom of enlightenment as, like madness, "out there." This kind of wisdom is not, however, to be dismissed as "worldly wisdom"; for those of us for whom Buddhist doctrine is mythology, these are the kinds of wisdom recorded in Pali texts that exist in and depict the real world. The purely textual characters that are Buddhas possess not only (to use a word Matthew would not) the highfalutin spiritual wisdom evinced at the culmination of the Bildungsromans of their careers. On their way to being celebrities of that sort, they are in the birth stories also culture heroes, exemplifying all manner of wise exploits and sayings. I have found the exploration of these kinds of wisdom to be of great interest and profit, and I hope that the results of my lengthier exploration, when published, will be found so by others as well. I wouldn't have started on that journey without Matthew's remark, and I thank him for it.

Works Cited

Aklujkar, Ashok. 2001. "Paṇḍita and Pandits in History." In *The Pandit: Traditional Scholarship in India*, edited by Axel Michaels, 17–40. New Delhi: Manohar Publishers.

Appleton, Naomi, and Sarah Shaw. 2015. *The Ten Great Birth Stories of the Buddha: The Mahānipāta of the Jātakatthavaṇṇanā*. Chieng Mai, Thailand: Silkworm Press.

Bechert, Heinz, and H. Braun, eds. 1981. *Pāli Nīti Texts from Burma*. London: The Pali Text Society.

Collins, Steven. Forthcoming. *Civilization, Wisdom, Practices of Self: Theravāda Buddhism Seen Anew*. New York: Columbia University Press.

Cone, Margaret, and Richard Gombrich. 1977. *The Perfect Generosity of Prince Vessantara*. Oxford: Oxford University Press. (Reprinted 2011, Bristol: The Pali Text Society).

Laing, R. D. 1969. *The Divided Self.* New York: Pantheon.

Shaw, Sarah. 2006. *The Jātakas: Birth Stories of the Bodhisatta*. India: Penguin.

Szasz, Thomas. 1961. *The Myth of Mental Illness: Foundations of a Theory of Personal Conduct*. New York: Harper & Row.

The Consort/Spell Observance (*Vidyāvrata*) and the Rite Bestowing It (*Dānavidhi*): Developments in Esoteric Buddhist Initiation

Christian K. Wedemeyer

TO HAVE HAD Matthew Kapstein as a teacher and mentor—and to thus find my work in the company of the eminent scholars who contribute to this volume celebrating his work—is a humbling experience. Confronted with the immense learning that Professor Kapstein wears so lightly and shares so freely, one cannot but feel the poverty of one's own knowledge and insights. Yet, in the eighteen years that I have had the pleasure of working with him, the experience has simultaneously been tremendously elevating. One always felt invited: drawn in to join a delightful feast of inquiry and discovery, philosophical, historical, sociological, psychological, orthographical, musicological . . . an encyclopedic festival. To witness Professor Kapstein's thought, whether in writing or in person, is to experience a kind of miraculous display; accordingly, I here offer a piece that I first presented on an auspicious full-moon day of *cho 'phrul dus chen*, when the Tibetan world celebrates a display of miracles by the Buddha. The paper seemed doubly (or triply) appropriate insofar as the *place* where it was first presented was the University of California, Berkeley, one of Kapstein's early intellectual homes and also the home (just a few years prior) of the Free Speech Movement. This latter, it may be recalled, was described at the time by a rather cynical administration as a "civil rights panty raid." Were we to be equally cynical, the topic of my paper today, the *prajñājñānābhiṣeka* and *vidyāvrata* (the wisdom-gnosis initiation and the consort/spell-observance) of the later Buddhist Tantras, might well (and rather more legitimately, insofar as they involve ritualized sexual behavior) be called a "gnostic insight panty raid," though the prurient details of these rites are not at issue in what follows.

What is important here, rather, is the manner in which these two rites were woven together into a common fabric by the liturgical craftsmen of the late first—and early second—millennia in India. That is, we are concerned to explore a ritual sequence and its alteration over time. Briefly, then, we will present some materials touching on the ritual sequence of these two rites—rites that seem to have been independent in their origins yet became associated, juxtaposed, and even conflated in later practice. As we shall see, the liturgical details of these rituals vary, particularly over the issue of whether there is to be a separate ritual of bestowing the consort/spell observance, the *vidyāvratadānavidhi*. The record reflects what I believe are two major paradigms for the developed ritual structure: one in which bestowing the observance appears as a separate rite (after the [third] wisdom-gnosis initiation or after the [final] fourth initiation in those sources that include it), and another in which the *vidyāvrata* is integral, even identical, to wisdom-gnosis initiation. I will briefly review the prehistory of this rite in more dualistic esoteric sources before turning to an examination of its later scriptural sources in the *Guhyasamāja* and its *Uttara Tantra*. I will then review a variety of initiatory sequences and observe the location of the elements of the *vidyāvrata* liturgy therein, before essaying some very tentative, speculative, and unsatisfying hypotheses and considering some of the questions these facts raise for future study of the *abhiṣeka* ritual.

As my earlier work (esp. "Locating Tantric Antinomianism") has stressed, I believe that greater attention to the role that temporary, supererogatory ritual observances, or *vrata*, play in the esoteric traditions is a desideratum. In esoteric Buddhism, and especially in the later tantras, these undertakings come into greater prominence. In earlier Buddhism, *vrata* appears as an element in religious practice but is comparatively restricted in scope. In general Buddhist sources, this term refers to what is clearly *the* preeminent supererogatory Buddhist ritual: the one-day vows of temporary, virtual cenobitic asceticism, or *poṣadha*. In some later Newar sources, the ritual of going forth from home to homelessness, or *pravrajyā*, is also referred to as a *vrata*, but this would seem to be an extension of the *poṣadha* paradigm, insofar as the Newar ritual of going forth shares more or less the same vows (the *poṣadha* vows are nearly identical to those of the novice monk) and is, like the *poṣadha*, a kind of temporary ascetic practice (though there are differences of opinion as to how temporary it may or may not be).

When new, named *vrata*s begin to appear in the early Buddhist esoteric literature, they are likewise (and in line with the essential feature of such observances across the Indic world) temporary ascetic practices, supererogatory in nature, generally intended for the ambitious (rather than the "workaday") practitioner. In this regard, they are similar in certain respects to the *vratas* that appear in contemporaneous Śaiva literature, where, for instance, in the *Niśvāsa Guhyasūtra*, one reads of a number of observances, such as the *mithyā-, śmaśāna-, gaṇa-, loṣṭuka-, kāṣṭha-, vīra-,* and *asidhārā-vrata*s (See, e.g., *Niśvāsatattvasaṃhita, Guhyasūtra* 3: 30–40).

In both Bauddha and Śaiva traditions, one of the most prominent of the new concepts is that of the *vidyāvrata,* or observance of the spell or knowledge (*vidyā*). The twenty-first chapter of the Śaiva *Brahmayāmala* or *Picumata* describes fourteen different observances, which are all subsumed under the general category of *vidyāvrata* (*Brahmayāmala/Picumata* XXI.1–3, 98r4–5). It is not clear to me whether the term has a similar, general application in the Buddhist context, as I have not had the time to explore systematically the earlier esoteric literature in which the *vidyāvrata* first appears.

Of especial importance for later esoterism, a *vidyāvrata* occupies prominent place in the *Mahāvairocana Sūtra* (D 494), wherein an entire chapter (the fifteenth) is dedicated to this observance. Like the general ritual protocol of this and related esoteric works, the practice involves maintaining proper purity strictures and engaging in a sequence of ascetical meditative practices, with restricted diets correlated to the meditative object. It is said to last for six months and to result in buddhahood. Likewise, a *vidyāvrata* appears prominently in the esoteric scripture translated into Tibetan as the *Rdo rje rtse mo* (D 480). Therein, details are in short supply, but there are numerous references, and the practice is clearly marked by dualistic purity strictures, avoiding sinful conduct, recollecting the buddha (*buddhānusmṛti*), performing conventional offerings (maṇḍala worlds, etc.), and disciplined recitation of mantric formulae. Like the *Mahāvairocana Sūtra*'s *vidyāvrata,* and as quite standard for *vrata*s in general, it is said to last for one, six, or twelve months.

While the further development of Śaiva *vrata*s entailed increasing levels of transgressive, funerary accoutrements, to my (very limited) knowledge, no Śaiva *vidyāvrata* so-called seems to have innovated in the particular way the Buddhist *vidyāvrata* did: that is, to sexualize the ritual through reinterpreting the term *vidyā* as "consort" rather than "spell." It seems that in this regard, as in so many other ways, we have the *Guhyasamāja Tantra* to thank for this rather radical shift in the Buddhist conception of the observance. As so often in the development of the Buddhist traditions, we see well-established older terms revalued and redeployed in accordance with new ideological valences. Henceforth, the *vidyā* of the observance was not construed as a mantra but as a woman. The locus classicus of this would seem to be the very end of *Guhyasamāja* chapter 16, which describes such a *vidyāvrata,* undertaken with a sixteen-year-old female, of either divine, magical serpent, dryad, semidivine, or human birth (*Guhyasamāja Tantra* 16.91–104). Like the *vidyāvrata* of the *Mahāvairocana,* this too promises quick buddhahood (*evaṃ buddho bhavec chīghraṃ, Guhyasamāja Tantra* 16.97a). Of particular note are the injunctions to perform so-called secret worship (*guhyapūjā*) and that cosmic failure will result if one transgresses the strictures of the observance (*atikramed yadi vajrātmā nāśaṃ vajrākṣaram bhavet* | *Guhyasamāja Tantra* 16.102cd).

The further ritual elaboration of this concept may be observed in the *Guhyasamāja Uttaratantra*, and it is here that one first sees the *vidyāvrata* mentioned in connection (or, at least, juxtaposition) with the initiation ritual rather than as a separate, supererogatory rite. In the opening salvo of queries by the bodhisattvas, one reads the following:

> How is initiation bestowed? How the *vidyāvrata*, too?
>
> abhiṣekaṃ kathaṃ deyaṃ kathaṃ vidyāvrataṃ tathā |
> (*Guhyasamāja Uttaratantra* v. 19ab)

It is worth noting at this point that the consumption of polluting substances, the five ambrosias and the like, are mentioned immediately thereafter ("How are the five ambrosias to be consumed?" *pañcāmṛtaṃ kathaṃ bhakṣyaṃ*). The complicated relationship of this antinomian gustatory practice to the *vidyāvrata* will be of ancillary interest as we proceed.

The answer to these questions will be found in the *Uttaratantra* verses 124–27. Here we will not be concerned with the answer to the question about initiation but will focus solely upon the immediately subsequent response to the *vidyāvrata* question, which reads as follows:

> The teacher, the *vajrin*, should take that very goddess, the *vidyā*,
> and place [her] hand in the hand [of the student], calling the tathāgatas to witness.
> Placing his hand on the head of the student, the teacher, the *vajrin*, says,
> "There is no other means for buddhahood than this excellent *vidyā*.
> All things are nondual though indicated by (or known through) duality.
> Hence, one should never separate [from her as long as] the life cycle [lasts].
> This is the unexcelled *vidyā* observance (*vidyāvrata*) of all the buddhas.

The fool who transgresses this will not have the highest success."[1]

tām eva devatāṃ vidyāṃ gṛhya śiṣyasya vajriṇaḥ |
pāṇau pāṇiḥ pradātavyaḥ sākṣīkṛtya tathāgatāṇ ||
hastaṃ dattvā ṣire śiṣyam ucyate guruvajriṇaḥ |
nānyopāyena buddhatvaṃ tasmād vidyām imāṃ varām||
advayāḥ sarvadharmās tu dvayabhāvena lakṣitaḥ |
tasmād viyogaḥ sāṃsāre na kāryo bhavatā sadā ||
idaṃ tat sarvabuddhānāṃ vidyāvratam anuttamam |
atikramati yo mūḍhaḥ siddhis tasya na cottamā ||

What seems reasonably clear from the above is this: the *Uttaratantra* presents an initiation, which is then followed by a further rite in which the student is joined to a fellow student of the opposite sex with the injunction never to leave her, and that this is called the (or, at least, a) *vidyā* observance.[2]

This presentation would seem to conform, more or less, to the elaboration of the ritual given in the *Vajrāvalī* of Abhayākaragupta (see appendix A, "Ritual Structures," no. 1). There, we see a complete wisdom-gnosis initiation, a fourth initiation (the practice of giving which Abhaya accepted), followed thereafter by a sequence of three *vratadānavidhi*-s: those of the *vidyā-*, *vajra*, and *caryā-vratas*. The sequence of Abhaya's presentation has served as the source for most later traditional (and some modern) presentations of the initiation ritual; the liturgy for the schematic elements given for each source in appendix A (marked by roman numerals I through VII) may be found in appendix B ("Liturgical Elements").

The first two liturgical elements (I and II) form the basis for Abhaya's presentation of the wisdom-gnosis initiation. The student requests the initiation

1. One is tempted here to translate this a bit more colloquially, as: "The moron who screws this up will not do well at all."

2. There is a legitimate question as to where the preceding discussion of the *prajñājñānābhiṣeka* should be construed to end and the *vidyāvrata* discussion to begin. The *Uttaratantra* is clear that there are three initiations, the last being the *prajñājñāna-* (*Uttaratantra* v. 113). The passage just anterior to the one translated culminates in a sequence of anointings (*niḥṣeka*) by a sequence of goddesses, culminating in the initiand becoming Prajñājñāna (niḥsekād jñānadhārābhiḥ prajñājñānaḥ svayaṃ bhavet); hence, my breaking it where I do. However, it is worth noting that the subcommentary of Thagana asserts that the section on the *vidyāvrata* does not begin until "All things are nondual" (*Guhyasamājatantravivaraṇa*, D 1845, 236a), construing the *vidyāvrata* merely as never separating from the consort. But this is contradicted by the ritual as presented by Abhaya and others (see below, where the *vidyāvrata* begins with the placing of the student and consort hand in hand).

from the teacher. Then the *vidyā* is bestowed upon him with the *dhāraṇī* verse (I)—note the reference to the *vidyā* here by another feminine term for spell, *dhāraṇī*:

This, your *dhāraṇī*-woman, is to be delighted [and] served;
[she is] appointed by all the buddhas.
By the procedure of the sequence of wheels (*cakra*), taste the true bliss.

iyaṃ te dhāraṇī ramyā sevyā buddhaiḥ prakalpitā |
cakrakramaprayogeṇa samāsvādaya satsukham ||

The naked, fragrant *vidyā* then addresses the student, with the *padma* verse (II):

O! My lotus is endowed with all bliss.
I stand before the one who serves [it] properly.
Do in the lotus what is to be done—adoration of all the buddhas and so on.
The king of great bliss itself [is] always situated here.

aho madīyaṃ padmaṃ sarvasukhasamanvitam |
yaḥ sevayati vidhānena tasyāham agrataḥ sthitā ||
kuru padme yathākāryaṃ sambuddhārādhanādikam ||
svayaṃ mahāsukho rājā atraiva hi sadā sthitaḥ ||

In some versions, including Abhaya's, this is followed by the mantra, *bha[ñ] ja mokṣa hoḥ*. There then follows the rite of the student and consort uniting in ritual sexual union and the consumption of the so-called bodhicitta produced therefrom.

In Abhaya's ritual, this is then followed by the fourth initiation; and it is only after the completion of the fourth that the rite of bestowing the *vidyāvrata* takes place. The ritual formulae of this are as follows: the teacher places the hand of the *vidyā* in the hand of the student and, holding the two with his left hand, places his right hand, holding a vajra, on the top of his head. This is articulated in Abhaya as found in Liturgical Element III. You will recall that this is likewise the first element of the *Uttaratantra*'s *vidyāvrata* rite. So, too, is this followed in Abhaya by calling the tathāgatas to witness this transaction, saying "You are witnesses here: she is made over by me to him." Abhaya concludes this rite with the liturgy taken directly from the *Uttaratantra* (elements V and

VI), omitting only the line about the nondual nature of reality, the final line of which identifies this liturgical element as part of the eponymous *vidyāvrata*:

> There is no other means for pure buddhahood in this triple
>   world.
> Hence, don't separate from her ever!
> This is the *vidyāvrata* of all the buddhas, unexcelled.
> That fool who transgresses this [will] not have the highest success.

Essentially the same liturgy for the *vidyāvrata* is to be found in the *Kriyāsamuccaya* of Darpaṇācārya (appendix A, 1A), which is not terribly surprising, given that his work was based upon that of Abhaya. It, too, features a separate wisdom-gnosis initiation and *vidyāvratadānavidhi*, with a fourth initiation intervening.

In this, Abhaya and Darpaṇa would seem to follow a precedent set in the quite early Guhyasamāja initiation rite set forth by Dīpaṃkarabhadra and further elucidated by Vitapāda[3] (appendix A, 3 and 4). Neither of these authors describes a fourth initiation, but both present sequential and separate rites of initiation and *vidyāvrata*. Dīpaṃkarabhadra's ritual text is rather terse liturgically in this section, so I will focus on its unpacking by Vitapāda. His presentation is somewhat differently structured than that found in the *Uttaratantra* or in our later systematizers' works (though not markedly so). His ritual begins the wisdom-gnosis initiation with the rite of joining hands, which in the other rituals is unmistakably the first element of the *vidyāvrata*.[4] The second liturgical element of his wisdom-gnosis initiation, however, has not been seen in what we have reviewed so far. It is a fascinating call-and-response exchange between the *vidyā* and the student, in which she tests his willingness to transgress purity strictures in a nondual practice: testing, in a sense, his yogic chutzpah (appendix B, VII). She asks:

> Can you handle eating feces, urine and the like, my dear?
> Blood? Semen? Meat, too? The supreme devotion to women—
> kissing the vaginal lotus? Speak, my dear, as you please.

3. Catherine Dalton's forthcoming dissertation (UC–Berkeley) will present serious arguments for believing this author is better known as Vaidyapāda rather than Vitapāda. I retain the older usage here for the time being. Thank you to Catherine for this information (personal communication).

4. Hence, his/this presentation is in accord with the interpretation given in Thagana's commentary on the *Uttaratantra*, as noted above.

He, then, the bold yogin, is supposed to reply:

> Goddess, how could I not bear eating feces, semen, and so on?
> The devotion to women is to be done always—even kissing the vagina.

Whereupon she addresses and commands him:

> O! My lotus is endowed with all bliss!
> I stand before him who serves it properly.
> Do in the lotus as is to be done—adoration of buddhas and the like.
> The king of great bliss himself stands right here always.

The precise source from which Vitapāda (or his teachers) drew this liturgy is not entirely clear, but it is worth noting that a very similar call-and-response passage occurs in the *Caṇḍamahāroṣaṇa Tantra*. The last verse, it should be noted, is equivalent to element II, the *padma* verse, which appears as the second part of Abhaya's initiation rite. Note also that integrated here are elements from the rite that immediately follows the *vidyāvrata* in the *Uttaratantra*: the consumption of the five impure "ambrosias."

Immediately thereafter, in Vitapāda's presentation, follows the rite of bestowing the *vidyāvrata*, in the order found in the *Uttaratantra*. The only divergence is that this initiation liturgy begins with element III, calling the buddhas to witness, as the joining of the hands (II) has taken place at the beginning of the preceding initiation rite. Following the witnessing (IV), come the *nānyopāya* verse and the *vidyāvrata* verse (V and VI).

Thus there seems to have been a well-established, early ritual structure in the Guhyasamāja traditions of three initiations, concluding in the wisdom-gnosis initiation, followed immediately by the bestowing of the *vidyāvrata*. The only deviation from this is that Abhaya added the *dhāraṇī* verse (whose first attested occurrence is in Dīpaṃkarabhadra's *Guhyasamājamaṇḍalavidhi*); and he abbreviated Vitapāda's call and response, including only the concluding *padma* verse.

This is all well and good; and the matter could rest there, were it not for a fact that there is another divergent tradition, attested at least as early as the late-tenth / early-eleventh-century works of Vāgīśvarakīrti, contemporary or slightly earlier than Abhaya. This alternative tradition, exemplified in ritual structures 5 through 11 (like the first four, these sources are not numbered in any particular order), does not feature a separate *vidyāvratadānavidhi* but essentially collapses any distinction between it and the rite of the wisdom-gnosis initiation: an odd choice, seemingly, given the clear attestation of the *vrata* in the *Uttaratantra* (but perhaps not so odd, given the lack of clarity concerning the distinction between it and the initiation evident in Vitapāda). The most common ritual structure among these authors is that found in Vāgīśvarakīrti's *Saṃkṣiptābhiṣekavidhi* (appendix A, 5), itself an influential articulation of the ritual protocols of the Guhyasamāja. His wisdom-gnosis initiation rite begins just the way Vitapāda begins his: with the joining of hands that in the *Uttaratantra* marks the beginning of the *vidyāvrata*. Vāgīśvara follows this with the *dhāraṇī* verse with which Abhaya begins his wisdom-gnosis initiation. Then follow liturgical elements V and VI, *nānyopāya* and *vidyāvrata*, concluding finally with the elaborate call and response (element VII) found in Vitapāda's wisdom-gnosis initiation, and which comprehends the more extensive rite of consuming impure substances, abbreviated by Abhaya to only the concluding verse about the lotus (i.e., *not* including consumption of other impure substances).

This structure, III–I–V–VI–VII, is found in sources 6 through 8: Advayavajra's *Saṃkṣiptābhiṣekaprakriyā*, Kṛṣṇācārya's *Guhyasamājamaṇḍalopāyikā*, and Kuladatta's *Kriyāsaṃgrahapañjikā*. Kumāracandra's *Ratnāvalī* commentary on the *Kṛṣṇayamāri Tantra* (which, it is worth bearing in mind, is heterogeneous, insofar as it is *not* a Guhyasamāja text) includes the witnessing element (IV) after the initial joining of the hands, conforming to the *Uttaratantra* and the Abhaya/Darpaṇa rites (but *not* Vitapāda). Two further outliers are the rites of the two Prajñā-s, Gupta and Śrī, with both omitting the "giveaway" *vidyāvrata* verse (VI), the former abbreviating the *nānyopāya* element (V) and the latter omitting it altogether.

The *sākṣin* element (IV) is conspicuously absent from the sources in this second initiatory tradition. Only the (heterogeneous) Yamāri text includes it. Its total omission is a little odd, and yet its inclusion in the initiation (rather than *vidyāvrata*) by Kumāracandra makes some sense. Depending on how one construes the text, there is a case that it fits better in the *prajñājñānābhiṣeka*. For the phrase *samarpiteyam asmai mayā*, rendered above as "she is made over by me to him," might just as well be understood as "she is restored to him by me," since she was first given by the student to the teacher in the context of the preceding secret initiation. So, it would be natural for the teacher to indicate formally his returning her to the student in the rite wherein those two are ritually united. On the other hand, it might equally be construed as essential to evoking the quasi-*vaivāha*, or marital, character of the *vidyāvrata*, insofar as *pāṇigrahana* is a stock element of South Asian marriage rites—a character accentuated perhaps by the rite of "calling to witness" insofar as Agni is called to witness in some versions of the *vivāha*. Interestingly, contemporary Newar initiatory practice, presumably due to the influence of Kuladatta's *Kriyāsaṃgrahapañjikā*, conforms to "tradition 2" and Vitapāda, insofar as it lacks a separate *vidyāvratadānavidhi* and features a wisdom-gnosis initiation in which the married partners' hands are placed together.

The omission of the line about the nondual nature of reality from *every* source except the *Uttaratantra* and Vitapāda is likewise a bit odd conceptually, given that it might seem especially suitable in the context of the wisdom-gnosis initiation (in the form it takes in "tradition 2"), insofar as this rite aims to give a foretaste of the view of reality (*tattvadṛṣṭi*). Abhaya's latter-day "tradition 1" liturgy conforms in this regard to the other, later sources of "tradition 2," omitting any explicit reference here to nonduality.

At this point in the paper I would ideally offer a learned and innovative hypothesis to account for the divergences I have so diligently documented for you in the foregoing. Unfortunately, I am not sure that at the present state of my research I can offer much in that regard. One possibility I entertained briefly early on in my explorations is that the lack of a separate *vidyāvratadānavidhi* might correspond to that (or those) sub-traditions that do not bestow a fourth initiation. As can be seen from appendix A, however, where those works that include a fourth initiation are marked with an asterisk (*) after their number, there is no apparent correlation between the variants between the two "traditions." The early testimony of the *Uttaratantra* (at least as unpacked by Jñānapāda authors like Dīpaṃkāra and Vitapāda [3 and 4]) does not feature a fourth initiation but nonetheless sets the *vidyāvrata* apart as a distinct rite. Among those that do not so distinguish, contrary to this hypothesis, most do in fact accept a fourth, the one outlier among Guhyasamāja authors being Kṛṣṇācārya, whose ritual ends with the hybrid wisdom-gnosis/*vidyāvrata* rite.

I will, however, essay one possible interpretation of what took place when Abhaya formulated his rite. His ritual structure may be said to be "conservative" in that it separates the initiation and the consort observance, according thereby both with the *Uttaratantra* and with the other authors in tradition 1. Abhaya innovates, however, in a number of other ways. For one, he creatively formulates a trio of observance-bestowing rites (*vratadānavidhi*) that occupy the place of the *vidyāvrata* rite: these being the *vidyāvrata*, *vajravrata*, and *caryāvrata-dānavidhi*s. To do so, he had to relocate the *vajravrata*, a virtually universal esoteric rite in which the student is commanded to wield the vajra just like Vajrasattva. In the received tradition, as found in the tradition 2 works, this rite occurs in conjunction with the earlier master initiation (*ācāryābhiṣeka*), with which it has a conceptual connection, insofar as one must bear the vajra to serve as an *ācārya/purohita* for clients. Abhaya discerned, I speculate, some conceptual coherence between this and the *vidyāvrata*, insofar as both entail the constant possession of an object, a vajra and a consort, respectively. Presumably due to the increasing prominence of the *caryāvrata*, or practice observance, in later Tantras, Abhaya added a further innovation—the *caryāvrata-dānavidhi*, with its transgressive, funereal accoutrements—to this pair. (In practice, the conceptual associations could have happened in either order, or simultaneously, to Abhaya; it is immaterial to my hypothesis.)

There is further evidence to suggest that Abhaya's innovations followed this ritual logic. Insofar as (a) the *vajravrata* typically occurred in a cluster of rites that came at the end of the older, esoteric ritual, including the prophecy (*vyākaraṇa*), permission (*anujñā*), and encouragement (*āśvāsa*), and (b) these rites, too, were moved to a position after the three *vratadānavidhi*s, one can see further evidence of a correlative conceptual sense behind Abhaya's thoroughgoing revision of the initiation rite, creating a new conceptual coherence out of the patchwork of inherited and gradually revised and resequenced rituals.

Ritual structures, it may be said, develop in part based upon inheritance (that is, prior practice), in part upon novel conceptual reformulation, and essentially through some expedient bricolage, synthesizing these two. In Abhaya's initiation ritual, then, one sees a conceptual reformulation of the entire initiation rite in which the *vidyāvrata* was restored to its early status as a separate rite, while simultaneously rectifying the awkward place of the *vajravrata*, *anujñā*, *āśvāsa*, and *vyākaraṇa* rites, which had been retained after the first (vase/*kalaśa*) initiation even after further, higher initiations were added. Having moved the initiation-concluding rites of *vajravrata*, *vyākaraṇa*, *anujñā*, and *āśvāsa* to a place at the conclusion of the new sequence of three (or four) initiations, and after the *vidyāvrata*, the *vidyāvrata* and the *vajravrata* became adjacent to one another in the new structure. It was an easy, further step, then, to add a special *dānavidhi* for the spectacular and preeminent rite of the *caryāvrata*, resulting in an elegant set of three such *dānavidhi*s, followed by the concluding trio of *vyākaraṇa*, *anujñā*, and *āśvāsa*. In the process, the integration of the higher three initiations with the earlier structure that had become designated by the corporate term "vase initiation" (*kalaśābhiṣeka*) was effected in a more elegant and conceptually coherent way than had previously been the case.

There are many curious features of these variants of ritual protocol that call for further reflection in light of a broader range of questions, but I think for now I will leave the issue here. The materials surveyed herein provide some tentative landmarks as research progresses on the fluid (re)formulations of esoteric rituals, as well as some insight into the specific processes of change and adaptation they underwent at the hands of their exponents. As is generally the case with questions worth exploring, "further research is a desideratum." As I look forward to further research in this (and other) area(s), I am ever grateful to Professor Kapstein for his warm collegiality, for his thoughtful support for me and other younger scholars, for his dedication to scholarship and its institutions, and for his superlative work, which stands as an inspiration for those of us laboring alongside him and an epitome to which we might aspire.

Appendix A: Ritual Structures

Asterisks (*) after the number indicate the source accepts a/the fourth initiation.

"Tradition 1": Vidyāvratadānavidhi Separate from Prajñājñānābhiṣeka

1*. Abhayākaragupta, *Vajrāvalī* (VĀ)

P/J initiation • fourth init. • *vidyāvratadānavidhi* • vajravrata- • caryāvrata- • vyākaraṇa/anujñā/āśvāsa

Prajñājñāna (P/J) initiation: I (dhāraṇī) • II (padma)

Vidyāvratadānavidhi: III (hasta) • IV (sākṣin) • V (nānyopaya) • VI (vidyāvrata)

1a*. Darpaṇācārya, *Kriyāsamuccaya* (As per VĀ, but abbreviated [based on / derived from VĀ])

P/J initiation: unique/idiosyncratic rite

Vidyāvratadānavidhi: III (hasta) • IV (sākṣin) • V (nānyopāya) • VI (vidyāvrata)

2. *Guhyasamāja Uttaratantra* [*Uttaratantra*, 124–27]

Initiations • *vidyāvrata* • samaya

Vidyāvrata: III (hasta) • IV (sākṣin) • V (nānyopāyena, incl. advaya) • VI (vidyāvrata)

3. Dīpaṃkarabhadra, *Guhyasamājamaṇḍalavidhi*

P/J initiation with separate *vidyāvrata*: explicit liturgy only includes: I (dhāraṇī)

4. Vitapāda, Commentary on Dīpaṃkarabhadra's *Maṇḍalavidhi* (Tōh. 1873)

P/J initiation followed immediately by *vidyāvrata*

P/J initiation: III (hasta) • VII (call/response)

Vidyāvrata: IV (sākṣin) • V (nānyopāya, incl. nondual line) • VI (vidyāvrata) [*Uttaratantra*, 124–27]

"Tradition 2": No Separate Vidyāvratadānavidhi

5*. Vāgīśvarakīrti, *Saṃkṣiptābhiṣekavidhi*
III (hasta) • I (dhāraṇī) • V (nānyopāya) • VI (vidyāvrata) • VII (call/response)

6*. Advayavajra, *Samkṣiptābhiṣekaprakriyā* (D 2244)
III (hasta) • I (dhāraṇī) • V (nānyopaya) • VI (vidyāvrata) • VII (call/response)

7. Kṛṣṇācārya, *Guhyasamājamaṇḍalopāyikā* (D 1819)
III (hasta) • I (dhāraṇī) • V (nānyopāya) • VI (vidyāvrata) • VII (call/resp.; no *kuru padme*)

8*. Kuladatta, *Kriyāsaṃgrahapañjikā*
III (hasta UT 124) • I (dhāraṇī) • V (nānyopāya) • VI (vidyāvrata) • VII (call/response)

9. Kumāracandra, *Ratnāvalī* commentary on *Kṛṣṇāyamāri Tantra*
III (hasta) • IV (sākṣin) • I (dhāraṇī) • V (nānyopaya) • VI (vidyāvrata)

10*. Prajñāśrī, *Abhiṣekavidhi* (D 1269)
III (hasta) • I (dhāraṇī) • VII (call/response)

11*. Prajñāgupta, *Abhiṣekaratnāloka* (D 1333)
III (hasta) • I (dhāraṇī) • Vab (nānyopāya) • VII (call/response)

Appendix B: Liturgical/Ritual Elements (Rites)

I. *Dhāraṇī* verse	
iyaṃ te dhāraṇī ramyā sevyā buddhaiḥ prakalpitā | cakrakramaprayogeṇa samāsvādaya satsukham ||	This your dhāraṇī-woman is to be delighted [and] served; [she is] appointed by all the buddhas. By the procedure of the sequence of wheels, taste the true bliss.

II. *Padma* verse	
aho madīyaṃ [yaṃ] padmaṃ sarvasukhasamanvitam | yaḥ sevayati vidhānena tasyāham agrataḥ sthitā ||	O! My lotus is endowed with all bliss. I stand before the one who serves [it] properly.

kuru padme yathākāryaṃ sambuddhārādhanādikam || svayaṃ mahāsukho rājā atraiva hi sadā sthitaḥ || bha[ñ]ja mokṣa hoḥ |	Do in the lotus what is to be done—adoration of all the buddhas and so on. The king of great bliss itself [is] always situated here.

III. *Hasta* element [joining of hands] [cf. *Uttaratantra* 125ab]	
tadanantaraṃ tasyāḥ prajñāyāḥ pāṇiṃ śiṣyapānau dattvā taddvayaṃ svavāmakareṇa dhṛtvā savajrasvyakaraṃ śiṣyaśirasi dattvā	Immediately thereafter, putting that wisdom-woman's hand in the hand of the student, and holding both with one's own left hand, place one's right hand with the vajra on the student's head.

IV. *Sākṣin* element [calling buddhas to witness]	
sākṣiṇo yūyam atra samarpiteyam asmai mayā || iti tathāgatān sākṣīkṛtya	Call the tathāgatas to witness, [saying,] "You are witnesses here: she is made over by me to him."

V. *Nānyopāya* verse [cf. *Uttaratantra* 125cd and 126]	
nānyopāyena buddhatvaṃ śuddhaṃ cedaṃ jagattrayam | [advayaḥ sarvadharmās tu dvayabhāvena lakṣitaḥ |] tasmād viyogam anayā mā kārṣīs tvaṃ kadācana ||	There is no other means for pure buddhahood in this triple world. [All things are nondual but characterized by dualities.] Hence, don't separate from her ever!

VI. *Vidyāvrata* verse [*Uttaratantra* 127]	
idaṃ tat sarvabuddhānāṃ *vidyāvratam* anuttaram | atikrāmati yo mūḍhaḥ siddhis tasya na cottamā ||	This is the *vidyāvrata* of all the buddhas, unexcelled. That fool who transgresses this [will] not have the highest success.

VII. Call-and-response element [querying śiṣya's nondual yogic chutzpah]	
kiṃ utsahase vatsa viṅmūtrādibhakṣaṇaṃ | raktaṃ śukraṃ tathā māṃsaṃ strīṇāṃ bhaktiṃ paraṃ | cumbanaṃ bhagapadmasya brūhi vatsa yathāsukham ||	Can you handle eating feces, urine, and the like, my dear? Blood? Semen? Meat, too? The supreme devotion to women—kissing the vaginal lotus? Speak, my dear, as you please.

kiṃ cāhaṃ notsāhe devi viṭśukrādibhakṣaṇam | kārya bhaktiḥ sadā strīṇāṃ cumbanaṃ bhagam eva ca ||	How, goddess, could I not bear eating feces, semen, and so on? The devotion to women is to be done always—even kissing the vagina.
[= II. padma verse] aho madīyaṃ [yaṃ] padmaṃ sarva- sukhasamanvitam | yaḥ sevati vidhānena tasyāham agrataḥ sthitā || kuru padme yathā kārya saṃbuddhārādhanādikaṃ | svayaṃ mahāsukho rājā atraiva hi sadā sthitaḥ ||	O! My lotus is endowed with all bliss! I stand before him who serves it properly. Do in the lotus as is to be done— adoration of buddhas and so on. The king of great bliss himself stands right here always.

Work Cited

Bahulkar, S. S., ed. 2010. *Śrīguhyasamājamaṇḍalavidhiḥ of Ācārya Dīpaṃkarabhadra*. Sarnath: Central University of Tibetan Studies.

Brahmayāmala/Picumata. Unpublished manuscript in Nepal National Archives, NAK 3-370, NGMPP A42/2; palm leaf; Newari script; 1052 CE.

Matsunaga, Yukei. 1978. *The Guhyasamāja Tantra*. Osaka: Toho Shuppan.

Mori, Masahide. 2009. *Vajrāvalī of Abhayākaragupta: Edition of Sanskrit and Tibetan Versions*, vol. 2. Tring, UK: The Institute of Buddhist Studies.

Moriguchi, Mitsutoshi. 1990. "Ācāriyakriyāsamuccaya Kanjō(bon) Tekisuto to Wayaku (II-1)." In *Shūkyō to Bunka: Saito Akitoshi Kyōju Kanrekikinen Ronbunshū*, edited by Saitō Akitoshi Kyōju Kanrekikinenronbunshū Kankōkai, 876–44. Tokyo: Ko-bianshobō.

———. 1991. "Ācāriyakriyāsamuccaya Kanjō(bon) Tekisuto to Wayaku (I-1)." In *Ju Butsu Dō Sankyō Shisō Ronkō: Makio Ryōkai Hakase Kiju Kinen*, edited by Makio Ryōkai Hakase Kijukinen Ronshū Kankōkai, 107–33. Tokyo: Sankibō Busshorin.

———. 1992. "Ācāriyakriyāsamuccaya Kanjō(bon) Tekisuto to Wayaku (I-2): Ryakujutsukyō 'Hosshikishidai' Kaigi." *Chisan Gakuhō* 41: 1–31.

Rinpoche, Samdhong, and Vrajvallabh Dwivedi, eds. 1992. *Kṛṣṇayamāritantram with Ratnāvalī Pañjikā of Kumāracandra*. Sarnath: Central Institute of Higher Tibetan Studies.

Sakurai, Munenobu. 1996. *Indo Mikkyō Girei Kenkyū: Kōki Indo Mikkyō no Kanjō Shidai*. Kyoto: Hōzōkan.

Wedemeyer, Christian K. 2011 [2012]. "Locating Tantric Antinomianism: An Essay toward an Intellectual History of the 'Practices/Practice Observance' (*caryā/caryāvrata*)," *Journal of the International Association of Buddhist Studies* 34.1–2: 349–419.

The Base of the Natural State according to the *Gter snying rin po che spungs pa'i rgyud* of the Spyi ti Yoga Tradition

Jean-Luc Achard (CRNS, CRACO)

Introduction

The base (*gzhi*) of the natural state of the individual is probably the theme most central to Dzogchen literature. It is also among the topics that have given rise to the most misconceptions, among both indigenous Tibetan authors and Westerners. These misconceptions revolve around the notion of *kun gzhi*, or universal base. In Tibetan Buddhist literature more generally, *kun gzhi* is simply shorthand for *kun gzhi rnam shes* (Skt. *ālayavijñāna*), the store consciousness in which karmic impregnations are stockpiled. But in Dzogchen literature, it becomes the universal base of both saṃsāra and nirvāṇa, sometimes described in positive terms as akin to the absolute body. Due to philological misinterpretation, some individuals apprehend *kun gzhi* as merely the store consciousness,[1] but Dzogchen literature clearly distinguishes *kun gzhi* (as the store consciousness) from the absolute body.

Several Dzogchen tantras are dedicated to this distinction, and one finds passages on the subject in Longchenpa's *Theg mchog mdzod* (1:14) and *Tshig don mdzod* (chap. 4). Misconceptions by Westerners tend to relate to the idea of a cosmic consciousness, "the base of all," which, when taken literally, is interpreted as a single ocean-like cosmic consciousness into which all individual consciousnessesses will eventually merge. Such a conception has nothing to do with any Buddhist idea, much less any Dzogchen conception.[2]

This essential notion of base is of course the first element of the famed triad of base, path, and fruit, in which the *base* refers to the true nature of the mind expressed according to the three wisdoms (see below), while the *path* stands for the core teachings of the view, meditation, and conduct. The *fruit* refers to

1. See the relevant discussion in Karmay 1988, 181–84.

2. See on this subject Achard 2010, 19n14.

the full measure of enlightenment expressed in terms of its bodies (*sku*), wisdoms (*ye shes*), and activities (*phrin las*).

The Base According to the Classical Man ngag sde Literature

Since the topic of the base is frequently discussed in the texts of the precepts series (*man ngag sde*), several ways of explaining it have developed. The most common approach consists in defining it according to its three wisdoms, namely its essence (*ngo bo*), its nature (*rang bzhin*), and its compassion (*thugs rje*).[3] On this subject, the *Rig pa rang shar gyi rgyud* (529) says:

> Before I even existed,
> the base was abiding in the following way:
> this base, called the great primordial purity,
> abided in the triple mode of essence, nature, and compassion;
> the immutable wisdom of its essence
> was called "the abiding mode of the youthful vase body,"
> unceasingly blazing.

This abstract is replete with philological information. The "I" who utters these lines is none other than Vajradhara, the emanation of Samantabhadra at the level of the *saṃbhogakāya*. What he describes is the base, or original state, of the mind before the unfolding epiphany (*gzhi snang*) of the base in various sounds, lights, and rays.[4] This state is called a *base* in the sense of a potential that is likely to manifest as a base of delusion (*'khrul gzhi*) or as a base of liberation (*grol gzhi*), depending on one's realization of the nature of its epiphany. In this sense, the base is expressed in terms of emptiness (*stong*) and clarity (*gsal*)—that is, in typical Dzogchen lexicon, primordial purity (*ka dag*) and spontaneity (*lhun grub*).

The notion of the great primordial purity (*ka dag chen po*), which is introduced as qualifying the base in particular, is meant to highlight the base's expression in terms of its three wisdoms. In other words, this great primordial purity is the actual sum of these wisdoms and their undivided expression. The essence of this state is defined as immutable precisely because it is empty and therefore primordially pure. If it were not pure from the beginning, it could

3. On these, see Deroche and Yasuda 2015, passim.

4. On this epiphany, see Achard 2016.

be tainted by stains and would lose its original purity. Therefore it is styled as immutable, not alterable by anything.[5]

The next crucial representation mentioned in the above abstract is that of the youthful vase body. I have already discussed it elsewhere,[6] but it might be helpful to clarify it again, despite its nearly total absence in the Spyi ti corpus of tantras.[7] Lopön Tenzin Namdak Rinpoche explains: "It is a *body* (*sku*) because it encapsulates a state which is that of the mind. It is a *vase* (*bum*) because it contains its own natural dynamism (*rang rtsal*); the dynamism is not expressed outwardly, since this vase is fastened with a seal (*rgya*) until it is broken by a spontaneous wind (*rlung*). It is *youthful* (*gzhon nu*) because it stands before time and does not know the aging due to passions."[8] A similar explanation is given in the oral transmission accompanying the *Spros bral don gsal*, the root tantra of the Yang ti category discovered by Gu ru Chos dbang (1212–70). In a sense, this youthful vase body illustrates the inner clarity (*nang gsal*) of the mind prior to the epiphany of the base. In this condition, mind is not static, as one may wrongly imagine; its natural luminosity is simply displayed inwardly, in a mode in which its natural dynamism remains as potential.

The explanation of the primordially pure original base (*ka dag gi ye gzhi*) fundamentally amounts to explaining awareness (*rig pa*), the knowledge of the natural state of the mind. This state is clearly equated with self-arisen wisdom (*rang byung ye shes*) in numerous tantras and exegetical works,[9] in which several other technical expressions are used as synonyms, for example:

- Primordially empty original absolute body (*ye stong thog ma'i chos sku*)
- Absolute truth of space (*dbyings don dam pa'i bden pa*)

5. Thus one should always keep in mind when encountering descriptions of the "essence of the base" in Dzogchen texts that (1) the absence of change or immutability and (2) the state of being empty and pure from the beginning are actually synonyms and can be used interchangeably.

6. Achard 1999, 158n3.

7. Its single appearance within the seventeen Spyi ti tantras of the *Rnying ma'i rgyud 'bum* is at the beginning of the *Dri med ka dag gi rgyud*. It is used to describe the state in which the Buddha 'Od mi 'gyur ba (the primordial Lord Samantabhadra) abides before he started to teach that tantra. This state is defined as the great primordial suchness (*ye ji bzhin pa chen po*), which is simply another way of describing the base before its epiphany. It is the same in the rest of the *man ngag sde* literature in which the state of the youthful vase body precisely refers to the base before its epiphany. The notion of youthful vase body is also present in the secret cycle (*gsang skor*) of the *mngag sde* tantras, for instance in the *Thig le kun gsal chen po'i rgyud* (see Karmay 1988, 185n57).

8. Private conversation with the author, Paris, 1996.

9. See Longchenpa, *Tshig don mdzod*, 170.

- Abiding mode of reality blazing with lights (*chos nyid 'od gsal ba'i gnas lugs*)[10]

The state that is thus referred to as the *base* is also defined as being beyond dualities such as saṃsāra and nirvāṇa, bliss and suffering, existence and non-existence, liberation and delusion, and awareness and ignorance. Basically, it is free from delusion, as is stated in the *Mu tig phreng ba* (460):

> In the primordial purity of the origin itself,
> There is nothing that can merely be said to be "delusion."
> Similarly, how can there be no delusion?
> For this reason, there is no delusion since the beginning.

According to the commentary on this tantra (170–71), there is a primordially pure state of the mind existing before the advent of realized buddhas and unrealized sentient beings. It is therefore a state totally devoid of ignorance (*ma rig pa*).[11] Within this primordial purity, the mere expression of "delusion" (*'khrul pa*) is never experienced, and therefore its formal verbalization does not even exist. It is thus also not through words that one reaches buddhahood.[12] The notion that delusion is completely alien to this state means that its essence is not fragmented and that it still abides as a primordial wisdom

10. Longchenpa, *Tshig don mdzod*, 170. Each of these expressions should be correctly understood as pointing to the base—the natural state of the mind. For instance, *ye stong* implies that it has never been soiled by anything whatsoever. *Thog ma* means that it abides as it is, before any fragmentation of the unity of the mind into various conditioned states of consciousness. *Chos sku* refers to its being the actual, abiding mode of the mind (*sems nyid*). In the second expression, *dbyings* refers to the primordial space, which is nothing other than the celestial nature of mind abiding in its original emptiness and endowed with its self-awareness (*rang rig*). *Don dam pa'i bden pa* simply means that it is not an ordinary space or relative dimension but the absolute, space-like expression of one's nature. Finally, in the third expression, *chos nyid* refers to the actual reality of the mind (that is, its primordial purity and its spontaneity). *'Od gsal ba* clearly demonstrates that this state is not affected by the darkness of ignorance but blazes with its own natural lights—the spontaneous expression of its dynamism. Finally, *gnas lugs* directly points to the fact that all the elements of this expression are not self-existing entities but are obviously related to the natural state of the mind.

11. It is de facto devoid of ignorance because the status of sentient beings is subsequent to the arising of ignorance at the time of the epiphany of the base. In this perspective, ignorance is perfectly justified as the first of the twelve links of interdependency.

12. This statement is certainly not a denial of theoretical knowledge and a rejection of the riches of the Dzogchen lexicon. However, in the perspective of the experience of buddhahood, words are corruptions, just as ignorance has become the queen of corruptions. It is buddhahood's inexpressibility that makes it not rely on words. This inexpressibility is a leitmotif throughout

(*ye shes*). Though one's present condition is characterized by delusion, one's essence has never been obscured by such delusion, precisely because wisdom can never experience delusion. It is naturally free from the latter. Owing to the special key points of Dzogchen, it is possible, through contemplating the vision of manifest reality (*chos nyid mngon sum*), to see this essence directly and, from then on, to avoid regressing into the three realms.[13]

The Base in the Practice Texts of Spyi ti Yoga

In the practice-oriented works of the Spyi ti category, teachings associated with the base are mostly found in the precepts dealing with the practice known as *cutting through rigidity* (*khregs chod*). There, instructions follow the standard approach of the *man ngag sde* literature and do not show peculiar traits that one could isolate as characteristics of the Spyi ti tradition. Rather, these teachings are fairly standard in terms of their vocabulary and objective. One such famous example is that of the instructions revealed by Spa ro Gter ston (sixteenth century), which have come down to us owing to their inclusion in the ninetieth volume of the *Rin chen gter mdzod*. In his *Spyi ti'i ka dag lhun grub kyi nyams len gnad du 'dus pa*, Padmasambhava is said to have declared (407–8):

> In brief, what is designated as the freedom of one's mind
> does not [undergo] passing from one state to the other:
> since [mind] is perfect [at the level of] the base, it is without fluctuations.
> It is not found through analysis and is without cause or characteristics.
> One cannot find in it any foundation or source, because it abides as emptiness and clarity;
> expressed as a natural clarity, mind itself
> is not meditated upon as being solid, but it increases as an awareness.[14]

Dzogchen literature, but such inexpressibility should not be considered a rejection of formal teachings.

13. Desire, form, and formless realms.

14. In other words, when one meditates on the true nature of the mind, one realizes that the latter is insubstantial and devoid of materiality. One thus comes closer to its authentic expression, which is that of awareness itself.

The five doorways [of the senses] are naturally relaxed and do not disperse outwardly.
All that arises becomes the display of reality,
and everything is then integrated into the absolute body.
By meditating thusly, the intensification
of experiences of discursiveness that arise
constitute the many displays of wisdom.
Mind, whose essence is free from concepts,
thus abides in the state of primordial purity.
These [instructions] form the practice of cutting through rigidity. Samaya!
Seal! Seal! Seal!

In the *Sgra thal 'gyur* commentary (2:714–15), the related instructions are described as focused on the liberation mode (*grol lugs*) of the mind or, in other words, what actually happens when the mind discovers and abides in its own nature. Thus the ultimate nature of the mind is defined as non-artificial in the sense of not being contrived by anything, despite the state of ignorance that characterizes ordinary deluded beings. Its "freedom" (*grol ba zhes bya*) refers to the fact that this state is *naturally free* (*rang grol*) because it is beyond antidotes (*gnyen po*). It is also defined as *primordially free* (*ye nas grol ba*) since there is no basis or need to re-enact the entire process of liberation (because of its being free from the beginning). It is furthermore already free since it is *established* (*bzhag pa*), or left exactly as it is, without corrections, transcending anything to accept or reject and so forth. It is also *thoroughly free* (*yongs su grol ba*) in the sense that it never experiences falling into extremes. Finally, it is *free through naked seeing* (*gcer mthong grol ba*)—through seeing it directly in its nakedness in its entire purity. All these various modalities of freedom justify why this state does not fluctuate from one condition to another.

As far as other practice-oriented texts of the Spyi ti tradition are concerned, I have not been able to identify any particular approach taken by the Spyi ti tradition in defining the base in the practice texts of the Bdud 'dul rdo rje and Klong gsal snying po collections of rediscovered teachings, but this needs more research.

The Chapter on the Base in the Gter snying rin po che spungs pa'i rgyud

In this section, I first present the transliteration of the second chapter of the *Gter snying rin po che spungs pa'i rgyud* followed by a lightly annotated translation. These are followed by a detailed commentary on this chapter based on the root text of the Spyi ti corpus.

The notion of *base* as described in this tantra is contained in its chapter 2. It is exceedingly short in all the versions at my disposal. The transliteration below follows the critical edition of the tantra:

> ||de nas shes rig rgyal po yis| |sngon thog spyi phud sangs rgyas la| |gzhi 'khrul rtsad gcod rtogs thabs gang | |zhes zhus pa dang | ston pas 'khor la bka' stsal pa| |gzhi ni ming ma thogs pa la| |dngos med ka dag blo las 'das| |dpe med tshig med tha snyad med| |lhun grub kun ldan gang yang med| |mi 'gyur kun gzhi phyogs med klong | |zhes gsungs so| |gter snying rin po che spungs pa'i rgyud las| gzhi bstan pa'i le'u ste gnyis pa'o||.[15]

This translates as follows:

> Then, the Lord of Knowing Awareness
> asked the buddha Primordial Sublimity:
> "What are the methods for investigating and realizing the base
> and delusion?"
>
> The revealer declared to his entourage:
> "The base to which no name can be applied
> is the unsubstantial primordial purity that transcends the
> intellect.
> It is without example, without words, and without designation.
> It is spontaneously accomplished, possesses all qualities, and is
> nothing (in particular).
> It is the impartial expanse of the immutable universal base."
>
> From the *Tantra of the Precious Heap Containing the Treasure Quintessence*, the second chapter, explaining the base.

Interestingly, some of the key conceptions in this chapter are actually discussed in some of the subsequent chapters of the tantra, although those explanations are not explicitly described as commentary. At best, they are textually connected clarifications deepening the correct understanding the reader should have of the technical terms associated with the base. Several other themes

15. See Achard 2013, 116.

are discussed in the remainder of the tantra, some of which are connected with the contents of the question that begins the chapter. Among these is the notion of delusion (*'khrul pa*), another crucial subject heavily discussed in Dzogchen literature.[16]

The chapter itself is structured as a dialogue in three main parts: (1) the introductory section containing the question formulated by the Lord of Knowing Awareness (Shes rig gi rgyal po), (2) the answer enunciated by the buddha Primordial Sublimity, and (3) the summary.

The Question of the Lord of Knowing Awareness

Lord Shes rig is a *saṃbhogakāya* manifestation of the buddha Sngon thog spyi phud. His name "knowing awareness" or "discerning awareness" (*shes rig*) underscores the nature of the mind as being naturally free from the ordinary mind's dualistic grasping. In the opening of this tantra, he is portrayed as an expression of the dynamic radiance (*rtsal zer*) of the Primordial Buddha, defined here as the buddha Sngon thog spyi phud.[17] As a *saṃbhogakāya* manifestation, Shes rig rgyal po is designated as a "lord" or "king" (*rgyal po*) because he reigns over all functions and capacities of the mind without being altered or stained by them, just like one's own awareness (*rang rig*) is experienced as abiding beyond the functions of the mind, unstained by discursiveness, and so forth.

As a *dharmakāya* manifestation, the buddha's name, Sngon thog spyi phud, is to be understood as follows. *Sngon thog* (Primordial)[18] refers to the primordial purity of the natural state (the emptiness aspect [*stong cha*] of this state), while the *spyi phud* (Sublimity)[19] points to the spontaneity (*lhun grub*, its clarity aspect [*gsal cha*]). The buddha himself therefore abides in the undifferentiated mode of emptiness and clarity (*stong gsal dbyer med*), the twofold

16. See chapter 3 of the tantra.

17. As shown in Achard 2013, 106n10, the technical term *rtsal zer* is quite widespread among the tantras of both Spyi ti and Yang ti. It seems that it is not to be found in the other tantras of the *man ngag sde* literature (including the *Rgyud bcu bdun*), nor in Longchenpa's works, so far as I can tell. I have suggested elsewhere (Achard 2013) that in the Yang ti tradition of Nyang ral Nyi ma 'od zer (1124–92), the expression *rtsal zer* can be related to the dynamic effulgence of the natural state expressed in what is technically known as the base's epiphany. The distinction between the base and its epiphany are crucial for understanding the explanation of the arising of delusion, which is the very subject of the inquiry formulated here by the Lord of Knowing Awareness.

18. Literally "prior" (*sngon*) and "former" (*thog*, for *thog ma*).

19. Literally "generic" (*spyi*) and "apex" (*phud*).

expression of the natural state. The entire tantra thus appears as an imaginary dialogue between the primordial state and its knowledge, personified by a *dharmakāya* buddha and his *saṃbhogakāya* emanation.

In this dialogue, Lord Shes rig asks the buddha Sngon thog spyi phud about the methods one can use to investigate the base of the natural state and the delusion that arises if one fails to realize the nature of this base. Hence, delusion is understood as a consequence of ignorance, which is itself the incapacity to recognize the nature of the base's epiphany. Therefore, Shes rig rgyal po asks for instructions about yogic or meditative techniques that can enable one to realize one's own natural state and to therefore destroy delusion. In a certain sense, this is the object of Buddhist teachings in their entirety.

The Answer of the Buddha

We can divide the five-line answer of the primordial buddha into three parts. The first three lines refer to the essence of the base, the fourth line refers to its nature, and the fifth line explains its function (*rnam pa*), compassion. Clearly, the thematic answer of the Buddha is consistent with the presentation of the three wisdoms—essence, nature, and compassion. These are generally associated with the absolute body, but here they are explicitly connected with the abiding mode of the natural state.

The answer of the buddha starts by addressing the essence of the base:

> The base to which no name can be applied . . .

Designating as *base* a state to which no name can be applied amounts to labeling a state that (1) precedes any designation elaborated by the mind (precisely because it is itself the very essence of that mind), and (2) does not depend on any designation whatsoever. This base that precedes all labels is actually the natural state that has abided from primordial time (*thog ma'i dus*).[20] It is a condition of the mind that "existed" before (*sngon rol*) any differentiation[21] and before any name that the ordinary mind projected over its own essence. As stated in the *Nyi zla snying po* (705):

> Its depth and immensity are liberated from the objects of the intellect;

20. See *Nyi zla snying po*, 705.

21. This condition beyond differentiations clearly points to its abiding mode as the single *thig le* (*thig le nyag gcig*), a central conception of Dzogchen, on which see Karmay 1988, 118.

> it is unborn and transcends illustrations, verbalizations, and conceptions.[22]

The central idea behind the expression "not applying any name" (*ming ma thogs*) to the base is obviously that of the ineffability of a state that is itself beyond characterization. However, communicating the knowledge of this state during direct introduction (*ngo sprod*), for instance, demands the use of words conceived as pointers or indicators of a meaning that, in all evidence, transcends them.

The second line continues:

> . . . is the unsubstantial primordial purity that transcends the intellect.

In chapter 5 of the tantra, the buddha declares that the base is devoid of substantiality and abides in primordially purity. He does not explain why this is so, but the notion of insubstantiality (*dngos med*) is applied to the base because the latter is totally free from material characteristics (*mtshan ma*).[23] This insubstantiality also implies that it is not limited by material constraints; it abides in a state defined as "transparent" (*zang thal*). This transparent condition guarantees that nothing can actually affect the base itself, just as a mirror is not soiled by any reflections that may appear on its surface. The classical designation for such a pristine condition is that of *primordial purity*. This state of primordial purity is not an object of the intellect because, within its infinite scope, thoughts arise and vanish by themselves (*rang yal*) without any traces (*rjes med*), therefore never affecting its unsoiled expression.[24] This pure transparency experienced during realization is an inner condition known as "the contemplation of the buddhas" (*sangs rgyas kyi dgongs pa*), which is precisely described in the *Nyi zla snying po* as "transcending the intellect" (*blo 'das*) and as being free from intention (*rtsis gdab med pa*).[25]

In conclusion, the third line says:

22. *Nyi zla snying po*, 705. The very same kind of explanations appears in the *Snang srid kha sbyor*, 174.

23. For instance, in Vimalamitra, *Seng ge rtsal rdzogs* (e.g., 261 and 267).

24. See also Longchenpa's *Zab mo bcud bsdus*, 287.

25. *Nyi zla snying po*, 706. This is a very good reason explaining why *dgongs pa* cannot be rendered as "intention" (and certainly not "intentionality"). See the discussion of this term here: http://www.wikidz.artremy.com/wiki/Contemplation.

> It is without example, without words, and without designation.

This line clearly echoes a verse from the *Rig pa rang shar* tantra where the originally pure nature of the absolute body is described as "without example, without illustrative (words), it cannot be explained."[26] The three terms—example, words, and designation—are evidently related to one another and basically refer to the inexpressible abiding mode of the base. A brief analysis of each of these terms will demonstrate that they follow a sequential scheme:

- The essence of the base is conceived as impossible to illustrate through any example simply because it stands beyond any description or comparison.
- Being impossible to describe, it cannot be defined either with specific words, because its original abiding mode is not something that one can define as "this is it" (*'di yin*) or "this is not it" (*'di min*).
- Consequently, designations cannot be applied to it to explain or label it correctly, though diachronic language can still point to it indirectly.

In summary, the essence of the base is described, as in chapter 5 of the tantra, in terms of a primordial radiance (*ye gdangs*)—or a profound clarity (*gting gsal*)—which, despite the baroque lexicon of Dzogchen, simply stands beyond any terminology.

To present the *nature of the base* described by the Buddha, the fourth line reads as follows:

> It is spontaneously accomplished, possesses all (qualities), and
> is nothing (in particular).

Here again, three aspects are put forward: spontaneity (*lhun grub*), naturally possessing all (*kun ldan*) liberating qualities, and being nothing whatsoever (*gang yang med*). They clearly derive from the inexpressible essence of the base described above.

Spontaneous accomplishment is the classical definition of the nature of the primordial state. It implies that the latter is not produced from a cause or because of specific conditions but that it abides as *already* accomplished as it is, in utter spontaneity. This spontaneous nature expresses itself in the display of the fivefold lights of awareness.

The fact that the base is—again—*already* endowed with all the qualities of the natural state implies that it does not need anything to abide in its own

26. Vimalamitra, *Rig pa rang shar gyi rgyud*, 661.

pristine perfection. In other words, it is already perfect as it is, in its twofold mode of emptiness and clarity.

The last aspect related to the nature of the base, its being nothing in particular, points again to its inexpressible essence. Indeed, were the base something specific, it would be endowed with distinctive, conditioned characteristics and would therefore be conditioned. Since, this is not the case by definition, then tautologically, the natural state of the base cannot be anything in particular—or anything except a luminous, empty quintessence. This expression occurs in multiple contexts in the Great Perfection tradition, such as "transcending existence and nonexistence, eternalism and nihilism" (*yod med rtag chad las 'das pa*), implying that nothing can be asserted about it (*khas len gang yang med*). We are thus returned to the inexpressible essence of the base.

Eventually, in the last line of the response, the buddha defines the compassion of the base:

> It is the impartial expanse of the immutable universal base.

Compassion (*thugs rje*) in Dzogchen texts is generally defined as all-embracing and unceasing, as well as abiding in discerning (*rig*) or ignorant (*ma rig*) modes. It abides in a discerning mode (*rig tshul*) if one recognizes the nature of the epiphany of the base and in an ignorant mode (*ma rig tshul*) if one lacks such recognition. In the present context, the buddha describes the true feature (*rnam pa*) of the base and, as specialists in the field know, *feature* and *compassion* are interchangeable terms within the scheme of the three wisdoms of Dzogchen. The present line enumerates three central aspects that characterize this feature: its total absence of partiality, its immutability, and its abiding as a vast, infinite expanse.

The base itself—and therefore its compassion—is defined as devoid of partiality because it abides in a mode of wisdom (*ye shes*) that naturally performs activities impartially.[27]

The base is also conceived as being immutable, since it does not depend on the conceptions of past, present, and future. Its immutable aspect furthermore relies on the fact that it abides as the all-embracing wisdom of the emanation body, which is linked to compassion in the scheme of the three wisdoms.[28]

Finally, this compassion does not exist by itself but as a modality of the natural state of the individual. It displays itself within the infinite expanse of the

27. This is actually the definition used by Longchenpa in his *Tshig don mdzod* (226–27) that explains the function of compassion. See Achard 1999, 119–20.

28. On this, see Longchenpa, *Theg mchog mdzod*, 1:563.

base, in which its twofold features (impartiality and immutability) express themselves in an unceasing mode.

Thus, despite any explicit mention of compassion and its otherwise usual features as described in Dzogchen texts, we see that the lexicon used by the buddha Primordial Sublimity maintains the interpretation of this last line within the actual scope of compassion itself, thus completing the traditional definition of the base as the "threefold pile of wisdom" (*ye shes sum brtsegs*).

The Summary

> From the *Tantra of the Precious Heap Containing the Treasure Quintessence*, this has been the second chapter, explaining the base.

In most *man ngag sde* exegetical literature, the closing repetition of the tantra's title followed by the chapter title is described as a "summary" (*mdor bsdus*) or as an "abridged explanation" (*mdor bstan pa*). This is conceived as a synthesis that encapsulates the entire contents of a chapter, highlighting its actual theme(s) as well as its doxographical affiliation.

Conclusion

There is an obvious doctrinal harmony among the various abstracts and specific chapters of the Spyi ti tantras dedicated to explicating the base. This is probably because most of these rely heavily on the *Snang srid kha sbyor* corpus that is composed of a root tantra and its suite (*phyi ma*). This coherence is also certainly because the revelation of these texts is the discovery of a single *gter ston* (Snye mo zhu yas). As far as I have been able to determine, there are no other discoverers of Spyi ti tantras.[29]

The central conception associated with the base in these tantras is that of primordial purity, which includes such notions as being unborn (*skye ba med pa*), empty (*stong pa*), and so forth. As we have seen, the topic of spontaneity (*lhun grub*) is not absent from explanations related to the base, whose overall definition therefore obviously fits perfectly with the way it is defined in the *man ngag sde* literature. It is thus consistent with the other subdivisions of this doxographical category. By investigating the chapter of the *Gter snying rin po che'i rgyud* translated in this paper, we have seen that the definition of *base* in Spyi ti literature is not limited to the notion of primordial purity, as

29. I limit this statement to tantras (*rgyud*) properly speaking, not to Spyi ti cycles that are practice oriented.

is often thought, but that it complies with the orthodox definition given by Longchenpa in his *Theg mchog mdzod*: emptiness *cum* clarity. In some of his works, such as in the *Tshig don mdzod*, Longchenpa discusses seven mistaken or partial approaches to the base, known as the "seven affirmations about the base" (*gzhi'i 'dod lugs bdun*). There, he concludes that the definition of the base as primordial purity is the sole acceptable definition, whereas in his *Theg mchog mdzod*, he revises his position and affirms that the only correct definition is that which expresses the base as being primordially pure *and* spontaneously accomplished. As shown in the chapter translated here, both primordial purity and spontaneity are central conceptions defining the actual abiding mode of the base, and in this perspective, one cannot but conclude that the Spyi ti tradition aligns with the rest of the *man ngag sde* tradition.

Works Cited

Achard, Jean-Luc. 1999. *L'Essence Perlée du Secret*. Brepols.

———. 2010. *The Precepts in Eight Chapters*. Naldjor Institute.

———. 2013. "Le Tantra du Précieux Amoncellement exprimant la Quintessence des Trésors—analyse thématique & édition critique." *Revue d'Etudes Tibétaines* 27: 103–25.

———. 2016. *Le Mode d'Emergence du Réel*. Sumène: Editions Khyung-Lung.

Deroche, Marc-Henri, and Yasuda, Akinori. 2015. "The *rDzogs chen* Doctrine of the Three Gnoses (*ye shes gsum*): An Analysis of Klong chen pa's Exegesis and His Sources." *Revue d'Etudes Tibétaines* 33: 187–230.

Dri med ka dag gi rgyud. Snga 'gyur rgyud 'bum phyogs bsgrigs, 3:623–38. Beijing: Mi rigs dpe skrun khang, 2009.

Gu ru Chos dbang (1212–70). *Spros bral don gsal: Spros bral don gsal chen po'i rgyud. Snga 'gyur rgyud 'bum phyogs bsgrigs*, 1:1–272. Beijing: Mi rigs dpe skrun khang, 2009.

Karmay, Samten G. 1988. *The Great Perfection*. Leiden: Brill.

Longchenpa (1308–64). *Theg mchog mdzod.* In *Klong chen mdzod bdun*, vols. *ga–nga*. Gangtok, Sikkim: Khentse Labrang, 1983.

———. *Tshig don mdzod.* In *Klong chen mdzod bdun*, vol. *ca*, pp. 155–519. Gangtok, Sikkim: Khyentse Labrang, 1983.

———. *Zab mo bcud bsdus.* In *Zab mo yang tig*, 1:285–88. Delhi: T. Tsewang, 1975.

Nyi zla'i snying po'i rgyud. Snga 'gyur rgyud 'bum phyogs bsgrigs, 3:639–718. Beijing: Mi rigs dpe skrun khang , 2009.

Rnying ma'i rgyud 'bum, 36 volumes. Gting skyes edition. Thimphu: Dingo Khyentse Rinpoche, 1975.

Rnying ma'i rgyud 'bum, 46 volumes. Unpublished Gangteng "b" manuscript.

Snga 'gyur rgyud 'bum phyogs bsgrigs, 58 volumes. Beijing: Mi rigs dpe skrun khang, 2009.

Spa gro gter ston (sixteenth cent.). *Spyi ti'i ka dag lhun grub kyi nyams len gnad du 'dus pa. Rin chen gter mdzod*, 90:405–10. Paro: Dingo Khyentse Rinpoche, 1976.

Thig le kun gsal chen po'i rgyud: Rin po che spyi gnad skyon sel thig le kun gsal gyi rgyud, Rnying ma'i rgyud 'bum, Mtshams brag, 10:614–24. Thimphu: National Library of Bhutan.

Vimalamitra (eighth cent.). *Rnying ma'i rgyud bcu bdun* [Seventeen Tantras]. New Delhi: Sanje Dorje, 1989.

———. *Mu tig phreng ba*, 2:417–537.

———. *Rig pa rang shar gyi rgyud*, 1:389–855.

———. *Seng ge rtsal rdzogs chen po'i rgyud*, 2:245–415.

———. *Sgra thal 'gyur*, 1:1–205.

———. *Mu tig phreng ba* commentary: *Rdzogs pa chen po mu tig phreng rgyud gsal byed. Bka' ma shin tu rgyas pa*, vol. 112. Chengdu: Kaḥ thog mkhan po 'jam dbyangs, 1999.

———. *Sgra thal 'gyur* commentary: *Paṇ chen dri med bshes gnyen gyi dgongs nyams sgron ma snang byed 'bar ba'i gsang rgyud*, 2 vols. *Bka' ma shin tu rgyas pa*, vols. 110–11. Chengdu: Kaḥ thog mkhan po 'jam dbyangs, 1999.

A Brief Analysis of Jonang Choklé Namgyal's *Pointing-Out Instruction on the Foundation, Path, and Fruit*

Klaus-Dieter Mathes

THE HONOREE OF THIS volume, among his many other accomplishments, opened up what is still a comparatively new field of Tibetology, namely Jonang studies, by making available in 1992, for the first time, the entire works of Dölpopa Sherab Gyaltsen (Dol po pa Shes rab rgyal mtshan), and this was followed by a number of groundbreaking articles and conference papers on the subject. My own research in this and other areas of common interest has profited considerably from a continuous exchange of ideas with Matthew. I thus offer here a contribution on Choklé Namgyal (Phyogs las rnam rgyal), one of Dölpopa's heart disciples, by way of felicitating a good and long-time friend.

Jonang Choklé Namgyal (1306–86),[1] a.k.a. Mnga' ris Chos kyi rgyal po, started his scholarly career by strongly advocating a *rang stong*[2] view, reflecting his education at the monasteries of Sa skya and Brag ram. In 1333 he met Dölpopa Sherab Gyaltsan (1292–1361) at Jonang and was immediately impressed by this charismatic teacher's interpretation of Buddhist philosophy. Having received from him a Kālacakra empowerment and teachings on the *Vimalaprabhā*, Choklé Namgyal furthered his Kālacakra studies under Dölpopa's disciples Kun spangs Chos grags dpal bzang (ca. 1283–ca. 1376) and Sa bzang Ma ti Paṇ chen Blo gros rgyal mtshan (1294–1376).[3] In 1354 he succeeded Bla ma Lo tsā ba Blo gros dpal (1299–1354) on the Jonang abbatial throne[4] and became one of Dölpopa's most important interpreters of Kālacakra and *gzhan stong*.[5]

1. Not to be confounded with the famous Bo dong Phyog las rnam rgyal (1376–1451).

2. The mode of emptiness according to which everything lacks an own nature.

3. Stearns 2008.

4. Van der Kuijp 2016, 124.

5. The validity of *rang stong* being restricted to the level of relative truth, the ultimate is only

Within the Collection of Jonang Texts (*Jo nang dpe tshogs*)—that is, the Jonang material presently available—the works of Choklé Namgyal are found in volumes 21 and 22. Volume 21 contains our text of interest, the *Pointing-Out Instruction on the Foundation, Path, and Fruit* (*Gzhi lam 'bras bu'i ngo sprod*), which is a systematic *gzhan stong* presentation of the Buddhist doctrine. It is based not only on the Tathāgatagarbha Sūtras and the Maitreya works, but also on tantric literature, most particularly the *Laghukālacakratantra* and its commentary, the *Vimalaprabhā*. Volume 22 contains a work on buddha nature, namely the *Conqueror of Delusion: An Ornament of Buddha Nature* (*Bde gshegs snying po'i rgyan gyi 'khrul 'joms*), and seven texts on the preliminary practices and the six yogas of Kālacakra. Apart from these, Choklé Namgyal richly annotated the Jonang translations of the *Laghukālacakratantra* and *Vimalaprabhā*, versions of which are spread over various volumes of the Collection of Jonang Texts.[6] The numerous detailed annotations show the importance that Choklé Namgyal (and the Jonang tradition in general) attached to Kālacakra.[7]

In the following, I will provide a short analysis of Choklé Namgyal's *Pointing-Out Instruction on the Foundation, Path, and Fruit*. Throughout the text, Kālacakra material is adduced especially in support of the Jonangpas' equation of buddha nature with a fully enlightened buddha (i.e., the *dharmakāya*), which cannot be unequivocally established in the Yogācāra-dominated *Ratnagotravibhāga*, as it restricts the equation of buddha nature with the enlightenment of a buddha to the level of stainless nonduality.[8] The full equation finds better support, though, from the concept of an *ādibuddha* as developed in the Kālacakra. To illustrate the contrast with the Yogācāra-dominated Maitreya works, in one of the Yogācāra texts belonging to the five

---

taken to be empty of other (*gzhan stong*), which are the adventitious stains of ordinary consciousness extrinsic to the ultimate. See Mathes 2016, 4–8.

6. Some of the Jonang translations of *Vimalaprahbā* texts contain a mixture of annotations by Choklé Namgyal, Dölpopa, and possibly other commentators. Thanks are due to Filippo Brambilla for a preliminary survey. In a future project, we plan to check these annotated texts in order to find out whether Dölpopa and his immediate disciples had their own *gzhan stong*–based understanding of the Kālacakra material.

7. Of interest is here also the biographical information that insight into *gzhan stong* dawned in Dölpopa's mind during a Kālacakra retreat at Jonang (Stearns 1995, 829–31).

8. Takasaki 1966 and Schmithausen 1971 showed that the *Ratnagotravibhāga* consists of different, chronological layers. For a recent discussion of these layers and the Yogācāra interpretation of the final version of the *Ratnagotravibhāga* and its *vyākhyā*, see Mathes 2015, 119–40. 'Gos Lo tsā ba Gzhon nu dpal, for one, followed this strategy in his commentary on the *Ratnagotravibhāgavyākhyā* (Mathes 2008, 317–50).

Maitreya works (*Byams chos sde lnga*), namely, *Mahāyānasūtrālaṃkāra* 9.77, the possibility of an ādibuddha is excluded on the grounds that buddhahood is an individual achievement and is impossible without the accumulation of merit and wisdom.[9] In order to resolve this contradiction with an important Jonang source text, Choklé Namgyal adopts the common *gzhan stong* explanation that the accumulations of merit and wisdom do not create buddhahood but only remove the adventitious stains, thus revealing a primordially complete ādibuddha.[10] It is again with reference to Kālacakra material, namely, *Sekoddeśa*[11] 102–3, that Choklé Namgyal supports his disclosure model:

> Just as the waxing moon becomes
> gradually full along the phases,
> and its fullness is due to the elimination of the traces [of darkness]
> and not because it is cut off and made full [again], [102]
>
> so the waxing wisdom becomes
> gradually full along the bodhisattva levels,
> and its fullness is due to the elimination of defilements and so on,
> and not because it is cut off and made full [again].[12] [103]

Based on that, Choklé Namgyal concludes:

> This self-arisen coemergent wisdom, which abides in oneself throughout beginningless time, seems not to exist when hindered by adventitious stains and appears to become full or arise. This is

9. See also Wallace 2001, 17.

10. Phyogs las rnam rgyal 2008, 5: "In order to remove adventitious stains, one completes the accumulation of wisdom (i.e., the essence of the path), the accumulation of merit (i.e., the branches of the path), the ripening of sentient beings, the purification of buddha fields, and prayers. Then one actualizes the four *kāya*s, which are spontaneously present throughout beginningless time. This is called 'becoming a buddha.'" (*glo bur gyi dri ma sbyang ba'i don du| lam kyi ngo bo ye shes kyi tshogs dang lam gyi yan lag bsod nams kyi tshogs| sems can yongs su smin pa dang| sangs rgyas kyi zhing yongs su dag pa dang| smon lam yongs su rdzogs par byas nas| gdod nas lhun grub kyi sku bzhi mngon du byas pa la sangs rgyas thob pa zhes bya'o*).

11. The only surviving part of the original *Kālacakratantra*, which is on empowerment.

12. Phyogs las rnam rgyal 2008, 149: *ji ltar zla shar rim pa yis| |cha rnams kyis ni rdzogs par 'gyur| |grib ma nyams par rdzogs pa ste| |zla ba chad dang rdzogs pa min| |de bzhin ye shes shar rim pas| |sa rnams kyis ni rdzogs par 'gyur| |nyon mong la sogs nyams pas rdzogs| |ye shes chad dang rdzogs pa min|* (=*Sekoddeśa*, 88).

> because this wisdom gradually appears on the bodhisattva levels—Joyful and the rest—as the adventitious stains are being gradually removed by the remedy. This wisdom, however, is not cut off or nonexistent in sentient beings and made full along the bodhisattva levels. It is not newly created.[13]

For his hermeneutic strategy of fully equating buddha nature with the enlightened mind of a buddha, Choklé Namgyal finds further support from *Hevajratantra* 2.4.69ab, which identifies sentient beings with buddhas:

> All sentient beings are nothing but buddhas.
> They are covered, however, by adventitious stains.[14]

In his lengthy argument that mind's natural luminosity is the buddha's dharmakāya, Choklé Namgyal's main strategy is to bring in again the concept of an all-pervading ādibuddha. It should be noted that the Sāṃkhya ontology of primordial nature (*prakṛti*) and its modifications, which is adopted and slightly modified in the Kālacakra to describe relative truth,[15] is here included within the category of adventitious stains—thus effectively denying, in Yogācāra fashion, that relative truth has any material existence apart from the mind:

> The primordial nature—the five elements and so forth—and its twenty-four modifications are the adventitious stains, that which is pervaded. In their middle abides the pervading vajra-holder, the *ādibuddha*. Primordially free from the mental imprints of saṃsāra, he belongs to the mind of natural luminosity and not to the mind of adventitious stains. As opposed to saṃsāric mind, the mind of the natural nirvāṇa truly exists.[16]

13. Phyogs las rnam rgyal 2008, 149: *rang byung lhan skyes kyi ye shes rang nyid la ye nas bzhugs pa de'ang glo bur gyi dri mas bsgribs pa na med pa lta bu dang gnyen pos glo bur gyi dri ma rim gyis zad par byas pa las rab tu dga' ba la sogs pa'i sa rnams su ye shes de rim gyis shar bas rdzogs pa'am skyes pa lta bur snang ba yin gyi| ye shes de sems can la chad pa ste med pa dang sa rnams kyis rdzogs pa ste gsar du bskyed pa ma yin no|*.

14. Phyogs las rnam rgyal 2008, 5: *sems can rnams ni sangs rgyas nyid| |'on kyang glo bur dri mas bsgribs|* (*Hevajratantra*, 154: *sattvā buddhā eva kiṃ tu āgantukamalāvṛttāḥ*).

15. See Wallace 2001, 56–60.

16. Phyogs las rnam rgyal 2008, 161: *khams lnga la sogs pa rang bzhin dang rnam 'gyur nyi shu rtsa bzhi ni khyab bya glo bur gyi dri ma yin la de'i dbus na khyab byed rdo rje can dang po'i sangs rgyas bzhugs pa de ni 'khor ba'i bag chags las gdod ma nas grol ba rang bzhin 'od gsal gyi sems yin*

Of interest is also that the ādibuddha, *qua* natural luminosity, includes here the reflections of emptiness:[17]

> Mahāmudrā wisdom, namely the reflections of emptiness (i.e., the ten signs and so forth), is the very Buddha, the dharmakāya. . . . As for the meaning of signs and characteristics, which are like smoke and the rest, they are mahāmudrā, coemergent wisdom, buddha, dharmakāya, the ādibuddha. These abide on their own, in ourselves, without effort, throughout beginningless time.[18]

The reflections of emptiness are, like the emptiness that contains all supreme forms, taken as proof that the transmundane ultimate is not a mere nothingness but endowed with qualities:

> If one asks what the essence of mind's natural luminosity is, its essence must be internalized, as clearly stated in Ārya Lokeśvara's (i.e., Kalkin Puṇḍarīka's) *Vimalaprabhā*. What is taught as ultimate truth is the transmundane, endowed with all supreme aspects. In order to realize the accomplishment of mahāmudrā, the fruit is conferred in accordance with the yogins' wish for self-awareness, the luminosity of mind, directly manifesting in the sky, just like virgins seeing magical reflections in divination mirrors. The fruit is the mind of unchangeable blissful wisdom.[19]

---

pas glo bur gyi dri ma'i sems ma yin gyi rang bzhin gyis mya ngan las 'das pa'i sems 'khor ba'i sems las gzhan bden par yod pa'i sems te|. . . .

17. The reflections of emptiness are pure images emerging in nonconceptual meditation and should not be confounded with ordinary saṃsāric appearances. They appear to the adept in a nonconceptual way, like images in a divinatory mirror. See *Sekoddeśa*, verses 28–29.

18. Phyogs las rnam rgyal 2008, 214: *rtags bcu la sogs pa stong pa nyid kyi gzugs 'di nyid kyi phyag rgya chen po'i ye shes sangs rgyas chos kyi sku nyid yin ... 'dir rtags dang mtshan ma'i don ni du ba lta bu la sogs pa 'di dag phyag rgya chen po lhan cig skyes pa'i ye shes sangs rgyas chos kyi sku dang po'i sangs rgyas de rang nyid la gdod ma nyid nas rang chas lhun gyis grub par bzhugs pa la. . . .*

19. Phyogs las rnam rgyal 2008, 163: *sems kyi rang bzhin 'od gsal ba de'i rang gi ngo bo nyid gang yin zhe na| 'di yi ngo bo ni| 'phags pa 'jig rten gyi dbang phyug gis dri ma med pa'i 'od du gsal bar gsungs pa ltar| khong du chud par bya ste| ji skad du| gang don dam pa'i bden pas bstan pa de ni 'jig rten las 'das pa rnam pa thams cad kyi mchog dang ldan pa| phyag rgya chen po'i dngos grub bsgrub pa'i slad du rang gi sems kyis yongs su brtags pa'i chos dang bral ba gzhon nu ma rnams kyis me long la sogs pa la pra phab pa bzhin du rnal 'byor rnams kyis rang rig sems kyi 'od gsal mngon sum du nam mkha' la snang ba 'dod pa'i don gyis 'bras bu ster ba ste 'bras bu ni 'gyur ba med pa'i bde ba'i ye shes kyi sems so|.*

In other words, the reflections of emptiness are taken as a revelation of the ultimate to the yogin, who without superimposition directly realizes what is really there. Thus they stand for the manifestation of mind's luminous nature:

> Self-arisen, coemergent wisdom abides as the pervader in the pervaded, the bodies of all sentient beings. As for the nature of this wisdom, it is the manifestation of mind's luminous nature, like the reflections of emptiness (smoke, a mirage, and so on) experienced by the yogin.[20]

This raises the issue of the third of the three reasons laid out by the *Ratnagotravibhāga* for the presence of buddha nature in all sentient beings, namely that the fruit is only used as a metaphor for the buddha potential. Choklé Namgyal takes the latter to be everybody's naturally present potential and equates it with the buddha's ten strengths and so forth, namely, the qualities of the dharmakāya:

> Because all sentient beings possess the naturally present potential, which consists of a buddha's ten strengths and so forth, they are constantly endowed with the nature of a perfect buddha.[21]

In order to back up his understanding, Choklé Namgyal[22] refers to the *Avataṃsakasūtra* example of the silk cloth with a painting of the universe on a 1:1 scale inside an atom. Just as every atom is said to have such a silk cloth in itself, so all sentient beings possess the immeasurable buddha-qualities in an already fully developed state.[23] Following the earliest layers of the *Ratnagotravibhāga*, which accord with the original intent of the Tathāgatagarbha Sūtras, Choklé Namgyal interprets all remaining parts of the final version of this standard Indian treatise on buddha nature as meaning that all sentient beings are already a complete buddha. As mentioned above, this strategy finds support in

20. Phyogs las rnam rgyal 2008, 148: *khyab bya sems can thams cad kyi lus la rang byung lhan cig skyes pa'i ye shes khyab byed du gnas pa yin la| ye shes de'i ngo bo ni rnal 'byor pas nyams su myong ba'i stong pa nyid kyi gzugs du ba lta bu dang smig sgyu lta bu la sogs pa sems kyi rang bzhin 'od gsal ba'i snang ba 'di nyid do|*.

21. Phyogs las rnam rgyal 2008, 152: *sangs rgyas kyi stobs bcu la sogs pa'i rang bzhin gyi rigs sems can thams cad la yod pa'i phyir sems can thams cad rtag tu rdzogs pa'i sangs rgyas kyi snying po can yin no|*.

22. Phyogs las rnam rgyal 2008, 153.

23. See Takasaki 1966, 189–92.

the tantras propagating the doctrine of an ādibuddha, which is to say, the full equation of sentient beings with buddhas, as professed in the *Hevajratantra*.[24]

This distinction between the ultimate reality of a primordial buddha and the relative reality of adventitious stains prepares the ground for Choklé Namgyal's own version of the *gzhan stong* view. Based on the formulaic definition of emptiness—"something is empty of that which does not exist in it, and whatever remains exists permanently"[25]—Choklé Namgyal defines it in the following way:

> The *dharmatā*-luminosity of sentient beings is not empty of its own nature but empty of other things, namely the conditioned and the adventitious. Thus it is taken as the great emptiness, also known as *gzhan stong*."[26]

Even though the term *gzhan stong* is used only once in the entire treatise, it is clear that it refers to the ultimate described in a positive fashion, *dharmatā*-luminosity being frequently equated with other ultimate categories, such as buddha nature or ādibuddha. The distinction between the basis of this *gzhan stong* emptiness and its *negandum* goes so far that the ultimate is exempted from dependent arising:

> The relative is dependent arising; the ultimate, self-arisen wisdom. The relative is the ground consciousness; the ultimate, ground wisdom. The relative must be abandoned; the ultimate, attained. The relative is adventitious stains; the ultimate, buddha nature. The relative obscures the dharmakāya; the ultimate is the final dharmakāya. The relative is the imagined and dependent; the ultimate, the unchangeable perfect.[27]

24. It should be noted that other scholars, such as 'Gos Lo tsā ba Gzhon nu dpal (1392–1481), maintained that there is a more substantial difference between the buddha potential and its fruit and read this distinction into the original parts of the *Ratnagotravibhāga*, which represent the Tathāgatagarbha Sūtras more literally (see Mathes 2008, 11).

25. This definition is already found in the *Cūḷasuññatasutta* (*Majjhima-nikāya*, 121) and is also adapted in the explanations of the emptiness found in the *trisvabhāva* and buddha-nature doctrines (see Mathes 2012, 191–98).

26. Phyogs las rnam rgyal 2008, 170: *sems can gyi chos nyid 'od gsal ba 'di rang gi ngo bos mi stong zhing gzhan 'dus byas glo bur pa rnams kyis stong pas na stong pa nyid chen po gzhan stong zhes bya yin par bzhed do|.*

27. Phyogs las rnam rgyal 2008, 337–38: *kun rdzob ni rten cing 'brel 'byung ste| |don dam ni rang byung ye shes yin| |kun rdzob ni kun gzhi rnam shes| |don dam ni kun gzhi ye shes yin| |kun rdzob*

It should be noted that the perfect (*pariniṣpanna*, *yongs grub*) in the sense of being unmistaken is not included in the ultimate here, as this perfect consists in wisdom cultivated on the path and thus something dependently arisen.[28] Nor, in Choklé Namgyal's system, are the two truths one in essence but rather defined according to the *Madhyāntavibhāga*[29] and *Dharmadharmatāvibhāga*[30] as neither identical nor different:

> Thus both the naturally luminous mind and the mind of adventitious stains are, in terms of their essence, neither identical nor different, given that they are phenomena (*dharmin*) and phenomena's true nature (*dharmatā*). . . . One cannot say that they are in essence either identical or different. In general, they only differ in the sense of their identity being negated.[31]

The extent to which Choklé Namgyal goes against the common Madhyamaka notion that the two truths are inseparable becomes clear from the way he understands Nāgārjuna's *Mūlamadhyamakakārikā* 25.20, as expressed at the end of his elucidation of the foundation in the *Pointing-Out Instruction on the Foundation, Path, and Fruit*:

---

ni spang bar bya ba ste| |don dam ni thob par bya ba yin| |kun rdzob ni glo bur dri ma ste| |don dam ni bde gshegs snying po yin| |kun rdzob ni chos sku'i sgrib byed de| |don dam ni mthar thug chos sku yin| |kun rdzob ni kun brtags gzhan dbang ste| |don dam ni 'gyur med yongs grub yin|.

28. See also Mathes 2004, 312–13.

29. *Madhyāntavibhāgabhāṣya*, 23: Therefore it is the characteristic [of emptiness] to be neither separate from nor identical with false imagining. If it were separate, the *dharmatā* would be different from *dharmas*, and this is not acceptable. It is just as [the *dharmas*' characteristics of] impermanence and suffering. If it were identical, it would not be an object of purification, sharing the same characteristic [as false imagining]. Therefore the characteristic of being neither identical nor separate has been taught (*tasmād abhūtaparikalpān na pṛthaktvaikalakṣaṇaṃ || pṛthaktve sati dharmād anyā dharmateti na yujyate | anityatāduḥkhatāvat | ekatve sati viśuddhyālambanaṃ* (del. *jñānaṃ*) *na syāt sāmānyalakṣaṇañ ca | etena tattvānyatvavinirmuktaṃ lakṣaṇaṃ paridīpitam bhavati |*).

30. *Dharmadharmatāvibhāgakārikā*, 105: "The two (i.e., *dharmas* and *dharmatā*) are neither identical nor different" (*gnyis po dag ni gcig nyid dang| |so so ba yang ma yin te|*). It should be noted that in the *Dharmadharmatāvibhāga*, *dharmas* are equated with false imagining and relative truth, and *dharmatā* with ultimate truth.

31. Phyogs las rnam rgyal 2008, 162: *de ltar rang bzhin 'od gsal gyi sems dang glo bur dri ma'i sems gnyis ngo bo gcig ma yin zhing| ngo bo tha dad pa yang ma yin te| chos can dang chos nyid yin pa'i phyir ro| . . . ngo bo de nyid dang gzhan du brjod du med pa yin la| spyir ni gcig pa bkag tsam gyi tha dad yin no|.*

> It is totally confused to maintain that [one is stuck in] saṃsāra if one does not recognize its nature, but that when its nature is recognized, saṃsāra itself turns out to be the buddha. Ārya Nāgārjuna thought that the suchness of saṃsāra does not differ from the suchness of nirvāṇa. This follows from the following verse:
>
> The limit of nirvāṇa
> is the limit of saṃsāra.[32]
> Between the two, there is not the slightest difference,
> not even a subtle one.[33]
>
> "Limit" refers here to the limit of reality (i.e., the true nature) of saṃsāra and nirvāṇa, the very dharmadhātu. Therefore, since there is a big difference between saṃsāra and the true nature of saṃsāra, one needs to be very skillful when it comes to analyzing the meaning [of this verse] so as not to be attached to the mere words "equality of saṃsāra and nirvāṇa."[34]

Finally, it is worth noticing that Choklé Namgyal indirectly responded to Candrakīrti's argument against the Yogācāra hermeneutics of the *Sandhinirmocanasūtra* (on which *gzhan stong* views heavily rely), according to which the *Laṅkāvatārasūtra* classifies buddha nature as a teaching of provisional meaning. Even though the *Laṅkāvatārasūtra*'s doctrinal position is not always consistent, it is safe to say that it mainly upholds the Yogācāra doctrine and, in particular, equates buddha nature with the Yogācāra version of emptiness, in a way similar to the identification of buddha nature with the suchness accompanied by stains that is developed in the *Mahāyānasūtrālaṃkāra*.[35]

32. That is, taking *saṃsaraṇa* as a synonym of *saṃsāra*, chosen *metri causa*.

33. *Mūlamadhyamakakārikā* (25.20), 458: *nirvāṇasya ca yā koṭiḥ koṭiḥ saṃsaraṇasya ca | na tayor antaraṃ kiṃ cit susūkṣmam api vidyate ||*.

34. Phyogs las rnam rgyal 2008, 159: *'khor ba'i rang gi ngo bo ngo ma shes pa na 'khor ba yin la| ngo shes pa na 'khor ba nyid sangs rgyas su bzhugs pa yin no| |zhes smra ba yang ches cher 'khrul ba yin te| 'phags pa klu sgrub kyis ni 'khor ba'i de bzhin nyid dang myang 'das kyi de bzhin nyid khyad par med pa la dgongs pa yin te tshigs su bcad pa de nyid kyi rjes su| mya ngan 'das mtha' gang yin pa| |de ni khor ba'i mtha' yin te| |de gnyis khyad par cung zad ni| |shin tu phra ba'ang yod pa ma yin| |zhes gsungs te| mtha' zhes pa ni 'khor 'das kyi yang dag pa'i mtha' chos kyi dbyings nyid do| |de bas na 'khor ba dang 'khor ba'i chos nyid ni khyad par shin tu che bas na| 'khor 'das mnyam pa nyid kyi ming tsam la mngon par ma zhen par don gyi rnam par dbye ba la shin tu mkhas par bya'o|*.

35. In the *Mahāyānasūtrālaṃkāra* (9.37) buddha nature is only suchness accompanied by stains (*samalā tathatā*), thus linking the *Ratnagotravibhāga*'s Yogācāra interpretation of buddha

In his *Madhyamakāvatārabhāṣya*, Candrakīrti quotes the dialogue featuring Mahāmati's objection that the teaching of buddha nature is similar to the heretical teaching of a self (*ātman*). The Buddha's reply is that buddha nature is emptiness, the limit of reality, nirvāṇa, nonorigination, signlessness, and wishlessness.[36] Choklé Namgyal argues, however, that the teaching of buddha nature is not classified as being of provisional meaning (*neyārtha*) in this passage, where by "emptiness" is meant the positively understood Yogācāra variety of it. A closer look at the *Laṅkāvatāra* passage quoted in the *Madhyamakāvatāra* shows that Candrakīrti leaves out precisely the sentence that Choklé Namgyal adduces to argue against the attempt to take buddha nature as *neyārtha*. The relevant part of the *Laṅkāvatāra* quote is as follows:

> Mahāmati, it is as follows: A potter produces various pots with his hands, his ingenuity, a pole, water, string, and effort—all from the same lump of clay molecules. Likewise, Mahāmati, the tathāgatas teach this same essencelessness of phenomena, which is beyond any conceptual characteristic, with—like a potter—manifold insight and skillful means, but in his case with a variety of words and verbal expressions in connection with buddha nature or essencelessness.[37]

The *Laṅkāvatārasūtra* then follows with the sentence that is not quoted by Candrakīrti:

> In a like manner, O Mahāmati, they teach buddha nature in order to attract, through the teaching of buddha nature, heretics who cling to the teaching of a self.[38]

Candrakīrti reads instead (against both the Sanskrit and Tibetan of the *Laṅkāvatārasūtra*):

---

nature with the three Yogācāra texts among the Maitreya works (i.e., the *Mahāyānasūtrālaṃkāra*, the *Madhyāntavibhāga*, and the *Dharmadharmatāvibhāga*).

36. See Mathes 2008, 17–19.

37. *Laṅkāvatārasūtra* 78: *tadyathā mahāmate kumbhakāra ekasmān mṛtparamāṇurāśer vividhāni bhāṇḍāni karoti hastaśilpadaṇḍodakasūtraprayatnayogāt | evam eva mahāmate tathāgatās tad eva dharmanairātmyaṃ sarvavikalpalakṣaṇavinivṛttaṃ vividhaiḥ prajñopāyakauśalyayogair garbhopadeśena vā nairātmyopadeśena vā kumbhakāravac citraiḥ padavyañjanaparyāyair deśayante |*.

38. *Laṅkāvatārasūtra*, 79: *evaṃ hi mahāmate tathāgatagarbhopadeśam ātmavādābhiniviṣṭānāṃ tīrthakarāṇām ākarṣaṇārthaṃ tathāgatagarbhopadeśena nirdiśanti.* For Tibetan, see note 45 below.

Therefore, O Mahāmati, they teach buddha nature in this way.[39]

Candrakīrti's quote of the *Laṅkāvatārasūtra* continues again in a correct way:

> How else would those with the disposition of somebody who has alighted upon the view of a false[40] self, but who verge on the disposition of someone who has alighted upon the experiential object of the three doors of liberation, swiftly awaken to complete enlightenment?[41]

Candrakīrti then jumps back to an earlier sentence in the *Laṅkāvatārasūtra*:

> Mahāmati, this defining characteristic of emptiness, nonarising, nonduality, and essencelessness is found in all sūtras of all the buddhas.[42]

From these quotations Candrakīrti concludes:

> Since, with the help of this canonical passage,[43] all parts of sūtras with similar content that the Vijñānavādins claim to be of definitive meaning (*nītārtha*) have been shown to [really] be of provisional meaning (*neyārtha*), the commentary now will turn to elucidating how the same meaning is reached by analysis.[44]

Choklé Namgyal comes to the opposite conclusion, interestingly, by elaborating on the sentence Candrakīrti omitted ("In a like manner, O Mahāmati,

39. *Madhyamakāvatāra*, 198: *de ltar de'i phyir blo gros chen po de bzhin gshegs pa'i snying po ston te* |.

40. The Tibetan has "genuine" (*yang dag pa'i*) instead of "false" (*Madhyamakāvatāra*, 198).

41. *Laṅkāvatārasūtra*, 79: *kathaṃ batābhūtātmavikalpadṛṣṭipatitāśayā vimokṣatrayagocarapatit āśayopetāḥ kṣipram anuttarāṃ samyaksaṃbodhim abhisaṃbudhyerann iti. . . .*

42. *Laṅkāvatārasūtra*, 77: *etad dhi mahāmate śūnyatānutpādādvayaniḥsvabhāvalakṣaṇaṃ sarvabuddhānāṃ sarvasūtrāntagatam* |.

43. I.e., from the *Laṅkāvatārasūtra.*

44. *Madhyamakāvatāra*, 198: *rnam pa de lta bu'i mdo sde rnam par shes par smra ba rnams kyi nges pa'i don nyid du khas blangs pa thams cad drang ba'i don nyid yin par lung 'dis mngon par gsal bar byas nas| rigs pas drang ba'i don nyid du gsal bar bya ba'i phyir bshad pa*|.

the tathāgatas teach buddha nature in order to attract, through the teaching of buddha nature, heretics who cling to the teaching of a self"):[45]

> Even though some claim that the teaching of buddha nature by the Illustrious One has provisional meaning, not definitive meaning, it is not outside of the reality taught by the Illustrious One. "In order to attract" expresses the necessity of teaching buddha nature, but it does not express [the notion] that it has provisional meaning.[46]

In order to fully understand Choklé Namgyal's argument, one needs to read between the lines: a positively understood Yogācāra emptiness is taught for what it truly is, namely buddha nature, in order to attract a certain group of potential disciples. This is most clear in the *Conqueror of Delusion*, where Choklé Namgyal explains that emptiness in the above-quoted *Laṅkāvatāra* passage is identical with buddha nature, not the emptiness of all phenomena being empty of an own nature.[47] It should be noted that Choklé Namgyal also profits here from indirectly hinting at Candrakīrti's mistake of not quoting canonical sources correctly, leaving out an important part of the sūtra passage that in Choklé Namgyal's eyes sheds a different light on the issue.[48]

45. Phyogs las rnam rgyal 2008, 159: *blo gros chen po de ltar de bzhin gshegs pa rnams ni mu stegs byed bdag du smra ba la mngon par zhen pa rnams drang ba'i phyir| de bzhin gshegs pa'i snying po bstan pas de bzhin gshegs pa'i snying po ston te|* = *Laṅkāvatārasūtra*, 79. For the Sanskrit see above.

46. Phyogs las rnam rgyal 2008, 159: *bcom ldan 'das de bzhin gshegs pa'i snying po bstan pa ni drang ba'i don yin gyi* (text: *gyis*) *nges pa'i don ma yin no zhes smra ba rnams kyang| bcom ldan 'das kyis bstan pa'i de kho na nyid las phyi rol tu gyur pa ma yin te| drang ba'i phyir zhes pa ni bde gshegs snying po ston pa'i dgos pa bstan pa yin gyi* (text: *gyis*) *drang don du ston pa ni ma yin no|*.

47. Phyogs las rnam rgyal 2010, 47–48: "He did not teach buddha nature with an intentional provisional meaning. It has been said that emptiness, the limit of reality, nirvāṇa, and so forth have been taught as buddha nature. . . . The emptiness that is buddha nature is not the emptiness that is each phenomenon's lack of an own nature." *de bzhin gshegs pa'i snying po gsungs pa dgongs pa can gyi drang don du ma bstan te| stong pa nyid yang dag pa'i mtha' dang mya ngan las 'das pa la sogs pa rnams la de bzhin gshegs pa'i snying por bstan zhes gsungs la| . . . bde bzhin gshegs pa'i snying po yin pa'i stong pa nyid ni chos thams cad rang rang ngo bos stong pa'i stong pa nyid de ma yin gyi|. . . .*

48. Notice that in the same enterprise of ascribing provisional meaning to the third *dharmacakra* Candrakīrti had to quote *Laṅkāvatārasūtra* 2.123 out of context. Taken on its own, the verse (*Laṅkāvatārasūtra*, 49: "Just as a physician provides medicine for each patient, | so the buddhas teach mind-only (*cittamātra*) to sentient beings" *āture āture yadvad bhiṣag dravyaṃ prayacchati | buddhā hi tadvat sattvānāṃ cittamātraṃ vadanti vai ||*.) indeed suggests that the *cittamātra* teaching has provisional meaning. But the following verse (*Laṅkāvatārasūtra* 2.124, 49), which is not quoted by Candrakīrti, sheds a different light on the issue: "[This *cittamātra*

Conclusion

With support from the Kālacakra concept of an ādibuddha and the *Hevajratantra*'s equation of sentient beings with buddhas, Choklé Namgyal interprets Yogācāra texts and parts of the Maitreya works in light of the original Tathāgatagarbha Sūtras. The result is a *gzhan stong* view, in which the basis of negation is an unconditioned ultimate that is not subject to dependent arising, the latter being fully included in the *negandum*. As for the three natures theory, Choklé Namgyal, in a way quite typical of the Jonangpas, restricts the perfect nature to its unchangeable aspect, thus confining everything conditioned within the *negandum*. In his discussion of the *Laṅkāvatārasūtra* passage of equating emptiness with buddha nature, Choklé Namgyal not only has a minor issue with Candrakīrti's interpretation of a sūtra passage but also attempts to lay axe to the project of ascribing provisional meaning (*neyārtha*) to the teaching of buddha nature and, by extension, to the entire third *dharmacakra*.

Works Cited

Dharmadharmatāvibhāgakārikā (Tibetan translation). See Mathes 1996, 104–14.

Hevajratantra. See Tripathi and Negi 2001.

Johnston, Edward H., ed. 1950. *Ratnagotravibhāgavyākhyā* (includes the RGV). Patna: The Bihar Research Society.

La Vallée Poussin, Louis de, ed. 1992. *Madhyamakāvatāra*. Bibliotheca Buddhica 9. Reprint (first published in 1907–12). Delhi: Motilal Banarsidass.

Laṅkāvatārasūtra. See Nanjio 1923.

Madhyamakāvatāra. See La Vallée Poussin 1992.

Madhyāntavibhāgabhāṣya. See Nagao 1964.

Mathes, Klaus-Dieter. 1996. *Unterscheidung der Gegebenheiten von ihrem wahren Wesen (Dharmadharmatāvibhāga)*. Indica et Tibetica 26. Swisttal-Odendorf: Indica et Tibetica Verlag.

———. 2004. "Tāranātha's "Twenty-One Differences with Regard to the Profound Meaning": Comparing the Views of the Two *gŹan stoṅ* Masters Dol po pa and Śākya mchog ldan." *Journal of the International Association of Buddhist Studies* 27.2: 285–328.

———. 2008. *A Direct Path to the Buddha Within: Gö Lotsāwa's Mahāmudrā Interpretation of the Ratnagotravibhāga*. Studies in Indian and Tibetan Buddhism. Boston: Wisdom Publications.

———. 2012. "The *Gzhan stong* Model of Reality: Some More Material on Its Origin,

teaching] is an object neither of philosophers nor of śrāvakas. | The masters teach it by drawing on their own experience" *tārkikāṇām aviṣayaṃ śrāvakāṇāṃ na caiva hi | yaṃ deśayanti vai nāthāḥ pratyātmagatigocaram ||*. See Mathes 2008, 18–19.

Transmission, and Interpretation." *Journal of the International Association of Buddhist Studies* 34.1–2: 187–226.

———. 2015. "The Original *Ratnagotravibhāga* and Its Yogācāra Interpretation as Possible Indian Precedents of *Gzhan stong* ("Empti[ness] of Other")." *Hōrin* 18: 119–40.

———. 2016. "The *Rang stong / Gzhan stong* Division." *Journal of Buddhist Philosophy* 2: 4–8.

Mūlamadhyamakakārikā. See Ye 2011.

Nagao, Gadjin M., ed. 1964. *Madhyāntavibhāgabhāṣya*. Tokyo: Suzuki Research Foundation.

Nanjio, Bunyiu, ed. 1923. *The Laṅkāvatāra Sūtra*. Bibliotheca Otaniensis 1. Kyoto: Otani University Press.

Orofino, Giacomella. 1994. *Sekoddeśa: A Critical Edition of the Tibetan Translation.* Serie Orientale Roma 72. Rome: Istituto Italiano per il Medio ed Estremo Oriente.

Phyogs las rnam rgyal, Jo nang. 2008. *Pointing-Out Instruction on the Foundation, Path, and Fruit. Gzhi lam 'bras bu'i ngo sprod.* In *Jo nang dpe tshogs*, vol. 21. Beijing: Mi rigs dpe skrun khang. TBRC.org ID: W1PD95815.

———. 2010. *Conqueror of Delusion: An Ornament of Buddha Nature. Bde gshegs snying po'i rgyan gyi 'khrul 'joms.* In *Jo nang dpe tshogs*, 22:1–116. Beijing: Mi rigs dpe skrun khang. TBRC.org ID: W1KG9015.

Ratnagotravibhāgavyākhyā. See Johnston 1950.

Schmithausen, Lambert. 1971. "Philologische Bemerkungen zum Ratnagotravibhāga." *Wiener Zeitschrift für die Kunde Südasiens* 15: 123–77.

———. 1973. "Zu D. Seyfort Rueggs Buch 'La Théorie du Tathāgatagarbha et du Gotra' (Besprechungsaufsatz)." *Wiener Zeitschrift für die Kunde Südasiens* 22: 123–60.

Stearns, Cyrus. 1995. "Dol-po-pa Shes-rab rgyal-mtshan and the Genesis of the *gzhan stong* Position in Tibet." *Asiatische Studien* 49.4: 829–52.

———. 2008. "Chokle Namgyel." In: *Treasury of Lives https://treasuryoflives.org/biographies/view/Chokle-Namgyel/2812.* Visited March 10, 2018.

Sekoddeśa. See Orofino 1994, 54–122.

Takasaki, Jikido. 1966. *A Study on the Ratnagotravibhāga (Uttaratantra) Being a Treatise on the Tathāgatagarbha Theory of Mahāyāna Buddhism.* Serie Orientale Roma 33. Rome: Istituto Italiano per il Medio ed Estremo Oriente.

Tripathi, Ram Shankar, and Thakur Sain Negi, eds. 2001. *Hevajratantra*. Bibliotheca Indo-Tibetica 48. Sarnath: Central Institute of Higher Tibetan Studies, 2001.

Van der Kuijp, Leonard. 2016. "Reconsidering the Dates of Dol po pa Shes rab rgyal mtshan's (1292–1361) *Ri chos nges don rgya mtsho* and the *Bka' bsdu bzhi pa'i don.*" *Journal of Tibetology* 14: 115–59.

Wallace, Vesna. 2001. *The Inner Kālacakratantra: A Buddhist Tantric View of the Individual.* Oxford: Oxford University Press.

Ye, Shaoyong, ed. 2011. *Mūlamadhyamakakārikā*. Beijing: Research Institute of Sanskrit Manuscripts & Buddhist Literature.

Classifications of Perception (*Saṃjñā*) in Buddhist Āgama and Abhidharma Treatises

Seiji Kumagai

Introduction[1]

The concept of perception (*saṃjñā*) is a key notion in Buddhism, frequently but not exclusively addressed in the context of the discussion of the five aggregates (*pañcaskandha*) in multiple sources. Being relevant in Buddhist āgama and abhidharma texts, the definition of perception is often given,[2] but its various classifications have never been systematically treated in a comparative fashion.[3] This paper thus represents the first attempt to present an overview of the development of the typology of the aggregate of perception (*saṃjñāskandha*) found in āgama and abhidharma texts. It aims to explain and analyze three different classifications according to the elements they comprise: (1) a threefold classification of perception, (2) a fourfold classification of perception, and (3) a combination of twofold and fourfold classifications of perception.

1. I had the chance to attend Professor Kapstein's lectures and seminars held at EPHE when I studied in Paris between 2008 and 2009. Learning research methodology in Buddhist studies and Tibetology from such a leading figure had a great impact in my formative years. I am therefore particularly honored and happy to participate in this collection celebrating Professor Kapstein's career.

2. See *Abhidharmakośa* (1.14cd, Ejima 1989, 16.4) *saṃjñā nimittodgrahaṇātmikā*. *Abhidharmakośabhāṣya* (1.14cd, Ejima 1989, 16.5–6): *yan nīla-pīta-dīrgha-hrasva-strī-puruṣa-mitrāmitra-sukha-duḥkhādi-nimittodgrahaṇam asau saṃjñā-skandhaḥ*.

3. In a previous paper (Kumagai 2017), I explained the theory of perception in Bön, the "indigenous religion" in Tibet. The paper pointed out that Bön also defends the idea that perception is one of the five aggregates. The Bön tradition proposes a threefold classification of perception different from the one found in Buddhist sources. It does not propose either a fourfold classification of perception or an articulation of twofold and fourfold classifications.

A Threefold Classification of Perception

The threefold classification of perception is already found in ancient Buddhist scriptures and treatises. For example, in his *Prakaraṇapāda* (*Apidamo pinlei zu lun*, 阿毘達磨品類足論), one of the Six Abhidharma Treatises (六足論) of the Sarvāstivādin school, Vasumitra (世友, fl. ca. second century BCE) postulates three perceptions: small perception (小想), great perception (大想), and boundless perception (無量想).[4] He does not, however, give any explanation regarding the nature of each perception and how they differ from one another. The *Zhong shifen apitan lun* (衆事分阿毘曇論), the oldest Chinese translation of *Prakaraṇapāda*, provides a slightly different translation of the terms: few perceptions (少想) and many perceptions (多想), instead of small perception (小想) and great perception (大想).[5] The *Mahāprajñāpāramitāsūtra* (*Dabore boluomiduo jing*, 大般若波羅蜜多経) also mentions the three categories of perception but does not explain their details.[6]

These three types of perception were interpreted variously in later periods. The *Mahāparinirvāṇasūtra* (大般涅槃経) correlated the three (small, great, and boundless perceptions) to the three realms (desire, form, and formless realms), respectively.[7] We will call this approach "type A" hereinafter.

In his *Abhidharmāvatāra* (入阿毘達磨論), Skandhila (塞建陀羅, fourth or fifth century CE) states that small, great, and boundless perceptions, respectively, apprehend small objects, extensive objects such as Mount Meru, and the field of infinite space and so on.[8] We will call this correlation "type B."

4. Taishō 1542.26.693a11–12: 想云何, 謂取像性. 此有三種, 謂小想大想無量想.

5. Taishō 1541.26.627b18: 云何想. 有三想, 謂少想, 多想, 無量想.

6. Taishō 220.7.495c15–18: 世尊, 云何菩薩摩訶薩常應圓滿遠離諸想. 善現, 若菩薩摩訶薩遠離一切小想大想及無量想, 是為菩薩摩訶薩常應圓滿遠離諸想.

7. Taishō 375.12.832a11-a28: 是想三種, 一者小, 二者大, 三者無邊. 小因縁故, 生於小想. 大因縁故, 生於大想. 無量縁故, 生無量想. 復有小想, 謂未入定. 復有大想, 謂已入定. 復有無量想, 謂十一切入. 復有小想, 所謂欲界一切想等. 復有大想, 所謂色界一切想等. 復有無量想, 謂無色界一切想等. *'Phags pa yongs su mya ngan las 'das pa chen po'i mdo* (trans. by Wang phub shun, Dge ba'i blo gros, and Rgya mtsho'i sde, Dergé 119, 392a6–b5): *'du shes de'ang rnam pa gsum ste / chung ngu dang / chen po dang / mtha' med pa'o // de la chung ba'i rgyus ni 'du shes chung ngur bskyed / che ba'i rgyus ni 'du shes chen por bskyed / mtha' yas pa'i rgyus ni 'du shes mtha' yas par bskyed do // yang 'du shes chung ngu yod de / 'di ltar ting nge 'dzin du ma zhugs pa'o // 'du shes chen po ni ting nge 'dzin du zhugs pa'o // yang mtha' yas pa'i 'du shes ni kun tu 'gro ba bcu'o // yang 'du shes chung ngu ni 'di lta ste / 'dod pa'i khams kyi 'du shes la sogs pa'o // yang 'du shes chen po ni gzugs kyi khams kyi 'du shes la sogs pa'o // yang mtha' yas pa'i 'du shes ni gzugs med pa'i khams kyi 'du shes la sogs pa ste / 'du shes rnam pa gsum 'gags na tshor ba'ang rang 'gag go //.*

8. *Rab tu byed pa chos mngon pa la 'jug pa* (Dergé 4098, 305a7–b2): *mtshan ma dang ming dang don dang brda zhes pa'i 'du shes te / sngon po dang / ser po dang / ring po dang / thung du dang /*

The third position attempted to merge the two previous ones. In his *Pañcaskandhaka*, Vasubandhu also refers to three perceptions, which he calls small, great, and boundless, without, however, commenting on them.[9] We can find some help in Sthiramati's (fl. ca. sixth century CE) commentary, the *Pañcaskandhakavibhāṣā*, where he explains that small, great, and boundless perceptions, respectively, correspond to the desire realm, the form realm, and the twofold fields of infinite space and infinite consciousness.[10] We will call this correlation "type C." In this approach, the small and great perceptions correspond to type A, while the boundless perception almost corresponds to type B. We need to note that Sthiramati does not include the field of nothingness or the field of neither perception nor nonperception, the two highest among the four fields of formless meditative absorption. Thus, the three perceptions do not completely correspond to the three realms. As we will see below, the three perceptions classified by Sthiramati are similar to the three perceptions articulated in the last theory that combines a twofold and a fourfold classification.

In sum, there are three different interpretations of the threefold classification of perception, as shown in the following chart:

dung dang / rnga dang / padma dang / sna ma'i me tog dang / uḍpa la'i dri dang / kha ba dang lan tshwa dang / 'jam pa dang rtsub pa dang / bud med dang skyes pa la sogs pa'i mtshan ma dang / ming dang don gcig tu shes pa'i chos gang yin pa de ni rnam par rtog pa'i rgyu ste / 'du shes zhes bya'o // de yang rnam par shes pa'i bye brag gis tshor ba bzhin du rnam pa drug go // yang chung ngu dang chen por gyur pa dang tshad med pa dang rnam pa gsum ste / de la yul chung ngu la dmigs pa ni chung ngu'o // ri rab la sogs pa la dmigs pa ni chen por gyur pa'o // nam mkha' mtha' yas skye mched la sogs pa dag la ni tshad med pa'o // 'du shes kyi dngos po'o //.

Its Chinese version presents the position of type A, which correlates the three perceptions to three realms, as well as the position of type B. Taishō 28.1554.981c20–26: 想句義者, 謂能假合相名義解. 即於青黃長短等色, 螺鼓等聲, 沈麝等香, 醎苦等味, 堅軟等觸. 男女等法相名義中假合而解. 為尋伺因故名為想. 此隨識別有六如受. 小大無量差別有三. 謂緣少境故名小想, 緣妙高等諸大法境故名大想, 隨空無邊處等名無量想. 或隨三界立此三名.

9. Li and Steinkellner 2008, 4.1–2: *sañjñā katamā / viṣaya-nimittodgrahaṇam / tat tri-vidham* ☒ *parīttaṃ mahad-gatam apramāṇaṃ ca //.*

10. Kramer 2013, 31.3–4: *parīttaṃ kāma-dhātuḥ / nikṛṣṭatvāt / mahad-gato rūpa-dhātuḥ / utkṛṣṭatvāt / apramāṇe ākāśa-vijñānānantyāyatane / aparyantatvāt /.*

THE THREEFOLD CLASSIFICATION OF PERCEPTION

	type A	type B	type C
small perception	desire realm	small objects	desire realm
great perception	form realm	extensive objects	form realm
boundless perception	formless realm	field of infinite space and so on	field of infinite space and field of infinite consciousness

A Fourfold Classification of Perception

The aggregate of perception was also interpreted as comprising four kinds of perception in āgama and abhidharma texts. In the *Madhyama Āgama* (*Middle-Length Discourses*), the *Shuo chu jing* (説処経)[11] and the *Diyi de jing* (第一得経)[12] refer to four perceptions: small, great, boundless perceptions, and perception of the field of nothingness (i.e., the third of the four formless absorptions). Except for the obvious last one, it is unclear what intentional object each of these types of perception has. We are left, once more, with doubts regarding what these perceptions are about.

We need to resort to the *Apidamo jiyimen zu lung* (阿毘達磨集異門足論, **Abhidharmasaṃgītiparyāyapādaśāstra*), one of the Six Abhidharma Treatises of the Sarvāstivādin school, to get an idea about what the nature of these perceptions is. In that text, Śāriputra makes connections between the four perceptions and certain kinds of objects. Small perception apprehends small objects, great perception apprehends extensive objects, boundless perception apprehends boundless objects, the fourth perception apprehends the field of nothingness. It thus means that the first two perceptions correspond to type B of threefold classification, while the third and fourth are different from any types of the threefold classification.[13]

11. Taishō 26.1.563b8–13: 阿難, 我本為汝説四想. 比丘者, 有小想, 有大想, 有無量想, 有無所有想. 阿難, 此四想, 汝當為諸年少比丘説以教彼. 若為諸年少比丘説教此四想者, 彼便得安隱, 得力得樂, 身心不煩熱, 終身行梵行.

12. Taishō 26.1.799c21–23: 復次, 有四想. 有比丘想小, 想大, 想無量, 想無所有. 衆生如是樂想意解者, 變易有異. 多聞聖弟子如是觀則厭彼. 厭彼已, 尚不欲第一. 況復下賤.

13. Taishō 1536.26.392a23–b6: 四想者, 一小想, 二大想, 三無量想, 四無所有想. 小想云何. 答, 作意思惟狹小諸色. 謂或思惟青瘀, 或思惟膿爛, 或思惟破壞, 或思惟膖脹, 或思惟骸骨, 或思惟骨鎖, 或思惟地, 或思惟水, 或思惟火, 或思惟風, 或思惟青, 或思惟黄, 或思惟赤, 或思惟白, 或思惟諸欲過患, 或思惟出離功徳. 與此俱行諸想等想, 現前等想, 已想, 當

THE FOURFOLD CLASSIFICATION OF PERCEPTION

small perception	small objects
great perception	extensive objects
boundless perception	boundless objects
perception of field of nothingness	field of nothingness

A Combination of the Twofold and Fourfold Classifications

In later periods, a new position developed that combined two interpretations: a twofold categorization, of which the first category is subdivided into four types of perception. The four, however, differ from the previously mentioned four types of perceptions given in the *Apidamo jiyimen zu lung* (阿毘達磨集異門足論).

The interpretation appears in the *Viniścayasaṃgrahanī* (摂決択分) section of Asaṅga's *Yogācārabhūmi*, where the two classifications are articulated together.[14] The "aggregate of perception" is divided into conceptual perception (*mtshan ma dang bcas pa'i 'du shes, *sanimitta-saṃjñā*) and nonconceptual perception (*mtshan ma med pa'i 'du shes, *animitta-saṃjñā*). The former is further subdivided into four: small perception (*chung ngu'i 'du shes*), great perception (*chen por gyur pa'i 'du shes*), boundless perception (*tshad med pa'i 'du shes*), and the perception of the field of nothingness (*ci yang med pa'i 'du shes*), which respectively correspond to the desire realm (*'dod pa['i khams]*), the form realm (*gzugs[kyi khams]*), the fields of infinite space and infinite consciousness (*nam mkha' dang rnam shes mtha' yas skye mched*), and the field of nothingness (*ci yang med pa'i skye mched*). Nonconceptual perception is

想. 是名小想. 大想云何. 答, 作意思惟廣大諸色而非無邊. 謂或思惟青瘀, 廣説如前. 是名大想.無量想云何. 答, 作意思惟廣大諸色其量無邊. 謂或思惟青瘀, 廣説如前. 是名無量想. 無所有想云何. 答, 此即顯示無所有處想.

14. Dergé 4038, 38a6–38b2: *'du shes gang zhe na / de yang snga ma bzhin du rnam pa drug go // de yang 'di lta ste / mtshan ma dang bcas pa'i 'du shes dang / mtshan ma med pa'i 'du shes dang / chung ngu'i 'du shes dang / chen por gyur pa'i 'du shes dang / tshad med pa'i 'du shes dang / ci yang med pa'i 'du shes so // de yang mdor bsdu na 'jig rten pa'i dang 'jig rten las 'das pa'i 'o // de la chung ngu'i 'du shes ni 'dod pa na spyod pa'i 'o // chen por gyur pa'i 'du shes ni gzugs na spyod pa'i 'o // tshad med pa'i 'du shes ni nam mkha' dang rnam shes mtha' yas skye mched na spyod pa'i 'o // ci yang med pa'i 'du shes ni ci yang med pa'i skye mched na spyod pa'i ste / de dag thams cad ni mtshan ma dang bcas pa'i 'du shes yin no // mtshan ma med pa'i 'du shes ni srid pa'i rtse mo'i 'du shes gang yin pa dang 'jig rten las 'das pa slob pa dang / mi slob pa'i thams cad de thams cad kyang kun du shes par byed pa'i mtshan nyid yin no //.*

defined as "that which is the perception of the pinnacle of existence, of supramundane states of learning and non-learning, and of omniscience" (*srid pa'i rtse mo'i 'du shes gang yin pa dang 'jig rten las 'das pa slob pa dang / mi slob pa'i thams cad de thams cad kyang kun du shes par byed pa*), which corresponds to the field of neither perception nor nonperception. Thus the classifications in two and four perceptions cover the totality of the three realms.

The *Jueding cang lun* (決定藏論), which is the partial Chinese translation of the *Viniścayasaṃgrahaṇī*, correlates nonconceptual perception with the field of neither perception nor nonperception (非想非非想処).[15]

Thus the four perceptions are equivalent to type C of the threefold classification with the addition of the perception of the field of nothingness. They thus differ from the four perceptions given in the *Apidamo jiyimen zu lung* (阿毘達磨集異門足論), which are similar to type B of the threefold classification.

This synthetic position is also attested in Asaṅga's *Abhidharmasamuccaya*.[16] Asaṅga divides the "aggregate of perception" into conceptual perception (*sanimitta-saṃjñā*) and nonconceptual perception (*animitta-saṃjñā*). The former is further subdivided into four: small perception (*parītta-saṃjñā*), great perception (*mahadgata-saṃjñā*), boundless perception (*apramāṇa-saṃjñā*), and perception of the field of nothingness (*akiñcana-saṃjñā*), which correspond, respectively, to the desire realm (*kāmadhātu*), the form realm (*rūpadhātu*), the fields of infinite space and infinite consciousness (*ākāśānantyāyatana* and *vijñānānantyāyatana*), and the field of nothingness (*ākiñcanyāyatana*). On the other hand, nonconceptual perception corresponds to the perception of "nonconventional virtue" (*avyavahāra-kuśala*), "meditation in the signless state" (*animitta-dhātu-samāpanna*), and the "pin-

15. *Jueding cang fen* (決定藏論), Taishō 1584.30.1029b17–23: 何者想相, 六種如前. 又六種生, 有相想, 無相想, 小想, 大想, 無量想, 無用想. 此一切想得二種異, 一者世間, 二出世間. 縁於欲界是名小想, 縁於色界是名大想, 縁空識處名無量想, 縁無所用處是無用想. 此欲界等是名有相想. 非想非非想是無相想. 出世間想, 謂諸學人及無學人. 是一切相分別想相.

16. *Abhidharmasamuccaya*, chap. 7 (Gohkale 1947, 15.21–28): [*saṃjñā-skandha-vyavasthānaṃ katamat / ṣaṭ saṃjñā-kāyāḥ / cakṣuḥ-saṃsparśajā saṃjñā śrotra-ghrāṇa*]*-jihvā-kāya-manaḥ-saṃsparśajā saṃjñā / yathā sanimittam api saṃjānāti, animittam api, parīttam api, mahadgatam api, apramāṇam api, nāsti kiñcid ity ākiñcanyāyatanam api saṃjānāti // sanimitta-saṃjñā katamā / avyavahāra-kuśalasyânimitta-dhātu-samāpannasya bhavāgrasamāpannasya ca saṃjñāṃ sthāpayitvā yāvad anyā saṃjñā // animitta-saṃjñā katamā / yā sthāpitā saṃjñā // parīttā saṃjñā katamā / yayā kāma-dhātuṃ saṃjānāti // mahadgatā saṃjñā katamā / yayā rūpa-dhātuṃ saṃjānāti // apramāṇa-saṃjñā katamā / yayā ākāśānantyāyatanaṃ vijñānānantyāyatanaṃ ca saṃjānāti // akiñcana-saṃjñā katamā / yayā ākiñcanyāyatanaṃ saṃjānāti //*.

nacle of existence" (*bhavāgra-samāpanna*). The same explanation is also found in Sthiramati's *Dacheng apidamo zaji lun* (大乘阿毘達磨雜集論).[17]

Combined twofold and fourfold classification of perception

<table>
<tr><td rowspan="4">conceptual perception</td><td>small perception</td><td>small objects</td></tr>
<tr><td>great perception</td><td>extensive objects</td></tr>
<tr><td>boundless perception</td><td>field of infinite space and field of infinite consciousness</td></tr>
<tr><td>perception of the field of nothingness</td><td>field of nothingness</td></tr>
<tr><td colspan="2">nonconceptual perception</td><td>field of neither perception nor nonperception</td></tr>
</table>

Conclusion

The concept of perception (*saṃjñā*) is a key notion in Buddhist doctrine, mentioned and investigated in multiple sources. It was especially developed in Buddhist āgama and abhidharma texts. Despite the relevance of this concept, its various classifications have never been systematically studied in a comparative fashion. This paper thus represents the first attempt to provide an overview of the development of the categorization of the aggregate of perception (*saṃjñāskandha*) found in Buddhist āgama and abhidharma texts. Three models emerged from this study: (1) a threefold classification of perception, (2) a fourfold classification, and (3) a combination of twofold and fourfold classifications.

17. Taishō 1606.31.696c19–697a4: 云何建立想蘊, 謂六想身. 眼觸所生想, 乃至意觸所生想. 由此想故或了有相, 或了無相, 或了小, 大, 無量, 或了無所有無所有處. 有相想者, 謂除不善言説無相界定及有頂定想所餘想. 無相想者, 謂前所除想. 小想者, 謂能了欲界想. 大想者, 謂能了色界想. 無量想者, 謂能了空無邊處, 識無邊處想. 無所有處想者, 謂能了無所有處想. 不善言説想者, 謂未學語言故, 雖於色起想而不能了, 此名為色故名無相想. 無相界定想者, 謂離色等一切相無相涅槃想故, 名無相想. 有頂定想者, 謂彼想不明利, 不能於境圖種種相故, 名無相想. 小者, 謂欲界下劣故. 大者, 謂色界增上故. 無量者, 謂空無邊處識無邊處無邊際故. 是故緣彼諸想亦名小大無量.

Works Cited

Ejima, Yasunori. 1989. *Abhidharmakośabhāṣya of Vasubandhu*. Tokyo: Sankibo Press.

Gohkale, V. V. 1947. "Fragments from the Abhidharmasamuccaya of Asaṅga." *Journal of the Royal Asiatic Society, Bombay Branch*, New Series 23: 13–38.

Kramer, Jowita. 2013. *Sthiramati's Pañcaskandhakavibhāṣā. Part 1: Critical edition*. Vienna: Austrian Academy of Sciences Press.

Kumagai, Seiji. 2016. "Bonpo Abhidharma Theory of Five Aggregates." *Journal of Indian and Buddhist Studies* 64.3: 150–57.

———. 2017. "The Bonpo Abhidharma Theory of Perception (*Saṃjñā*)." *Journal of Indian and Buddhist Studies* 65.3: 147–54.

Li, Xuezhu, and Ernst Steinkellner, eds. 2008. *Vasubandhu's Pañcaskandhaka*. Vienna: Austrian Academy of Sciences Press.

Mimaki, Katsumi, and Samten G. Karmay. 2007. *Bon sgo gsal byed (Clarification of the Gates of Bon): A Fourteenth Century Bon po Doxographical Treatise*. Kyoto: Graduate School of Letters of Kyoto University.

Pradhan, Prahlad, ed. 1967. *Abhidharmakośabhāṣya of Vasubandhu*. Patna: K. P. Jayaswal Research Institute.

Taishō: *Taishō Shinshū Daizokyō* 大正新脩大蔵経 (The Taishō-Era Revised Chinese Tripiṭaka), 100 volumes. Edited by Junjiro Takakusu. Tokyo: Taishō Issaikyō Kankōkai, 1924–32.

This research was funded in part by the Uehiro Foundation on Ethics and Education and a grant from the Japan Society for the Promotion of Science (No. 20140395).

Memory, Imagination, and the Culture of Religious Experience

Karin L. Meyers

The treasures are not exactly what they pretend to be, and yet they flow inexorably from the depths of the Tibetan cultural and religious system. Every discovery is also a memory. The treasures are exactly what they pretend to be.[1]

"WHAT DOES CREATIVITY look like when it is understood in terms of retrieval of the past?" This is the essence of a question I remember Matthew posing to a class of undergraduates at the University of Chicago some twenty years ago in an effort to help make the incredible (difficult to believe *and* marvelous) Tibetan phenomenon of "treasure" (*gter ma*) revelation plausible or, at least, imaginable. That question, with its historical, cultural, and phenomenological sensitivity to what is essentially a philosophical proposition about the nature of a religious experience, has been so productive for my own attempt to make sense of Tibetan Buddhism that I have often repeated it for my own students.

Readers of Matthew's work will readily recognize such rumination on memory, imagination, and the culture of religious experience as a significant and recurrent theme of his scholarship—even when not the explicit focus. In this essay I trace critical connections between these three topics through a somewhat idiosyncratic selection of Matthew's works—namely, those to which I have returned most often and that have had the most impact on my thinking. My aim is not to provide an authoritative interpretation of his views on these topics but to pull on several provocative threads of his thinking to weave together a theory of religious experience centered on the category of the *imaginal*. To my knowledge, Matthew has not expressed this theory himself.

1. Kapstein 2000, 137.

Thus the essay is—fittingly, I hope, for the topic and the occasion—an exercise in both retrieval and creative reappropriation.

Memory and Imagination

At the time when Matthew posed the question regarding Tibetan treasures to the class, he was in the final stages of editing *The Tibetan Assimilation of Buddhism*. There, however, the question is posed somewhat differently. In the context of criticizing the dichotomies of canonical versus apocryphal for classifying Buddhist literature, and authentic versus fraudulent for Tibetan treasures, Matthew explains with reference to Michael Aris's work on Padma gling pa (1450–1521):

> It is the apparent paradox of the fraud who is nonetheless genuinely inspired, and so becomes a *real* creator of culture, that interests me here. The question that we must ask, I think, is not so much whether the "treasures" were real or fake, but rather why it was that, in traditional Tibet, creativity so often masked itself as the retrieval of the past.[2]

On my reading, the question from class makes the provocative philosophical suggestion that creativity is a universal human experience with culturally distinct phenomenological presentations and interpretations. It thus speaks to the nature of the *imaginal* realm of Tibetan visionaries. By contrast, the question in the quote seems more a historical question about the formation of the Tibetan cultural *imaginaire*, about how Tibetans came to present, understand, and shape their world. There is an important distinction between the *imaginal* and *imaginaire* (see below), but they are intimately related. In the discussion that follows and elsewhere in Matthew's work, historical analysis of Tibetan culture (focused on the *imaginaire*) regularly gives way to phenomenological-philosophical reflection on the nature of religious experience (where the imaginal comes into play).

In answer to the historical question, Matthew suggests that because Tibetan Buddhism locates authority in the past and conceives of knowledge, talent, and creativity as the results of previous lives, it is plausible that for Tibetans the creative genius of the treasure revealer is itself a mark of authenticity "not entirely different" from "the authenticity which is claimed for the [historical] origin of these treasures," and that this may hold, "even if a present act of

2. Kapstein 2000, 137.

manufacture is involved."[3] There are, however, cultural constraints on such creativity and on the personality[4] of the creator. Elsewhere, Matthew explains that, as with aesthetic experience, only certain kinds of religious experience will be valued in a given "religious life-world":

> Religiously creative individuals, like creative artists, may sometimes challenge these limits, transgress them, and succeed in initiating their reconstruction, but such creativity derives its power in part from its relation to pre-given cultural frameworks and can never be entirely dissociated from them.[5]

This not only speaks to the conditions that enable Tibetans to understand treasures and their revealers as authentically linked to the past but also explains why modern Western-educated readers[6] have trouble seeing discovery as memory, and so may become preoccupied with the material-historical question regarding whether treasures are "real" or "fake." Matthew suggests that if his argument regarding the coincidence of discovery and memory in the Tibetan imagination appears sophistical, it is merely because we do not share the Buddhist conviction in rebirth and have a radically different conception of individual creativity.[7] He does not elaborate here, but I think the meaning is clear. Modern Western culture values progress and novelty over retrieval and continuity. Aside from not tending to believe in rebirth, we understand creativity as belonging to psychically and temporally bounded individuals—even if they have a special intuitive (or "visionary") relationship with the future. By contrast, Tibetans understand treasure revealers to have psyches that are in regular communication with other intelligences, beings that reside in other times and realms—including the revealer's own former personalities. Indeed, the revealer's authority depends to a large extent on the evaluation of these communications as evidence for a special relationship with the past.

Such cultural conditions not only inform the inter-subjective evaluation of religious experience but also plausibly its intra-subjective presentation. If this is right, then we might be able to imagine how what we call "creativity" could manifest with the phenomenological features of "memory" in the

3. Kapstein 2000, 136–37.

4. See Gyatso 1993 and Gyatso 1998.

5. Kapstein 2004, 280.

6. I beg the reader to forgive my overgeneralization here. Limited space prevents relevant qualifications.

7. Kapstein 2000, 137. Also see the epigraph at the opening of this essay.

Tibetan cultural context—as I recall Matthew suggesting to the University of Chicago students. We might even consider the possibility that *our* memories are regularly masked (or presented)[8] as novel discoveries. This is not to say that there is no distinction between discovery and memory, just that much of what we interpret as novel discovery—in artistic and intellectual endeavors alike—may, in a different cultural context, be plausibly interpreted as *re*-discovery and *re*-presentation. It is also possible that our cultural valorization of novelty and individuality not only affects how we interpret our moments of inspiration but also their phenomenological presentation, effectively "masking" (or psychologically repressing) our communications with other intelligences.

Given the discrepancy between the quote I remember from class with its more phenomenological orientation and the one memorialized in *The Tibetan Assimilation of Buddhism*, I am not certain if my own memory is, in fact, a confabulation or if I have perhaps read too much into Matthew's brief comments about the coincidence of memory and discovery in the Tibetan imagination. However, like the fabricated treasure that is meaningful and true (even if presently manufactured) in virtue of making good sense in its cultural context, I think the version of the question I remember makes good sense within the context of Matthew's works—especially when they venture beyond historical discussion of the Tibetan *imaginaire* to reflect upon the *imaginal*.

The Imaginaire and the Imaginal

The terms *imaginaire* and *imaginal* were introduced to English (from the French and Latin, respectively) to contend with the fact that the word *imaginary*[9] is associated with fiction, fantasy, and unreality. While neither *imaginaire* nor *imaginal* refers to something false or unreal, the terms have distinctly different meanings and ontological valences. In his masterwork on the Pali *imaginaire,* Steven Collins draws on the medieval historian Jacques Le Goff to explain the *imaginaire* as:

> . . . a nonmaterial, imaginative world constituted by texts, especially works of art and literature. Such worlds are by definition not the same as the material world, but insofar as the material world is

8. "Presented" may be preferable here, as "masked" might be taken to imply that the scholar wears no mask and is thus in a privileged position to reveal the true faces of others.

9. However, "imaginary" is sometimes used as a translation for *imaginaire*.

> thought and experienced in part through them, they are not imaginary in the sense of beings false, entirely made up.[10]

The suggestion here is that while products of the imagination are by definition unreal, they may have a kind of contingent reality insofar as they inform social and material facts.[11] *The Tibetan Assimilation of Buddhism* is primarily concerned with the Tibetan *imaginaire* in this sense—namely, with the transformations of memory and imagination involved in the assimilation of Buddhism by Tibet's cultural elite.[12] Arguably, it is also the *imaginaire* that Matthew has in mind when, as a historian, he refers to the "imaginal persistence of the empire"[13] or the "imaginal polity."[14] It is when he is writing as a historian *of religion*[15] that he begins to speak in terms of the *imaginal* proper.

The *imaginal* is a far more ontologically radical concept than the *imaginaire*—particularly in the version popularized by the scholar of Islamic mysticism Henry Corbin.[16] Corbin uses the term *imaginal* (or *mundis imaginalis*) to demarcate a realm of knowing and being that mediates between the sensible physical world and the world of the pure intellect in the Platonically inflected thought of Ibn 'Arabī. The imaginal has also become a comparative category. As such, it refers to a quasi-physical realm (or realms) of images in which vision, prophesy, dreams, alchemy, commerce with angels, myth, and symbol "take place."[17] It is accessed through the faculty of the "creative" or "active" imagination.[18] This is the same faculty that is at work in the social-cultural *imaginaire* as well as in individual creative work, but here it is "empowered" by spiritual vision and may be endowed with the various noetic

10. Collins 1998, 73. See Le Goff 1998, Introduction.

11. Although not addressed explicitly in the quote, an *imaginaire* not only informs the apprehension of existing social and material facts, but also the creation of new ones.

12. Kapstein 2000, vii.

13. Kapstein 2000, chapter 8.

14. Kapstein 2006, 83.

15. I refer here to the specialized study of religion as a distinct (even if not *sui generis*) phenomenon.

16. For an entertaining discussion of how the term made its way from the British Psychical Society to Theodore Flournoy's study of Swiss medium Catherine Elise Müller *From India to the Planet Mars* (1900) to Jung and then Corbin, see Kripal 2018, chapter 11.

17. Corbin 1989, xi–xii.

18. Corbin also borrowed this term from Jung.

and paranormal powers commonly associated with religious virtuosos (e.g., transcendent or transformative wisdom, clairvoyance, and psycho-kinesis).[19]

The imaginal realms accessed through such an empowered imagination are not imaginary, nor is their reality merely contingent on social and material facts. On the contrary, they are *more real* than the physical world known through the senses. Thus, while the *imaginaire* speaks to the power of the imagination to shape material facts, the *imaginal* speaks to the power of the imagination to transcend these facts and access a reality that is ontologically prior to them. As such, the *imaginal* denotes realms of knowing and being found in many human cultures but excluded from modern epistemologies and ontologies.

In *The Tibetan Assimilation of Buddhism*, Matthew makes passing reference to Corbin's *mundis imaginalis* in the context of discussing how Tibetans resolve tensions between novel visionary and conservative scholastic approaches to Buddhist teaching[20] and again when discussing how Great Perfection praxis relies on "the rich domain of symbolic forms" to mediate between "ordinary" experience and primordial reality.[21] This suggests that he takes the comparative category of the imaginal to have some theoretical purchase on Tibetan Buddhism, but he does not elaborate on this here, nor does he discuss the philosophical implications of Corbin's ontological prioritization of the imaginal over the sensible. But as I will attempt to demonstrate in the next two sections, the imaginal is directly relevant to Matthew's historiographic reflections on narratives about visionary experience as well as to his philosophical analysis of such experience.

The Historiographer and Imaginal History

A notable feature of Matthew's work is that he is not always in a hurry to a conclusion. (He even titles one conclusion, "In Search of a Conclusion.")[22] He seems to delight in raising a question and sketching possible routes to an answer before revealing that we do not know now or can never know the information necessary to arrive at that answer. Along the way, we learn as much about what information we do and do not have as about how our questions and concerns may be a mismatch for the data. One of the more striking exam-

19. Hollenback 1998.

20. Kapstein 2000, 87.

21. Kapstein 2000, 180.

22. Kapstein 2004, 150.

ples is a short essay in which he discusses the difficulty, nay impossibility, of developing a relative chronology to date the founder of the Shangpa (Shangs pa) Kagyü sect, Khyungpo Naljor (Khyung po rnal 'bjor),[23] on the basis of his hagiography.[24]

As was typical of the Tibetan genre in its early phase and of the early Shangpa Kagyü hagiographies in particular, Khyungpo is shown to glide seamlessly between dream, vision, and physical reality without notice, and with little respect for the historiographer on his tail[25] (except perhaps for an occasional playful wink back at him).[26] As Matthew makes clear, while later Tibetan hagiographers develop conventions for distinguishing between dream, vision, and physical reality—perhaps with the Tibetan historiographer's interests in mind—the fact that Khyungpo's do not is rather the point.

In the competitive atmosphere of the second dissemination of Buddhism, there were pragmatic reasons for Tibetan hagiographers to prioritize a saint's spiritual attainments and miraculous feats over his scholarly learning or the historical circumstances of his life.[27] Given the tenuous historical connection of the Shangpa lineage to India, and its specialization in the yogas of dream (*svapna*, *rmi lam*) and apparition (*māyākāya*, *sgyu lus*), it would have made particular sense to remain vague with regard to historical circumstance and advertise instead the founder's *polyphasic* virtuosity (i.e., his mastery of different states of consciousness).[28] While Matthew notes how these pragmatic concerns may have informed the hagiography, he is careful not to reduce its visionary content to them, and cautions us against reading it solely through the lenses of our own concerns and sensibilities. Aside from questioning whether we are entitled to read it as history,[29] he concludes the essay by noting that even when Tibetan hagiographers do take an interest in historical-material facts and their organization according to a linear, unidirectional flow of time, they persist in their enchantment, in their preoccupation with marvels, visions, and dreams.[30] In an earlier essay, Matthew suggests that the text is more properly described as "soteriography" (the story of an individual's

23. Traditionally said to have lived 150 years beginning in 978 or 990.

24. Kapstein 2005.

25. Kapstein 2005, 5.

26. Kapstein 2005, 10–11. See the discussion of Atiśa and the rotting texts.

27. Kapstein 2005, 5.

28. For this reason, they do sometimes announce that an event takes place in a dream.

29. Kapstein 2005, 4.

30. Kapstein 2005, 12.

salvation or liberation).[31] Referring to the episode in which Khyungpo meets his teacher, Niguma, he explains that, "The tale is constructed so as to overturn ordinary conceptions of reality, to introduce us to the luminous and magical realm in which Buddhist esoteric experience unfolds."[32] In other words, the meeting with Niguma is both a story about an initiation into an imaginal realm and a preliminary form of initiation into that realm. As such, it is what Corbin calls an "imaginal history," that is, a narrative indexed to events that take place in the imaginal rather than sensible, temporal realm. A few highlights from the episode should serve to illustrate this.[33]

The story begins with Khyungpo explaining[34] that he had traveled to India in search of a teacher with a direct transmission from a buddha. He learns that Niguma is such a person but that she no longer resides in bodily form. She has "become the stuff of rainbows" and now abides only in the pure bodhisattva stations, making her accessible only to those with pure vision.[35] Upon learning that she sometimes apparates[36] (presumably, to just such persons) in a particular charnel ground, Khyungpo makes his way there with great devotion. Eventually, Niguma appears in the sky and confers upon him the empowerments of dream and apparition. She then takes him on an aerial journey to a spectacular golden mountain. While hovering above the mountain, Khyungpo asks her where they might be in India or if the scene is a magical creation. Niguma responds by suggesting that all of saṃsāra can be realized as a golden isle and that all dharmas, even his own future buddhahood, are but apparitions. She then blesses and commands him, "Grasp your dreams!"[37] After this, by what appears to be his own power of supernormal locomotion,[38] Khyungpo travels to the realms of the gods and demigods. When a demigod swallows him whole, Niguma reappears and warns him not to wake up, whereupon she teaches him the entirety of the six yogas.

Given that this episode begins with what sounds like a physical journey to

31. Kapstein 1992, 195.

32. Kapstein 1997, 181.

33. See Matthew's translation in Kapstein 1992, 195–96.

34. While the text is narrated in the first person, the colophon clarifies that disciples compiled it. Kapstein 1992, 195.

35. Kapstein 1992, 195.

36. The Harry Potter neologism seems appropriate.

37. "Grasping" a dream means becoming aware of a dream as a dream and implies the kind of control such lucidity makes possible.

38. See Hollenback 1998 for a comparative discussion of this feature of the empowered imagination.

India but turns into a shamanic vision quest[39] and concludes in a lucid dream, it is not clear that any part of the journey should be interpreted as taking place in historical time or at a particular physical location. As Matthew suggests, such narratives can be read fruitfully by the historian as speaking to the *mentalités* (or *imaginaire*) of a particular time;[40] some episodes might be best read as fictions serving a particular apologetic end.[41] However, I think he would agree that it would be overly cynical to treat all such visionary narratives as *merely* apologetic fiction and rather unimaginative to consider their significance only in relation to historical fact.

Corbin's concept of imaginal history gives us another option. Because events of imaginal history are not (primarily)[42] indexed to historical time or physical geography, Corbin explains that it doesn't make sense to evaluate the narratives that give them meaning as true or false in relation to physical events and locations. In other words, they are not history in the ordinary sense of the term. Nor are they fiction.[43] As Matthew suggests, the point of the story about the meeting with Niguma is not to orient the reader in physical time and space but in an *imaginal* realm of experience. Arguably, the entirety of the Vajrayāna, and much of the Mahāyāna as well, is predicated on the soteriological efficacy of commerce in such imaginal realms. Both Mahāyāna and Vajrayāna practices make abundant use of the active imagination, and Mahāyāna sūtras often explicitly involve their hearers and preachers in the imaginal histories they describe.[44]

At first blush, the suggestion that Khyungpo's hagiography is indexed to *imaginal* rather than historical events is hardly controversial. Things get more interesting if we take seriously Corbin's insistence on the power of the imagination as a noetic faculty, and the reality, indeed, *hyper-* or *sur*-reality of the imaginal. And there may be good reasons for doing so, or at least, for not dismissing the idea out of hand. Modern Western academic cultures tend to be *monophasic*, that is, focused on a rather narrow bandwidth of sensory, rational, waking consciousness, and are heavily influenced by the view that only matter and material interactions are real. But we must remember that this is

39. Kapstein 1992.

40. Kapstein 2005, 5.

41. Such as the encounter with Atiśa; Kapstein 2005, 11.

42. While the physical and imaginal are largely discrete for Corbin, there is a great deal of permeability between the two in Tibetan Buddhist literature and practice, where events are often indexed to both physical and imaginal realms.

43. Corbin 1989, vii.

44. Gummer, Forthcoming.

a rather unusual way of being human. Most of the world's cultures have been *polyphasic*, inhabiting and attributing meaning and reality to multiple states of consciousness.[45] Given this situation, it is not surprising that we should find ourselves nonplussed when we intercept transmissions from the imaginal such as Khyungpo's visionary journey, but are we therefore justified in dismissing or deflating the reality of their contents? The fact that our materialistic monophasy has led to demonstrable technological success (often taken as testament to the truth of materialism) need not entail that other modes of knowing and being are invalid. Moreover, it is possible that these successes have come at some epistemic cost, that in erasing other dimensions of reality from public discourse and private concern, we have lost something of our human capacity to use our imaginations to participate in them. In other words, it is possible that our disenchantment has resulted in the disempowerment of our imaginations.

Matthew does not put matters in quite these terms. Nonetheless, when he contrasts modern materialist sensibilities to traditional Tibetan ones, attempts to make sense of Tibetan phenomena that defy our historical or scientific explanatory frameworks, and refuses to reduce or explain them away, he is pointing to the ways in which these frameworks, for all their value, may be incomplete—something he addresses more directly in his comparative and philosophical analysis of visionary religious experience.

Dual-Aspect Theory and the Imaginal

One reason we find it easy to dismiss imaginal journeys such as Khyungpo's as unreal or, at least, less real than physical journeys (even if personally or culturally meaningful), is that while the physical world appears to be independent of individual psychological or cultural influence (at least at the level of mid-sized objects), imaginal realms are clearly otherwise. This fact, combined with modernist commitments to the dualities of subject-object and mind-matter, and the ontological alignment and prioritization of the objective and material, makes it tempting to dismiss experiences or phenomena that do not comport with common-sense conceptions of the physical world as *merely* subjective, or to explain them reductively in terms of cultural construction or neural processes. In his edited volume on religious experiences of light, *The Presence of Light,*[46] Matthew discusses the limitations of such subjectivist and objectivist interpretations of visionary experience and proposes dual-aspect theory

45. Laughlin 2013.

46. Kapstein 2004.

as a more satisfactory alternative. Dual-aspect theory[47] maintains that while reality may be unitary, neither a mental nor material substance, our epistemic access to it is dualistic. This preserves subjective and objective epistemological perspectives without reducing one to the other. But as we will see, it cannot—without some tweaking—accommodate situations or phenomena that blur the boundary between the subjective and objective or the mental and material.

Curiously, Matthew's own contribution to the volume is focused on just such a phenomenon: the rainbow body.[48] While the primary focus of his essay is the historical and cultural conditions that contribute to the development of the rainbow body as a uniquely Tibetan religious experience, he argues that that it is deeply problematic to conclude from this history that the rainbow body is therefore a "cultural construction."[49] Part of the problem is descriptive. The rainbow body is, after all, purported to be a *physical* phenomenon. As such, "It belongs to the class of miracles."[50] A less metaphysically loaded word for this is "paranormal."[51] As Jeffrey Kripal puts it,

> A paranormal event is one in which a material event corresponds more or less precisely to a subjective event or mental state, thereby collapsing the assumed subject-object dualism of our ordinary cognitive and sensory experience and suggesting some deeper superreality that is neither simply mental nor material but somehow both.[52]

In other words, a paranormal event is an event in which the imaginal crosses over into the sensible domain. In the case of the rainbow body, the subjective experience of the yogi (cultivated through imaginal work with the subtle body) initiates a physical transformation. (A placebo and the use of visualization to heal one's body are arguably similar, though admittedly less dramatic, examples of an empowered imagination at work.) While aspects of the

47. There are several versions of this. Here I follow the broad outlines of the one Matthew cites (Nagel 1986).

48. Kapstein 2004, chap. 6.

49. Kapstein 2004, 151.

50. Kapstein 2004, 151.

51. While "miracle" implies a break with natural law, "paranormal" only means something extraordinary or supernormal, something not explicable according to current scientific theory but not necessarily contrary to natural law.

52. Kripal 2018, 241.

rainbow body may be amenable to naturalistic explanation,[53] and the idea of a body disappearing into light is not unimaginable,[54] the phenomenon as a whole defies current scientific explanation. However, as Matthew suggests, this is not sufficient reason to declare it a physical impossibility or a mere cultural construction. This, he says, would require "some rather strong assumptions on our part about physical possibility . . . Who are we to say that it never occurs?"[55] Like many paranormal phenomena that bear the marks of culture but are also physical in nature, the rainbow body is not confined to the hazy literary past but enjoys contemporary witnesses.[56]

While Matthew does not dismiss the paranormal character of the rainbow body, he does not say much about how we should understand it other than to suggest that any explanation of it in terms of the physical properties of light must be complemented by a story about the religious nature of light in the Tibetan cultural context—a context in which a variety of ideas work together to make it plausible.[57] In the concluding essay to the volume, however, he elaborates on this, suggesting that the capacity to have religious experiences of light might be understood as an emergent property of our physical bodies,[58] or that such experiences might supervene upon physical systems or other kinds of experiences, such as aesthetic ones.[59] Both theories help mediate between constructivist and perennialist interpretations of religious experience (a central concern of the volume). While the physical properties of light and human physiology account for common patterns in religious experiences of light across cultures, cultural context accounts for differences. Ultimately, however, Matthew endorses dual-aspect theory, which has the added virtue of placing the reality of the subjective aspects of religious experience on equal footing with objective physical processes and preempts any attempt to reduce the subjective to the objective (or vice versa). The problem with dual-aspect theory is that while its power to fend off reductionism lays in its epistemic isolation of the subjective and objective aspects of experience, if one insists too

53. Kapstein 2004, 151.

54. See Matthew's comments on the Star Trek transporter. Kapstein 2004, 122 and 151.

55. Kapstein 2004, 151.

56. Matthew opens the essay with examples of contemporary accounts of rainbow body. Also see Tiso 2016.

57. Kapstein 2004, 152.

58. He does not use the term *emergent property* but speaks of religious experience as a "potential" or "capacity" of a physical system and as emerging from a complex skein of conditions (which include cultural and physical conditions); Kapstein 2004, 289.

59. Kapstein 2004, 151 and 288.

strongly on this isolation, it cannot account for (or will be contradicted by) instances in which the imaginal breaks into the sensible world—as in the case of the rainbow body, the yogas of dream and apparition, and many of the phenomena surrounding treasure revelation (e.g., precognitive dreams or the synchronistic discovery of material artifacts).[60]

If, like Matthew, we are not inclined to dismiss the possibility of such paranormal events and processes out of hand, and are also not satisfied with a purely descriptive or historical account of them, then we will need to modify dual-aspect theory with something like Kripal's theory of the empowered imagination.[61] As was hinted at above, according to this theory, paranormal events reveal the limitations of our ordinary dualistic cognitions and expose the mysterious super-reality (for Kripal, this is consciousness) that underlies them.[62] Given their participation in the imagination, such events are culturally conditioned, but just as Matthew maintains with respect to the rainbow body, they are not only cultural constructs. They are also something More.[63]

Notably, the basic metaphysics of Kripal's theory is not entirely dissimilar to the Dzokchen idea of a primordial mind or awareness that is ontologically and epistemically prior to dualistic experience. As mentioned above, Matthew notes that access to this primordial mind is regularly mediated by "the rich domain of symbolic forms" that is the imaginal. I have further suggested that many phenomena in Tibetan Buddhism may be usefully interpreted as paranormal intrusions of the imaginal into the sensible world and would further venture that much of the alchemical practice of Vajrayāna Buddhism precisely concerns the imaginal transformation of the sensible world. Given the appearance of the various threads of this theory in Matthew's works, perhaps something like this idea of the *imaginal* has been weaving its way through them. Maybe that is where my understanding of it came from in the first place.[64] Or, perhaps I just imagined it there.

60. See Gyatso 1993 and Gyatso 1998.

61. Jorge Ferrer's theory of participation (Ferrer 2017), which rejects the entire edifice of subject-object dualism in interpreting religious experience, is another option.

62. See Kripal 2018, chapters 9–14.

63. On the idea of "More," see Kripal et al. 2014.

64. Kripal and Hollenback are also influences.

Works Cited

Collins, Steven. 1998. *Nirvana and Other Buddhist Felicities: Utopias of the Pali Imaginaire*. Cambridge: Cambridge University Press.

Corbin, Henry. 1989. *Spiritual Body and Celestial Earth: From Mazdean Iran to Shī'ite Iran*. Translated by Nancy Pearson. Princeton, NJ: Princeton University Press.

Ferrer, Jorge. 2017. *Participation and the Mystery: Transpersonal Essays in Psychology, Education, and Religion*. Albany: State University of New York Press.

Gummer, Natalie. 2020. "Sūtra Time." In *The Language of the Sūtras*, edited by Luis O. Gómez and Natalie Gummer. Berkeley: Mangalam Press.

Gyatso, Janet. 1993. "The Logic of Legitimation in the Tibetan Treasure Tradition." *History of Religions* 33.2: 97–134.

———. 1998. *Apparitions of the Self: The Autobiography of a Tibetan Visionary*. Princeton, NJ: Princeton University Press.

Hollenback, Jess Byron. 1998. *Mysticism: Experience, Response, and Empowerment*. University Park: Pennsylvania State University Press.

Kapstein, Matthew T. 1992. "The Illusion of Spiritual Progress: Remarks on Indo-Tibetan Buddhist Soteriology." In *Paths to Liberation: The Mārga and Its Transformations in Buddhist Thought*, edited by Robert E. Buswell Jr. and Robert M. Gimello, 193–224. Honolulu: University of Hawaii Press.

———. 1997. "The Journey to the Golden Mountain." In *Religions of Tibet*, edited by Donald Lopez, 178–87. Princeton, NJ: Princeton University Press.

———. 2000. *The Tibetan Assimilation of Buddhism: Conversion, Contestation, and Memory*. New York: Oxford University Press.

———. 2004. *The Presence of Light: Divine Radiance and Religious Experience*. Chicago: University of Chicago Press.

———. 2005. "Chronological Conundrums in the Life of Khyung Po Rnal 'byor: Hagiography and Historical Time." *Journal of the International Association of Tibetan Studies* 1: 1–14.

———. 2006. *The Tibetans*. Malden, MA: Blackwell Publishing.

Kripal, Jeffrey J., Ata Anzali, Andrea R. Jain, and Erin L. Prophet. 2014. *Comparing Religions: Coming to Terms*. Hoboken, NJ: Wiley Blackwell.

Kripal, Jeffrey J. 2018. *Secret Body: Erotic and Esoteric Currents in the History of Religions*. Chicago: University of Chicago Press.

Laughlin, Charles D. 2013. "Dreaming and Reality: A Neuroanthropological Account." *International Journal of Transpersonal Studies* 32: 64–78.

Le Goff, Jacques. 1998. *The Medieval Imagination*. Translated by Arthur Goldhammer. Chicago: University of Chicago Press.

Nagel, Thomas. 1986. *The View From Nowhere*. New York: Oxford University Press.

Tiso, Francis. 2016. *Rainbow Body and Resurrection: Spiritual Attainment, the Dissolution of the Material Body, and the Case of Khenpo A Cho*. Berkeley: North Atlantic Books.

Buddhist Philosophy as a Way of Life: Perspectives on the "Three Wisdoms" from Tibet and Japan

Marc-Henri Deroche

Philosophical discourse must be understood from the perspective of the way of life of which it is both the expression and the means. Consequently, philosophy is above all a way of life, but one that is intimately linked to philosophical discourse.

—Pierre Hadot[1]

Separated from our actual "here and now" existence, the study of doctrines becomes mere speculation. In Buddhism, speculation apart from existence is called vain discourse (prapañca).

—Keiji Nishitani[2]

Introduction: From Paris to Palri to Kyōto

Paraphrasing the beginning of Matthew Kapstein's paper in honor of Gene Smith,[3] I shall say that, in the 2000s, I was one of those who came strongly under the influence of Matthew Kapstein, in this very filiation of the academic study of the so-called *ris med* or "impartial" approach, with an initial focus on its eclectic model of the main lineages of Tibetan Buddhist meditation and yoga, the "eight great conveyances that are vehicles of attainment"

1. Hadot 2002, 3–4. Original French 1995, 19: [. . .] *le discours philosophique doit être compris dans la perspective du mode de vie dont il est à la fois le moyen et l'expression et, en conséquence, que la philosophie est bien avant tout une manière de vivre, mais qui est étroitement liée au discours philosophique.*

2. Nishitani 1984, 22. Original Japanese 1967, 25:「今ここ」という現実の実在を離れては、教理の考究は思弁になる。実在を離れた思弁は、仏教でいう戯論である。

3. Kapstein 2007, 110.

(*sgrub pa'i shing rta chen po brgyad*). This formed the core topic of my graduate studies (2003–11) under Matthew Kapstein's supervision at the École Pratique des Hautes Études in Paris. My research focused on the original author to whom this model was attributed, Prajñāraśmi ('Phreng po gter ston Shes rab 'od zer, 1518–84), the founder of a major monastic institution of the Nyingmapas in 'Phyongs rgyas, central Tibet: the Mahāyāna Monastery of the Glorious Mountain (*dpal ri theg chen gling*). Palri (Dpal ri), the "glorious mountain" referred to here, is the pure land of Padmasambhava. While this monastery had become almost forgotten by the tradition and was largely unknown in academia, I demonstrated that it was actually pivotal for the successive revivals of the Nyingmapas beginning in the sixteenth century and for the emergence of the *ris med* approach in the nineteenth.[4]

In this short essay, I will focus on the underlying ideals for these successive Tibetan Buddhist premodern revivals and how they can be related to the contemporary question of the "potentialities" of Buddhist philosophy raised by Matthew Kapstein in reference to Pierre Hadot's redefinition of ancient *philosophia*.[5] We will consider first how the study of the Tibetan traditions of "spiritual instructions" (*gdams ngag*), defined as "the quintessential Tibetan 'technologies of the self,'"[6] offer a privileged perspective to envision the living, soteriological and transformative dimensions of Buddhism. We will see then how they are to be understood as the orientation and apex of the progression of the three layers of wisdom (*shes rab*, *prajñā*)—born from study (*thos pa*, *śruta*), reflection (*bsam pa*, *cintā*), and cultivation (*sgom pa*, *bhāvanā*)—a defining paradigm for Buddhist philosophy as a way of life.[7]

Finally, having spent the last ten years researching, then teaching at Kyōto University, and being since 2015 appointed in a graduate school that refers in its name and secular program to these "three wisdoms" (*san-e* 三慧, born respectively from *mon shi shu* 聞思修),[8] I will present and discuss some Japanese contemporary perspectives in connection to the philosophy of the Kyōto School (*kyōto gakuha*京都学派). I hope thus to offer a modest contribution to the cross-cultural project of a "Buddhist philosophy," elaborated in both East and West, and reflect upon Matthew Kapstein's extraordinary breadth of scholarship. In parallel to the Buddhist model discussed here, I could call his three wisdoms

4. Deroche 2011, Deroche 2013, and Deroche, Forthcoming(a).

5. Kapstein 2001.

6. Kapstein 1996, 276.

7. For another recent discussion of this idea based on Vasubandhu's *Abhidharmakośa*, see Fiordalis 2018.

8. The *Shishukan* 思修館, "Institute for Study and Practice."

those born from (1) philological and historical in-depth investigation, (2) philosophical clarification, and (3) anthropological direct observation.

Tibetan Technologies of the Self

Matthew Kapstein's articles on "Tibetan Technologies of the Self" (1996, 2008) focused on the model and general content of the *Treasury of Spiritual Instructions* (*Gdams ngag mdzod*), a compilation by 'Jam mgon Kong sprul (1813–1899/1900) of the main systems of "spiritual instructions" (*gdams ngag*, *upadeśa*) reportedly transmitted from India to Tibet, and guiding the practice of yoga. Matthew Kapstein wrote:

> In this context, *gdams ngag* refers essentially to the immediate, heartfelt instructions and admonitions of master to disciple concerning directly liberative insight and practice. *gDams ngag* in this sense is, in the final analysis, a product solely of the interrelationship between master and disciple; it is the non-repeatable discourse event in which the core of the Buddhist enlightenment comes to be manifestly disclosed.[9]

This category forms a specific genre of literature at the heart of Tibetan Buddhist contemplative life. We shall note the importance of the intersubjective dimensions: advice comes from the experienced master to the disciples to instruct. It has a prescriptive character, stating how one ought to live and act, emerging in vibrant response to specific circumstances and singular needs. When Tibet began to absorb Buddhism from India through an immense industry of transmission and translation, Buddhism had become by then a very elaborate and diverse set of schools and doctrines, with a sophisticated scholasticism. The traditions of "spiritual instructions" can be seen then as pragmatic means to synthetize this whole, to actually put it into concrete practice—literally, "to bring [it] into experience" (*nyams su len pa*). Atiśa (982–1154), who played a central role in the second diffusion of Buddhism in Tibet, seems to reflect upon this situation, within the Indian context as well, when he writes in the autocommentary of his *Lamp for the Path to Awakening* (*Bodhipathapradīpa*):

> Nowadays, sentient beings, time, passions,
> views, and life are subject to degeneration.

9. Kapstein 1996, 275.

Since there is no need to learn [all] the texts,
cultivate the yoga of the essential meaning.

Nowadays, there is no time to learn the vast texts
that are like ships [for crossing the ocean of cyclic existence].
So abandoning all that disturbs the mind,
cultivate only the instructions of holy people.

Life is short and there are many things to know.
But since we do not even know the duration of our lives,
like the swan that extracts milk from water,
select [carefully] among the objects of your desires.[10]

In Tibet, distinct Buddhist "schools" (*chos lugs*) actually emerged around the holders of such yogic "lineages" (*brgyud*), retrospectively seen as the founders of these schools. In this way, it can be said that most of the contemplative life of Tibetan Buddhism revolved around such lineages, including institutional and scholastic aspects. The interest of Prajñāraśmi's model of the eight lineages, later used by Kong sprul for organizing his *Treasury of Spiritual Instructions*, was that in times of intensified sectarianism, it promoted (1) a return to the lineages of "spiritual instructions" while showing their common intent, and (2) a trans-sectarian genealogy of Tibetan Buddhism, since these lineages could circulate across the instituted schools and communities that practiced and transmitted them. These two aspects are reflected in the fact that Prajñāraśmi gives for each lineage a summary of its system of instructions and then of its historical ramifications. The relation between school and lineage appears to be a kind of hylomorphism: the school being like the physical body and the lineage its animating soul. Then, in Kong sprul's project:

> *gDams ngag*, essentially the pithy expressions of contemplative experience, thus become the basis for renewed dogmatic system-building.... The products of these and other similar doctrinal syn-

10. Atiśa, *Lamp for the Path to Awakening*, 236: *deng sang sems can dus dang nyon mongs dang // lta ba tshe'i snyigs mar gyur pa ste // gzhung rnams mnyan par dgos pa med pas na // snying po don gyi rnal 'byor bsgoms par bya // ding sang dus su gzings dang 'dra ba yi / gzhung rnams rgya chen mnyan pa'i dus med pas // yid 'khrug byed pa thams cad spangs byas la // dam pa'i nyer bstan 'ba' zhig bsgom par bya // tshe ni yun thung shes bya'i rnam pa mang // tshe yi tshad kyang 'di tsam mi shes pas // ngang pas chu las 'o ma len pa ltar // 'dod pa'i dngos po dang las blang bar bya //*. Translation is mine.

> theses certainly represent some of the most creative developments of Tibetan Buddhist thought.[11]

Matthew Kapstein notes as precedents the philosophical elaborations of the Great Perfection (*rdzogs chen*) of the Nyingmapas, of the Great Seal (*phyags chen, mahāmudra*) of various Kagyüpas, or the Gradual Path (*lam rim*) of the Kadampas that was then expanded by the Gelukpas. Philosophical writing, if oriented toward the practice of such spiritual instructions, has then to fulfill the duty of justifying them and organizing them in a meaningful and rationally compelling way. It has a function of clarification and systematization that, by providing a coherent set of clear goals, ideas, and means, is of central importance for memorization and then application or integration within the life of the individual.

The emphasis on "spiritual instructions" in the contemplative revival promoted by the *ris med* approach and its waves of precedents in the history of Tibetan Buddhism points to an interesting parallel with the role of "spiritual exercises" in Pierre Hadot's efforts to rediscover the ancient ideal of *philosophia* and explore the possibilities of its re-actualization. In both cases, we see the common ideal of wisdom relativizing the differences among schools[12] and giving a general orientation for the conduct of both life and philosophical discourse. Because of this affinity, such Tibetan traditions represent a privileged perspective to envision Buddhism in Hadot's terms. But it is the paradigm of the "three wisdoms" that gives the full articulation of the different dimensions of "spiritual exercises" in Tibetan Buddhist contexts, in its institutions and communities.

The Threefold Quest of Wisdom in Tibetan Buddhism

The original source for the model of the eight lineages was a twofold epistle by Prajñāraśmi. In the first epistle, the *Ambrosia of Listening and Reflection* (*Thos bsam 'chi med kyi bdud rtsi*), he presented the "ten pillars that established the lineages of exegesis," and in the *Ambrosia of Cultivation* (*Sgom pa 'chi med kyi bdud rtsi*), he presented the "eight pillars that established the lineages of attainment."[13] Study and reflection are thus gathered into the rubric of "exegesis" (*bshad*), and cultivation corresponds to practice or "attainment" (*sgrub*). This distinction informs deeply the social realities of scholastic and yogic

11. Kapstein 1996, 281.

12. Hadot 2002, 189–90 and 276; original French 1995, 291 and 415.

13. Deroche 2009, Deroche, Forthcoming(a), and Deroche, Forthcoming(b).

curricula within the "colleges of exegesis" (*bshad grwa*) and the "colleges of yogic practice" (*sgrub grwa*) or "hermitages" (*ri khrod*) mainly focused on the systems of spiritual instructions considered above. The first type of institution leads to being a "scholar" (*mkhas pa, paṇḍita*), while the second aims at training an ascetic (*rnal 'byor pa, yogin*) or ideally a saint or adept (*grub pa, siddha*). But it is precisely the conjunction of both (*mkhas grub*) that best describes the ideal fixed by the Tibetan tradition inherited from India.[14] The two aspects are thus to be integrated along the path of a single individual. And from the perspective of the society, scholastic and yogic communities are living in close dependence upon each other.

If explicit quotations of the threefold wisdom are rare in the Pāli canon, the *Saṅgārava Sutta* (*Majjhima-nikāya* 100) seems to present major ideas in connection to this model. There, the Buddha Śākyamuni distinguishes three types of teachers: the "traditionalists" (*anussavikā*), the "rationalists and speculators" (*takkī vīmaṃsī*), and finally the "experimentalists," who have "directly known the dharma for themselves" (*sāmaṃ yeva dhammaṃ abhiññāya*), regarding himself in this last category considered as supreme.[15] Bhikkhu Anālayo (2003, 44–46) considers this to represent the "early Buddhist approach to knowledge," the three types of teachers being distinguished according to their privileged sources for valid cognition (*pramāṇa*): received tradition, logical reasoning, and direct perception. If, on one hand, direct perception, especially yogic perception that cognizes absolute truth, is considered supreme in Buddhism, on the other hand, meditative experiences, however astonishing as they might sound first, can also be misleading and sources of potential confusion, errors or pitfalls. They thus have to be checked against what the tradition says about them, that is to say according to the records and warnings accumulated by the past generations of experienced meditators, and critically investigated in conjunction with a qualified teacher. While the three grades of wisdom are not identical to the three sources for valid cognition, they nonetheless appear to establish the relations among them along the soteriological path. For in Buddhism, soteriology is deeply connected with epistemology, since the liberation from suffering is obtained ultimately through an insight into its nature. Vasubandhu's discussion of the three wisdoms as three types of certainty (*niścaya*) based, respectively, on reliable scriptures,

14. Prajñāraśmi was reportedly a *dge bshes* in the Sakya and Geluk traditions and a yogin and *gter ston* ("treasure revealer") in the Nyingma and Kagyü traditions. He represents thus the trans-sectarian version of the ideal conjunction of exegesis and contemplation (Deroche 2011 and Deroche, Forthcoming(a)).

15. Chalmers 1977, 211.8–22. Translated by Ñāṇamoli and Bodhi 1995, 820.

reasoning, and contemplation seems also to establish such correlations with epistemological categories.[16] As for the so-called epistemological tradition of Dignāga and Dharmakīrti, Matthew Kapstein (2013) has also shown its connection with soteriology, which, if complex in Indian contexts, can still be directly observed in its contemporary Tibetan living exegetes and successors.

Along a way of life, and on the basis of ethics (*Abhidharmakośa* 6.5a–b), the three wisdoms describe the process of spiritual maturation of an individual. Listening to a teacher or studying texts can be seen as the first input of relevant information from outside, which begins to reorient one's own priorities, interests, and attention through learning from the wisdom accumulated by past generations, especially the Buddha. Nevertheless, there is then the need to go from the words to the meaning, from what ancient sages meant in their own time, place, culture, and language to what it can mean to the individual *hic et nunc*, and from the abstract universal message to the concrete individual life. This is the role of personal reflection, of crucial importance, as pointed out by Kong sprul:[17]

> The meaning of what has been studied just once, a theoretical understanding, does not get applied into one's own continuum and is lost. Thus, reflect on it again and again, examining it in detail. In this way, the attachment to thoughts related to this life will be reversed from the depths, and an uncommon mind that aspires to the highest good in the future will arise.

Repetition can access the deeper or subconscious layers of the mind, leading to an internalization or assimilation of the teachings, thus bringing a deeper sense of conversion, unification, and conviction. But such result, still unstable, is then to be fully achieved through cultivation. By its function of repeated training with embodied methods, cultivation is said to overcome the mechanistic reactivity of our karmic imprints, subconscious tendencies, passions,

16. *Abhidharmakośabhāṣya*, commentary to 6.5a–b. Pradhan 1967, 334. La Vallée Poussin 1925, 4:142–43.

17. From the catalogue (*dkar chag*) of the *Treasury of Instructions*, 18:392.3–4: *thos pa'i don yang lan re tsam gyi go yul du shor na rgyud la mi 'byor bas yang nas yang du bsam mno shib par dpyad / des tshe 'di'i snang shas la shen pa gting nas log ste phyi ma'i nges legs don gnyer gyi blo thun mong ma yin pa skye bar 'gyur la /*. For the Indian context, in relation to Buddhist epistemology, see Eltschinger 2009.

and create new virtuous habits and states of being.[18] Prajñāraśmi concludes his epistle on scholarship, writing:

> Having reached the perfection of study and reflection upon the fields of knowledge,
> for these objects of study to have a meaning or purpose,
> make great effort in the cultivation of absorption (*samādhi*) and
> mature the continuum of your own [conscious experience] in a solitary place![19]

Cultivation thus brings full maturity to the "mental continuum," proceeding from intellectual understanding to the person as a whole, fully embodied. Following the Buddhist tantric approach, cultivation in Tibet is conceived according to the threefold dimension: body (*lus, kāya*), speech (*ngag, vāc*), and mind (*sems, citta*). If cultivation also involves discursive or analytical practices, it fully involves the body, sensations, feelings, emotions, memories, and thoughts, all directly recognized, with the deepening of mindfulness and meta-awareness (*dran pa dang shes bzhin, smṛti-saṃprajanya*). The jump from logical reasoning to supra-sensorial perception, or the direct perception of emptiness, is actually patiently prepared or carefully accompanied by a systematic training and refinement of direct perception as a whole, including common sensitivity and sensibility.[20]

If, in "Heidegger's view," as pointed out by Matthew Kapstein (2001, 6), there has been in Greek philosophy "a rupture, whereby thinking became fatefully unhinged from being," it is noteworthy that *cultivation*, with the Sanskrit *bhāvanā* literally meaning "bringing into being," can be seen as bridging this existential gap between the opposing notions of reason/emotion, mind/

18. Discursive reason, or the wisdom born from reflection, cannot alone transform such subconscious reactivity. We may have here a similar problem to the one addressed by Aristotle in his *Nicomachean Ethics* where he distinguishes moral virtues, defined explicitly as habits, and intellectual virtues. If observing ethical rules is a prerequisite for the progression of the three wisdoms, then internalized or sublimated morality, based on the deepening of self-awareness, may be said to be their fruit.

19. Prajñāraśmi, *Ambrosia of Listening and Reflection*, 240.4–5: *rig pa'i gnas la thos bsam mthar phyin nas // thos pa'i don rnams don yod bya ba'i phyir // ting 'dzin sgom pa'i bya ba lhur blangs nas // dben pa'i gnas su rang rgyud smin par mdzod //.*

20. Anālayo 2003, 46, referring to the *Saḷāyatana Saṃyutta*, states that the four applications of mindfulness (body, feelings, mind, and dharmas) represent the way to train an undistorted direct perception of the whole spectrum of our lived experience.

body, subject/object, and so on. But for discussing what such ancient techniques can mean for our contemporary times and philosophy, and considering how then to bridge the past/present, East/West gaps, we now turn to Japan.

Walking on Kyōto's "Path of Philosophy"

As remarked by Matthew Kapstein, the solutions to our contemporary problems cannot be found ready-made in ancient Buddhist sources or traditions. And "one of the hallmarks of philosophy is that it must forever renew itself in response to the specificities of place and time. . . ."[21] The so-called Kyōto School represents in the twentieth century such a Japanese project to reconsider the potentialities of ancient Asian and Buddhist traditions within a cross-cultural and critical philosophical framework in order to adapt to modernity, or to "overcome" it, especially when negatively seen as the spread of nihilism. Following the inspiration of his teacher Kitarō Nishida (西田 幾多郎, 1870–1945), retrospectively the founder of the school, Keiji Nishitani (西谷 啓治 1900–90) explicitly contributed to the critical project of a Buddhist philosophy, remaining as well, during all his lifetime, a devoted lay practitioner of the traditional Rinzai 臨済/臨濟 school of Zen. In his "religious philosophy," the frontiers between religion and philosophy are indeed not rigidly demarcated,[22] since it is mainly concerned with self-transformation through self-knowledge—that is, the radical Zen "investigation of the self" (*koji kyūmei* 己事究明). And such "wisdom" is neither reducible to faith (religion) or to reason (philosophy). Actually, I would suggest that the three wisdoms of Buddhism could be seen as an integrated procession from (1) faith in the tradition, to (2) critical reason, then to (3) embodied wisdom. If rational thinking is critical to Nishitani's project, it is as a means but not as an end. The investigation of forms of intuition and self-awareness becomes then the heart of the project, both of his philosophical writings and living engagement, from "the standpoint of Zen."[23]

As for the question of the re-actualization of ancient wisdom traditions, like Hadot on *philosophia*, Nishitani re-envisions Buddhism with the concept of the "way of life" (*ikikata* 生き方). In reference to Buddhist methods of cultivation, he wrote:

21. Kapstein 2001, 20.

22. Hadot's redefinition of *philosophia* also blurred some modern distinctions between philosophy and religion, implying even a "conversion" of the individual.

23. Nishitani 1984.

> These religious practices were given as a way of life itself. It is very important to bring this way of life back again to the place in which it originated. To "bring back" means to render this way of life capable of being a "lived form" in the real sense. In this way, it again becomes a way by means of which, or through which, we live our lives.[24]

The approach of Nishitani (2006) was to recognize the importance of the accumulated wisdom of traditions and to conscientiously avoid the destruction that would lead to nihilism, a major concern in his personal trajectory. But for Nishitani, mere conservation is not the ultimate answer. He strove to deconstruct traditions in order to bring them back to their original meaning as "ways of life." Only then can we reconstruct or revitalize them through our own ways of life, here and now. Nishitani's approach was thus both from inside and outside the tradition. Here we see again a parallel with the Buddhist model of the three wisdoms: (1) learning from the tradition, (2) critically inquiring into its original intention, and (3) fully living it. In this way, the tradition can be rediscovered and renewed in each generation.

In the context of Zen, cultivation has also been phenomenologically described as a form of learning through the body, or the whole human being, with the acquisition of spontaneity through repeated practice:

> This means that we have come to know them [i.e., philosophical and religious higher truths] by means of our body instead of our head—that is, by becoming a human being as a whole. It is not until we acquire knowledge in this way that we come to appropriate it truly, that is, to embody it in our body—or rather, I should say, if the term "body" leads to some misunderstanding, in the whole of us, including body and mind. "To embody" (*mi ni tsuku* 身につく) means that it is first of all given life in such a manner that it comes to be realized in one's way of living. When we gain knowledge in this way, something makes its appearance in one way or another in our everyday life.[25]

Japanese Buddhism, and Zen in particular, are celebrated for the diffusion of their ideals of cultivation (*shugyō* 修行) into everyday life, through the arts

24. Nishitani 2006, 26; original Japanese, 1982, 14. Here and below, I have modified the English translation on the basis of the original Japanese.

25. Nishitani 2006, 57; original Japanese, 1982, 63.

(tea, flower, calligraphy), or "ways" (道 *dō*), that manifest refined forms of living. In this sense, philosophy as a way of life can lead to the re-creation of a "culture" understood as the "cultivation of life": *la culture est la culture de la vie.*[26]

Conclusion: A Cosmopolitan Love of Wisdom

Let us finally consider how the questions asked by Hadot about the re-actualization of the ancient ideal of *philosophia*, including a remarkable opening to Asian traditions, can be connected with the potentialities of "Buddhist philosophy" by using the Buddhist model of threefold wisdom.

Hadot mentions two risks for the philosopher understood as a "lover of wisdom": (1) being satisfied with philosophical discourse, or worse, (2) thinking that one can do without philosophical discourse, which leads to potential aberrations.[27] As we saw, the Buddhist model of the three wisdoms shows a clear articulation designed to avoid those two pitfalls. Then, as Hadot explains, ancient traditions can be re-actualized only if they are reduced to their most profound significance, detached from antiquated elements.[28] We have seen how Nishitani has described such a solution, beyond the extremes of mere conservation and mere destruction, and how we can interpret it according to the model of the three wisdoms.

Then, "ancient philosophy teaches us . . . [to] try to live following the norm of the Idea of wisdom,"[29] and indeed, the Buddhist three wisdoms define explicitly such an orientation. But there is here a fundamental difference. If Greek *philosophia* tends toward wisdom without ever attaining it, the Buddhist progression to wisdom intends to fully realize it. And it is to be done precisely with various methods of "cultivation," still practiced now in living traditions and lineages of transmission.[30] While I would suggest that the general Western philosophical restraint from the claims of having definitely attained perfect wisdom is a sure ethical and epistemological safeguard for the cosmopolitan philosopher, Buddhism has nonetheless a lot to offer to Western

26. Henry 1987, 38.

27. Hadot 2002, 279–80; original French, 1995, 421–22.

28. Hadot 2002, 277–78; original French, 1995, 418.

29. Hadot 2002, 281; original French, 1995, 424.

30. As considered above with the model of the lineages of exegesis and practice, in Tibet the need for direct transmission from a teacher belonging to a lineage is strongly emphasized. For ancient Western philosophy, Hadot's works insist too on the importance of the collective context of schools and communities living together around a teacher.

philosophy regarding methods of "self-cultivation" or refinement of direct perception, since we do not find exact equivalents in Western traditions, or not to the same extent. The Buddhist model of the three wisdoms can thus also serve as a cross-cultural heuristic tool: the step of logical reflection as a way to control one's own mind has been especially emphasized in Greek and Western philosophy, while the step of yogic practice or cultivation has been systematically explored in Indian and Buddhist traditions. But, if we are to speak of a "Buddhist philosophy," the question is then how to articulate and integrate those two aspects in the dialectical process of the "path."

In this aim, we thus have to consider the overall philosophical coherence for which the model of the three wisdoms is paradigmatic. For example, *mindfulness* in Buddhism is not only a meditative skill or technique (wisdom born from cultivation) but also the capacity to properly learn and retain valuable information (wisdom born from listening/studying) as well as to sustain deep reflections (wisdom born from reflection). Not unlike the Stoic *prosokhê*, it means both to cultivate a "presence of mind" and to "keep in mind" the philosophical principles according to which one chooses to live. If the mission, essential yet endangered, of world humanities and classics is the very "cultivation of humanity," the threefold paradigm of Buddhist philosophy discussed here can certainly contribute to a reexamination of the ethical act of self-knowledge that opens the way to the good life.

To conclude, Pierre Hadot's work clearly articulated two levels of academic research: (1) objective historical and philological work that investigates what was philosophy in its ancient context, and (2) truly philosophical reflection on what it might mean to us, as subjects situated *hic et nunc* in our contemporary context. Without distinguishing, we might end up projecting our own preconceptions onto an idealized past, or inversely, we might impose obsolete or inauthentic ways of thinking upon our present situation. I remain deeply grateful to Professor Matthew Kapstein for having transmitted to us, his students, in the inspiration of Pierre Hadot, such a twofold rigorous discipline of the *logos*, (1) historical objective detachment and (2) philosophical existential engagement, applied especially to the academic study of the wisdom traditions of Tibet.

Works Cited

Anālayo, Bikkhu. 2003. *Satipaṭṭhāna: The Direct Path to Realization*. Cambridge: Windhorse.

Atiśa (982–1054). *Lamp for the Path to Awakening. Bodhipathapradīpa. Byang chub lam gyi sgron ma'i dka' 'grel*. Edited from Peking and Dergé versions in Sherburne 2000.

Chalmers, Robert. 1977 (1896). *The Majjhima-Nikāya*, vol. 2. London: The Pāli Text Society.

Deroche, Marc-Henri. 2009. "'Phreng po gter ston Shes rab 'od zer (1518–84) on the Eight Lineages of Attainment: Research on a *Ris med* Paradigm." In *Contemporary Visions in Tibetan Studies: Proceedings of the First International Seminar of Young Tibetologists,* edited by Brandon Doston, Kalsang Norbu Gurung, Georgios Halkias, and Tym Myatt, 319–42. Chicago: Serindia Publications.

———. 2011. "Sherab Wozer (1518–1584)." https://treasuryoflives.org/biographies/view/Sherab-Ozer/8964.

———. 2013. "History of the Forgotten Mother Monastery of the Ancients' School: The dPal ri Monastery in the Valley of the 'Tibetan Emperors.'" *Bulletin of Tibetology* 49.1: 77–112.

———. Forthcoming(a). *Une quête tibétaine de la sagesse: Prajñāraśmi (1518–1584)*. Louvain: Brepols, Bibliothèque de l'École des Hautes Études, Sciences religieuses.

———. Forthcoming(b). "Along the Middle Path, in Quest for Wisdom: The Great Madhyamaka in Rimé Discourses." In *The Other Emptiness: Perspectives on the Zhentong Buddhist Discourse in India and Tibet*, edited by Klaus-Diether Mathes and Michael Sheehy. New York: State University of New York Press.

Eltschinger, Vincent. 2009. "Studies in Dharmakīrti's Religious Philosophy: 4. The *cintāmayī prajñā*." In *Logic and Belief in Indian Philosophy*, edited by Piotr Balcerowicz, 565–603. Warsaw Indological Studies 3. Delhi: Motilal Banarsidass.

Fiordalis, David V. 2018. "Learning, Reasoning, Cultivating: The Practice of Wisdom in the *Treasury of Abhidharma*." In *Buddhist Spiritual Practices: Thinking with Pierre Hadot on Buddhism, Philosophy, and the Path*, edited by David Fiordalis, 245–89. Berkeley: Mangalam Press.

Hadot, Pierre. 2002. *What Is Ancient Philosophy?* Translated from the French by Michael Chase. Cambridge, MA: Belknap Press of Harvard University Press. (French original: *Qu'est-ce que la philosophie antique?* Paris: Gallimard, 1995.)

Henry, Michel. 1987. *La barbarie*. Paris: Presses Universitaires de France.

Kapstein, Matthew T. 1996. "*gDams ngag*: Tibetan Technologies of the Self." In *Tibetan Literature: Studies in Genre*, edited by José Cabezón and David Jackson, 275–89. Ithaca, NY: Snow Lion Publications.

———. 2001. "Introduction: What Is Buddhist Philosophy?" In *Reason's Traces: Identity and Interpretation in Indian and Tibetan Buddhist Thought*, 3–26. Boston: Wisdom Publications.

———. 2007. "Tibetan Technologies of the Self, Part II: The Teachings of the Eight Great Conveyances." In *The Pandita and the Siddha: Tibetan Studies in Honour of E. Gene Smith*, edited by Ramon N. Prats, 110–29. Dharamsala, India: Amnye Machen Institute.

———. 2013. "'Spiritual Exercise' and Buddhist Epistemologists in India and Tibet." In *A Companion to Buddhist Philosophy*, edited by Steven Emmanuel, 270–89. Chichester, UK: John Wiley & Sons.

La Vallée Poussin, Louis de, trans. 1923–31. *L'Abhidharmakośa de Vasubandhu*, 6 vols. Paris: Paul Geuthner; and Louvain: J.-B. ISTAS, Société belge d'études orientales.

Ñaṇamoli, Bhikkhu, and Bhikkhu Bodhi, trans. 1995. *The Middle Length of Discourses of the Buddha: A New Translation of the Majjhima Nikāya*. Wisdom Publications: Boston.

Nishitani, Keiji. 1984. "The Standpoint of Zen." Translated by John C. Maraldo. *The Eastern Buddhist* 17.1: 1–26. (Original Japanese: Nishitani Keiji西谷 啓治. "Zen no tachiba"「禅の立場」. In *Kōza Zen*『講座禅』, edited by Nishitani Keiji, 1:5–28. Tōkyō: Chikuma Shobō, 1967.)

———. 2006. *On Buddhism*. Translated by Seisaku Yamamoto and Robert E. Carter. New York: State University of New York Press. (Original Japanese: Nishitani Keiji 西谷 啓治. *Bukkyō ni tsuite*『仏教について』. Tōkyō: Hōzōkan, 1982.)

Prajñāraśmi ('Phreng po gter ston Shes rab 'od zer, 1518–84). *Ambrosia of Cultivation. Sgom pa 'chi med kyi bdud rtsi*. In *Gsung 'bum*, 1:243–66. Gangtok: Gonpo Tseten, 1977.

———. *Ambrosia of Listening and Reflection. Thos bsam 'chi med kyi bdud rtsi*. In *Gsung 'bum*, 1:231–42. Gangtok: Gonpo Tseten, 1977.

Pradhan, Prahlad. 1967. *Abhidharmakośabhāṣya of Vasubandhu*. Tibetan Sanskrit Works Series 8. Patna: Kashi Prasad Jayawal Research Institute.

Sherburne, Richard. 2000. *The Complete Works of Atīśa Śrī Dīpaṁkara Jñāna, Jo-bo-rje: The Lamp for the Path and Commentary, Together with the Newly Translated Twenty-Five Key Texts (Tibetan and English Texts)*. New Delhi: Aditya Prakashan.

Treasury of Spiritual Instructions = 'Jam mgon Kong sprul Blo gros mtha' yas (1813–99). 1979–81. *Gdams ngag mdzod: A Treasury of Precious Methods and Instructions of All of the Major and Minor Buddhist Traditions of Tibet, Brought Together and Structured into a Coherent System*. 18 vols. Paro, Bhutan: Lama Ngodrup and Sherab Drimay.

Part 4
Reason's Traces

Plate 1. From left: Matthew Kapstein, Tulku Pema Tharchin, Khenpo Sangyé Tenzin, and Kurt Schwalbe at Serlo Monastery in Junbesi in 1975.
Photo courtesy of Tulku Pema Tharchin

Plate 2. Matthew Kapstein.
Photo courtesy of Christine Mollier

Plate 3. The author at Phajoding Temple northwest of Thimphu, Bhutan.

Plate 4. Sorting book pages in Yagang Temple near
Mongkar in the east of Bhutan.

Plate 5. Digitization in Gangteng.
Photo courtesy of Bjorn Henriksen

Plate 6. From traditional poti to pixels.

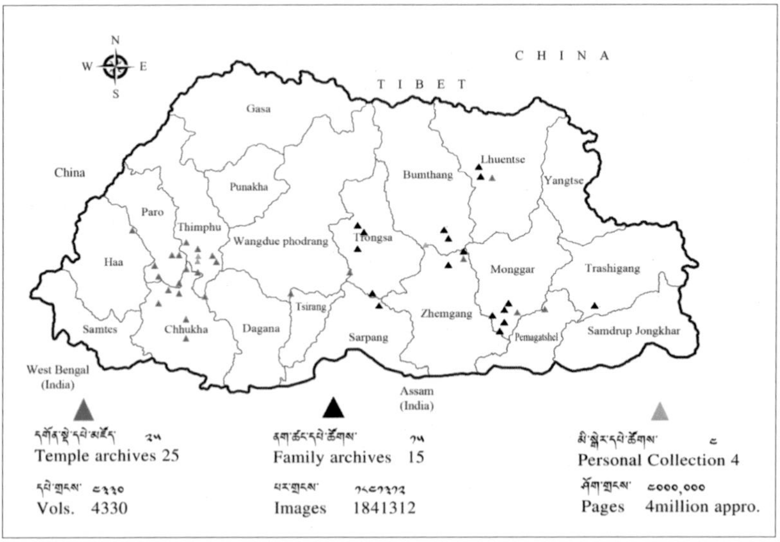

Plate 7. The extent of the digitization project in Bhutan.

Plate 8. Zhang zhong Monastery.
Photo by Michael Sheehy

Plate 9. Jog mda' 'Chad kha Monastery.
Photo by Michael Sheehy

Plate 10. Ri bo che Stūpa.
Photo by Michael Sheehy

Plate 11. A lineage portrait thangka of the ninth and tenth abbots of Ngor Monastery, Tibet, late sixteenth century, pigments and gold on cotton, 85.7 x 76.3 cm. See key on page 145.
Photo courtesy of Bonham's Auction

Plate 12. Portrait of Grags pa blo gros, P19 (detail).

Plate 13. Portrait of Mus chen, P12 (detail).

Plate 14. Portrait of the Sakya hierarch Ngag dbang bsod nams dbang phyug, Tibet, seventeeth century, cast brass, 10 x 9 x 7 cm, MG 24 472.
Photo courtesy of the Musée Guimet (Réunion des Musées Nationaux)

Plate 15. Portrait of Ngag dbang bsod nams dbang phyug, back. MG 24 472.

Why Did the Buddha Come to Earth? Monastic Lineage, Interreligious Polemics, and Philosophy

Vincent Eltschinger[1]

IN A RECENT PAPER, Seishi Karashima (2015) examines the original meaning of scriptures designated as *vaitulya*, *vaipulya*, and so on and the early Buddhist attitudes toward them. In Karashima's opinion, these texts were termed *vaitulya* (**vedulla*) due to their unconventional, unusual nature (*vi-tulya*, "not of the same kind") as "scriptures consisting of repeated questions and answers," and were regarded as "incomparable, peerless" by their authors.[2] On the basis of earlier research,[3] Karashima suggests that these texts (the *Aṣṭasāhasrikā Prajñāpāramitā*, the *Saddharmapuṇḍarīka*, the *Samādhirājasūtra*, the *Mahāparinirvāṇa Mahāsūtra*, the *Daśabhūmika*, and so on) most likely originated in a Mahāsāṅghika or related environment (Andhakas, Aparaśailas, Pūrvaśailas, etc.) and were not labeled *mahāyānasūtras* before the fourth century. These scriptures are abundantly quoted by putative Mahāsāṅghika authorities such as the Mādhyamika scholars Nāgārjuna (ca. 200 CE?), Candrakīrti (between 550 and 650), Śāntideva (early eighth century), and Dīpaṅkaraśrījñāna (Atiśa, 982–1054). According to Karashima, then, much of early Mahāyāna literature originated in Mahāsāṅghika circles, to which the most prominent personalities of Indian Madhyamaka (with the notable exception of the likely Mūlasarvāstivādins Śāntarakṣita [725–88] and Kamalaśīla [740–95]) belonged by their ordination lineage (*nikāya*, or "monastic order"). These *vaitulya/vaipulya/mahāyāna* scriptures often

1. Most sincere thanks are due to Hélène de Brux, Jens-Uwe Hartmann, Isabelle Ratié, and John Taber for their precious help. Phyllis Granoff deserves my heartfelt gratitude for allowing me to present a preliminary version of this paper at Yale University (February 22, 2018).

2. See Karashima 2015, 132–38; for earlier scholarship on this issue, see Karashima 2015, 132n56.

3. For references, see Karashima 2015, 139–40n82.

criticize key Sarvāstivāda ideas, such as the existence of all *dharmas* in the past, the present, and the future.

Paul Demiéville's pioneering work (1954) on early Yogācāra literature revealed close connections between early—not yet and/or partially "mahāyānized"—Yogācāra literature and Sarvāstivāda circles of meditation specialists (*yogācāra*). The earliest and most prominent figure of this movement was likely the monk poet Aśvaghoṣa (around 100 CE),[4] whose *Saundarananda* was much quoted, together with other early Sarvāstivādin authorities (Upagupta, Pārśva, Vasumitra, Kumāralāta, Saṅgharakṣa, Saṅghasena, etc.), by Kumārajīva (350–409 CE?) in his *Sūtra on the Concentration of Sitting Meditation* (Taishō 614, 坐禪三昧).[5] And indeed, most of the canonical scriptures quoted in the *Yogācārabhūmi*, the Qyzyl "*Yogalehrbuch*," and the works of Vasubandhu (350–430?), reflect Mūlasarvāstivāda recensions.[6] The most orthodox Sarvāstivādins vehemently criticized the Vaitulikas and the Mahāyāna; in particular, the Mahāyāna "convert" Vasubandhu, though himself a (Mūla)sarvāstivādin, was accused by the Dīpakāra of "lead[ing] people toward the texts of the Vaitulikas" and of being himself "a Vaitulika who dropped out of the Sarvāstivāda (school)."[7] Similarly, the *Bodhisattvabhūmi*, a comparatively early witness of the "mahāyānized," albeit still pre-idealistic, Yogācāra, strongly criticized wrong conceptions of emptiness that are clearly reminiscent of the Mādhyamikas, accused of being *sarvavaināśika*s, "universal deniers."[8]

There are thus some reasons to hypothesize connections between ordination lineage / monastic order and doctrinal/philosophical orientation, and this beyond the ordinary scale of Abhidharma dogmatics—the traditional repository of "sectarian" doctrinal identities—that is, at the level of doctrines that have hitherto been widely regarded as sect-independent or "super-sectarian." Karashima indeed assumes "that the original background of the Madhyamaka school, founded by Nāgārjuna, might have been the Mahāsāṃghikas, while

4. See Yamabe 2003.

5. See Yamabe and Sueki 2009, xv–xviii.

6. Concerning the *Yogācārabhūmi*, see Schmithausen 1977, 928–29n24, and Schmithausen 1987, 305, 377, and 380; concerning the "*Yogalehrbuch*," see Schmithausen 1970, 112n257 (see also Yamabe 2006, 326); in the same footnote, Schmithausen terms Vasubandhu's *Abhidharmakośa* "ein Mūlasarvāstivāda-Werk."

7. *Abhidharmadīpa*, 101,3–8 and 282,1 (translation Karashima 2015, 143; see also 144n116).

8. *Bodhisattvabhūmi*, 47–48; see Seyfort Ruegg 1969, 319–46, and Eckel 2008, 65–66.

that of the Yogācāra school, founded by Vasubandhu and Asaṅga, may have been the Sarvāstivādins."[9]

In the same paper, Karashima draws attention to a remarkable passage from the *Mahāvaitulya-Mahāsannipāta* (Taishō 397, 大方等大集經). In a prophetic mood, Śākyamuni spells out the respective characteristics of the future *nikāyas*. The aim of the passage is to praise the Mahāsāṅghikas for acknowledging the *vaitulya/vaipulya* scriptures and correlatively to blame the other monastic orders for rejecting them. The Sarvāstivādins are described as follows:

> After my *parinirvāṇa*, O Kauṇḍinya, there will be my disciples, who will receive, hold, read, recite, and copy the twelve categories of the Tathāgata's teachings. They will also read, recite, copy, and speak about non-Buddhist texts (外典), receive [the doctrine] concerning the existence of [the *dharmas*] of the three time periods [past, present, and future] and of internal and external [*dharmas*]. They will refute heretics, be good at arguing, and maintain that all kinds of beings are able to receive the precepts. They will be able to answer (√*vad*) correctly all (*sarva*) intricate questions. Therefore they will be called the Sarvāstivādins.[10]

Considering the polemical purpose and the rhetorical strategy (etymologies) of the passage, one should be wary of overestimating its reliability as a historical document. The text's portrayal of the Sarvāstivādins, however, provides a fairly true picture of this order's characteristic doctrines and inclinations. In particular, the description of the Sarvāstivādins as being "able to answer correctly all intricate questions" and "being good at arguing" is abundantly corroborated by the impressive exegetical and theological skills displayed in Sarvāstivāda Abhidharma literature.

What is more striking about this account is its insistence on the Sarvāstivādins' commitment to learn about and to criticize non-Buddhists. Contrary to other monastic orders, the prophecy says, they "will read, recite, copy, and speak about non-Buddhist texts" and "will refute heretics" (外道, [*anya*]*tīrthya*, [*anya*]*tīrthika*). This may look surprising in view of the truly marginal role played by anti-*tīrthika* controversy in Abhidharma literature as a whole, including Vasubandhu's *Abhidharmakośa*, where the targets of the Sarvāstivādin and/or Vaibhāṣika intellectuals are overwhelmingly (more

9. Karashima 2015, 148.

10. T. 397.13.159a16–21; translation Karashima 2015, 138–39.

than 95 percent) Buddhist.[11] This, however, is in keeping with the very nature of Abhidharma, which ultimately consists in the immaculate discernment of the factors (*dharmapravicaya*) and thus entails a strong exegetical component.

Sarvāstivāda Abhidharma may not be the only or even the most relevant type of literature to examine, however. The monk poet Aśvaghoṣa, himself a noted specialist of Buddhist doctrine and a gifted philosopher, provides a paradigmatic—and perhaps the earliest—example of a Sarvāstivāda intellectual engaged in "interconfessional" polemics. That Aśvaghoṣa, in spite of his proto-Sautrāntika leaning, was a Sarvāstivādin is strongly suggested by persistent legends about him and made entirely clear, I think, by close scrutiny of his canonical sources.[12] The poet and dramatist engaged in a large-scale apologetic entreprise on behalf of the Buddhist dharma[13] in which he systematically criticized all major actors (and competitors) on the religio-philosophical stage of first- to second-century northern India: the Sāṅkhya, his favorite target, but also brahmanical asceticism and ritualism, "penitential" asceticism, meditation practices, and various cosmological, metaphysical, and soteriological doctrines concerning the Self, Nature, God, Time, Fate, and so on as the ultimate principles of the universe.[14]

Kumāralāta's (third century CE?) *Kalpanāmaṇḍitikā Dṛṣṭāntapaṅktiḥ* (Taishō 201, 大莊嚴論經),[15] the breviary of the so-called Darṣṭāntikas, provides another example of a Sarvāstivāda narrative work replete with Buddhist apologetics and various polemics against non-Buddhists.[16] Whereas its first chapter attempts to demonstrate the Buddha's superiority over the Hindu gods, and thus forms the model of works such as Udbhaṭasiddhasvāmin's *Viśeṣastava* and Śaṅkarasvāmin's *Devātiśayastotra*,[17] its second chapter is a systematic critique of Sāṅkhya and Vaiśeṣika tenets. Obviously, those among the Sarvāstivādins who were most commited to anti-*tīrthika* polemics were not the Ābhidharmikas but the philosophically educated specialists of *kāvya*,

11. See Eltschinger 2014, 174–89.

12. See Eltschinger 2012 and Eltschinger 2013.

13. See, e.g., Olivelle 2008, xxiv–xlix.

14. See Eltschinger 2014, 6–12.

15. See Hahn 1983.

16. *Dṛṣṭāntapaṅkti*, v. 2ac (ed. Hahn 1983, 321): "Having faithfully paid reverence to the various Sarvāstivāda hierarchs [in the persons of] Pūrṇa, Pārśva, Mecaka, and so on, I am going to expound this 'Garland of Parables.'"

17. See Schneider 1993 and Schneider 2014, respectively.

avadāna, and perhaps *jātaka* literature.[18] The so-called Paravāda section of the *Yogācārabhūmi* provides an early example of (Mūla)sarvāstivādin polemics against non-Buddhists in a non-narrative literary framework.[19] In this short text, sixteen "allodoxies" (*paravāda*), many of which go back to the *Brahmajālasūtra* of the *Dīrghāgama*, are presented and criticized in a systematic manner. This early Yogācāra document includes polemics against the Jainas, the Sāṅkhyas, and orthodox brahmanical conceptions of caste, purity, ritual violence, and so on, as well as—and this is noteworthy—the orthodox Sarvāstivāda doctrine of the existence of the *dharma*s in the three times,[20] thus likely testifying to intrasectarian dissensions, possibly at the level of regional specificities.

The (Mūla)sarvāstivādins were thus apparently famed for their critical engagement with the non-Buddhists, and although they cannot be said to have had monopoly on this type of polemics, definite segments of their literature clearly exhibit such tendencies. One feels therefore justified in asking if this inclination could perhaps be reflected, legitimated, and even encouraged, in extant (Mūla)sarvāstivāda canonical sources. I think it clearly is, and this in one of the most venerable canonical sources of the (Mūla)sarvāstivādins, the *Saṅghabhedavastu* of the *Mūlasarvāstivāda-vinaya*, which contains an extensive narrative of the Buddha legend and innumerable examples of the (future) Buddha's polemical interaction with the non-Buddhists. The passage I have in mind concludes the well-known episode of the Bodhisattva's four or five "examinations" (*[vy]avalokana*, *[mahā]avalokita*) while still abiding in the Tuṣita Heaven, and immediately precedes—not to say justifies—his descent (*avatāra*) to Jambudvīpa.[21] Interestingly enough, this passage has no counterpart in its *Lalitavistara* and *Mahāvastu* parallels and thus can be considered a specifically (Mūla)sarvāstivāda elaboration.

From his fivefold examination, the Bodhisattva concludes that he should be reborn as a *kṣatriya* in Jambudvīpa at a time in cosmic (d)evolution in which

18. Unfortunately, nothing is known of Āryaśūra's (early fourth cent. CE?) monastic affiliation; see Hahn 1985, 253–55. There is no reason to believe that the *Prātimokṣasūtrapaddhati* (D 4104), a commentary on the (Mūla)sarvāstivāda *Prātimokṣasūtra* ascribed to Dpa' bo (Skt. Śūra), is an authentic work of Āryaśūra.

19. See Eltschinger 2015.

20. See Eltschinger 2015, 206–7 and Dhammajoti 2017.

21. See *Saṅghabhedavastu* 1:36,1–38,18 (D 1, *ga* 225a7–227a6), *Lalitavistara*, 19,6–29,13 (Foucaux 1884, 20–29), *Mahāvastu* 2:1,1–3,20 (Jones 1952, 1–4). While the *Lalitavistara* and the *Mahāvastu* list (in slightly different orders) four examinations (as to time [*kāla*], space [*deśa*], continent [*dvīpa*], and family [*kula*]), the *Saṅghabhedavastu* knows of five (*vy*)*avalokana*s (caste [*jāti*], space [*deśa*], time [*kāla*], family/lineage [*vaṃśa*], and woman/mother [*strī*]).

buddhas can teach profitably (when humans' life expectancy ranges between 80,000 and 100 years), in Śuddhodana's family (*kula*) among the Śākyas, and with Mahāmāyā as his mother. The passage begins as follows:

> Then the Bodhisattva, having carried out the five examinations, thrice proclaimed [the following] to the six [classes of] gods dwelling in the realm of desire: "Friends, leaving (*cyutvā*) this Tuṣita group of gods, I will take rebirth among humans in the womb of the chief queen of King Śuddhodana. Having become his son, I will obtain immortality. He among you who is striving for immortality should take rebirth among humans, as a rule in the Madhyadeśa."[22]

The gods, however, are reluctant to let him go and try to dissuade the Bodhisattva by informing him about the nasty circumstances in Jambudvīpa:

> The Bodhisattva should know that, at present, the world is sullied by depravities,[23] that the creatures have pernicious dispositions, and that Jambudvīpa is led astray by six reasoners (*tārkika*), six traditionalists (*ānuśravika*), and six meditators (*samāpattṛ*). Among them, who are the six reasoners? They are Pūraṇa Kāśyapa, Maskarin Gośālīputra, Sañjayin Vairaṭṭīputra, Ajita Keśakambala, Kakuda Kātyāyana, [and] Nirgrantha Jñātiputra. Who are the six traditionalists? They are the brahman Kūṭatāṇḍya, the brahman Śroṇatāṇḍya, the brahman Caṅgin, the brahman Brahmāyus, the brahman Puṣkarasārin, [and] the brahman Lohitya. Who are the six meditators? They are Udraka Rāmaputra, Arāḍa Kālāma, the religious mendicant Subhadra, the brahman youth Sañjayin, the *ṛṣi* Asita, and the matted-hair ascetic Uruvilvākāśyapa. But here [in Tuṣita Heaven], a twelve-league seat(/throne) has been prepared for the Bodhisattva so that [we can] listen to the dharma. So we think: Listening to the dharma that the Bodhisattva will teach us [while] dwelling in the Tuṣita abode, we will practice [it] exactly in such a way that it will be for our profit, for our sake, and for our bliss forever.[24]

22. *Saṅghabhedavastu*, 1:38,18–23 (D 1, *ga* 227a6–b1).

23. As the Tibetan version *sdig pa*(*s gos pa*) suggests, *kali* is here to be understood as "evil" or "depravity" and not in the sense of "quarrel" or "strife" (Tib. *rtsod pa*) that it usually has in the prophetic, eschatological, and apocalyptic context of the *kaliyuga*.

24. *Saṅghabhedavastu*, 1:38,24–39,12 (D 1, *ga* 227b1–6) Read *caṅgī* for *cogī* (*bzang ldan* ↔

Far from being tempted to stay, however, the Bodhisattva adopts a resolutely martial tone and *ipso facto* transforms the final segment of a long "spiritual" journey into a military campaign:

> "Therefore, friends, beat all musical instruments!" [And] all musical instruments were beaten by the deities of the Tuṣita class. The Bodhisattva himself, having blown into a conch shell, spoke [as follows]: "Friends, which among them is the loud[est] sound?"
>
> "The sound of the conch-shell, O Blessed One!" [replied the gods].
>
> "Friends, just as the sound of the conch shell is stronger than all musical instruments, I, having descended to Jambudvīpa, will defeat the six reasoners, the six traditionalists, and the six meditators [and] then obtain immortality. I will delight[/satiate] the world with immortality[/ambrosia]. I will blow the conch of impermanence. I will beat the kettledrum of emptiness. I will roar the lion's roar of selflessness." Having said so, he uttered [the following] stanza:
>
> A single lion harasses a multitude of wild beasts,
> a single thunderbolt strikes multiple mountain peaks,
> Śakra alone (*eka*) defeats many chiefs of the demons,
> a single sun disperses abundant darkness.[25]

Obtaining final liberation and awakening has become, as it were, a marginal concern. According to some at least among the (Mūla)sarvāstivādins, crusading against the *tīrthika*s is an essential dimension of the Bodhisattva's *avatāra*, hence possibly of their own self-understanding as the truest sons of the Buddha.

The gods' tripartition of the non-Buddhists is likely modeled on the *Sandakasutta*[26] (*Majjhima-nikāya* 1:513–24) in which Ānanda expounds the "four ways that negate the living of the holy life" (*cattāro abrahmacariyavāsā*)

---

caṅga ["handsome"] + *in*), *brahmāyur* for *brāhmāyur*, and *samāpattāraḥ* for *pratipattāraḥ* (*snyoms par 'jug pa*).

25. *Saṅghabhedavastu*, 1:39,13–25 (D 1, *ga* 227b7–228a4). On *prahaṇyantām*, see Renou 1984, §§17–18; read *tāḍayiṣyāmi* for *tāḍayiṣyāmīti*, and *vaditvā* for *viditvā* (*smras nas*; see Waldschmidt 1973 s.v. √*vad*, and Edgerton 1953, §§35.2–28).

26. For a translation, see Ñāṇamoli and Bodhi 1995, 618–28; for a study of the fragmentary Sanskrit parallels, see Anālayo 2011, 1:413–16. The sūtra has no Chinese counterpart.

and the "four kinds of holy life without consolation" (*cattāri anassāsikāni brahmacariyāni*). Whereas the four ways that negate the living of the holy life consist in the doctrines ascribed in the *Sāmaññaphalasutta* (*Dīgha-nikāya* 1:47–85) to Ajita Kesakambalin, Pūraṇa Kassapa, Makkhali Gosāla, and Pakudha Kaccāyana / Makkhali Gosāla,[27] the four kinds of holy life without consolation consist of (1) claims to omniscience (ridiculed in the sutta), (2) traditionalism, (3), ratiocination, and (4) eel wriggling.[28] The sutta does not mention any representative of these four ways but provides interesting explanations of what is meant by traditionalism and ratiocination, two of the three categories referred to in the *Saṅghabhedavastu* (the *Sandakasutta* has no equivalent of the *Saṅghabhedavastu*'s *samāpattṛ*). A traditionalist (*anussavika*) is a teacher "who regards oral tradition as truth; he teaches a Dhamma by oral tradition, by legends handed down, by what has come down in scriptures."[29] As for the reasoner (*takkī*), he is "an inquirer. He teaches a Dhamma hammered out by reasoning, following a line of inquiry as it occurs to him."[30]

Most of the eighteen *tīrthika*s listed in the *Saṅghabhedavastu* are well-known figures of the Buddha's legend and preaching ministry. The six *tārkika*s—"reasoners" or "libres penseurs"—are paradigmatic "allodox" thinkers and rival teachers who appear several times in the *Mūlasarvāstivāda-vinaya* and originate in the *Śrāmaṇyaphalasūtra*.[31] Pūraṇa Kāśyapa teaches a blend of nihilism and materialism and accordingly denies post-mortem existence of any kind (in the *Saṅghabhedavastu*, 1:220,11–227,10, this doctrine is labeled *nāstitā*, "nonexistence"). The doctrine of Maskarin Gośālīputra, the alleged founder of Ājīvikism, can be roughly characterized as fatalism; according to him, man is not in the capacity to influence his present condition and future destiny (*ahetutā*, "fortuitism"). Sañjayin Vairaṭīputra denies merit and demerit (*akriyā*, "nonaction"). Ajita Keśakambalin teaches predestination and "automatic" purification by going through the most varied forms of existence during 84,000 great eons (*saṃsāraśuddhatā*, "purification through saṃsāra"). Kakuda Kātyāyana has no doctrine of his own and practices "eel wriggling,"

27. See Anālayo 2011, 1:414–15.

28. On the doctrine or, rather, the attitude of the eel wrigglers (*amarāvikkhepika*), see Eltschinger 2015, 215–17, and below.

29. *Majjhima-nikāya*, 1:520. Translation Ñāṇamoli and Bodhi 1995, 624. For a parallel formula, see Eltschinger 2015, 200n43.

30. *Majjhima-nikāya*, 1:520. Translation Ñāṇamoli and Bodhi 1995, 624. On this formula and its parallels, see Eltschinger 2015, 200–201.

31. For a detailed study of the "six heretics," see Vogel 1970, to whom the Sanskrit of the *Saṅghabhedavastu* was not yet available.

or equivocation, refusing to commit himself to any position or to contradict his interlocutors. Finally, Nirgrantha Jñātiputra—the founder of Jainism, or at least its main representative in the Buddha's time—preaches the atonement of former bad actions by penances (*tapas*) and the nonproduction of new karma by refraining from any action (*akaraṇa*, a doctrine that is phrased *pūrvakṛtahetutā*, "being caused by past action"). In a famous episode,[32] the six *tārkika*s make alliance against the Buddha and challenge his magical powers; the Blessed One's answer is none other than the "great miracle" at Śrāvastī, which leaves the allodox teachers flabbergasted—and even dead, in the case of Pūraṇa. Toward the end of the supernatural display, the Buddha utters the following stanza: ". . . the reasoners shined as long as the Tathāgata didn't arise, but when the Perfectly Awakened One shined in the world, the reasoners no longer shined, nor did their disciples."[33]

The *Saṅghabhedavastu*'s six followers of tradition (*ānuśravika*) are paradigmatic brahmans playing important roles as interlocutors (and virtual converts) of the Buddha in the *Dīgha-* and the *Majjhima-nikāya* as well as their Chinese and (fragmentary) Sanskrit equivalents. All of them are presented as powerful brahmans ruling over royal domains granted by Kings Prasenajit or Bimbasāra. More importantly, all of them are paragons of Vedic learning and practice characterized by the following formula: "He was a master of the Three Vedas with their vocabularies, liturgy, phonology, and etymology, and the histories as a fifth; skilled in philology and grammar, he was fully versed in natural philosophy and in the marks of a Great Man."[34] Kūṭatāṇḍya (Pāli Kūṭadaṇḍa) is the protagonist of a sūtra in which the Blessed One criticizes blood sacrifices by referring to the normative practices of a king of the past and by promoting a moral and spiritual reformation of sacrifice.[35] Śroṇatāṇḍya was forced by the Buddha to reduce the criteria of true brahmanity to (Buddhist) morality and insight.[36] The brahman youth Kāmaṭhika (Pāli Kāpaṭhika) is the main protagonist of the *Caṅgīsūtra* (*Cankīsutta*);[37] for him, "in regard to the ancient brahmanic hymns that have come down through oral transmission

32. *Divyāvadāna*, 143–66, chapter 12; translation Rotman 2008, 253–87.

33. *Divyāvadāna*, 163,7–9; translation Rotman 2008, 280, with "reasoners" substituted here for "sophists." In a story told at *Avadānaśataka*, 47,1–49,9, it is a "miracle" (*prātihārya*) that decides who, between Pūraṇa (with the five other teachers) and the Buddha, is truthful.

34. *Majjhima-nikāya* 2:133 (and passim); translation Ñāṇamoli and Bodhi 1995, 743.

35. See *Dīgha-nikāya*, 1:127–49; translation Rhys Davids 1899, 1:173–85.

36. *Dīgha-nikāya*, 1:111–26; translation Rhys Davids 1899, 1:144–59.

37. *Majjhima-nikāya*, 2:164–77; translation Ñāṇamoli and Bodhi 1995, 775–85. On the *Cankīsutta* and its (fragmentary) Sanskrit parallels, see Anālayo 2011, 2:557–63.

and in the scriptural collections, the brahmans come to the definite conclusion 'Only this is true, anything else is wrong.'"[38] The Buddha opposes to this belief a vitriolic critique of faith in tradition, compared to a line of blind men and regarded as groundless (*amūlika*). Like his student Uttara, the old Mithilā brahman Brahmāyus was in doubt about two of the Buddha's thirty-two marks of a great man;[39] the Buddha magically revealed to them that his male organ was enclosed in a sheath and that his tongue was exceptionally large. Ambaṭṭha, a disciple of Pokkharasādi (Skt. Puṣkarasārin), scorned the Buddha and the Śākyas for their low birth; the sermon quickly turns to a critique of (pride in) caste.[40] As for the brahman Lohitya (Pāli Lohicca), his egoistic and pessimistic thoughts on the uselessness of sharing one's attainments with others triggered a sermon of the Buddha concerning bad teachers and their opposite, the Tathāgata that arises in the world.[41]

With the exception of the *māṇava* Sañjayin, the *samāpattṛ*s are well-known figures of the Buddha legend as told in (Mūla)sarvāstivāda circles. After the brahman soothsayers had predicted that the newborn Bodhisattva would become either a universal ruler (*cakravartin*) or a perfect buddha, the *ṛṣi* Asita ascertained that he would be a buddha.[42] Arāḍa Kālāma and Udraka Rāmaputra were the Bodhisattva's first teachers for brief periods after he left home, instructing him about the stages of nothingness (*ākiñcanyāyatana*) and neither-ideation-nor-non-ideation (*naivāsañjñānāsañjñāyatana*).[43] Uruvilvākāśyapa, a matted-hair ascetic performing austerities on the bank of the Nairañjanā river together with his two brothers and their thousand disciples, was one of the most important early converts of the Buddha, who converted him to the dharma after a series of magical exploits.[44] The identity of the *māṇava* Sañjayin is more obscure. The most famous Sañjayin in the Buddha legend is the former teacher of the Buddha's "great disciples" Upatiṣya (= Śāriputra) and Kolita (= Maudgalyāyana). According to an early stage of the legend, this Sañjayin was none other than the above-mentioned *tārkika* Sañja-

38. *Majjhima-nikāya*, 2:169; translation Ñāṇamoli and Bodhi 1995, 779.

39. *Majjhima-Nikāya*, 2:133–46; translation Ñāṇamoli and Bodhi 1995, 743–54. The Pāli sutta knows of two Chinese parallels (T. 26.1.685a–690a and T. 76.1.883b–886a); for references to Sanskrit fragments, see Anālayo 2011, 2:527–45.

40. *Dīgha-nikāya*, 1:87–110; translation Rhys Davids 1899, 10–136.

41. *Dīgha-nikāya*, 224–34. Translation Rhys Davids 1899, 288–97.

42. *Saṅghabhedavastu*, 1:46,18–47,21 and 52,17–57,8.

43. On Arāḍa Kālāma, see *Saṅghabhedavastu*, 1:97,4–98,2 and 130,16–131,2; on Udraka Rāmaputra, see *Saṅghabhedavastu*, 1:98,3–32 and 131,3–13.

44. *Saṅghabhedavastu*, 1:217,1–234,11 [appendix II] and 154,1–157,5.

yin Vairaṭīputra and strongly opposed his two pupils' wish to follow the Buddha.[45] As shown by Lamotte, however, a later stage of the legend presents him as a Kauṇḍinya brahman (hence the epithet *māṇava*?) whose teaching somehow foreshadowed the Buddha's. Given that this later phase of the legend is well represented in (Mūla)sarvāstivāda sources, and that it is very unlikely that the eighteen-name list of the *Saṅghabhedavastu* introduces twice the same person under different labels, it is plausible that this second Sañjayin is the one alluded to in the present context.[46] Finally, the *(anyatīrthika)parivrājaka* Subhadra is famous for being the Buddha's last pupil and convert.[47]

As we can see, the *Saṅghabhedavastu* quite eloquently presents the Bodhisattva's last existence as being aimed primarily at defeating a host of independent philosophers, Vedic brahmans, and experts in meditation as well as ascetic and mantic practices. As their very number (18) suggests, these persons can be said to symbolically stand for all the non-Buddhist challengers humiliated in magical contests, rebuked by words and arguments, and surpassed by higher spiritual attainments. In doing so, the Buddha was represented as freeing the world from powerful obstacles to liberation in the form of wrong discourses and practices. The absence of the Sāṅkhyas, likely the most threatening challengers of Buddhism in the early centuries of the Common Era, can plausibly reflect the authors/compilers' sense for anachronism and their willingness to restrict the list to canonically attested personalities. Considering that defeating the non-Buddhists is the Bodhisattva's mission statement at the time of leaving Tuṣita Heaven, it is hardly surprising that some (Mūla)sarvāstivādins at least regarded polemics against the *tīrthika*s as a fundamental component of their own identity. This might explain in turn why the *Mahāvaitulya-Mahāsannipāta* pictured this (group of) sect(s) as specializing, among other things, in philosophical controversy against non-Buddhists.

45. Sañjayin's disciples derided and scorned the Buddhist monks in the marketplace in Rājagṛha, telling them: "The Buddha has reached Rājagṛha, Magadha's foremost city, [but] all [here] are [already] guided by Sañjayin; who else are you going to guide?" (*Catuṣpariṣatsūtra*, §28f3).

46. See Lamotte 1949, 623–30, esp. 623–627n2.

47. *Mahāparinirvāṇasūtra*, §§40.1–48. For another Subhadra *parivrājaka*, see *Divyāvadāna*, 152,22–153,20; translation Rotman 2008, 266–67.

Works Cited

Abhidharmadīpa = Padmanabh S. Jaini. 1977. *Abhidharmadīpa with Vibhāṣāprabhāvṛtti*. Patna: Kashi Prasad Jayaswal Research Institute.

Anālayo. 2011. *A Comparative Study of the Majjhima-nikāya*. 2 vols. Taipei: Dharma Drum Publishing.

Avadānaśataka = J. S. Speyer. 1902–6. *Avadānaçataka: A Century of Edifying Tales Belonging to the Hīnayāna*. Saint Petersburg: Académie Impériale des Sciences.

Bodhisattvabhūmi = Unrai Wogihara. 1930–36 (1971). *Bodhisattvabhūmi: A Statement of the Whole Course of the Bodhisattva (Being the Fifteenth Section of Yogācārabhūmi)*. Tokyo: Sankibo Buddhist Bookstore.

Catuṣpariṣatsūtra = Ernst Waldschmidt. 1962. *Das Catuṣpariṣatsūtra: Eine kanonische Lehrschrift über die Begründung der buddhistischen Gemeinde*, vol. 3. Berlin: Akademie-Verlag.

Demiéville, Paul. 1954. "La Yogācārabhūmi de Saṅgharakṣa." *Bulletin de l'École française d'Extrême-Orient* 44.2: 339–436.

Dhammajoti, K. L. 2017. "Yogācāra Refutation of Tritemporal Existence." *Journal of Buddhist Studies* 14: 235–47.

Dīgha-nikāya = T. W. Rhys Davids and J. E. Carpenter, eds. 1890–1911. *Dīgha-Nikāya*. 3 vols. London: The Pali Text Society.

Divyāvadāna = Edward B. Cowell and Robert A. Neil. 1886. *The Divyāvadāna: A Collection of Early Buddhist Legends*. Cambridge: The University Press.

Eckel, Malcolm David. 2008. *Bhāviveka and His Buddhist Opponents*. Cambridge, MA: Department of Sanskrit and Indian Studies, Harvard University.

Edgerton, Franklin. 1953. *Buddhist Hybrid Sanskrit Grammar and Dictionary, vol. 1: Grammar*. New Haven, CT: Yale University Press.

Eltschinger, Vincent. 2012. "Aśvaghoṣa and His Canonical Sources II: Yaśas, the Kāśyapa Brothers and the Buddha's Arrival in Rājagṛha (*Buddhacarita* 16.3–71)." *Journal of the International Association of Buddhist Studies* 35.1–2: 171–224.

———. 2013. "Aśvaghoṣa and His Canonical Sources I. Preaching Selflessness to King Bimbisāra and the Magadhans (*Buddhacarita* 16.73–93)." *Journal of Indian Philosophy* 41.2: 167–94.

———. 2014. *Buddhist Epistemology as Apologetics: Studies on the History, Self-Understanding and Dogmatic Foundations of Late Indian Buddhist Philosophy*. Vienna: Austrian Academy of Sciences Press.

———. 2015. "The *Yogācārabhūmi* against Allodoxies (*paravāda*), 1: Introduction and Doxography." *Wiener Zeitschrift für die Kunde Südasiens* 55: 191–234.

Foucaux, P. E. 1884. *Le Lalitavistara: L'histoire traditionnelle de la vie du Bouddha Çakyamuni, traduit du sanscrit*. Paris: Ernest Leroux.

Hahn, Michael. 1983. "Kumāralātas Kalpanāmaṇḍitikā Dṛṣṭāntapaṅkti Nr. 1: Die Vorzüglichkeit des Buddha." *Zentralasiatische Studien* 16: 309–36.

———. 1985. "Vorläufige Überlegungen zur Schulzugehörigkeit einiger buddhistischer Dichter." In *Zur Schulzugehörigkeit von Werken der Hīnayāna-Literatur*, edited by Heinz Bechert, 1:239–57. Göttingen: Vandenhoeck & Ruprecht.

Jones, J. J. 1952. *The Mahāvastu: Translated from the Buddhist Sanskrit*, vol. 2. London: Luzac & Company.

Karashima, Seishi. 2015. "Who Composed the Mahāyāna Scriptures? The Mahāsāṃghikas and *Vaitulya* Scriptures." *Annual Report of the International Institute for Advanced Buddhology at Soka University (for the Academic Year 2014)* 18: 113–62.

Lalitavistara = Salomon Lefmann. 1902. *Lalita Vistara: Leben und Lehre des Çâkya-Buddha*. Halle: Verlag der Buchhandlung des Waisenhauses.

Lamotte, Étienne. 1949. *Le Traité de la Grande Vertu de Sagesse de Nāgārjuna* (*Mahāprajñāpāramitāśāstra*), vol. 2. Louvain: Institut Orientaliste.

Mahāparinirvāṇasūtra = Ernst Waldschmidt. 1950–51. *Das Mahāparinirvāṇasūtra: Text in Sanskrit und Tibetisch, verglichen mit dem Pāli nebst einer Übersetzung der chinesischen Entsprechung im Vinaya der Mūlasarvāstivādins*. 3 vols. Berlin: Akademie-Verlag.

Mahāvastu = Émile Senart. 1890. *Mahāvastu Avadānaṃ: Le Mahāvastu, texte sanscrit publié pour la première fois, accompagné d'introductions et d'un commentaire*, vol. 2. Paris: Imprimerie nationale.

Majjhima-nikāya = V. Trenckner. 1935. *The Majjhima-Nikāya*, vol. 1. London: The Pali Text Society. Robert Chalmers. 1898. *The Majjhima-Nikāya*, vol. 2. London: The Pali Text Society.

Ñāṇamoli, Bhikkhu, and Bhikkhu Bodhi. 1995. *The Middle Length Discourses of the Buddha: A Translation of the Majjhima Nikāya*. Boston: Wisdom Publications.

Olivelle, Patrick. 2008. *The Life of the Buddha by Aśvaghoṣa*. New York: New York University Press, JJC Foundation.

Renou, Louis. 1984. *Grammaire sanscrite, tomes I et II réunis*. Paris: Librairie d'Amérique et d'Orient Adrien Maisonneuve.

Rhys Davids, T. W. 1899. *Dialogues of the Buddha*, vol. 1. London: Pali Text Society.

Rotman, Andy. 2008. *Divine Stories: Divyāvadāna, Part I*. Boston: Wisdom Publications.

Saṅghabhedavastu = Raniero Gnoli. 1977–78. *The Gilgit Manuscript of the Saṅghabhedavastu, Being the 17th and Last Section of the Vinaya of the Mūlasarvāstivādin*. 2 vols. Rome: Istituto Italiano per il Medio ed Estremo Oriente. (Tibetan: D 1, *ga* 255b1–*nga* 302a1.)

Schmithausen, Lambert. 1970. "Zu den Rezensionen des Udānavargaḥ." *Wiener Zeitschrift für die Kunde Südasiens* 14: 47–124.

———. 1977. "Zur buddhistischen Lehre von der dreifachen Leidhaftigkeit." *Zeitschrift der Deutschen Morgenländischen Gesellschaft*, Supplement III,2: 918–31.

———. 1987. "Beiträge zur Schulzugehörigkeit und Textgeschichte kanonischer und postkanonischer buddhistischer Materialien." In *Zur Schulzugehörigkeit von Werken der Hīnayāna-Literatur*, edited by Heinz Bechert, 2:304–435. Göttingen: Vandenhoeck & Ruprecht.

Schneider, Johannes. 1993. *Der Lobpreis der Vorzüglichkeit des Buddha: Udbhaṭasiddhasvāmins Viśeṣastava mit Prajñāvarmans Kommentar, nach dem tibetischen Tanjur herausgegeben und übersetzt*. Bonn: Indica-et-Tibetica Verlag.

———. 2014. *Eine buddhistische Kritik der indischen Götter. Śaṃkarasvāmins Devātiśayastotra mit Prajñāvarmans Kommentar, nach dem tibetischen Tanjur herausgegeben und übersetzt*. Vienna: Arbeitskreis für tibetische und buddhistische Studien Universität Wien.

Seyfort Ruegg, David. 1969. *La Théorie du Tathāgatagarbha et du Gotra: Études sur la Sotériologie et la Gnoséologie du Bouddhisme*. Paris: École française d'Extrême-Orient.

Vogel, Claus. 1970. *The Teaching of the Six Heretics according to the Pravrajyāvastu of the Tibetan Mūlasarvāstivāda Vinaya*. Wiesbaden: Deutsche Morgenländische Gesellschaft, Kommissionsverlag Franz Steiner.

Waldschmidt, Ernst, and Jens-Uwe Hartmann. 1973–2015. *Sanskrit-Wörterbuch der buddhistischen Texte aus den Turfan-Funden und der kanonischen Literatur der Sarvāstivāda-Schule*. Göttingen: Vandenhoeck & Ruprecht.

Yamabe, Nobuyoshi. 2003. "On the School Affiliation of Aśvaghoṣa: 'Sautrāntika' or 'Yogācāra'?" *Journal of the International Association of Buddhist Studies* 26.2: 225–54.

———. 2006. "Fragments of the 'Yogalehrbuch' in the Pelliot Collection." In *Dieter Schlingloff: Ein buddhistisches Yogalehrbuch, Unveränderter Nachdruck der Ausgabe von 1964 unter Beigabe aller seither bekannt gewordenen Fragmente*, edited by Jens-Uwe Hartmann and Hermman-Josef Röllicke, 325–47. Düsseldorf: EKŌ Haus der Japanischen Kultur.

Yamabe, Nobuyoshi, and Fumihiko Sueki. 2009. *The Sutra on the Concentration of Sitting Meditation*. Berkeley: Numata Center for Buddhist Translation and Research.

Gyaltsab Darma Rinchen and the *Rigs gter dar ṭik*, an Exegesis of Sakya Paṇḍita's *Tshad ma rigs pa'i gter**

Leonard W. J. van der Kuijp

Some five years ago, Matthew T. Kapstein brought his eloquent pen to bear on a folio of a xylographed text, which he rightly identified as having come from an early xylograph edition of a commentary by Gyaltsab Darma Rinchen (Rgyal tshab Dar ma rin chen) on Dharmakīrti's (ca. 600–ca. 660) *Pramāṇavārttika* that carries the subtitle *Thar lam gsal byed.*[1] Given Matthew's omnivorous scholarly interests, I am happy to contribute this very modest paper on Rgyal tshab, a major figure at the very beginning of what came to be called the Geluk school, to a volume in celebration of his seventieth birthday.

This essay focuses on the part of this learned monk's oeuvre that specifically addresses the interpretation of the logic and epistemology (*tshad ma*) of the Indian Buddhist thinkers Dignāga (ca.480–ca.540) and Dharmakīrti, and their major Indian exegetes. Judging from his extant *oeuvre*, we can unequivocally state that Gyaltsab's intellectual energies focused on the explication of both Madhyamaka thought[2] and *tshad ma*, and that his main ambition in life was to write exegeses of virtually all the basic texts of the Indian Buddhist *pramāṇavāda* literature of Dignāga and Dharmakīrti. In fact, the only works for which he did not seek to provide explanations, or at least

* When not indicated otherwise, all references to Rgyal tshab's *Collected Works* are from the 1897 Lhasa Zhol xylograph edition of his writings that were published in Rgyal tshab Dar ma rin chen 1982.

1. Kapstein 2013. It turned out to be a folio from printing blocks that were carved in 1449, for which see Rgyal tshab Dar ma rin chen 1449 and now van der Kuijp n.d. A translation of Rgyal tshab's comment on the second chapter of his *Thar lam gsal byed* is found in Jackson 1993, and the entire *Thar lam gsal byed* was translated into Japanese by Khang dkar and Fujinaka 2010–13. My thanks to Dr. Sh. Mekata for this information.

2. See his commentary on Āryadeva's *Catuḥśataka* in Sonam 2004, his work on the *Ratnāvalī* in Eda 2005, and now also his commentary on the *Uttaratantra* in Jiang 2017.

on which he did not leave behind commentaries, were Dharmakīrti's *Hetubindu*, *Santānāntarasiddhi*, and *Vādanyāya*. In the history of Tibetan exegetical scholarship on Dignāga and Dharmakīrti and in terms of the depth and breadth of his contributions to *tshad ma* studies, he stands second only to Dar ma rgyal mtshan (1227–1305), alias Bcom ldan rig[s] pa'i ral gri, Rong ston Shākya rgyal mtshan (1367–1449), and Stag tshang Lo tsā ba Shes rab rin chen (1405–77).

Early historians of the Geluk school include Gyaltsab's commentary on Sakya Paṇḍita's (Sa skya Paṇḍita Kun dga' rgyal mtshan, 1181–1252) celebrated *Tshad ma rigs pa'i gter* in his bibliography.[3] Owing to Gareth Sparham's generosity, Shunzo Onoda and Georges Dreyfus were able to reprint a late Bla bang Bkra shis 'khyil Monastery xylograph of the *Tshad ma rigs pa'i gter gyi rnam bshad legs par bshad pa'i snying po*, a work that is attributed to Gyaltsab, to which Dreyfus added an informative introduction.[4] For reasons that will become clear below, I will henceforth [and only tentatively] refer to it as the *Rigs gter dar ṭik*. Supplementing Dreyfus's introduction, I provide a capsule history of the xylograph itself, and I conclude this essay with a brief discussion of what appears to be an explicit reference to it by Sera Jetsun (Se ra Rje btsun Chos kyi rgyal mtshan, 1469–1544/46).

There is so far no airtight proof for the view that the *Tshad ma rigs pa'i gter* commentary attributed to Gyaltsab by Las chen Kun dga' rgyal mtshan (1432–1506)—this is in the latter's 1494 chronicle of the Kadam tradition,[5] which includes a sketch of Gyaltsab's life and works—is the same work that, almost four centuries later, the authorities at Bla brang had committed to the printing block. But it goes without saying that those of us working in the rather arcane area of *tshad ma* studies welcomed the publication, now already twenty-four years ago, of this Bla brang xylograph of what was then *alleged* to be Gyaltsab's *Tshad ma rigs pa'i gter* commentary. Dreyfus's introductory remarks shed much valuable light on the text itself and its historical context. Nevertheless, one cannot always readily assent to the veracity of the information given by him or to some of his interpretations thereof, especially regarding the attribution of the authorship of the work to Gyaltsab. The following notes are thus intended to bring the text-historical dimension of this work into a somewhat sharper relief. That said, there is no question that the earliest evidence for the ascription of a *Tshad ma rigs pa'i gter* commentary to Gyal-

3. For the various editions of Sa skya Paṇḍita's work, see most recently Hugon 2008, 363–69.

4. In Dreyfus 1994, 1n2, Dreyfus thanks Matthew for having first brought the existence of this xylograph to his attention.

5. Las chen Kun dga' rgyal mtshan 1972, 476, and 2003, 724.

tsab is explicitly found toward the second half of the fifteenth century in the work of the Las chen.

The printer's colophon (*par byang*) of the xylograph edition, composed by a certain Btsun gzugs Shes rab rgya mtsho, relates that, although it had not been included in prior xylograph editions of Gyaltsab's collected oeuvre, two manuscripts of this work were available at Bla brang.[6] One had belonged to 'Jam dbyangs rgya mtsho of Mog kya, an earlier abbot of Dpal 'khor sde chen legs bshad sgrog pa'i tshal Monastery in Rgyal mkhar rtse, who may, but only may, be identified as the third abbot of its Gser khang gong pa seminary.[7] If so, then he must have flourished sometime toward the end of the fifteenth century. This manuscript was apparently so rife with omissions (*chad*) and unwarranted additions (*lhag*) that it could not be responsibly used by Dkon mchog rgya mtsho and Chos kyi rgya mtsho, the editors of this xylograph edition. Instead, they based their text on a better exemplar that had been earlier procured by Kun mkhyen bla ma 'Jam dbyangs bzhad pa. Now we know that 'Jam dbyangs bzhad pa'i rdo rje I Ngag dbang brtson 'grus (1648–1722), Bla brang's founder, seems to have been among the relatively few Gelukpa scholars to have made use of the text. He quotes it in his undated survey of Buddhist epistemology (*blo rigs*) as well as in his grand doxography, the *Grub mtha' chen mo* of 1699, and refers to it with the abbreviated title of *Rigs gter dar ṭik* in both these studies.[8] Unfortunately, neither his biography written by his disciple Bse tshang I Ngag dbang bkra shis (1678–1738), nor the somewhat "sanitized" one by his subsequent re-embodiment 'Jam dbyangs bzhad pa'i rdo rje II Dkon mchog 'jigs med dbang po (1728–91), nor even his own incomplete "record of teachings heard" (*gsan yig*) indicate under whom or where he might have studied this work, let alone the *Tshad ma rigs pa'i gter*. Less probable, but not altogether impossible, would be that the designation "Kun mkhyen bla ma 'Jam dbyangs bzhad pa" refers to Dkon mchog 'jigs med dbang po. This would then indicate that this manuscript, too, may have resulted from the manuscript buying spree he conducted in Central Tibet in the mid-1780s.[9]

6. Rgyal tshab Dar ma rin chen 1994, 151b, and Rgyal tshab Dar ma rin chen 2016, 226.

7. Sde srid Sangs rgyas rgya mtsho 1989, 245.

8. See, for example, 'Jam dbyangs bzhad pa'i rdo rje I vol. *ba*, 25b, and vol. *pha*, 175b–176a. In connection with the meaning of *dar ṭik* or *dar ṭīk*, we cannot of course follow Stcherbatsky 1962, 325n1, who suggested that it means something like **vistaraṭīkā*; *dar* [*ma* < Skt. *dharma*] is simply an abbreviation of Rgyal tshab's name in religion, so that *dar ṭik* or its variants simply means "commentary written by Dar ma rin chen."

9. Gung thang Dkon mchog bstan pa'i sgron me (1762–1823) described this venture in his 1799 biography of Dkon mchog 'jigs med dbang po, for which see Gung thang Dkon mchog bstan pa'i sgron me 1990, 333ff. and 368ff.

The next issue that needs to be raised is the identity of Btsun gzugs Shes rab rgya mtsho, the printer's colophon. Of course, "Shes rab rgya mtsho" is hardly an uncommon name, and at least three scholars with the same ordination name have left their mark in Bla brang during the last hundred and fifty years or so. If our Btsun gzugs Shes rab rgya mtsho is to be identified as the famous intransigent, and perhaps even tragic, Rdo sbis (or: Klu 'bum) Dge bshes Shes rab rgya mtsho (1884–1968), then the blockprint itself may date from the second or early third decade of the previous century. Rdo sbis Dge bshes was, inter alia, responsible for the printing of Rngog Lo tsā ba Blo ldan shes rab's (ca. 1059–ca. 1109) short study of the *Uttaratantra.*[10] On the other hand, it is also possible that Btsun gzugs was the name used by Gung thang tshang, the erstwhile abbot of Bla brang, who seems to have flourished from 1851 to 1928 or 1930, for he is associated with a good number of other printing projects of such rarities as Rngog Lo tsā ba's commentary on the *Abhisamayālaṃkāra* and probably Nya dbon Kun dga' dpal's (fourteenth cent.) large exegesis of the *Abhisamayālaṃkāra* of 1371.

All things considered, however, there can be no doubt that our Shes rab rgya mtsho must be identified with A khu Shes rab rgya mtsho (1813–75), a former abbot of Bla brang and the well-known author of a listing of rare books, the philosophical section of which seems largely based on the holdings of Bla brang's monastic library. That he had printing blocks prepared for the *Rigs gter dar ṭik* in 1873 is confirmed by the entry for this year in Grags pa rgya mtsho's 1927 study of the life of Zhwa dmar Paṇḍita Dge 'dun bstan 'dzin rgya mtsho (1852–1912), a close disciple of A khu Shes rab rgya mtsho.[11] For there we learn that Zhwa dmar had assisted his master with reading the proofs for the xylograph edition of this text. In the course of preparing what amounted to the first printed edition of the text, A khu pointed out to the young Zhwa dmar that printing blocks for a number of Gyaltsab's writings were never carved because their content did not agree with the views of the Lord Master (*rje bla ma*)—that is, Tsong kha pa Blo bzang grags pa (1357–1419). And even though, he remarked, the *Rigs gter dar ṭik* was in thorough agreement with Tsong kha pa's *oeuvre*, it was not included in such editions of his collected writings as the

10. See now Kano 2016.

11. Grags pa rgya mtsho 1990, 125. It is unfortunate that the editors of the Lhasa Zhol xylograph edition of A khu's writings of 1943 in seven volumes, which were reissued in New Delhi in 1974, did not include his biography by 'Jam dbyangs bzhad pa'i rdo rje IV Blo bzang skal bzang thub bstan dbang phyug (1856–1915/16), for which see Sun Wenjing 1989, 142. I do not know whether the other xylograph edition of his oeuvre (eight volumes issued from the printing blocks of Mdzod dge sgar gsar Monastery in Amdo) did include this biography. See Chandra 1964, 302.

Bkra shis lhun po xylograph. This is a curious anomaly, since, to be sure, text-internal evidence indicates that, if anything, this work must have been written after Gyaltsab had met Tsong kha pa, regardless of whether or not Gyaltsab was its author. It also appears that for some reason, the oral *lung* and teaching transmissions for the text seem to have been lost, since as far as I have been able to determine, none of the later Geluk *gsan yig*-s, including the one of A khu himself (compiled shortly before his passing in 1875), mention its line of transmission.[12]

The *Rigs gter dar ṭik* is not available in any of the four xylograph editions of Gyaltsab's collected writings. We must therefore conclude that its omission was either due to conscious editorial policy, meaning that the editors felt that the text was a forgery, or that it did not sufficiently conform to what they and the Geluk establishment felt Gyaltsab's position to have been or should have been. This might have been due to the fact that the colophon expresses the author's intellectual debt to Red mda' ba Gzhon nu blo gros (1348–1413), which is strange when we consider that Red mda' ba *and* Tsong kha pa are mentioned in each and every one of Gyaltsab's "authenticated" *tshad ma* writings—only his exegeses of the *Pramāṇavārttika*, *Pramāṇaviniścaya*, and the *Tshad ma'i lam khrid* [= *Tshad ma'i lam bsgrigs*] mention a certain Kun dga' dpal alongside these two men.[13] That said, the author's colophon of the *Rigs gter dar ṭik* has it that it was written by "Dar ma rin chen who theorizes about logic" at Dga' ldan Monastery, which was founded in 1409. Hence, this fact, too, indicates that it was written well after Gyaltsab had met Tsong kha pa. In addition to the explicit information provided by the colophon, Dreyfus has pointed out that it must have then been one of Gyaltsab's later ventures in this area, for in it the author refers to a *Pramāṇavārttika* and a *Pramāṇaviniścaya* commentary, which he identified, respectively, as his *Thar lam gsal byed* and *Dgongs pa rab gsal* exegeses.[14] But this is not all. Reading through the *Rigs gter dar ṭik* in its entirety, we notice that the text also refers to Gyaltsab's *'Brel brtag*

12. For the listing of Rgyal tshab's works for which he received the *lung*, see A khu Shes rab rgya mtsho 1998–99, 142–45; his *lung* for the *Mngon sum le'u'i brjed byang* is listed on 131–32.

13. See, respectively, *Collected Works*, vol. *cha*, 873, *Collected Works*, vol. *nya*, 520, and *Collected Works*, vol. *ca*, 553. In the second, Kun dga' dpal is noted as having been one under whom he had specifically studied the *Pramāṇaviniścaya* and related texts (*cha lag dang bcas pa*), whereas in the third he is noted as having also been a disciple of Tsong kha pa.

14. Dreyfus 1994, 2, *ad* Rgyal tshab Dar ma rin chen 1994, fols. 9a, 20b, 56a–b, 82b, 98b, 119b, and 120b, and Rgyal tshab Dar ma rin chen 2016, pp. 12, 29, 81, 122, 148, 179, and 180. However, the author simply refers to these as "explanations" (*rnam bshad*) of the *Rnam 'grel* (*Pramāṇavārttika*) and *Tshad ma rnam nges* (*Pramāṇaviniścaya*) and *not* by their subtitles of *Thar lam gsal byed* and *Dgongs pa rab gsal*.

gi rnam bshad and *'Gal 'brel gyi rnam bzhag nges par byed pa bstan bcos.*[15] Of course, it should be noted that none of these references are qualified as "having been written by me/us," a self-referential qualification so frequently used by Tibetan authors. This would seem to hold for all the text-internal references he has made to his other writings.

This same colophon also has it that three people requested Gyaltsab to write this work: a certain *dka' bcu pa* Blo gros dpal bzang, Grags pa bkra shis, and a Sakya nephew (*sa skya dbon po*) Nyi ma rgyal mtshan. Dreyfus did not identify these men, and I was myself at pains to do so for a long time. Fortunately, further digging has proved successful for the first two. Blo gros dpal bzang can most probably be identified as Gyaltsab's disciple who is sometimes referred to by his sobriquet Rigs gter ba, "the one with expertise in the *Tshad ma rigs pa'i gter.*" He was to become the third abbot of Gsang sngags mkhar,[16] a monastery founded either by Tsong kha pa and his patron Brag dkar nang so Rin chen lhun po in 1419, or only by the latter shortly after Tsong kha pa's passing. Grags pa bkra shis, on his part, figures in Paṇ chen Bsod nams grags pa's listing of Gyaltsab's students.[17]

Now a feature of Gyaltsab's writings in general is that none are dated, save two. The two are the series of notes he took when Tsong kha pa lectured on tantric practice of the mother tantras (*ma rgyud*) in Se ra chos sdings, which is dated to the winter of a pig year (1407/8), and the other one that took place in Gong dkar in the winter of a rat year (1409/10).[18] And an additional two works that had come from his pen can be dated with some precision but only by way of consulting the studies of Tsong kha pa's life. Thus the biography of Tsong kha pa written by Gnas rnying Kun dga' bde legs (1446–96) suggests that Gyaltsab completed his *Abhisamayālaṃkāra* exegesis in 1403[19] and that his notes on Tsong kha pa's lectures on *tshad ma*, the *Rje'i gsung zin bris tshad ma'i*

15. Rgyal tshab Dar ma rin chen 1994, 52b/53b and 64b, and Rgyal tshab Dar ma rin chen 2016, 75/77 and 94.

16. Sde srid Sangs rgyas rgya mtsho 1989, 145.

17. Paṇ chen Bsod nams grags pa 1977, 67.

18. The first is the *Rdzogs rim dpyid kyi thig le'i zin bris, Collected Works*, vol. *ka*, 790: *'di ni phag lo dgun gnas snel bas bteg nas se ra chos sdings su bzhugs dus /*. The colophon states that these notes were written down by a certain "Mi bskyod rdo rje." As in the case of Red mda' ba [and many others], Mi bskyod rdo rje may have been his "tantric" name, one that presumably derived from his initiation into the mysteries of the Guhyasamāja, on which he composed several works. The second is the *Rdzogs rim dpyid kyi thig le*, Rgyal tshab Dar ma rin chen 1982, vol. *ka*: 835.

19. He is cited to this effect in Rgyal dbang chos rje Blo bzang 'phrin las rnam rgyal's superb 1845 study of Tsong kha pa's life that is based on a careful assessment of a large number of earlier biographies; see Rgyal dbang rje 1981, 283–84.

brjed byang chen mo, date from 1404. He composed his *Pramāṇavārttika* and *Uttaratantra* commentaries in Gnas rnying Monastery.[20] Aside from the former and the *Tshad ma'i lam khrid*, which he wrote in Po ta ri, Gyaltsab wrote or had begun all his other contributions to *tshad ma* at Dga' ldan Monastery, and these must therefore necessarily postdate the year 1409. His rewarding work on the *Pramāṇasamuccaya* can now also be more or less dated, for it was petitioned by, inter alia, Thu btsun Bsod nams rnam rgyal, who must of course be identified as Byams gling Paṇ chen Bsod nams rnam rgyal ba'i sde (1400–75). It was written sometime between 1424 and 1432.[21]

Several of his compositions contain references to his earlier works, so that we can venture to sketch their relative chronology numerically, whereby the first [1] is referred to by the second [2] and so on. Both the *Nyāyabindu* and *Pramāṇasamuccaya* commentaries as well as the *Rigs gter dar ṭik* refer to Gyaltsab's work on the *Pramāṇavārttika* and *Pramāṇaviniścaya*, so that the first three must postdate the last two. His study of the *Pramāṇaviniścaya* is posterior to his study of the *Pramāṇavārttika*, since the former mentions the latter. The undated study of the difficult portions of the first chapter of Gyaltsab's *Pramāṇavārttika* commentary, which is based on Sera Jetsun's remarks, suggests a close exegetical affinity among his exegeses of the *Pramāṇavārttika*, *Pramāṇaviniścaya*, and *Nyāyabindu*, which suggests in turn that the distance between their compositions could turn out to be rather insignificant.[22] That being said, his *Nyāyabindu* commentary makes references to his exegeses of the *Pramāṇavārttika* and *Pramāṇaviniścaya* and then cites in passing the *Pramāṇasamuccaya* without referencing his commentary.[23] This absence of reference to his own commentary leads me to suspect that he wrote the latter subsequent to his work on the *Nyāyabindu*. The *Rigs gter dar ṭik* seems to refer to Gyaltsab's commentary on the *Pramāṇasamuccaya* on some three separate occasions.[24] Further, while Gyaltsab does not mention any of the above

20. The colophon of the latter states that Gung ru Rgyal mtshan bzang po (1383–1450) had requested him to write it; see Gung ru 2007, 461. As G.yu pa Brtson 'grus bzang po indicates in his brief study of Gung ru's life, his subject had studied with Rgyal tshab prior to his ordination as a monk in 1412 during which the latter officiated as the "confessor"; see G.yu pa 2011, 6. G.yu pa authored his work in 1454 at Se ra theg chen gling.

21. For this, see van der Kuijp and McKeown 2013, xcvi–viii.

22. Se ra Rje btsun 2006, 56.

23. See the *Tshad ma rigs thigs kyi 'grel pa legs bshad snying po'i gter* in Rgyal tshab Dar ma rin chen 1982, vol. *nya*: 548 and 615.

24. Rgyal tshab Dar ma rin chen 1994, fols. 13a, 120b, and 139a, and Rgyal tshab Dar ma rin chen 2016, pp. 18, 180, and 208. Rgyal tshab's commentary is styled a *Rnam bshad*, as opposed to Dignāga's autocommentary and Jinendrabuddhi's (eighth-century) study, which he refers to

in his *'Gal 'brel gyi rnam bzhag*, a study of contraries and relations, he does cite in this work his exegeses of the *Uttaratantra* and *Abhidharmasamuccaya*. And since the latter quotes his *Pramāṇaviniścaya* commentary, we can be sure that the *'Gal 'brel gyi rnam bzhag* belongs to his middle or late period.[25] Similarly, he also references his work on the *Abhidharmasamuccaya* in his *Pramāṇasamuccaya* commentary.[26]

Given the above data, we can now come up with the following relative chronology of Gyaltsab's works on *tshad ma*:

1. *Pramāṇavārttika* commentary
2. *Pramāṇaviniścaya* commentary
   ? *'Gal 'brel gyi rnam bzhag*
   ? *Sambandhaparikṣā* commentary
3. *Pramāṇasamuccaya* commentary

If the *Rigs gter dar ṭik* turns out to be a bona fide work of his, it would have to figure at the very end of this list. Only Gyaltsab's commentary on the *Sambandhaparīkṣā* contains a unique reference to the *Tshad ma rigs pa'i gter* and defends Sakya Paṇḍita against a critcism by Chu mig pa Seng ge dpal (ca. 1220–ca. 1280).[27]

A relative chronology of an author's oeuvre may prove to be of some use to gain an insight into his intellectual and spiritual development. With few exceptions such as Tsong kha pa and Gser mdog Paṇ chen, the very idea of such a development is usually not even considered by native Tibetan scholarship. The prevalent conception is rather that great scholars and masters are not inclined to change their minds or mature intellectually.

We have seen that the earliest listings of Gyaltsab's oeuvre provide fairly solid circumstantial evidence that he had in fact authored an exegesis of the *Tshad ma rigs pa'i gter*. But it nonetheless remains to be determined, not least

as, respectively, the *'grel pa / rang 'grel* and the *'grel bshad*. See his *Tshad ma kun las btus pa'i rnam bshad mthar 'dzin gyi tsha gdung ba 'joms byed rigs pa'i rgya mtsho*, Rgyal tshab Dar ma rin chen 1982, vol. *nga*: 352 and 355.

25. See the *Legs par bshad pa'i chos mngon rgya mtsho'i snying po*, Rgyal tshab Dar ma rin chen 1982, vol. *ga*: 672. It is of interest that, on page 562, he does not refer to Tsong kha pa's youthful work on the notion of fundamental awareness (*ālayavijñāna*) for a detailed analysis of this concept (see Sparham 1993) but rather to Red mda' ba's *Abhidharmasamuccaya* commentary.

26. *Tshad ma kun las btus pa'i rnam bshad mthar 'dzin gyi tsha gdung ba 'joms byed rigs pa'i rgya mtsho*, Rgyal tshab Dar ma rin chen 1982, vol. *nga*: 556.

27. *'Brel pa brtag pa'i rnam bshad nyi ma'i snying po*, Rgyal tshab Dar ma rin chen 1982, vol. *ca*: 494–95.

because of the inordinate editorial lapse of time between the alleged autograph and the xylograph, whether the manuscript(s) that formed the basis of the Bla brang xylograph was in fact Gyaltsab's work—or whether its ascription to Gyaltsab was accidental or purposive, thereby turning it into a forgery, a phenomenon not altogether unknown to Tibetan literary history. If one of the later editors of Gyaltsab's works had had any slight suspicion that the latter scenarios had been the case, it would go a long way in explaining why he would have been loath to include the text in any of the later "editions" of his collected oeuvre. Indeed, it would appear that all the references to the manuscript[s] and xylograph of this work are in one way or another connected to Bla brang and Amdo in general, and thus date from the early 1700s and 1800s.

So far so good. But we should also be aware that references to Gyaltsab as a *Dar ṭik pa* in the *Tshad ma rigs pa'i gter* literature do not always assure that these in fact point to the *Rigs gter dar ṭik*. An instance of this is found in Go rams pa Bsod nams seng ge's (1429–89) *Tshad ma rigs pa'i gter* commentary of 1471, where he cites "the author of the Dar ṭik."[28] Go rams pa's citation is not found in the relevant section of the *Rigs gter dar ṭik*[29] or, for that matter, anywhere else in the text. Instead, we more or less find this citation in the said passage [note 37 above] of Gyaltsab's commentary on the *Pramāṇavārttika*. To my limited knowledge, Sera Jetsun is the oldest authority who might come to our aid in establishing whether, at least by the end of the fifteenth and the beginning of the sixteenth centuries, the text that came to be printed in Bla brang as Gyaltsab's work one to two hundred years later was the same one with which he was familiar. For he cites the *Rig*[*s*] *gter dar ṭik*, if only once.[30] The passage in question is concerned with Gyaltsab's supplementary considerations regarding *Pramāṇavārttika* 1.169 in his *Pramāṇavārttika* commentary. In this text, Gyaltsab first unpacks the verse and then gives an account of the formation of concepts known as other-exclusion (*gzhan sel*, *anyāpoha*) and its typology.[31] He isolates three distinct types of exclusions:

28. Go rams pa 1969, vol. *ga*: 180a, *ad* Sa skya Paṇḍita 1284, 122b–124b, Sa skya Paṇḍita 1968, vol. *da*: 151a–152b, and Sa skya Paṇḍita 2007, 302–5; see also *Pramāṇavārttika* 3.301–319; see Miyasaka 1971/72, 82–85. Not surprisingly, we find the very same puzzling proverb used by Go rams pa in Rgyal tshab's *Pramāṇavārttika* commentary in his *Collected Works*, vol. cha: 585, in the section where he briefly discusses the three alternative conceptualizations of *tshad 'bras* (585–86).

29. Rgyal tshab Dar ma rin chen 1994, 99b–101b, and Rgyal tshab Dar ma rin chen 2016, 50.

30. Se ra Rje btsun 2006, 200–201.

31. Rgyal tshab Dar ma rin chen 1982, vol. *cha*: 166–68, and Rgyal tshab Dar ma rin chen 1449, 47b–48a.

1. Object-based exclusion (*don gi gzhan sel*): "the exclusion of a jug from what is not a jug" (*bum pa bum ma yin las ldog pa*)
2. Cognition-based exclusion (*blo'i gzhan sel*): "the sensum that has emerged in a conceptual cogniton of a jug, which appears to be contrary to what is a jug" (*bum 'dzin rtog pa la shar ba'i rnam pa bum ma yi las log par snang ba*)
3. Nonexistence-based exclusion (*med dgag gi gzhan sel*): "the absence of what is not a jug at the locus of a jug" (*gzhi bum pa la bum pa ma yin med pa*)

After referencing several Indian commentators, he focuses on a classification of negation, which he takes to be synonym of other exclusion, and gives the following definitions:

1. Absolute negation (*med par dgag pa*):[32] an explicit exclusion of the negandum in which it is denied that there is no other phenomenon that is implied.
2. Implicative negation (*ma yin pa'i dgag pa*): negating something without implying that there is no other phenomenon.

Gyaltsab then cites an unidentified verse on the subject that in fact Sera Jetsun happily identified as deriving from Avalokitavrata's (ca. 700) extensive commentary on Bhāviveka's (sixth-century) *Prajñāpradīpa* gloss on Nāgārjuna's *Mūlamadhyamakārikā*'s first *pāda*, in which are isolated as many as four different types of implicative negation.[33] At the outset of his deliberations, Sera Jetsun cites Gyaltsab's two main types of negation. He comments that this is quite fine (*shin tu legs pa*) and proceeds to analyze these, whereby he provides two subtypes in the first of them: the absolute negation of what are and what are not possible knowable objects, respectively—for instance, a jug and the horns of a hare.[34] Sera Rje btsun then writes (see note 30 above), referencing the *Rigs gter dar ṭik*:

The explanation in the *Rig*[*s*] *gter dar ṭik* that the meaning of the

32. For the Tibetan terms for two types of negation are of course interpretive translations of Sanskrit *paryudāsa-* and *prasajyapratiṣedha*; on these, see the long note in Seyfort Ruegg 2002, 19–24, note 6.

33. See, respectively, Bhāviveka 1994–2008, 913, and Avalokitavrata 1994–2008, 1018.

34. The latter would of course be an instance of an "empty subject term"; see, with some reservations, the otherwise rewarding essay of Yao 2009.

> statement in the *Rig[s] gter* about the exclusion of what exists and the exclusion of what does not exist is an absolute negation of what is to be negated (namely, what exists as knowable) and an absolute negation of what is to be negated (namely, what does not exist as knowable) is the ultimate intent of [Dharmakīrti's] basic text . . .

Sera Jetsun appears to point to the passage in the fourth chapter of the *Tshad ma rigs pa'i gter* that deals with "exclusion of the other" (*gzhan sel*, *anyāpoha*), wherein we read the following in the verse text and autocommentary[35]:

> Exclusion is twofold on account of
> the negandum's existence and nonexistence.

> Since exclusion does not have a real essence, it is twofold when classified on account of what is to be excluded—that is, what is to be excluded that exists as a knowable object, such as there is no jug and so on, and what does not exist as a knowable object, such as there are no rabbit horns and there is no eternal thing and so on.

The *Rigs gter dar ṭik* comments on this passage:[36]

> Exclusion of the other has two types because there are two types on account of a phenomenon that is to be negated, such as a jug that exists among knowable objects, and a phenomenon that is to be negated, such as the horns of a hare that do not exist among knowable objects. Those who claim that the point of the basic text is to support the idea that existence entails impermanence are quite intellectually naïve . . .

While the basis to reach a firm conclusion furnished by this single item is far too narrow, it would appear that the manuscript of the *Rigs gter dar ṭik* Sera Jetsun had in his possession may have been based on the work for which printing blocks were carved at Bla brang in 1873. It is in this context certainly not irrelevant to point out that, to my knowledge, not a single one of the very well-read commentators of the *Tshad ma rigs pa'i gter* who belonged to the rival Sakya school, such as Gser mdog Paṇ chen, Glo bo Mkhan chen Bsod nams lhun grub (1456–1532), Mang thos Klu sgrub rgya mtsho (1523–1596), and his disciple Mkhan chen Ngag dbang chos grags (1572–1641), makes any mention

35. Sa skya Paṇḍita 1284, 29b, Sa skya Paṇḍita 1968, vol. *da*: 57a, and Sa skya Paṇḍita 2007, 110.

36. Rgyal tshab Dar ma rin chen 1994, 36b, and Rgyal tshab Dar ma rin chen 2016, 53.

of Gyaltsab having written a commentary on Sakya Paṇḍita's work, let alone explicitly mentioning a treatise called the *Rigs gter dar ṭik*.

A few final observations: In connection with Gyaltsab's *tshad ma* oeuvre, I can see one minor and two main immediate tasks for future studies. The minor one will be to investigate to what extent the *Rigs gter dar ṭik* departs from Sakya Paṇḍita's thoroughgoing nominalism. Dreyfus contends that the text did do so,[37] but I am not prima facie convinced of this. On the other hand, the first major task, as I see it, will be to evaluate to what extent, if any, the relative chronology of Gyaltsab's writings that was outlined above can provide an insight into his intellectual development and understanding of Dharmakīrti's work in particular. The second outstanding task is to investigate to what degree, if any, his oeuvre was able to wield a measure of influence over subsequent generations of commentators on the work of Dignāga, Dharmakīrti, and Sakya Paṇḍita. It remains to be shown how Gyaltsab's views may contrast with the cognate writings on *tshad ma* of Mkhas grub, his student and handpicked successor to Dga' ldan Monastery's abbatial throne, whose oeuvre, which shows so many distinctive traits that mark many departures from Gyaltsab, appears to have been less immediately influential.

37. Dreyfus 1994, 11–13.

Works Cited

A khu Shes rab rgya mtsho. 1998–99. *Thog mtha' bar du dge ba'i dam pa'i chos kyi thob yig mdo sngags zab rgyas bdud rtsi'i mtsho las skra rtses blangs pa'i chu thigs. Collected Works*, vol. 6. Lhasa: no publisher named.

Avalokitavrata. 1994–2008. *Prajñāpradīpaṭīkā*. In *Bstan 'gyur* [*dpe sdur ma*], vol. 58. Edited by Krung go'i bod kyi shes rig zhib 'jug lte gnas kyi bka' bstan dpe sdur khang. Beijing: Krung go'i bod kyi shes rig dpe skrun khang.

Bhāviveka. 1994–2008. *Prajñāpradīpa*. In *Bstan 'gyur* [*dpe sdur ma*], vol. 57. Edited by Krung go'i bod kyi shes rig zhib 'jug lte gnas kyi bka' bstan dpe sdur khang. Beijing: Krung go'i bod kyi shes rig dpe skrun khang.

Chandra, Lokesh. 1964. "Tibetan Buddhist Texts Printed by the Mdzod-dge-sgar-gsar Monastery." *Indo-Iranian Journal* 7: 298–306.

Dreyfus, Georges B. J. 1994. *Introduction*. In Rgyal tshab Dar ma rin chen 1994, 1–18.

Eda, Akimichi. 2005. *Untersuchungen zur Nāgārjunas Ratnāvalī unter besonderer Berücksichtigung des Kommentars des Rgyal tshab*. PhD dissertation. Marburg: University of Marburg.

Go rams pa Bsod nams seng ge. 1969. *Tshad ma rigs pa'i gter gyi dka' ba'i gnas rnam par bshad pa sde bdun rab gsal* [Sde dge xylograph]. *Sa skya bka' 'bum*, vol. 12. Compiled by Bsod nams rgya mtsho. Tokyo: The Toyo Bunko.

Grags pa rgya mtsho. 1990. *Rje zhwa dmar dge 'dun bstan 'dzin rgya mtsho'i rnam thar*. Edited by Rdo rje tshe ring. Xining: Mtsho sngon mi rigs dpe skrun khang.

Gung ru Rgyal mtshan bzang po. 2007. *Theg pa chen po rgyud bla ma'i bstan bcos 'grel pa dang bcas pa'i rnam par bshad pa rgyal ba'i ring lugs pa chen po. Collected Works*, vol. *ga* [3]. Edited by Dpal brtsegs bod yig dpe rnying zhib 'jug khang. Beijing: Krung go'i bod rig pa dpe skrun khang.

Gung thang Dkon mchog bstan pa'i sgron me. 1990. *Kun mkhyen 'jigs med dbang po'i rnam thar*. Edited by Mkha' 'gro skyabs. Lanzhou: Kan su'u mi rigs dpe skrun khang.

G.yu pa Brtson 'grus bzang po. 2011. *Mtshungs med chos kyi rje thams cad mkhyen pa rgyal mtshan dpal bzang po'i rnam thar mdor bsdus dad pa'i rol mtsho, Gung ru rgyal mtshan bzang po'i stong thun dang nam thar*. Edited by Ser gtsug nang bstan dpe rnying 'tshol bsdu phyogs sgrig khang. Lhasa: no publisher named.

Hugon, Pascale. 2008. *Trésors du raisonnement. Sa skya Paṇḍita et ses prédécesseurs tibétains sur les modes de fonctionnement de la pensée et le fondement de l'inférence. Édition et traduction annotée du quatrième chapitre et d'une section du dixième chapitre du Tshad ma rigs pa'i gter*, vol. 2. Wiener Studien zur Tibetologie und Buddhismuskunde 69.2. Vienna: Arbeitskreis für Tibetische und Buddhistische Studien Universität Wien.

Jackson, Roger R. 1993. *Is Enlightenment Possible? Dharmakīrti and Rgyal tshab rje on Knowledge, Rebirth, No-Self, and Liberation*. Ithaca, NY: Snow Lion Publications.

'Jam dbyangs bzhad pa'i rdo rje I Ngag dbang brtson 'grus. *Blo rig*[*s*] *kyi rnam gzhag nyung gsal legs bshad gser gyi phreng mdzes. Collected Works* [Bla brang xylograph], vol. *ba* [15].

———. *Grub mtha' chen mo. Collected Works* [Bla brang xylograph], vol. *pha* [14].

Jiang, Bo. 2017. *The Sublime Continuum and Its Explanatory Commentary . . . with The Sublime Continuum Supercommentary*. New York: The American Institute of Buddhist Studies et al.

Kamalaśīla. 1994–2008. *Tattvasaṃgrahapañjikā*. In *Bstan 'gyur* [*dpe sdur ma*], vol. 107. Edited by Krung go'i bod kyi shes rig zhib 'jug lte gnas kyi bka' bstan dpe sdur khang. Beijing: Krung go'i bod kyi shes rig dpe skrun khang.

Kano, Kazuo. 2016. *Ratnagotravibhāga from India to Tibet*. Wiener Studien zur Tibetologie und Buddhismuskunde 91. Vienna: Arbeitskreis für Tibetische und Buddhistische Studien Universität Wien.

Kapstein, Matthew T. 2013. "A Fragment from a Previously Unknown Edition of the *Pramāṇavārttika* Commentary of Rgyal tshab rje Dar ma rin chen (1364–1432)." In *Nepalica et Tibetica. Festgabe für Christoph Cüppers*, edited by Franz-Karl Ehrhard and Petra Maurer, 1:315–24. Andiast: International Institute for Tibetan and Buddhist Studies.

Khang dkar Tshul khrims skal bzang and Takashi Fujinaka. 2010–13. *A Study of Buddhist Logic-Epistemology in Tibet* [in Japanese]. 4 vols. Research Institute for Humanity and Nature (RIHN), Kyoto.

van der Kuijp, Leonard W. J. n.d. "On the 1449 Xylograph of Rgyal tshab Dar ma rin chen's (1364–1432) *Pramāṇavārttika* Commentary." On academia.edu.

van der Kuijp, Leonard W. J., and Arthur P. McKeown. 2013, *Bcom ldan ral gri (1227–1305) on Indian Buddhist Logic and Epistemology: His Commentary on Dignāga's Pramāṇasamuccaya*. Wiener Studien zur Tibetologie und Buddhismuskunde 80. Vienna: Arbeitskreis für Tibetische und Buddhistische Studien Universität Wien.

Las chen Kun dga' rgyal mtshan. 1972. *Bka' gdams chos 'byung gsal ba'i sgron me*, vol. 2. New Delhi: Jamyang Norbu.

———. 2003. *Bka' gdams chos 'byung gsal ba'i sgron me*. Edited by Mig dmar rgyal mtshan. Lhasa: Bod ljongs mi rigs dpe skrun khang.

Miyaska, Yushō, ed. 1971/72. *Pramāṇavārttikakārikā*. *Acta Indologica* II. Narita: Naritasan Shinshoji.

Paṇ chen Bsod nams grags pa. 1977. *Bka' gdams gsar rnying gi chos 'byung yid kyi mdzes rgyan, Two Histories of the Bka' gdams pa Tradition*. Gangtok: Gonpo Tseten.

———. 1998. *Rgyas pa'i bstan bcos tshad ma rnam 'grel gyi dka' 'grel dgongs pa rab gsal*. Edited by Mig dmar. Beijing: Krung go'i bod kyi shes rig dpe krun khang.

Rgyal dbang chos rje Blo bzang 'phrin las rnam rgyal. 1981. *'Jam mgon chos kyi rgyal po tsong kha pa chen po'i rnam thar* [based on the Lhasa xylograph]. Edited by Grags pa rgya mtsho et al. Xining: Mtsho sngon mi rigs dpe skrun khang.

Rgyal tshab Dar ma rin chen. 1449. *Tshad ma rnam 'grel gyi tshig le'ur byas pa'i rnam bshad thar lam phyin ci ma log par gsal bar byed pa* [xylograph]. TBRC.org ID: W00KG03841.

———. 1982. *Collected Works*, vols. *ka–a* [1–8]. New Delhi: Mongolian Lama Guru Deva.

———. 1994. *A Recent Discovery: Rgyal tshab's Rigs gter rnam bshad*. Edited by Georges B. J. Dreyfus in collaboration with Shunzo Onoda. Biblia Tibetica 3. Kyoto: Nagata Bunshodo.

———. 2016. *Rigs gter rnam bshad*. Edited by Ser gtsug nang bstan dpe rnying 'tshol bsdu phyogs sgrig khang nas bsgrigs. Lhasa: no publisher named. [Based on the xylograph, the manuscript on which this typed work is based apparently had 130 folios.]

Sa skya Paṇḍita Kun dga' rgyal mtshan. 1284. *Tshad ma rigs pa'i gter rang gi 'grel pa* [1284 Dadu xylograph]. TBRC.org ID: W1CZ2047.

———. 1968. *Tshad ma rigs pa'i gter rang gi 'grel pa* [Sde dge xylograph]. *Sa skya bka' 'bum*, vol. 5. Compiled by Bsod nams rgya mtsho. Tokyo: The Toyo Bunko.

———. 2007. *Tshad ma rigs pa'i gter rang gi 'grel pa*. *Collected Writings* [*Dpe sdur ma*], vol.

3. Edited by Dpal brtsegs bod yig dpe rnying zhib 'jug khang. Beijing: Krung go'i bod rig pa dpe skrun khang.

Sde srid Sangs rgyas rgya mtsho. 1989. *Dga' ldan chos 'byung baiḍūrya ser po*. Edited by Rdo rje rgyal po. Xining: Krung go bod kyi shes rig dpe skrun khang.

Se ra Rje btsun Chos kyi rgyal mtshan. 2006. *Rgyas pa'i bstan bcos tshad ma rnam 'grel gyi don 'grel rgyal tshab dgongs pa rab gsal mgul rgyan*. *Collected Works*, vol. 1. Edited by 'Jigs med bsam grub. Beijing: Krung go'i bod rig pa dpe skrun khang.

Seyfort Ruegg, David. 2002. *Two Prolegomena to Madhyamaka Philosophy* (*Studies in Indian and Tibetan Madhyamaka Thought, Part 2*). Wiener Studien zur Tibetologie und Buddhismuskunde 54. Vienna: Arbeitskreis für Tibetische und Buddhistische Studien Universität Wien.

Sonam, Ruth, trans. and ed. 2004. *Yogic Deeds of Bodhisattvas: Gyeltsap on Aryadeva's Four Hundred*. Commentary by Geshe Sonam Rinchen. Ithaca, NY: Snow Lion Publications.

Sparham, Gareth, trans. 1993. *Ocean of Eloquence: Tsong kha pa's Commentary on the Yogācāra Doctrine of Mind*. Albany: State University of New York Press.

Stcherbatsky, Theodore. 1962. *Buddhist Logic*, vol. 2. New York: Dover Publications.

Sun Wenjing, ed. 1989. *Mi rigs dpe mdzod khang gi dpe tho las gsung 'bum skor gyi dkar chag shes bya'i gter mdzod*. Bar cha [vol. 2]. Beijing: Mi rigs dpe skrun khang.

Śākyabuddhi. 1994–2008. *Pramāṇavārttikaṭīkā*. In *Bstan 'gyur* [*dpe sdur ma*], vol. 98. Edited by Krung go'i bod kyi shes rig zhib 'jug lte gnas kyi bka' bstan dpe sdur khang. Beijing: Krung go'i bod kyi shes rig dpe skrun khang.

Thar shul Blo bzang bstan pa rgya mtsho and Dge 'dun bstan pa dar rgyas. 1994. *Rje dge 'dun chos skyong rgya mtsho'i rnam thar*. Edited by 'Phrin las don grub. Xining: Mtsho sngon mi rigs dpe skrun khang.

Tsong kha pa Blo bzang grags pa. 1978–79. *Yid dang kun gzhi'i dka' ba'i gnas rgya cher 'grel pa*. *Collected Works* [of Tsong kha pa, Lhasa Zhol xylograph], vol. *tsha* [18]. New Delhi: Mongolian Lama Guru Deva.

Yao, Zhihua. 2009. "Empty Subject Terms in Buddhist Logic: Dignāga and his Chinese Commentators." *Journal of Indian Philosophy* 37: 383–98.

The Traces of the World in the Tracks of the Philosophers

Sonam Kachru

So, too, reason's traces call upon us to imagine, and imagine ourselves journeying within, unfamiliar worlds of thought, conversation, and practice.

—Matthew T. Kapstein

So much as look at my copy of *Reason's Traces* and it is likely to fall open to page 161, where you will find that the following paragraph is adjoined by marks, inscribed by various implements, dating back as far as my time as an undergraduate, long before it could have seemed plausible that I would one day study with the author of these words:

> The study of Indian Buddhist philosophy has, for the most part, been connected closely to the study of the Buddhist religion . . . [T]his may bias in certain respects our perceptions of Buddhist thought: we are drawn to focus on those issues which lend themselves to discussion in the contexts of contemporary Religious Studies or Philosophy of Religion, perhaps neglecting topics which have no immediate bearing on the concerns of those disciplines.[1]

In tribute to Matthew Kapstein, whose essays exemplify the art of imaginative crossings into worlds only superficially assessed as being either familiar or unfamiliar, I here want to consider three examples from Vasubandhu's *Treasury of Metaphysics* (*Abhidharmakośa*) that demand of us similar imaginative crossings—three occasions wherein one can find that worlds (natural, social, and historical) have left traces among the philosophical tracks of the ancients.

The traces I have in mind are unlikely to show up on the maps with which our

1. Kapstein 2001, 161.

contemporary disciplines would have us orient ourselves. My examples involve Vasubandhu's entertaining such facts as these: that humans are normally born with a pair of eyes; that the way an arrow falls resists easy description; that a curious and entertaining report concerning the behavior of large marine creatures, perhaps specifically female turtles, warrants philosophical and philological attention. Though the latter example is distinctive for requiring that we attend to a more widely connected historical world within which philosophers such as Vasubandhu lived and thought, what links these examples, in addition to their affording us a glimpse of large-scale concerns that only closely realized detail affords, is the fact that each has the potential of expanding our sense of what Buddhist philosophers of antiquity thought about, and how.

In a way, each of my examples provides us with ways in which traces of the world show up in the reasons of past philosophers. I will conclude by considering the very image of reason's traces, taking up all too briefly with both Matthew Kapstein and Kamalaśīla the intrinsic sociality of thought and the virtues enjoined on us as students of the history of philosophy.

Eyes

It is often suggested that Buddhist philosophers are innocent of the concept of *teleology*. Sometimes the suggestion is a matter of omission, though one can also meet with explicit disavowal.[2] And yet, to take an example almost at random, consider Vasubandhu's engagement with an issue raised early in the first chapter of the *Treasury of Metaphysics*: "But the production of a pair [of eyes] is for the sake of beauty (*śobhārthaṃ tu dvayodbhavaḥ*, 1.19d)." This is said, in part, to counter the idea that the faculty of sight involves not one *kind* of visual organ but distinct visual organs to be counted as *two* (as though each eye represents a distinct faculty). Against this idea, Vasubandhu maintains that eyes come into being pairwise and so should be counted as realizing the exercise of a single faculty. The question implied by this verse, however, is why eyes should occur pairwise at all.

Vasubandhu's comment glosses the verse thus:

> Despite the fact that the sensory faculties, such as the visual faculty, count as a single factor, they occur pairwise *for the sake of the*

2. Consider, e.g., Lusthaus 1997, 44, and Harris 2014, 125. If one distinguishes commitments to teleological description from a narrower commitment to final (and backward) causation, as I think one should, my comments below need not be in tension with the conclusions of Bronkhorst 2000, though I would assess those conclusions differently.

> *beauty* of the physical locus (*āśraya*) [of the faculties]. Otherwise, given the occurrence of only a single physical basis (*adhiṣṭhāna*) for the eye, ear, or a single nostril, there would be considerable deformity.[3]

We have two eyes, Vasubandhu here says, not in order that we may *see* better but in order that we may *be seen* in a certain light by others of our kind.[4] Flourishing is easier when we do not find one another repulsive, given that our intersubjective horizon is basic to our life as individuals.

This is not the only adaptive function recognized by Buddhist philosophers as served by our having a pair of eyes. Later in the same chapter, Vasubandhu recognizes the possibility that our having two eyes makes another contribution to visual functioning: binocular vision. The value of binocular vision, the argument runs, is evident in the fact that distinctness or clarity (an object's being *vyakta* or *pariśuddha*) is increased when a subject sees with both eyes and diminished if for any reason one eye is unavailable.[5] In the hands of some philosophers, such as Saṃghabhadra, the function of enabling increased clarity provides an implicit argument for why we have a pair of eyes.[6]

Granted, even Vasubandhu's second answer does not fully capture the adaptive functions we would list today (among which we might highlight such factors as the role of stereopsis in enabling depth perception, the variable width of our field of vision, and the possibility of surviving damage to one eye). Nevertheless, it is important that Vasubandhu should have asked the question at all. What's more, it is striking that he should have sought to answer it in teleological terms; and what's most salient here, I would suggest, is not the precise function attributed by Vasubandhu but the fact that such explanations are extremely common in his work. Indeed, not only does Vasubandhu not eschew teleological explanations, but we find him entertaining the necessity of arguing that there can be *causes* that are not *adaptations*[7]—

3. Translated from Pradhan 1975, 12–13. All translations from Sanskrit, unless otherwise marked, are my own.

4. Cf. Hall 1983, 91, for a discussion of Yaśomitra's recognition of the significance of this observation.

5. See *Abhidhamakośabhāṣya* 1.43ab and commentary, Pradhan 1975, 31; see Sangpo 2012, 1:447n537.

6. Sangpo 2012, 1:396n237.

7. See Hall 1983, 123–24. By "adaptation" here I mean "a function that has come to be because it serves a purpose." In Yaśomitra's commentary to the *Abhidharmakośabhāṣyaṃ*, there is a

a metaphysical description of the world that requires that one make theoretical room for speaking of causes even in the absence of purposes served by their effects is perhaps not quite the mechanistic one we have become accustomed to reconstructing on Vasubandhu's behalf.

Arrows

If we read the *Treasury of Metaphysics* with the foregoing in mind, it can come to seem a rather different work than the one we've allowed familiarity to make of it. In this light, it becomes possible to be struck by the fact that this is a book invested in questions like "Why does an arrow, once shot, fall to the ground?" What's more, it becomes possible to appreciate that the question matters. For Vasubandhu the answer affords us a paradigm for bringing natural phenomena under a causal description.

Let us, then, re-describe the familiar with Vasubandhu. When shot, an arrow is set into motion with a certain capacity or power (*śakti*), to use Vasubandhu's preferred term for power properties or dispositions. The arrow flies for a certain time, and unless it strikes something, it gradually and inevitably falls to the ground. We want to make sense of the variation in speed (*śīghra*) through the flight and also of the falling (*patana*). Among other things, should the initial power that propels the arrow be understood as somehow remaining present, as an occurrent particular, at each moment of the arrow's flight? To think so would be to think of the sequence of moments in the arrow's flight as *punctuated*, with each moment a metaphysically discrete instant that itself enjoys an independent connection with the antecedent moment (or with its *motion*, taken by philosophers such as the Vaiśeṣikas to be a property particular, inhering in the arrow at every moment of its flight).[8]

If that's right, however, we could not (Vasubandhu argues) explain why the arrow exhibits the variation in speed over its trajectory and fall:

> But some maintain that the relevant causal factor is some kind of quality-particular that arises in the arrow, and that it is by virtue of this that an arrow is in flight until it falls. On account of this quality-particular's being unitary, and on account of the consequent

complicated discussion involving the concepts of *purpose* (*prayojana*) and *cause* (*kāraṇa*); it is noteworthy that the conclusion for which Yaśomitra argues (which is that there can be causes that are not purposes) has to be argued for. (See Hall 1983, 124.) Notably, this discussion evinces concern with whether talk of adaptations presupposes the concept of a beneficiary thereof.

8. See Mishra 1936, 218.

> fact that no change in the quality-particular is possible, there could be no variation in speed over time and across space, and no such thing as the fall of the arrow. If one says that the flight of the arrow is checked by wind, then given that there is no special variation in the wind over the duration of the flight of the arrow, this would have the consequence that the arrow falls at the outset, just when it's shot, or else that once shot, it will never fall.[9]

Vasubandhu argues for a view that is almost the opposite of the modern principle of inertia. Instead of understanding a body as having a tendency to resist change, Vasubandhu would have change be treated as intrinsic to the possibility of (what we register as) motion. In particular, his view of a directed phenomenon exhibiting momentum is that the "power" or "capacity" in play constitutes a process that can be reconstructed as being a sequence of directed and intrinsic change. Insofar as the *explanandum*, flight, is thus modeled as a particular variety of process, no further causal explanation is required, either for the sequence as a whole or for any phase therein.

The difference this makes is stark. On the first picture, the arrow's flight is explained by separable and occurrent property particulars, according to which flight involves distinct causes for each moment in the flight—treated as a separable particular—as well as for the arrow's finally falling. Vasubandhu, instead, argues that it is only the phenomenon of flight taken *as a whole* that can make sense of the arrow's fall, here treated as the final event to which the entire process is directed; there are no atomic "moments" here, nor are the events in the sequence "stitched together" (whether by extrinsic relations or by the inherence of separable quantities).

Significantly, Vasubandhu considered all this in the context of considering what must figure in descriptions of life and of living processes.[10] And his thought is that these are best understood when brought under the particular kind of causal description we've just considered. Integral to such a description, on Vasubandhu's view, as Matthew Kapstein translates him, is that any effect arises "from the distinctive feature of the transformation of that continuum;

9. Translated from Pradhan 1975, 74; cf. Sangpo 2012, 1:578.

10. He appeals to such metaphors when articulating the difference it makes to think of any instance of "life" not as a concrete particular (a separate "substance") but instead as a process forming a connected sequence. See, for example, *Abhidhamakośabhāṣya* ad 2.45ab; Sangpo 2012, 1:578. For another context, in which the examples of an arrow in flight and the growth of plants from seeds are used together, see Lamotte 1987, 65.

from the completion of the sequence of sprout, stem, leaf, etc., culminating in the flower which transforms into the fruit."[11]

It is in his *Pudgalapratiṣedha* that Vasubandhu thus speaks of an effect's being related to its cause in terms of "the distinctive feature of the transformation of that continuum." His reference here to a "continuum" (*santāna*) represents a provocative way of characterizing the connections of dependence (distinct from "real" relations) obtaining between "moments" in a sequence; these are to be understood not as distinct from the continua they comprise but as aspects or phases of a single directed process—and that is perhaps the most basic thought behind anything we might call a *teleological* form of description.[12] For it is not some occult variety of "final causation" but this idea, with its evocation of directedness and finality, that ultimately sets teleological forms of description apart.[13]

The Curious Case of Turtles

The use made of certain examples can help us not only get a grip on what the world *was* like for the ancients but what it *could possibly have been* like: it can show us how they understood and tested modal intuitions. An illustrative case of this comes from chapter 3 of the *Treasury of Metaphysics*, wherein Vasubandhu tries to make sense of how thought (*manaḥ-saṃcetanā*) can serve as sustenance (*āhāra*) for a living being even in the absence of food. He adduces three scenarios in this regard, of which we will here consider only the third, which Vasubandhu takes from one of the earliest works of Buddhist scholasticism:

> And the *Saṃgītiparyāya* states: "Large sea creatures, ascending the beach from out of the water, lay their eggs on the shore, bury them in the sand, and return again to the ocean. If the mother remembers the eggs, the eggs will not perish. But if the mother forgets the eggs, they will perish."[14]

Here, "large sea creatures" stand in for all the creatures listed in the *Saṃgītiparyāya* as exemplifying the sustaining power of thought: "Fish, tur-

11. Kapstein 2001, 374.

12. Cf. Thompson 2012, 78.

13. Cf. Des Chene 1996, 168–200.

14. *Abhidhamakośabhāṣya* ad 3.41a; Pradhan 1975, 154; see La Vallée Poussin 1926, 125, and Sangpo 2012, 2:1037.

tles, crocodiles, and [the still unidentified creatures whose name in Chinese is recorded as] Pu-lu-chias."[15]

While Vasubandhu has, then, abbreviated what's given in his source text, he is nevertheless scrupulous with respect to the reported behaviors in this natural-historical example. Among the reported behaviors, consider just one again: "If the mother remembers the eggs . . ." We might capture the metaphysical possibility ostensibly exemplified by this natural-historical report in the following schematic way:

> (A) A certain psychological activity ϕ, in a bounded physical locus S, can directly have a physical effect in a set of separate and bounded physical loci S1, S2, S3, . . . Sn, given that these are genetically connected with S and the activity ϕ on the part of S has S1, S2, S3, . . . Sn, as its content.

The phenomenon in question, then, is a striking one: a psychological activity on the part of one being, a mother, can keep other beings, her children, alive, even when these beings, once generated from her, are now physically insulated from her—behind the walls, as it were, of their individual shells. It is with such a wonder that the text seeks to exemplify the category of "mental sustenance."

Before considering the metaphysical possibility exemplified by this natural-historical report, it is important to note that the example is not a parochial one. Pliny the Elder (d. 79 CE) thought it necessary to add to his account of turtles in book 9 of his *Natural History* a very similar report: "Some persons are of the opinion that [turtles] hatch their eggs by means of the eyes, merely by looking at them (*quidam oculis spectandoque ova foveri ab iis putant*)."[16] "Looking" at the eggs, I would venture—or, better yet, "cherishing their eggs"[17]—ought to be read as variants for the kind of psychological activity the natural-historical report is taken to exemplify in the *Saṃgītiparyāya* and functionally equivalent to Vasubandhu's "remembering."

There are, no doubt, stories to be told that might link Pliny's cursory "looking" or "cherishing" and Vasubandhu's "remembering." Better understanding the different historical vectors for these different uses of the same example might help us flesh out the still-elusive context for philosophy in a connected world, in which Pliny's Rome enjoyed, after all, some commerce with Vasubandhu's Peshawar. Such an account is likely to be forthcoming, however, only

15. *Saṃgītiparyāya* on *Saṃgītisūtra* 4.22, after Stache-Rosen 1968, 105.

16. *Natural History* 9.12, after Pliny 1893, 10.

17. As in Pliny 1940, 189.

if we keep in view not only the varieties of evidence for what Kapstein characterizes as the "difficult question of mutual influence" between Greek and Indian philosophers[18] but also the smallest details of the world that could become, for the likes of Vasubandhu and Pliny, objects of wonder, curiosity, and reasoning. That is, the sense their respective intellectual projects make may depend on our considering what Pliny, in his dedication to the *Natural History*, called "the nature of things, and life as it actually exists . . . and often the lowest department of it."[19]

Neither the (ultimately historically variable) attention to life "as it actually exists" or the nature of things, nor the recovery of it from descriptions, however, is ever quite straightforward. To see this, let us turn now from the example of the report of turtle behavior construed as a variety of historical object in circulation—or even as an "object of translation," to borrow a felicitous phrase from Finbarr Flood[20]—to the use made of the example by Vasubandhu and the philosophical salience of the use of such examples more generally. Vasubandhu, for one, might have tut-tutted were he to have encountered Pliny's straightforward use of the example of the wondrous behavior of turtles; for in fact, Vasubandhu did go on to stress that the received scriptural account of the behavior of turtles cannot be correct. At least, the Sautrāntikas, Vasubandhu tells us, take it that the wording cannot be that "the thought of another is sustenance for the life of some other being." That's impossible, they say. Therefore the text must be emended to say that "If the eggs think of the mother, they will not perish; if they forget the mother, they will perish."[21]

To appreciate the difference this bit of textual criticism might make, consider, schematically, the difference between the possibility enshrined in scenario A and the following:

> (B) Tokens of a certain psychological activity ϕ, occurring within members of a set of bounded physical loci (S1, S2, S3 . . . Sn), exert a direct physical effect on the relevant individuals in that set only if these individuals are biologically generated by S and the activity ϕ has S as its content.

A world in which A is possible is rather different from a world where, as in B

18. Kapstein 2013, 114n5.

19. Pliny 1893, 4–5.

20. See Flood 2018, 8–10.

21. Sangpo 2012, 2:1037.

above, it is not. The use of the natural-philosophical report to exemplify A is likewise very different than the use made of it to exemplify the possibility in B: the former represents a wonder, a challenge to, and enlargement of our sense of what is possible; the latter merely creates an intriguing variation on what the audience for this example presumably already knew to be true of the psychosomatic powers of thought.

The significance of all this to the student of the history of philosophy comes down to this. We cannot gauge the conceptual distance between what constrains thought in our own time when compared to the orienting conditions for philosophers in antiquity—European or South Asian—if we do not have a sense of how they would assess the difference between the possibilities available to them in their own time—possibilities like those represented in scenarios A and B—and how to choose among them. The larger questions thrown up by any reconstruction of the past, then, are pragmatic: How is one to determine, in each particular case, the historically variable sense of what the world is possibly like? How did the ancients? What are the historically contingent conceptual connections between conceivability and possibility, and how might different realizations of such connections be assessed? The example of the behavior of turtles and others like it—examples where we can, as it were, catch Vasubandhu and his contemporaries *reading*—at least show us what tackling such questions might involve.

If, in relating how the Sautrāntikas would alter the received description of turtle behavior, Vasubandhu shows us an extraordinary instance of rational reconstruction driving philological criticism, this is not inconsistent with his larger hermeneutic commitments. The knowledge that comes down to us in a textual tradition must, Vasubandhu avers, always be subject to our understanding of what the world is possibly like. But the situation is not so simple. We have seen how natural-historical reports—even those found in scripture—are not to be treated as independent testimony of the nature of the world—independent, that is, of the modal intuitions developed through philosophical analysis. And yet, were we to try and reconstruct the systems of possibility within which Vasubandhu lived and thought—the quasi-historical and contingent system that makes *available* certain statements as truth-evaluable candidates—and were we to look for how Vasubandhu himself sought to assess what is possible and what is not, we would find him, even like his contemporary Augustine, referring us to the evidence of natural-philosophical accounts of the world.[22] There are times when "armchair" conceivability (or

22. For Vasubandhu's adverting to the case of what Aristotle knew as "flies born in fire" to make sense of Buddhist cosmological commitments, see Kachru 2017. For Augustine's invocation of

general concerns with *logical* possibility and impossibility) take a backseat, as it were, to the use made of the above variety of account that has gone missing in contemporary reconstructions of ancient philosophy of religion. Natural-philosophical reports, moreover, were notably taken by both Augustine and Vasubandhu to have the same evidentiary status with respect to our modal intuitions, and the same exploratory function with respect to our modal intuitions, as the more tendentious cosmological commitments to which each thinker was responsible.

Both these contexts for modal thinking—the ostensibly familiar concern with natural philosophy and the ostensibly unfamiliar and exotic concern with cosmology—are among the prime examples of what our current disciplinary preoccupations and sensibilities have allowed to fall to the wayside. And yet if we want to know not only what they thought, but how, we shall need to know more about how these thinkers oriented themselves to modality, for to recover their sense of the world will require of us reconstructing more than the facts and the truths to which each thinker might have assented.

Traces

The use made of natural-historical examples by philosophers in antiquity does not strike me as having been merely an academic exercise. Given time, one could argue that the use made of such examples to chart what is possible and what is not served to orient some of these thinkers to the tasks of analysis, or to the world and their place in it, perhaps even finally attuning some of them to unrealized possibilities at the level of their forms of life. Likewise, if I have here been stressing the significance of examples without emphasizing the arguments in which they figure, this is not because I do not agree with Kapstein that Vasubandhu's arguments merit "more thorough philosophical interpretation overall than [they] have received to date."[23] My point is that we must join to philosophical interpretation a concern for idiosyncratic detail and a sense of the different contexts for thought provided by the natural and historical world if we are to achieve the kind of understanding so eloquently evoked by Kapstein:

> When we begin to appreciate Vasubandhu's insights from the vantage point of our own philosophical understanding, what is most human about us leaps through centuries, rushes across continents,

---

the closely related reports of the salamander when considering the nature of punishment in hell, see book 21, chapter 4, of *City of God*, in Augustine 2003, 968.

23. Kapstein 2001, 197.

> and greets what is most human in what had formerly been alien. We meet Vasubandhu face-to-face . . .[24]

This eminently humanistic conception of understanding is integral to Kapstein's work. We find the same sentiment expressed at the close of his "Stoics and Bodhisattvas," where Kapstein particularly emphasizes the importance for this of what I would call *conditions for orienting oneself in a world*—conditions perhaps better captured in myths and cosmology than in arguments. He writes: "It is from this position [when we find our way to dwelling confidently within orienting philosophical myths, our own and those of others] that we may meet Epictetus and Śāntideva not just as our distant ancestors, but as challenging conversation partners, capable of shaking our lives even now."[25] Their seemingly eccentric examples, I have been arguing, their historical provenance and philosophical use, are among the things we must consider if we wish to reconstruct a sense of what it meant for these authors to be oriented in thought, what the-world-as-thought-by-them was like.

The humane and humanizing fusion of horizons so eloquently imagined by Kapstein can make a difference. As a once-young Kashmiri, I found my life changed by Kapstein's eloquent invitation to take up Vasubandhu and my countrymen, the Vaibhāṣikas, as conversational partners. When I first read them, Kapstein's words on Vasubandhu seemed to say to me: "There is a place from which you have come, and it is a place worth reaching." Faced later on with the choice whether to train as a chiseller of epitaphs to the mighty philosophical dead of Europe, I decided instead to heed Kapstein's call to follow the traces of the reasons of "our" forebears along the less parochial philosophical path that Kapstein has long labored to clear.

That phrase, "reason's traces," is one that Kapstein derives from a remark made by Kamalaśīla, who in turn uses it to introduce his commentary on his teacher Śāntarakṣita's magisterial *Gathering of Quiddities* (*Tattvasaṃgraha*). Kamalaśīla, as Kapstein translates him, says that he "could find no dialectical pathway that had not already been well-worn by earlier sages" (*kṣuṇṇo vā bahudhā buddhair arahaḥ ko 'sau na panthāḥ kvacit*).[26] Kamalaśīla here particularly exploits the single adjective *kṣuṇṇa*, "trampled," to suggest a humanistic emphasis not dissimilar to Kapstein's own practice as a historian of philosophy. Just as a path can be trampled into bits, so too can thoughts be gone over, reflected on, again and again—a sense also conveyed by *kṣuṇṇa*. Thus, when

24. Kapstein 2001, 197.

25. Kapstein 2013, 114.

26. See Kapstein 2001, 10; Sanskrit per Krishnamacharya 1926, 1.

Kamalaśīla asks, "What path is there which has not been trodden many times by the learned?"[27] he is also suggesting that, turn within philosophy as you might, even your thoughts may turn out to be the well-worn ways your predecessors have already taken.

If thinking involves potentially a repetition of the way-making thoughts of others, this might require of us an acknowledgment to the effect that knowing our *own* thoughts might involve a considered recapitulation of the meanings of past utterances of others.[28] The constitutively hermeneutic exercise of so situating oneself in an internal theater involving the recapitulation of the history of thought is powerful, particularly with Kapstein's sense that the promise of such critical reflection on recapitulated views lies "in the fact that they are not just *others'* views of *them*selves, but that potentially at least, they are views that any of us may harbor . . . with respect to *our*selves."[29]

What Kamalaśīla suggests with the help of the image of "reason's traces," then, implies a rather differently accented task for the philosopher than is suggested by Vasubandhu's valorization of the Buddha's teaching as "a path of reasons felicitously laid out" *(suvihita-hetu-mārga-śuddha)*, with its concomitant sense that philosophy then involves largely keeping the path of reasons clear of the faulty reasons of others.[30] For each of these philosophers, to be sure, philosophy involves the constitutively hermeneutic task that is making a tradition's views *one's own*—to make of what "comes down to us" (*āgama*, as the Buddhists denominate tradition) something that also "gets through to us" (*adhigama*), as Kapstein put it in explicating two of the words that orient Vasubandhu's *Treasury of Metaphysics*.[31] The differences between them, and

27. Jha 1937, 3.

28. Kamalaśīla's word "*tattvābhyāsa*" in 2.4 is intended to gloss the title of his teacher's work, *Tattvasaṃgraha*, underscoring thereby perhaps the recapitulation of reality through a constitutively hermeneutic endeavor. Compare Owen Barfield's saying in 1928 that "there is a very real sense, humiliating as it may seem, in which what we generally venture to call our feelings are really Shakespeare's 'meanings'" (Barfield 1973, 137).

29. Kapstein 2001, 15.

30. In the second of his concluding verses to the ninth chapter of the *Treasury of Metaphysics* (Pradhan 1975, 475).

31. Kapstein 2001, 335. There is a sense in which Kapstein might not wish for too great an emphasis on a difference between Kamalaśīla's sense of philosophy as a hermeneutic practice involving an internal dialogue and Vasubandhu's. As Kapstein notes elsewhere of Vasubandhu's *Pudgalapratiṣedhaprakaraṇa* (and the point might hold true of many other essays by Vasubandhu): "Though Vasubandhu's work clearly does betray its origins in earlier dialogic works, it seems to me that the dialogue here is by and large left implicit, and that many passages can best be interpreted as the internal dialogue of a single thinker" (Kapstein 2001, 349).

the availability of new possibilities in the history of Buddhism with respect to this hermeneutic task, will depend on two variables: the degree to which one internalizes the views recovered by philosophical reconstruction, and the degree to which the success of such an enterprise involves hewing closely to *the words* of concrete individuals and not just the generic statements with which doxographies express *the views* of indefinitely many others.

If, as with Kamalaśīla's use of the image, and Kapstein's constitutively humanistic praxis, *argument* is always, inevitably, *interpretation* of the views of concrete individuals and their contingent utterances[32]—and the meanings of which are taken to possibly constitute our own thoughts—philosophy, to that extent, ought not to be divorced from the virtues of humane scholarship, even as the virtues of scholarship ought not to be divorced from the virtues of solidarity with a more capaciously conceived past (and possible future) than philosophy today allows itself to imagine.

Reflections in this vein have me reflect, then, on Matthew Kapstein himself—scholar, philosopher, humane being, whom I am fortunate to count among my teachers, and for whose traces I count myself grateful.

If I find myself grateful it is because not everyone will choose to value Kamalaśīla's vision of philosophical praxis, or even the virtues of the history of philosophy more generally, given the degree to which one thereby seems committed to talking to the dead. To choose to try orienting oneself to the weight of the past with Kamalaśīla and his world crowded with predecessors is at the same time to call into question the self-evidence of another possibility too often held out as the norm for young philosophers. Consider the broad and easy way (crowded by other philosophers) eloquently eschewed in this verse:

> No one rides ahead,
> none behind: the path
> shows no more
> fresh tracks. Wait—
> am I alone? I think
> I see it now: the path
> the ancients cleared, now overgrown; and
> that other way, the broad and easy road
> I've surely left behind.[33]

32. As it is for Kamalaśīla, as was recognized by B. Bhattacharya in his introduction to Krishnamacharya 1926, xxiv. See McCrea 2013 for the view that it is with Dignāga that philosophers in South Asia first began engaging with the views of other philosophers by citing their utterances.

33. Vidyākara, *Subhāṣitaratnakośa*, verse 1729 (Kosambi and Gokhale 1957, 50.32): *vahati na*

Here again we find the word *kṣuṇṇa*, again in the second foot of the verse, used to show us the obliteration of any fresh tracks. This verse, one that Kamalaśīla might just have expected his auditors to hear echoed in his own, is attributed to Dharmakīrti and is quoted by that Buddhist connoisseur of Jagaddala, Vidyākara, in his *Treasury of Well-Turned Verse* (*Subhāṣitaratnakośa*). Here Dharmakīrti turns on its head a metaphorical association we might too easily bring to our consideration of the task of philosophy. The association I have in mind is one to which Seneca, for one, helps himself in his advice to Lucilius:

> Shall I not follow in the footsteps of my predecessors? I shall indeed use the old road, but if I find one that makes a shorter cut and is smoother to travel, I shall open the new road.[34]

Philosophy, as the pursuit of what Seneca called "mental independence," is here taken to involve the lonely and individualizing task of path-finding. In Dharmakīrti's hands, instead, the word *kṣuṇṇa* emphasizes the isolation potentially involved in re-tracing the path of the ancients and forgoing the broad and easy road taken by young philosophers who wish, absurdly, to set out in a crowd in which each considers themselves to be on their own. It seems to me that to orient oneself with Dharmakīrti's verse need involve no loss of autonomy. Cannot Dharmakīrti say with Seneca: "Men who have made these discoveries before us are not our masters, but our guides"?[35]

Notwithstanding the appeal of loneliness in both Seneca and Dharmakīrti, perhaps the more valuable concern each philosopher memorably captures in their image of their waiting for us ahead on their chosen path involves a quality of care for future lives. I think Dharmakīrti was right here (and surely never again as eloquent) to stress that care for those who are to follow can involve care for the traces of those who have gone before us, those whose traces can lead us to new paths we might acknowledge as our own. At least we might take away this much: it is surely not enough for the path of philosophy to have been found; it wants constant clearing, again and again set out upon. Dharmakīrti was right, moreover, to seek to find in the solidarity such clearings involve one of the great felicities of a life lived in response to the calls of reason. Think of this in connection with Kapstein's typically generous second-person and col-

---

puras kaścit paścāt na kas api anuyāti mām, na ca navapadakṣuṇṇas mārgas katham nu aham ekakas | bhavati viditam pūrvavyūḍhas adhunā khilatām gatas, sa khalu bahulas vāmas panthā mayā sphuṭam urjitas; cf. Ingalls 1965, 445.

34. *Ad Lucilium epistulae morales* 33.11, as translated in Gummere 1917, 241.

35. Gummere 1917, 241.

lective pronouns, which (as in the epigraph to this essay) sustain an air of *invitation* to a life of the mind that is conceived as eminently social. Indeed, put this book down and clear the way a bit; pick up anything by Matthew Kapstein and read it again. Then read, in turn, something by any of the innumerable thinkers he so carefully and humanely continues to read.

Works Cited

Aelien. 1959. *On Animals: Books 12–17*. Translated by A. F. Scholfield. Loeb Classical Library. Cambridge, MA: Harvard University Press.

Augustine, St. 2003. *Concerning the City of God against the Pagans*. Translated by Henry Bettenson. London: Penguin Books.

Barfield, Owen. 1973. *Poetic Diction: A Study in Meaning*. Middletown, CT: Wesleyan University Press.

Bronkhorst, Johannes. 2000. *Karma and Teleology: A Problem and Its Solutions in Indian Philosophy*. Tokyo: International Institute for Buddhist Studies.

Des Chene, Dennis. 1996. *Physiologia: Natural Philosophy in Late Aristotelian and Cartesian Thought*. Ithaca, NY: Cornell University Press.

Doody, Aude. 2010. *Pliny's Encyclopedia: The Reception of the Natural History*. New York: Cambridge University Press.

Flood, Finbarr B. 2018. *Objects of Translation: Material Culture and Medieval "Hindu-Muslim" Encounter*. Princeton, NJ: Princeton University Press.

Gummere, Richard Mott, trans. 1917. *Moral Letters to Lucilius* (*Epistulae morales ad Lucilium*) by Seneca, vol. 1. Loeb Classical Library. Cambridge, MA: Harvard University Press.

Hall, Bruce Cameron. 1983. "Vasubandhu on 'Aggregates, Spheres and Components': Being Chapter One of the Abhidharmakośa." PhD dissertation. Cambridge, MA: Harvard University.

Harris, Ian Charles. 2014. "Causation and 'Telos': The Problem of Buddhist Environmental Ethics." In *Environmental Philosophy in Asian Traditions of Thought*, edited by J. Baird Callicot and James McRae, 117–31. Albany: State University of New York Press.

Ingalls, Daniel H. H. 1965. *An Anthology of Sanskrit Court Poetry: Vidyākara's Subhāṣitaratnakoṣa*. Cambridge, MA: Harvard University Press.

Jha, Ganganatha, trans. 1937. *The Tattvasaṅgraha of Śāntarakṣita with the Commentary of Kamalaśīla*. 2 vols. Gaekwad's Oriental Series 53. Baroda, India: Oriental Institute.

Kachru, Sonam. 2017. "Things You Wouldn't Think to Look For in One Place: A Note on an All-Too Brief Example on Life and Matter in *Abhidharmakośabhāṣyam ad* 3.14c." *Journal of the American Oriental Society* 137.4: 669–78.

Kapstein, Matthew T. 2001. *Reason's Traces: Identity and Interpretation in Indian and Tibetan Buddhist Thought*. Boston: Wisdom Publications.

———. 2013. "Stoics and Bodhisattvas: Spiritual Exercise and Faith in Two Philosophical Traditions." In *Philosophy as a Way of Life: Ancients and Moderns*, edited by Michael Chase, Stephen R. L. Clark, and Michael McGhee, 99–115. Oxford: John Wiley and Sons.

Kosambi, D. D., and V. V. Gokhale, eds. 1957. *The Subhasitaratnakosa*. Harvard Oriental Series 42. Cambridge, MA: Harvard University Press.

Krishnamacharya, Embar. 1926. *Tattvasaṅgraha*, vol. 1. Gaekwad's Oriental Series 30. Baroda, India: Central Library.

La Vallée Poussin, Louis de. 1926. *L'Abhidharmakośa De Vasubandhu. Troisième Chapitre*. Paris: Paul Geuthner.

Lamotte, Étienne. 1987. *Karmasiddhiprakarana: The Treatise on Action by Vasubandhu*. Translated by Leo M. Pruden. Berkeley: Asian Humanities Press.

Lusthaus, Dan. 1997. "Critical Buddhism and Returning to the Sources." In *Pruning the Bodhi Tree: The Storm over Critical Buddhism*, edited by Jamie Hubbard and Paul L. Swanson, 30–56. Honolulu: University of Hawai'i Press.

McCrea, Lawrence. 2013. "The Transformations of Mīmāṃsā in the Larger Context of Indian Philosophical Discourse." In *Periodization and Historiography of Indian Philosophy*, edited by Eli Franco, 127–45. Vienna: Publications of the De Nobili Research Library.

Mishra, Umesha. 1936. *Conception of Matter According to Nyāya-Vaiśeṣika*. Allahabad: Allahabad Law Journal Press.

Pliny. 1893. *The Natural History of Pliny*, vol. I. Translated by John Bostock and H. T. Riley. London: George Bell and Sons.

———. 1940. *Natural History: Books 8–11*. Translated by H. Rackham. Loeb Classical Library. Cambridge, MA: Harvard University Press.

Pradhan, Prahlad, ed. 1975 (1967). *Abhidharmakośabhāṣyam of Vasubandhu*. Tibetan Sanskrit Works 8. Patna: K. P. Jayaswal Research Institute.

Sangpo, Gelong Lodrö, trans. 2012. *Abhidharmakośa Bhāṣya of Vasubandhu: The Treasury of the Abhidharma and Its (Auto) Commentary*. 4 vols. Annotated English translation of Louis de la Vallée Poussin's French translation. Delhi: Motilal Banarsidass.

Stache-Rosen, Valentina. 1968. *Dogmatische Begriffsreihen Im Älteren Buddhismus: Das Saṅgītisūtra und sein Kommentar Saṅgītiparyāya*. Berlin: Akademie-Verlag.

Thompson, Michael. 2012. *Life and Action: Elementary Structures of Practice and Practical Thought*. Cambridge, MA: Harvard University Press.

Reading, Yielding, Doubting: Passages of Reception in Indian Buddhist Literature

Richard F. Nance

IN THE MID-1990S, at an early stage of my time in graduate school, Matthew Kapstein began teaching at the University of Chicago. During his first year, he offered a small graduate course, among the readings for which was, as I recall, David Snellgrove's translation of the *Hevajra Tantra* (Snellgrove 1959). At one point during our discussion of the book, a student posed a question to Matthew about whether some key Sanskrit term could be found anywhere in the text. Matthew's response to this query—at once dryly humorous and deeply instructive—has lingered with me longer than anything else from that course. He reached across the table where the Snellgrove edition of the Sanskrit text lay, opened it, and began perusing its contents. Silence fell across the room. After what seemed an eternity, he quietly flipped the page. More silence; another eternity. Flip. Another page. Flip. Another page. Flip. Finally, after several minutes of this, he raised his eyes from the volume, looked across the table at the questioner (who was now looking rather sheepish), paused for a beat, and quietly said, "No."

The response struck many of us as funny. It *was* funny. But it carried a serious message: if you want to know what a text says, there is no substitute for actually doing the work of *reading* that text. Since that time, the field of Buddhist studies has made great strides in creating text-searchable digital corpora. Students who want to know whether a term appears in a particular edition of a Buddhist text can now avail themselves of vast searchable archives housed at various sites on the Internet. Such technological advances might seem to undermine the relevance of (what I take to have been) Kapstein's point during that class session long ago—namely, that there is no shortcut to the hard work of reading. In fact, however, such advances only add to the significance of his point. For although it is now comparatively easy to know *that* a term appears in a particular text, such knowledge does not, by itself, tell us much about *what* the term is being used in context to communicate. And I suspect that it was actually the latter concern—a concern less lexical than hermeneutic—that motivated the question posed to Matthew so many years ago.

It is in a spirit of gratitude for Matthew Kapstein's continuing insistence on the importance of the hermeneutic dimensions of Buddhism (see, for example, Kapstein 1988, Kapstein 2001, and Kapstein 2014, chapter 5) that I offer this brief contribution on the subject of Buddhist reading practices. In attempting to put together this contribution, however, I have repeatedly found myself with the peculiar sense that there is at once far too much to deal with and far too little to go on. Too much, in the sense that there are just too many different terms, in too many different languages, in too many different Buddhist texts, for it to be easy to pick out references to what are reasonably counted as practices of *reading*. Too little, in the sense that the English term *reading* doesn't provide much guidance as to what to rule in and what to rule out when doing this counting. To *read* can be to do any number of different things: to repeat a succession of poorly understood syllables, for example, or to chant memorized verses in unison with others, or to squint at marks on a page in an effort to make out words, or to offer a sophisticated interpretation of a transmitted text, or something else—and an account of "Buddhist reading practices" focused on what is going on when monastic novices sound out syllables that they do not yet find meaningful is unlikely to be adequate to the question of what is going on when highly educated commentators work their magic. When we're talking about *reading*, therefore, we need to be clear on just what it is that we're talking about. And there is a lot that we might be talking about: The English term *reading* can be used both verbally and nominally; it can name actions as well as the outcomes of those actions; and it can range over practices that would seem to be wildly heterogeneous, from noisy declamation to silent attentiveness, with lots in between.

A similar point might also be made about relevant terms in Buddhist source languages. Consider, as just one example, the family of Sanskrit terms deriving the root √*vac* as prefixed by the upasarga *anu-*, for which Apte's dictionary offers the following definition: "to say or speak after or for one; to repeat, recite, reiterate; learn, study; to concede the point, assent to, yield; to name, call." And, in the causative, "to cause to recite; to read to oneself (before reading aloud); often used in dramas."[1] We have not ventured beyond a single Sanskrit verb, and already we are faced with profound heterogeneity.

There are, then, many ways to read. But one theme lies buried in Apte's definition of *anu* + √*vac* that can be understood as a kind of ostinato, one that runs not only through the other senses of *anu* + √*vac* but also through the

1. Apte 1965, 73.

various practices that we might think of as constitutive of, or contributing to, reading: the theme of *yielding*. The term *yield* is itself, of course, also polysemic in English. It might mean, among other things, to pay, repay, requite; to give or put forth, produce, furnish, exhibit, bear, or generate; to break down; to present, offer, give, or allow; to render obedience or service; to perform a promise; to state, declare, communicate or report; to give way; to comply, assent, surrender, submit, succumb; to be dedicated or devoted to.[2] I want to exploit this polysemy in what follows—to suggest, that is, that this whole field of meanings is useful for thinking about reading practices in Buddhist India.

In suggesting this, I recognize that I have shifted very quickly from reflecting on a *Sanskrit* term to encouraging reflection on the range of connotations that might be borne by *one* candidate translation *in English* for that term. This would be bad form if adopted as a general procedural principle. (The Sanskrit *nīla* is often rendered, in English, as *blue*, and the English term *blue* can connote sadness, but we're not likely to understand the Sanskrit *nīla* better by reflecting on what it means to be sad.) Yet a procedure that is not readily generalizable may still be well suited to isolated cases—and this, I think, is one such case. Even so, not all senses of *yielding* will be in play in every reading practice. Just which senses end up being included or excluded, downplayed or emphasized, will shift depending on the nature of the reading practice under consideration.

Before addressing forms of yielding, therefore, we need to take a closer look at reading practices per se. What might we be getting at when we speak of "reading a text" or "offering a reading of a text"? I want to suggest that we, as well as traditional Buddhists, are typically pointing to practices that fall into three types. The first type of reading aims, in the main, at determining the particular words present in a given text: its phrasing, or *vyañjana* (Pali *byañjana*, Tib. *tshig 'bru*). There are many ways to be worried over phrasing, and many different contexts in which worries of this sort loom large. A monastic novice repeats a verse to memorize it; a paleographer puzzles over a faded birchbark manuscript; a scholar peruses her journal submission at the proofing stage. In all these scenarios, what is crucial is pinning down not what is (or has been, or should be) *meant* (that is, the *content* some marks or noises can be understood to convey), but rather what is (or has been) *said*, in the sense of just what those marks and noises *are* (or were). This sense of "reading" thus covers the various practices that aim at fixing marks and noises into patterns of intelligibility: patterns that make sense for making sense.

A second sort of "reading a text" names another family of practices in which

2. "yield, v." OED Online, January 2018. http://www.oed.com/view/Entry/231851.

what is most crucial is pinning down meaning, where I here have in mind at least some of what is picked out by the Sanskrit *artha* (Pali *attha*, Tib. *don*). When reading is understood in this sense, the focus is not so much on the "signal" as on what is signaled—on what is typically taken to be intended by the speaker responsible for the marks and noises at issue. This is the sense of reading at work when a senior monk paraphrases a passage for the purpose of instructing his pupils; when a commentator offers synonyms for an obscure term in his root text; when a student struggles to understand what Nāgārjuna is saying about conditions in the first chapter of the *Mūlamadhyamakakārikā*.

The third type of reading comprises, in effect, what is left out by the other two senses. Even if we take ourselves to have a good grip on matters of *vyañjana* and *artha*, many questions about a text may still remain unanswered. And they are questions that practices of reading may help to answer. Who is speaking or writing these words, and to whom? When, where, and why are these words being spoken or written? What is going on here? Why these words and not others? By what means or media have these words been transmitted or received? These are questions that have to do with speakers or promulgators (*vaktṛ*, *pranetṛ*), purposes (*prayojana*), grounds (*nimitta*), and discursive framing (*nidāna*). In grouping these together, I do not want to deny their heterogeneity but to suggest that we might think of them as forming a family of concerns over aspects of *context*: the circumstances in and through which words and meanings come to be invoked.

I'm suggesting, then, that we think of reading as coming in three broad kinds, respectively targeting *phrasing*, *meaning*, and *context*. These kinds of reading may weave together in complex ways, as one sort of reading may be, and often is, pressed into the service of another. We might, for example, imagine a scribe tasked with copying out a manuscript. As he is busy with his work, he happens upon a textual lacuna: a portion of his manuscript has gone missing. That absence raises a question of phrasing (the first sense of reading): What has been lost? In hazarding an answer, the scribe might appeal to his understanding of what the text is saying more generally (the second sense of reading) as well as his familiarity with stylistic proclivities of the text's author (the third sense of reading). Or consider a commentator who happens upon a thorny textual passage. In order to address questions of meaning (sense 2), he might triple-check his text (sense 1) and also reflect on the kind of text it is, its intended audience, and so on (sense 3). Or consider a monk who is deliberating over whether to count a text as *buddhavacana* (sense 3). He might ponder whether the words it contains are akin to those found elsewhere in the canon (sense 1) or whether their meanings veer wide of what he already takes to be acceptable (sense 2). While they are distinguishable, then, these three kinds of reading often work together to facilitate the understanding of texts.

Now, how might these three forms of reading involve forms of *yielding*? When issues of *phrasing* loom particularly large, one form of yielding in play might take the form of a felt obligation to do justice to the text that is before one: to what it says, irrespective of what one might wish it to say. In forms of reading concerned with getting at *meaning*, the yielding in play might pertain mainly (though again, not exclusively) to a felt obligation to interpret the text within the bounds of what is taken to be acceptable within the community from which (and perhaps also for which) one speaks, whether those bounds be determined by the dictates of reason, or by tradition, or by what one thinks one's immediate teachers wish to hear. Finally, when matters of *context* are salient, yielding might involve giving oneself over to a particular sort of *doubt* that, I want to suggest, at least some Buddhist texts actively court in their readers.

Now, the claim that Indian Buddhist texts court *any* sort of doubt may itself seem rather doubtful, given the traditional understanding of doubt (Skt. *vicikitsā*, alt. *kaṅkhā*, *saṃśaya*, Tib. *the tshom*) as pernicious; doubt, Buddhists typically held, is a negative mental state, to be classed among such other limitations as the five hindrances, the six (or fourteen) unwholesome mental factors, or the ten fetters. Doubt is problematic insofar as it places the practitioner at risk of wandering away from the path and so is clearly not a good thing. Even so, not all forms of uncertainty are viewed by Buddhist authors as problematic. Consider, for example, the stress routinely placed upon the point that conditioned things are—that life itself is—unstable or uncertain.[3] If one seeks a path to overcoming suffering, then coming to acknowledge the full extent of this instability is crucially important. In doing so, however, one must come to question many things one had previously taken for granted. One must, in other words, come to have certain doubts about what one previously took oneself to know. Such doubts are hardly hindrances to the development of insight; if anything, they can be understood as spurs to greater effort in practice—even if, in the end, such practice is presented as a means by which those same doubts may be resolved.

We see this sort of thing in a passage from the *Saṃyutta-nikāya* that purports to recount a conversation between the Buddha and Pāṭaliya the headman. Pāṭaliya, having tried to make sense of a welter of discordant teachings from different teachers, has ended up in a state of perplexity and doubt (*kaṅkhā*, *vicikicchā*). He confesses this to the Buddha, who responds, "It is

3. The relevant terms here are *adhruva* (Tib. *brtan med g.yo ba*) and *aniyata* (Tib. *ma nges pa*).

fitting for you to be perplexed, headman, fitting for you to doubt (*alañhi te, gāmaṇi, kaṅkhituṃ, alaṃ vicikicchituṃ*). Doubt has arisen in you about a perplexing matter . . ."

Pāṭaliya responds, "I have confidence in the Blessed One thus: 'The Blessed One is capable of teaching me the Dhamma in such a way that I might abandon this state of perplexity.'"[4]

Passages like this recur in various canonical Pali suttas and beyond.[5] If doubt may be, on certain occasions, "fitting" or "appropriate" (*alam*), if it is a response that even the Buddha will endorse as suitable to the world as one finds it, then it would be too simple to think of doubt in exclusively negative terms. Doubt can be a good thing: for Pāṭaliya, doubt brings him to the Buddha—and that can only be a good thing.

In the passage from the *Saṃyutta-nikāya*, Pāṭaliya's finally productive perplexity and doubt is engendered by non-Buddhist teachers propounding mutually contradictory claims. But Buddhist traditions also at times, if more subtly, register the possibility that salutary forms of doubt can be engendered even by claims attributed to the Buddha. This, at least, is a plausible way of reading the opening of the famous "Questions of Paramārthasamudgata" chapter of the *Saṃdhinirmocanasūtra*.[6] This chapter presents the Buddha in dialogue with the bodhisattva Paramārthasamudgata, who is troubled by an apparent discrepancy between two teachings that he supposes both come from the Buddha: one that would seem to affirm the existence of certain phenomena and another that would seem to deny the existence of those same phenomena. In the sūtra, Paramārthasamudgata asks after the Buddha's intentions regarding the second of these teachings, effectively asking why he would deny what he previously appeared to affirm. The Buddha, noting that Paramārthasamudgata's question has been posed out of a concern to bring benefit and happiness to other beings, identifies his line of inquiry (or, more precisely, his thought—his *sems kyi yongs su rtog pa*, or **cittaparikalpa*) as "good and virtuously arisen" (*dge ba tshul bzhin skyes ba*, **kuśala, yoniśa utpanna*) and then offers his famous teaching of the three turnings of the wheel of Dharma.

A prima facie plausible way of understanding what is going on in this exchange is that the Buddha is working to quell Paramārthasamudgata's doubts about the teaching. But we need to exercise caution here, inasmuch as Paramārthasamudgata does not say that he is afflicted with doubt about the

4. *Saṃyutta-nikāya* IV.8.13, translation Bodhi 2000, 1366–67.

5. In the opening book of the *Vyākhyāyukti*, a nearly identical passage is adduced by Vasubandhu to illustrate one of the meanings that the term *alam* can bear. See Nance 2012, 137.

6. Powers 1995, 94–99; cf. Lamotte 1935, 65–67 and 192–93.

Buddha's intentions and the Buddha does not attribute doubt to him. Given that there is no *explicit* admission of perplexity or doubt in the text, should we assume that Paramārthasamudgata *isn't* doubtful or perplexed by the issue he is raising? Certain Tibetan commentators have understood the text in this way, in order to guard against the attribution of any form of ignorance to Paramārthasamudgata—a being whom they understand to be a tenth-stage bodhisattva.[7] Yet the sūtra does not explicitly say that Paramārthasamudgata is a tenth-stage bodhisattva. What it says—in its opening pages, or *nidāna*—is that he is among those who have achieved one of the stages of irreversibility (that is, the *phyir mi ldog pa'i sa*, **avaivartikabhūmi*), nomenclature traditionally reserved for the eighth *bhūmi* and beyond.[8] It is, moreover, not at all clear how much weight one should place on what the *nidāna* says about the bodhisattvas who serve as the interlocutors for the Buddha in the *Saṃdhinirmocana*, for this portion of the text also insists that Paramārthasamugata is "free from all thoughts" (*yongs su rtog pa thams cad dang bral ba*)—a point that would seem to undermine the Buddha's later description of him as a being whose thought is virtuous.

I would prefer to say that the text leaves Paramārthasamudgata's state of mind as a questioner open to speculation. And while such speculation might in the end prove idle (who knows what lurks in the minds of the bodhisattvas of yore?), it's not idle to attend to the rhetoric of the text, and to our own responses as readers or hearers of the sūtra. That rhetoric is clearly tailored to inculcate a certain sort of doubt in its readers or hearers. It hands them a mystery: A buddha, contradicting himself? How could that be? Any audience who understands the dilemma this poses is likely to find its attention piqued, and to want that mystery solved. And here comes a buddha with a teaching that purports to solve it.

Once one begins to reflect on Buddhist hermeneutic strategies and devices—the great recourses (*mahāpadeśas*), the reliances (*pratisaraṇa*), the *neyārtha/nītārtha* distinction, talk of skillful means or ingenuity (*upāyakauśalya*), and so on—it becomes clear that many can be understood as ways of responding to forms of doubt regarding aspects of the tradition: doubts as to whether a particular teaching ought to be understood as the teaching of a buddha; doubts as to what or whom one should rely on; doubts as to how to understand a particular Buddhist teaching. These strategies presuppose the possibility of doubt and offer ways of dealing with it.

Of course, it's one thing to say that Buddhist traditions recognize that

7. See Hopkins 2002, 112–13.

8. Powers 1995, 8–11; cf. Lamotte 1935, 34 and 168–69.

doubts are possible and that they provide some means by which they may be addressed (and, ideally, resolved). It's quite another thing to say that these traditions ever portray doubt as genuinely salutary, something to be actively *courted*. And it might be objected that what we have seen thus far provides support for the first claim but not the second. That is, the passage from the *Saṃyutta-nikāya*, the passage from the *Saṃdhinirmocana*, and the various hermeneutic strategies I've just listed can all be understood as ways of responding to doubt, but in each case, what is aimed at is the *removal* of doubt. *That* is what is salutary—not the doubt that is removed. (The removal of an illness is a good thing; illness itself is not.) If doubt may, on occasion, be a fitting response to the world, this is only because the world itself is unfit. So the idea that some forms of doubt have been understood as salutary cannot be effectively supported by passages that endorse its removal. If any case for the latter claim is to be made, it will need to be made by other means.

I think such a case can be made. The means for doing so can be found scattered among the *nidāna*s, the frame stories, that wrap Buddhist sūtra texts. These frame stories achieve their most elaborated form in certain Mahāyāna sūtras, and they are crafted in a way that stokes a particular form of uncertainty in their audience—an uncertainty as to their source, and as to the relation that should be understood to obtain between their *immediate* source and their *ultimate* source.

As an exemplary Mahāyāna *nidāna*, I want to consider the frame story that surrounds a text whose title has been translated into Tibetan as *De bzhin gshegs pa'i skye ba 'byung ba'i bstan pa* (**Tathāgatotpattisambhavanirdeśa-sūtra*).[9] I have selected this particular text not for its outstanding literary merit but because its frame story nicely exemplifies a structure that manifests itself, with certain variations, in other Mahāyāna sūtra texts. Similar observations might be made, *mutatis mutandis*, about any of the texts in which this structure, or something similar, shows up.

Here, then, is a condensed account of the events of the frame story. The reader's attention is directed first to the figure of the Buddha, who, we are told, emits a great beam of light from his head; this courses through the universe and returns to enter the head of a bodhisattva in the vicinity, who bears the name "Radiance Manifesting in the Family of the Tathāgatas" (Tib. *De bzhin gshegs pa'i rigs su byung ba'i dpal* ≈ **Tathāgatakulodbhavaśrī*). The display is

9. See Hamar 2007a, Hamar 2007b, and Hamar 2014. This text shows up for us today incorporated into the vast *Avataṃsakasūtra*. For an English translation (from the Chinese of Śikṣānanda), see Cleary 1993, 970–1021. The relevant Tibetan runs from D. Phal chen *nga* 102b6–197b5, with the portion of the *nidāna* recounted here at 104a2–106a4.

said to portend the giving of a great teaching by the Buddha himself. But this doesn't quite happen. Tathāgatakulodbhavaśrī does *request* a teaching, but the Buddha responds to this request by emitting yet another beam of light that, having circled the universe just like the first, returns to the scene and enters into the mouth of yet another bodhisattva—identified as Samantabhadra—who then begins to teach.

Readers who continue past the frame story are thus encountering the teaching of Samantabhadra. Or are they encountering the teaching of the Buddha? Is the Buddha speaking *through* Samantabhadra, as he might through a ventriloquist's dummy? (The text nowhere *says* he is.) Or is the Buddha's illumination (*'od*, **pratibhā*) simply a more florid way of speaking of Samantabhadra's inspiration (*spobs pa*, **pratibhāna*)?[10] Are Samantabhadra's words his own, or are they the Buddha's? The sūtra doesn't say. And while it is hazardous to speculate on the rationale for its remaining silent on this score, perhaps this silence is no accident.[11] The scenario here imagined can be read as a way of depicting the unavoidable messiness of transmission: its ambiguities, ambivalences, and opportunities. Perhaps the scenario is intended, that is, as an idealized account not only of the circumstances that led to an initial act of teaching but also of the circumstances that allow successive generations of Buddhists to continue to encounter that teaching.

Imagine that you are listening to a person who tells you that the teaching he or she is relaying is ultimately sourced in the figure of the Buddha. Do you believe this person? If you do, how do you understand the relation between the ultimate source of the teaching and the person before you? Whose words are you hearing? Are you hearing the Buddha's words? An inspired paraphrase? Something else? What is required for you to take the teaching you are hearing to be authoritative, for it to prompt you, at the limit, to change your life? Or perhaps to recognize that your life has already changed? After all, in the sūtra it is not only Samantabhadra's *teaching* that is somehow illuminated by the Buddha but also the request to which that teaching serves as a response; it seems we are to understand Tathāgatakulodbhavaśrī's question, too, as somehow inspired by the Buddha. Pondering the latter fact, one might begin to wonder: what brought me to this teacher, the one before whom I now find myself? Was this my choice? Was something working within me that I do not

10. On *pratibhāna*, see Harrison 2003 and the sources cited therein. See also Nance 2012, chapter 2.

11. Collins 2010, 58–60, offers provocative normative remarks on the scholarly treatment of silences in Buddhist texts—a view that appears to diverge from one taken by Buddhist commentators (cf. Nance 2012, 126).

yet fully understand? All of these are questions that open on to the doctrine of dependent arising, and all can be opened up for us in pondering this frame story and others like it.

The fact that these questions can be opened up for us does not mean that they *were* opened up for traditional Buddhist readers in centuries past. There are, it must be noted, very few explicit admissions of doubt or uncertainty in Indian Buddhist texts. What we generally find instead is something like the opposite: an increasing stress placed on certainty or definite determination (*niścaya*) as a *sine qua non* for successful action.[12] Such insistence can, of course, be read in more than one way: as suggesting that Indian monastic elites were blissfully free from doubt or, alternatively, as suggesting a form of rhetorical overcompensation. Whatever the motivation, it would seem that the perceived cost of explicitly admitting doubt was high.

If we are looking for places where Buddhist authors grapple with uncertainty, we may therefore need to look beyond explicit admissions of doubt. But once we widen our focus in this way, we can begin to see uncertainty surfacing all over the place. A sūtra commentator facing down an intractable passage might throw up his hands and insist on the Buddha's inconceivability. Alternatively, he might introduce a welter of divergent voices into the text without expressing a clear preference for one over another. Or again, he might busy himself with making analytic distinctions that complicate notions of authorship—e.g., the distinction between "promulgator" and "speaker" invoked in the *Madhyāntavibhāga* corpus.[13] Or again, he might appeal to mental techniques that suffice to secure the continuity of the teaching, like the so-called "stream-of-doctrine" (*dharmasrotas*, *chos rgyun*) samādhi traditionally taken to have granted Asaṅga access to Maitreya. These strategies can all be understood as different ways of responding—of *yielding*—to doubts about sourcing. Such responses may vary from individual to individual, or from community to community.

A final point in closing. Doubt is often understood as carrying with it an attitude of suspicion: to *doubt* a person's claim, often, just is to be *suspicious* of that claim. If we are to get a grip on the sort of uncertainty that I have been working to sketch here, we need to decouple it from the idea of suspicion. This is not to say that forms of Buddhist reading *cannot* borrow certain aspects from what Paul Ricoeur has famously called the "hermeneutics of suspicion."

12. Among later Indian Buddhist philosophical thinkers, Kamalaśīla (fl. 8th–9th cent.) offers a rare and refreshing exception to the general rule in the opening pages of his *Tattvasaṃgrahapañjikā*. For a translation of the relevant passage, see Jha 1937, 3–24.

13. See especially the opening of the *Madhyāntavibhāgaṭīkā* (Pandeya 1999; translation Friedmann 1937, 1–2).

They may, that is, aim at "demystification . . . [or] reduction of the illusions and lies of consciousness."[14] Such illusions and lies are, of course, legion, and suspicion toward them may surely help to counter forms of ignorance that masquerade as false certainties.

But there are also forms of doubt quite compatible with modes of reading that Ricoeur terms the "hermeneutics of faith"—modes oriented, as he puts it, to "the manifestation and restoration of a meaning addressed to me in the manner of a message."[15] To see a text as requiring *manifestation* or *restoration* is to see it as requiring *interpretive work*; what the text seems to say, or the idea that what it seems to say is all that might be said about it, is called into question. We are brought up short by a text, made to pause over it, to reread it, to consider its source and audience, to weigh alternative ways of making sense of what it says, to consider potential objections to it, to assess the cogency of those objections, perhaps to respond to them. All of these ways of responding to a text have traditionally been held to be appropriate for aspiring Buddhist commentators.[16] All seem to me quite appropriate for contemporary scholars of the tradition as well. It would seem to me misleading, however, to characterize the forms of doubt that prompt such responses as varieties of *suspicion*. I would say, rather, that they are necessary preconditions for the successful transmission of Buddhist tradition itself, and that they are to that extent not modes of mistrust but harbingers of hope.

14. Ricoeur 1970, 27 and 32.

15. Ricoeur 1970, 27.

16. See, for example, the recommendations made in Vasubandhu's *Vyākhyāyukti*, discussed in Nance 2012, chapter 4.

Works Cited

Apte, V. S. 1965 [1890]. *The Practical Sanskrit-English Dictionary: Revised and Enlarged Edition*. Delhi: Motilal Banarsidass.

Bodhi, Bhikkhu, trans. 2000. *The Connected Discourses of the Buddha: A New Translation of the Saṃyutta Nikāya*. Boston: Wisdom Publications.

Cleary, Thomas, trans. 1993. *The Flower Ornament Scripture: A Translation of the Avatamsaka Sutra*. Boston: Shambhala Publications.

Collins, Steven. 2010. *Nirvana: Concept, Imagery, Narrative*. Cambridge: Cambridge University Press.

Friedmann, David. 1937. *Sthiramati Madhyāntavibhāgaṭīkā: Analysis of the Middle Path and the Extremes*. Utrecht: Utr. Typ. Ass.

Hamar, Imre. 2007a. "The Manifestation of the Absolute in the Phenomenal World: Nature Origination in Huayan Exegesis." *Bulletin de l'Ecole française d'Extrême-Orient* 94: 229–250.

———. 2007b. "The History of the Buddhāvataṃsaka-sūtra: Shorter and Larger Texts." In *Reflecting Mirrors: Perspectives on Huayan Buddhism*, edited by Imre Hamar, 151–79. Wiesbaden: Harrassowitz.

———. 2014. *The Buddhāvataṃsaka-sūtra and Its Chinese Interpretation: The Huayan Understanding of the Concepts of Ālayavijñāna and Tathāgatagarbha*. Budapest: Hungarian Academy of Sciences.

Harrison, Paul. 2003. "Mediums and Messages: Reflections on the Production of Mahāyāna Sūtras." *The Eastern Buddhist* 35.1/2: 115–51.

Hopkins, Jeffrey. 2002. *Reflections on Reality: The Three Natures and Non-Natures in the Mind-Only School: Dynamic Responses to Dzong-ka-ba's* The Essence of Eloquence, vol. 2. Berkeley: University of California Press.

Jha, Ganganatha, trans. 1937. *The Tattvasaṅgraha of Śāntarakṣita with the Commentary of Kamalaśīla*. 2 vols. Gaekwad's Oriental Series 53. Baroda, India: Oriental Institute.

Kapstein, Matthew. 1988. "Mi-pham's Theory of Interpretation." In *Buddhist Hermeneutics*, edited by Donald Lopez, 149–74. Honolulu: University of Hawaii Press.

———. 2001. *Reason's Traces: Identity and Interpretation in Indian and Tibetan Buddhist Thought*. Boston: Wisdom Publications.

———. 2014. *Tibetan Buddhism: A Very Short Introduction*. Oxford: Oxford University Press.

Lamotte, Étienne. 1935. *Saṃdhinirmocanasūtra: L'Explication des Mystères*. Paris: Adrien Maisonneuve.

Nance, Richard F. 2012. *Speaking for Buddhas: Scriptural Commentary in Indian Buddhism*. New York: Columbia University Press.

Oxford English Dictionary. 2018. Online at www.oed.com. Oxford: Oxford University Press.

Pandeya, R., ed. 1999. *Madhyānta-vibhāga-śāstra Containing the Kārikā-s of Maitreya, Bhāṣya of Vasubandhu and Ṭīkā by Sthiramati*. Delhi: Motilal Banarsidass.

Powers, John. 1995. *Wisdom of Buddha: The Saṃdhinirmocana Sūtra*. Berkeley: Dharma Publishing.

Ricoeur, Paul. 1970. *Freud and Philosophy: An Essay on Interpretation*. New Haven, CT: Yale University Press.

Snellgrove, David. *The Hevajra Tantra: A Critical Study*. 2 vols. London Oriental Series 6. London: Oxford University Press.

Who Practices the Path? Persons and Dharmas in Mind-Only Thought

Joy Cecile Brennan

THIS EXPLORATORY ESSAY arises from a simple yet startling insight. In early Yogācāra-Vijñānavāda texts, the concept "mind only" arises not as an assertion about what kinds of things exist or as a reflection on the relationship between mental and material elements. Instead, even before Vasubandhu provides the first argument intended to establish the mind-only claim, the assertion "mind only" already referred to a theoretical description of one point or station on a soteriological path process. Returning to the earliest texts in which the assertion appears, we find that it has in them a pragmatic function.

My consideration of that function occurs by way of reflection on the relationship between two central and related features of early Yogācāra-Vijñānavāda thought: the three-natures path theory and what I call the mind-only dialectic. The former is a formulation, found almost universally in presentations of the three-natures theory, that applies three processes described as stages on the path to liberation—thoroughly knowing, abandoning, and directly realizing—to the constructed, dependent, and perfected natures, respectively. The latter central feature is a movement, also construed in our texts as a path movement, from the acceptance of the reality of objects, through the recognition of their nonexistence, itself constitutive of the positing of mind-only, and finally to the realization of or entry into no-mind. This dialectic is likewise nearly universally found as a feature of Yogācāra-Vijñānavāda treatments of the idea that the triple world is mind only. These two formulations are moreover conceptually paralleled to one another in a number of key texts, notably Asaṅga's *Mahāyānasaṃgraha* and Sthiramati's *Madhyāntavibhāgaṭīkā*. Despite their prevalence in these early texts, these two formulations have not received due consideration, and consequently the philosophical significance of both their individual meanings and their parallels have not been explored. I should like to here propose that the parallel between these two formulations proffers a resolution to the persistent problem within Buddhist path theory of how the concept of the person—on the one hand the apparent subjective agent of the normative path practices but on the other hand analyzed into a collocation of apparently impersonal elements—relates to the practices of the path.

The significance of the three-natures path theory emerges from a consideration of how three processes used in canonical treatments of the āryas' four truths are adopted and adapted in the three-natures theory. According to standard accounts of the four truths, suffering is the object of thorough knowledge, dependent arising is the object of abandonment, and cessation is the object of direct realization. The three-natures theory adopts and adapts these processes, such that the constructed nature becomes the object of thorough knowledge, the dependent nature becomes the object of abandonment, and the perfected nature becomes the object of direct realization. In canonical recitations of the four truths, these three processes are never referred to as "path stages." Indeed, their differentiation from the path is signaled by the presence alongside them of a fourth process, cultivation, which takes the truth of the path as its object. While it is true that in some sense the four truths together are framed by a conception of path insofar as they identify a problem and propose the route to its resolution, in accounts of the āryas' four truths, the language of path and the process of cultivation of the path is reserved for the fourth truth alone.[1]

Moreover, of the four processes described in those accounts of the four truths, only the process of cultivation refers to activities whose agents may be intuitively understood as persons. It is persons who choose among livelihoods and thus can choose right livelihood over wrong; it is persons who say words and thus may speak either harmful and deceptive language or skillful, truthful language, and so on. The relationship of the person to the other three processes is not clear. The states of affairs described by the other three truths—suffering, its arising, and its cessation—may seem to rely on a notion of the person, but they are described in the seemingly impersonal terms of dharma analysis, not the person-level terms that describe the practices of the path. The language of path is therefore restricted in descriptions of the four truths to the practices of cultivation undertaken by people, while the nature of the agent or subject of the other processes remains unclear.

Yogācāra-Vijñānavāda literature absorbs this set list of the first three processes, and yet it adapts them by changing their objects. Certain Yogācāra-

1. Piyadassi 2013 writes about thoroughly knowing, abandoning, directly realizing, and cultivating as four functions that take the four truths as their respective objects in his translation of the *Dhammacakkappavattana Sutta* (*Saṃyutta-nikāya* 56.11).

Vijñānavāda texts introduce the three-natures theory precisely as an answer to the question: what are the objects of these processes? For example, in his commentary on the *Mahāyānasaṃgraha*, Asvabhāva proposes discerning the objects of these three processes as a motivating force behind postulating the three natures.[2] Sthiramati makes the point more directly in his subcommentary on the *Madhyāntavibhāga*, citing "teaching the entities of abandonment, thorough knowledge, and direct realization with the intention of separating from the obstacles of the bodhisattvas" as one of four reasons for teaching the three natures.[3] This text, unlike the *Dhammacakkappavattana Sutta* in which the truth of the path (*mārga-satya*) refers exclusively to the cultivation practices undertaken by people, actually identifies the three-natures path theory as a full description of the truth of the path itself.[4] Here and elsewhere, the three-natures path formulation is the truth of the path because it describes the process of the path not at the personal level, as the eight practices of the fourth truth do, but at the seemingly impersonal level of dharma analysis.[5]

But here we may ask, to what end? By incorporating the notion of the dharma into its account of the causes and resolutions of the problem of suffering, the Yogācāra-Vijñānavāda school appears to embrace the spirit of dharma analysis already present in the four truths' account of suffering, its arising, and its cessation: that the person and her world can be analyzed in terms of impersonal constituent elements. But this school then transforms the language of path, which is reserved in the four truths for the activities a person as agent undertakes as a means to liberation, by applying the concept of the "truth of the path" not just to the dharmas as impersonal elements but to the three distinct natures of those impersonal elements. For what reason does Yogācāra-Vijñānavāda thought transform the language of path and adapt the objects of the three path processes from suffering to the constructed nature, from the arising of suffering to the dependent nature, and from cessation to the perfected nature? What justifies applying the seemingly person-level language of

2. Verse 1 of chapter 2 lists the constructed, dependent, and perfected as the three natures of dharmas. Asvabhāva comments: "These are three in number because with regard to every dharma there must be that which should be thoroughly known, that which should be abandoned, and that which should be directly realized." Taishō 1598.31.398c17–18.

3. *Madhyāntavibhāgaṭīkā*, chapter 3, subcommentary on verse 3. Pandeya 1971, 85.

4. *Madhyāntavibhāgabhāṣya* and *ṭīkā*, chapter 3, commentary and subcommentary on verse 9. Pandeya 1971, 92.

5. Paramārtha in his *San wuxing lun* likewise identifies the truth of the path with this three-natures path formulation. Taishō 1617.31.872c18–24.

path to the elements of reality originally proposed precisely to give an impersonal account of it?

To approach answers, let us work backward, starting with the changes effected by the three-natures theory itself. The purport of the three-natures path theory is that the three natures themselves are—like the first three truths—intended to provide a full account of the nature of the problem that characterizes sentient life, the cause of its arising, and the possibility of its cessation or resolution. This point is confirmed by prevalent definitions of each of the three natures, for which, generally speaking, the constructed nature is the sign or appearance of the problematic condition, the dependent nature is its cause, the perfected nature its cessation. In some early texts, the constructed nature is defined simply as the distinguishing characteristics (*svabhāva* and *viśeṣa*) of individual dharmas, but other texts make clear that these are the signs of the problematic existential condition, here usually explained in terms of delusion rather than the first truth's suffering. The dependent nature is sometimes defined as dependent arising, and even when it is not so defined, the function of giving rise to delusion, in particular the delusion that the constructed nature is real, is attributed to it. And the perfected nature is everywhere described, like nirvāṇa, as pure and absolute.

Given that the first three truths and the three natures share this explanatory function, the shift from the explanation proffered by the ārya truths to that provided by the three-natures theory is, in the first place, a change in scope. The first three truths take dharmas either in aggregate or considered in their relationships to one another as their objects. Suffering is described as either a characteristic of an aggregation of dharmas or as a shared characteristic of all dharmas. The arising of suffering is described in the first place as rooted in the dharma of thirst and subsequently elaborated into the links of the chain of dependent arising, whose scope is dharmas as they are causally related, which could also be considered an aggregation of dharmas causally connected over time. And cessation also takes as its scope an aggregation of dharmas, since the goal is to bring about the cessation of saṃsāra itself, understood as the whole mass of dharmas, all "on fire with suffering," as the metaphor sometimes goes. The three natures, on the other hand, are three distinct features belonging to each individual dharma. The transition to these three distinct features as the objects of the three processes renders the problematic condition, its arising, and its cessation internal to each and every dharma, where "internal" simply means that these three features are indexed to every dharma as an individual rather than either describing relations among dharmas or serving as characteristics of an aggregation of dharmas.

The second major effect of the three-natures theory is consequent to this internalization. Having made the function of the arising of suffering a feature of every individual dharma, the three natures theory decouples the distinguishing characteristics (*svabhāva* and *viśeṣa*) of dharmas from that function, in effect putting the latter unavailable to our ordinary means of cognition. Dependent arising as a set of causal relations among dharmas rests on the notion that dharmas, understood as individuals with distinguishing features, possess causal efficacy as such. This idea assumes that things *as they appear to the mental faculty* are causally efficacious in the arising of suffering by virtue of their possession of that distinguishing characteristic. For the three-natures theory, by contrast, a dharma's distinguishing characteristic taken as causally efficacious is just its constructed nature. And the existence of the constructed nature is denied precisely to deny that distinguishing characteristics do indeed possess causal efficacy, which is instead attributed to the dependent nature. The latter in turn is out of view, unavailable to the cognitive faculty, precisely because it has been dissociated from the dharmas' distinguishing characteristics.

With this move, the three-natures theory critiques the notion that the mental faculty is a transparent apprehender of dharmas in their relations to one another, and in particular of dharmas as they participate in the arising of delusion. The theory's association with the mind-only position strengthens this critique, for the Yogācāra-Vijñānavāda school's notion of mind as threefold (as comprising the storehouse consciousness, the *manas* or ego function, and the six faculties of cognition) makes the same critique through a consideration not of the nature of dharmas but of the nature and support of the mental faculty itself. Whereas dharma analysis begins with the assumption that dharmas *as they appear* to the cognitive faculty of a person figure in to the causal arising of suffering, therefore seemingly encouraging the view that the faculty of cognition is a transparent vehicle for the correct apprehension of reality, the mind-only position assesses the mind to be both multilayered and essentially delusional. Because the operations of the mental faculty are supported by and embedded within the storehouse and ego-making consciousnesses, that mental faculty is viewed as neither transparent nor a vehicle for the apprehension of reality. It is instead shaped by the historicity of the storehouse consciousness and the self-making and self-strengthening functions of the *manas*.[6]

If the mental faculty were such a transparent apprehender of dharmas,

6. On the historicity of the storehouse consciousness, or its function as a "transmitter of karmic effects," see Waldron 2003, 45 and passim. The self-making and self-strengthening functions—or, together, the ego-function—of the *manas* are my gloss of the functions commonly attributed to it in, e.g., *Mahāyānasaṃgraha* 1.6; Lamotte 1973, 16.

particularly of their causal roles in the arising of suffering, then it could plausibly be understood as the agent of the three path processes. But given its critique of this view of the mental faculty, how can the three-natures theory account for the agent of these processes? For the three-natures path theory, *who* or *what* thoroughly knows the constructed nature, abandons the dependent nature, and directly realizes the perfected nature?

The mind-only dialectic's parallel to the three-natures path theory answers just this question. While this parallel is made only contextually in a number of texts,[7] it is explicitly drawn in other texts, including the *Mahāyānasaṃgraha* and the *Madhyāntavibhāgabhāṣya* and *ṭīkā*.[8] The context of both texts' discussions of the two formulations is revealing. Each text clearly distinguishes between the nature of dharmas on the one hand and the entry into those natures on the other: the nature of dharmas is described through the three-natures theory and path formulation, while entry into those natures occurs by means of the mind-only dialectic, whose three positions (objects, mind only, and no-mind) are paralleled to the three natures themselves. These two approaches to the path can be characterized as having, respectively, object and subject orientations. An *object orientation* starts from the concept of dharmas as mental objects discernable by means of their distinguishing characteristics and adopts the subject position of the mental faculty, the faculty that takes an object-oriented approach in seeking to mentally apprehend the theory of the three natures of dharmas. But since only those distinguishing characteristics (the constructed nature) are "in view" or available to the conceiving powers of a person's mental faculty, this object orientation can provide only a theoretical understanding. It cannot bring about abandonment of the dependent nature or direct realization of the perfected. A *subject orientation* on the other

7. For example, this parallel is made only contextually in the *Mahāyānasūtrālaṃkāra* corpus, where the mind-only dialectic appears in 6.6–10 (Lévi 1911, 52–54), while the three-natures path theory appears in the *bhāṣya* commentary to 11.13 (Lévi 1911, 108). This text introduces the mind-only dialectic as the mode of the bodhisattva's entry into ultimate realization and the three-natures path formulation as part of the objective investigation of dharmas. The conceptual connection provided by context is simply that both movements describe the attainment of realization of the ultimate.

8. *Mahāyānasaṃgraha* 3.7–9 and commentary; Lamotte, 1973, 2:161–65. *Madhyāntavibhāga* 1.6–7 commentary and subcommentary; Pandeya 1971, 19–20. Paramārtha's *San wuxing lun* also explicitly connects the mind-only dialectic to the three-natures path formula, at Taishō 1617.31.871c27–872a15. Paramārtha's presentation introduces two novel aspects. First, he distinguishes the Hīnayāna's embrace of the idea that the twelve *āyatana*s are not distorted from the Mahāyāna view that they too are distorted, which accords with my point that the three-natures theory critiques a notion of the mental faculty as transparent. Second, he replaces the idea of no-mind with that of pure consciousness.

hand articulates the person's relationship to those objects, starting from the recognition that a person's mental faculty itself is also a dharma and thus is also a target of the object-oriented analysis given in the three-natures theory. In a preliminary sense then, the three-natures theory occurs at the impersonal level of dharmas, while the mind-only dialectic occurs at the level of discourse about persons.[9]

Moreover, the problem that necessitates the articulation of the mind-only dialectic is revealed by this shift from an object-oriented investigation to a subjective one. Dharma analysis in systematic Buddhist thought consistently recognizes the mind faculty as one among the list of dharmas. An object-oriented analysis of the three natures would then naturally include it as one of the objects analyzed. But the analysis of dharmas proffered by means of the three-natures theory does not account for the fact that the mental faculty is commonly *experienced* as subject and even agent of both cognition generally and any analytic process in particular. In failing to describe how to perform the object-oriented analysis of the three natures on that dharma which is experienced as subject, the three-natures theory leaves room for a lazy exemption of the mental faculty from the analysis provided by the theory itself.

As a response to this problem, the mind-only dialectic leaves no such room. It describes a sequence in which the subjectively experienced mental faculty is itself made object of analysis, or in which a person's inclination to exempt the mental faculty from the object analysis provided by the three-natures theory—and thereby to reify the mental faculty as agentive subject or self—is faced head on. Its first step is to transform the language of the three-natures theory from the terms *constructed*, *dependent*, and *perfected* to *objects*, *mind only*, and *no-mind*. Just as the three-natures theory denies the existence of the constructed nature, so the mind-only dialectic denies the existence of objects. Just as the three-natures path theory admonishes us to thoroughly know the constructed nature "in its mereness," which is to say, as just the distinguishing characteristics by which dharmas are recognized and referred to in language but not as causally efficacious, so too objects must be known as nonexistent. Attendant upon this thorough knowing of objects as nonexistent, the mind-only dialectic posits "mind only," in parallel to the recognition that the causal support of the constructed nature is just the activity of the dependent nature.

9. The *Mahāyānasaṃgraha* explicitly treats the mind-only dialectic as a discourse about persons: it is introduced to answer the questions "*Who* enters into the natures of the knowables?" and "By what cause and how does *the bodhisattva* enter into the natures of the knowables?" The bodhisattva is subject and agent of the dialectic, and the dialectic itself is the manner of entry into the natures of the knowables (*jñeya*, defined in chapter 1 as all dharmas, pure and impure), the three natures themselves. See 3.3 and 3.7 in Lamotte 1973, 155 and 161.

And just as the dependent nature is the cause of the arising of the false constructed nature—which is to say, it is the cause of the arising of the delusion that brings about suffering—so is mind the cause of this delusion.

This is the key moment of the dialectic, for it is here that the dialectic forces the mental faculty to count itself among the objects of the analysis provided by the three-natures theory. The three-natures theory diagnoses the human condition as mistaking the distinguishing characteristic of dharmas for their causally efficacious aspect, which is another way of saying to mistake things as they appear to the mental faculty to be the way things are. This mistake is the source of the problem, the cause of delusion, and indeed the nature of delusion itself. The theory thus expects that the person who undertakes the mind-only dialectic will begin from within this delusion. When the mind-only dialectic asserts "mind only," it does so assuming that the person who has undertaken the movement described in the dialectic will intend or hold the concept "mind only" with precisely the mental faculty that takes the world as it appears to be real, which is to say with precisely the mental faculty that does not understand, or has not entered into, "mind only." It is because the content or referent of the concept "mind only" is unavailable to the mental faculty that apprehends it that the moment of confronting the concept is productive. Holding this concept, the mental faculty is faced with its own limitations, indeed its own opacity. If the concept's content is understood, the mental faculty has no choice but to relinquish its self-granted status as the subject and agent of discernment of truth by means of its cognitions of distinctions among dharmas. This relinquishment is precisely the abandonment of the very concept "mind only" in favor of the final position of the dialectic, no-mind, a movement that parallels the abandonment of the dependent nature and direct realization of the perfected nature.

This use of the concept "mind only" to confront and work past the limitations of the mental faculty as an agent of the path is perhaps nowhere expressed more vividly or viscerally than in Vasubandhu's *Triṃśikā*. That text's rendition of the second and third positions of the mind-only dialectic reads:

> Even if one apprehends the idea "this is nothing but mind,"
> this too is an apprehension.
> Therefore, placing something in front of one,
> one does not rest in that only.
>
> But when cognition no longer apprehends objects,
> it rests in mind-only,
> because of that not being grasped
> when there is no graspable object.

This is nonapprehension and no-mind,
and this cognition is super-mundane.
The revolution of the basis takes place
because of the abandonment of the two kinds of defilements.[10]

Here the paradox of the mind-only assertion is clear: the concept "mind only" is an obstacle to resting in mind only, which is itself no-mind. This text's vividness derives from its use of a spatial metaphor to describe apprehending a concept as "placing something in front of one" and to describe the abandonment of it as "rest[ing] in that only." This spatial metaphor implies a philosophically fruitful equivocation between the mental faculty that apprehends objects and the embodied person among whose aggregates that mental faculty occurs. This equivocation in turn gestures toward the subtler idea that the three-natures theory critiques: that the mental faculty is a transparent apprehender of dharmas. But this equivocation suggests that the idea of mind as transparent apprehender is neither accidental nor trivial. Instead, only through the identification of mental faculty as self is it plausible to build a systematic analysis of the nature of suffering, its cause, and the possibility of its cessation that takes as constituent elements the features of the world as it appears to the mental faculty. This identification of this faculty as transparent apprehender of dharmas is then not just an obstacle on the way to understanding the natures of dharmas but also the essence of delusion itself.

The concern that motivates analysis of dharmas is to provide a description of persons and worlds that lays bare the fact that none of those components constitute a self in the relevant philosophical sense. And yet the force of this critique is that non-Mahāyāna dharma analysis appears to rest on the assumption that dharmas *can* actually be individuated based on their chief distinguishing characteristic, where that is none other than how they appear to a person's cognitive faculties. Thus, although the very idea of describing a person and her world in terms of dharmas appears intended to be an impersonal description, it is in fact hinged precisely on the way that a person apprehends the elements of herself and her world within cognition.

The three-natures theory identifies this very tension between personal and impersonal in our considerations of what we are and what the world is as the heart of the matter. The constructed nature of any dharma is the way that dharma appears *taken as real*, which is to say taken as causally efficacious. And a dharma's dependent nature is unavailable as an object of cognition but refers nevertheless to the reality of that process of *taking as real*. It is therefore

10. *Triṃśikā* verses 27–29; Buescher 2007, 134–38.

agentive in the way we are conventionally inclined to think persons are and yet entirely out of view of persons conventionally understood. According to the three-natures theory, the causal system that brings suffering into being is always out of view of persons, for it is now internal to the dharmas that constitute persons and that are known to persons only in their false aspect. The world is, at base, not as it appears to persons, and yet persons somehow still bear responsibility for transforming themselves into beings who understand the world as it is. The three-natures theory draws us in by granting, like the forms of dharma analysis it critiques, that dharmas are individuated by the characteristics by which they are known to persons. But what it gives with one hand it takes away with the other, for the theory divorces these characteristics from any causal role and identifies the persistent inclination to attribute to them a causal role as the very nature of false construction or grasping. In this way the three-natures theory exploits the tension between the personal and impersonal aspects of the very idea of the dharma within dharma analysis to arrive at a new understanding of the nature of delusion.

The parallel between the three-natures theory and the mind-only dialectic introduces and answers a question about who or what can undertake the three processes associated with the first three of the āryas' four truths just by exposing the instability of the personal/impersonal distinction that those four truths appear to introduce. The three-natures theory proffers no place for the original path activity of cultivation, apparently ceding that it is entirely a person-level activity, one that does not even depend on a false identification of person with the mental faculty. And the objects of the other three processes have been streamlined: all are internal to every dharma; taken together they account for the process of delusion, the appearance of delusion, and the possibility of its cessation, and all are impersonal insofar as they are object oriented. But it is the parallel mind-only dialectic that makes room for persons, where to be a person is just to be in the delusional state of identifying mind with self. Such persons undertake the path, they seek to enter into the characteristics of the knowable, and they start from where they are: from delusion itself. Instead of using delusion as a leaping-off point for realization, they use it as the medium of realization, for on this account only entering into delusion leads to realization.

In considering how the mind-only assertion functions within the mind-only dialectic, as the seat of delusion and the object of abandonment that is available to persons to conceptualize, we might add another alternative to Matthew Kapstein's categorization of idealisms into two broad sorts, eliminative and non-eliminative.[11] In light of the foregoing discussion of the mind-only dialectic and its parallels to the three-natures path theory, the "mind only" of these early Yogācāra-Vijñānavāda texts may best be deemed a *pragmatic idealism*. A pragmatic idealism makes a claim that itself appears to amount to either an eliminative or non-eliminative idealism. But it does so because this claim itself, when taken up as a concept, functions to free the person from entrapment in the state of affairs described by that eliminative or non-eliminative idealism. The claim functions pragmatically in a robust Jamesian sense: if "God is real since he produces real effects," then the mind-only claim describes a true state of affairs because this description has a real effect.[12] The twist however is not accounted for by James's pragmatic theory of the reality of the objects of religious experiences: the real effect produced by the concept "mind only" is its own dissolution, and with it the dissolution of the state of affairs that it describes. And this dissolution of the entrapment within the historicity and self-making functions of the mind writ large happens to persons, because it is persons who mistakenly identify the mental faculty as self and who therefore require the antidote that "mind only" provides.

Works Cited

Asaṇga. *Mahāyānasaṃgraha*, with a *Bhāṣya* by Vasubandhu. Chinese translation by Xuanzang in *She da sheng lun shi*. Taishō 1597.31.321a12–380a17.

Asvabhāva. *Mahāyānasaṃgrahopanibandhana*. Chinese translation by Xuanzang in *She da sheng lun shi*. Taishō 1598.31.380a20–449b26.

Buescher, Hartmut, ed. 2007. *Sthiramati's Triṃśikāvijñaptibhāṣya: Critical Editions of the Sanskrit Text and Its Tibetan Translation*. Vienna: Verlag der Österreichischen Akademie der Wissenschaften.

James, William. 2002. *The Varieties of Religious Experience*. Mineola, NY: Dover Publications.

Kapstein, Matthew T. 2014. "Buddhist Idealists and Their Jain Critics on Our Knowledge of External Objects." *Royal Institute of Philosophy Supplement* 74: 123–47.

Lamotte, Étienne, trans. 1973. *La Somme Du Grand Véhicule D'Asaṅga (Mahāyānasaṃgraha)*, vol. 1. Louvain-La-Neuve, Belgium: Université de Louvain Institut Orientaliste.

Lévi, Sylvain. 1911. *Mahāyāna-sūtrālaṃkāra*, vol. 2. Paris: Librairie Honoré Champion.

Pandeya, Ramchandra. 1971. *Madhyāntavibhāgaśāstra* of Maitreya, with a *Bhāṣya* by Vasubandhu and a *Ṭīkā* by Sthiramati. Delhi: Motilal Banarsidass.

11. Kapstein defines *eliminative idealisms* as those that "seek to remove all but minds and mental entities from their ontologies, their inventories of what is," while he defines *non-eliminative idealisms* as those that "accept that the universe really does include at least some non-mental things, but insist nevertheless that mind (or spirit, or reason) in some sense takes precedent over those others." Kapstein 2014, 125–26.

12. James 2002, 517.

Paramārtha. *San wuxing lun*. Taishō 1617.31.867b2–878b26.
Piyadassi Thera, trans. 2013. *Dhammacakkappavattana Sutta: Setting in Motion the Wheel of Truth*. http://www.accesstoinsight.org/tipitaka/sn/sn56/sn56.011.piya.html.
Waldron, William S. 2003. *The Buddhist Unconscious: The Ālaya-vijñāna in the Context of Indian Buddhist Thought*. London: RoutledgeCurzon.

What's Not in the Texts? Vasubandhu on Attainments (*Adhigama*)

Jonathan C. Gold

What use is it to flash a mirror at the lodestar? With little hope of discharging my debt of light to Matthew Kapstein, I tender these incendiary bits.

EVERY YEAR IN BEGINNING Buddhism courses I teach the *Setting the Wheel of Dharma in Motion Sūtra* (*Dharmacakrapravartana-sūtra*), which affords the occasion to explain the idea of the "wheel of Dharma" and provides a primary source for discussion of the four noble truths. I always call attention, of course, to the fact that after the Buddha has explained his own realization of the four truths, his disciple Kauṇḍinya is described as having had his "Dharma eye" opened to the truth that "What is subject to origination is subject to cessation"—upon which the gods, reading Kauṇḍinya's mind, rejoice that the wheel of Dharma has been set into motion.[1]

As I was preparing for one such class last year, it first occurred to me to be puzzled at the relation between the Buddha's teaching and Kauṇḍinya's realization. After all, the realization is essentially the doctrine of impermanence, stated in terms that do not appear in the teaching given by the Buddha. Furthermore, across the sūtras, a wide range of students attain the Dharma eye in the presence of the Buddha and have their experience of realization narrated in exactly the same terms. The realization is generally said to be the attainment called the path of seeing (*darśana-mārga*), whereby an ordinary person

1. I generally teach from Thanissaro Bhikkhu's (1993) or Bhikkhu Bodhi's (2005) accessible translations from the Pāli, but this article is primarily a study of Vasubandhu, who read and composed in Sanskrit, so for relative simplicity, I'm using Sanskrit terms, names, and titles in the discussion.

becomes a noble (*ārya*).[2] And, as occurs with Kauṇḍinya, the realization is most often followed by the student's admission to the Buddha's monastic community. In contemplating this scriptural moment when the wheel is first set in motion, the great Abhidharma scholastic Vasubandhu (fourth century) lays out the Vaibhāṣika school's view that literally equates the path of seeing with the wheel of Dharma and the eightfold path. To say that the wheel of Dharma *turns*, on this view, is just to say that a disciple of the Buddha traverses the path of seeing. The wheel is a symbol of royal sovereignty and power for Buddhists, so perhaps their point is that it is only on the stages of the path of seeing that the dharma in fact establishes sovereignty in the mind. In his critical intervention in this discussion, however, Vasubandhu argues that the so-called turning of the wheel is better understood not as the path of seeing itself but as a metaphorical expression for the way in which the Buddha's teachings effectively transform a given listener's intellect. On his view, the "turning of the wheel" refers to the whole process whereby the Buddha's teachings *cause* (or condition) the person to traverse the stages of the path of seeing.[3]

With this reading perhaps in the back of my mind, I was wondering what, exactly, the scripture meant to say had *happened* at this moment of mental transformation—a transformation that, directly or indirectly, constituted the occasion as the initial turning of the Dharma wheel. How did Kauṇḍinya, though taught only the four noble truths by the Buddha, realize that "what is subject to origination is subject to cessation"? That is to say, how did he get impermanence from the four noble truths? And why is this, specifically, highlighted as the first, perhaps even paradigmatic, event of Buddhist instruction? What does it say about the nature of the Buddha's Dharma and its potential to establish sovereignty in the mind? What, finally, are the specific cause and result that are metaphorically designated "the turning of the wheel of Dharma"?

As I pondered the text before class, I realized that among the puzzles here is that Kauṇḍinya's vision of impermanence seems to reflect only a part of the teaching (i.e., of the four truths) that prompts it; for the first truth alone (that of suffering) would seem to comprise the truth of impermanence, since surely it is the impermanence of the individual—human mortality—that is at the root of the unsatisfactory nature of existence.[4] Granted, it would be impres-

2. Asaṅga's *Abhidharmasamuccaya*, for instance, equates the Dharma eye with the path of seeing; Rahula 1971, 109.

3. *Abhidharmakośabhāṣya* 6.54.

4. This point is helpfully summarized by Siderits 2007, 20. In some texts, not only the Buddha, but also his peer renunciants, are depicted as pursuing, centrally, "the deathless state." See, for instance, the story of Sāriputta and Kolita (i.e., Maudgalyāyana) in Nyanaponika 1994.

sive enough that the Buddha had stimulated, through language, a kind of replication of his own existential crisis, which came about as a result of the four sights. That revelation set the Buddha on his own path. Yet it was not sufficient to grant him liberation, and it is not a full expression of his recently discovered dharma. What needs explanation, then, is that the gods rejoice when Kauṇḍinya sees how the doctrine of impermanence follows from *all four* of the four noble truths.

Thus having framed the problem, I realized that indeed the doctrine of impermanence—"what is subject to origination is subject to cessation"—could, in fact, be taken to follow from the combination of the four truths. The fact that conditioned existents are subject to cessation accounts not only for decay and suffering but also for the possibility of nirvāṇa. Suffering itself is conditioned (as detailed in the second truth), and therefore it too is subject to cessation (the third truth), via the method of the path (the fourth truth). Nirvāṇa is possible because everything in saṃsāra is impermanent, and therefore saṃsāra itself (including of course "my" saṃsāra, my impurities), as nothing but a mass of conditioned things, is impermanent as well. Kauṇḍinya's amazing and amazed understanding, I saw, might have been that nirvāṇa is possible because liberation is an *instance* of impermanence.

A cascade of ideas followed. The universal nature of impermanence might suggest that nothing binds or constitutes or contains living beings but the mass of conditioned things itself, always changing. Since impermanence applies to saṃsāra, the absence of "self" that is entailed by impermanence applies not just to the individual, personal soul, but to a purported universal soul as well. On another track, these thoughts resonate with Nāgārjuna's famous claim that, contrary to the idea that emptiness prevents the path, emptiness in fact makes nirvāṇa possible—because non-empty entities would never change. I had always considered this an instance where Nāgārjuna cleverly turned the tables on his adversary's appeal to common sense. Now, it appeared anew as a strategic application of philosophical dialectic to disclose and illuminate a neglected but core Buddhist principle. This, furthermore, suggested to me a new perspective on disputes over the nature of the *ālayavijñāna*, which had better not be considered a stable "background" reality, lest it preclude the psychological effectiveness of the truth that impermanence makes nirvāṇa possible.

Now removed from the immediacy of these pre-class realizations, I think it is likely that the *Setting the Wheel of Dharma in Motion Sūtra* pairs the Buddha's teaching with Kauṇḍinya's realization in what had already become a stereotyped expression for the opening of the Dharma eye, and that the text itself therefore implies no logical relation between the four truths and impermanence per se. And even if I did chance upon a deep pattern in Buddhist thought, I promise you that my realization was *not* the attainment of the path of seeing. No gods rejoiced in my attentive preparation for lecture. But *I* did. As a votary of the liberal arts, I take joy in intellectual adventure and the potential for self-understanding. A question posed of a text, pursued with diligence, led to an opening onto new ground, and new questions.[5] I don't remember if I got chills, but I sometimes do at such moments. Funny to think of getting chills from a naïve, wrong reading. But that's the way it goes (*tathāgata*).

I have narrated my mental causal story, and my projection into Kauṇḍinya's story, because it dramatizes for me the question of whether my goals—liberal arts goals—hinder me from understanding the Buddha's teachings in a way that is only available to those whose eye is focused on the path of seeing and beyond. Does the fact that I'm not working to attain stream entry mean that I am destined to fail, in some way, to truly understand the Dharma? Buddhists, as well as those familiar with academic Buddhist studies, know well the distinction between intellectual and direct understanding. It is one thing to study Buddhism, we are told, and something else entirely to practice it. This is a key distinction for all Buddhists, it would seem, yet it is not always clear what the distinction means or entails. Frankly, I'm not sure which of these characterizations applies to the luminous joy of learning for learning's sake, though perhaps the question is otiose, given that we are working with different paradigms. Yet a proper examination will need a good deal more information about how premodern Buddhists articulated the problem. While scholars working on the question of religious "experience" have critiqued claims to the unmediated and unitary nature of mystical states, and have called into doubt the centrality of meditation for premodern Buddhists,[6] it remains an open question just how Buddhist traditions have understood what is distinctive, and especially valuable, about the knowledge attained through practice. Buddhist traditions are numerous, and the question deserves extensive treatment. This first foray seeks a preliminary answer from Vasubandhu.

At the risk of giving away the ending, I feel obliged to mention, and set aside, an obvious answer to the question of what is special about Buddhist

5. My interest in and attention to the different modes of scholarship in traditional scholastic Buddhism and the modern academy was first stimulated by Griffiths 1999, an essential work that remains a touchstone. Nonetheless, where Griffiths levels a trenchant critique of what he terms rampant "consumerist reading" in the modern academy, I find my own academic explorations are motivated not by a consumerist approach to knowledge but rather by the "immeasurable" values that Delbanco 2012, 184, argues are admittedly under threat but still surviving in the modern college: "intellectual adventure, joy in learning, self-understanding."

6. Sharf 1998, McMahan 2008, and sources cited therein.

practice as opposed to study, which is that it leads to nirvāṇa. We can grant that nirvāṇa is something special and that Buddhist practice is geared toward its attainment, but this hardly justifies claims, on the part of ordinary meditators (i.e., those who are not āryas), that they have access to an understanding that ordinary scholars do not. But what knowledge, distinctive to Buddhist practice, can arise before stream entry? This is the question we are posing to Vasubandhu.

Another obvious possibility to set aside is the suggestion that *any* practices performed on the path, to the degree that they have an experiential component, yield knowledge that is distinct from merely hearing about them. It would be difficult to deny the general salience of the difference between cognitive and experiential knowledge in Buddhism. Indeed, this point can be made about any experience. No matter how much I learn about roller coasters and the people who ride them, there's something I will know differently once I ride the roller coaster: *what it's like* to ride a roller coaster. This point deserves fuller discussion in a Buddhist philosophical context than I can give it here. But we can set it aside as irrelevant insofar as our question concerns what is distinctive of Buddhist experiences that is only known through practice.

An example will make the point clear. As is well known, the Buddha taught of three sense domains (*dhātu*) that interact to create visual experience: a sensory organ (the eye), a visible object, and a distinctive kind of consciousness—a visual consciousness. Now, suppose someone points out that a blind person lacks *experiential* knowledge of the Buddha's teachings on the sensory domains—only sighted people have a direct understanding of visual sensation. Surely we would want to say that this is a trivial point, irrelevant to the question of the special value of Buddhist practice. Blind people do not miss out on the true import of the Buddha's *dhātu* system simply because they are unacquainted with the visual experience it explains. And why not? Clearly because the Buddha did not teach the *dhātu* system in order to *generate* the described sensations; he was simply explaining the causal structure of well-known experiences. There is nothing *Buddhist* about ordinary seeing. We are looking, then, for evidence of something in the experience of the Buddhist path—before stream entry—that the Buddha recommends and that is not general knowledge.

For Vasubandhu's Abhidharma, this issue, like every issue, is a technical one. Our point of departure is the passage from the final verses of the *Commentary on the Treasury of Abhidharma*, in which Vasubandhu distinguishes scriptural from practical knowledge.[7] The key terms are well known: The true

7. *Abhidharmakośabhāṣya* 8.39; Pradhan 1975, 459.

dharma (*saddharma*) is described as twofold, including *āgama* (scriptural tradition) and *adhigama* (attainments). In glossing these, Vasubandhu tells us that *āgama* includes *sūtra, vinaya*, and *abhidharma* and that it is maintained by teachers, while *adhigama* includes the *bodhipakṣya-dharma*s (dharmas that contribute to awakening) and is maintained by practitioners.

Although Vasubandhu does not cite it, this assemblage of terms and topics resonates strongly with famous passages from the *Great Scripture on the Parinirvāṇa* (*Mahāparinirvāṇa-sūtra*), where the Buddha is charging the monastic community with upholding the Dharma after he is gone.[8] In this sūtra passage as in Vasubandhu's text, the discussion is framed by the question of whether the Dharma might endure after the Buddha's passing (and if so, *how* it will endure, and for how long). In the sūtra, the Buddha tells the monks that, in order to maintain the Dharma, they should first learn, practice, and develop dharmas that he has himself attained and taught. Once they have grasped and "mastered" (*paryavāpya*)[9] these dharmas, they should teach them. What, specifically, are the dharmas that must be mastered? The Buddha lists the "seven sets" that add up to thirty-seven individual dharmas, which is what Vasubandhu is referring to as the *bodhipakṣya-dharma*s. As long as people are mastering and teaching these, he says, the true *dharma* will endure.[10] Vasubandhu cites the prediction that the Dharma will pass away after one thousand years and comments that this refers to *adhigama*; thus the continued occurrence of "attainments" will cease then, while the *āgama* might have more time.

Notice that it is the continued achievement of practical mastery that constitutes the continuity of the true Dharma. In case we did not know it already, attainment through practice is not here valorized as a tool for gaining knowledge or even liberation; it is valorized as a tool for protecting the teachings and maintaining them through time. It is reasonable to conclude, then, that the Buddha and Vasubandhu were suggesting that practical mastery of the seven sets provides an internal guide or corrective—an epistemic ground—for the teachings that it authorizes. "Experience" and "mastery" are valorized because they allow a monk to be among the Dharma's guardians. It is these that ensure

8. As discussed by Gethin 1991, 229–33.

9. In the Sanskrit cited by Gethin 1991, 213.

10. This discussion provides a nice example of how the word *dharmas*, used in the plural to refer to items listed within the Buddha's teachings, is often difficult to distinguish in meaning from *dharma*, singular, in the sense of the Buddha's teachings ("the Dharma"). On this important, often misunderstood, point, see Gethin 1991, 147–54.

that the Buddhist tradition continues, not just as a series of doctrines but as a practical method for the liberation of sentient beings.[11]

While this appears to be the Buddha's point, a legitimate alternative reading would emphasize that the *adhigama* attainments—the mastery of the *bodhipakṣya-dharma*s—are not just a means whereby monks can check their understanding and so help to liberate sentient beings; rather, the *adhigama* attainments *instantiate* the liberative results of the dharma, properly applied. If mastery of the *bodhipakṣya-dharma*s entails the attainment of the path of seeing and the opening of the Dharma eye, then the *adhigama* is as much a result as it is the cause of the Dharma's continued success. So we might read a kind of tautological or definitional meaning here, such that the Buddha is saying the Dharma will last as long as people are teaching it and reaching attainments. This works as encouragement to the Buddha's disciples not to give up after his passing, but it may also seem almost Yogi Berra–like ("It ain't over till it's over")—or like the elderly pizza man who, when asked how long he would keep making pizzas, said he would stay open "as long as there are pizzas coming out of that oven." Read this way, *āgama* and *adhigama* legitimate one another and are not hierarchically arranged. The Buddha might be saying that the Dharma is the true Dharma because it works to produce realizations, that it is the true Dharma because realized beings authorize it, or both.

To settle this question, we must ask just what are these *bodhipakṣya-dharma*s, these thirty-seven "dharmas that contribute to awakening" that are ostensibly capable of validating the Dharma. When Vasubandhu equates these with *adhigama*, could he have it in mind that some of them pertain to attainments on the path before stream entry? In fact, the seven sets do include dharmas that are cultivated before stream entry. For readers who haven't memorized them, the seven sets are (using Gethin's translations):

1. The four establishings of mindfulness
2. The four right endeavors
3. The four bases of success
4. The five faculties
5. The five powers

11. This reading may find support in Vasubandhu's declaration (7.47) that teaching the Dharma is the best kind of "miracle" (*prātihārya*), one that depends upon the attainment of the transcendent knowledge of the destruction of the defilements (Pradhan 1975, 424.10: *āsravakṣayābhijñā*). But this attainment issues in full awakening, not just in stream entry. That passage, then, may be limited to the Buddha, or even to the Buddha's special magical methods of teaching the Dharma. See Fiordalis 2010 for an interesting discussion of "miracles" in this and other Buddhist contexts.

6. The seven factors of awakening
7. The eightfold noble path

The first set, the four establishings of mindfulness, includes, along with its fourth item—that of establishing (4) mindfulness of dharmas—three practices establishing mindfulness that are regularly sought by ordinary MBSR[12] and Vipassana practitioners: (1) mindfulness of the body, (2) mindfulness of feeling, and (3) mindfulness of the mind. The second set, that of the four right endeavors, consists in effortful, deliberate cultivations of proper patterns of behavior—they refer, that is, to the work involved in cultivating wholesome qualities. Such effort is reasonably taken as meant to figure in every meditation session, and perhaps in every aspect of effortful moral restraint (such as the decision not to lie). So there is preliminary evidence that these are experiences early on the path that the tradition understood to represent as a special kind of knowledge, attainable only through practice.

Yet the other passages where Vasubandhu uses the term *adhigama* in the *Treasury* seem to be making reference only to advanced attainments. At 6.45, Vasubandhu uses the term *adhigama* to refer to "sequential attainments,"[13] where he is clearly referring to the once-returner and the nonreturner. At 6.58, in a short sentence introducing a quotation by saying, "And the attainment, through wisdom, of the first and last fruit by nobles only,"[14] Vasubandhu is again using the term *adhigama* to refer to transcendent (*lokottara*) attainments. Asaṅga's *Abhidharma Compendium* also uses the term *adhigama* to name attainments on the path of seeing.[15] If this is the basic meaning of "attainments" (*adhigama*), Vasubandhu's division of true Dharma into texts and attainments surely valorizes practice but should not be taken to imply that there are any meaningful practical attainments before stream entry. To underline the point, the attainments associated with the term *adhigama* seem to be, in each case, realizations that arise *specifically* at stream entry. Vasubandhu seems to be saying that the true Dharma consists in (1) text traditions and (2) the path of seeing.

Is there a way to match the more capacious list of the thirty-seven

12. Mindfulness-Based Stress Reduction, designed by Jon Kabat-Zinn, is the most widely taught form of meditation in America today.

13. Pradhan 1975, 366.5: *anupūrvādhigamaṃ pratyevam ucyate.*

14. Pradhan 1975, 375.12: *ādyantayoś ca phalayor āryayâiva prajñayâdhigamaḥ*. Note that this phrase was not translated by La Vallée Poussin, so it may not have been in Xuanzang's Chinese translation. It does not appear in Yaśomitra's commentary either.

15. Rahula 1971, 110.

bodhipakṣya-dharmas with the idea that there is no *adhigama* before stream entry? Here it will help to turn to Vasubandhu's detailed discussion of the *bodhipakṣya-dharmas*.[16] For in 6.67–69, he writes that while there are thirty-seven dharmas listed among the seven sets, in fact only ten of those thirty-seven really count as distinct, substantial dharmas. This is important for our question of what counts as *adhigama*, since one might reasonably say that no merely conventional—as opposed to substantial—dharma could count as a proper state of attained knowledge or awareness of the sort that only religious practice could bring about. We will return to the question of whether there might be merely conventional realizations below. For now, let's examine the effect and the method of the reduction from thirty-seven to ten.

So how does Vasubandhu get from thirty-seven to ten? Some of it is by eliminating repetition. Many of the dharmas are repeated in multiple lists. In fact, two of the lists—the five faculties and the five powers—list the very same dharmas. The other key move is to reduce each of the first three lists of four to one dharma, *each of which is also one of the five faculties/powers.*

four establishings of mindfulness	are reduced to *prajñā*
four right endeavors	are reduced to *vīrya*
four bases of success	are reduced to *samādhi*
five faculties/powers: *śraddhā, vīrya, smṛti, samādhi, prajñā*	

Next, Vasubandhu notes that four of the latter five are repeated as parts of the seven factors of awakening (reading *prajñā* as equivalent to discrimination of dharmas, *dharmapravicaya*) and, given the right twist, as parts of the eightfold path:

vīrya	is equivalent to right endeavor (*samyakvyāyāma*)
smṛti	is equivalent to right mindfulness (*samyaksmṛti*)
samādhi	is equivalent to right concentration (*samyaksamādhi*)
prajñā	is equivalent to right view (*samyakdṛṣṭi*)

That leaves us with the five faculties, plus three of the seven factors of awakening not yet accounted for (joy [*prīti*], pliancy [*praśrabdhi*],[17] and equanimity [*upekṣā*], which he accepts as is) and the four remaining dharmas on the eightfold noble path: right intention (*samyaksaṃkalpā*) and the three categories of moral behavior—right speech, right action, and right livelihood. In

16. Pradhan 1975, 383ff.

17. Pradhan 1975, 383.10. Alt. *prasrabdhi*, as 397.22.

disagreement with the Vaibhāṣikas, who take bodily and vocal action to be distinct, Vasubandhu declares these last three to be reducible to *śīla* (moral behavior) alone. Thus, from the thirty-seven, Vasubandhu gets the following ten substantial dharmas: *śraddhā, vīrya, smṛti, samādhi, prajñā, prīti, praśrabdhi, upekṣā, samyaksaṃkalpā*, and *śīlāṅgāni*. These are the ten dharmas whose attainment signals the continuity of the teachings.

We are now in a position to consider whether it is a principle of the reduction that only transcendent—*lokottara*—versions of these dharmas count as properly substantial *bodhipakṣya-dharmas.* I'd like to argue that it is. Consider, for instance, the removal of the duplication of the five faculties and the five powers. Yes, they are the same listed dharmas. But, as Gethin has shown at some length and as a glance at Vasubandhu confirms, the five powers represent the five faculties made maximally strong.[18] If Vasubandhu had intended to include the distinctive stages of cultivation of the five faculties *before* stream entry within the *bodhipakṣya-dharma*s, he would not have reduced the more general faculties to the narrowly transcendent powers. Consider the dharma of *smṛti*, or mindfulness. It is hardly necessary to mention, today, that there are many ways to understand and apply the notion of mindfulness. In the five faculties, it can refer to a variety of cultivations. Yet as one of the powers, it is clearly the perfect mindfulness that is equivalent to one of the seven factors of awakening—the mindfulness that leads directly to stream entry. The same can be said of *śraddhā* (faith), which need not always be perfect but which has a perfected identity as a "power" and is declared to be pure when considered as one of the factors of awakening.

A similar logic is in play, but even more decisively, in Vasubandhu's reduction of the four establishings of mindfulness to *prajñā*. The four establishings are the most "worldly" (*laukika*) and universal of the seven sets. One of the reasons it is called the "singular path," in a famous phrase, is that it is possible to access this liberative method from anywhere.[19] It is an advanced method, but it can also be taught to beginners. Furthermore, since *smṛti* is present in so many lists—the five faculties, the five powers, the seven factors of awakening, and the eightfold noble path—and is not going to be reduced away, it would be a natural choice to reduce the four establishings of mindfulness to mindfulness (*smṛti*). Why, then, does Vasubandhu instead claim that the substantial aspect of the four establishings of mindfulness is *prajñā*? Surely the point is that, *when perfected,* mindfulness is equivalent to pure "discrimination of

18. Gethin 1991, 140–45. Pradhan 1975, 384.9: *kasmād indriyāṇy eva balāny uktāny | mṛdvadhimātrabhedād avamardanīyānavamardanīyatvāt.*

19. Gethin 1991, 59–66.

dharmas" (*dharmapravicaya*), the "awakening insight" that is the definition of *prajñā* with which Vasubandhu opens the *Treasury*.[20]

Does the same principle, to include only the *lokottara* among the substantial *bodhipakṣya-dharma*s, hold for the reduction of the four right endeavors to *vīrya*? I believe it does, though Vasubandhu does not treat these terms at length. The Buddha often used the right endeavors as an explanation of the cultivation of *vīrya*, so surely there is no proper line to draw between them. But the right endeavors are described as "where a monk generates desire, endeavors, activates persistence, upholds, and exerts his intent" to cultivate positive qualities and to abandon negative ones.[21] Perfected as a power, the heroic willpower that is *vīrya* involves hardly any vestige of the effortful project of making the right decision, which is significant earlier on the path.

It might seem obvious that the factors of awakening (*sambodhyaṅga*) are transcendent experiences, but Vasubandhu's staging of a debate on the topic of one of these terms, *pliancy* (*praśrabdhi*, commentary to 2.25), helpfully illuminates the distinction between substantial and conventional dharmas as they pertain to the factors (see 6.68, 6.71a)—and thus as they pertain, in turn, to the *bodhipakṣya-dharma*s. The issue under debate centers around the fact that, as suggested by a sūtra citation, there are two kinds of pliancy—bodily and mental pliancy. Are both to be considered factors of awakening? Or, as seems more sensible, is only mental pliancy one of the factors of awakening? The commentary of Yaśomitra glosses the concern as being that bodily senses are unsuitable to the state of awakening, since they are "not absorbed" (*asamāhitatvāt*)—meaning, ostensibly, that awakening takes place in a state of concentration that allows no bodily consciousness.[22] This means that the pliancy that is a constituent of this absorption must be mental only. Yet Vasubandhu prefers not to throw away the scripturally founded notion that bodily pliancy is a factor of awakening.

The resolution to the conundrum comes from a hermeneutical analysis of the interpretive principle that elements are often designated, in scripture, in terms of what they cause. Listing a few examples of this idea, Vasubandhu concludes that *bodily* pliancy is metaphorically called a "factor of awakening" because it is conducive to *mental* pliancy. We may note that this hermeneutical principle typifies the pattern of Vasubandhu's reductions from thirty-seven to ten *bodhipakṣya-dharma*s. Insofar as they contribute causally to the attainment of the path of seeing, all thirty-seven may rightly be considered

20. Pradhan 1975, 2.4: *tatra prajñā dharmapravicayaḥ*.

21. Thanissaro 1996.

22. Śāstrī 2008, 1:149.22.

*bodhipakṣya-dharma*s, but in terms of being present in and partaking in the attainment itself, perhaps only ten are truly *bodhipakṣya-dharma*s.

In the end, then, the only remaining possibilities of *bodhipakṣya-dharma*s with a *laukika* experiential component are right intention (*samyaksaṃkalpā*)—which means proper moral intent—and the combined aspects of moral behavior (*śīlāṅgāni*). In fact, these constitute a very interesting exception that proves the rule.

Needless to say, moral behavior, especially following the monastic rule, is lauded across Buddhist traditions. In fact, there is reason to believe that moral behavior is the *basic* meaning of the "practice" that is deemed superior to learning. To take just a few examples, at *Aṅguttara-nikāya* 4:6, the Buddha says that learning a bit and putting it into practice is superior to learning a great deal without applying it—but he specifies that "application" of such knowledge *just is* virtuous behavior. Similarly, at *Aṅguttara-nikāya* 10:97 the Buddha declares that learning is the second of the ten qualities that make a monk worthy of gifts—the first being that he follows the monastic rule. And, perhaps most importantly, the Buddha's teaching to the Kālāmas, widely cited as evidence that the Buddha was an epistemic rationalist, is in fact an argument that deduces the excellence of his teachings from the evident moral behavior of his disciples.[23] All of these sources suggest not just that good Buddhists ought to act morally but that their *reliability* is evident in their *morality*.[24]

I cannot elaborate the discussion here, but I do believe that moral behavior is, in fact, the main—perhaps the only—Buddhist practice that is defended as having a strong benefit that precedes those that arise upon stream entry. Yet as John Holt has argued, the Vinaya narratives and monastic rituals seem to imply, structurally (in defense of the purity and authenticity of the sangha), that monastics disciplined by the *prātimokṣa* are, at least in the ideal, envisioned as nobles.[25] Vasubandhu's reduction of the three dharmas dealing with morality on the eightfold path to one—*śīlāṅgāni* alone—may also be taken to suggest a noble's generalized perfection of discipline as it pertains to any moral concern. So, the proper mastery of discipline may be in direct parallel with—may even be (at least symbolically) the same attainment as—the path of seeing.

23. Thanissaro 1994.

24. To switch contexts and millennia, when the thirteenth-century Tibetan scholar Sakya Paṇḍita is defending his polemical approach against opponents who think he should refrain from controversy, their criticism is that his intellectual expertise has not prevented him from being hostile and jealous. The implication is that a proper exponent of the Buddhist teachings should be constitutionally averse to combative stances. See Rhoton 2002, 178–79.

25. Holt 2015.

Or, to say almost the same thing, *śīla* proper cannot actually be maintained until one has had the *dṛṣṭi* of the path of seeing.

Our analysis would appear to show, then, that on Vasubandhu's reading, there are indeed elements of the true dharma that are only accessible via "experience," but that the experience in question is transcendent (*lokottara*) in the technical sense that only noble beings (*ārya*) attain it. There are no dharmas accessible only to experience before stream entry. As critical humanists, we should note the rhetorical power of a statement that "you can't really understand it until you get there." We may, furthermore, wonder whether monastic discipline, if it came to stand in for meditative attainments, pushed the latter into ever further reaches of unattainability.[26] But this exclusivity of experience pertains only to the teachings taken in a strict sense. In a broader, more capacious and metaphorical, sense, all aspects of the teachings and practices that are *causal conditions* for attainment of the path of seeing ought to be counted among the *bodhipakṣya-dharma*s. This is why there are thirty-seven, and why these include the impure versions of dharmas such as ordinary faith and everyday mindfulness.

Yet if we thus include the causal conditions as part of the true dharma known by experience, we need to allow for Vasubandhu's more capacious, figurative, *conventional* understanding of the Dharma wheel as well—as referring not just to the mental events that liberate the nobles but also to the words that trigger such mental events. And if *discursive teachings* are counted as integral to the transformation that takes place within the mind of another, we lose the obvious difference between *āgama* and *adhigama*—between study and practice. After all, Vasubandhu opens his commentary on the *Treasury* with the statement that, in a strict sense, the Abhidharma is "pure" (*amalā*)—that is to say, transcendent—*prajñā*. His own work, therefore, is (like all scholarship) only and figuratively "Abhidharma," insofar as it, though not itself pure wisdom, is nonetheless a potential causal condition thereof.[27]

This allows us to make the point more clearly: The Buddha's true Dharma comes in two forms—namely, the teachings themselves and the experience toward which these point. The experience toward which the teachings point is first realized on the path of seeing; there is more to experience beyond, but until the path of seeing, there is nothing of intrinsic value. Everything in the texts of the Dharma thus derives its value, its identity, and its truth from the

26. Lopez 1992 also suggests that ideological considerations might have pushed the possibility of enlightenment into an inaccessible future. Thanks to Dan Arnold for suggesting this reference.

27. *Abhidharmakośabhāṣya* 1.2; Pradhan 1975, 2.3–5.

transcendent attainments. This was true when the Buddha first spoke the Dharma to Kauṇḍinya, and it remains true throughout the Dharma's history: it is not the doctrine or the practice but the liberation of beings—initiated on the path of seeing—that justifies and exemplifies the truth of the Buddha's teachings and associated practices. Nevertheless, any activity—study or practice or foosball—that, intentionally or not, causes a change in the intellect that conduces to the path of seeing is, figuratively and conventionally, an instance of the true Dharma. This would seem to leave room for my revelations, generated for the love of learning alone, to have a potential basis on the path. In this late age, far beyond the thousand-year limit, it is doubtful that anyone can attain the Dharma eye, let alone someone doubting its possibility. But if through my studies I should happen upon it, they will deserve to be called "true Dharma" as much as any monastic recitation.

Yet if the true Dharma as text is only "true" to the extent the words *cause* the realization that opens the Dharma eye, then by the figurative logic of Abhidharma, of the worldly *bodhipakṣya-dharma*s, of bodily pliancy, and of the turning of the Dharma wheel, it must be that *all* of the textual Dharma is "true" only metaphorically. But who would dare to say such a thing? In fact, none other than Vasubandhu himself says something very much like this in the famous opening verse of his masterful Yogācāra treatise the *Thirty Verses*. The opening line of that text refers to the first kind of true Dharma—Dharma as text—saying "the metaphors of self and dharmas operate in various ways"—and goes on to add that they all operate on the transformation of consciousness.[28] Then, after thirty verses of technical dharma analysis, the very last line of the text refers to the *second* kind of true Dharma, Dharma as realization: "Happy, that liberated body called Dharma is the great sage."[29] The logic of metaphors in the *Treasury* has been extended only a short, but luminous, bit in each direction to suit a Mahāyāna context. Before, to say that dharmas were metaphorically true meant that various teachings of the Buddha put into practice became conditions for a disciple's Dharma eye opening on the path of seeing. Now, to say that the dharmas that constitute the textual aspect of the true Dharma are metaphorical is to say that they are only called Dharma because they act on the minds of sentient beings as conditions for the attainment of the Dharma body. Like the other metaphorical predications, the Dharma gets its name from its causal result: in this case, the Dharma body of a fully enlightened buddha. But of course, since this is a realization *as described in a text*, not

28. *Triṃśikāvijñaptikārikā* 1; Lévi 1925, 13: *ātmadharmopacāro hi vividho yaḥ pravartate.*

29. *Triṃśikāvijñaptikārikā* 30; Lévi 1925, 14: *sukho vimuktikāyo 'sau dharmākhyo 'yaṃ mahāmuneḥ.*

a realization itself, even the ostensibly final result is acknowledged to be only a figurative expression: not the Dharma body, but the "body *called* Dharma."

Works Cited

Abhidharmasamuccaya = Rahula 1971.

Abhidharmakośabhāṣya = Pradhan 1975.

Bodhi, Bhikkhu. 2005. *The Connected Discourses of the Buddha: A Translation of the Saṃyutta Nikāya.* Boston: Wisdom Publications.

Delbanco, Andrew. 2012. *College: What It Was, Is, and Should Be.* Princeton, NJ: Princeton University Press.

Gethin, Rupert. 1991. *The Buddhist Path to Awakening.* Oxford: Oneworld.

Griffiths, Paul J. 1999. *Religious Reading: The Place of Reading in the Practice of Religion.* Oxford: Oxford University Press.

Fiordalis, David V. 2010 (2011). "Miracles in Indian Buddhist Narratives and Doctrine." *Journal of the International Association of Buddhist Studies* 33.1–2: 381–408.

Holt, John Clifford. 2015 (first edition 1981). *Discipline: The Canonical Buddhism of Vinayapiṭaka.* Delhi: Motilal Banarsidass.

Lévi, Sylvain. 1925. *Vijñaptimātratāsiddhi: Deux traités de Vasubandhu, Viṃśatikā (La Vingtaine) accompagnée d'une explication en prose, et Triṃśikā (La Trentaine), avec le commentaire de Sthiramati.* Paris: Librairie Ancienne Honoré Champion.

Lopez, Donald S., Jr. 1990. "Paths Terminable and Interminable." In *Paths to Liberation: The Mārga and Its Transformations in Buddhist Thought*, edited by Robert E. Buswell Jr. and Robert M. Gimello, 147–83. Honolulu: University of Hawai'i Press.

McMahan, David. 2008. *The Making of Buddhist Modernism.* New York: Oxford University Press.

Nyanaponika Thera. 1994. *The Life of Sariputta: Compiled and Translated from the Pali Texts.* https://www.accesstoinsight.org/lib/authors/nyanaponika/wheel090.html.

Pradhan, Prahlad, ed. 1975 (first edition 1967). *Abhidharmakośabhāṣyam of Vasubandhu.* Tibetan Sanskrit Works 8. Patna: K. P. Jayaswal Research Institute.

Rahula, Walpola, ed. and trans. 1971. *Le compendium de la super-doctrine (philosophie) (Abhidharmasamuccaya) d'Asaṅga.* Paris: L'École Française d'Extrême-Orient.

Rhoton, Jared, trans. 2002. *A Clear Differentiation of the Three Codes: Essential Distinctions among the Individual Liberation, Great Vehicle, and Tantric Systems. The sDom gsum rab dbye and Six Letters by Sakya Pandita Kunga Gyaltshen.* New York: State University of New York Press.

Śāstrī, Dwārikā Dās, ed. 2008. *The Abhidharmakośa & Bhāṣya of Ācārya Vasubandhu with Sphuṭārtha Commentary of Ācārya Yaśomitra.* 2 vols. Varanasi: Bauddha Bhāratī.

Sharf, Robert. 1998. "Experience." In *Critical Terms for Religious Studies*, edited by Mark C. Taylor, 94–116. Chicago: University of Chicago Press.

Siderits, Mark. 2007. *Buddhism as Philosophy: An Introduction.* Indianapolis: Hackett Publishing.

Sphuṭārtha = Śāstrī 2008.

Thanissaro Bhikkhu. 1993. "Dhammacakkappavattana Sutta: Setting the Wheel of Dhamma in Motion." https://www.accesstoinsight.org/tipitaka/sn/sn56/sn56.011.than.html.

———. 1994. "Kalama Sutta: To the Kalamas." https://www.accesstoinsight.org/tipitaka/an/an03/an03.065.than.html.
———. 1996. "Magga-vibhanga Sutta: An Analysis of the Path." https://www.accesstoinsight.org/tipitaka/sn/sn45/sn45.008.than.html.
Triṃśikāvijñaptikārikā = Lévi 1925.

From Exegesis to Hermeneutics: Rongtön and the Hidden Meaning (*sbas don*) of Perfect Wisdom

Pierre-Julien Harter

THERE CAN BE NO doubt that Matthew Kapstein is an impressive scholar, learned in multiple cultures, civilizations, languages, and fields. He has advanced scholarship in many ways: studies, editions, translations. Those who have worked with him cannot help being overwhelmed, at some point, with *awe* by the extent and depth of his interests and knowledge. Those who have been fortunate enough to study with him, though, often know him to be even more impactful as a teacher, as a director of research. In classes and conversations, he has suggested many leads that flourished into research projects and new insights. One such lead encouraged me to look into the literature of the *Abhisamayālaṃkāra*, and especially the work of a commentator whom few Western and even Tibetan scholars have read—the great G.yag ston Sangs rgyas dpal (1349–1414). Tibetan scholars with whom I have worked have sometimes wondered why I was so intent on reading such a tedious and forgotten (if nevertheless respected) commentator. Matthew had, however, the intuition that this figure was central to the history of Tibetan exegesis of the *Abhisamayālaṃkāra*. Considering the work of his many predecessors in light of his commentaries, one can appreciate that something of the entire ocean of texts constituting the *Abhisamayālaṃkāra* literature can be accessed through G.yag ston's work, so great was his almost complete command over the commentarial literature preceding him. Considering developments subsequent to him, one can gain, through his works, an orientation to the philosophically fascinating fifteenth century in Tibet, since G.yag ston inaugurated an impressive lineage of masters and disciples. I didn't perceive at the time the potential of Matthew's seemingly insignificant remark, but I am glad I followed it. It has guided me to great discoveries.

Matthew's lead also came, though, with the twofold demand imposed by the example set by his own work throughout his career, a demand that few can meet (and that too few appreciate)—the demand at once for philological rigor (which remains the fuel of the fields of Buddhist studies), and for philosophically imaginative engagement that sees in philology the tool for accomplishing much more than mere repetition. I offer this article as an homage to the pair of virtues Matthew and his work have embodied so uncompromisingly, with the hope that the generations of students he has trained, and those beyond, will cultivate them with care and a sense of duty.

In a previous publication,[1] I analyzed the growth and transformation of the exegetical tradition of the *Abhisamayālaṃkāra* (henceforth *Ornament*) in India, with a particular focus on the ways in which commentators interpreted the relationship between that text and the Perfect Wisdom (*prajñāpāramitā*) Sūtras. I argued that the *Ornament*'s commentators gradually drove a wedge between the *Ornament* and the Perfect Wisdom Sūtras by elevating perfect wisdom above its textual existence, coming to understand it instead as primarily denoting the wisdom of the buddhas, which is to say ultimate reality itself. To that extent, the *Ornament* came increasingly to be associated with the meaning or essence of "perfect wisdom," in its non-textual dimension rather than with the actual texts from which it supposedly emerged. This shift from a literal relationship to a semantic one allowed for great freedom and creativity in elaborating distinctive doctrines about the path. Haribadhra (ca. 735–810) played a crucial part in this story, along with one of his major commentators, Dharmamitra (ca. ninth century).

In the present article, I propose to follow the sequel of the story as it developed in Tibet to show how the exegetical literature on the *Ornament* transformed from the typical commentarial work into a complete philosophical hermeneutic of the Buddhist tradition. This transformation took place in Tibet, where the concept of the "hidden meaning" (*sbas don*) of perfect wisdom became central. The process of development I have in mind saw its final stage with the Tibetan scholar Rong ston Shes bya kung rig (1367–1449, henceforth Rongtön).

It is widely held among both Western and Tibetan scholars that commentators had all along resorted to the concept of "hidden meaning" in interpreting the *Ornament*.[2] As I aim to show, however, ready appeal to this exegetical expe-

1. Harter 2014.

2. Sparham in Vimuktisena and Haribhadra 2006, xx, ascribes this approach to Dharmamitra, probably following Tsong kha pa, even though the expression cannot be found in Indian commentaries. This absence is noted by Brunnhölzl 2010, 690, which makes it all the more so surprising that Brunnhölzl, 2010, 35 and 64, seem to take the interpretation of the *Ornament* as manifesting a hidden meaning as a fact. See also Apple 2008, 26, and for a Tibetan contemporary example see Thrangu Rinpoche 2001, 14.

dient becomes the norm only in the fifteenth century, as the result of a long exegetical process. The origins of this hermeneutic are to be found, as can be rightfully expected, in India, both within the exegetical corpus of the *Ornament* and elsewhere. Dharmamitra seems to be the first Indian commentator to refer to two distinct approaches to perfect wisdom, those of Nāgārjuna and Maitreya, albeit without specifying their respective functions.[3] Reference to these luminaries was a way for Dharmamitra to address a problem that faced all commentators on the *Ornament*: how can the *Ornament* be thought to *explain* perfect wisdom when Nāgārjuna's works were already taken to have provided the definitive account thereof? It was necessary, then, to say that the tradition required two different approaches to perfect wisdom: the one epitomized by Nāgārjuna's Madhyamaka and the one traditionally associated with Maitreya, elaborated by the *Ornament*. However, the basis for the diverging approaches was never systematically formulated by Indian commentators. Far from simply rehashing what Indian thinkers had elaborated, Tibetan scholars of this literature identified the issues (e.g., the seeming contradiction between Nāgārjuna's and Maitreya's texts). Exploiting the under-determined character of the distinction between these, they elaborated the concept of a "hidden meaning" of perfect wisdom, taking this as the hermeneutical key for at once distinguishing and harmonizing the two exegetical traditions. The result was a veritably complete hermeneutic of the Buddhist tradition.

The phrase "hidden meaning" had already appeared in South Asian literature, albeit limitedly. Jonardon Ganeri indicates that some non-Buddhist authors used the Sanskrit equivalent *guḍhārtha* by way of emphasizing that their own commentaries were able to extract the hidden meaning of a text whereas rival commentaries were deemed to be concerned only with the obvious meaning.[4] The idea seems, however, completely absent from the Indian exegetical literature on the *Ornament*.[5] Moreover, when the expression "hidden meaning" starts to appear in Tibetan commentaries on the *Ornament*, it first has a very modest function. Early adopters of the phrase seem to have been making a limited philological point, paraphrasing the word *instruction* (*man ngag*, *upadeśa*), as it occurs in the full title of the *Ornament*, with the phrase "hidden meaning" (*sbas don*). The first commentators to use this expression seem to have been 'Bre Shes rab 'bar (eleventh century) and Khyung Rin chen grags pa (eleventh to twelfth centuries); that is, at any rate, what Nya dbon

3. Harter 2014, 371–77.

4. Ganeri 2008, 191–92.

5. The expression is largely used in Tibet to comment on tantric material as well, but it is unclear to me whether the term can be found in Indian tantric literature.

Kun dga' dpal (1285–1379) asserts in his commentary, the *Remover of Mental Obscurities* (*Yid kyi mun sel*). Nya dbon writes that the *Ornament* is called an *instruction* because, as 'Bre and Khyung had explained, *instruction* properly clarifies a meaning "as if it were hidden."[6] Nya dbon is careful and subtle here: the meaning had not actually been "hidden" but *seems* to have been so in light of the clarity brought out by the commentator. The instruction clarifies a potential obscurity, but it does not uncover a secret. This suggests that for Nya dbon (and 'Bre and Khyung by implication), the hermeneutical sense of the expression does not yet involve the paradigm of "revealing" a genuinely esoteric meaning. On this reading, accordingly, the attribution of different aspects of the corpus to Nāgārjuna and Maitreya did not track any distinction between manifest and hidden meanings.

Notably, no other commentators on the *Ornament* in the twelfth and thirteenth centuries seem to have used the same expression at all. Neither Rngog Blo ldan shes rab (1059–1109) nor Ar Byang chub ye shes (ca. 1050–1150) considered it useful to explain either the title of the *Ornament* or its purpose with reference to the idea of "hidden meaning." Bu ston (1290–1364), for his part, mostly repeats the same interpretation of the word *instruction* introduced by 'Bre and Khyung; he adds, however, that an *instruction* communicates a meaning that had actually been "hidden," which represents a step toward the later hermeneutic.[7] Nevertheless, this modification leads to no major shift in the overall interpretation. What is perhaps most notable about Bu ston's use of "hidden meaning" is that he could have pushed the interpretation in the direction taken by scholars a century later, since he also offered a historical-doctrinal picture of the interpretation of perfect wisdom. Indeed, only two pages before using the phrase "hidden meaning," Bu ston succinctly presents the great founders (*shing rta chen po'i srol bzhi*) of the interpretation of perfect wisdom: Nāgārjuna, Maitreya, Dignāga, and Daṃṣṭrāsena.[8] But he makes no connection between this historical-doctrinal perspective and the concept of a hidden meaning. This "missed opportunity" suggests that it was not inevitable that these would become linked, and that other factors must therefore explain how Rongtön came to his final elaboration.

6. Nya dbon 2007, 9: *tshegs chung ngus dgos pa rgya chen po sgrub pa'am sbas pa lta bu'i don gsal bar byed pas man ngag ces rim bzhin 'bre khyung 'chad de.*

7. Bu ston 1971, 11: *gnyis pas man ngag ni/ shes par bya ba'i yul myur du khong du chud par byed pa ste. Mdo don rgya chen rtogs par byed pa'i thabs nyung 'dus sam sbas pa'i don ston pa'o.*

8. Bu ston 1971, 9. This passage owes much to Dharmamitra, both in content and in form. Bu ston only adds Dignāga and Daṃṣṭrāsena, whom he considers to be the author of the great commentary (*'Bum gyi ṭīk*). See Sparham 2001, 199–201.

The fourteenth and fifteenth centuries saw a period of intense reflection and debate on how best to systematize the architecture of Buddhist textual and spiritual traditions (*āgama* and *adhigama*). The debates of this period did not much concern the status of Madhyamaka (which had already come to be recognized as the tradition's culminating philosophical position); debates centered, rather, on considering Madhyamaka in its relationship with other Buddhist philosophical positions, particularly those associated with texts (such as the *Ornament*) considered to have been authored by Maitreya. The problem was as much philosophical as exegetical, since the determination of a rationally acceptable and convincing Madhyamaka position entailed rethinking its relations with other philosophical positions and thus the readjustment of the frame in which other textual corpora were interpreted and understood. It is this intertwined relationship between the philosophical and the exegetical that demands the kind of "hermeneutic" I here have in mind—one that consists in assimilating the interpretation and comprehension of *texts* to that of the nature of things (*yathābhūta*), where the achievement of that comprehension depends on rightly interpreting scripture (*āgama*).[9]

It is in this context that Tsong kha pa Blo bzang grags pa (1357–1419) turns out to be an important character in our story. When it comes to the *Ornament*, Tsong kha pa's commentary, the *Golden Garland of Eloquence* (*Legs bshad gser phreng*), did not strike the thinkers of his time as particularly original. If it shows a vast mastery of the Indian and Tibetan literature on the subject, it nevertheless remained largely indebted to "mainstream" interpretations.[10] What is of interest to us in this work, however, is not the general interpretive position of Tsong kha pa but a point of detail that, although apparently unnoticed by contemporaneous scholars, represents a decisive step toward the kind of complete hermeneutic that Rongtön accomplished.

Thus, at the beginning of his commentary, Tsong kha pa offers a general presentation of the Perfect Wisdom literature, which he takes to represent the definitive teaching of the Buddhist Dharma. He reminds his readers of

9. Kapstein sheds light on this particular sense of hermeneutics in a Buddhist context: "We began this inquiry by considering Buddhist hermeneutics to be the explicit theory guiding Buddhist scriptural interpretation, and we have followed its course as it has merged with Buddhist philosophy as a general framework for Buddhist exegesis and practice." Kapstein 2001b, 332.

10. The Geluk school generally adduces biographical considerations to justify its own neglect of Tsong kha pa's work on the *Ornament*. It is fairly well established that the *Golden Garland* was written before 1398—the year in which Tsong kha pa was said to have attained awakening, which thus marked an important shift in his thought. His commentary on the *Ornament* was, then, taken to represent his earlier thinking and thus an inferior view compared to the post-1398 works. See Apple 2008, 38–39.

the four founders of the exegetical traditions that expound perfect wisdom, thus adopting Bu ston's classification.[11] Taking an important step beyond Bu ston, however, he rearranges this history by reducing all the exegetical traditions concerning perfect wisdom to two: that of Nāgārjuna (which includes both Nāgārjuna's works and the *Paddhati* of Darṃṣtrāsena) and that of Maitreya (which encompasses all of Maitreya's works and Dignāga's *Prajñāpāramitā-piṇḍārtha*).[12]

Remarkably, Tsong kha pa accomplishes this reduction by invoking Dharmamitra, quoting the specific passage alluded to above to justify his interpretation. But Tsong kha pa completes Dharmamitra in his effort of clarification:

> Two ways of explaining perfect wisdom came about, that of the Lord [Maitreya] and that of the revered Nāgārjuna. Dialectical works present the meaning of emptiness as it is directly taught, and the *Ornament* presents the series of realizations produced in the mental continuum of disciples when emptiness is explained as it is indirectly taught.[13]

Tsong kha pa presents this passage as a quotation from Dharmamitra, although it does not, in fact, appear in the Tibetan translation of Dharmamitra's *Dazzling Words*.[14] This is, rather, a free elaboration on Dharmamitra's text, to which Tsong kha pa adds something significant. Dharmamitra had only indicated that Nāgārjuna presented the "essential meaning" (*snying po'i don*), whereas Maitreya expounded the "meaning of realizations" (*mngon par rtogs pa'i don*).[15] Tsong kha pa takes a further step in determining how these two kinds of meaning complement one another by relating them to, respectively, an explicit and an implicit meaning.[16] Significantly, these need

11. See Sparham 2001, 203–5.

12. Tsong kha pa 1986, 3–8; Tsong kha pa 2008, 5–10.

13. Tsong kha pa 1986, 8: *yang na dngos bstan stong nyid kyi don rigs tshogs dang, shugs bstan stong nyid bshad pa na gdul bya'i rgyud la mngon rtogs skyes pa'i rim pa rnams rgyan gyis bkral bas, rje btsun dang klu sgrub zhabs gnyis kyi sher phyin 'grel tshul gnyis su byung ngo.*

14. The full title of Dharmamitra's commentary is *Abhisamayālaṃkārakārikāprajñāpāramitopadeśaśāstraṭīkāprasphuṭapadā*, but some editors of the Tibetan canon present a variation with *-prasannapadā*.

15. Harter 2014, 375–76.

16. In addition, it is important to remember that in the introductory verses of his *Golden Garland* (Tsong kha pa 1986, 1), Tsong kha pa explains that the meaning of perfect wisdom has

not be opposed or contradictory, even if they present the same texts (the Prajñāpāramitā Sūtras), or the same reality, in very different terms. It is crucial to emphasize that it is only with Tsong kha pa that reference to these two layers of meaning starts to be widely in use in the literature on the *Ornament*, signaling a new phase in the history of its exegesis. We are now very close to a full-blown "hermeneutic of the hidden meaning," even though Tsong kha pa did not go quite so far. On Tsong kha pa's reading, the *Ornament* is revelatory not just because its title represents it as providing "instruction" (which, recall, had earlier been defined as revealing a hidden meaning, though Tsong kha pa does not refer to this definition despite his extended acquaintance with past Tibetan commentaries). Rather, it is revelatory because the purpose of the *Ornament* is to disclose to readers of the Perfect Wisdom Sūtras what is not obvious: the gnoselogical, moral, and soteriological progress that they can count on as practitioners of perfect wisdom. By thus specifying the proper purpose and object of the *Ornament*, Tsong kha pa redefines the overall hermeneutic of Tibetan thought: the *Ornament* and the Madhyamaka treatises are now taken as together covering the totality of true and final philosophical positions, without either repeating or contradicting each other.

Remarkably, this innovation seems to have gone unnoticed by Tsong kha pa's direct and more famous disciples, none of whom developed this idea. Rgyal tshab, who was highly regarded by the Geluk tradition, employs the phrase "hidden meaning" with reference to the *Ornament* in his *Ornament of the Essence* (*Rnam bshad snying po'i rgyan*)—but he does so almost incidentally, and without opposing that to an "explicit meaning."[17] Mkhas grub dge legs dpal bzang (1385–1438), for his part, skirts around the topic in his *Light on Difficult Issues* (*Rnam bshad rtogs dka'i snang ba*) but never does formulate the idea.

Strangely, it is in the writings of one of Tsong kha pa's first adversaries that his ideas on the two exegetical lineages and their significance are picked up and conjoined with an interpretation of the "hidden meaning" to produce in fully realized form a "hermeneutic of the hidden meaning." The adversary in question was Rongtön, who is remembered as one of the fiercest among the first opponents of Tsong kha pa and his successors and one of the most important scholars of the Sakya school, especially for his exegesis of Madhyamaka texts.

---

been uttered "in a hidden fashion" (*sbas pa'i tshul gyis*), even though he does not use the phrase *sbas don*. But the fact that this idea surfaces in the introduction and then again within the commentary indicates that it certainly corresponded to a consistent vision in Tsong kha pa's hermeneutics.

17. Rgyal tshab 2002, 6: *mdo rgyas 'bring bsdus gsum gyi sbas don khong na gnas pa gsal bar ston par byed do.*

Rongtön's opposition to the Gelukpas was arguably owing to the fact that he saw the novelty of the interpretations of Tsong kha pa and his followers as a danger.[18] Rongtön was strongly committed to the *Ornament*, and more generally to the Five Treatises of Maitreya (*byams chos sde nga*), as the Tibetans came to call them; indeed, he is among the very few Tibetan scholars to have produced commentaries on each of these five texts.[19] On the Perfect Wisdom literature more generally, he wrote several texts, including two commentaries on the *Ornament* itself,[20] a full commentary on the *Śatasahāsrikāprajñāpāramitā*, and two smaller texts expanding on the practice of perfect wisdom. The breadth of Rongtön's scholarship is impressive, and his available complete works attest to his diverse interests and areas of expertise. More than just displaying his talent, though, the all-encompassing perspective reflected in his range of interests suggests something of Rongtön's efforts to rethink the entire hermeneutical framework of the Buddhist tradition—an effort, I am arguing, that was exemplified in his treatment of the concept of the "hidden meaning" of the *Ornament*.

This concept appears in his largest commentary on the *Ornament*. Rongtön begins this work by presenting the Buddha's intention to liberate all beings from suffering, his attainment of awakening, and his turning of the wheel of the Dharma. This gives him an opportunity to reflect on what the Dharma is and on its different forms:

> The most profound of these [teachings] is that of perfect wisdom. Its meaning has two aspects: the meaning of emptiness, which is its direct teaching, and the series of realizations, which is its hidden meaning. The first one is to be found in the teachings clearly expounded in the Madhyamaka dialectical works of Ārya

18. For biographical elements about Rong ston, see Jackson 1989, Jackson 2007, and (of particular interest here) Jackson 1988. Rong ston's most obvious opposition to Tsong kha pa might be found in his Madhyamaka commentaries, in particular his *Dbu ma rigs pa'i tshogs kyi dka' ba'i gnad bstan pa rigs lam kun gsal*, where he discusses two issues of particular interest to Tsong kha pa: the status of the object of negation (*dgag bya*) and the distinction between Svātantrikas and Prāsaṅgikas.

19. On the five treatises of Maitreya, see Brunnhölzl 2012, 15–19.

20. The title of his detailed commentary, whose abbreviated form is *Tshig don rab tu gsal ba*, bears an interesting resemblance to the title of Dharmamitra's commentary, which was translated into Tibetan as *Tshig rab tu gsal ba*. It is worth asking whether this was a way for Rong ston to compete, on the one hand, with Tsong kha pa (who heavily referenced Dharmamitra), and, on the other hand, to claim to be himself a sort of Tibetan Dharmamitra—which is to say, a faithful disciple of Haribhadra, of whom Rong ston (in agreement with his master G.yag ston) was a fierce defender (in contrast to Dol po pa). See Jackson 1988, vi, on Rong ston's dream.

> Nāgārjuna; the second one is the series of realizations,—the subjective side corresponding to the objective side that emptiness is, as taught by Ārya Maitreya.[21]

In this passage, Rongtön reclaims the expression "hidden meaning" that had figured in older Tibetan commentaries, but he substitutes a hermeneutical understanding for a more limitedly philological one (as exemplified by Nya dbon).[22] "Hidden meaning" no longer denotes simply the content of the instruction that the *Ornament* is supposed to provide, but one of the two aspects of perfect wisdom itself. "Perfect wisdom" stands for the discourse on emptiness but also encompasses the "vast" aspect of the teaching—namely, the path and its complex and detailed categories. The discourse on the path, Rongtön tells us, corresponds to (*sbyar*) the discourse on emptiness, by which he means that the two types of discourses, however distinct they might seem, remain in harmony: one is the object of the analytical investigation determining the nature of things as being insubstantial (the "objective side"), while the other analyzes the appropriation of this discourse from the point of view of the practitioner who transforms himself or herself on the path (the "subjective side"). Rongtön thus does not identify these two dimensions of perfect wisdom but rather posits a correspondence or a connection that allows them both to relate to a common basis. Specifically, Rongtön means that the eight realizations (*abhisamaya*, *mngon rtogs*) that provide the respective headings of the eight chapters of the *Ornament*—the realizations, that is, that constitute the different kinds of achievements on the path (whose order and relationships are the objects of much controversy)—represent the subjective side of the realization of emptiness, whereas emptiness itself represents the objective content of perfect wisdom. "Perfect wisdom" is, as it were, a coin, one of whose sides is the emptiness that this corpus takes as its guiding concern, and the other of which is the subjective character of the path's progressively deeper realizations

21. Rong ston 2008, 3:119, Jackson 1988, 2b: *De rnams kyi shin tu zab pa ni shes rab kyi pha rol tu phyin pa yin la. De'i don ni rnam pa gnyis te. dngos bstan stong pa nyid gyi don dang, sbas don mngon par rtogs pa'i rim pa'o. dang po ni, 'phags pa klu sgrub kyi* [Jackson: *kyis*] *dbu ma rigs pa'i tshogs kyis gsal bar bstan pa dag yin la. gnyis pa ni, 'phags pa byams pas yul stong pa nyid dang sbyar nas bstan pa'i yul can mngon par rtogs pa'i rim pa'o.*

22. This is not the only passage from his oeuvre where he resorts to both aspects. In his *Mngon par rtogs pa'i rgyan gyi brjod bya ma nor bar togs pa brgyad don bdun cu la sogs pa nyams su len pa'i tshul phyin ci ma log pa* (Rong ston 2008, 1:513), he also refers to these two aspects but calls them the "direct teaching" (*dngos su bstan pa*) and the "indirect teaching" (*shugs la bstan pa*). He then relates these to, respectively, the exegetical traditions of Nāgārjuna and of Maitreya.

of that. Hence, *perfect wisdom* denotes a totality that includes both objective and subjective aspects, which are not separated in reality, though they are presented distinctly for the benefit of those who are ignorant of the nature of perfect wisdom but who strive to realize it. It seems obvious to anybody familiar with the Prajñāpāramitā Sūtras that if these texts abundantly discuss the emptiness or insubstantiality (*niḥsvabhāvatā*) of phenomena, they remain rather evasive on the practical aspect of Buddhist thought—that is, on what one is supposed to "do" to realize this wisdom of emptiness and on what it is like to realize that. The purpose of the *Ornament*, according to Rongtön's synthesis, is precisely to reveal that the Prajñāpāramitā Sūtras were all along hiding references to the path—references to "what needs to be done" in order for the understanding of emptiness to become fully realized and to what it is like to realize that. There is thus no need to oppose the "evident" and the "hidden" meanings of these texts; indeed, the whole point is to see how these can be different perspectives or expressions of the same reality.

Now, this shift in the conception of "hidden meaning" becomes the basis for a complete hermeneutic of the Buddhist tradition such as I have in mind only when combined with a historical-doctrinal perspective. Nāgārjuna and Maitreya, in this regard, had long been considered the founders and representatives of the two main exegetical traditions on perfect wisdom; Rongtön, following Tsong kha pa, particularly elaborates a view on which the orientations of these two traditions complement one another without contradiction. Nāgārjuna, in his dialectical works (excluding, that is, his hymns and letters) directly presents the definitive teaching as presented (if obscurely) in the Perfect Wisdom Sūtras; Maitreya's *Ornament* discloses the same sūtras' teachings, but as they relate to the path, which is not immediately evident when one reads the sūtras. In other words, Maitreya shows these sūtras as theorizing Buddhist practice in addition to presenting, more directly, the metaphysics of insubstantiality. Notice that both Nāgārjuna and Maitreya receive the same title (*ārya*, *'phags pa*), which emphasizes their equal status.[23] In thus harmoniz-

23. Maitreya generally receives other titles such as *rje btsun* (*nātha*) or *mi pham* (*ajita*). Despite these elevated epithets, his texts have been the subject of intense disagreements among Tibetan scholars, who often had to demote them to the lesser status of Cittamātra texts, given the place already occupied by Madhyamaka texts atop the scriptural hierarchy. In reevaluating Maitreya and his texts, Rongtön might have been influenced by his revered master G.yag ston. In his *Gsal gyi rin chen sgron me*, G.yag ston disagrees with scholars who think that Maitreya's works do not express a Madhyamaka position but rather a Cittamātra one, and he does not even agree with those who consider that at least the *Ornament* and the *Uttaratantraśāstra* are Madhyamaka (G.yag ston 1985, 595–96). He emphatically asserts (615) that all five of Maitreya's treatises are Madhyamaka, since Maitreya himself is a perfect buddha, and his texts therefore all represent the words of a buddha.

ing what earlier interpreters had taken to be two divergent traditions of exegesis regarding perfect wisdom (one Madhyamaka, one Yogācāra), Rongtön was perhaps reacting against a century of conflict between, on one hand, Jonangpas like Dol po pa, who considered Asaṅga (traditionally, Maitreya's direct disciple) to have surpassed Nāgārjuna, and, on the other, the diverse group of thinkers from Gsang phu or Sa skya (led most recently by Red mda' ba) who took Asaṅga's Yogācāra to represent a finally provisional teaching relative to the definitive interpretation expressed in Nāgārjuna's Madhyamaka.[24] Rongtön changes this narrative by changing the hermeneutics of perfect wisdom, offering a more comprehensive synthesis that recognizes both exegetical lineages as equally valuable insofar as each gives a true account of one of the two essential aspects of perfect wisdom—and thus, in a sense, expanding the meaning of Madhyamaka to include also the discourse on the path and the Maitreya texts.[25]

Conclusion

Philosophical destinies are sometimes surprising: who would expect that two of the most famously adversarial opponents on the Tibetan philosophical stage (Tsong kha pa and Rongtön) might be so closely connected? Not only did they share some doctrinal-historical principles that were foundational for both but also a desire to systematically rethink the essential unity of the Buddhist philosophical tradition. More fundamentally, perhaps, their common desire is rooted in the idea, much emphasized by Matthew Kapstein, that hermeneutics in Tibet is invariably a philosophical, and not merely an exegetical or philological, endeavor.[26] The innovations of both Tsong kha pa and Rongtön figured in producing one of the most widely accepted hermeneutical frameworks in the Tibetan world. By using the hermeneutics of the hidden meaning, Tibetan scholars have been able to affirm the authoritativeness of disparate texts that seem to recommend contradictory views. In this sense, hermeneutics was a tool for creating space for multiple and different but compatible texts and conceptions that are delimited by a common horizon, a horizon that stands both as a delimitation and as a goal—that of perfect wisdom.

24. See Wangchuk 2018, 83–87.

25. I do not subscribe to a teleological understanding of history, hence my argument here is merely that Rongtön's hermeneutical move is explainable from the perspective of a long series of interpretative shifts and decisions that could have gone another way. One of the alternatives is the interpretation of perfect wisdom by Dol po pa as presented in Kapstein 2001a.

26. Kapstein 2001b, 335–36.

The creation of such a space was also the result of a process of de-textualization," which started with the decoupling of perfect wisdom understood as denoting ultimate reality from the textual corpus of the Perfect Wisdom Sūtras.[27] With the hermeneutics of the hidden meaning, the process is advanced to the point that the original texts so denominated become increasingly less relevant. Indeed, there is a certain paradox in the idea of a hermeneutics of hidden meaning. *Hermeneutics* theorizes the recovery of meaning that is never self-evident, always requiring interpretation for its understanding. That does not imply, however, that hermeneutics has always to deal with a hidden meaning, such as in the "coded" poetry of the Renaissance "hermetic poetry" or of Stéphane Mallarmé's poems. By affirming the essential hiddenness of a text's meaning, the interpreter effectively affirms that access to the meaning cannot be only through the text; another means of access needs to be provided from outside the text in order for the full meaning to become intelligible. In this sense, hermeneutics is no longer a science of interpreting texts only through attention to texts; the relationship between the hermeneut and the text is mediated by a third term, which disrupts any possibility of an immediate grasp of the text. But this disruption, at the same time, opens up space for creativity: the interpreter is no longer simply subservient to the text, since any obvious meaning thereof may be no help in attaining the hidden meaning. Thus philosophical and doctrinal creativity become crucial—a fact clearly evident to anyone who has studied the exegetical tradition of the *Ornament*. Hermeneutics, this tradition shows, is thus not only fundamentally philosophical itself but also prepares the ground for the possibility of philosophy.

Works Cited

Apple, James. 2008. *Stairway to Nirvāṇa: A Study of the Twenty Saṃghas Based on the Works of Tsong kha pa*. Albany: State University of New York Press.

Brunnhölzl, Karl. 2010. *Gone Beyond: The Prajñāpāramitā Sūtras, the Ornament of Clear Realization, and Its Commentaries in the Tibetan Kagyü Tradition*, vol.1. Ithaca, NY: Snow Lion Publications.

———. 2012. *Mining for Wisdom within Delusion: Maitreya's Distinction between Phenomena and the Nature of Phenomena and Its Indian and Tibetan Commentaries*. Boston: Snow Lion Publications.

Bu ston Rin chen grub. 1971. *Shes rab kyi pha rol tu phyin pa'i man ngag gi bstan bcos mngon par rtogs pa'i rgyan ces bya ba'i 'grel pa'i rgya cher bshad pa lung gi snye ma*. In *Collected Works of Bu-ston*, vol. 18. New Delhi: International Academy of Indian Culture.

Ganeri, Jonardon. 2008. "Sanskrit Philosophical Commentary: Reading as Philosophy." *Journal of the Indian Council of Philosophical Research* 25.1: 107–27.

27. Harter 2014, 378–80.

G.yag ston. 1985. *Gsal gyi rin chen sgron me*. In *G.yag ston sher phyin ṭīkā* vol. *nga*: 593–691. Dehradun: Pal Ewam Chodan Ngorpa Centre.

Harter, Pierre-Julien. 2014. "Histoire de l'interprétation de *L'Ornement des Réalisations* (*Abhisamayālaṃkāra*): Réflexions sur l'idée de tradition philosophique." *Revue de l'histoire des religions* 231.3: 349–83.

Jackson, David P. 1988. *Rong ston on the Prajnāpāramitā Philosophy of the Abhisamayālaṃkāra, His Sub-Commentary on Haribhadra's "Sphuṭārthā": A Facsimile Reproduction of the Earliest Known Blockprint Edition, from an Examplar Preserved in the Tibet House Library, New Delhi.* Kyoto: Nagata Bunshodo.

———. 1989. *The Early Abbots of 'Phan-po Na-lendra: The Vicissitudes of a Great Tibetan Monastery in the 15th Century*. Vienna: Arbeitskreis für Tibetische und Buddhistische Studien, Universität Wien.

———. 2007. "Rong ston bKa' bcu pa: Notes on the Titles and Travels of a Great Tibetan Scholastic." In *Pramāṇakīrtiḥ: Papers Dedicated to Ernst Steinkellner on the Occasion of his 70th Birthday*, edited by B. Kellner, 1:345–60. Vienna: Arbeitskreis für Tibetische und Buddhistische Studien, Universität Wien.

Kapstein, Matthew T. 2001a. "From Kun-mkhyen Dol-po-pa to 'Ba'-mda' Dge-legs: Three Jo-nangs-pa Masters on the Interpretation of the *Prajñāpāramitā*." In *Reason's Traces: Identity and Interpretation in Indian and Tibetan Buddhist Thought*, 301–16. Boston: Wisdom Publications.

———. 2001b. "Mi-pham's Theory of Interpretation." In *Reason's Traces: Identity and Interpretation in Indian and Tibetan Buddhist Thought*, 317–43. Boston: Wisdom Publications.

Nya dbon Kun dga' dpal. 2007. *Bstan bcos mngon par rtogs pa'i rgyan 'grel ba dang bcas pa'i rgyas 'grel bshad sbyar yid kyi mun sel*. 2 vols. Beijing: Mi rigs dpe skrun khang.

Rgyal tshab Dar ma rin chen. 2002. *Shes rab kyi pha rol tu phyin pa'i man ngag gi bstan bcos mngon par rtogs pa'i rgyan gyi rtsa ba dang / de'i 'grel pa don gsal dang bcas pa'i rnam bshad snying po'i rgyan*. Mundgod, India: Drepung Loseling Library Society.

Rong ston Shes bya kung rig. 2008. *Rong ston gsung 'bum*, 10 vols. Khren tu'u: Si khron mi rigs dpe skrun khang.

Sparham, Gareth. 2001. "Demons on the Mother: Objections to the Perfect Wisdom Sūtras in Tibet." In *Changing Minds: Contributions to the Study of Buddhism and Tibet in Honor of Jeffrey Hopkins*, edited by Guy Newland, 193–214. Ithaca, NY: Snow Lion Publications.

Thrangu Rinpoche. 2001. *The Ornament of Clear Realization: A Commentary on the Prajnaparamita of the Maitreya Buddha*. Delhi: Sri Satguru Publications.

Tsong kha pa. 1986. *Shes rab kyi pha rol tu phyin pa'i man ngag gi bstan bcos mngon par rtogs pa'i rgyan 'grel ba dang bcas pa'i rgyan cher bshad pa legs bshad gser gyi phreng ba*. Mtsho sngon mi rigs dpe skrun khang.

———. 2008. *Golden Garland of Eloquence: Legs Bshad Gser Phreng*, vol. 1. Translated by Gareth Sparham. Fremont, CA: Jain Publishing.

Vimuktisena and Haribhadra. 2006. *Abhisamayālaṃkāra with Vṛtti and Ālokā*, vol. 1. Translated by Gareth Sparham. Fremont, CA: Jain Publishing.

Wangchuk, Tsering. 2018. *The Uttaratantra in the Land of Snows: Tibetan Thinkers Debate the Centrality of the Buddha-Nature Treatise*. Albany: State University of New York Press.

Is No-Self a Pathology?

Georges B. J. Dreyfus

IN RECENT YEARS there has been a growing interest among cognitive scientists in examining Buddhist ideas, particularly those concerning the nature of the self or its absence. This focus on no-self makes sense given the centrality of this concept in this Buddhist tradition, but it has often given rise to misunderstandings. Hence, there is ample room for further discussion of the self or of its absence from a Buddhist perspective in the light of some of the concepts of contemporary cognitive-scientific findings. This seems most appropriate in the context of a work dedicated to Matthew Kapstein, who has produced several insightful pieces connecting ancient Indian ideas about the self to contemporary philosophical discussions of the subject.[1]

I will, however, take an unusual approach to this topic. Rather than directly discuss the nature of the self, I will examine its opposite state, that of no-self, and ask: what happens when its absence is realized? To answer this question, I focus on what happens when people undergo what Buddhists describe as an experience of no-self and ask: how does this realization differ from states in which subjects suffer from a pathological loss of the self? This focus on the pathological will allow us to ask another important question: are there inherent differences between the various pathologies of the self and the realization of no-self sought by the various Buddhist traditions, and if so, what are they? These provocative questions are not just theoretical; they have pressing practical implications insofar as there are a number of people who seem to have experienced these pathologies of the self precisely in the course of attempting to realize no-self through meditation. This raises some obvious and difficult questions: what happened to these people? Have they failed in their practice? Or does their unfortunate experience show that the line between pathological and soteriological experiences may be less easy to draw than one may think? Such are the questions I examine in this essay.[2]

1. Kapstein 2001, 29–177.

2. I must thank W. Britton and J. Lindahl, whose important pioneering project, The Varieties

Self vs. No-Self

There are several ways to understand what Buddhists have meant by the concept of no-self (*anātma*). One of the primary ways in which this concept has been understood is metaphysical—as a claim regarding what really exists. This is the way that early Buddhist thinkers of the Abhidharma tradition interpreted the many passages of the early canon dealing with the self. Ābhidharmika interpretations are often described as exemplifying reductionism, according to which composite entities, being simply agglomerations of ultimately real components, do not exist ultimately. Composite wholes exist only as conglomerates of parts and hence are only conventionally real, whereas their ultimate components (the indivisible parts or *dharma*s posited in the Abhidharma literature) are ultimately real (which is to say, exist independently of our conceptual frameworks).

Nevertheless, this metaphysical approach raises a number of questions, such as what is the self that is negated, and what does it mean to say that it is not real? Here, rather than deal with these complex questions, I adopt another approach and transpose the concept of no-self into a phenomenological context. That is, rather than discuss whether there is a self in reality, I focus on our experience or sense of self. The question is not whether there is a self in reality but whether our sense of self is realistic or, as Susan Blackmore aptly suggests, is illusory.[3] A phenomenological approach has the great merit of providing a way to connect Buddhist concepts with contemporary discussions of the self taking place in various fields such as psychology, cognitive science, and neuroscience. It also locates the discussion of no-self in the domain of experience and hence connects this concept to Buddhist practice, a central concern of the tradition. I follow this phenomenological approach here as it offers a good basis for the discussion of my topics: the comparison of the various pathologies of the self with some of the effects of meditative experiences of no-self.

Furthermore, this phenomenological way of understanding no-self provides a valuable way to question and expand the Buddhist view of no-self. Often, the Buddhist tradition seems quite content to consider our sense of self simply as an obstacle to be eliminated, the root of our suffering. Although this is perhaps ultimately true, this way of understanding the self leaves out a number of important functions performed by the sense of self. The sense of self is not just an obstacle; it is also at the center of our ordinary affectivity and as

---

of Contemplative Experiences, has inspired this work. I also thank Joe Cruz, Evan Thompson, Jay Garfield, Sonam Kachru, David Germano, and Tomm Kohut for their valuable suggestions.

3. Baggini 2011, 149.

such is a crucial part of our subjectivity. It is this sense of self that is the basis of many of our affective responses, of our sense of what is desirable and what is not, of what is to be obtained and what is to be feared. The centrality of our sense of self explains why its eradication might be a more delicate enterprise than is often supposed. But before we can go into this question, we need to get a more precise grip on this "sense of self" to which I have been referring.

Three Levels of Self-Construction

Each of us feels that he or she is a self, a sharply bounded entity by virtue of which we are who we are: one possessed of agency and enduring so as to effect both continuity over time and unity across various sensory modalities. It is this sense that gives us the impression that we are unique beings clearly separated from others, enabling us to act in the world as though we are in charge of the body-mind complex and hence in control of our actions. Given the sense of unity and control conveyed by our sense of self, it may be tempting to assume that there is just one clearly delineated "sense of self." This is a mistake, however, for a brief phenomenological inquiry reveals that our sense of self is layered and highly complex. Sometimes we see ourselves as the body, sometimes as the mind. At still other times, we see ourselves as social beings or else as isolated individuals. Our sense of self is, then, multiple, operating in a variety of ways and at a multiplicity of levels.

Indeed, the multiplicity of our sense of self makes a lot of sense in the context of the no-self view. The basic Buddhist idea found in the Abhidharma tradition is not that the self is completely nonexistent, only that it is not found among the ultimate building blocks of reality (the *dharmas*). The self exists only as the object of a construction, which is produced in dependence upon innumerable causes and conditions. Given that the self is not given in reality but constructed in experience, it makes sense that it would appear in a multiplicity of ways depending on the variety of experiences; it is as we should expect. The constructed nature of the self is also reflected in the cognitive-scientific literature, which speaks of a multiplicity of ways to understand the self, sometimes going so far as to list as many as twenty-five types of self, such as ecological self, working self, social self, interpersonal self, private self, bodily self, and so on.[4]

Rather than deal with such complexity, I suggest we base our inquiry on a simpler typology, such as the one I offered in an earlier essay that distinguishes

4. Gallagher and Zahavi 2008, 197.

between minimal self, core self, and extended self.[5] In my interpretation, which partially follows Albahari's insightful discussion (2006), the *minimal self* is constituted by the continuum of momentary mental states with their first-personal self-given-ness. That is, rather than being given anonymously and appropriated retrospectively as "mine," mental states are given immediately in my experience as already self-referring. When I undergo an experience, this experience is not given as an impersonal element in a complex flux that I appropriate conceptually; rather, it is already given (phenomenologically) as happening to an I, immediately and without any possibility of mistake or doubt (immunity from misidentification). The psychologist Daniel Stern (2000) calls this minimal level of subjectivity the *emergent self* and argues in developmental terms that it forms at around the age of two months, when experiences achieve a minimal level of coherence. This minimal self represents a kind of sense of self only in that it involves an element of self-reference. I would argue, however, that this is not the self that basic Buddhist practice targets; this is not the bounded entity with which we identify and that we take to serve as the seat of our deepest affects (desire, fear, aversion, and so on). Indeed, it is hard to imagine to what extent a person deprived of such a minimal self could still be a subjective being at all—that is, a person undergoing an experience from a certain perspective, a subject for whom, or in reference to whom, an experience is taking place.[6]

The *core self* is quite different from this minimal self; it is, in particular, an illusory reification of subjectivity hypostatized as being a bounded agent enduring through time rather than a complex flow of fleeting, self-specified experiences. This kind of illusion is based on a mechanism of identification through which the subject creates a boundary, appropriating and identifying itself with elements of the mind-body complex (the Buddhist tradition's five aggregates), thus separating itself from everything else. For example, when I feel really healthy, I identify with the body. It is as if the experiencing subject becomes fused with the body felt as healthy and separated from everything else. In this way, the subject is imagined as an enduring, bounded entity, a kind of phenomenal avatar to which various qualities are attributed on the basis of the identification with the various parts of the body-mind complex so as to separate itself from the rest of the world.[7] This is what I call the *core self*,

5. Dreyfus 2011.

6. The question of whether such level of subjectivity becomes the target of practice in some Buddhist traditions remains for me an open question. Many Yogācāra texts suggest so, but it is hard to imagine what a person would be like without this minimal level of awareness.

7. Metzinger 2005.

which arises transiently, being constantly regenerated anew for every activity in which we are engaged throughout our lives. It does not depend on conventional memory, language, or reasoning and hence is not exclusively human.

I would argue that this *core self* represents the sense of self that is mainly targeted by Buddhist practice. This is the sense of the self as the boss or CEO in charge of leading the mind-body complex, and also the sense of self involved in the simple actions in which we engage in daily life (grabbing a chair, holding a pot, going to a place, and so on). With respect to such simple actions, we typically feel that we are in command, freely deciding to initiate actions that we try to bring to successful conclusions. Of course, the results of our actions are often not in our control, but acting itself is. Or so we think; the reality is quite different. Although we have some control over some of our actions, most of them result from habits, automatisms, and unconscious (or only partly conscious) desires. Moreover, as we will suggest later, the various functions that this self is experienced as performing can occur, in fact, without any reference to the self, as Suzanne Segal's case illustrates (more on this shortly). Hence, our sense of being a self in control is largely illusory; that is, it is misleading, both cognitively and affectively. This is not how we actually function but merely the way we experience ourselves functioning.[8] Nevertheless, it is this sense of self that is involved in our instinct for survival; hence, it is this sense of self that needs to be addressed by Buddhist practice if one wants to be freed from the conditioning of these deeply habituated affects.

The core self, represented by memory and language, is then extended in relation to others. Coan has argued that an important aspect of the self-construction process consists of the incorporation of relational patterns in the representation of the self.[9] We are constantly assessing how we are doing in relation to others, how much we can rely on them to deal with potential risks and share burdens. This constant preoccupation is not just a central concern of ours but is a vital aspect of the process of self-construction that develops from a very young age. Tomasello has argued that this construction of an "expanded sense of self" is rooted in the process of joint attention through which the very young infant learns how to play and cooperate with others.[10] This expanded sense of self further develops through the construction of oneself as an agent able to play varied social roles that are based on the expectation of having

8. R. Wright (2017) speculates that this sense of self can be explained as providing an evolutionary advantage.

9. Coan and Sbarra 2015. Thanks to David Germano for drawing my attention to this very helpful way to understand the way in which the self is socially extended.

10. Tomasello 2009.

access to relationships involving reciprocity and shared goals. It is also this expanded sense of self that is at work in the often-destructive distinctions that we make between our group and others, with all the affective and cognitive biases that this distinction entails.

Finally, the core self becomes a full-blown *extended self* when we develop the narrative ability to understand ourselves over longer periods of time. It is the sense of self that is closely connected to our identity: I am a Swiss man, a professor, a Buddhist, and so on. Although we often think of this sense of self as being our own ("It is I who am Swiss"), it is in fact born out of our interactions with others. This extended sense of self is also the target of Buddhist practice inasmuch as it is the seat of social emotions such as pride, shame, remorse, and the like; it is not, however, the main target inasmuch as it is not the seat of the most basic affects that Buddhism seeks to eliminate (desire, aversion, fear). To be really freed from suffering, not only does one need to be free from emotions such as pride and jealousy, but also one must be able to remain unaffected by the greatest dangers and ordeals, and hence to be free of the deepest affects such as attachment to oneself, fear concerning one's survival, aversion to what is seen as other, and so on associated with the core self. This is the state of the arhat, who is described as being free not only of desire and aversion but also of fear; only thus will one be unmoved by death.

What Happens When the Self Goes?

Now that we have gained some understanding of the various senses of self, and the ways in which these senses of self might for various reasons be at issue in Buddhist practice, we can proceed to ask the central questions of this essay: what can happen when these various senses of self are undermined? We might wonder at the question; isn't it the case that concepts of the ultimate goal of Buddhist practice (enlightenment, the condition of arhathood or buddhahood) are normative and as such cannot be empirically assessed? And if so, what is the point of asking what happens when practitioners eliminate their sense of self? It is obviously true (but perhaps bears repeating) that no amount of scientific inquiry can decide whether a person is enlightened, but the claimed merits of Buddhist practices are not limited to these normative goals. Buddhists also claim that their practices have observable effects, that they transform the person in ways that can be experienced and observed, that they can free people from attachment to a sense of self and hence allay from fear, and in other ways make them into better persons (more compassionate, more patient, less affected by ordeals). Hence, there is ample scope for empirically based inquiries into the results of the various practices recommended by the tradition, and into the ways in which these affect the sense of self in particular.

To understand what happens when various senses of self are impaired, it may be useful to look at pathologies that variously affect these senses of self, and whether or how the symptoms of such pathologies differ from the desired effects extolled by Buddhist traditions. Of particular interest is the Depersonalization Syndrome Disorder (henceforth DSD), which is a good example of impairment of the core sense of self and which presents some thought-provoking similarities with the soteriological realization of no-self. In this condition, which is recognized by the *Diagnostic and Statistical Manual of Mental Disorders*, the person loses her sense of owning a body, her sense of stability and security in life, and the ability to feel that she is connected to reality as a coherent self. At times, the person may feel that she is floating outside her body, or that she is located in her body but unable to own it ("this is my head," "this is my hand"). Actions seem somehow to happen, with no sense of oneself as their owner or agent. As we know, the categories of the DSM are not exactly set in stone (homosexuality was once described as a psychological disorder). Nevertheless, these symptoms are thought to represent a real syndrome, one particularly relevant to our topic (the effects of the disappearance of the sense of self through meditation); for this syndrome shows a *negative* reaction to the feeling of loss of the self. It seems to make sense, then, to ask whether or how this pathological condition differs from the soteriological realization of no-self, wherein the same loss is experienced as a *positive* development.

These symptoms are also interesting in that they show the precarious and delicate nature of the self. The sense of ownership of the body-mind complex is not as robust as we may think. We have the sense that we are solidly anchored in our body and mind, which we take as self-evidently ours to control. But this strong sense of self is in part an illusion (if at times a useful one) that can evaporate relatively easily given its constructed nature. The self is not a self-evident entity existing independently of our perceptual and conceptual constructions; it is the result, rather, of cognitive and affective tricks (what Baggini aptly calls the *ego trick*) that conjure the impression of a stable entity that appears to be in control of our actions, whereas in fact the control is much more diffused throughout the entire cognitive and affective systems that make up our psyche (and even beyond).[11] I would not go so far as to argue that our sense of agency is entirely illusory or due entirely to a retrospective attribution, but it seems undeniable that agency is not the province of a self-entity as we imagine it to be. The sense of unity and control that we experience as a self-entity may be

11. See Menary 2012.

useful in bringing some degree of order and coordination to the mind-body complex; nevertheless, it is largely illusory and hence fragile.

The above-described symptoms of depersonalization should sound familiar to those with meditative experience. Many have undergone, at least temporarily, similar experiences: sensations of being a detached observer of one's thoughts and actions, having the impression of being in a dream, floating away from one's body, feeling fear while experiencing a loss of the sense of self, and so on. When these symptoms remain for only a short period, they are not pathological but simply momentary obstacles that represent a normal part of the intensive practice of meditation; they may, indeed, even signal progress in the practice. But when they remain for an extended period of time and seriously impair the people who experience them, these experiences become the symptoms of what has to be seen as a pathological state, either temporarily or durably so.

Suzanne Segal's story illustrates the experience that people suffering from DSD undergo as well as the proximity of such a pathology with the soteriological experience of no-self.[12] She was an ordinary housewife who practiced TM (Transcendental Meditation) and as a result had to struggle for many years to come to term with her experience of depersonalization. She describes her struggles in her fascinating book, *Collision with the Infinite*, where she provides an excellent phenomenology of DSD symptoms while also demonstrating the fragility of the distinction between pathological and normal cases. She describes how she experienced suddenly the complete loss of her sense of self, the disappearance of her sense of identity, and the loss of the usual reference points in relation to which everything else had been meaningful. She also describes her temporary out-of-body experiences and her persisting difficulties in feeling ownership of her body. Nevertheless, she was never delusional and was able to function normally (she raised a daughter), despite her inner distress. After seeking help from various psychologists and spiritual teachers, she came to see her experience, under the influence of reading Ramana Maharshi's dialogue with his students, as a realization of what she called "Vastness" (not unlike the *Brahman* of Maharshi's Vedānta). Fear was still there, like other emotions, but it had no hold on her, as she saw it as the expression of the Vastness in which she felt living.[13] It is in this spirit that she wrote her book and started to lecture as a spiritual teacher. Unfortunately, her health deteriorated, and it was revealed that she had a brain tumor. She succumbed shortly after.

One may be tempted to follow Baggini and dismiss her experience as the

12. Segal 2009.

13. Segal 2009, 119.

expression of a disease (brain tumor);[14] that would be a mistake. Although Segal was sick, she always remained lucid in her abilities to assess external reality and her experiences accurately. Hence, we have to take her description of her experiences of the loss of the sense of self seriously (that is, as being a subjective experience of the absence of a sense of self), regardless of the etiology of her condition. Her case is all the more relevant given that similar cases of DSD have been observed in several meditators by the Varieties of Contemplative Experiences project (henceforth VCE).[15] In this study, Jared Lindahl and his colleagues describe the cases of over seventy Western meditators durably impaired (that is, for anywhere from one to ten years) by the practice of meditation. Although the pathologies of these meditators vary, DSD figures prominently as one of the observed syndromes among people not affected by any obvious physical ailment such as brain tumor. The study also describes these cases as pathological in the sense that these people were negatively affected for years. Some were unable to function altogether, whereas others were just deeply distraught by their experiences, as was Segal.[16]

The dismissal of Segal's experience seems to be based on the mistaken idea that there is an intrinsic difference between the experiences of recognized mystics and pathological cases. I think this way of understanding the distinction is deeply flawed. It piously isolates religious experiences as some kind of sui generis category that cannot be understood by science. It also fails to recognize that her experiences seem to resemble those of recognized spiritual masters—particularly her sense of having no self, her sense of not owning her body but still being connected to it and able to function. It is also the case that many of the recognized mystics undergo years of ordeals described by the literature of several traditions. Hence, I do not see why we should exclude Segal's experience as not being a genuine case of having an experience of no-self, despite its negative effects.

What emerges from this is that the line between the pathological and the soteriological might not be as robust as one may think. The line separating those who come out of a meditative retreat seriously impaired and those who have greatly benefited is thin and resists an easy explanation, as multiple

14. Baggini 2011, 28.

15. Lindahl et al. 2017.

16. I have been looking for similar cases in traditional contexts. In the extended version of this essay (in progress), I mention the case of Jay Sherab Senge, who upon realizing no-self, was gripped by fear (Pabongka 1997, 695). Similarly, Hubert Decleer brought to my attention the case of the Third Yulmo Tulku, who reports for many days not noticing the existence of his body (Bogin 2014, 331–32).

factors are involved. Hence, we should not succumb to the pious temptation of assuming that there is a clear line separating positive from negative outcomes, that there are the people who really undergo the soteriological experience of no-self whereas others are just undergoing pathological delusions. We should also keep in mind that the line between positive and negative outcomes is changing. Individuals may undergo long and trying experiences but have a positive outcome in the long run, whereas positive experiences might transform into much more negative situations.

Works Cited

Albahari, Miri. 2006. *Analytical Buddhism: The Two-Tiered Illusion of Self.* New York: Palgrave Macmillan.

Baggini, Julian. 2011. *The Ego Trick: What Does It Mean to Be You?* London: Granta Books.

Bogin, Benjamin. 2014. "The Red and Yellow War: Dispatches from the Field." In *Himalayan Passages: Tibetan and Newar Studies in Honor of Hubert Decleer*, edited by Benjamin Bogin and Andrew Quintman, 319–41. Boston: Wisdom Publications.

Coan, James, and David Sbarra. 2015. "Social Baseline Theory: The Social Regulation of Risk and Effort." *Current Opinion in Psychology* 1:87–91.

Dreyfus, Georges. 2011. "Self and Subjectivity: A Middle Way Approach" In *Self, No Self? Perspectives from Analytical, Phenomenological, and Indian Traditions*, edited by Mark Siderits, Evan Thompson, and Dan Zahavi, 114–56. Oxford: Oxford University Press.

Gallagher, Shaun, and Dan Zahavi. 2008. *The Phenomenological Mind: An Introduction to Philosophy of Mind and Cognitive Science.* Oxford: Routledge.

Kapstein, Matthew. 2001. *Reason's Traces: Identity and Interpretation in Indian and Tibetan Buddhist Thought.* Boston: Wisdom Publications.

Lindahl, J. R., N. E. Fisher, R. K. Rosen, and W. Britton. 2017. "The Varieties of Contemplative Experience: A Mixed-Methods Study of Meditation-Related Challenges in Western Buddhists." *PLoS ONE* 12.5. https://doi.org/10.1371/journal.pone.0176239.

Menary, Richard, ed. 2012. *The Extended Mind.* Cambridge, MA: Bradford Book.

Metzinger, Thomas. 2005. "Being No One." *Psyche* 11: 1–35.

Pabongka Rinpoche. 1997 (1991). *Liberation in the Palm of Your Hand.* Boston: Wisdom Publications.

Segal, Suzanne. 2009 (1996). *Collision with the Infinite: A Life Beyond the Personal Self.* Delhi: Blue Dove Press.

Stern, Daniel. 2000 (1985). *The Interpersonal World of the Infant.* New York: Basic Books.

Tomasello, Michael. 2009. *Why We Cooperate.* Cambridge, MA: MIT Press.

Wright, Robert. 2017. *Why Buddhism Is True: The Science and Philosophy of Meditation and Enlightenment.* New York: Simon & Schuster.

Tabula Gratulatoria

Yael Bentor
José Cabezón
Cathy Cantwell
Jake Dalton
Brandon Dotson
Peter Faggen
Holly Gayley
David Germano
Steven Goodman
Janet Gyatso
Agnieszka Helman-Wazny
Dan Hirshberg
Pascale Hugon
Roger Jackson
Berthe Jansen
Ngawang Jorden
Thierry Lamouroux
Robert Mayer
Carmen Meinert
Françoise Pommaret
Andrew Quintman
Kurtis Schaeffer
Peter Schwieger
Marta Sernesi
Jan-Ulrich Sobisch
Alice Travers
Vesna Wallace
Shen Weirong

Dissertations Directed by Matthew Kapstein

University of Chicago Divinity School

Daniel Arnold. 2002. Mīmāṃsakas and Mādhyamikas against the Buddhist Epistemologists: A Comparative Study of Two Indian Answers to the Question of Justification.

Jonathan C. Gold. 2003. Intellectual Gatekeeper: Sa-Skya Paṇḍita Envisions the Ideal Scholar.

Richard F. Nance. 2004. Models of Teaching and the Teaching of Models: Contextualizing Indian Buddhist Commentary.

Karin Meyers. 2010. Freedom and Self-Control: Free Will in South Asian Buddhism.

Joy Brennan. 2015. Like a Lotus in Muddy Water: Achieving Purity in an Impure World according to the Yogācāra-Vijñānavāda Three Natures Theory.

Pierre-Julien Harter. 2015. Buddhas in the Making: Path, Perfectibility, and Gnosis in the *Abhisamayālaṅkāra* Literature.

École Pratique des Hautes Études, Paris

Marc-Henri Deroche. 2011. Prajāraśmi ('Phreng po gter Shes rab 'od zer, Tibet, 1518–1584): Vie, oeuvre, et contributions à la tradition ancienne ("Rnying ma") et au mouvement non-partisan ("Ris med").

Sandy Hinzelin. 2016. « La nature de Bouddha » dans le *Traité qui montre la nature de Bouddha* du 3e Karmapa Rangjoung Dorjé.

Cécile Ducher. 2017. A Lineage in Time: The Vicissitudes of the rNgog pa bka' brgyud from the 11th through 19th Centuries.

Peter Kersten. 2018. Biographies of the First Karma-pa Dus-gsum-mkhyen-pa, Critical Edition and Translation of Two Biographical Works, and an Overview of the Dus-gsum-mkhyen-pa Collection.

About the Contributors

Jean-Luc Achard is a researcher at the Centre National de la Recherche Scientifique (CNRS, National Center for Scientific Research) in Paris and a member of the Centre de Recherches sur les Civilisations de l'Asie Orientale (CRCAO). He is also the creator and editor of the *Revue d'Etudes Tibétaines* (RET), a free online journal of Tibetan studies available on the Digital Himalaya website hosted by Cambridge University. His main fields of research are the studies of the Bönpo and Nyingmapa traditions in general, and their specific Dzogchen lineages and teachings in particular.

Dan Arnold is associate professor of philosophy of religions at the University of Chicago Divinity School. He is the author of *Buddhists, Brahmins, and Belief: Epistemology in South Asian Philosophy of Religions* (2005), which won an American Academy of Religion Award for Excellence in the Study of Religion; and of *Brains, Buddhas, and Believing: The Problem of Intentionality in Classical Buddhist and Cognitive-Scientific Philosophy of Mind* (2012), which won the Numata Book Prize in Buddhism. He is currently working on an anthology of original translations from India's Madhyamaka tradition of Buddhist philosophy.

Joy Brennan is assistant professor of Buddhism and East Asian religions at Kenyon College. Her scholarship focuses on Yogācāra, Huayan, and Zen Buddhist theories of human transformation.

Steven Collins was the Chester D. Tripp Professor in the Humanities at the University of Chicago, where he was affiliated with the department of South Asian Languages and Civilizations and with the Divinity School. Educated at Oxford University, he taught at Bristol University, Indiana University, and Concordia University before joining the University of Chicago faculty in 1991. He was one of the world's leading scholars of Pali Buddhist literature and helped spearhead the Theravāda Civilizations Project. Among his many works are *Selfless Persons: Imagery and Thought in Theravāda Buddhism*

(1982) and *Nirvana and Other Buddhist Felicities: Utopias of the Pali Imaginaire* (1998). At the time of his death in 2018, he had completed a manuscrip entitled *Civilization, Wisdom, Practices of Self: Theravāda Buddhism Seen Anew*, which is to be published by Columbia University Press.

Ronald M. Davidson is professor of religious studies at Fairfield University. He received his AB (1971), MA (1980), and PhD (1985) from the University of California, Berkeley, specializing in Indian and Tibetan Buddhist studies, although also trained in Chinese Buddhist documents. He arrived at Fairfield in 1990, after having taught at the Graduate Theological Union, the Institute of Buddhist Studies, and Santa Clara University. He was the inaugural director of the Humanities Institute, College of Arts and Sciences, and is currently codirector of Fairfield's Digital Humanities Consortium. He was awarded research fellowships from Fulbright, American Institute of Indian Studies, ACLS, NEH, ASIANetwork, the Numata Foundation, and the American Academy of Religion. His area of expertise is in the social and linguistic dynamics of Buddhist ritual, particularly associated with the use of mantras, dhāraṇīs, and tantrism, and he has translated texts from Sanskrit, Tibetan, and Chinese. He has published five single-authored or edited volumes, most notably *Indian Esoteric Buddhism: A Social History of the Tantric Movement* and *Tibetan Renaissance: Tantric Buddhism in the Rebirth of Tibetan Culture* (both with Columbia University Press), as well as dozens of articles, recently including a series on the mantra-dhāraṇī literature of Buddhism in the Gupta-Vākāṭaka and early medieval periods.

Karl Debreczeny is senior curator at the Rubin Museum of Art, New York. He completed a double-masters in art history and Tibetan studies at Indiana University (1994) and a PhD in art history at the University of Chicago (2007). He was a Fulbright-Hays fellow (2003–2004) and a National Gallery of Art CASVA Ittleson fellow (2004–2006). His research interests focus on exchanges between Tibetan and Chinese artistic traditions, and he has conducted field research in various locations along the Sino-Tibetan border. His publications include: *Faith and Empire: Art and Politics in Tibetan Buddhism* (ed., 2019); *The Black Hat Eccentric: Artistic Visions of the Tenth Karmapa* (2012); *The Tenth Karmapa and Tibet's Turbulent 17th Century* (ed. with Tuttle, 2016); *The All-Knowing Buddha: A Secret Guide* (with Pakhoutova, Luczanits, and van Alphen, 2014); *Situ Panchen: Creation and Cultural Engagement in 18th-Century Tibet* (ed., 2013); and *Wutaishan: Pilgrimage to Five Peak Mountain* (2011).

JETSUN DELEPLANQUE is a doctoral candidate at the University of Chicago Divinity School's program in the history of religions. He is currently completing his dissertation, tentatively entitled *Visions of Theocracy: The Rise of Ecclesiastical Power in Tibet and the Founding of the Bhutanese State.* He received a BA in the study of religions and Tibetan from the School of Oriental and African Studies in London and a Master of Theological Studies from Harvard University's Divinity School.

MARC-HENRI DEROCHE is associate professor at Kyōto University (Shishu-Kan), Japan, where he teaches Buddhist studies and cross-cultural philosophy. His doctoral dissertation (École Pratique des Hautes Études, Paris, 2011), forthcoming as a book and a series of articles, investigated the life, works, and legacy of Tibetan author Prajñāraśmi (1518–84) for the successive revivals of the Nyingma school and the emergence of the nineteenth-century so-called "impartial" (*ris med*) movement. He is also the coeditor of *Revisiting Tibetan Religion and Philosophy* (2012). More recent publications have focused on the Great Perfection (*rdzogs chen*), especially its philosophy of mind, meditation manuals, and association with the ideal of impartiality. A current research grant project (JSPS, 2017–20) investigates the various forms of mindfulness in the Great Perfection, their exercises, and relation with pure awareness (*rig pa*). He is a collaborator of the Dzokchen Initiative (University of Virginia) and a Fellow of the Mind & Life Institute.

GEORGES DREYFUS spent fifteen years in Buddhist monasteries before receiving in 1985 the title of *geshe*, the highest degree conferred by Tibetan monastic universities. He then entered the University of Virginia, where he received his MA and PhD in the history of religions. He is currently a professor in the Department of Religion at Williams College. He has published five books, including *Recognizing Reality: Dharmakīrti and his Tibetan Interpreters* (1997), *The Svātantrika-Prāsaṅgika Distinction* (coedited with Sara McClintock, 2003), and *The Sound of Two Hands Clapping: The Education of a Tibetan Buddhist Monk* (2003), as well as many articles on various aspects of Buddhist philosophy and Tibetan culture. He has been chair of the Department of Religion at Williams College and chair of the Tibetan and Himalayan Religions group of the American Academy of Religion. He is the recipient of various awards, such as a grant from the National Endowment for the Humanities.

CÉCILE DUCHER defended her dissertation on the history of the Ngokpa Kagyü lineage in December 2017 in Paris under the supervision of Matthew Kapstein. She is a research fellow at the École Pratique des Hautes Études / PSL (Paris), within the ANR "Social Status in the Tibetan World" (TIBSTAT). Author of a book on Marpa's biographies, she is particularly interested in the history of the early Kagyü lineage and the specificities of the tantric transmissions coming from Marpa.

FRANZ-KARL EHRHARD is professor of Tibetan and Buddhist studies at Ludwig Maximilians University, Munich. He has published widely on the religious and literary traditions of Tibet and the Himalayas. His recent books include *Die Statue und der Tempel des Ārya Va-ti bzang-po* (2004) and *A Rosary of Rubies: The Chronicle of the Gur-rigs mDo-chen Tradition from South-Western Tibet* (2008).

VINCENT ELTSCHINGER is professor for Indian Buddhism at the École Pratique des Hautes Études, PSL Research University, Paris. His research focuses on the religious background, the apologetic dimensions, and the intellectual genealogy of late Indian Buddhist philosophy. His publications include numerous books and articles dedicated to various aspects of Indian Buddhists' polemical interaction with orthodox Brahmanism from Aśvaghoṣa to late Indian Buddhist epistemologists such as Śaṅkaranandana. Mention can be made of *Penser l'autorité des Écritures* (2007), *Caste and Buddhist Philosophy* (2012), *Buddhist Epistemology as Apologetics* (2014), *Self, No-Self and Salvation* (2013, with Isabelle Ratié). An editor of *Brill's Encyclopedia of Buddhism*, he has taught at various universities in Budapest, Lausanne, Leiden, Leipzig, Tokyo, Venice, Vienna, and Zurich.

GREGORY FORGUES is a university lecturer and researcher of Indian and Tibetan Buddhism at the University of Leiden. He works on the Open Philology research project with Professor Jonathan Silk, sponsored by the European Research Council. His PhD dissertation on Jamgön Mipham's two truths theory was reviewed by Professor Birgit Kellner and Professor Matthew Kapstein and was awarded distinction from the University of Vienna. Before joining Leiden University, he was a post-doctoral researcher at the University of Heidelberg and visiting professor of Buddhist studies at the University of Bochum. He has published on a wide variety of topics, including Mahāyāna sūtra translations, Tibetan tantric rituals, the *Rimé* tradition, Dzogchen teachings and history, and digital humanities methods.

JONATHAN C. GOLD is associate professor in the Department of Religion and director of the Program in South Asian Studies at Princeton University. A scholar of Indian and Tibetan Buddhist philosophy, he is especially interested in Buddhist approaches to language and the ethics of personal cultivation. He is the author of *The Dharma's Gatekeepers: Sakya Paṇḍita on Buddhist Scholarship in Tibet* (2007) and *Paving the Great Way: Vasubandhu's Unifying Buddhist Philosophy* (2015), as well as numerous articles, including the online Stanford Encyclopedia of Philosophy entries on Vasubandhu and Sakya Paṇḍita. He is coeditor, with Douglas S. Duckworth, of *Readings of Śāntideva's Guide to Bodhisattva Practice (Bodhicaryāvatāra)*, forthcoming from Columbia University Press. In his current work he is developing a Buddhist approach to contemporary problems in religion, politics, and social thought.

PIERRE-JULIEN HARTER is assistant professor of philosophy and the Robert H.N. Ho Family Foundation Professor of Philosophy in Buddhist Studies at the University of New Mexico. He specializes in Buddhist philosophy in India and Tibet. His research on the Buddhist concept of the path (especially in the exegetical Indian and Tibetan literature of the *Ornament of Realizations—Abhisamayālaṃkāra*) has nurtured his wide-ranging interests in different aspects of Buddhist thought, such as metaphysics and ontology, epistemology, and ethics. He frames his research in the larger context of philosophy by favoring conversations between different philosophical traditions and texts.

AMY HELLER is affiliated with the Institute for Religious Studies and Central Asia, University of Bern, and the Centre de Recherche pour les Civilisations de l'Asie Orientale (CRCAO), Paris. She is a Tibetologist and art historian.

FABIENNE JAGOU (PhD Paris, École des Hautes Études en Sciences Sociales), historian, is associate professor (with habilitation) at the École française d'Extrême-Orient. Her research focuses on Sino-Tibetan political and cultural relations from the eighteenth century to the present. She teaches at the École Normale Supérieure and at the Lyon Political Science Institute in Lyon. She is the author of *Le 9e Panchen Lama (1883–1937): Enjeu des relations sino-tibétaines* (2004), published in English under the title *The Ninth Panchen Lama (1883–1937): A Life at the Crossroads of Sino-Tibetan Relations* (2011). She is the editor of "Conception et circulation des textes tibétains" in *Cahiers d'Extrême-Asie* (2005); coeditor (with Paola Calanca) of "Border Officials" in *Sinologie française* (2007, in Chinese), and editor of *The Hybridity of Buddhism: Contemporary Encounters between Tibetan and Chinese Buddhism in*

Taiwan and the Mainland (2018). Her forthcoming book is entitled: *Gongga Laoren (1903–1997), Son rôle dans la diffusion du bouddhisme tibétain à Taïwan.*

Sonam Kachru is an assistant professor in the Department of Religious Studies, University of Virginia. He is a student of the history of philosophy, with a particular focus on the history of Buddhist philosophy and literature in South Asia. He is currently completing a monograph on the Buddhist philosopher Vasubandhu, *More and Less Than Human: Mind, Life, and World in Indian Buddhism.*

Klaus-Dieter Mathes is the head of the Department of South Asian, Tibetan and Buddhist Studies at the University of Vienna. His current research deals with Tibetan Madhyamaka, Yogācāra, and the interpretations of buddha nature from the fourteenth to the sixteenth century. He obtained a PhD from Marburg University with a translation and study of the Yogācāra text *Dharmadharmatāvibhāga* (published in 1996). His habilitation thesis was published by Wisdom Publications under the title *A Direct Path to the Buddha Within: Gö Lotsāwa's Mahāmudrā Interpretation of the Ratnagotravibhāga* (2008). Recent publications include *A Fine Blend of Mahāmudrā and Madhyamaka: Maitrīpa's Collection of Texts on Non-Conceptual Realization (Amanasikāra)* (2015).

Karin Meyers is currently a fellow at the Insight Meditation Society in Barre, Massachusetts, where she supports meditators on retreat. Until 2018 she was associate professor and director of the masters program in Buddhist studies at Kathmandu University's Center for Buddhist Studies at Rangjung Yeshe Institute in Nepal, and most recently held visiting positions at Princeton University and George Washington University. Her work focuses on free will and Buddhism, Buddhist psychology and contemplative practice, and philosophical and religious studies perspectives on traditional Buddhist worldviews.

Richard F. Nance is associate professor in the Department of Religious Studies at Indiana University–Bloomington. He is the author of *Speaking for Buddhas: Scriptural Commentary in Indian Buddhism* (2012) and has published work in various journals, including the *Journal of the American Academy of Religion*, the *Journal of Indian Philosophy*, the *Journal of the International Association of Buddhist Studies*, *Religion Compass*, and *Revue d'Études Tibétaines.*

LOPEN KARMA PHUNTSHO teaches Buddhism and Bhutan studies in Bhutan and abroad. He finished his full monastic training before he joined Balliol College, Oxford, to read Sanskrit and Classical Indian religions and pursue a D.Phil. in Oriental studies. He has worked as a researcher at Cambridge University, at CNRS, Paris, and at the University of Virginia. He is the author of over a hundred books and articles, including *The History of Bhutan* and *Mipham's Dialectics and Debates on Emptiness*. A spiritual and social thought leader and changemaker, his current work focuses on the study of Bhutan's written and intangible cultures. He is also the president of the Loden Foundation, a leading educational, entrepreneurial, and cultural initiative in Bhutan.

CHARLES RAMBLE is *directeur d'études* in the History and Philology Section of the École Pratique des Hautes Études, PSL University, Paris, and director of the Tibetan studies research team of the Centre for Research on East Asian Civilisations (CRCAO). From 2000 to 2010, he held the position of university lecturer in Tibetan and Himalayan studies, then recently established at the University of Oxford, with which he remains associated as a university research lecturer. From 2006 to 2013 he was president of the International Association for Tibetan Studies. He is currently director of the European Society for the Study of Himalayan and Central Asian Civilisations (SEECHAC), and codirector of the ANR/DFG-funded research project Social Status in the Tibetan World. His book publications include *The Navel of the Demoness: Tibetan Buddhism and Civil Religion in Highland Nepal* (2008) as well as three volumes in a series entitled *Tibetan Sources for a Social History of Mustang (Nepal)* (2008, 2015, 2019).

SEIJI KUMAGAI studied Buddhist philosophy and received his PhD in 2009 from Kyoto University. In 2011, he became an assistant professor at Hakubi Center for Advanced Research of Kyoto University. In 2012, he became a senior lecturer in Kyoto Women's University and an associate professor at Kokoro Research Center of Kyoto University. Since 2013, he has been *Uehiro* associate professor at Kokoro Research Center of Kyoto University, serving as a divisional director at Kokoro Research Center since 2017. He has been invited by many universities as a guest professor/researcher, including a stint as the Numata Visiting Professor at the University of Vienna in 2018. His field of research is Buddhist Madhyamaka and Abhidharma philosophy in India, Tibet, and Bhutan and also the Bon religion. He has also studied the history of Tibetan and Bhutanese Buddhism. His books include *The Two Truths in Bon* (2011), *Bhutanese Buddhism and Its Culture* (2014), and

Buddhism, Culture and Society in Bhutan (2018), and he has published many academic articles on the philosophy of Indo-Himalayan Buddhism and Bon religion.

Michael R. Sheehy, PhD, is the director of scholarship at the Contemplative Sciences Center and a research assistant professor in the Department of Religious Studies at the University of Virginia. He has conducted extensive literary preservation and fieldwork with monastic communities inside Tibet, including three years training in a Buddhist monastery in the Golok cultural domain of eastern Tibet. His translations and writings give attention to literary and philosophical histories of marginalized traditions of Tibetan Buddhism. His current research interests abide at intersections of the Tibetan contemplative traditions with the cognitive sciences, philosophy of mind, and cultural psychology. He is coeditor of *The Other Emptiness: Rethinking the Zhentong Buddhist Discourse in Tibet* (2019).

Leonard W. J. van der Kuijp is professor of Tibetan and Himalayan studies at Harvard University and chair of the Committee on Inner Asian and Altaic Studies. His scholarly interests focus on Indo-Tibetan Buddhist intellectual history, Tibetan Buddhism, biographies and the transmission of Tibetan Buddhist works and texts, and Tibetan-Mongol relations during the Yuan dynasty. He has won MacArthur and Guggenheim fellowships for his work. His CV and a select number of his publications can be found on academia.edu.

Sam van Schaik is head of the Endangered Archives Programme at the British Library. His research has focused on the early practices of Tibetan Buddhism based on the manuscripts from Dunhuang and other Silk Road sites, as well as the history and texts of the Sakya school and the early Zen tradition. Recent books include *Tibetan Zen* (2015); *The Sakya School of Tibetan Buddhism* (2016), a translation of Dhongthog Rinpoche's history; and *The Spirit of Zen* (2019), a translation of the early Zen history *The Masters and Students of the Lankavatara*.

Christian Wedemeyer is associate professor of the history of religions at the University of Chicago Divinity School, where he is also affiliated with the Department of South Asian Languages and Civilizations, the Committee on Southern Asian Studies, and the Center for East Asian Studies. He has published five single-authored or edited volumes, most notably *Āryadeva's Lamp that Integrates the Practices (Caryāmelāpakapradīpa): The Gradual Path of Vajrayāna Buddhism according to the Esoteric Community Noble Tradition* (2007) and *Making Sense of Tantric Buddhism: History Semiology, and Transgression in the Indian Traditions* (2013), winner of an American Academy of Religion Award for Excellence in the Study of Religion.

Books by Matthew Kapstein from Wisdom Publications

Buddhism Between Tibet and China
Edited by Matthew Kapstein

"This splendid book about the multifaceted Tibetan-Chinese interactions through Buddhism will quickly become established as path-breaking and authoritative in its field."—Colin Mackerras

Reason's Traces
Identity and Interpretation in Indian and Tibetan Buddhist Thought
By Matthew Kapstein

"An excellent book: lucid, well-written, and enjoyable to read."
—*Chicago South Asia Newsletter*

The Nyingma School of Tibetan Buddhism
Its Fundamentals and History
By Dudjom Rinpoche
Translated and edited by Gyurme Dorje and Matthew Kapstein

"A landmark in the history of English-language studies of Tibetan Buddhism."—*History of Religions*

Studies in Indian and Tibetan Buddhism
Titles Previously Published

Among Tibetan Texts
History and Literature of the Himalayan Plateau
E. Gene Smith

Approaching the Great Perfection
Simultaneous and Gradual Methods of Dzogchen Practice in the Longchen Nyingtig
Sam van Schaik

Authorized Lives
Biography and the Early Formation of Geluk Identity
Elijah S. Ary

Buddhism Between Tibet and China
Edited by Matthew T. Kapstein

The Buddhist Philosophy of the Middle
Essays on Indian and Tibetan Madhyamaka
David Seyfort Ruegg

Buddhist Teaching in India
Johannes Bronkhorst

A Direct Path to the Buddha Within
Gö Lotsāwa's Mahāmudrā Interpretation of the Ratnagotravibhāga
Klaus-Dieter Mathes

The Essence of the Ocean of Attainments
The Creation Stage of the Guhyasamāja Tantra according to Panchen Losang Chökyi Gyaltsen
Yael Bentor and Penpa Dorjee

Foundations of Dharmakīrti's Philosophy
John D. Dunne

Freedom from Extremes
Gorampa's "Distinguishing the Views" and the Polemics of Emptiness
José Ignacio Cabezón and Geshe Lobsang Dargyay

Himalayan Passages
Tibetan and Newar Studies in Honor of Hubert Decleer
Benjamin Bogin and Andrew Quintman

How Do Mādhyamikas Think?
And Other Essays on the Buddhist Philosophy of the Middle
Tom J. F. Tillemans

Jewels of the Middle Way
The Madhyamaka Legacy of Atiśa and His Early Tibetan Followers
James B. Apple

Luminous Lives
The Story of the Early Masters of the Lam 'bras Tradition in Tibet
Cyrus Stearns

Mipham's Beacon of Certainty
Illuminating the View of Dzogchen, the Great Perfection
John Whitney Pettit

Omniscience and the Rhetoric of Reason
Śāntarakṣita and Kamalaśīla on Rationality, Argumentation, and Religious Authority
Sara L. McClintock

Reason's Traces
Identity and Interpretation in Indian and Tibetan Buddhist Thought
Matthew T. Kapstein

Remembering the Lotus-Born
Padmasambhava in the History of Tibet's Golden Age
Daniel A. Hirshberg

Resurrecting Candrakīrti
Disputes in the Tibetan Creation of Prāsaṅgika
Kevin A. Vose

Scripture, Logic, Language
Essays on Dharmakīrti and His Tibetan Successors
Tom J. F. Tillemans

Sexuality in Classical South Asian Buddhism
José I. Cabezón

The Svātantrika-Prāsaṅgika Distinction
What Difference Does a Difference Make?
Edited by Georges Dreyfus and Sara McClintock

Vajrayoginī
Her Visualizations, Rituals, and Forms
Elizabeth English

About Wisdom Publications

Wisdom Publications is the leading publisher of classic and contemporary Buddhist books and practical works on mindfulness. To learn more about us or to explore our other books, please visit our website at wisdomexperience.org or contact us at the address below.

Wisdom Publications
199 Elm Street
Somerville, MA 02144 USA

We are a 501(c)(3) organization, and donations in support of our mission are tax deductible.

Wisdom Publications is affiliated with the Foundation for the Preservation of the Mahayana Tradition (FPMT).